Panic Scrip of 1893,
1907 and 1914

Panic Scrip of 1893, 1907 and 1914

An Illustrated Catalog of Emergency Monetary Issues

NEIL SHAFER *and* TOM SHEEHAN

Edited by Fred Reed

McFarland & Company, Inc., Publishers
Jefferson, North Carolina, and London

The authors' research was supported by a grant
from the Central States Numismatic Society.

Library of Congress Cataloguing-in-Publication Data

Shafer, Neil.
Panic scrip of 1893, 1907 and 1914 : an illustrated catalog of emergency monetary issues / Neil Shafer and Tom Sheehan ; edited by Fred Reed.
p. cm.
Includes bibliographical references and index.

ISBN 978-0-7864-7577-3
softcover : acid free paper ♾

1. Emergency currency—United States—Catalogs.
2. Money—United States—History. 3. Currency crises—United States—History. I. Title.

HG538.S43 2013 769.5'5—dc23 2013026690

British Library cataloguing data are available

On the cover: 2 Dollars (certificate of indebtedness), 1893, Atlanta Litho. Co.;
2 Dollars Draft to Mercantile National Bank of New York (1907);
1 Dollar, August 4, 1914, black, New York state seal at left.

Manufactured in the United States of America

McFarland & Company, Inc., Publishers
Box 611, Jefferson, North Carolina 28640
www.mcfarlandpub.com

To my dear wife, Edith,
without whose love, support, and assistance
in many ways this book could never have been achieved.

(Neil Shafer)

Table of Contents

Acknowledgments viii

Preface 1

How to Use This Book 3

Part I. Scrip from the Panic of 1893 7

Part II. Scrip from the Panic of 1907 57

Part III. Scrip from the Financial Crisis of 1914 337

Appendices:
A. 1907 Pseudo or Parody Scrip 353
B. Miscellaneous Scrip 356
C. The Clearing House Certificate as a Cash Substitute, 1857–1933
by Loren Gatch 368
D. G.B. DeBernardi Labor Exchange Scrip of 1895–1905
by Steven K. Whitfield 383

Bibliography 395

Index 397

ACKNOWLEDGMENTS

Fred Reed (www.fredwritesright.com) has done his usual outstanding job editing this reference work and providing its comprehensive index. Grateful thanks is extended to him on all fronts, as he has performed well beyond any normal expectations. We are very proud and pleased that he took on the enormous job. Douglas Corrigan rendered a great deal of special assistance through his compilation of 1907 scrip census listings over a period of years. His work proved to be extremely useful to the authors. Appendix C was masterfully written by professor Loren Gatch of Oklahoma. Appendix D was beautifully prepared by labor scrip specialist Steven K. Whitfield. Both of these contributions greatly enhanced the value of the catalog. The authors are also deeply appreciative of the kind assistance rendered over a period of years by the following individuals († deceased), organizations and benefactors (who provided essential financial support):

James H. Adams	Robin M. Ellis	Donald Kagin	John N. Rowe
John Bajema	Larry Falater	Russell Kaye	Herb Schingoethe†
Ron Benice	Don Fisher	Andrew Keene	Martha Schingoethe†
Herman L. Boraker†	James Garboni	Don Kelly	Fred Schwan
Angus E. Bruce	Loren Gatch	John Kleeberg	George Shamlin
William G. Bruce	Steve Goldsmith	Lyn F. Knight	Austin M. Sheheen, Jr.
Maurice M. Burgett†	Dick Hanscom	Chester L. Krause	Hugh Shull
J.W. "Doc" Carberry	Robert Hayes	A.T. Mallory	George W. Slade
Tom Carson	John Heleva	Douglas B. McDonald	Kent Smith
Robert Chapman	Shawn Hewitt	Mark Mullin	Steve Vesely
Rod Charleton II	Wayne K. Homren	Claud Murphy	Gerome Walton
Bradley Coleman	Richard Horst	Judith Murphy	Bill Webber
George Cuhaj	Ron Horstman	Eric P. Newman	Steven K. Whitfield
Lee DeGood	Lowell C. Horwedel†	Dean Oakes	John Wilson
Kaye Dethridge	Peter Huntoon	Gary W. Potter	Nancy Wilson
James Downey	Hermann Ivester	Lee Quast	Ross L. Woodman
Tom Durkin†	Art Kagin†	Bill Rindone	Jamie Yakes

... and thanks to any others who were not remembered as they should have been.

Organizations — American Numismatic Association, American Numismatic Society (Dr. Robert Hoge), Numismatic Education Society (Eric P. Newman), Smithsonian Institution (Dr. Richard G. Doty†).

Benefactors — Central States Numismatic Society, Milwaukee Numismatic Society, Numismatists of Wisconsin, South Shore Coin Club.

The Society of Paper Money Collectors provided a special grant during preparation of the manuscript to help with the cost of compiling this volume for publication. This assistance is very much appreciated.

Preface

There have been a number of economic downturns throughout the history of the United States. Our recent national economic hard times have focused interest on the monetary expedients employed in former times. Interest in these many and varied issues of emergency scrip issued during times of severe monetary stress in the past has reached a high level of importance to a growing number of collectors, researchers and historians. Yet — except for the period of the Great Depression of the 1930s — not until very recently has a serious attempt been made to gather information about such pieces in hopes of producing a comprehensive numismatic listing. We believed three periods of monetary uncertainty—1893, 1907, 1914 — could be managed in a single catalog.

This book has been "in preparation" since 1992, though preliminary discussions first took place as early as 1986 about the possibilities of trying to accomplish such a task. The necessary notes were widely scattered by then, so that it was very difficult to locate a large group in one place except for public collections, chiefly those of the American Numismatic Society and the Smithsonian Institution. Auction catalogs provided listings as well, but progress was slow in coming. Douglas Corrigan began a project a few years ago of putting together a census of 1907 panic issues, by serial number wherever possible. This very substantial listing has contributed greatly to the issues found in the present volume.

Several private collections turned out to be very important to this book. The late Maurice M. Burgett had a significant group, as well as Chet Krause, whose collection was sold through Lyn Knight Currency Auctions in 2003 and 2004. But the later availability of the magnificent Herb and Martha Schingoethe collection was paramount in the final unlocking of the door for this volume to emerge. Though they did not live to see it come to fruition, they were well aware of the true importance of their holdings to the success of this undertaking.

A special section covering a small number of scrip issues not directly associated with any of the three major periods is included as Appendix B. These pieces date from the approximate times of the scrip outpourings, and we felt that collectors might expect to find them listed in a reference such as this. We also believed that if such issues were not included here, there would really be no suitable place for them to be listed in the future.

It will be seen that every available source was used to try to supply as many listings, illustrations and information as possible. Some of these even come from contemporary newspaper accounts that showed only rather crude copies of notes, but in every case that was considered better than nothing. We urge everyone to scour all old auction sales catalogs and other references where panic scrip may be mentioned or listed, as there are certain to be a fair number that escaped our attention, so scattered are these pieces at present. We sincerely hope that collectors everywhere will enjoy this compilation, and we welcome contact with anyone who may have additions or corrections to share with us.

Scrip images are shown at about 60 percent to 90 percent of original size; each is marked as to the precise percentage, if not at 100 percent.

How to Use This Book

Issue Number Chart

Each section of the catalog has its own Issue Number range:

1893 Section: Issue Numbers from 100 to 400.
1907 Section: Issue Numbers from approximately 500 to 2400.
1914 Section: Issue Numbers from approximately 2500 to 2900.
Parodies: Letter P with the catalog number.
Miscellaneous Section: Issue Numbers from approximately 3000 up.

Catalog Numbers

A flexible and easily understood numbering system is used for this catalog. Each note cataloged starts with the official abbreviation for a given state, followed by the issue number, a dash line and then either a final number or Var, for variable. This final number or Var. indicates either the specific denomination or a note that could be made into various values as desired.

A few examples (contrived only to illustrate the use of the numbers) follow:

AL100-.25. This note is from Alabama, the issue number indicates a listing from the 1893 section, and the face value is 25 cents.

CT250-5. This piece is from Connecticut, the issue number indicates a listing from the 1893 section, and the face value is $5.

KS500-1. This issue is from Kansas, the issue number indicates a listing from the 1907 section, and the face value is $1.

MN650-5000. This piece is from Minnesota, the issue number indicates a listing from the 1907 section, and the face value is $5,000.

UT2650-Var. This note is from Utah, the issue number indicates a listing from the 1914 section, and the face value is variable.

WA3000-200. This issue is from Washington, the issue number indicates a listing from the Miscellaneous group, and the face value is $200.

This system allows newly discovered notes to be inserted easily, since the issue number is already fixed. Also, there are many issue number skips throughout the book, including some space before the lowest number now in each section. As new issues are found they can be placed in proper order without disturbing those numbers in place. New denominations of a known issuer will use the same issue number but add a new face value number or Var. at the end.

Types of Notes Listed

There were basically five types of emergency money issued during these periods of economic stress:

(1) *Clearing House Loan Certificates.* These are notes of high denomination made to be used only within the clearing house system, not to be issued to the public as a cash substitute. Issued in denominations from $500 to $100,000, they were released to a particular member bank by the Loan Committee after the bank had deposited collateral with the clearing house. The bank could substitute these certificates for cash during the normal clearing process. Collateral could be stocks, bonds, commercial paper, etc. The Loan Committee would generally allow the bank 50 percent to 75 percent of the face value of the collateral in the form of loan certificates. They paid 5 percent to 10 percent per annum and were the collective legal responsibility of the clearing house and its member banks.

In appearance, since they were designed only for bank use, loan certificates are very utilitarian: generally quite large in size, very plain and with text only. They are included in this catalog only because they are a part of the full economic story of the periods of panic under consideration. Their availability to collectors is sparse, though several issues appear on the market from time to time.

(2) *Clearing House Certificates.* These are low denomination notes made for public circulation as a money substitute and sponsored by the named clearing house or member bank. Usually they come in values from 25¢ to $20.00, but occasionally they go higher. Banks could secure a supply of such certificates through deposit of collateral or loan certificates with the clearing house. These notes paid no interest but were the legal liability of the clearing house and its member banks collectively.

In appearance such certificates will at times bear attractive designs, sometimes having been printed by a major security printing firm, and will otherwise be of a size that could circulate easily. Many are also rather plain since they may be check forms often hastily altered to circulate as emergency notes.

(3) *Clearing House Checks.* These are low face value pieces intended for public circulation as a money substitute, obtained by a bank through deposit of collateral. While their use was similar to clearing house certificates described above, they were a liability only of the bank named in the lower part of the check and not the clearing house.

(4) *Cashier's Checks.* These are low denomination notes issued to the public as a money substitute by individual banks. Usually these were not backed by any collateral deposited in a clearing house. They were legal liabilities of the bank named in the lower part of the check. Several variations of such checks bore wording such as Treasurer's Checks, Certificates of Deposit, Money Orders, Drafts Payable on New York Exchange, or similar wording.

(5) *Payroll Checks.* These are also low denomination pieces intended for public use as a cash substitute. They were issued by private businesses, generally without collateral on deposit with any clearing house. Payroll checks came one of two ways, Certified or Non-certified. Certification meant that the check was one for which a special account was provided by the issuer solely for the purpose of redeeming it. Such an account was backed by a non-revocable line of credit that made the check a liability of the bank as well as the company issuing the check. A non-certified check had no special redemption account and was the liability only of the issuing company. Most payroll checks were non-certified and were cashed as quickly as possible. Pittsburgh area businesses issued a great many payroll checks instead of clearing house certificates.

Types of Issues Not Included

Issues such as discount coupons, restricted-time coupons, special event scrip and other short-term use pieces do not constitute true panic scrip and are excluded from the main body of listings.

Note Descriptions

Description of each note begins with catalog number, denomination, usually the type of note (unless an obvious clearing house issue), and date (or ND for no date) followed by year of issue, if known. If the date is handwritten or stamped instead of being printed, that fact will be mentioned. When the basis for the listing is a black/white copy, the designation *b/w* in parentheses will show with that entry. If the note was found only as part of a bare listing, the word *list* in parentheses will be shown. Descriptions will include color and basic design (where known) if there is anything more than text or other wording.

Issuers' names are taken exactly as they appear on the notes. If the word *Certificate* is on the note as an integral part of the issuer's name or note title, that word will be included as such in the catalog. The same is true of the type designations; thus, if the note has wording *Cashier's Check* with apostrophe or *Cashiers Check* without, that difference will show in every applicable listing.

General Characteristics

Most notes listed are generally in a size approximating that of large U.S. paper money issues. Size will be mentioned only for those issues that deviate substantially from this standard.

States of Existence

A very important factor in the collecting of scrip contained in this book is the state of existence of a piece in question. The listings under each item cataloged will have one or more of the following designations:

a. Issued, not cancelled. As far as can be determined, such a note was fully prepared with all necessary validations allowing it to enter circulation, and was never cancelled either by hand, machine or any other way. In most cases issues in this state of existence are true rarities in an otherwise available series.

b. Issued, cancelled. This note entered circulation as described in paragraph a. Cancellation in various ways may include punched holes, perforation, bank stamping, piece(s) removed, lines drawn, handwritten or stamped *Paid, Cancelled, Void, Withdrawn, Souvenir*, etc.

c. Unissued, cancelled. Such a note normally does not have signatures or date unless printed as part of the original design. It may occasionally show some features required for actual use, but not all of them. Cancellation marks may be one or more of any of those listed under paragraph b.

d. Unissued, remainder. This is a note fitting the description of paragraph c. above, but without any kind of cancellation or other marking.

e. Sample. An example supplied (at times by the printer) for approval or personal reasons, not intended for circulation. The word SAMPLE will appear on the face of the note either in printed, stamped or handwritten form.

f. Specimen. Related to Sample, but generally with an all-zero serial number and printed or stamped "SPECIMEN" across the face. These are often made to show the finished design and color of a given issue, or for archival purposes. Specimen notes are never issued to circulation.

g. Proof, essay or otherwise unfinished note. A note showing the progression of a certain design, color or any other characteristic of a note in progress. Finished proof pieces are often uniface and on thin India paper for clarity of printing.

u. Unreported, unknown. This designation is used only when information about a note's true state of existence is incomplete or totally unknown. In some cases, even though the note is known to have been issued, it will receive the u designation if it cannot be determined whether or not the note was cancelled.

On Collecting Panic Scrip Notes

It is fair to say that the majority of issues listed in this catalog are scarce to extremely rare. An individual trying to build a collection will find it slow going, with a few notable exceptions. For the scrip issues of 1907, hoards of approximately 50 or more cancelled or unissued pieces exist from places such as Riverside and San Francisco, California; Fort Collins, Colorado; Augusta, Georgia; Illinois Central Railroad of Chicago, Illinois; Doe Run Lead Co. of Missouri; Wausa, Nebraska; Group 2 Ohio Bankers Association; Altoona, Pennsylvania and Richfield, Utah. Cancelled pieces from Bellingham, Washington, appear from time to time. The Los Angeles issue is also available on occasion.

Rarity Ratings and Values

The majority of issues included are of such rarity that a valid dollar estimate of market value cannot be provided. In such cases a rarity rating based on observed examples either in private or public collections, auction sales and reliable reports will be given. A number of issues do come up frequently enough for sale or in auctions that they can be properly evaluated. They will not have a rarity rating; instead, they will have standard types of values in various grades and states of existence as applicable.

It must be emphasized strongly that a high rarity may not indicate high value. One of the main factors to consider is condition. A very rare piece in low grade will ordinarily not do well on the market unless there is something special about it, such as place of issue, design, printer or some other feature. If the rarity comes from a group of similarly designed notes that are not particularly scarce, unless a collector feels he "must have" this particular issue, it may go for considerably less than another item of similar rarity but with more unique features.

On the other hand, a relatively available issue may engender a strong demand, again depending on its overall appeal for reasons stated, or perhaps some other characteristic peculiar only to that issue or example.

The table of rarity as used in this book is as follows:

R1: lowest rarity. Quite scarce but sometimes available; possibly 15 or 20 examples may exist.

R2: second level of rarity. Very scarce, seldom available; about 10 to 14 may be extant.

R3: a rare note, generally unavailable except on special occasions. Seven to 10 may exist.

R4: a very rare note; surviving examples are estimated at perhaps five or six pieces.

R5: highest rarity; fewer than five examples thought to exist.

SENC: a note listed but not fully described may receive this designation, meaning Surviving Example Not Confirmed. At times such a note is believed to have been printed, but no example is reported in any known collection. At other times the note is known to exist but has not been examined to determine its full state of existence.

Part I.
Scrip from the Panic of 1893

Historical Background

The Panic of 1893 began on May 4 and soon became the worst economic crisis to hit the nation in its history to that point. Like most major financial downturns, the depression of the 1890s was preceded by a series of shocks that had undermined public confidence and weakened the economy.

Causes of the panic were many and varied. Among them were unsteadiness in commodity and crop prices, a strong wave of European monetary instability that had a profound effect on the business climate in New York and elsewhere, a slowdown in railroad investment because of overextension and overbuilding in many areas, and a significant drain on gold reserves brought about in part by the Sherman Silver Purchase Act of 1890. This Act required the U.S. Treasury to purchase silver using notes backed by either silver or gold.

In the last days of the Harrison administration, the Philadelphia and Reading Railroad, a major eastern line, went into receivership. That collapse was soon magnified by the failures of hundreds of banks and businesses dependent upon the Reading and other railroads. Then the National Cordage Company (the most actively traded stock at the time) went into receivership because bankers called in their loans in response to rumors about the financial stability of the company.

The stock market reacted to all this activity with a dramatic plunge. Fearing further collapse, European investors pulled their funds from the United States, but depression soon gripped the other side of the Atlantic as well. An ongoing agricultural depression in the West and South deepened, spreading the misery to those regions.

A series of bank failures followed, and the price of silver fell. Several other major rail lines all failed. This was followed by the bankruptcy of many other companies. In total, an unprecedented 15,252 American businesses went into receivership, and 500 banks failed (a large number of them in the West). By the winter of 1893 about 12 percent to 18 percent of the national work force was unemployed. Those who remained at work found their wages slashed by an average of almost 10 percent.

A few weeks after President Grover Cleveland was sworn in, the nation's reserves dipped below $100 million, a psychological barrier whose breaching further weakened public trust. The U.S. Treasury was driven four times between 1894 and 1896 to resort to bond issues totaling $260 million to obtain specie to augment its reserve. The president had acted to rescue the gold standard, but in the process divided the Democratic Party and alienated the silver forces of the South and West.

Although thousands of businesses were ruined and more than four million people were left unemployed, President Cleveland did little. As most people then, he believed that business cycles should be left alone and not tampered with by politicians.

An extensive but incomplete business revival occurred in 1895. An upsurge of support for Democratic presidential nominee William Jennings Bryan on a free silver platform the following year contributed to a second downturn affecting only the United States. A return to normalcy began in earnest by 1896 with the election of William McKinley, but only by mid–1897 did recovery take hold, returning gradually over the next 12 to 18 months. Afterwards, confidence was fully restored and the economy began ten years of rapid growth until the Panic of 1907.

Catalog Listing

ALABAMA

Birmingham

BIRMINGHAM CLEARING HOUSE CERTIFICATE

A. Peoples Savings Bank & Trust Co.

AL100-.50 50 Cents Aug. 19, 1893 (stamped date and bank name). Black on green underprint. Countersigned by hand. Uniface. 160 × 69mm.

a. Issued, not cancelled. **R4**

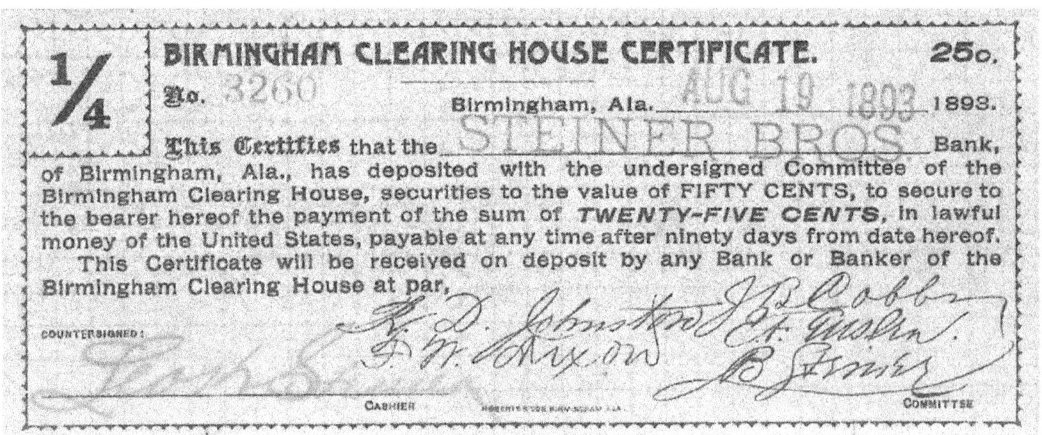

1/4 BIRMINGHAM CLEARING HOUSE CERTIFICATE. 25c.
No. 3260 Birmingham, Ala. AUG 19 1893 1893.
This Certifies that the STEINER BROS Bank, of Birmingham, Ala., has deposited with the undersigned Committee of the Birmingham Clearing House, securities to the value of FIFTY CENTS, to secure to the bearer hereof the payment of the sum of TWENTY-FIVE CENTS, in lawful money of the United States, payable at any time after ninety days from date hereof.
This Certificate will be received on deposit by any Bank or Banker of the Birmingham Clearing House at par.
COUNTERSIGNED: CASHIER COMMITTEE

B. Steiner Brothers Bank

AL105-.25 25 Cents Aug. 19, 1893 (stamped date and bank name). Black on dark orange underprint. Countersigned by hand. Uniface. 160 × 69mm. Imprint: Roberts & Son, Birmingham, Ala. (shown at 85%)

a. Issued, not cancelled. **Fine, 100. VF, 150.**

c. Unissued, cancelled. **R1**

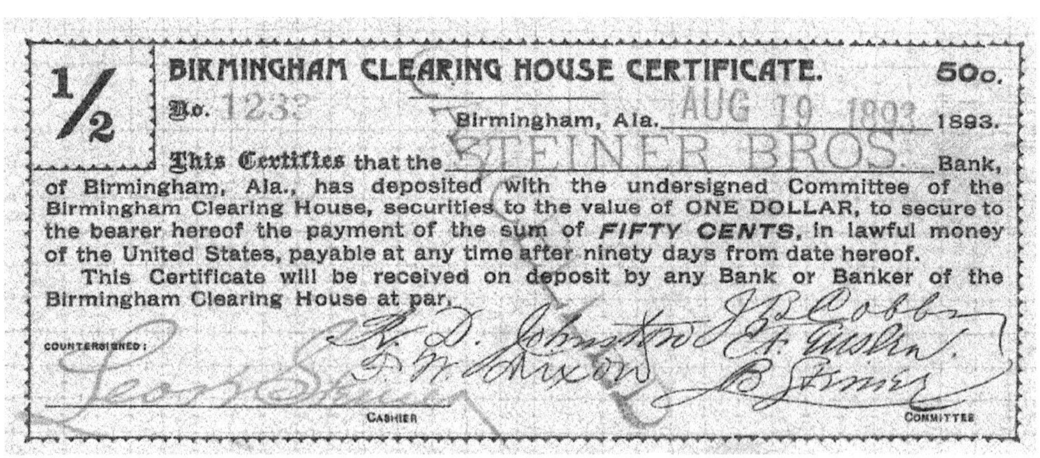

1/2 BIRMINGHAM CLEARING HOUSE CERTIFICATE. 50c.
No. 123? Birmingham, Ala. AUG 19 1893 1893.
This Certifies that the STEINER BROS Bank, of Birmingham, Ala., has deposited with the undersigned Committee of the Birmingham Clearing House, securities to the value of ONE DOLLAR, to secure to the bearer hereof the payment of the sum of FIFTY CENTS, in lawful money of the United States, payable at any time after ninety days from date hereof.
This Certificate will be received on deposit by any Bank or Banker of the Birmingham Clearing House at par.
COUNTERSIGNED: CASHIER COMMITTEE

AL105-.50 50 Cents Aug. 11, 19, 1893 (stamped date and bank name). Black on green underprint. As above, except without imprint. (shown at 85%)

b. Issued, cancelled. **Fine, 125. VF, 200.**
c. Unissued, cancelled. **R1**

Birmingham Clearing House Certificate

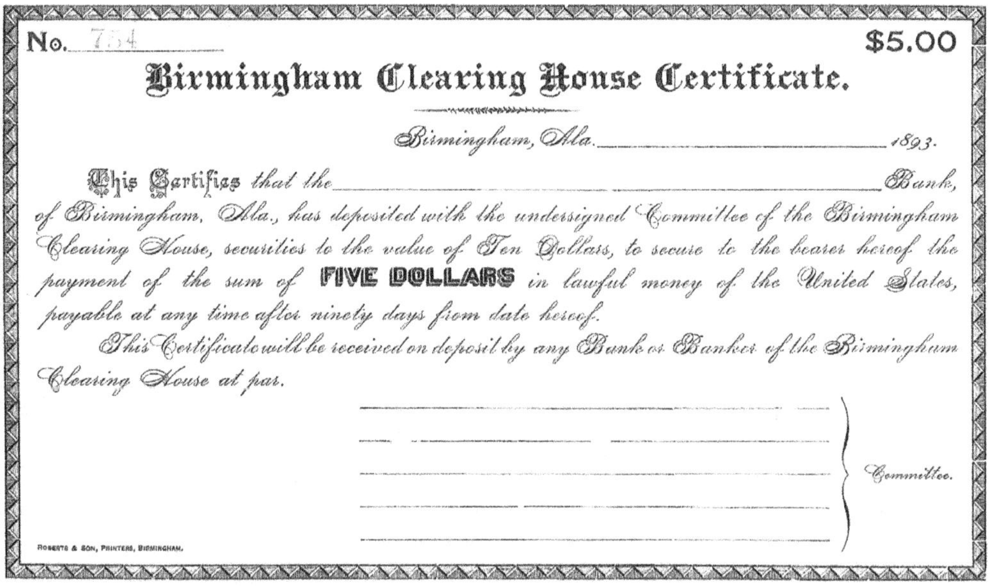
No. 754 $5.00

Birmingham Clearing House Certificate.

Birmingham, Ala. ______ 1893.

This Certifies that the ______ Bank, of Birmingham, Ala., has deposited with the undersigned Committee of the Birmingham Clearing House, securities to the value of Ten Dollars, to secure to the bearer hereof the payment of the sum of FIVE DOLLARS in lawful money of the United States, payable at any time after ninety days from date hereof.

This Certificate will be received on deposit by any Bank or Banker of the Birmingham Clearing House at par.

Committee.

Roberts & Son, Printers, Birmingham.

A. Larger size (ca. 225 × ca. 135mm.)

AL120-5. 5 Dollars 1893. Black. Spaces for signatures of five committee members at right. Uniface. Imprint: Roberts & Son, Printers, Birmingham. (shown at 61%)
d. Unissued, remainder. **R4**

AL120-50. 50 Dollars 1893. As above.
c. Unissued, cancelled. **R4**

AL120-100. 100 Dollars 1893. As above. Five hand signatures at right but unfinished date.
c. Unissued, cancelled. **R4**

AL120-500. 500 Dollars 1893. As above. (list)
c. Unissued, cancelled. **R4**

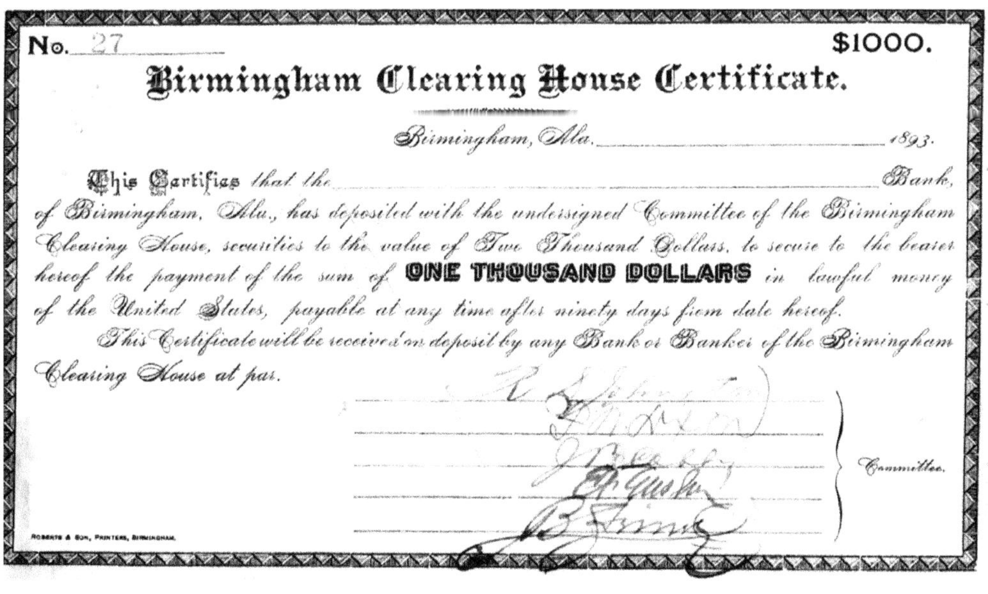
No. 27 $1000.

Birmingham Clearing House Certificate.

Birmingham, Ala. ______ 1893.

This Certifies that the ______ Bank, of Birmingham, Ala., has deposited with the undersigned Committee of the Birmingham Clearing House, securities to the value of Two Thousand Dollars, to secure to the bearer hereof the payment of the sum of ONE THOUSAND DOLLARS in lawful money of the United States, payable at any time after ninety days from date hereof.

This Certificate will be received on deposit by any Bank or Banker of the Birmingham Clearing House at par.

Committee.

Roberts & Son, Printers, Birmingham.

AL120-1000. 1,000 Dollars 1893. As above. (shown at 61%)
c. Unissued, cancelled. R4

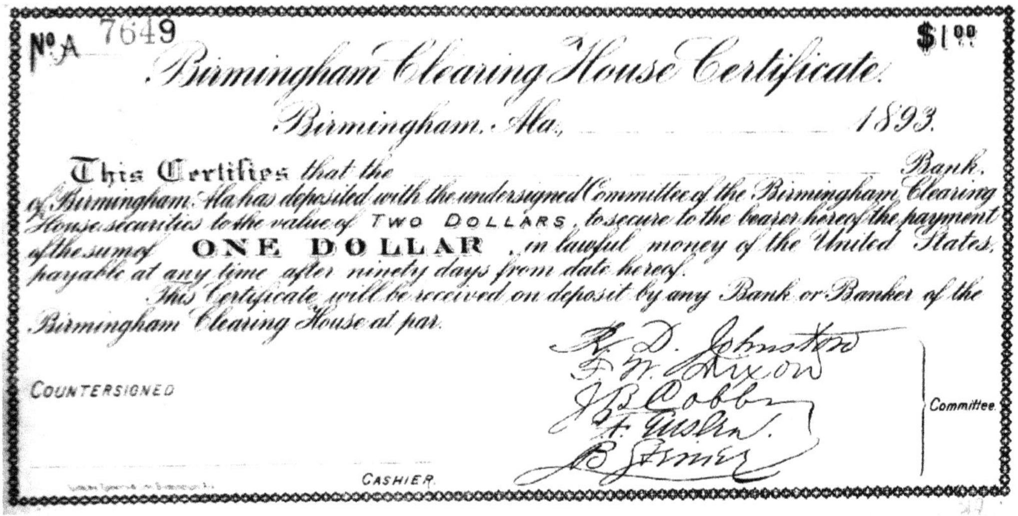
No A 7649 $1.00
Birmingham Clearing House Certificate.
Birmingham, Ala., 1893.
This Certifies that the Bank, of Birmingham, Ala has deposited with the undersigned Committee of the Birmingham Clearing House securities to the value of TWO DOLLARS, to secure to the bearer hereof the payment of the sum of ONE DOLLAR, in lawful money of the United States, payable at any time after ninety days from date hereof.
This Certificate will be received on deposit by any Bank or Banker of the Birmingham Clearing House at par.
COUNTERSIGNED
CASHIER
Committee

B. Smaller size (ca. 190 × 98mm.)
AL130-1. 1 Dollar 1893. Black. Five printed signatures at lower right. Uniface. Imprint: Lith. by Roberts & Son Birmingham Ala. (shown at 71%)
c. Unissued, cancelled. R4
d. Unissued, remainder. R4
AL130-2. 2 Dollars 1893. As above.
c. Unissued, cancelled. R4
AL130-5. 5 Dollars 1893. As above.
c. Unissued, cancelled. R4
AL130-10. 10 Dollars 1893. As above.
c. Unissued, cancelled. R4
d. Unissued, remainder. R4

ARKANSAS

Little Rock

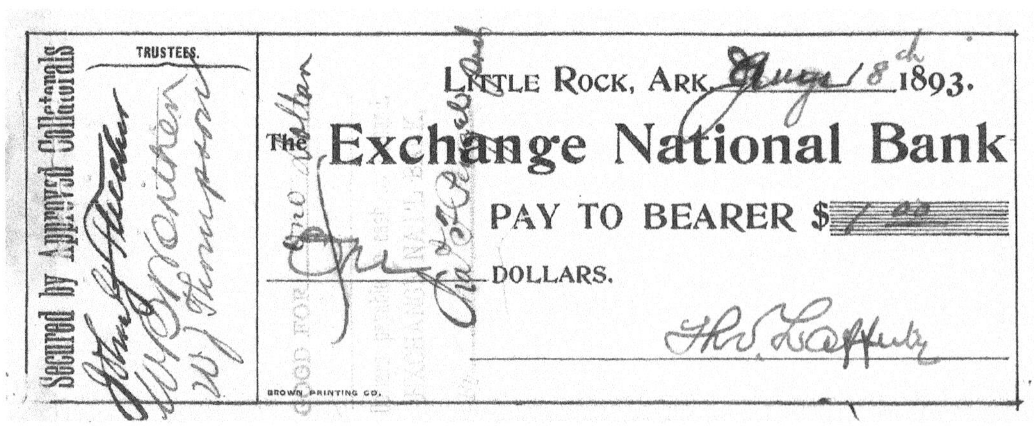
Secured by Approved Collaterals
TRUSTEES.
Little Rock, Ark. Aug 18th 1893.
The Exchange National Bank
PAY TO BEARER $
DOLLARS.
BROWN PRINTING CO.

THE EXCHANGE NATIONAL BANK

AR100-1. 1 Dollar Aug. 1, 1893 (handwritten over July 8 date). Bearer check with written denomination. Black on white paper. Vertical bank stamping and hand signature at left center. Uniface. (shown at 71%)

a. Issued, not cancelled. R5

b. Issued, cancelled (cut). R5

CONNECTICUT

Danbury

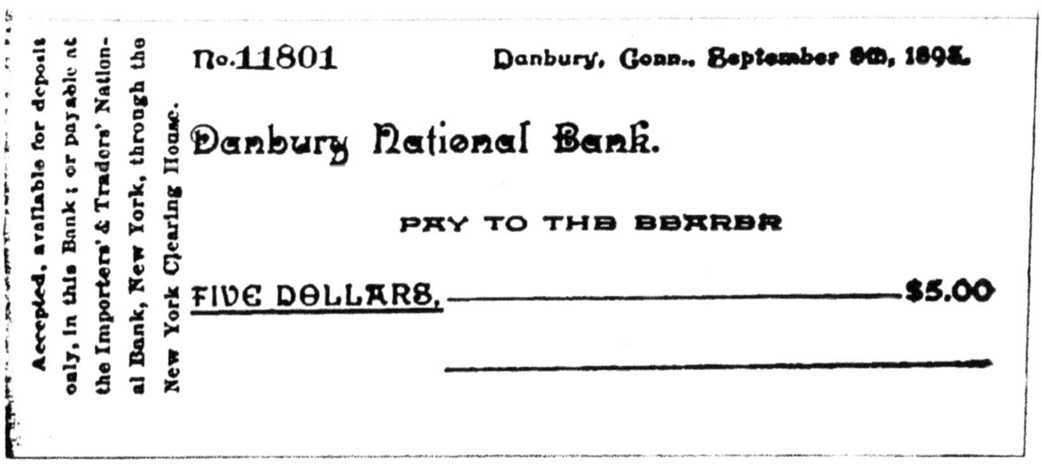
Accepted, available for deposit only, in this Bank; or payable at the Importers' & Traders' National Bank, New York, through the New York Clearing House.

No. 11801 Danbury, Conn., September 8th, 1893.

Danbury National Bank.

PAY TO THE BEARER

FIVE DOLLARS, $5.00

DANBURY NATIONAL BANK

CT100-5. 5 Dollars Sept. 8, 1893. Uniface. (b/w) (shown at 67%)

d. Unissued, remainder. R5

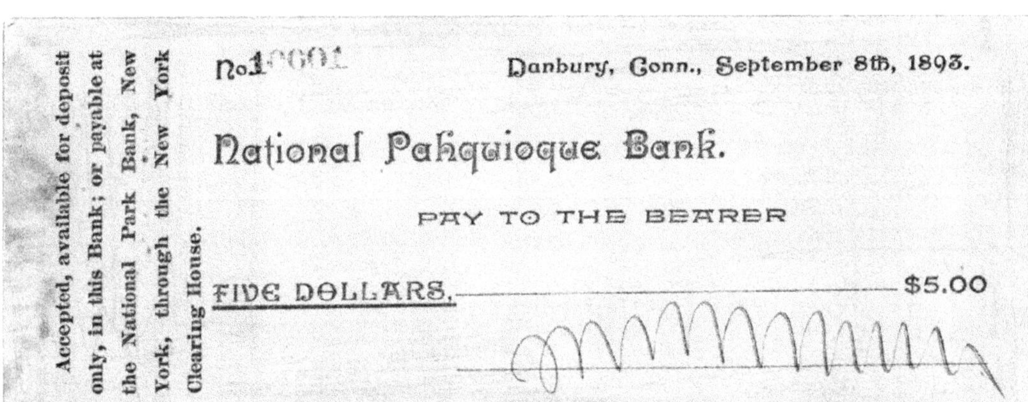
Accepted, available for deposit only, in this Bank; or payable at the National Park Bank, New York, through the New York Clearing House.

No. 1[illegible] Danbury, Conn., September 8th, 1893.

National Pahquioque Bank.

PAY TO THE BEARER

FIVE DOLLARS, $5.00

NATIONAL PAHQUIOQUE BANK

CT125-5. 5 Dollars Sept. 8, 1893. Red. Payable as stated at left. Uniface. (shown at 69%)

c. Unissued, cancelled. R5

d. Unissued, remainder. R5

Hartford

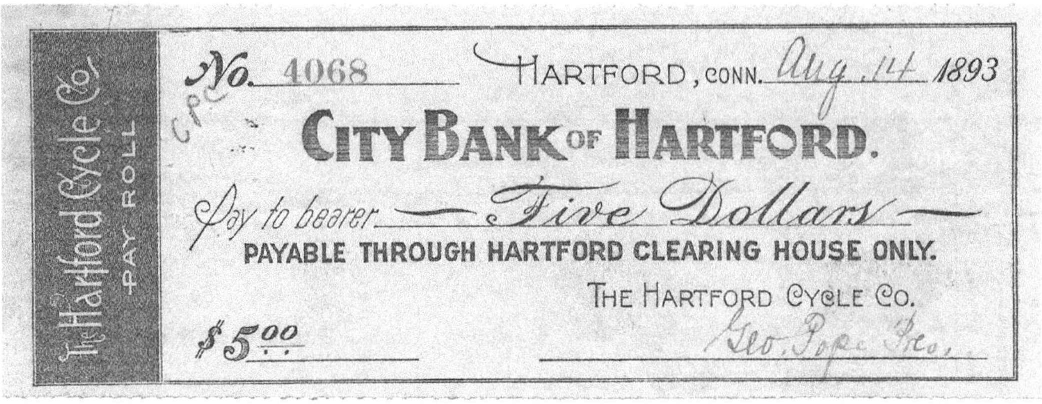

The Hartford Cycle Co./City Bank of Hartford

CT150-1. 1 Dollar Pay Roll Check Aug. 14, 1893. Black on orange paper. Uniface. (shown at 70%)
a. Issued, not cancelled. **R4**
CT150-2. 2 Dollars Aug. 14, 1893. As above. (b/w)
a. Issued, not cancelled. **R4**
CT150-5. 5 Dollars Aug. 14, 1893. Black on lilac paper. As above.
a. Issued, not cancelled. **R4**

Hartford Trust Company

CT175-1. 1 Dollar Pay Roll Check Aug. 12, 1893. Uniface. (b/w) (shown at 78%)
a. Issued, not cancelled. **R5**

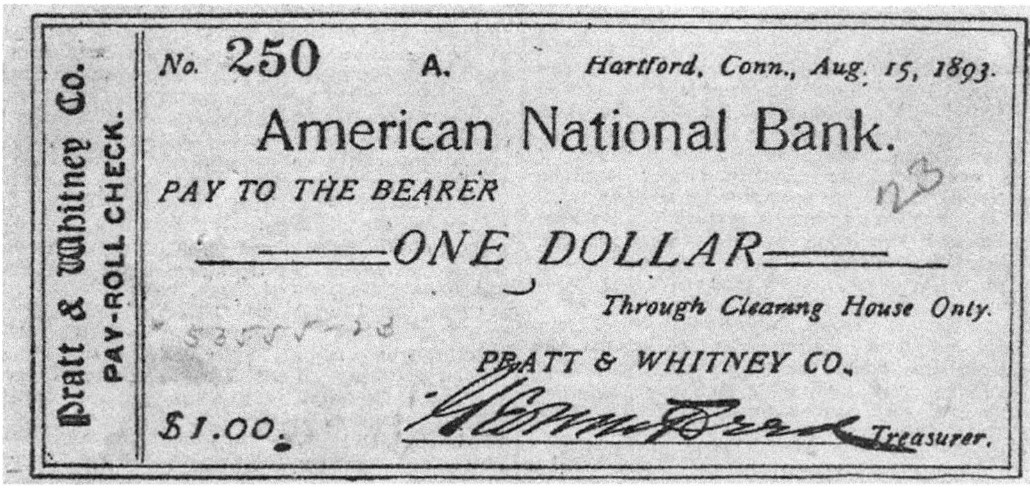
Pratt & Whitney Co.
PAY-ROLL CHECK.
No. 250 A. Hartford, Conn., Aug. 15, 1893.
American National Bank.
PAY TO THE BEARER
ONE DOLLAR
Through Clearing House Only.
PRATT & WHITNEY CO.,
$1.00. Treasurer.

Pratt & Whitney Co./American National Bank
CT200-1. 1 Dollar Pay-Roll Check Aug. 15, 1893. (b/w) (shown at 76%)
a. Issued, not cancelled. **R5**

Winsted

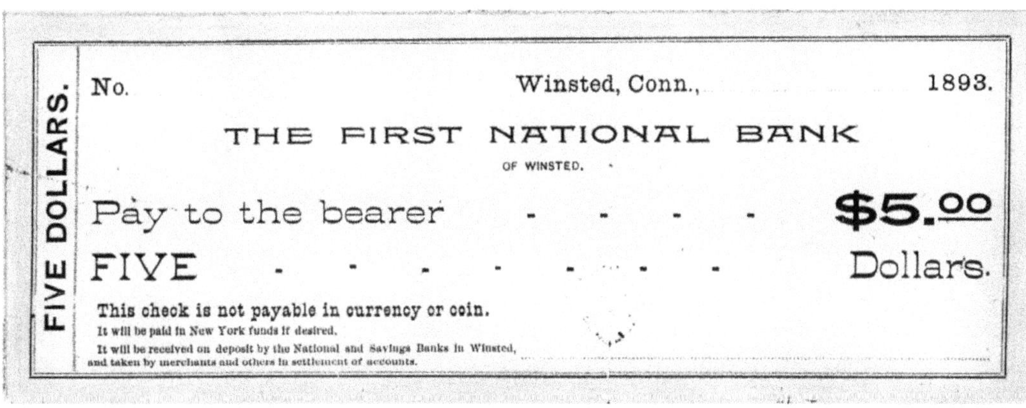
FIVE DOLLARS.
No. Winsted, Conn., 1893.
THE FIRST NATIONAL BANK
OF WINSTED.
Pay to the bearer - - - - $5.00
FIVE - - - - - - - - Dollars.
This check is not payable in currency or coin.
It will be paid in New York funds if desired.
It will be received on deposit by the National and Savings Banks in Winsted, and taken by merchants and others in settlement of accounts.

The First National Bank of Winsted
CT225-1. 1 Dollar 1893. (b/w) (shown at 70%)
d. Unissued, remainder. **R5**

GEORGIA

Albany

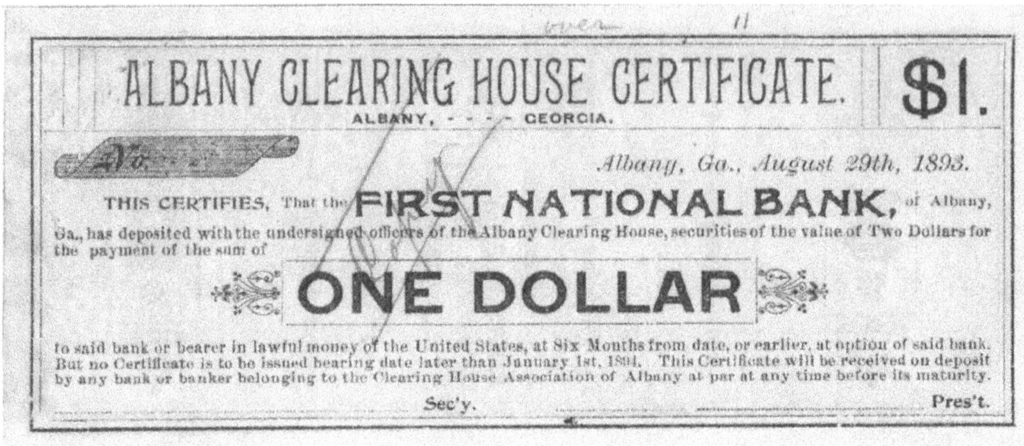

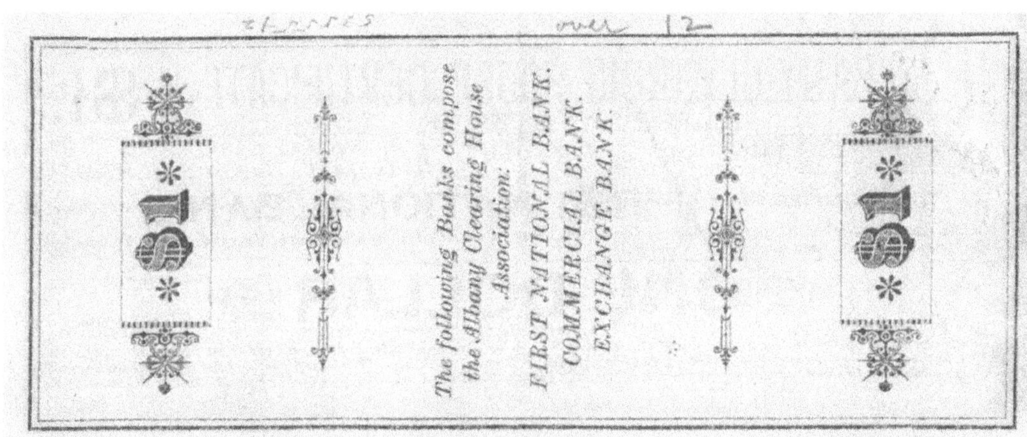

ALBANY CLEARING HOUSE CERTIFICATE

A. First National Bank

GA100-1. 1 Dollar Aug. 29, 1893. Dark blue on light green underprint. List of member banks vertically on back. (shown at 74%)

c. Unissued, cancelled. **R4**

GA100-5. 5 Dollars Aug. 29, 1893. (list)

c. Unissued, cancelled. **R5**

GA100-10. 10 Dollars Aug. 29, 1893. As above.

c. Unissued, cancelled. **R5**

B. Exchange Bank

GA120-5. 5 Dollars Aug. 29, 1893. Dark blue on light green underprint. As previous issue. (shown at 73%)
  c. Unissued, cancelled. R5

Atlanta

ATLANTA CLEARING HOUSE ASSOCIATION CERTIFICATE

GA140-5. 5 Dollars Aug. 15, 1893. Black on gray underprint. Large red outline denomination in words across center in underprint. Cotton plant at left. Back deep orange; list of member banks vertically. Series A. Imprint: Syl. Lester & Co Prs.
  d. Unissued, remainder. R3

GA140-10. 10 Dollars Aug. 15, 1893. As above. (shown at 65%)
  d. Unissued, remainder. R4

GA140-20. 20 Dollars Aug. 15, 1893. (Known to have been issued, but no example reported in any collection.) SENC

GA140-100. 100 Dollars Aug. 15, 1893. As above.
  d. Unissued, remainder. R5

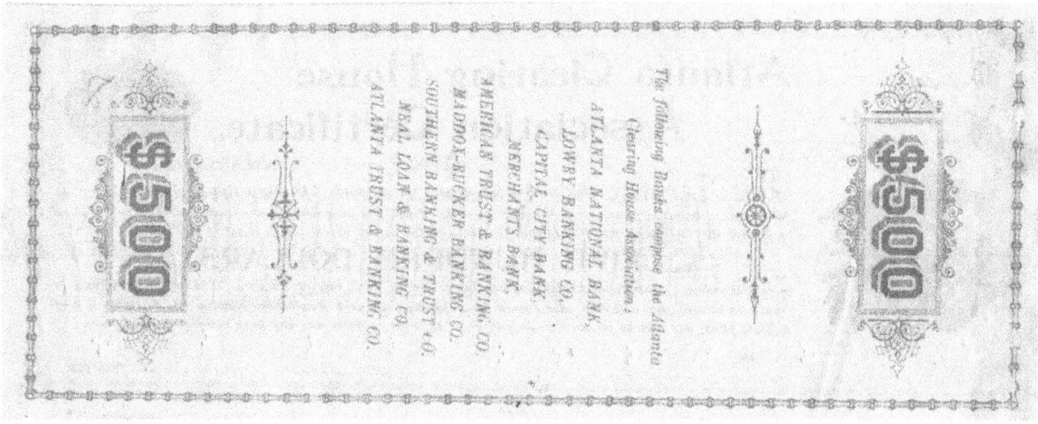

GA140-500. 500 Dollars Aug. 15, 1893. As above. (shown at 64%)

c. Unissued, cancelled. R5

d. Unissued, remainder. R5

NOTE: Atlanta certificates were issued to only 66⅔% of collateral deposited instead of the usual 75%. The largest amount outstanding at any one time was $127,000.00; all except about $20 was redeemed by Nov. 1.

Brunswick

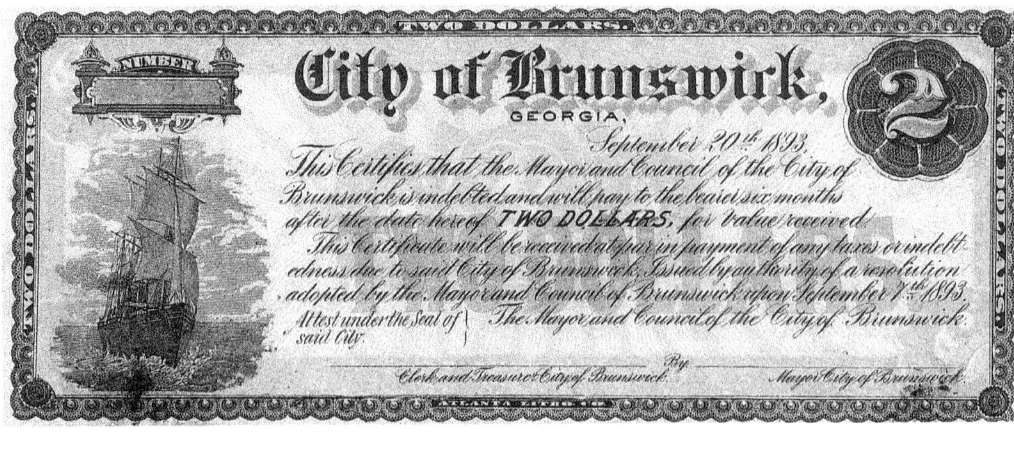

City of Brunswick

GA160-2. 2 Dollars (certificate of indebtedness) Sept. 20, 1893. Black on peach underprint. Sailing ship at left. Large denomination words in dark orange in underprint at right center. Back blue. Imprint (on both sides): Atlanta Litho. Co. (shown at 70%)
d. Unissued, remainder. **R2**

Carrollton

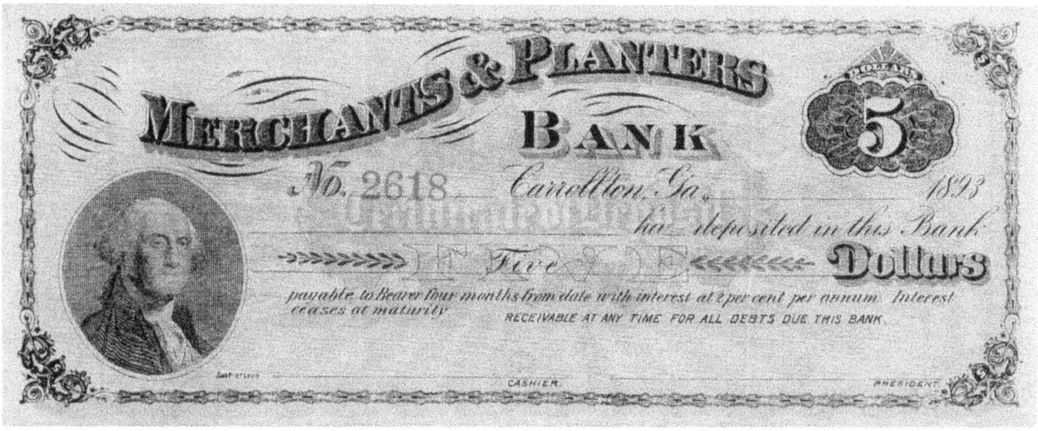

Merchants & Planters Bank

GA180-1. 1 Dollar Certificate of Deposit 1893. Black on light green underprint. Washington at left. Back green; vignette with three horses at center. Imprint: Gast—St. Louis.
 d. Unissued, remainder. R3

GA180-5. 5 Dollars 1893. As above. (shown at 73%)
 d. Unissued, remainder. R4

Columbus

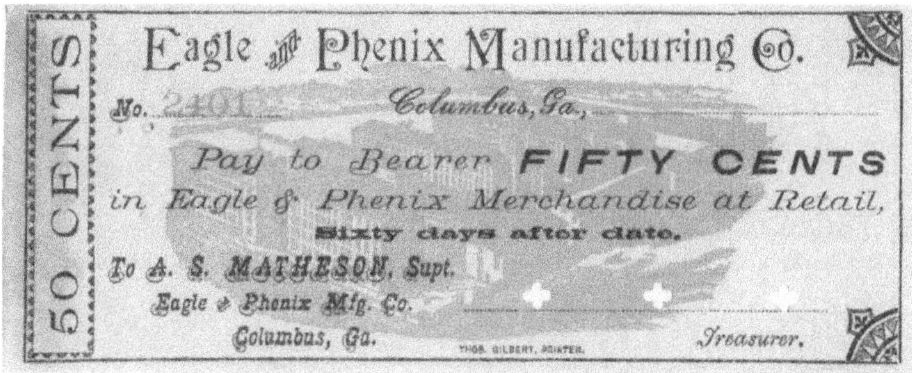

Eagle and Phenix Manufacturing Co.

GA200-.50 50 Cents ND (1893). Black on pink paper. Orange underprint design of large factory building at center. Back orange. Size: 143 × 60mm. Imprint: Thos. Gilbert, Printer. (shown at 85%)
 c. Unissued, cancelled. R5

GA200-1. 1 Dollar ND (1893). Black. As above. (shown at 63%)
 c. Unissued, cancelled. R5

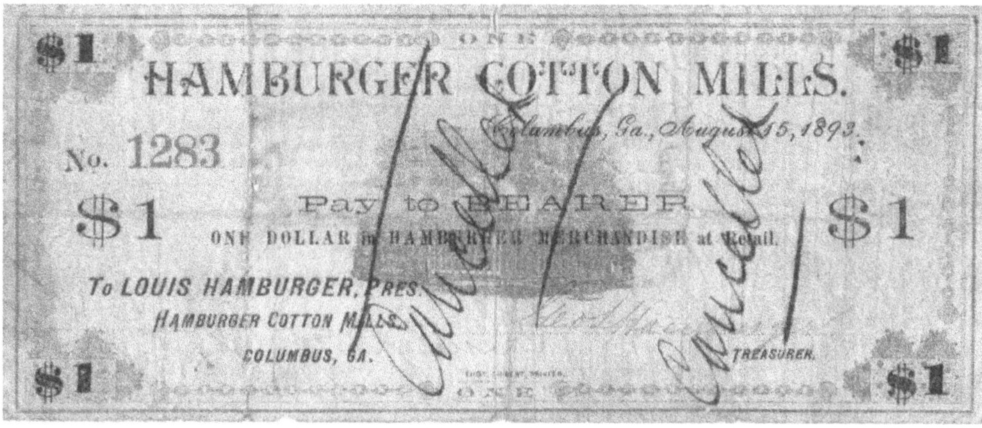

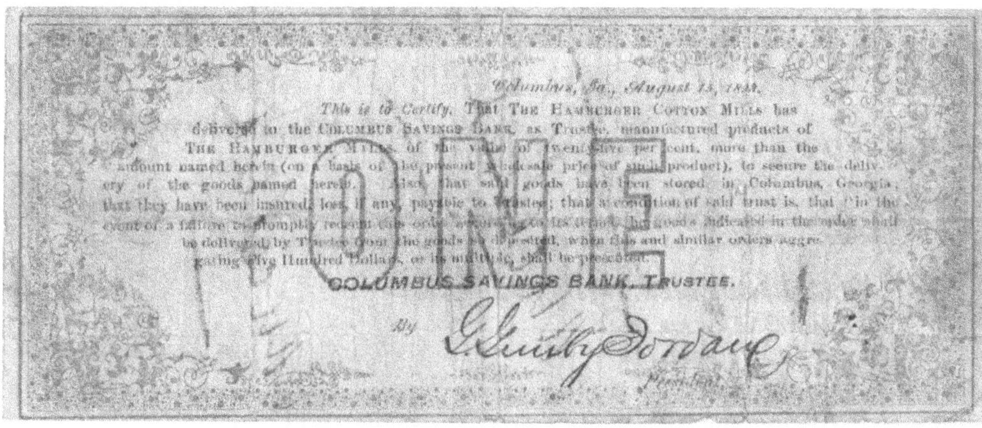

Hamburger Cotton Mills

GA220-1. 1 Dollar Aug. 15, 1893. Black and brown. Building at center. Long text on back relative to use of this certificate. Imprint: Thos. Gilbert, Printer. (shown at 70%)

b. Issued, cancelled. R5

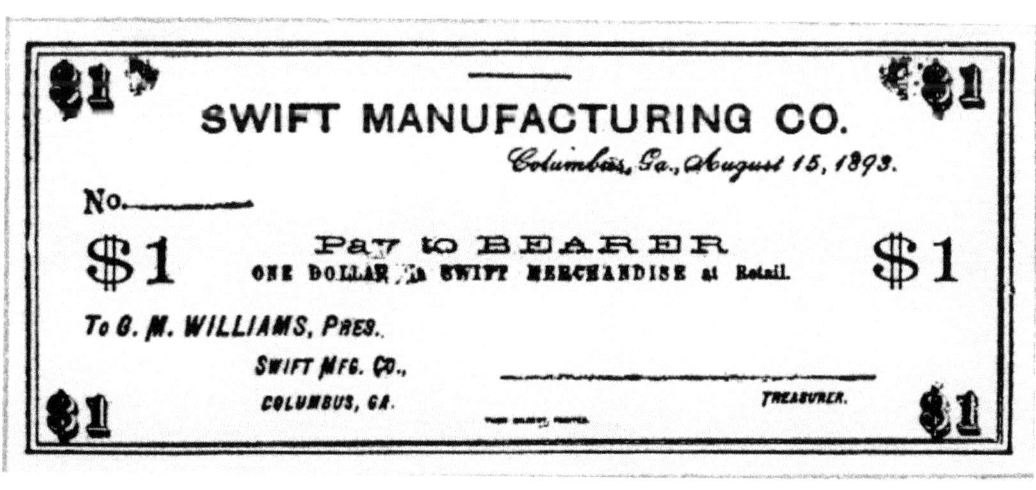

Swift Manufacturing Co.

GA240-1. 1 Dollar Aug. 15, 1893. (b/w) (shown at 88%)

d. Unissued, remainder. R5

Eatonton

The Middle Georgia Bank

GA260-1. 1 Dollar Certificate of Deposit 1893. Black. (b/w)
d. Unissued, remainder. **R5**

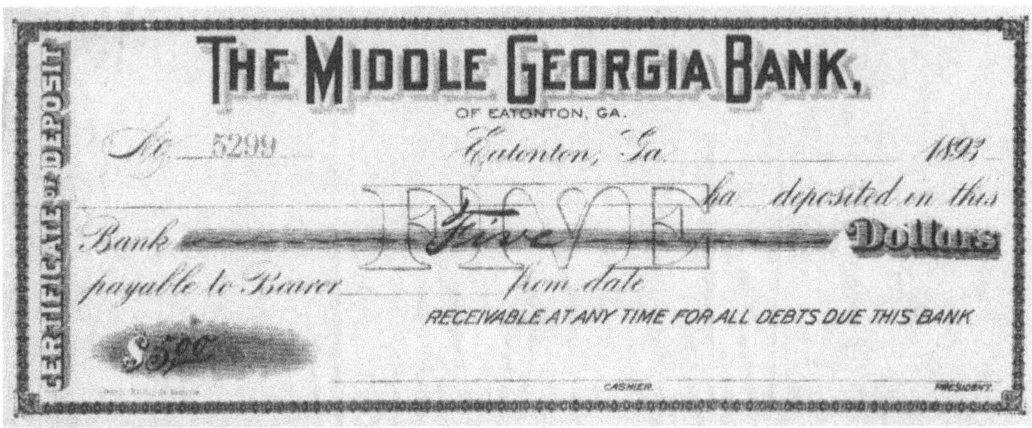

GA260-5. 5 Dollars 1893. Black on yellow paper. Uniface. Imprint: Brandon Printing Co. Nashville. (shown at 73%)
d. Unissued, remainder. **R5**

Elberton

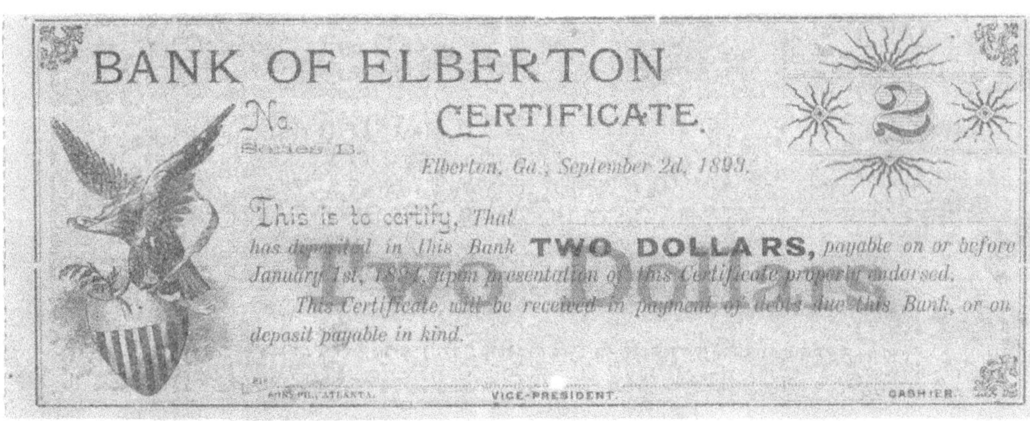

Bank of Elberton

GA280-2. 2 Dollars Sept. 2, 1893. Blue-black on green underprint. Eagle and shield at left. Red denomination words across lower center. Uniface. Series B. Imprint: Sisson, Pr., Atlanta. (shown at 70%)
d. Unissued, remainder. **R2**

GA280-5. 5 Dollars Sept. 2, 1893. As above. (Stub at left.) Series C.
c. Unissued, cancelled. **R4**

Macon

The Exchange Bank

GA300-1. 1 Dollar Certificate of Deposit Sept. 1, 1893 (stamped date). Black on light green underprint. Large denomination outline word in orange at center. Back orange with vertical text stating backing for the note. Imprint: Brandon Printing Co. Nashville. (shown at 65%)

a. Issued, not cancelled. R3

GA300-10. 10 Dollars (1893). As above.

d. Unissued, remainder. R4

GA300-20. 20 Dollars (1893). As above.

d. Unissued, remainder. R4

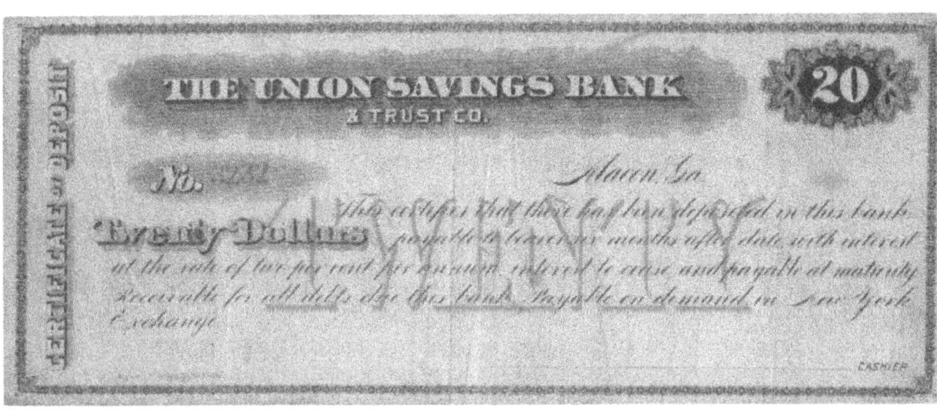

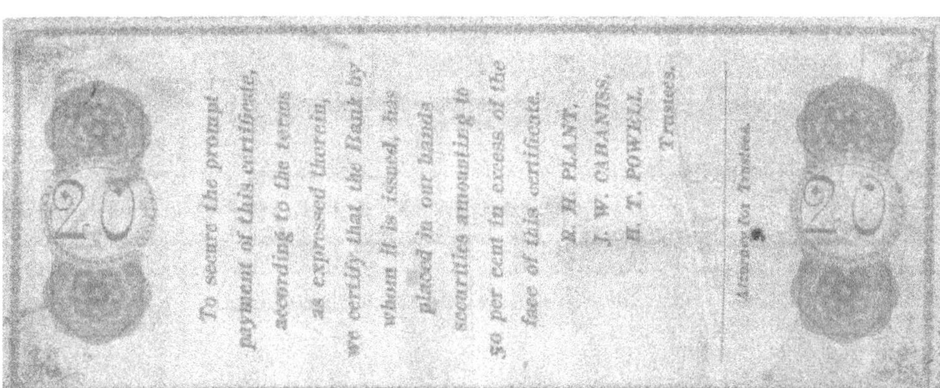

The Union Savings Bank & Trust Co.

GA305-20. 20 Dollars Certificate of Deposit (1893). Similar to GA300-20. (shown at 65%)
d. Unissued, remainder. **R4**

Newnan

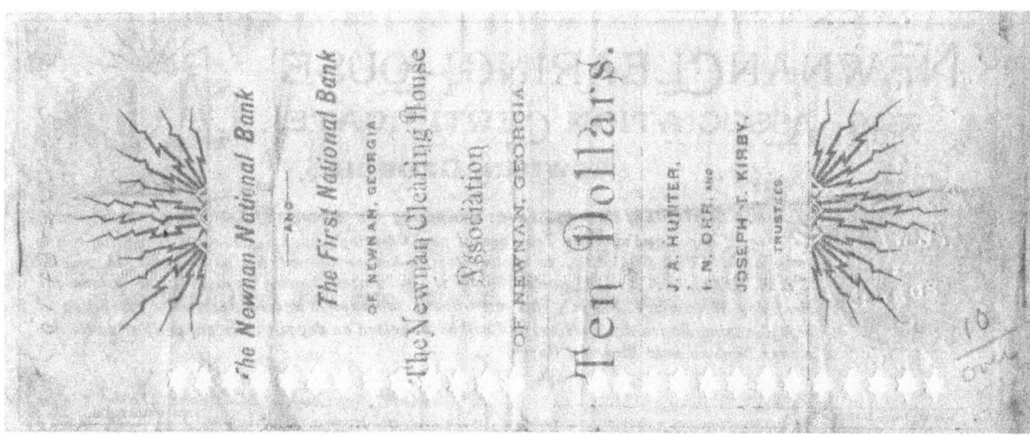

Newnan Clearing House Association Certificate

GA320-10. 10 Dollars ND. Payable on or before Jan. 1, 1894. Black on pink underprint. Red denomination words across center right. State seal at left. Back blue; vertical list of member banks. Imprint: Sisson, Pr., Atlanta. (shown at 73%)
b. Issued, cancelled. **R5**
c. Unissued, cancelled. **R5**

NOTE: A $1 and $5 are reported to have been part of the Newnan issue. Only the $10 has been verified; no details are known about the others at present.

Louisiana

New Orleans

Loan Committee of the New Orleans Clearing House Association

LA100-Var. Various Amounts 189_ (1893). Amount of certificate to be filled in at upper right. (b/w)
d. Unissued, remainder. **R5**

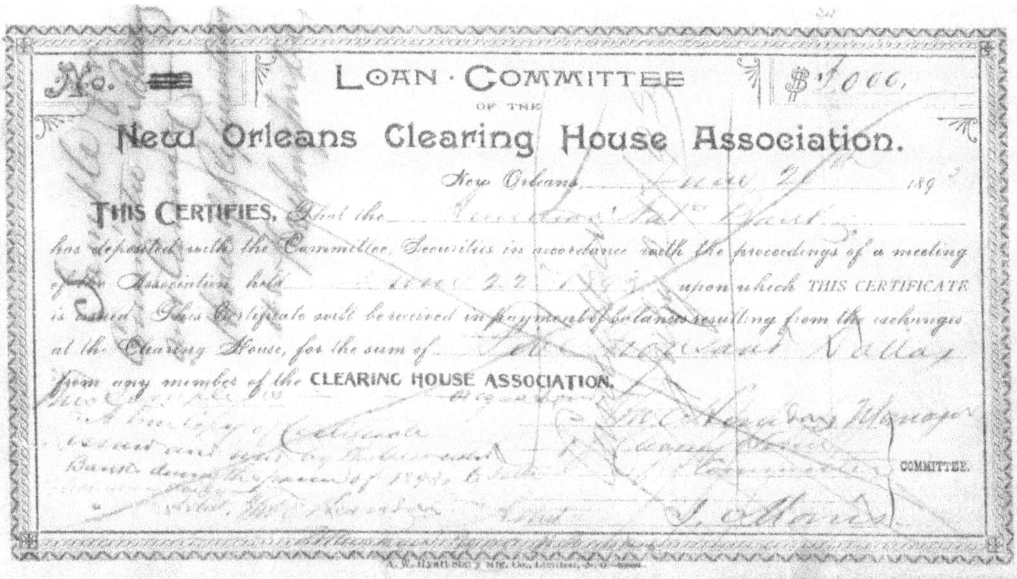
No.

LOAN · COMMITTEE

OF THE

New Orleans Clearing House Association.

$1000,

New Orleans 189

THIS CERTIFIES, That the

has deposited with the Committee, Securities in accordance with the proceedings of a meeting of the Association held upon which THIS CERTIFICATE is issued. This Certificate will be received in payment of balances resulting from the exchanges at the Clearing House, for the sum of

from any member of the CLEARING HOUSE ASSOCIATION.

Manager

COMMITTEE.

LA100-5000. 5,000 Dollars Loan Certificate June 26, 1893. Black. Issued in the name of the American National Bank. Imprint: A.W. Hyatt Stat'y Mfg. Co., Limited, N.O. Large size. (shown at 57%)

b. Issued, cancelled. **R5**

d. Unissued, remainder. **R5**

NOTE: Handwritten inscription vertically in red at upper left, "Sample for Committee on Banking and Currency, House of Representatives U.S., Washington, D.C." One report mentions an issue of clearing house certificates for New Orleans ranging from "$500 to $10,000." Another indicates use of lower-value certificates in denominations of $5, $10, $50 and $100. Information is clearly needed here.

In 1896 this association issued loan certificates to a total of $399,000.00.

MARYLAND

Baltimore

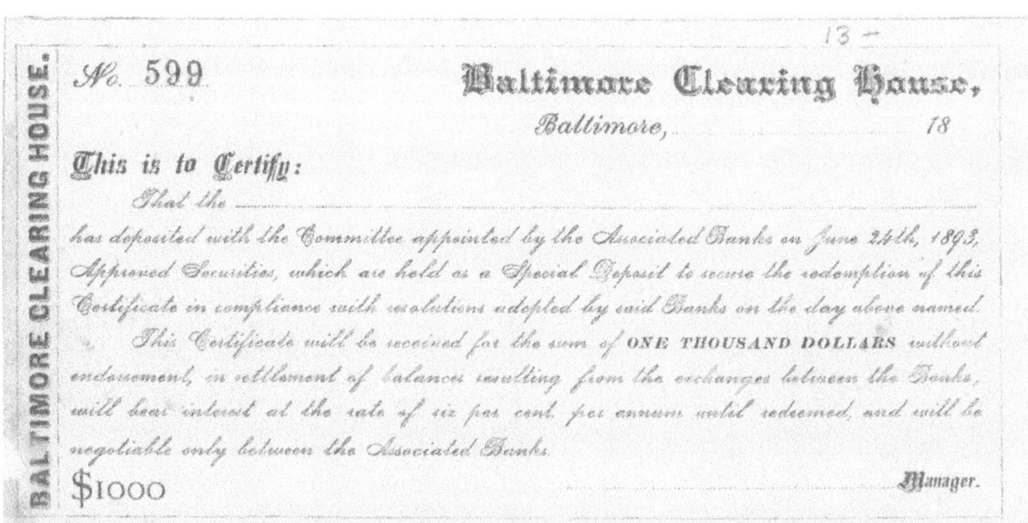
BALTIMORE CLEARING HOUSE.

No. 599

Baltimore Clearing House,

Baltimore, 18

This is to Certify:

That the

has deposited with the Committee appointed by the Associated Banks on June 24th, 1893, Approved Securities, which are held as a Special Deposit to secure the redemption of this Certificate in compliance with resolutions adopted by said Banks on the day above named.

This Certificate will be received for the sum of ONE THOUSAND DOLLARS without endorsement, in settlement of balances resulting from the exchanges between the Banks, will bear interest at the rate of six per cent. per annum until redeemed, and will be negotiable only between the Associated Banks.

$1000

Manager.

Baltimore Clearing House

MD100-1000. 1,000 Dollars June 24, 1893. Black. Uniface. Larger size. (shown at 68%)
  d. Unissued, remainder. **R5**
MD100-3000. 3,000 Dollars ND (1893). Black. As above.
  d. Unissued, remainder. **R5**
MD100-6000. 6,000 Dollars ND (1893). Black. As above.
  d. Unissued, remainder. **R5**

Massachusetts

Boston

Loan Committee of the Boston Clearing House Association

MA100-5000. 5,000 Dollars June 26, 1893. Black. Large size.
  c. Unissued, cancelled. **R5**

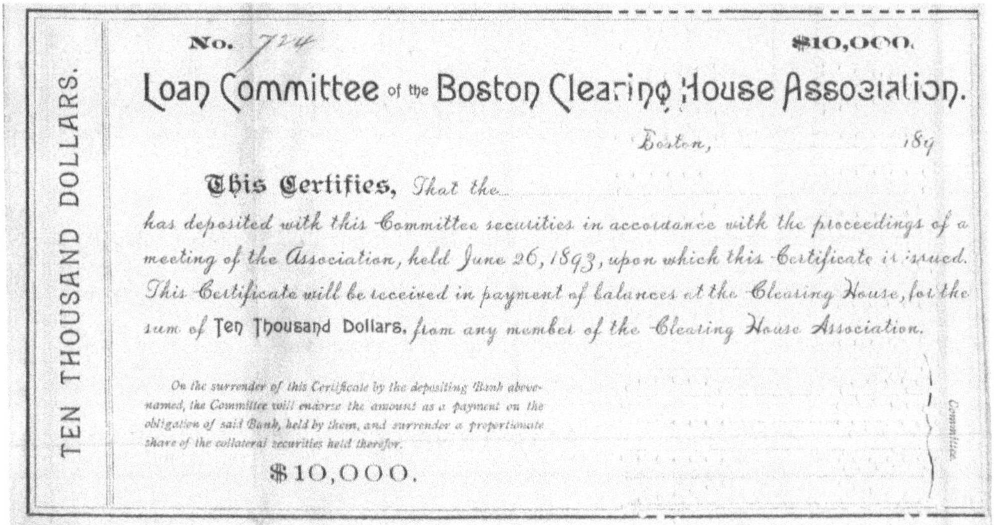
TEN THOUSAND DOLLARS.
No. 724 $10,000.
Loan Committee of the Boston Clearing House Association.
Boston, 189
This Certifies, That the
has deposited with this Committee securities in accordance with the proceedings of a meeting of the Association, held June 26, 1893, upon which this Certificate is issued. This Certificate will be received in payment of balances at the Clearing House, for the sum of Ten Thousand Dollars, from any member of the Clearing House Association.
On the surrender of this Certificate by the depositing Bank above-named, the Committee will endorse the amount as a payment on the obligation of said Bank, held by them, and surrender a proportionate share of the collateral securities held therefor.
$10,000.
Committee.

MA100-10,000. 10,000 Dollars June 26, 1893. Black. As above. (shown at 50%)
  c. Unissued, cancelled. **R5**
NOTE: The Boston Clearing House Association also issued loan certificates in 1895 to a total of $235,000.00.

Fall River

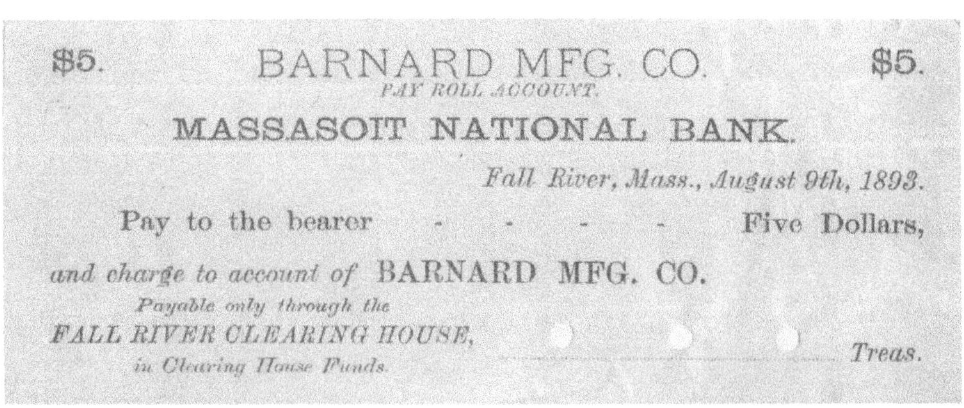
$5. BARNARD MFG. CO. $5.
PAY ROLL ACCOUNT.
MASSASOIT NATIONAL BANK.
Fall River, Mass., August 9th, 1893.
Pay to the bearer - - - - Five Dollars,
and charge to account of BARNARD MFG. CO.
Payable only through the
FALL RIVER CLEARING HOUSE,
in Clearing House Funds.
Treas.

BARNARD MFG. CO./MASSASOIT NATIONAL BANK

MA140-5. 5 Dollars Pay Roll Account check Aug. 9, 1893. Black on light tan paper. Uniface. (shown at 70%)
c. Unissued, cancelled. **R5**

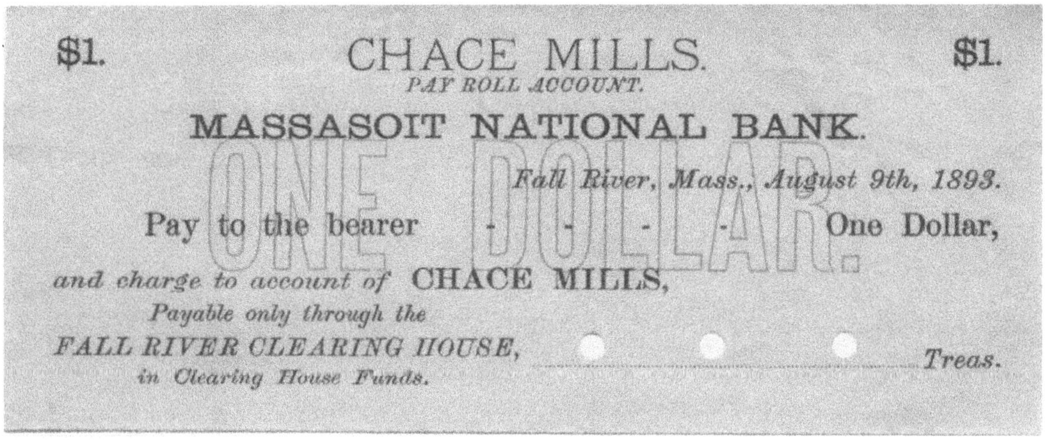

CHACE MILLS/MASSASOIT NATIONAL BANK

MA160-1. 1 Dollar Pay Roll Account check Aug. 9, 1893. Black on dull peach paper. Red outline value in words across center. Uniface. (shown at 75%)
c. Unissued, cancelled. **R5**

MA160-2. 2 Dollars Aug. 9, 1893. As above (newspaper illustration).
u. Issued.... **SENC**

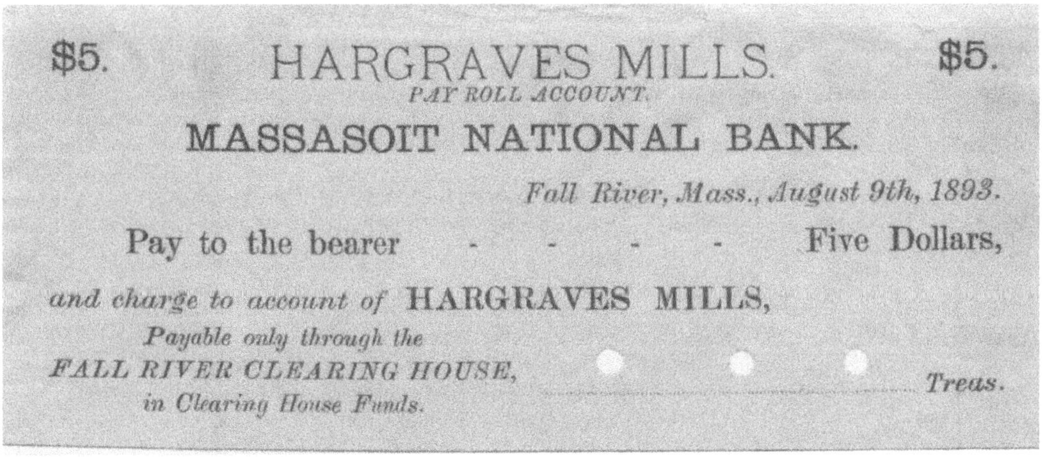

HARGRAVES MILLS/MASSASOIT NATIONAL BANK

MA180-5. 5 Dollars Pay Roll Account check Aug. 9, 1893. As MA140-5. (shown at 78%)
c. Unissued, cancelled. **R5**

Tecumseh Mills/Massasoit National Bank

MA200-2. 2 Dollars Pay Roll Account check Aug. 9, 1893. Black on blue paper. Uniface. (shown at 75%)
c. Unissued, cancelled. R5

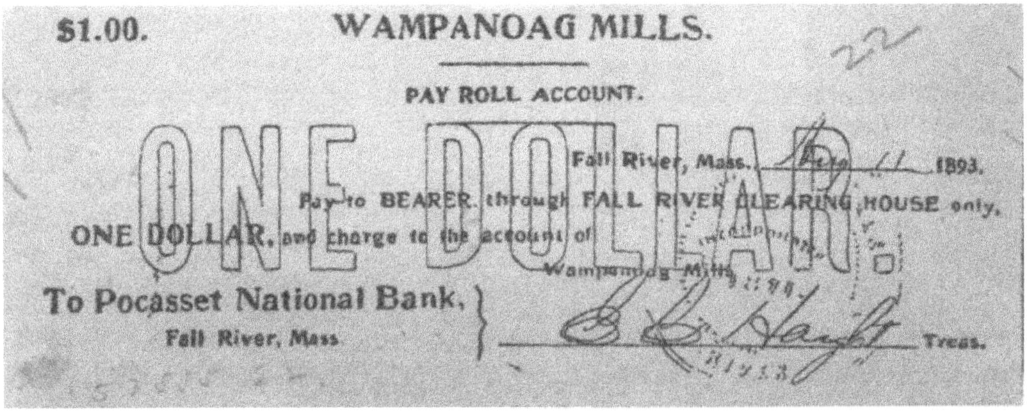

Wampanoag Mills/Pocasset National Bank

MA220-1. 1 Dollar Pay Roll Account check Aug. 11, 1893. Embossed seal at lower right (newspaper illustration). (shown at 75%)
u. Issued. SENC

New Bedford

Howland Mills Corporation

MA250-1. 1 Dollar Pay Roll Account check Aug. 11, 1893. Black on pink paper. Uniface. Redemption stamping on back. (shown at 75%)
b. Issued, cancelled. R5

MA250-2. 2 Dollars Aug. 11, 1893. Blue. As above.
b. Issued, cancelled. R5

MA250-5. 5 Dollars Aug. 11, 1893. Red. As above.
b. Issued, cancelled. R5

MA250-10. 10 Dollars Aug. 11, 1893. Blue-green. As above.
b. Issued, cancelled. R5

New Bedford Manufacturing Co.

MA270-1. 1 Dollar Pay Roll Account check Aug. 10, 1893. Black on yellow-green paper. Uniface. Redemption stamping on back.
b. Issued, cancelled. R5

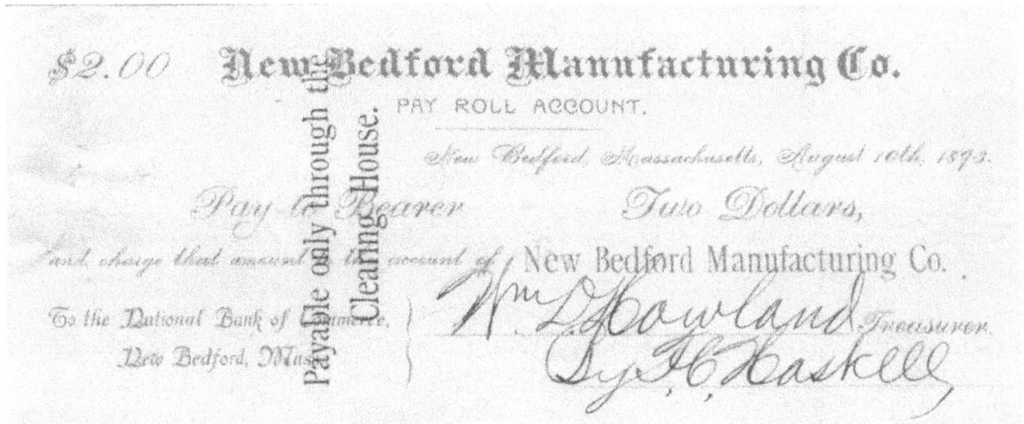

MA270-2. 2 Dollars Aug. 10, 1893. Blue. As above. (shown at 74%)
b. Issued, cancelled. R5

MA270-5. 5 Dollars Aug. 10, 1893. Red. As above.
b. Issued, cancelled. R5

MA270-10. 10 Dollars Aug. 10, 1893. Blue-green. As above.
b. Issued, cancelled. R5

Rotch Spinning Corporation

MA290-1. 1 Dollar Pay Roll Account check Aug. 10, 1893. Black on blue paper. Uniface. Redemption stamping on back. (shown at 75%)
b. Issued, cancelled. R5

MA290-2. 2 Dollars Aug. 10, 1893. Blue. As above.
b. Issued, cancelled. **R5**
MA290-5. 5 Dollars Aug. 10, 1893. Red. As above, but without stamping on back.
a. Issued, not cancelled. **R5**
MA290-10. 10 Dollars Aug. 10, 1893. Blue-green. As MA290-2.
b. Issued, cancelled. **R5**

North Adams

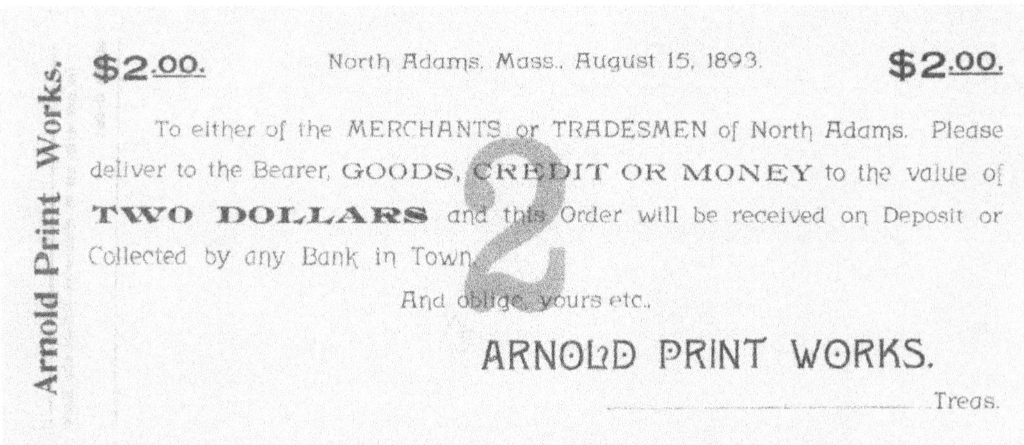

Arnold Print Works

MA325-2. 2 Dollars (payroll check) Aug. 15, 1893. Black. Green value numeral at center. One line of vertical text on back. (shown at 68%)
a. Issued, not cancelled. **R4**
d. Unissued, remainder. **VG, 90. VF, 185.**
MA325-5.A 5 Dollars Aug. 15, 1893. As above. Dark blue value numeral at center. Value in larger black type at upper left and right.
a. Issued, not cancelled. **R4**
d. Unissued, remainder. **VG, 150. VF, 225.**

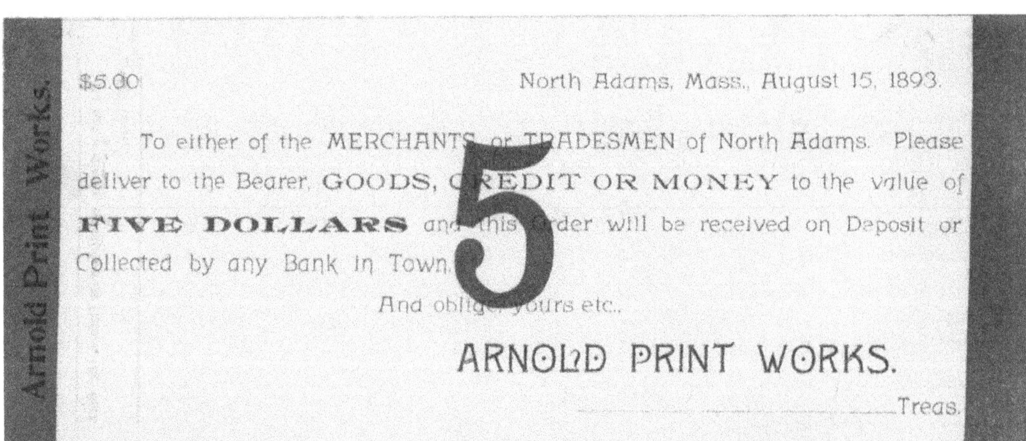

MA325-5.B 5 Dollars Aug. 15, 1893. Text and color as above. Dark blue strip at left and right borders. Value in smaller numerals but only at upper left. (shown at 66%)
c. Unissued, cancelled. **R1**
MA325-10.A 10 Dollars Aug. 15, 1893. Large value numeral at center. (b/w)
c. Unissued, cancelled. **R4**

MA325-10.B 10 Dollars Aug. 15, 1893. Black on light yellow paper. Pink value numerals and strips in style as 5.B.

c. Unissued, cancelled. **R4**

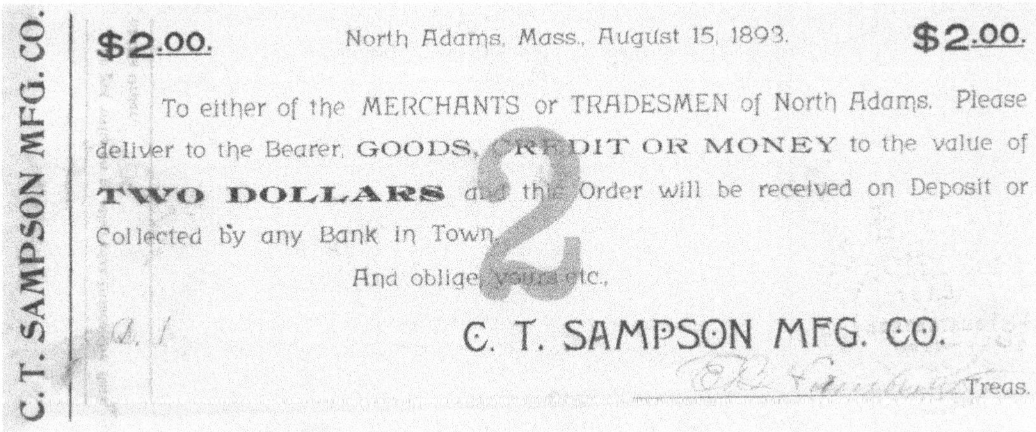
C. T. SAMPSON MFG. CO.

$2.00. North Adams, Mass., August 15, 1893. $2.00.

To either of the MERCHANTS or TRADESMEN of North Adams. Please deliver to the Bearer, GOODS, CREDIT OR MONEY to the value of TWO DOLLARS and this Order will be received on Deposit or Collected by any Bank in Town.

And oblige, yours etc.,

C. T. SAMPSON MFG. CO.

Treas.

C. T. Sampson Mfg. Co.

MA360-2. 2 Dollars (payroll check) Aug. 15, 1893. Black. Large value numeral in aqua at center. Embossed seal at lower right. (shown at 69%)

b. Issued, cancelled. **R5**

MICHIGAN

Detroit

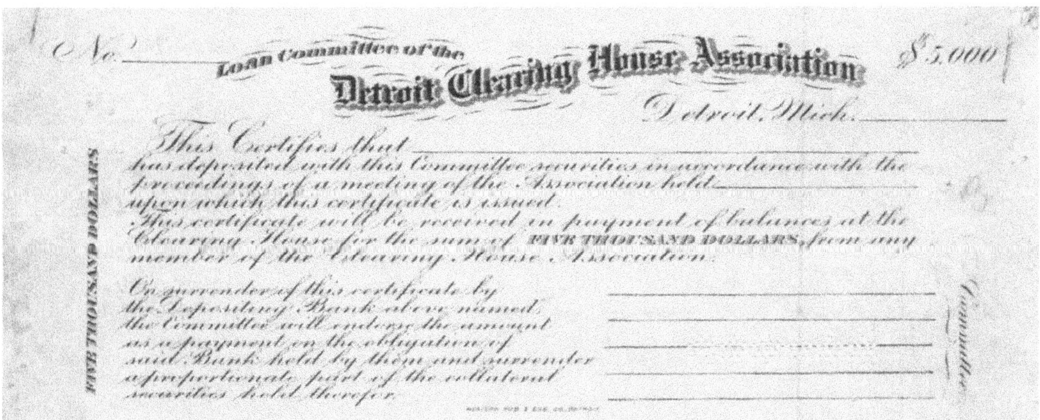
No. ____ Loan Committee of the Detroit Clearing House Association $5,000

Detroit, Mich. ____

This Certifies that ____ has deposited with this Committee securities in accordance with the proceedings of a meeting of the Association held ____ upon which this certificate is issued.

This certificate will be received in payment of balances at the Clearing House for the sum of FIVE THOUSAND DOLLARS, from any member of the Clearing House Association.

On surrender of this certificate by the Depositing Bank above named, the Committee will endorse the amount as a payment on the obligation of said Bank held by them and surrender a proportionate part of the collateral securities held therefor.

Committee

FIVE THOUSAND DOLLARS

Detroit Clearing House Association

MI100-5000. 5,000 Dollars Loan Certificate ND (1893). Black. Uniface. Imprint: Western Pub. & Eng. Co. Detroit. (shown at 66%)

c. Unissued, cancelled. **R4**

MINNESOTA

Minneapolis

JAS. JOHNS & CO./BROOKS-GRIFFITHS CO.

MN125-10. 10 Dollars (payroll check) Sept. 1, 1893. Design and printer similar to MN150-5. (b/w)
- d. Unissued, remainder. **R5**

MINNEAPOLIS & NORTHERN ELEVATOR CO.

MN150-5. 5 Dollars (payroll check) Sept. 1, 1893. Black on light blue and pink underprint. Back maroon; state seals of North Dakota, Minnesota and South Dakota across. Imprint at center (on face only): Northwestern Lith. & Pub. Co. Minneapolis. (shown at 72%)
- a. Issued, not cancelled. **R5**
- b. Issued, cancelled. **R4**
- c. Unissued, cancelled. **R4**

THE MINNEAPOLIS THRESHING MACHINE CO.

MN175-1. 1 Dollar (payroll check) Sept. 1, 1896 (stamped over original date of Sept. 10, 1896). Design as MN150-5. (b/w)
- a. Issued, not cancelled. **R5**

VICTORIA ELEVATOR CO.

MN200-2. 2 Dollars 189_ (1893). Design similar to MN200-5. (b/w)
- d. Unissued, remainder. **R5**

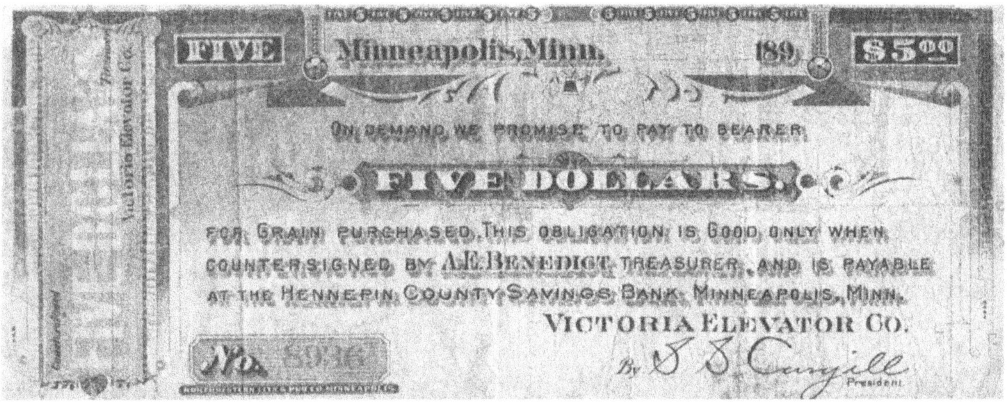

MN200-5. 5 Dollars 189_ (1893). Face black on gray paper, otherwise colors, design and imprint as MN150-5. Imprint appears at left on face, at center on back. (shown at 70%)

a. Issued, not cancelled. R5

c. Unissued, cancelled. R5

Red Wing

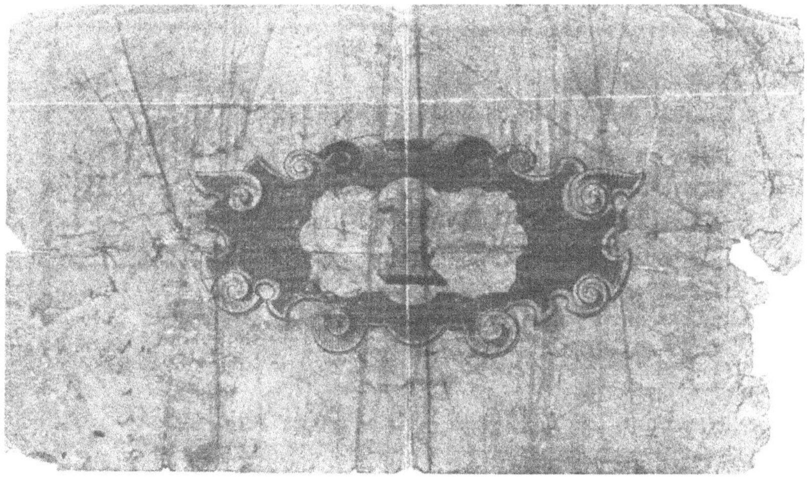

Red Wing Stoneware Company

MN240-1. 1 Dollar (payroll note) ND (1893). Black on blue paper. Payable until March 1, 1894. Small size note (113 × 70mm). (shown at 60%)
a. Issued, not cancelled. R5

Mississippi

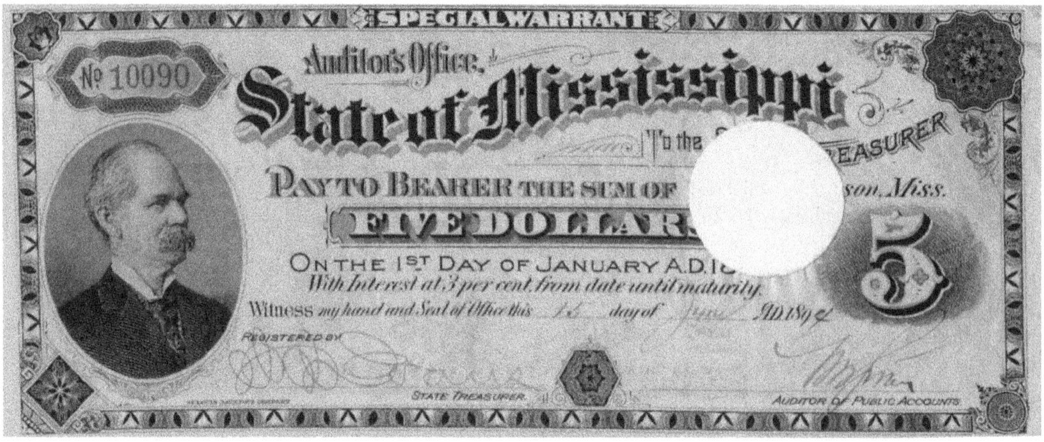

1894 Issue, State of Mississippi

MS100-5. 5 Dollars 3% Special Warrant June 15, 1894 (handwritten date). Black on light green paper. Portrait of Governor John M. Stone at left. Back green; large elk head at left. Imprint: St. Louis Bank Note Company. (shown at 76%)
b. Issued, cancelled. **VF, 60. Unc., 175.**
p. Proof or trial piece. Uniface back in red-brown. **R2**

MS100-10. 10 Dollars June 15, 1894 (handwritten date). Black. Back brown. Design and printer as above.
b. Issued, cancelled. **VF, 110. Unc., 225.**

MS100-20. 20 Dollars June 15, 1894 (handwritten date). Black. Back green. Design and printer as above.
b. Issued, cancelled. **VF, 225. Unc., 400.**

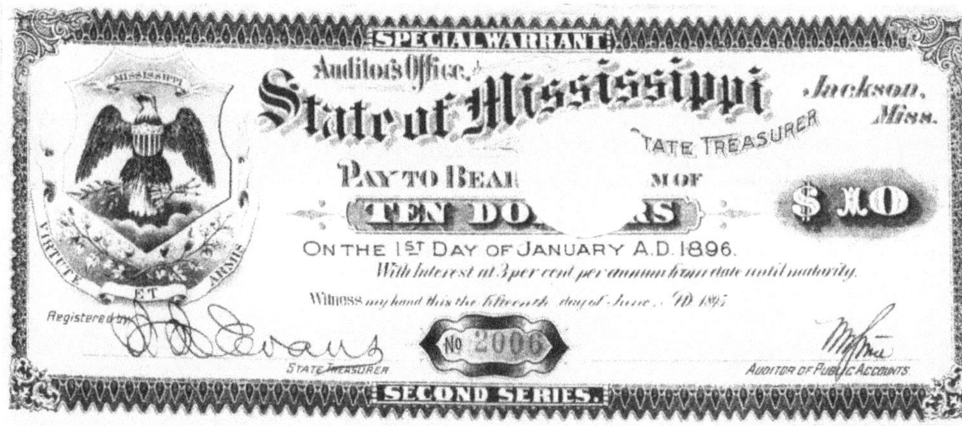

1895 Issue, State of Mississippi

MS120-10. 10 Dollars 3% Special Warrant June 15, 1895. Black. State seal at left. Back brown; field hands picking cotton at center. Imprint: S.C. Toof & Co. Memphis. (shown at 65%)

b. Issued, cancelled. **VF, 100. Unc., 225.**

Nevada

Carson City

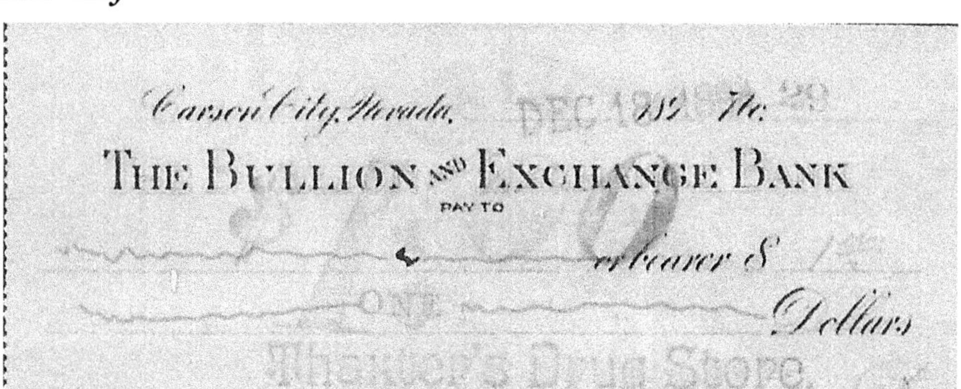

Thaxter's Drug Store

NV125-1. 1 Dollar bearer check Dec. 18, 1894 (stamped date). Black text on dull green paper. Large denomination in purple on face, also in word below. Drawn on account with the Bullion and Exchange Bank. (shown at 76%)

a. Issued, not cancelled. R5

New York

Amsterdam

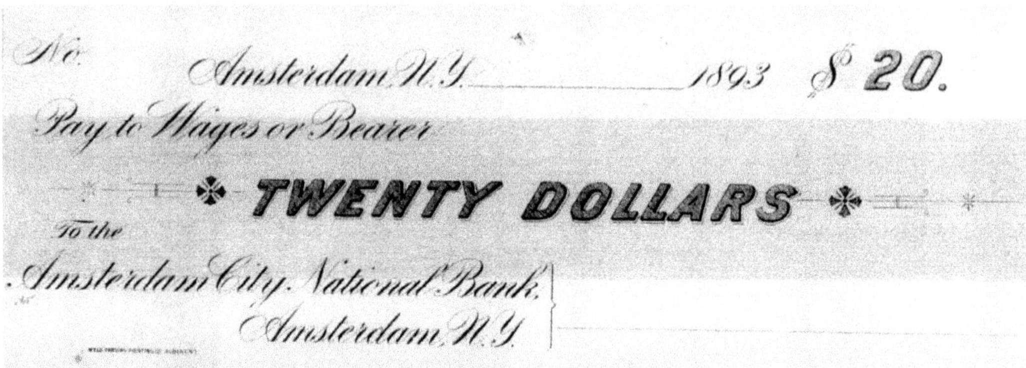

Amsterdam City National Bank

NY100-20. 20 Dollars (pay check) 1893. Black and green. Uniface. Imprint: Weed Parsons Printing Co. Albany, N.Y. (shown at 74%)

c. Unissued, cancelled. R4
d. Unissued, remainder. R4

Buffalo

NOTE: Reportedly all associated banks in Buffalo took out clearing house certificates for amounts of $1,000 and $5,000 but not all banks issued them. No further details are known at present. See also the listing in Appendix B.

Marine Bank

NY150-5. 5 Dollars Pay-Roll Check 1893. Black on white paper. Uniface.

c. Unissued, cancelled. R5
d. Unissued, remainder. R5

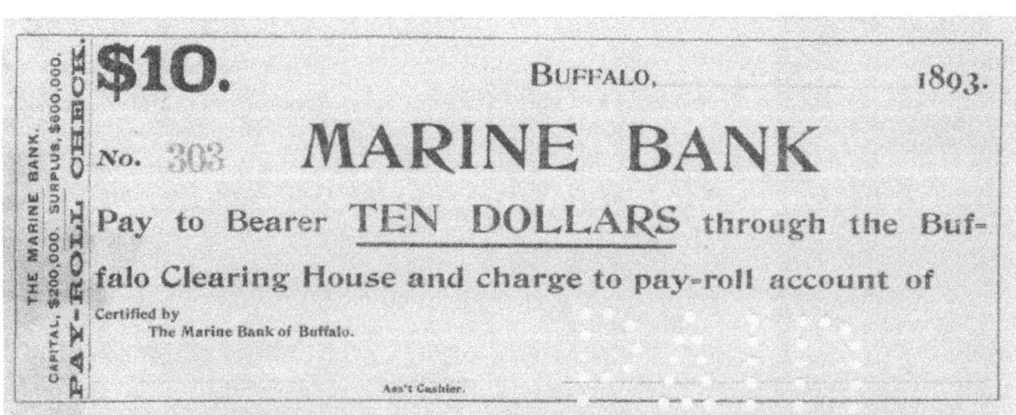

NY150-10. 10 Dollars 1893. Black on light green paper. As above. (shown at 66%)
c. Unissued, cancelled. R5

New York City

Loan Committee of the New York Clearing House Association

NY200-5,000. 5,000 Dollars June 15, 1893. Black on gold paper. Large size. (shown at 54%)
c. Unissued, cancelled. R5
NY200-10,000. 10,000 Dollars June 15, 1893. Black on white paper. As above.
c. Unissued, cancelled. R5
NY200-20,000. 20,000 Dollars June 15, 1893. Black on pink paper. As above.
c. Unissued, cancelled. R5

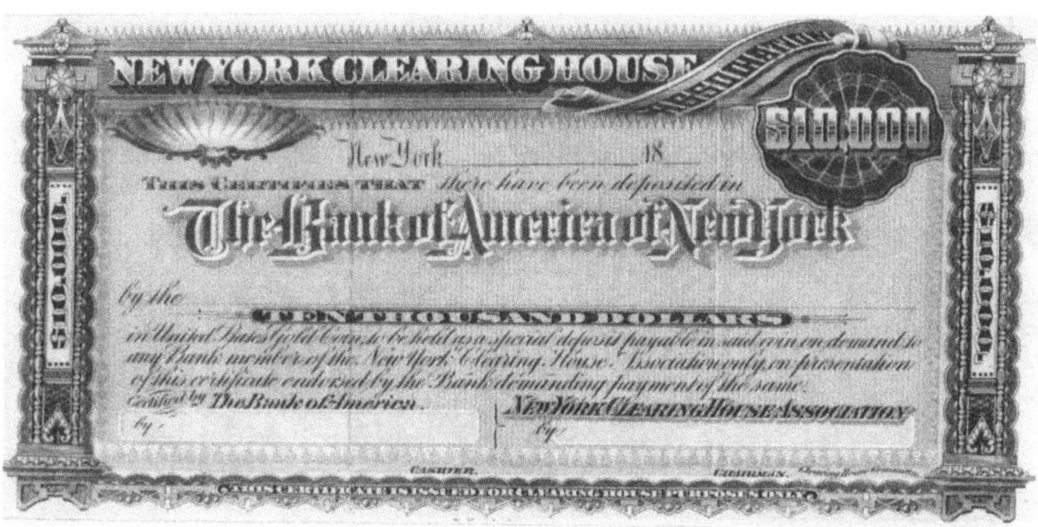

New York Clearing House/The Bank of America of New York

NY225-10,000. 10,000 Dollars (certificate of deposit) 18__. Payable in United States Gold Coin. Black on light brown underprint. (shown at 63%) R5

NEW YORK, LAKE ERIE & WESTERN RAILROAD COMPANY/
NATIONAL BANK OF THE REPUBLIC

NY250-20. 20 Dollars Pay Roll Draft Aug., 1893. Black. Train and buildings at left. Uniface. Imprint: American Bank Note Co. New York, Litho. (shown at 66%)
p. Proof. R5

OHIO

Akron

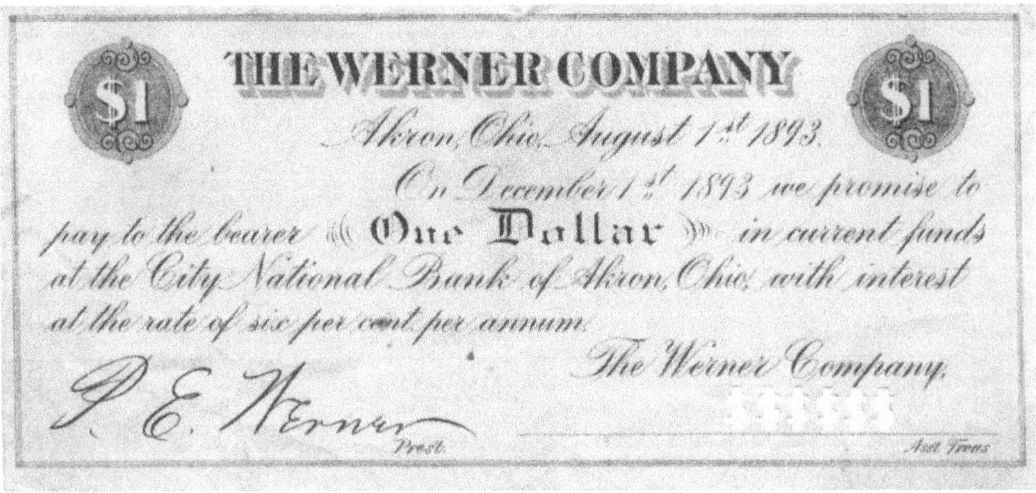

THE WERNER COMPANY

OH100-1. 1 Dollar (payroll check) Aug. 1, 1893. Dark blue on yellow paper. Uniface. (shown at 80%)
c. Unissued, cancelled. R5

Cincinnati

CLEARING HOUSE CERTIFICATE

OH150-10,000. 10,000 Dollars (loan certificate) 1893. Four signature lines at lower right.
d. Unissued, remainder. R5

Cleveland

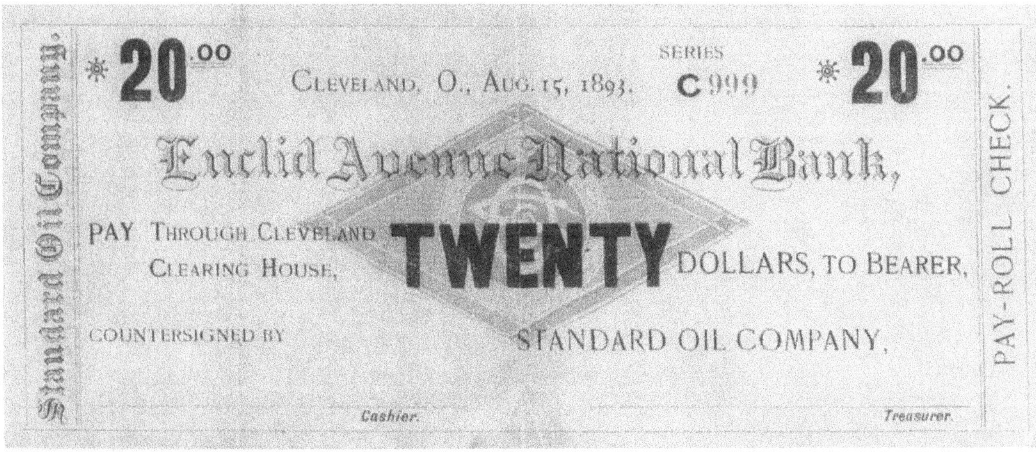

STANDARD OIL COMPANY/EUCLID AVENUE NATIONAL BANK

OH200-20. 20 Dollars Pay-Roll Check Aug. 15, 1893. Dark blue on light blue-gray paper. Company emblem in brown diamond design as underprint at center. One text line on back. (shown at 76%)
d. Unissued, remainder. R4

Massillon

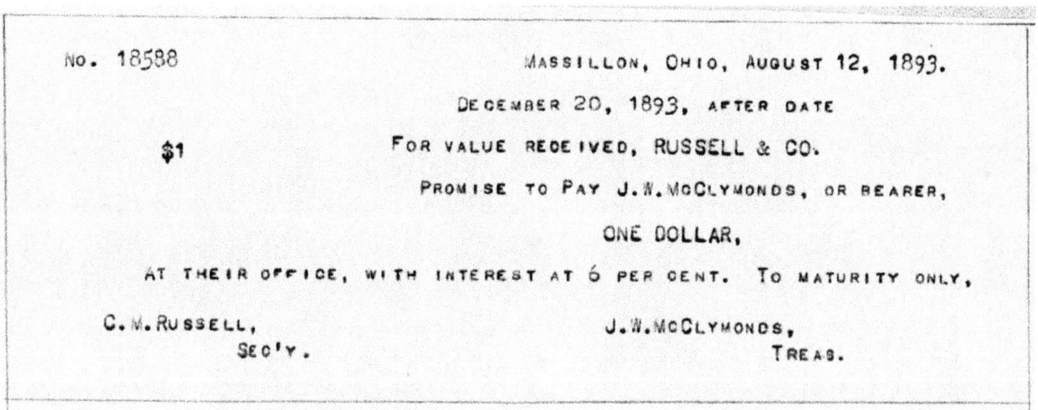
No. 18588 MASSILLON, OHIO, AUGUST 12, 1893.

DECEMBER 20, 1893, AFTER DATE

$1 FOR VALUE RECEIVED, RUSSELL & CO.

PROMISE TO PAY J.W.McCLYMONDS, OR BEARER,

ONE DOLLAR,

AT THEIR OFFICE, WITH INTEREST AT 6 PER CENT. TO MATURITY ONLY,

C.M.RUSSELL, SEC'Y. J.W.McCLYMONDS, TREAS.

RUSSELL & CO.

OH250-1. 1 Dollar (6% interest-bearing note) Aug. 12, 1893. (word copy) (shown at 82%)
u. Issued? SENC

Oklahoma

Kingfisher City

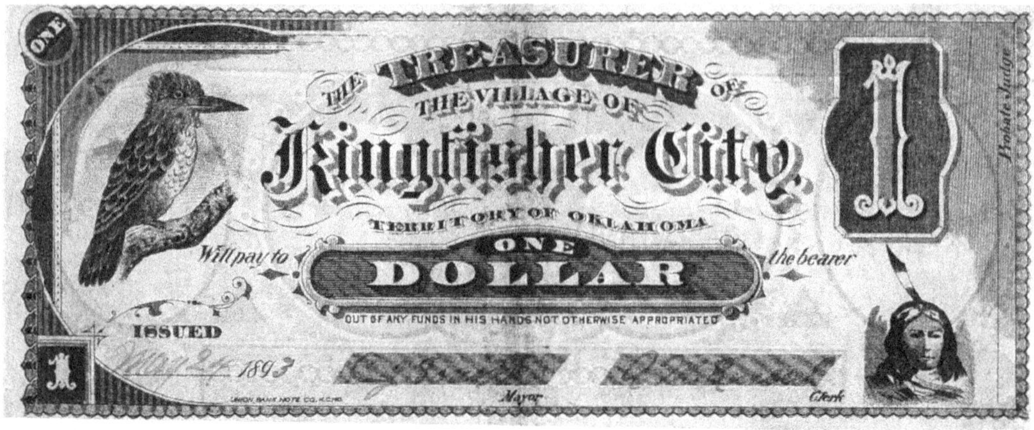

Village of Kingfisher City

OK100-1. 1 Dollar (treasury note) May 24, 1893 (handwritten date). Black on tan paper. Kingfisher at left, value and Indian head at right. Back brown; large eagle at center flanked by urban and rural scenes. Imprint: Union Bank Note Co. K.C. Mo. (shown at 75%)

a. Issued, not cancelled. **R4**

OK100-2. 2 Dollars May 24, 1893. As above.

a. Issued, not cancelled. **R4**

NOTE: An example of OK100-2. hand dated Dec. 9, 1891 was offered in the R. M. Smythe Memphis Sale of July, 2007 (lot 1572).

PENNSYLVANIA

Johnstown

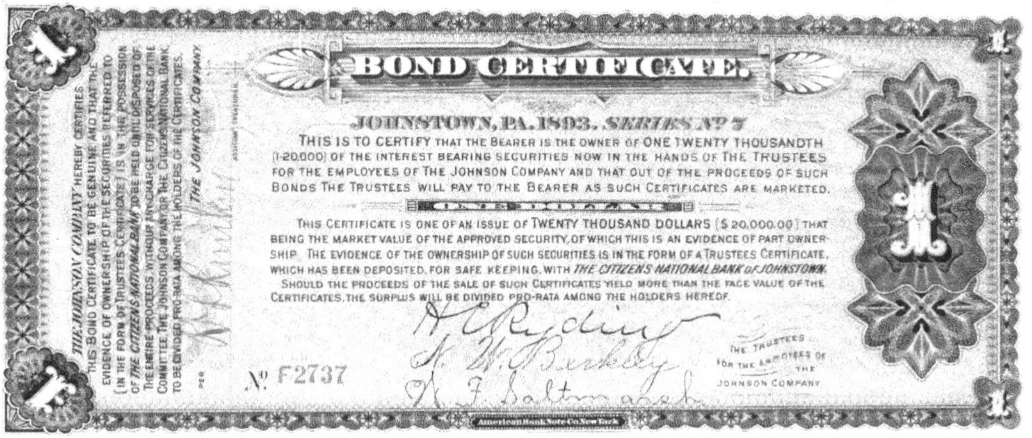

THE JOHNSON COMPANY/
THE CITIZENS NATIONAL BANK OF JOHNSTOWN

PA100-1. 1 Dollar Bond Certificate 1893. Black on red-brown underprint. Back red-brown. Imprint: American Bank Note Co. New York. (shown at 66%)

a. Issued, not cancelled. R4

b. Issued, cancelled. R2

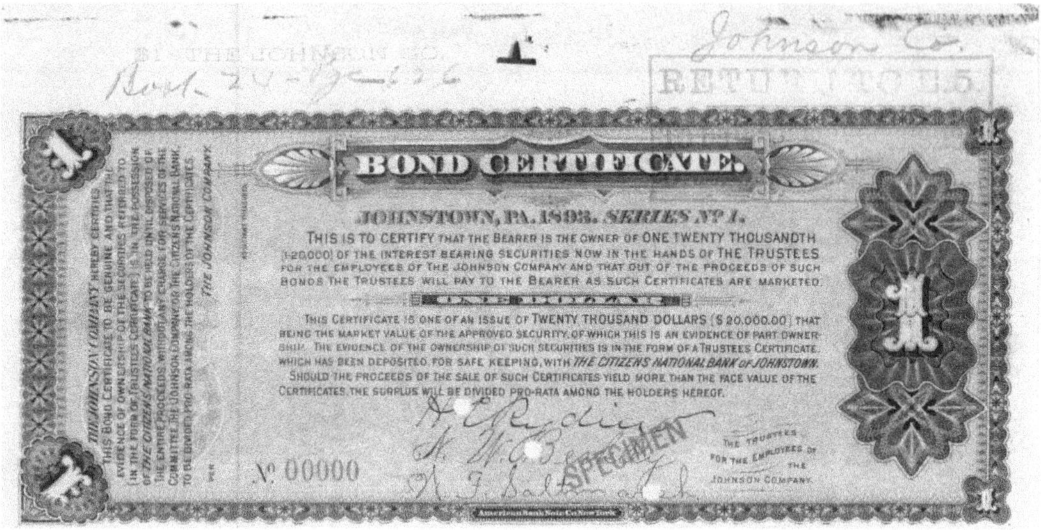

f. Specimen. (shown at 64%) R2

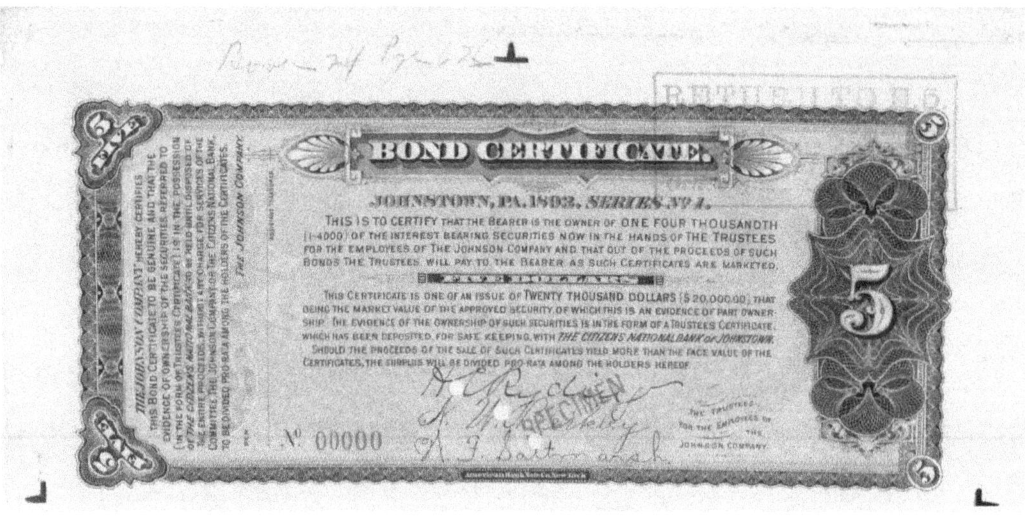

PA100-5. 5 Dollars 1893. Black on brown underprint. Back brown. As above. (shown at 58%)
f. Specimen. **R3**

NOTE: The Johnson Steel Street Rail Company was the original name of this firm. In 1888 it was changed to The Johnson Company.

Philadelphia

Loan Committee of the Philadelphia Clearing House Association

PA150-5000. 5000 Dollars 1893. (list)
u. Unissued. **R5**

NOTE: In 1895 the Philadelphia Clearing House Association issued a total of $8,220,000.00 in certificates.

The Pennsylvania Railroad Company

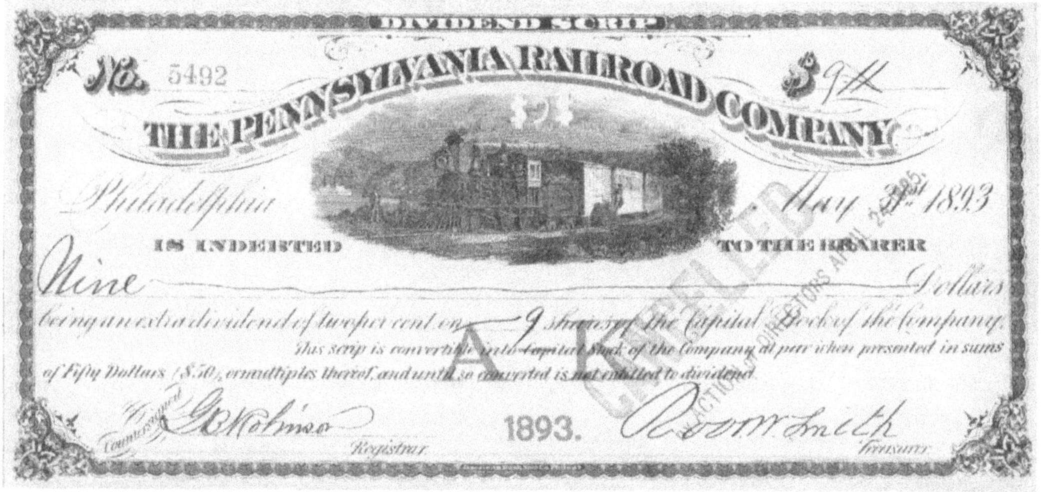

PA200-Var.A. Various Amounts Dividend Scrip May 31, 1893. Black. Freight train at center. Red year date and letters at lower center. Uniface. Imprint: American Bank Note Co. Philada. (shown at 61%)
b. Issued, cancelled. **R5**

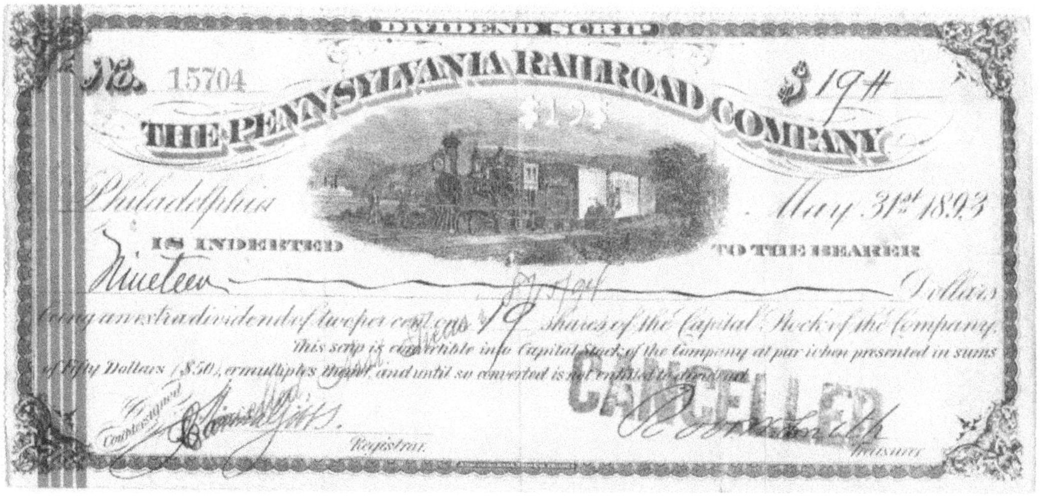

PA200-Var.B. Various Amounts May 31, 1893. As above except for addition of four vertical red bars at left and removal of red date and letters at center. (shown at 61%)
b. Issued, cancelled. **R5**

The Seventeenth National Bank

PA225-Var. Various Amounts 189_ (1893). To Seventh National Bank. (b/w)
 d. Unissued, remainder. R5

Pittsburgh

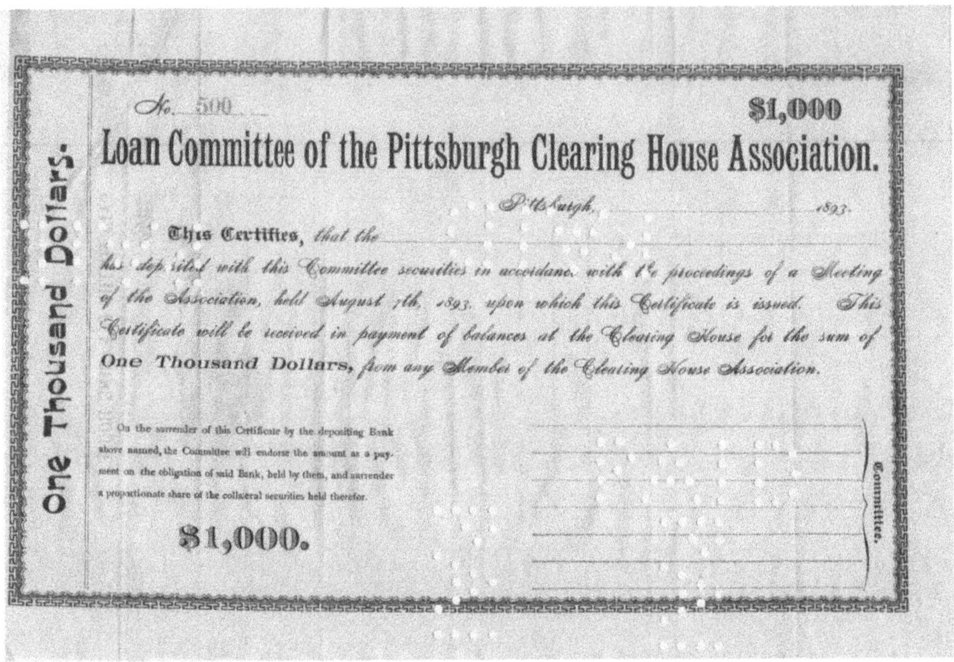
No. 500 $1,000
Loan Committee of the Pittsburgh Clearing House Association.
Pittsburgh, 1893.
This Certifies, that the
has deposited with this Committee securities in accordance with the proceedings of a Meeting of the Association, held August 7th, 1893, upon which this Certificate is issued. This Certificate will be received in payment of balances at the Clearing House for the sum of One Thousand Dollars, from any Member of the Clearing House Association.
On the surrender of this Certificate by the depositing Bank above named, the Committee will endorse the amount as a payment on the obligation of said Bank, held by them, and surrender a proportionate share of the collateral securities held therefor.
$1,000.
Committee.
One Thousand Dollars.

Loan Committee of the Pittsburgh Clearing House Association

PA300-1000. 1000 Dollars Aug. 7, 1893. Black on yellow paper. One text line on back, with lines for signatures beneath. Large size. (shown at 50%)
 c. Unissued, cancelled. R5
PA300-5000. 5000 Dollars Aug. 7, 1893. Black on pink paper. As above.
 c. Unissued, cancelled. R5
PA300-10,000. 10,000 Dollars Aug. 7, 1893. As above.
 c. Unissued, cancelled. R5

Rhode Island

Providence

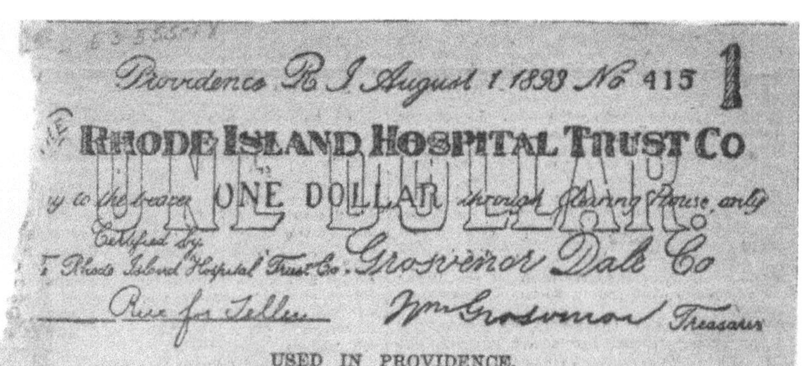
Providence R.I. August 1 1893 No 415 1
The Rhode Island Hospital Trust Co
Pay to the bearer ONE DOLLAR through Clearing House only
Certified by
The Rhode Island Hospital Trust Co. Grosvenor Dale Co
Rice for Teller Wm Grosvenor Treasurer
USED IN PROVIDENCE.

Grosvenor Dale Co./Rhode Island Hospital Trust Co.

RI100-1. 1 Dollar (pay check) Aug. 1, 1893. Large denomination letters across center (from newspaper illustration copied from a note). (shown at 88%)

u. Unissued? SENC

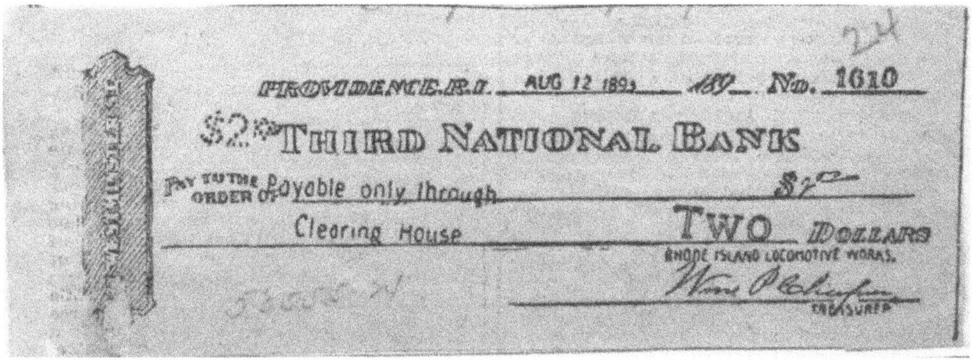

Rhode Island Locomotive Works/Third National Bank

RI125-2. 2 Dollars (pay check) Aug. 12, 1893 (from newspaper illustration copied from a note). (shown at 100%)

u. Unissued? SENC

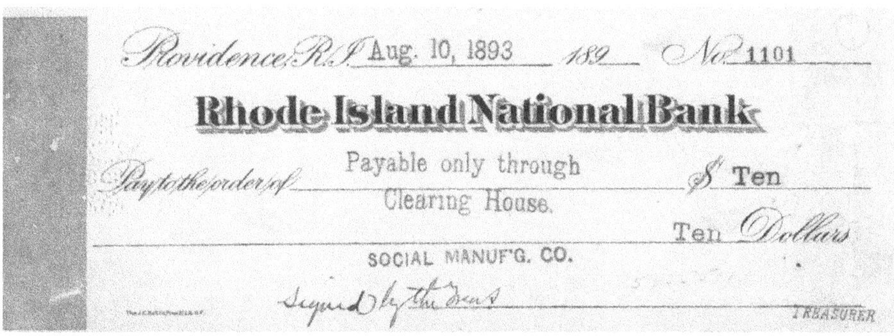

Social Manuf'g. Co./Rhode Island National Bank

RI150-10. 10 Dollars (pay check) Aug. 10, 1893. Black, with gray panel at left. Uniface. Imprint: The J.C. Hall Co. Prov.R.I. & S.F. (shown at 55%)

c. Unissued, cancelled. R5

South Carolina

Abbeville

Abbeville Mercantile Association

SC100-2. 2 Dollars (certificate of deposit) Aug. 24, 1893. Black on green underprint. Boy harvesting corn at left. Large red outline denomination words across center. Uniface. Imprint: Syl. Lester & Co. Atlanta. (shown at 78%)

c. Unissued, cancelled. R5

Charleston

Carolina Savings Bank

SC120-10. 10 Dollars Sept. 1, 1893. Bank building at left.

b. Issued, cancelled. R5

Chester

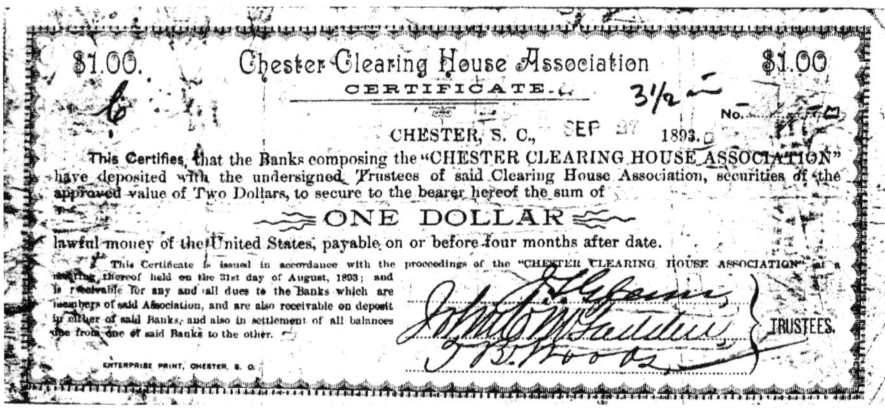

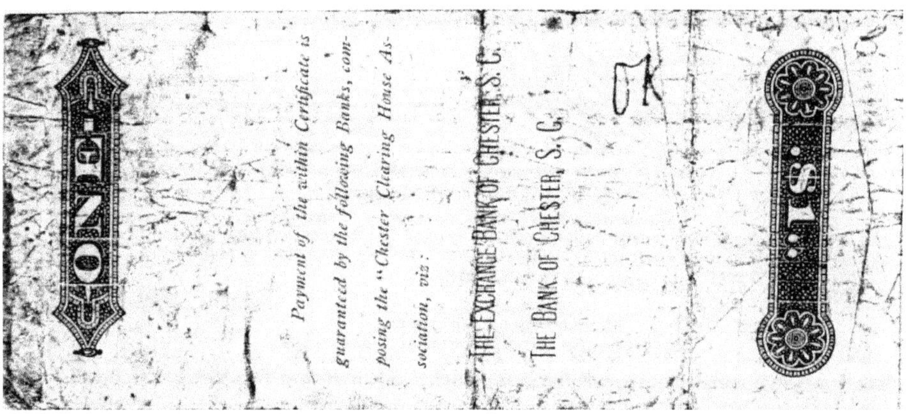

Chester Clearing House Association

SC150-1. 1 Dollar Sept. 27, 1893 (stamped date). Black. Member banks listed on back. Imprint: Enterprise Print, Chester, S.C. (shown at 77%)

a. Issued, not cancelled. R5

NOTE: A $5 and $10 were reportedly issued in Chester, but no details about these two values are presently known.

Columbia

Columbia Clearing House Association

First Issue—small denomination numerals at upper corners. Three written signatures.

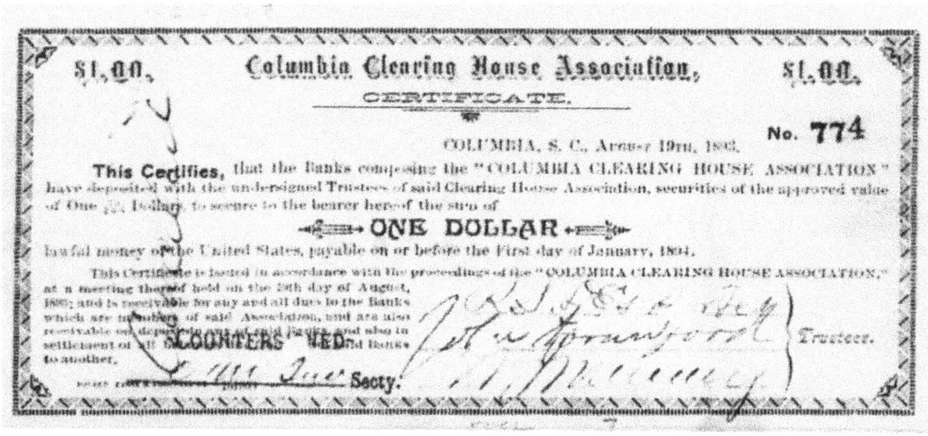

SC200-1. 1 Dollar Aug. 19, 1893. Black. List on back in black of member banks. Imprint: Walker, Evans & Cogswell Co. (shown at 100%)
b. Issued, cancelled. **R4**
SC200-5. 5 Dollars Aug. 19, 1893. Black. As above.
b. Issued, cancelled. **R4**
SC200-10. 10 Dollars Aug. 19, 1893. Black. As above.
b. Issued, cancelled. **R4**
Second Issue — large denomination numeral at upper right only. Three printed signatures.

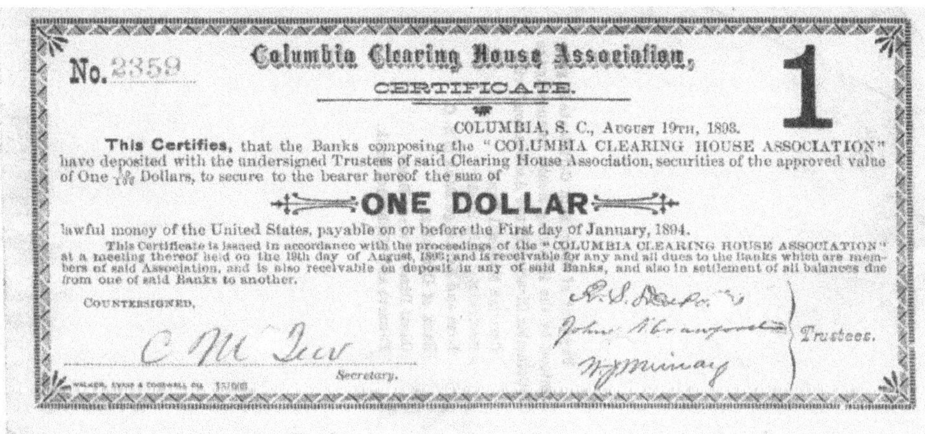

SC225-1. 1 Dollar Aug. 19, 1893. Black. Back and imprint as above. (shown at 70%)
b. Issued, cancelled. R4
SC225-5. 5 Dollars Aug. 19, 1893. Brown, otherwise as above.
b. Issued, cancelled. R4
SC225-10. 10 Dollars Aug. 19, 1893. Blue, otherwise as above.
b. Issued, cancelled. R4
SC225-20. 20 Dollars Aug. 19, 1893. Red, otherwise as above.
b. Issued, cancelled. R4
SC225-50. 50 Dollars Aug. 19, 1893. Green, otherwise as above.
b. Issued, cancelled. R4
NOTE: A $2 denomination is reported to have been issued in Columbia, but no details are presently known.

Rock Hill

Associated Banks of Rock Hill, S.C.

SC250-1. 1 Dollar Clearing House Certificate Sept. 4, 1893. Black. Yellow denomination words at center. Imprint: A. Hoen and Co., Lith.-Richmond,Va.
a. Issued, not cancelled. R5
SC250-2. 2 Dollars Sept. 4, 1893. Black denomination words at center, otherwise as above.
c. Unissued, cancelled. R5

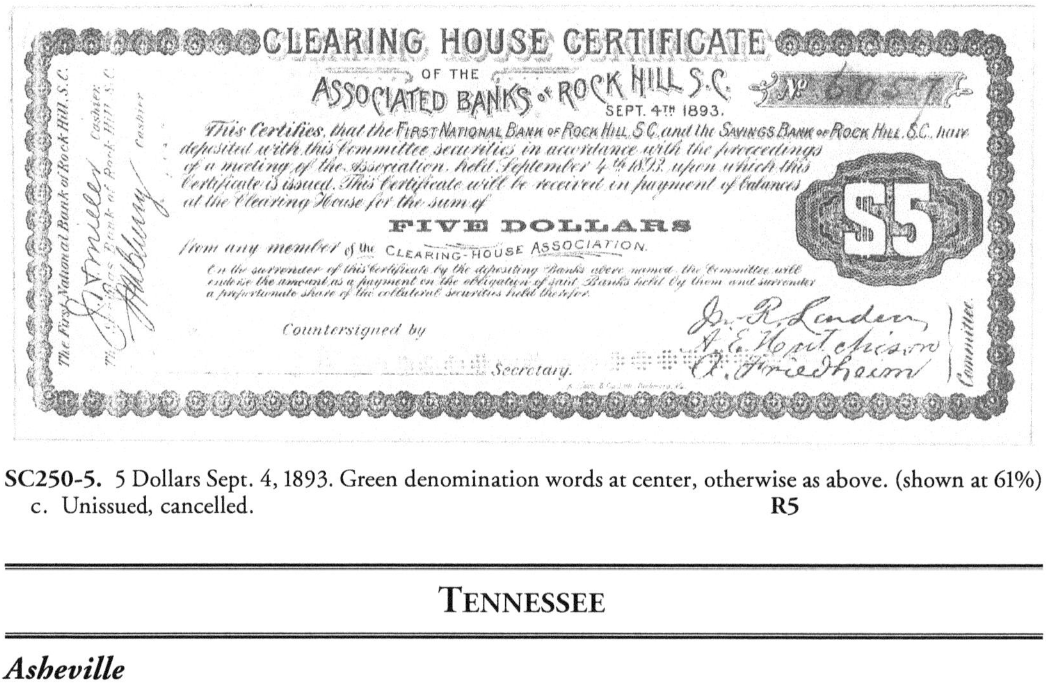

SC250-5. 5 Dollars Sept. 4, 1893. Green denomination words at center, otherwise as above. (shown at 61%)
c. Unissued, cancelled. R5

Tennessee

Asheville

Union Bank & Trust Co.

TN100-5. 5 Dollars Certificate of Deposit 1893. Black on dull gold paper. Uniface. Imprint: Brandon Printing Co. Nashville.
c. Unissued, cancelled. R4

Chattanooga

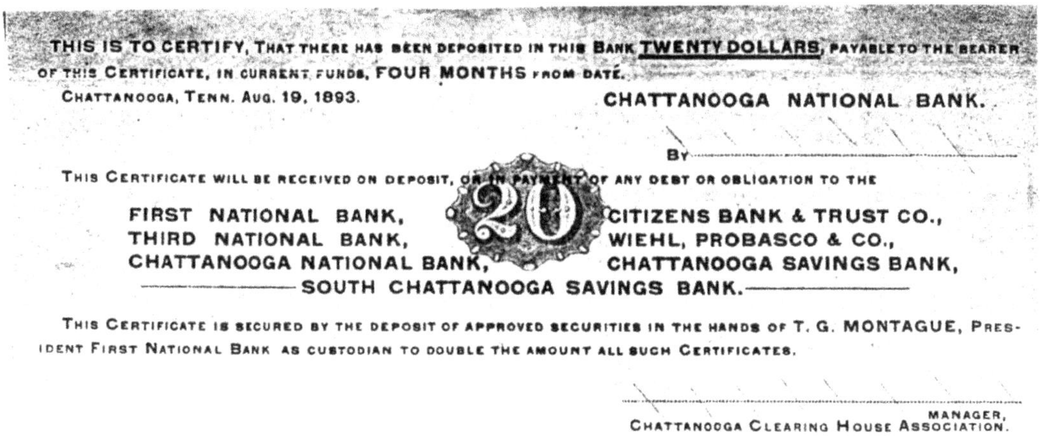
THIS IS TO CERTIFY, THAT THERE HAS BEEN DEPOSITED IN THIS BANK TWENTY DOLLARS, PAYABLE TO THE BEARER OF THIS CERTIFICATE, IN CURRENT FUNDS, FOUR MONTHS FROM DATE.

CHATTANOOGA, TENN. AUG. 19, 1893. CHATTANOOGA NATIONAL BANK.

BY

THIS CERTIFICATE WILL BE RECEIVED ON DEPOSIT, OR IN PAYMENT OF ANY DEBT OR OBLIGATION TO THE

FIRST NATIONAL BANK, 20 CITIZENS BANK & TRUST CO.,
THIRD NATIONAL BANK, WIEHL, PROBASCO & CO.,
CHATTANOOGA NATIONAL BANK, CHATTANOOGA SAVINGS BANK,
SOUTH CHATTANOOGA SAVINGS BANK.

THIS CERTIFICATE IS SECURED BY THE DEPOSIT OF APPROVED SECURITIES IN THE HANDS OF T. G. MONTAGUE, PRESIDENT FIRST NATIONAL BANK AS CUSTODIAN TO DOUBLE THE AMOUNT ALL SUCH CERTIFICATES.

MANAGER,
CHATTANOOGA CLEARING HOUSE ASSOCIATION.

CHATTANOOGA NATIONAL BANK

TN150-20. 20 Dollars Aug. 19, 1893. Black. Center value in red. Back green pattern without devices. (shown at 75%)

c. Unissued, cancelled. **R4**

TN150-50. 50 Dollars Aug. 19, 1893. Black. As above, but with added vertical text in red at left. Value in red at center.

c. Unissued, cancelled. **R4**

NOTE: On back of a b/w copy of TN150-50., a handwritten notation reading as follows refers to above two notes plus other denominations not listed: "The notes are in bank. One had note written in 1912 that these 2 plus a set of 10, 20, 50, 100 were all that were not destroyed. Cpt Lyerty president 1st Natl had the 4. No one has seen. Must have been 8 notes in set w & w o overprints. Lyerty was president of 1st Chatt Natl became president of 1st National when merger in 1905."

FIRST NATIONAL BANK

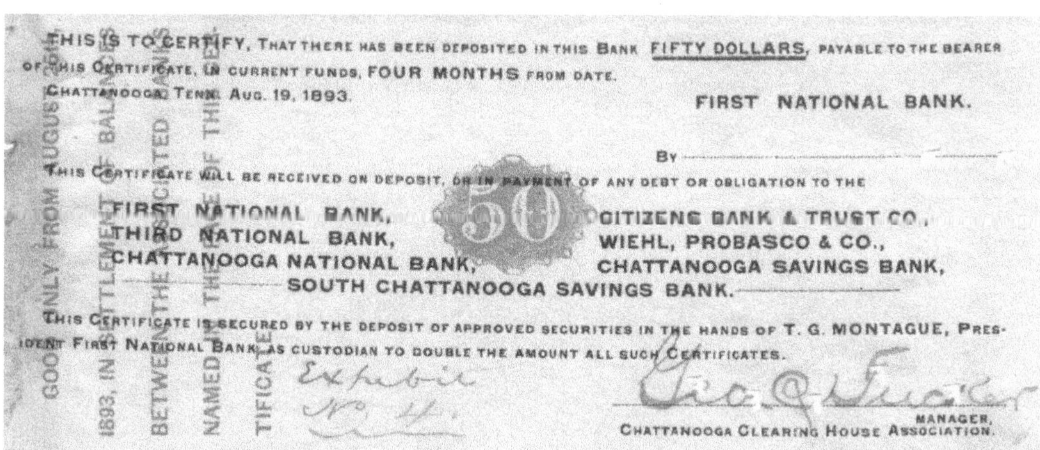
THIS IS TO CERTIFY, THAT THERE HAS BEEN DEPOSITED IN THIS BANK FIFTY DOLLARS, PAYABLE TO THE BEARER OF THIS CERTIFICATE, IN CURRENT FUNDS, FOUR MONTHS FROM DATE.

CHATTANOOGA, TENN. AUG. 19, 1893. FIRST NATIONAL BANK.

BY

THIS CERTIFICATE WILL BE RECEIVED ON DEPOSIT, OR IN PAYMENT OF ANY DEBT OR OBLIGATION TO THE

FIRST NATIONAL BANK, 50 CITIZENS BANK & TRUST CO.,
THIRD NATIONAL BANK, WIEHL, PROBASCO & CO.,
CHATTANOOGA NATIONAL BANK, CHATTANOOGA SAVINGS BANK,
SOUTH CHATTANOOGA SAVINGS BANK.

THIS CERTIFICATE IS SECURED BY THE DEPOSIT OF APPROVED SECURITIES IN THE HANDS OF T. G. MONTAGUE, PRESIDENT FIRST NATIONAL BANK AS CUSTODIAN TO DOUBLE THE AMOUNT ALL SUCH CERTIFICATES.

Exhibit No. 4.

MANAGER,
CHATTANOOGA CLEARING HOUSE ASSOCIATION.

TN175-50. 50 Dollars Aug. 19, 1893. As TN150-50. (shown at 75%)

c. Unissued, cancelled. **R4**

THE LOOMIS & HART MFG. CO.

TN200-1. 1 Dollar Pay-Roll Check Aug. 19, 1893. Black on yellow paper. Embossed seal at left. Uniface. Small size, 136 × 70mm. Imprint: The Bradt Printing Co., Chattanooga, Tenn.

b. Issued, cancelled. **R5**

TN200-2. 2 Dollars Aug. 19, 1893. Black on pink paper, otherwise as above.
b. Issued, cancelled. **R5**

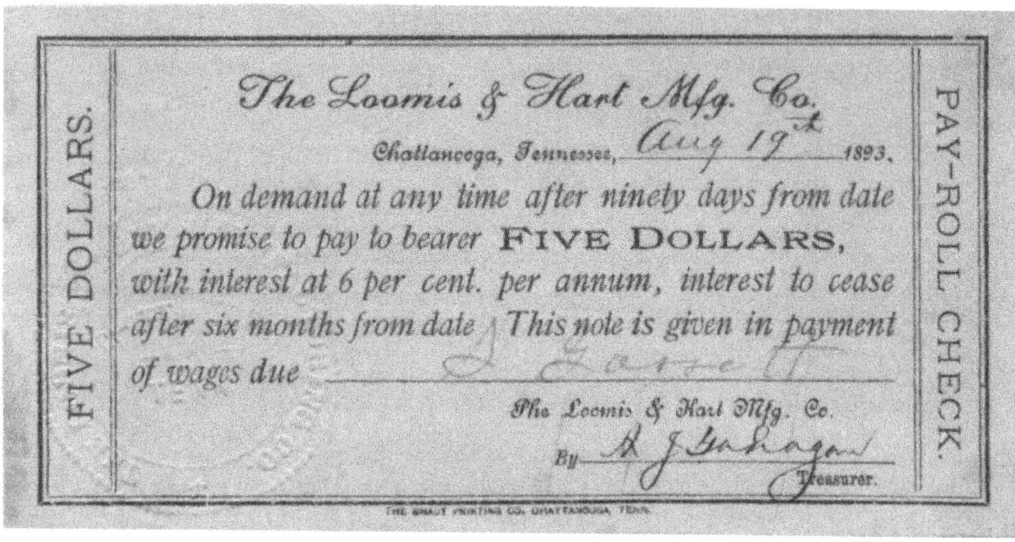

FIVE DOLLARS.

The Loomis & Hart Mfg. Co.

Chattanooga, Tennessee, Aug 19th 1893.

On demand at any time after ninety days from date we promise to pay to bearer FIVE DOLLARS, with interest at 6 per cent. per annum, interest to cease after six months from date. This note is given in payment of wages due

The Loomis & Hart Mfg. Co.

By A J Gahagan Treasurer.

PAY-ROLL CHECK.

TN200-5. 5 Dollars Aug. 19, 1893. Black on blue paper, otherwise as above. (shown at 100%)
b. Issued, cancelled. **R5**

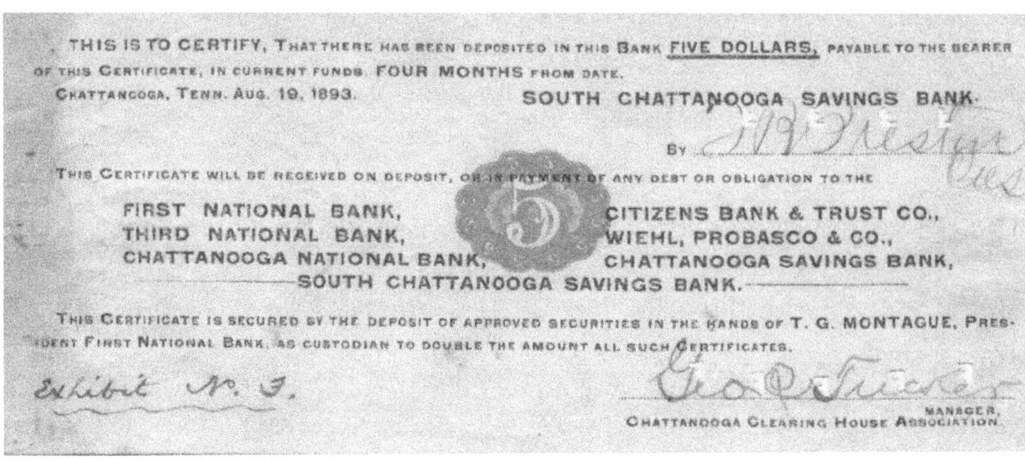

THIS IS TO CERTIFY, THAT THERE HAS BEEN DEPOSITED IN THIS BANK FIVE DOLLARS, PAYABLE TO THE BEARER OF THIS CERTIFICATE, IN CURRENT FUNDS FOUR MONTHS FROM DATE.

CHATTANOOGA, TENN. AUG. 19, 1893.

SOUTH CHATTANOOGA SAVINGS BANK.

BY

THIS CERTIFICATE WILL BE RECEIVED ON DEPOSIT, OR IN PAYMENT OF ANY DEBT OR OBLIGATION TO THE

FIRST NATIONAL BANK,
THIRD NATIONAL BANK,
CHATTANOOGA NATIONAL BANK,
CITIZENS BANK & TRUST CO.,
WIEHL, PROBASCO & CO.,
CHATTANOOGA SAVINGS BANK,
SOUTH CHATTANOOGA SAVINGS BANK.

THIS CERTIFICATE IS SECURED BY THE DEPOSIT OF APPROVED SECURITIES IN THE HANDS OF T. G. MONTAGUE, PRESIDENT FIRST NATIONAL BANK, AS CUSTODIAN TO DOUBLE THE AMOUNT ALL SUCH CERTIFICATES.

Exhibit No. 3.

MANAGER,
CHATTANOOGA CLEARING HOUSE ASSOCIATION.

South Chattanooga Savings Bank

TN250-5. 5 Dollars Aug. 19, 1893. Colors and design similar to TN150. (shown at 74%)
b. Issued, cancelled. **R5**

Nashville

Fourth National Bank

TN300-5. 5 Dollars Certificate of Deposit 1893. Black. Uniface. Imprint: Brandon Printing Co. Nashville.
c. Unissued, cancelled. **R5**

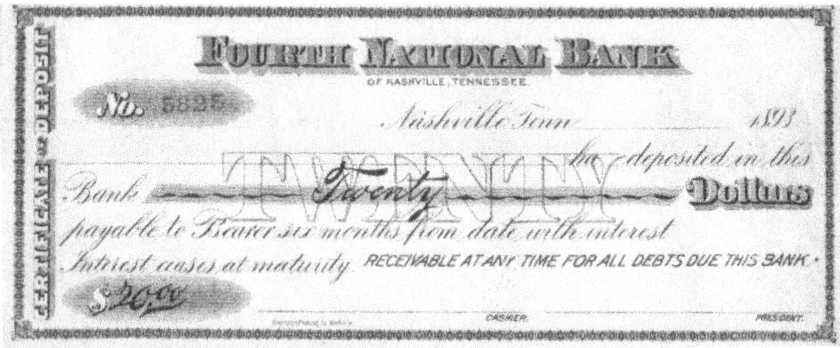

TN300-20. 20 Dollars 1893. As above. (shown at 60%)
c. Unissued, cancelled. **R5**

UNION BANK & TRUST CO.

TN325-5. 5 Dollars Certificate of Deposit 1893. Black on yellow paper. Imprint: Brandon Printing Co. Nashville. (shown at 60%)
c. Unissued, cancelled. **R5**

Warner

SOUTHERN IRON WORKS

An issue of scrip for this company is reported, but no details have been confirmed.

VIRGINIA

Danville

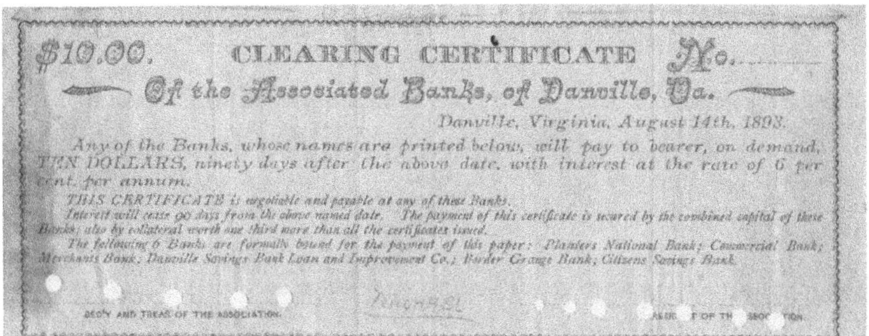

The Associated Banks of Danville, Va.

VA100-10. 10 Dollars Clearing Certificate Aug. 14, 1893. Black on pale pinkish paper. Uniface. (shown at 55%)

c. Unissued, cancelled. **R5**

NOTE: An issue consisting of denominations ranging from $1.00 to $100. is reported to have been made for use in Danville. Only the $10 denomination has been seen; no details about any other value are known at present.

Richmond

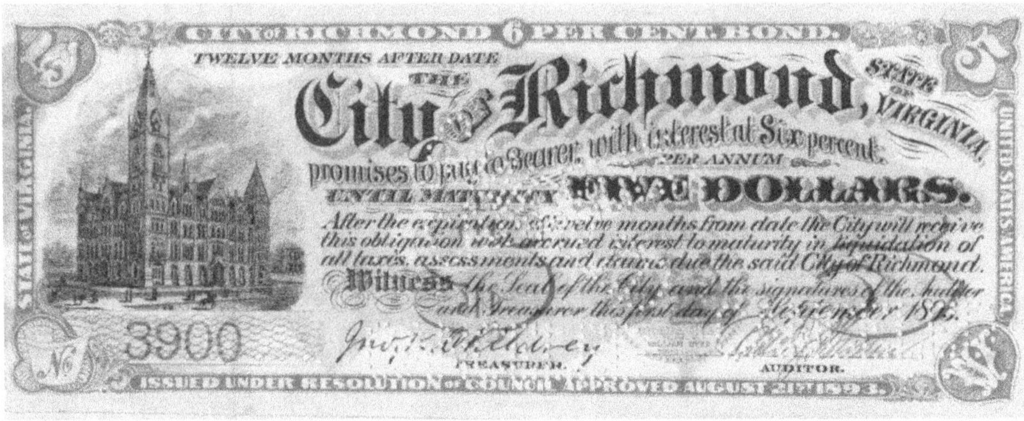

City of Richmond

VA150-5. 5 Dollars 6% Bond Sept.1, 1893. Black and blue. Church at left. Red seal at lower right center. Back brown; value in ornate guilloche at center. (shown at 66%)

b. Issued, cancelled. **R5**

VA150-10. 10 Dollars Sept. 1, 1893. Face black and green, otherwise as above. Back blue; design as above.

b. Issued, cancelled. **EF, 200. Unc. 400.**

NOTE: A small group of about 25 pieces of VA150-10. was located in the Richmond area in recent years.

Richmond Locomotive & Machine Works

VA200-1. 1 Dollar (wage certificate) Aug. 12, 1893. Black. Train sideways at left. Uniface.

b. Issued, cancelled. **R5**

VA200-2. 2 Dollars Aug. 12, 1893. Black. Eagle with wings folded at left. As above. (shown at 52%)
b. Issued, cancelled. **R5**
VA200-5. 5 Dollars Aug. 12, 1893. Black. Liberty standing at left holding pole to cap in left hand, sword in right hand. As above.
b. Issued, cancelled. **R5**
VA200-10. 10 Dollars Aug. 12, 1893. Black. Justice standing with scales at left. As above.
b. Issued, cancelled. **R5**

VA200-20. 20 Dollars Aug. 12, 1893. Black. Three women, child and river steamer at left. As above. (shown at 52%)
b. Issued, cancelled. **R5**

WASHINGTON

Mt. Vernon

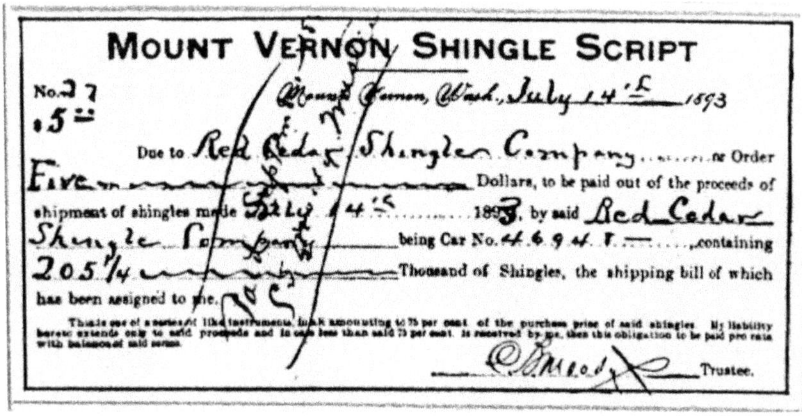

Mt. Vernon Shingle Script/Red Cedar Shingle Company

WA100-5. 5 Dollars July 14, 1893. Black. (shown at 64%)
b. Issued, cancelled. R5

Port Angeles

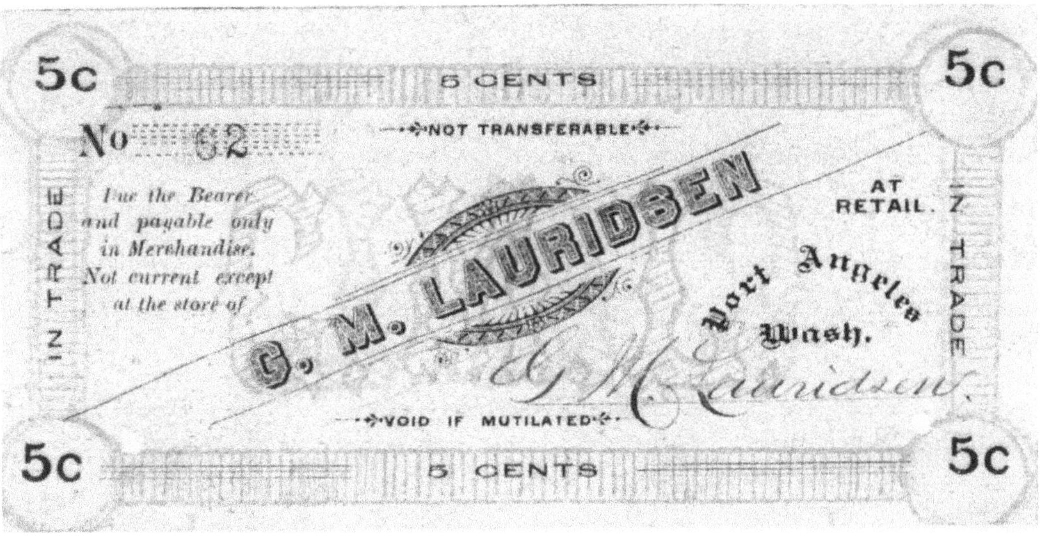

G. M. Lauridsen

WA125-.05 5 Cents (trade certificate) ND (1893). Black on light olive green underprint containing large letters G.M.L. across center. Back blue-gray; large letters G.M.L. across center. (shown at 100%)
b. Issued, cancelled. R4

WA125-.10 10 Cents ND (1893). Black on gold underprint as above.
b. Issued, cancelled. R4

WA125-.25 25 Cents ND (1893). Black on orange underprint as above.
a. Issued, not cancelled. R4

WA125-.50 50 Cents ND (1893). Black on orange underprint as above.
a. Issued, not cancelled. R4

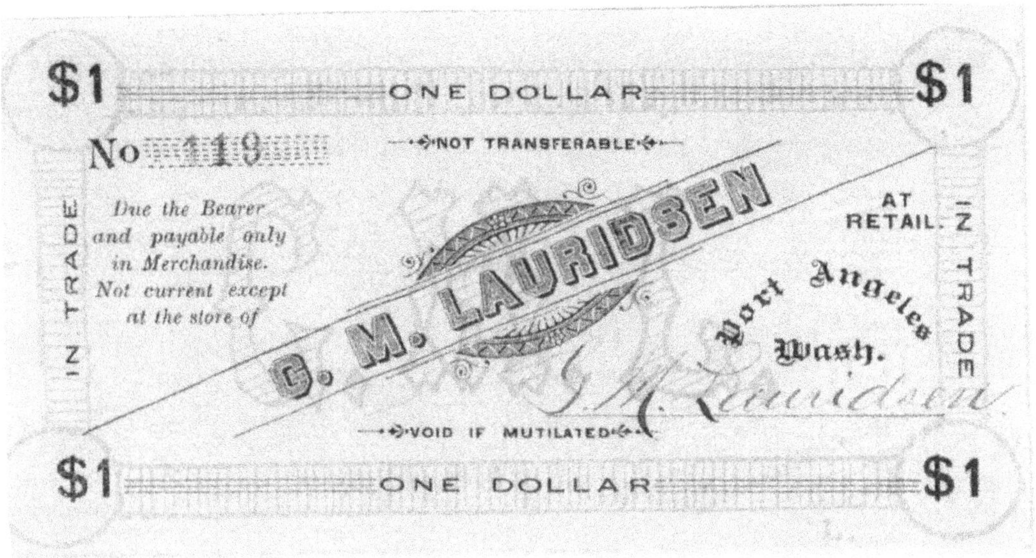

WA125-1. 1 Dollar ND (1893). Black on light gold underprint as above. (shown at 100%)
a. Issued, not cancelled. **R4**
WA125-5. 5 Dollars ND (1893). (list)
u. Issued. **SENC**

Seattle

FIRST NATIONAL BANK OF SEATTLE

WA150-5. 5 Dollars Certified Check Oct. 25, 1893. Black on yellow paper. Bank emblem at upper left. Certified stamping vertically at left center. Uniface. Imprint: Leo D. Burnard & Co. St. Louis. (shown at 66%)
a. Issued, not cancelled. **R5**

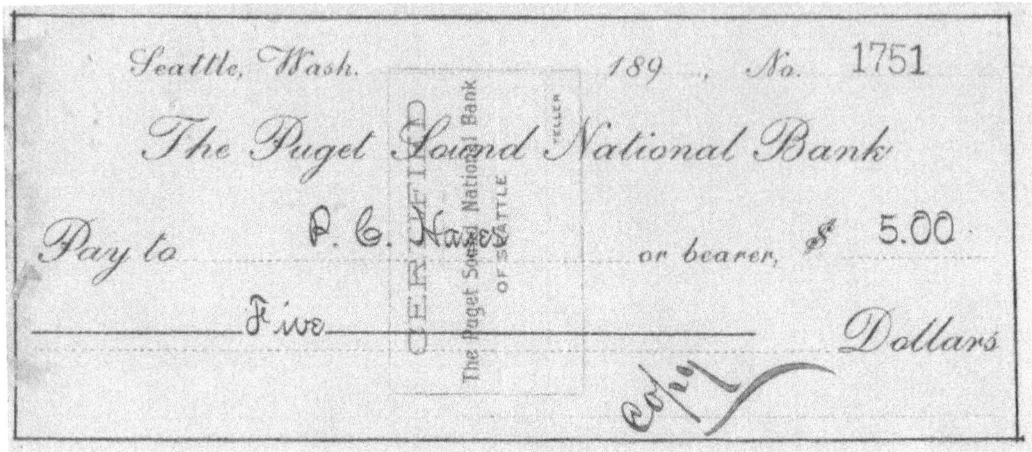

THE PUGET SOUND NATIONAL BANK

WA200-5. 5 Dollars (certified check) 189_ (1893). Black on light green paper. Red CERTIFIED, bank name and line for teller's signature vertically at center. Uniface. (shown at 86%)

c. Unissued, cancelled. **R5**

d. Unissued, remainder. **R5**

Spokane

SCHOOL WARRANT

WA250-1. 1 Dollar 189_ (1893). Green and brown with black text. Black text on back. Imprint: The Shaw-Borden Co., Spokane. (shown at 70%)

c. Unissued, cancelled (handwritten Sample Copy Series "A"). **R5**

NOTE: Red handwritten lines on the above note indicate that higher values of 2, 5 and 10-dollar notes were issued. None are reported at this time.

Tacoma

CITY COUNCIL OF THE CITY OF TACOMA

WA300-1. 1 Dollar Sept. 18, 1893 (stamped date). Payable to the Tacoma Bituminous Paving Company or bearer. Brown on green underprint. Large denomination words in white across center. Back orange; G. Washington portrait at center. Imprint: The Blatchly Co. Tacoma. (shown at 63%)

a. Issued, not cancelled. **R5**

Part II.
Scrip from the Panic of 1907

History of the "Rich Man's Panic"

On the last day of 1899 the *New York Times* carried an article that heralded the innovations of that century. The steam engine, railroads, electric lights and telephones were all new to the world. The new century brought forth optimism and hope for even better things to come. Prosperity was everywhere. A new sofa was less than $10.00, and in fact, most quality furniture was priced similarly. President McKinley's slogan was "The Full Dinner Pail." Even the great earthquake that leveled San Francisco could not stifle the positive attitude of the times. April 18, 1906, was the beginning of a new San Francisco. Times had certainly been good, but the next year would bring everyone back to earth.

In 1907 business slumped. The stock market declined because of a lack of buying. This was the first bad year in many people's memories. President Theodore Roosevelt laid blame on the investors who had manipulated railroad and other companies' shares. He later referred to these people as "malefactors of great wealth."

The stock market, though, did play a central role in the coming panic. Its volume had increased from 1904 to 1906 by a factor of 50 percent and the dollar value of the transactions essentially doubled. The country had been going through a period of exuberance, but the growth was too great and too fast; New York banks began to restrict their loans. The so-called country banks, i.e. the banks away from "the city," continued to lend funds to satisfy the demand for growth. They did not heed the message the New York banks were sending to reduce their loans. Meanwhile the stock market had gone through a correction from the beginning of the year. Margin loan rates were allowed to decline to try to keep the market up.

Trust companies were financial institutions engaged in the business of administering wills, estate and other personal financial matters. They had emerged because that type of business was forbidden to the national and state banks at the time. The trust companies did not enjoy the best of reputations. All too often they were involved in speculative ventures and naturally many did not work out. Bankers Trust was established in 1903 by Thomas W. Lamont and Pomeroy Davison. Their idea was that the House of Morgan would refer business to them and once the trust business was completed the customers would return to Morgan. Though these types of relationships were not unusual, they would add to the concern of depositors.

Heinze and the Development of the Panic

F. Augustus Heinze and C. F. Morse were relative newcomers to Wall Street. *Kings View of Wall Street*, published in 1897, containing more than a thousand photos of Wall Street brokers and bankers, bore no mention of either man. Certainly had they been important and well established in 1907 there would have been some recognition given as they began their careers ten years earlier. They did have a reputation as fast wheelers and dealers.

Heinze came to Wall Street with a history as a copper speculator. He and his brother jointly ran a brokerage firm but Heinze individually had just become the president of the Mercantile National Bank. The belief that he was a speculator caused many depositors to withdraw their funds. When depositors of the Knickerbocker Trust learned of the relationship between its president Charles T. Barney and Heinze, they grew concerned for the safety of the bank and their money. The National Bank of Commerce refused to clear for the Knickerbocker. Fear spread quickly; in an effort to shore up confidence in the bank Barney was forced to resign, but to no avail. The Knickerbocker had 18,000 depositors, but in short order there was a run on the firm and it was forced to close its doors. This action occurred October 21, 1907, and the Panic of 1907 had begun.

Unfounded fear rapidly spread across the country. Banks in various cities experienced runs on their cash reserves by frightened depositors. Country banks withdrew money from city banks; they in turn tried to replenish their money supplies from New York banks. Telegrams flooded New York requesting additional funds to meet the severe demands.

The national banking system that had begun in 1863 proved unable to provide necessary supplies of cash to maintain any semblance of public confidence. Chief criticism was its inability to allow quick expansion or contraction of paper currency supplies. At no time did this inadequacy show itself so strongly as during the Panic of 1907.

The oft-stated axiom about the use of locally provided emergency currency is simply this: Whenever a government fails to provide an adequate supply of currency to maintain commercial trade, the people will step in and provide their own to fill the vacuum. At the point where people all over the country felt the monetary restriction in 1907, there was an immediate move to fill the gap through monetary instruments made for local circulation in place of the vanished government paper money.

In various states the governor proclaimed a bank holiday, sometimes for a rather extended period. In other places state officials stretched laws to allow banks to pay out only minimal amounts to depositors while still claiming solvency. Money substitutes such as certified or cashier's checks, bank drafts and clearing house certificates were officially sanctioned as emergency measures. Many firms also issued payroll scrip in various denominations for their workers because cash was so scarce.

Clearing houses and businesses across the country quickly stepped in to fill the void by issuing their own emergency currencies in these forms. It is estimated that nearly $500 million in currency substitutes circulated during this several-month period.

Intercession of J. Pierpont Morgan

J. P. Morgan was a 70-year-old man at the time and not very active in Wall Street. He was more occupied in organizing his vast collections and engaging in activities with his church. This was to change in the last quarter of 1907.

He had been watching the events and was content to let the Knickerbocker fail, but he knew that the panic had to be stopped. He gathered several bankers and Treasury Secretary George Cortelyou for a meeting. Cortelyou pledged $25,000,000 in government funds. As these funds began to run short the easy money of low margin rates reversed and shot up 150 percent. Yet more money was necessary to prop up several of the brokerage firms. They could not be allowed to fail; any such failure would perpetuate the panic.

Morgan met with Ransom H. Thomas, president of the New York Stock Exchange, on October 24. Thomas wanted to close the exchange because funds were short and several brokerage firms were in danger of failing. Morgan told him not to close the exchange, and an hour before the close at 2:00 P.M. he summoned the bank presidents and gave them just minutes to pledge $25,000,000. With less than 45 minutes to the close, Morgan sent a team to the exchange to announce that call money was available for 10 percent. This action satisfied the market for the moment.

On Friday evening, October 25, Morgan had many of the city's religious leaders come to a meeting where he asked them to preach for calmness in their Sunday sermons. The next day

Morgan led a group that gave New York City a loan of $30,000,000 to cover its obligations. Normally foreign investors would have provided funds for the city, but in that situation they were unwilling to release their resources.

The following weekend things came to a head. The Trust Company of America and the Lincoln Trust were still on shaky ground, and a speculative brokerage named Moore and Schley had an outstanding debt of $25,000,000. Morgan again assembled banking leaders, with the commercial bankers in one room and trust bankers in another room. No one was allowed to leave until a plan had been devised and agreed upon. Morgan presented a plan that would save the brokerage and help him out as well. The brokerage controlled a major block of stock that would send the market down if it were sold openly. He proposed to buy it himself if the bankers would come up with another $25,000,000 to prop up the weak trust banks. The bankers all signed off on it at 5:00 A.M.

Morgan's U.S. Steel would buy the stock of Tennessee Coal which normally would not have been allowed, but President Roosevelt was swayed at the last minute not to interfere. By acting as a virtual one-man federal reserve bank, Morgan literally saved the day. By February of 1908 public confidence had been restored and the panic was brought to an end.

Aftermath of the Panic

After the panic there was a widespread demand for changes in the banking community. In 1908, the Aldrich-Vreeland Currency Act created a Monetary Commission to study changes in the banking system. The Commission looked at banking systems in several European countries. J. P. Morgan favored patterning the central bank after that of the Bank of England. Aldrich proposed a central bank to Congress in 1910 only to be blocked by the Democrats. After extensive changes to the 1910 plan a Virginia Democrat, Carter Glass, proposed the Federal Reserve Act in 1913. President Wilson saw to it that the bill was pushed through Congress and the Federal Reserve Bank System was born. It called for twelve regional banks that could control the money supply, allowing one region to borrow from another region when its supply was running short. An elastic money supply is necessary when different parts of the country have varying times and levels of production, whether they are agricultural or manufacturing. This system provided the needed elasticity.

Catalog Listing

ALABAMA

Bessemer

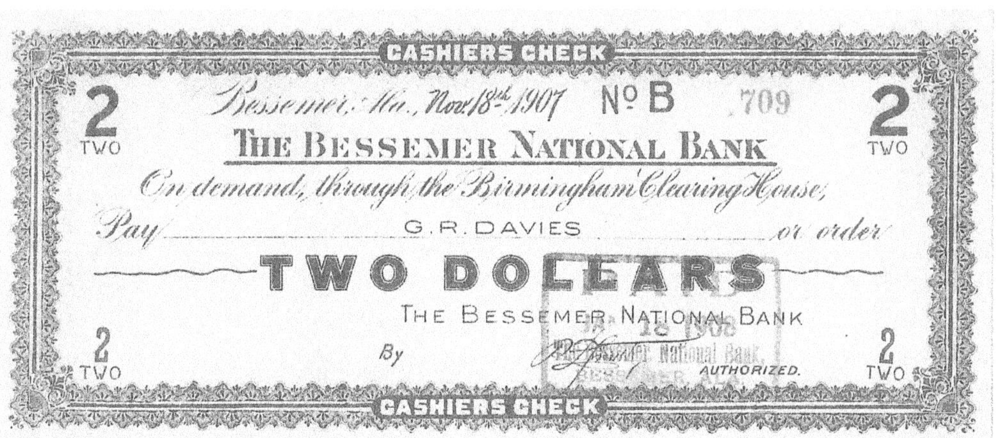

The Bessemer National Bank

AL500-2. 2 Dollars Cashiers Check Nov. 18, 1907. Payable to G.R. Davies. Brown text and border. Back green, with shield at each corner. Imprint: Roberts & Son Lith. Birmingham. (shown at 72%)
b. Issued, cancelled. R3

Birmingham

American Trust & Savings Bank

AL520-1. 1 Dollar Cashiers Check Nov. 18, 1907. Payable to Frank Stevens. Green text and border on beige paper. Back green; design similar to AL500-2. (shown at 76%)
b. Issued, cancelled. R4

Birmingham Trust & Savings Co.

AL550-5. 5 Dollars Cashiers Check Nov. 18, 1907. Payable to J.H. Hine. Blue text and border. Back green; design similar to AL500-2. (shown at 76%)
b. Issued, cancelled. R3

Commercial State Bank

AL580-2. 2 Dollars Cashiers Check Nov. 18, 1907. Payable to J.B. Greene Jr. Brown text and border. Back green; design similar to AL500-2.
b. Issued, cancelled. R3

AL580-5. 5 Dollars Nov. 18, 1907. Payable as above. Dark blue. Back green; design as above. (shown at 65%)
b. Issued, cancelled. **VG 175. VF 400.**

The First National Bank of Birmingham, Ala./ The Chase National Bank

A. Draft in New York Exchange on Chase National Bank. Payable to J.P. Brandewie.

AL600-5. 5 Dollars Dec. 2, 1907. Brown text and border, face and back. Shield in each corner on back.
b. Issued, cancelled. **R3**
c. Unissued, cancelled. **R3**

AL600-10. 10 Dollars Dec. 2, 1907. As above.
b. Issued, cancelled. **R3**
c. Unissued, cancelled. **R3**

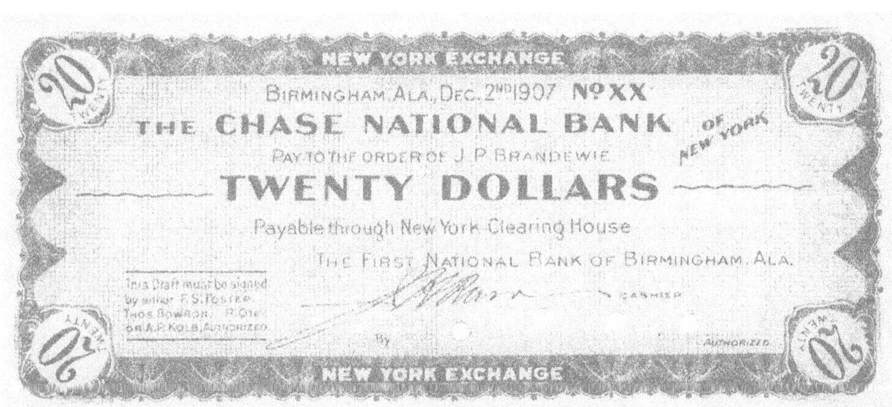

AL600-20. 20 Dollars Dec. 2, 1907. As above. (shown at 64%)
  b. Issued, cancelled. R4
  c. Unissued, cancelled. R4

B. Pay Check. Payable to J.P. Brandewie.
AL620-5. 5 Dollars Nov. 1, 1907. (b/w)
  b. Issued, cancelled. R5
AL620-10. 10 Dollars Nov. 1, 1907. (b/w)
  b. Issued, cancelled. R5
AL620-20. 20 Dollars Nov. 1, 1907. (b/w)
  b. Issued, cancelled. R5

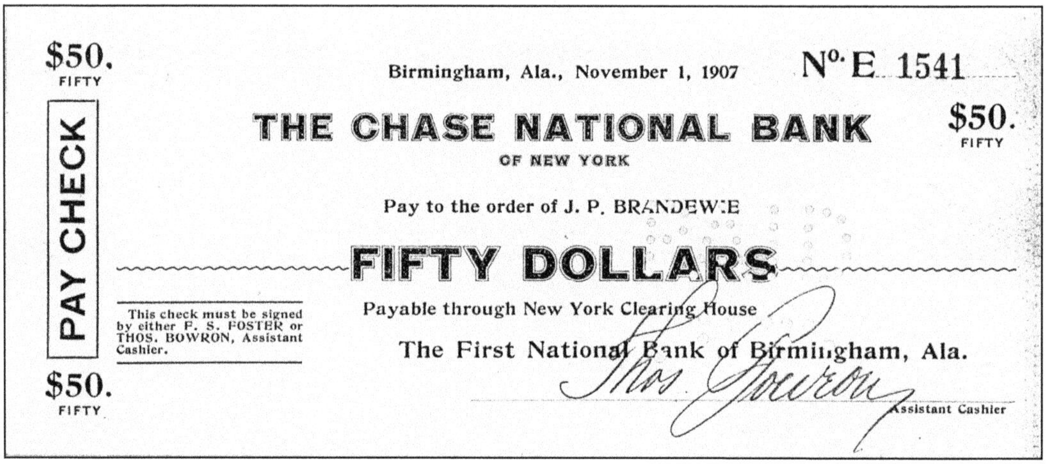

AL620-50. 50 Dollars Nov. 1, 1907. (b/w) (shown at 75%)
  b. Issued, cancelled. R5

THE FIRST NATIONAL BANK OF BIRMINGHAM

A. Cashiers Check

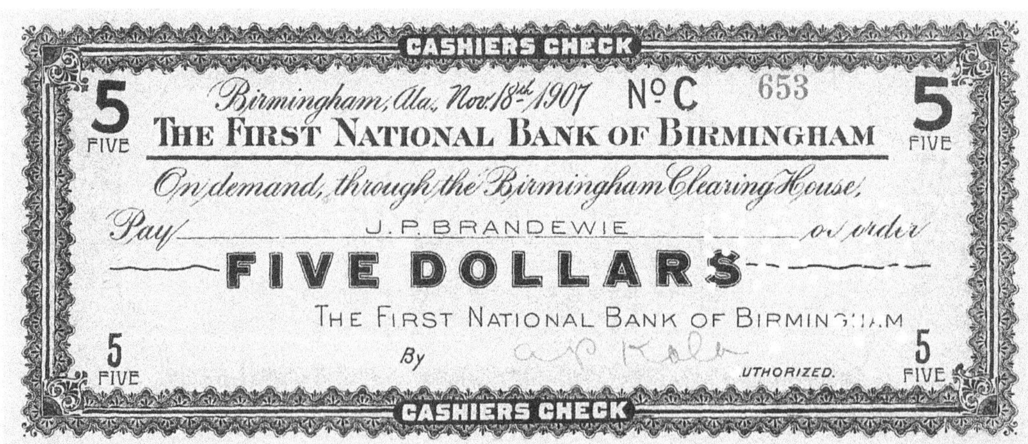

AL630-5. 5 Dollars Cashiers Check Nov. 18, 1907. Payable to J.P. Brandewie. Dark blue face. Back green; design similar to AL500-2. (shown at 74%)
b. Issued, cancelled. R3

B. Pay Check

AL650-1. 1 Dollar Nov. 1, 1907. Payable to J.P. Brandewie. (b/w) (shown at 65%)
b. Issued, cancelled. R5

Jefferson County Savings Bank

AL700-1. 1 Dollar Cashiers Check Nov. 18, 1907. Payable to S.N. Wilson. Green face and back. Designs and printer similar to AL600-2.
b. Issued, cancelled. VG, 175. VF, 400.

AL700-2. 2 Dollars Nov. 18, 1907. Brown text and border on face. Back green; as above. (shown at 65%)
b. Issued, cancelled. **R3**

Peoples Savings Bank & Trust Co.

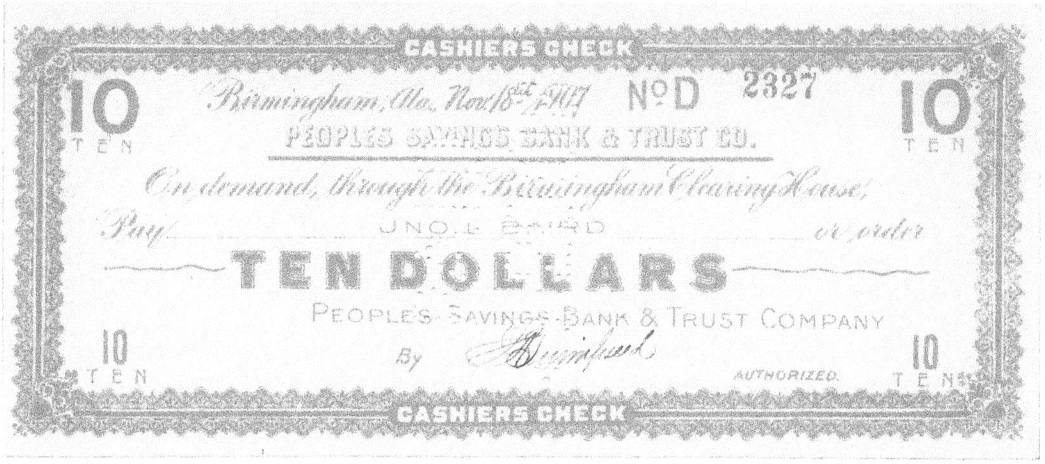

AL720-10. 10 Dollars Cashiers Check Nov. 18, 1907. Payable to Jno. L. Baird. Deep orange face, dark green back. Design and printer similar to above. (shown at 74%)
b. Issued, cancelled. **R3**
u. Unissued. **SENC**

AL720-20. 20 Dollars Nov. 18, 1907. Red face, green back, otherwise as above.
b. Issued, cancelled. **VG, 175. VF 400.**

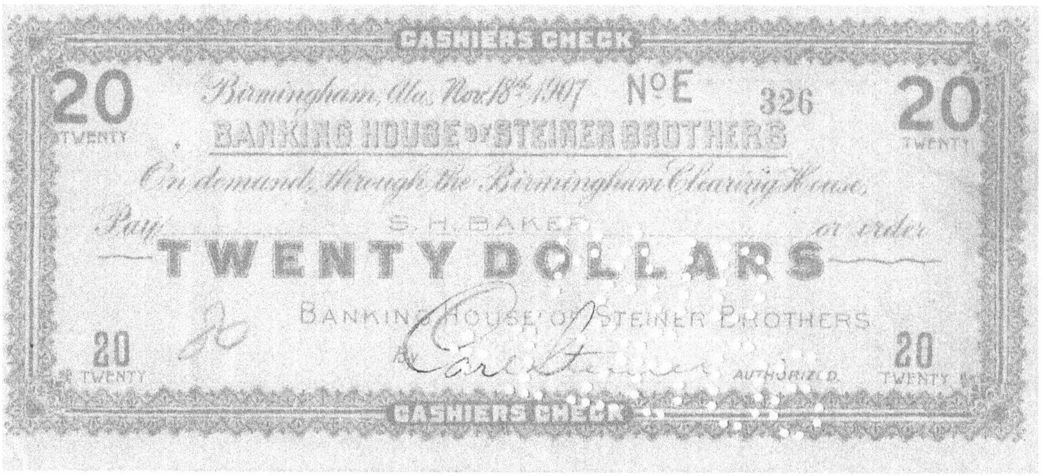

Steiner Brothers, Banking House of

AL740-20. 20 Dollars Cashiers Check Nov. 18, 1907. Payable to S.H. Baker. Red text and border on face. Back green; design similar to above. (shown at 76%)
b. Issued, cancelled. **R4**

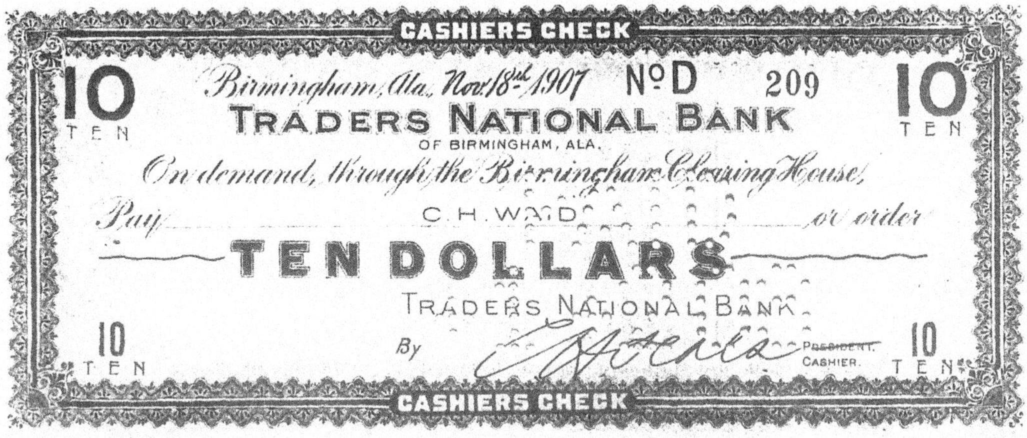

TRADERS NATIONAL BANK

AL760-10. 10 Dollars Cashiers Check Nov. 18, 1907. Payable to C.H. Waid. (b/w) (shown at 75%)
 b. Issued, cancelled. **R5**

AL760-20. 20 Dollars Nov. 18, 1907. As above. (b/w)
 b. Issued, cancelled. **R5**

Dothan

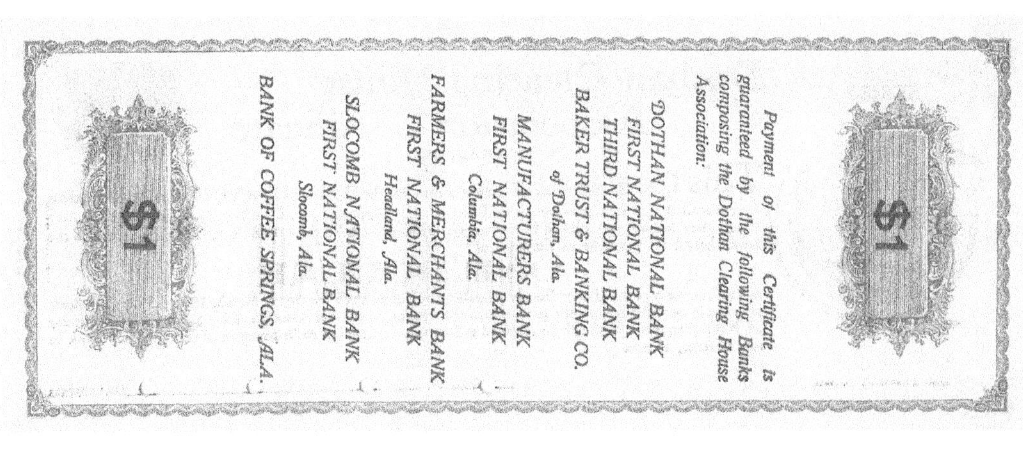

Dothan Clearing House Association Certificate

AL800-1. 1 Dollar Nov. 18, 1907. Black and green, red outline value at lower right center. Eagle on mountain top at left. Vertical list of participating banks of local clearing house on back. Imprint: Foote & Davies Co. Atlanta (imprint on both sides, the one on back with GA. at end). (shown at 64%)
c. Unissued, cancelled. **VG, 125. VF, 300.**

Ensley

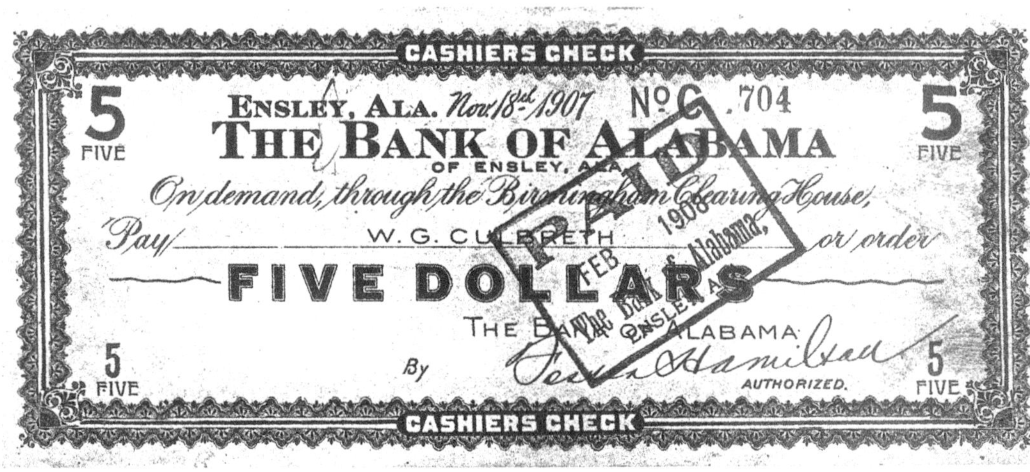

The Bank of Alabama

AL830-5. 5 Dollars Cashiers Check Nov. 18, 1907. Payable to W.G. Culbreth. (b/w) (shown at 75%)
b. Issued, cancelled. **R5**

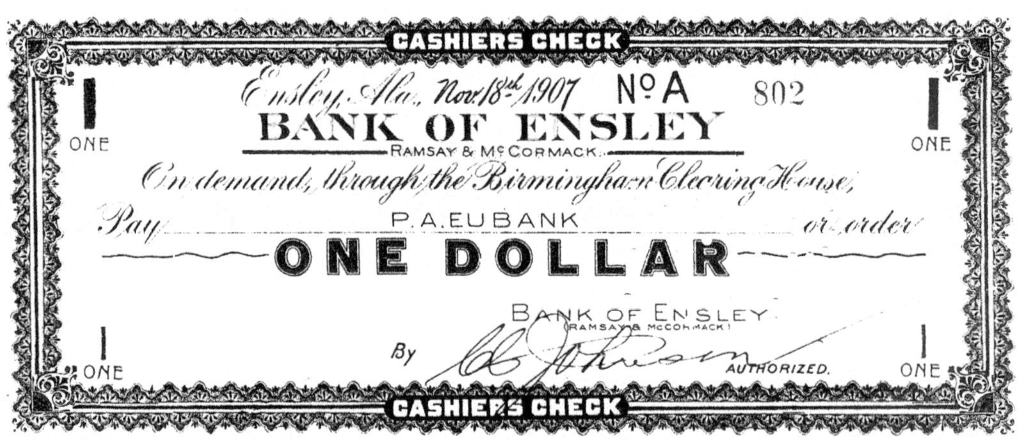

Bank of Ensley

AL850-1. 1 Dollar Cashiers Check Nov. 18, 1907. Payable to P.A. Eubank. (b/w) (shown at 74%)
b. Issued, cancelled. **R5**

AL850-5. 5 Dollars Nov. 18, 1907. As above. (b/w)
b. Issued, cancelled. **R5**

GUARANTY TRUST COMPANY OF NEW YORK/BANK OF ENSLEY

AL870-5. 5 Dollars Draft in New York Exchange Dec. 2, 1907. Payable to Peyton A. Eubank. Brown face and back. Design like AL600-2. (shown at 74%)

c. Unissued, cancelled. R4

f. Specimen. R5

Gadsden

GADSDEN CLEARING HOUSE ASSOCIATION CERTIFICATE

AL910-1. 1 Dollar ND (1907). (list)

u. Unissued. SENC

AL910-10. 10 Dollars Nov. 2, 1907. Series B, otherwise as AL910-20. (b/w)

c. Unissued, cancelled. R3

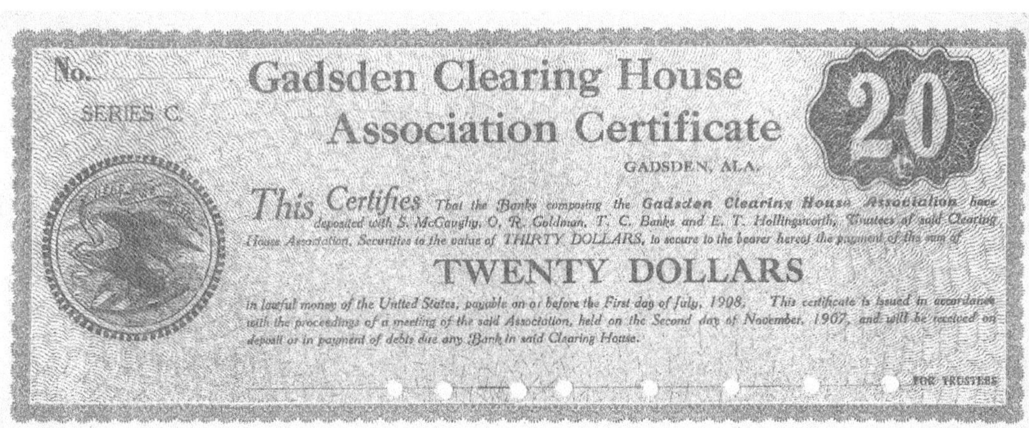

AL910-20. 20 Dollars Nov. 2, 1907. Black and green. Eagle on shield at left. Printer as AL800-1. but with back imprint only. (shown at 65%)

c. Unissued, cancelled. R2

Montgomery

MONTGOMERY CLEARING HOUSE CERTIFICATE/ THE NEW FARLEY NATIONAL BANK

AL930-.25 25 Cents Nov. 15, 1907 (stamped date). Black on off-white paper. Stamped name in purple of The New Farley National Bank (on issued notes). Red text line across bottom. Uniface. Handwritten cancellation and bank stamping with signature on back. Imprint: Brown Printing Co., Montgomery, Ala. (shown at 74%)

b. Issued, cancelled. **VG, 150. VF, 250.**

d. Unissued, remainder. **VF, 150. EF, 250.**

AL930-.50 50 Cents Nov. 15, 1907 (stamped date and bank as above). Black on peach paper, otherwise as above, including printer.

b. Issued, cancelled. **VG, 150. VF, 250.**

d. Unissued, remainder. **VF, 150. EF, 250.**

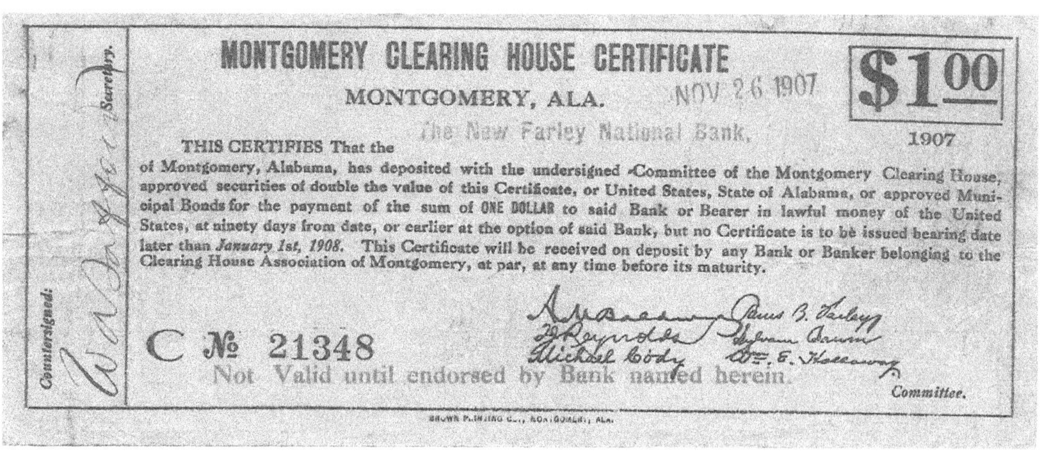

AL930-1. 1 Dollar Nov. 26, 1907 (stamped date). Bank name as above. Black on blue paper, otherwise as above. (shown at 74%)

b. Issued, cancelled. **VG, 150. VF, 250.**

AL930-2. 2 Dollars Oct. 31, 1907 (stamped date). Bank name as above. Black on gold paper, otherwise as above.

b. Issued, cancelled. **VG, 150. VF, 250.**

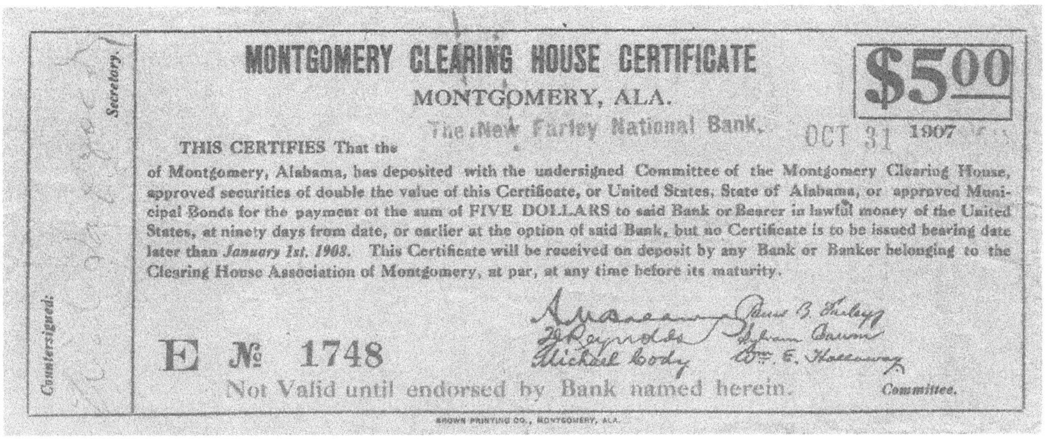

AL930-5. 5 Dollars Oct. 31, 1907 (stamped date). Bank name as above, but printed in blue. Black on blue paper, otherwise as above. (shown at 74%)
b. Issued, cancelled. **VG, 150. VF, 250.**
AL930-10. 10 Dollars Oct. 31, 1907 (stamped date and bank name as above). Black on light pinkish paper, otherwise as above.
b. Issued, cancelled. **VG, 150. VF, 250.**
AL930-50. 50 Dollars ND (1907). Design as above. (b/w)
d. Unissued, remainder. **R5**

ALASKA

Fairbanks

THE CALIFORNIA/SALCHAKET TRADING POST AND ROADHOUSE

AK500-.25 25 Cents ND (1907). Red on light tan safety paper. Hand signature of Wm. Munson at lower right. Back dark brown on tan background. Two hand signatures at bottom. Red serial number on face and back. 115 × 70mm. (shown at 100%)
a. Issued, not cancelled. **R5**

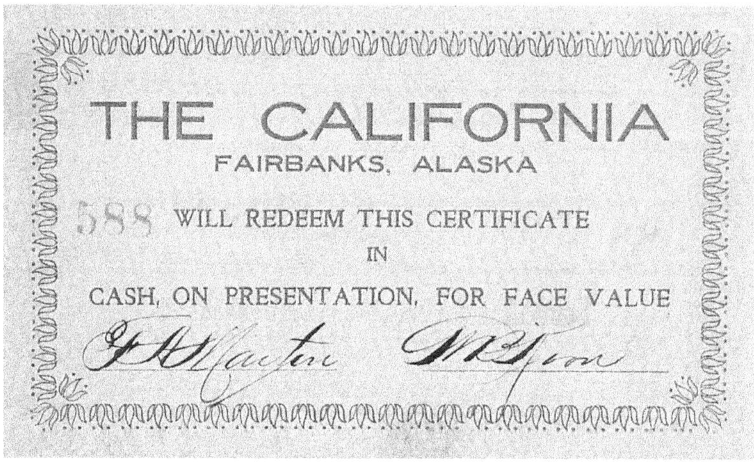

AK500-.50 50 Cents ND (1907). Description as above. (shown at 90%)

a. Issued, not cancelled. **R5**

NOTE: Salcha is located at the mouth of the Salcha River, 33 miles southeast of Fairbanks. The village was first reported in 1898 by the U.S. Geological Survey as "Salchaket," an Indian word meaning "mouth of the Salcha." The trading post was established some time before 1907. It was reportedly destroyed by fire in 1927.

FAIRBANKS BANKING CO. OF FAIRBANKS

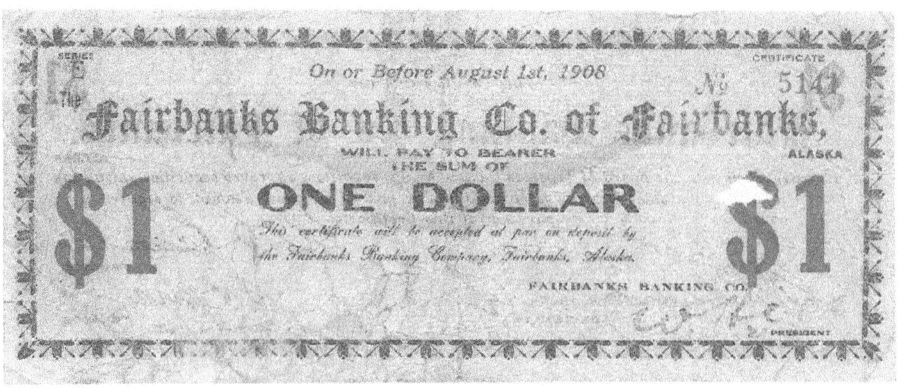

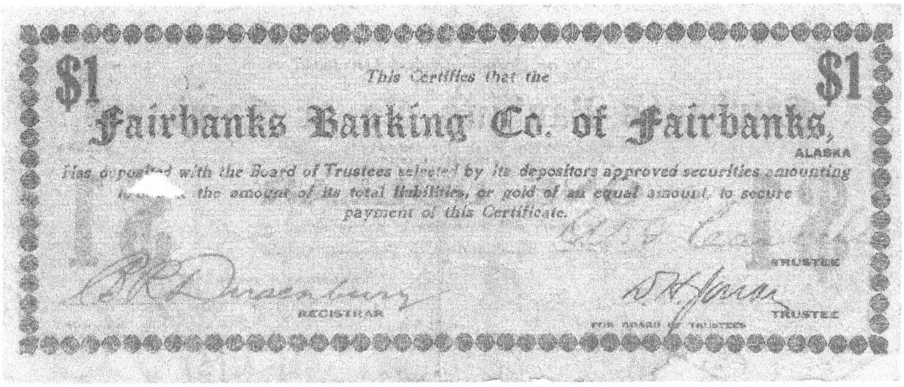

AK520-1. 1 Dollar ND (1907). Payable on or before Aug. 1, 1908. Black with red denomination on yellow paper. Green eagle at center in underprint. Single signature at lower right. Back black on green underprint. Three signatures (handwritten and printed) at bottom. (shown at 65%)
a. Issued, not cancelled. R5

First National Bank of Fairbanks

AK540-1. 1 Dollar ND (1907). Payable as above. Green on orange background. Large red denomination at center in underprint. Single signature at lower right. Back green with red numerals of value at upper corners. Orange eagle at center in underprint. Three signatures at bottom (one left, two right).
a. Issued, not cancelled. R5

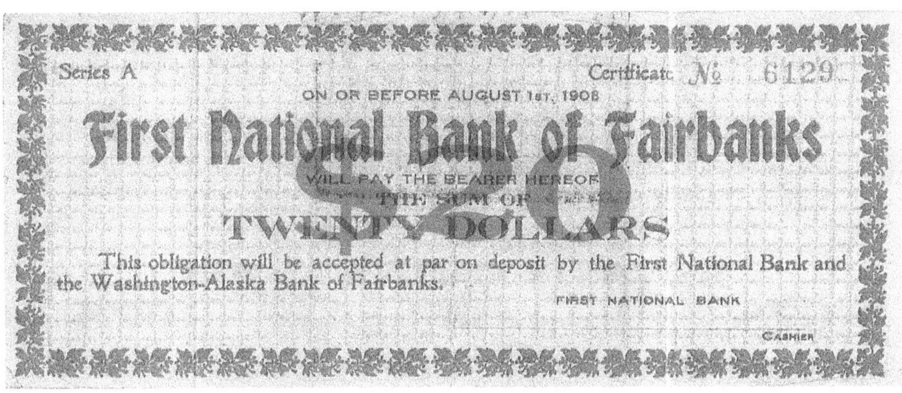

AK540-20. 20 Dollars ND (1907). Description as above. (shown at 65%)
d. Unissued, remainder. R5

AK540-50. 50 Dollars ND (1907). As above. (list)
u. Unissued. SENC

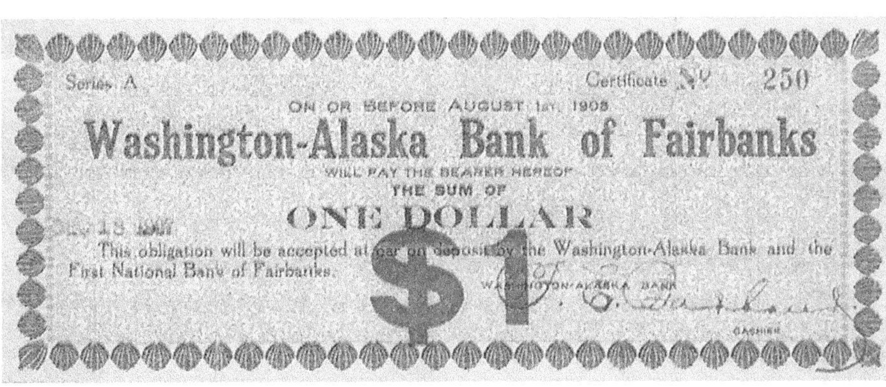

WASHINGTON–ALASKA BANK OF FAIRBANKS

AK545-1. 1 Dollar Dec. 18, 1907 (stamped date). Payable on or before Aug. 15, 1908. Black on pale red underprint. Eagle at center in underprint on back. (shown at 90%)
- d. Unissued, remainder. **R5**
- u. Unissued. **SENC**

AK545-3. 3 Dollars ND. Black on light lime green underprint. Design as above.
- d. Unissued, remainder. **R5**

AK545-5. 5 Dollars ND. Black on dull orange underprint. Design as above.
- d. Unissued, remainder. **R5**

AK545-10. 10 Dollars ND. Black on light blue underprint. Design as above.
- d. Unissued, remainder. **R5**

AK545-20. 20 Dollars ND. Black on pale red underprint. Design as above.
- d. Unissued, remainder. **R5**

AK545-50. 50 Dollars ND. Black on light lime green underprint. Design as above.
- d. Unissued, remainder. **R5**

AK545-100. 100 Dollars Dec., 1907. Black on dull orange underprint. Design as above.
- d. Unissued, remainder. **R5**

Nome

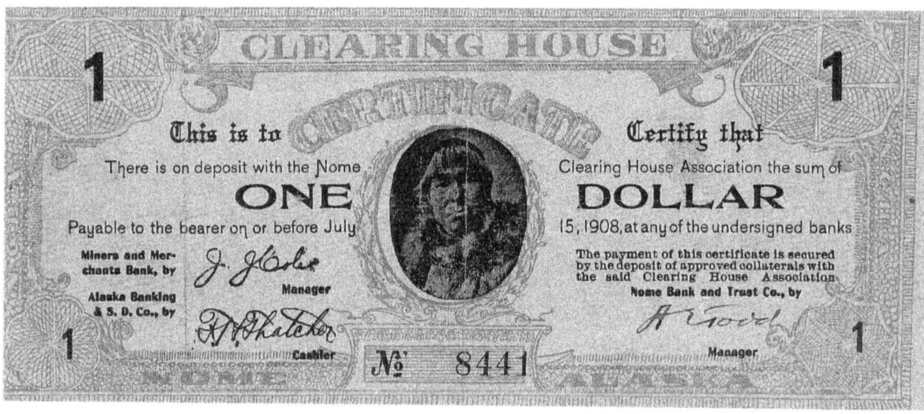

CLEARING HOUSE CERTIFICATE

AK590-1. 1 Dollar ND (1907). Payable on or before July 15, 1908. Green and black on light green paper. Eskimo portrait at center. Back light olive green; large text of clearing house across center. (shown at 70%)
- a. Issued, not cancelled. **R5**
- b. Issued, cancelled. **R5**

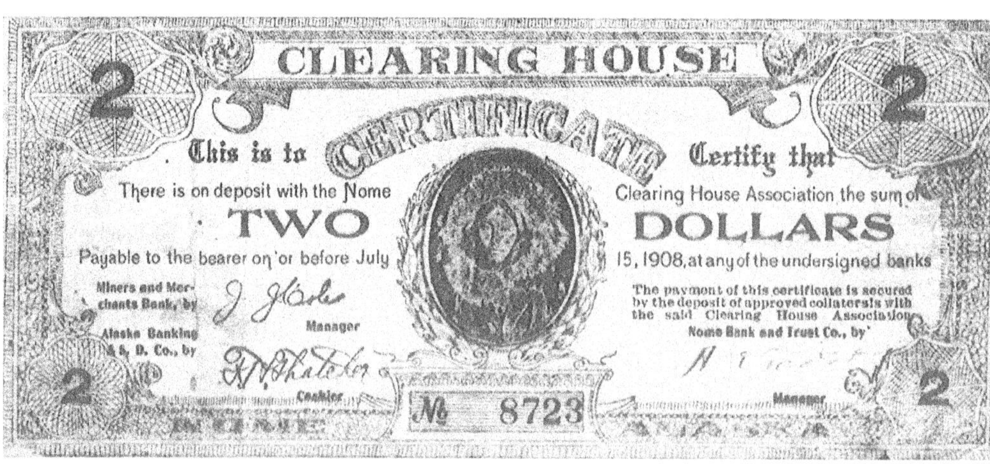

AK590-2. 2 Dollars ND (1907). Green with black portrait and wording on light green paper. Eskimo woman at center. Payable as above. (shown at 72%)

a. Issued, not cancelled. R5

b. Issued, cancelled. R5

AK590-5. 5 Dollars ND (1907). Light green and black on white paper. Moose at center. Payable as above. (shown at 65%)

b. Issued, cancelled. R5

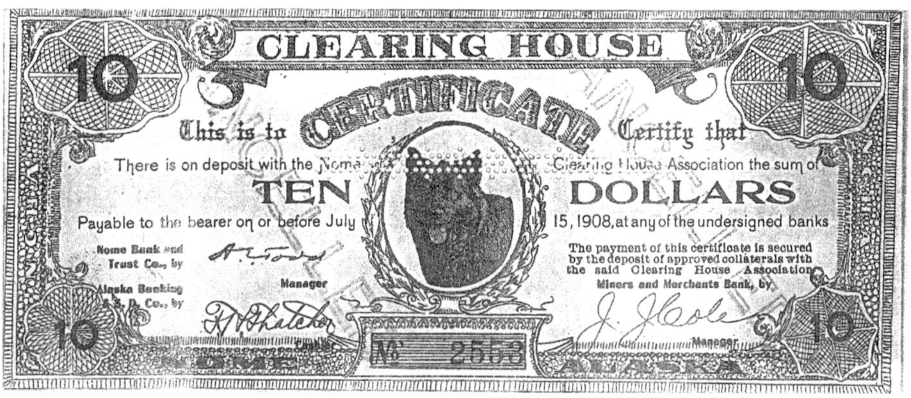

AK590-10. 10 Dollars ND (1907). Colors and text as above. Wolf at center. Payable as above. (shown at 67%)

b. Issued, cancelled. R5

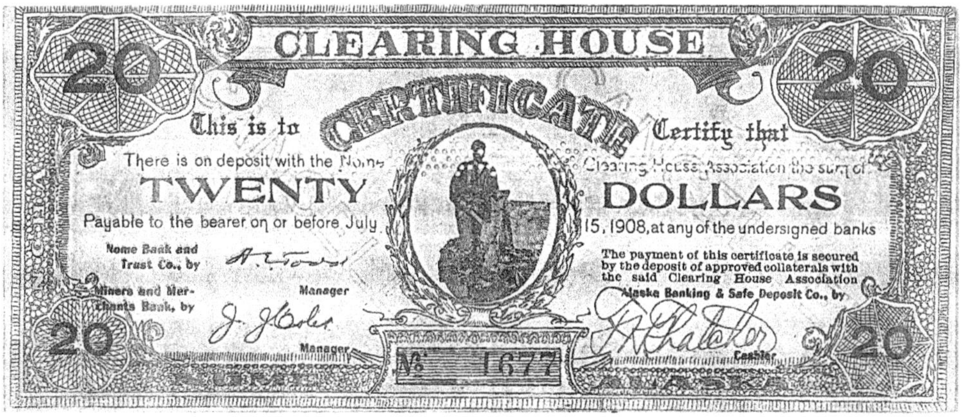

AK590-20. 20 Dollars ND (1907). Colors and text as above. Man with skins at center. Payable as above. (shown at 71%)

b. Issued, cancelled. **R5**

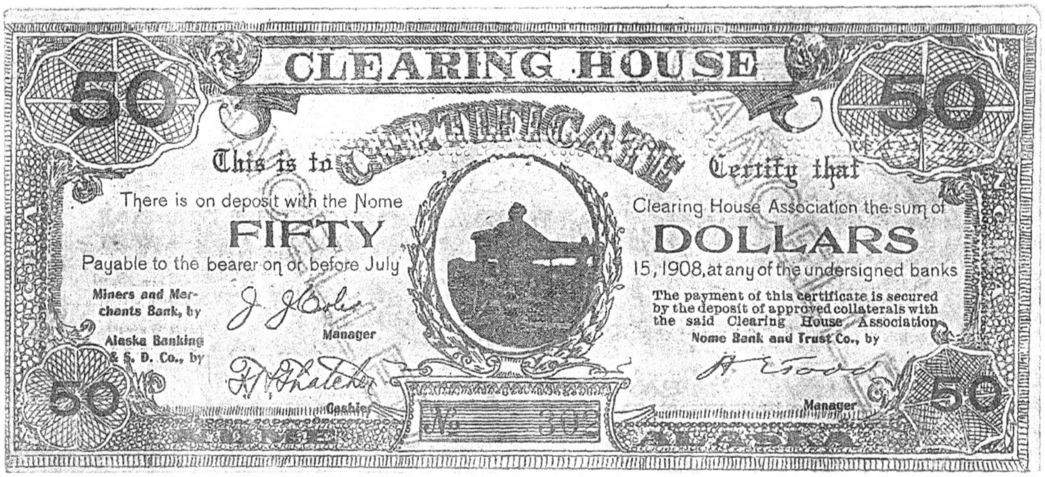

AK590-50. 50 Dollars ND (1907). Colors and text as above. Eskimo in kayak at center. Payable as above. (shown at 78%)

b. Issued, cancelled. **R5**

AK590-100. 100 Dollars ND (1907). Colors and text as above. Gold nugget at center. Payable as above. (shown at 78%)

b. Issued, cancelled. **R5**

NOTE: Every certificate had a representative facsimile signature from each of the three member banks at the bottom. Locations of these bank names and their respective signatures were sometimes switched so that the signature at lower right might be from any of the three banks.

ARIZONA

Benson

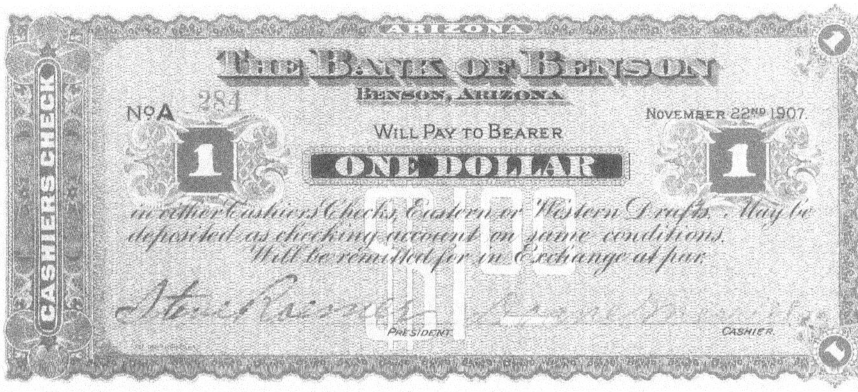

THE BANK OF BENSON

AZ500-1. 1 Dollar Cashiers Check Nov. 22, 1907. Face black and green. Back green; standing allegory of Liberty with flag at center in circle, shield at left and right. Imprint: The Union Litho. Co., L.A. (shown at 60%)

a. Issued, not cancelled. **R4**

Bisbee

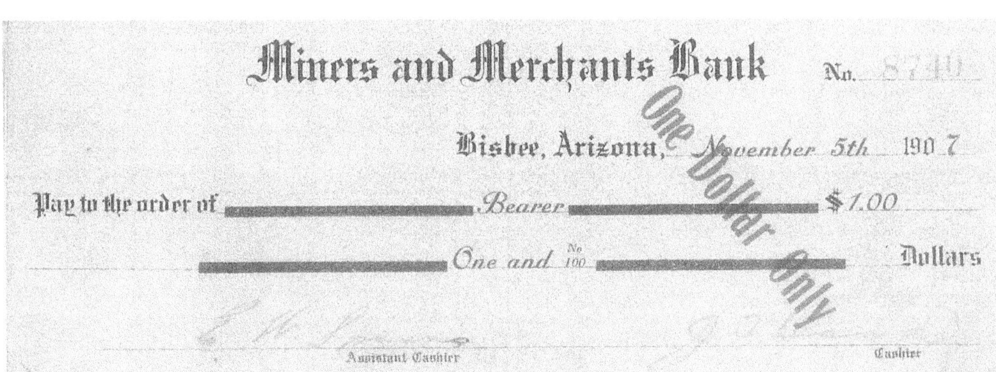

Miners and Merchants Bank

AZ520-1. 1 Dollar (cashier's check) Nov. 5, 1907. Black on gray underprint, yellow paper. Red value in words diagonally at right center. Altered bank check format. Uniface. Imprint: Stephens Litho & Eng. Co. St. Louis. (shown at 65%)
a. Issued, not cancelled. R5

Douglas

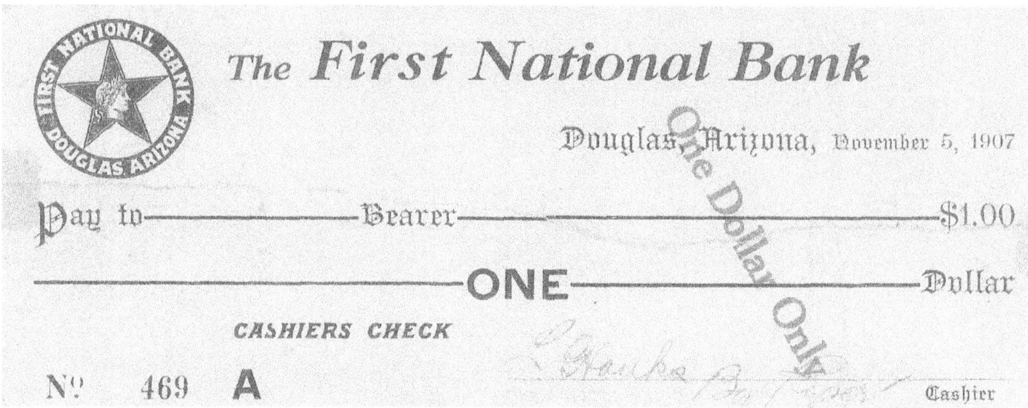
FIRST NATIONAL BANK DOUGLAS ARIZONA
The First National Bank
Douglas, Arizona, November 5, 1907
Pay to——Bearer——$1.00
——ONE——Dollar
One Dollar Only
CASHIERS CHECK
No. 469 A
Cashier

The First National Bank

AZ540-1. 1 Dollar Cashiers Check Nov. 5, 1907. Black on light tan paper. Bank emblem at upper left. Red value in words diagonally at right center. Bearer check format. Uniface. (shown at 68%)
a. Issued, not cancelled. R5

Globe

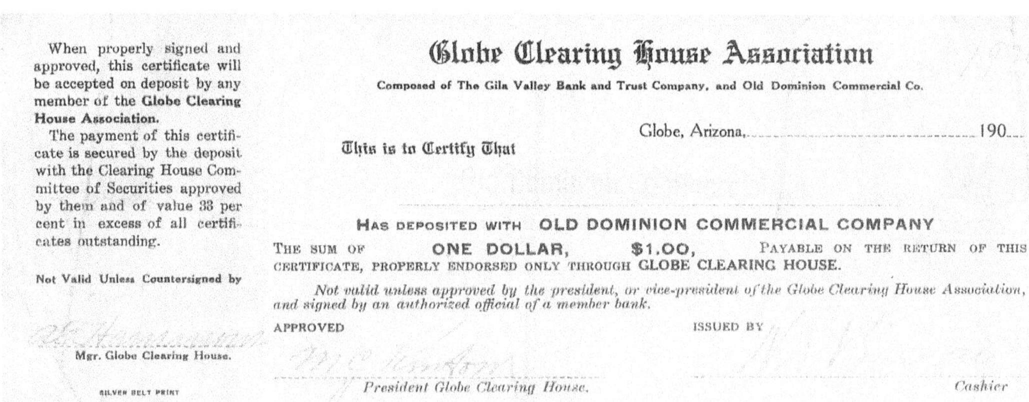
When properly signed and approved, this certificate will be accepted on deposit by any member of the Globe Clearing House Association.
The payment of this certificate is secured by the deposit with the Clearing House Committee of Securities approved by them and of value 33 per cent in excess of all certificates outstanding.
Not Valid Unless Countersigned by
Mgr. Globe Clearing House.
SILVER BELT PRINT

Globe Clearing House Association
Composed of The Gila Valley Bank and Trust Company, and Old Dominion Commercial Co.
Globe, Arizona, ... 190...
This is to Certify That
HAS DEPOSITED WITH OLD DOMINION COMMERCIAL COMPANY
THE SUM OF ONE DOLLAR, $1.00, PAYABLE ON THE RETURN OF THIS CERTIFICATE, PROPERLY ENDORSED ONLY THROUGH GLOBE CLEARING HOUSE.
Not valid unless approved by the president, or vice-president of the Globe Clearing House Association, and signed by an authorized official of a member bank.
APPROVED ISSUED BY
President Globe Clearing House. *Cashier*

Globe Clearing House Association/
Old Dominion Commercial Co.

AZ560-1. 1 Dollar Certificate of Deposit Dec. 19, 1907. Black on yellow paper. Stamped name of Old Dominion Commercial Co. along with printed name at center. Uniface. Imprint: Silver Belt Print. (shown at 65%)
a. Issued, not cancelled. R5

Tombstone

The First National Bank

AZ600-1. 1 Dollar Cashier's Check Dec. 14, 1907 (stamped date). Denomination filled in by hand. Payable to "Any one." One hand signature at bottom right. NOT OVER FIVE DOLLARS 5 stamped across face at right.

a. Issued, not cancelled. **R5**

Tucson

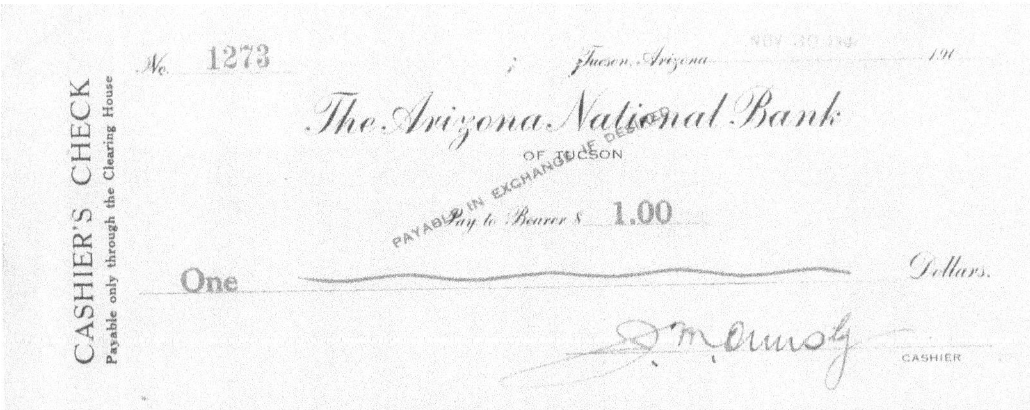

The Arizona National Bank

AZ620-1. 1 Dollar Cashier's Check Nov. 30, 1907 (stamped date). Black on yellow paper. Diagonal red text line at center, red value in word and numerals. Uniface. (shown at 75%)

a. Issued, not cancelled. **R5**

Consolidated National Bank

AZ640-1. 1 Dollar Cashier's Check Nov. 17, 1907. Pink paper. Design and format as above.

a. Issued, not cancelled. **R5**

Arkansas

Forrest City

Bank of Eastern Arkansas

AR500-1. 1 Dollar Bank Certificate Nov. 4, 1907. Green face and back. Red value in outline letters across center. Same design with arms on both sides. Serial no. B-99314.

d. Unissued, remainder. **VG, 100. VF, 300.**

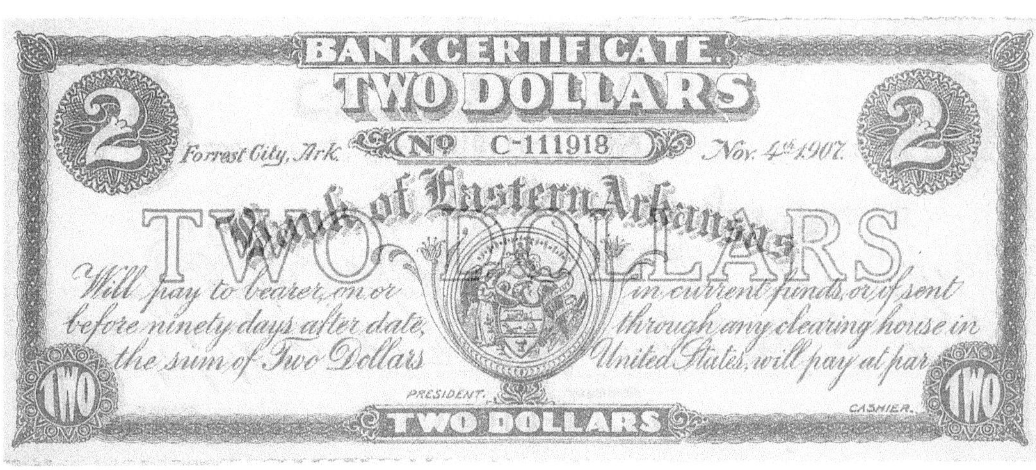

AR500-2. 2 Dollars Nov. 4, 1907. As above. Serial no. C-111918. (shown at 74%)
d. Unissued, remainder. **VG, 100. VF, 300.**
AR500-5. 5 Dollars Nov. 4, 1907. As above. Serial no. D-16871.
d. Unissued, remainder. **VG, 100. VF, 300.**
AR500-10. 10 Dollars Nov. 4, 1907. As above. Serial no. E-100013.
d. Unissued, remainder. **VG, 100. VF, 300.**
NOTE: It appears that each denomination of the above issue has a particular serial number that appears on all known examples of that value. No facts have been found to explain this strange situation. Though most known examples show what appear to be indications of usage, these notes were reportedly not issued to circulation.

BANK OF FORREST CITY

AR505-.50 50 Cents Cashier's Check. Nov. 15, 1907. Black on greenish gray underprint. Denomination and check designation in violet. Pay to "E.A. Rolfe or bearer..." Small size. (shown at 100%)
a. Issued, not cancelled. R5

Fort Smith

MERCHANTS NATIONAL BANK

FIRST ISSUE

AR520-1. 1 Dollar Cashier's Check Nov. 7, 9, 11, 1907 (stamped date). Black on white paper. Red numeral 1 near upper left corner. Two hand signatures. Vertical text with instructions on use and redemption at left. Uniface. Imprint: Weldon, Williams & Liew, Ft. Smith, Ark. (shown at 74%)
a. Issued, not cancelled. R5
b. Issued, cancelled. R5

c. Unissued, cancelled. (shown at 72%) R3
AR520-2. 2 Dollars ND (1907). As above. Without imprint. (b/w)
c. Unissued, cancelled. R5
AR520-5. 5 Dollars ND (1907). As above. Without imprint. (b/w)
c. Unissued, cancelled. R5
AR520-10. 10 Dollars ND (1907). As above. Without imprint. (b/w)
c. Unissued, cancelled. R5

Second Issue

AR525-1. 1 Dollar (1907). Light green safety paper. Similar to AR520-1. but instructions at left with unspecified differences. Uniface. Not issued. (shown at 73%)
c. Unissued, cancelled. R5

AR525-2. 2 Dollars (1907). Similar to AR525-1. (shown at 72%)
c. Unissued, cancelled R5

AR525-5. 5 Dollars (1907). Similar to AR525-1. (shown at 72%)
c. Unissued, cancelled. R5
AR525-10. 10 Dollars (1907). Similar to AR525-1.
c. Unissued, cancelled. R5

Little Rock

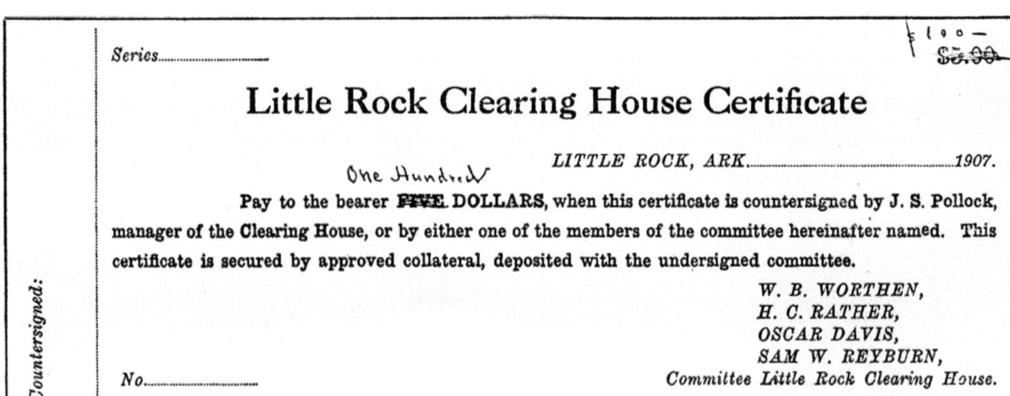

Little Rock Clearing House Certificate

AR560-5. 5 Dollars Clearing House Certificate 1907. (b/w) (shown at 75%)
 d. Unissued, remainder. **R5**

NOTE: The example shown has its denomination altered by hand from $5 to $100. in numerals and wording.

Pine Bluff

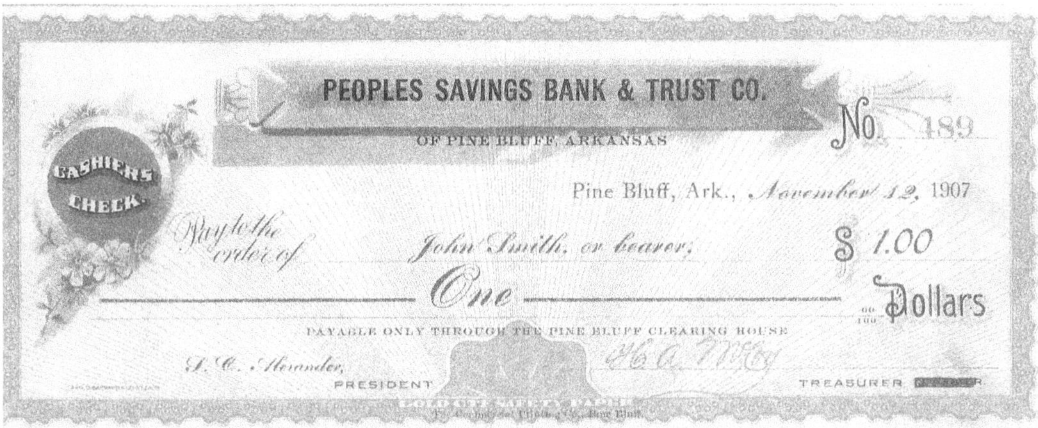

Peoples Savings Bank & Trust Co.

AR600-1. 1 Dollar Cashiers Check Nov. 12, 1907. Black and orange on yellow paper. Uniface. Imprints: Geo. D. Barnard & Co. St. Louis/The Commercial Printing Co., Pine Bluff. (shown at 66%)
 a. Issued, not cancelled. **R5**

California

Berkeley

The First National Bank of Berkeley

A. First Issue — Uniface

CA500-5. 5 Dollars Certificate of Deposit Nov. 9, 1907. Red text and border on cream paper. Uniface. (shown at 71%)

b. Issued, cancelled.	**R5**
c. Unissued, cancelled.	**R3**

CA500-10. 10 Dollars Nov. 5, 1907. Black text and border. As above.

b. Issued, cancelled.	**R5**
c. Unissued, cancelled.	**R3**

CA500-20. 20 Dollars Nov. 5, 1907. Blue text and border. As above.

b. Issued, cancelled.	**R5**
c. Unissued, cancelled.	**R4**

B. Second Issue — Two-sided

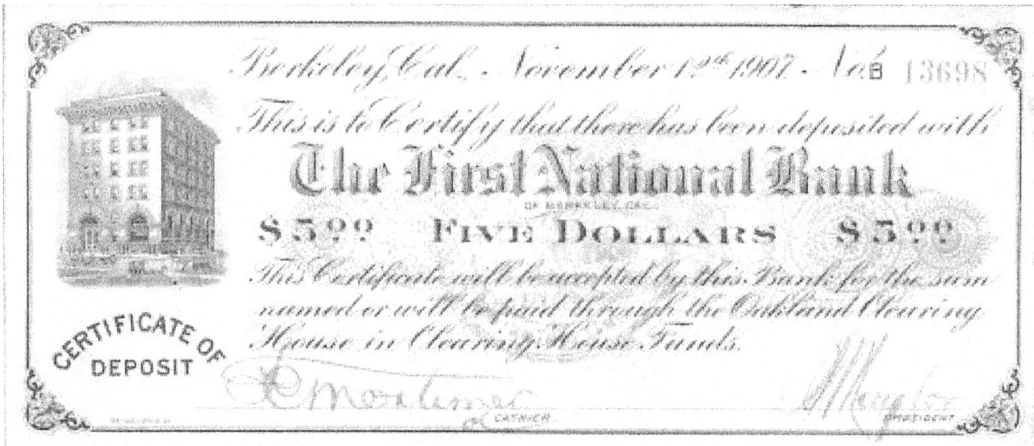

CA520-5. 5 Dollars Certificate of Deposit Nov. 12, 1907. Black on orange underprint. Bank building at left. Back brownish orange. Imprint: The Union Litho. Co. S.F. (shown at 75%)

b. Issued, cancelled. **VG, 300. VF 650.**

C520-10. 10 Dollars Nov. 12, 1907. As above. Black on green underprint. Back green.

b. Issued, cancelled. **VG, 300. VF, 650.**

Fresno

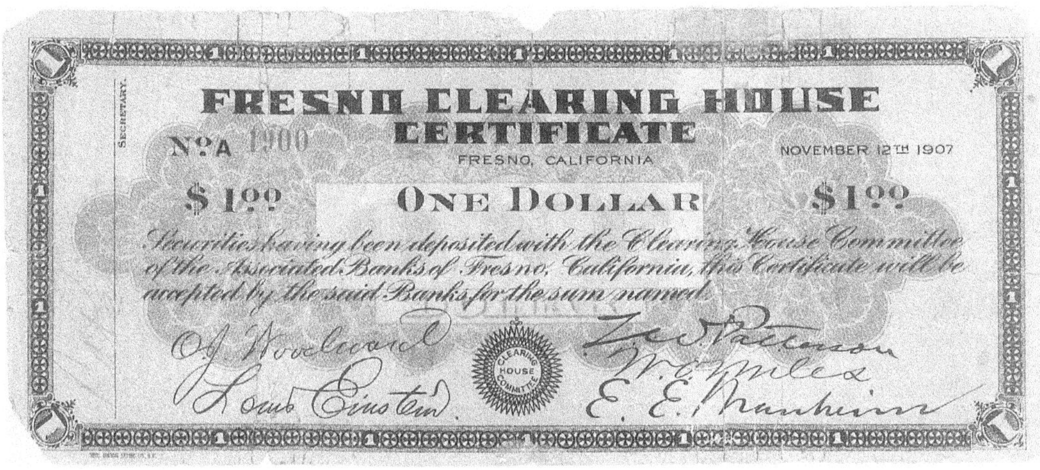

FRESNO CLEARING HOUSE CERTIFICATE

CA540-1. 1 Dollar Nov. 12, 1907. Black text and border on reddish brown underprint. Five signatures at lower portion, one vertically at left. Back reddish brown. Imprint: The Union Litho. Co. S.F. (shown at 70%)

a. Issued, not cancelled. **VG, 300. VF, 700.**

CA540-2. 2 Dollars Nov. 12, 1907. Black text and border on blue underprint. Generally as above.

b. Issued, cancelled. **R5**

Los Angeles

LOS ANGELES CLEARING HOUSE CERTIFICATE

A. Uniface Issue

CA600-1. 1 Dollar Nov. 5, 1907. Blue text on cream paper. Imprint: The Union Litho. Co. L.A. (shown at 70%)

a. Issued, not cancelled. **VG, 125. VF, 300.**

u. Issued. **SENC**

CA600-10. 10 Dollars Nov. 5, 1907. As above.

b. Issued, cancelled. **VG, 150. VF, 400.**

CA600-20. 20 Dollars Nov. 5, 1907. (list)

b. Issued, cancelled. **VG, 150. VF, 400.**

u. Unissued. **SENC**

B. Two-sided Issue

CA610-1. 1 Dollar Nov. 5, 1907. Black and green on light green underprint. White value in numerals in underprint at center. Back green; eagle with flag at center. Imprint: The Union Litho. Co. L.A.

a. Issued, not cancelled. **VG, 50. VF, 100.**

b. Issued, cancelled. **VG, 40. VF, 85.**

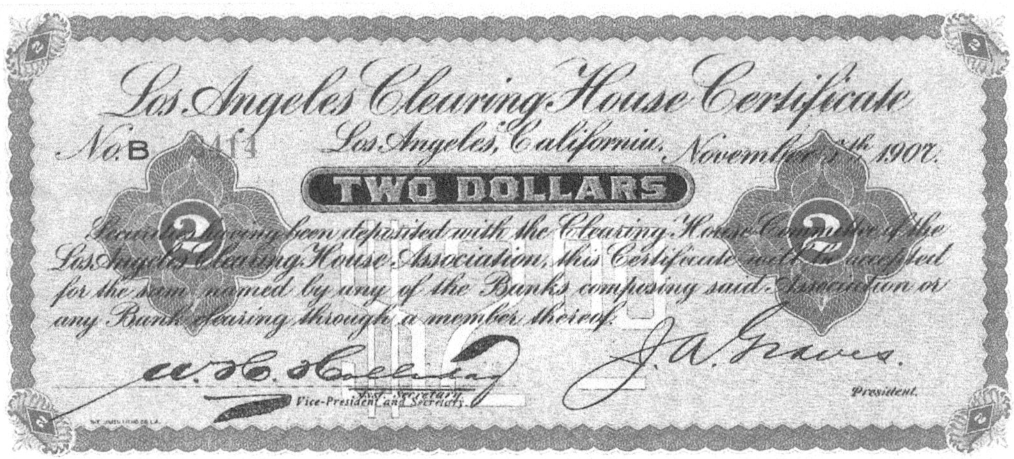

CA610-2. 2 Dollars Nov. 5, 1907. Black and blue on light blue underprint. Back blue. As above. (shown at 70%)

a. Issued, not cancelled. **VG, 140. VF, 300.**

b. Issued, cancelled. **VG, 75. VF, 150.**

CA610-5. 5 Dollars Nov. 5, 1907. Black and brown on light brown underprint. Back brown. As above.

a. Issued, not cancelled. **VG, 200. VF, 500.**

b. Issued, cancelled. **VG, 100. VF, 200.**

CA610-10. 10 Dollars Nov. 5, 1907. Black and tan on light gold underprint. Back tan. As above.

a. Issued, not cancelled. **SENC**

b. Issued, cancelled. **VG, 140. VF, 300.**

NOTE: A variant of CA610-1, 5 and 10.a exists with title "Assistant Secretary" crossed out and new title "Vice-President and Secretary" placed below.

CA610-20. 20 Dollars Nov. 5, 1907. (list)

b. Issued, cancelled. **VG, 200. VF, 400.**

ERROR NOTE: Illustrated is an example of CA610-1.a that received the black face text and red serial number in an upside down position. In a CAA auction of September 2005, this note sold for $425.00. (shown at 72%)

Oakland

Oakland Clearing House Certificate

CA640-1. 1 Dollar Nov. 1, 1907. Black on light brown underprint. Back brown; denomination at center. Imprint: The Union Litho. Co., S.F. (shown at 69%)

a. Issued, not cancelled. **VG, 120. VF, 250.**

CA640-10. 10 Dollars Nov. 1, 1907. Black on green underprint. Back green. As above.

c. Unissued, cancelled. **VG, 175. VF, 375.**

CA640-20. 20 Dollars Nov. 1, 1907. Black on brown underprint. Back brown. As above.

c. Unissued, cancelled. **R4**

Riverside

Associated Banks of Riverside, California

CA680-1. 1 Dollar Nov. 25, 1907. Black on green frame. White numerals of value in underprint. Back green; woman with shield at center. Imprint: The Union Litho. Co. L.A.

a. Issued, not cancelled. **R2**

b. Issued, cancelled. **EF, 50. Unc., 85.**

c. Unissued, cancelled. **EF, 50. Unc., 85.**

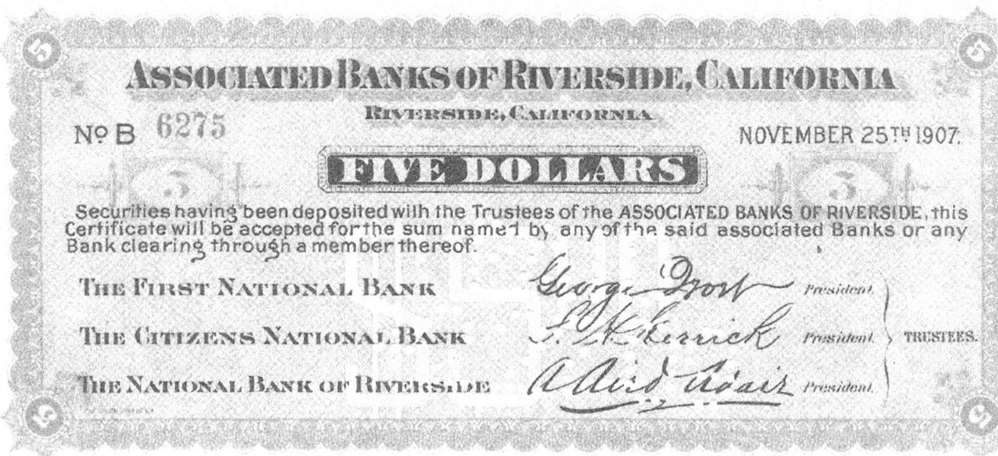

CA680-5. 5 Dollars Nov. 25, 1907. Black on brown frame. Back brown. As above. (shown at 71%)

b. Issued, cancelled. **EF, 65. Unc., 100.**

CA680-10. 10 Dollars Nov. 25, 1907. Black on purple frame. Back purple. As above.

b. Issued, cancelled. **EF, 100. Unc., 175.**

CA680-20. 20 Dollars Nov. 25, 1907. Black on orange frame. Back orange. As above.
b. Issued, cancelled. **EF, 125. Unc. 200.**

Sacramento

Sacramento Clearing House Certificate

CA700-1. 1 Dollar ND (1907). Black on cream paper. Uniface.
a. Issued, not cancelled. **R5**

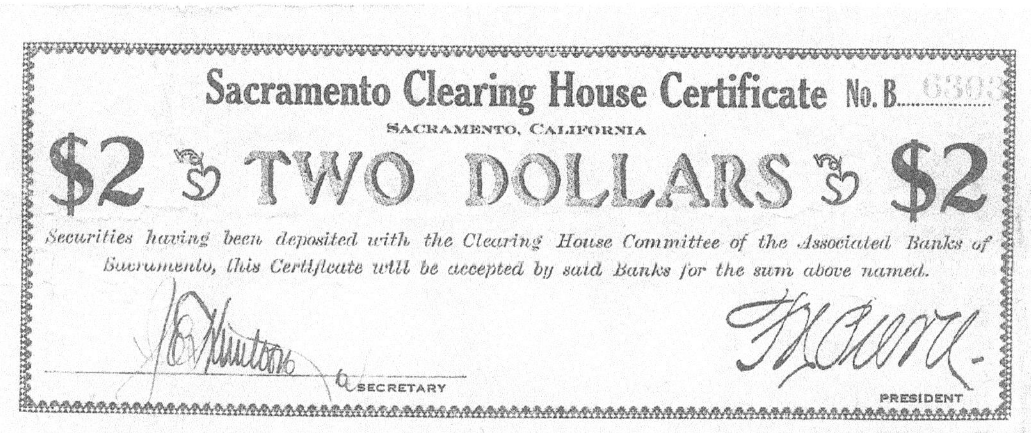

CA700-2. 2 Dollars ND (1907). As above. (shown at 73%)
a. Issued, not cancelled. **R5**

San Francisco

San Francisco Clearing House Certificate

A. Uniface Issue

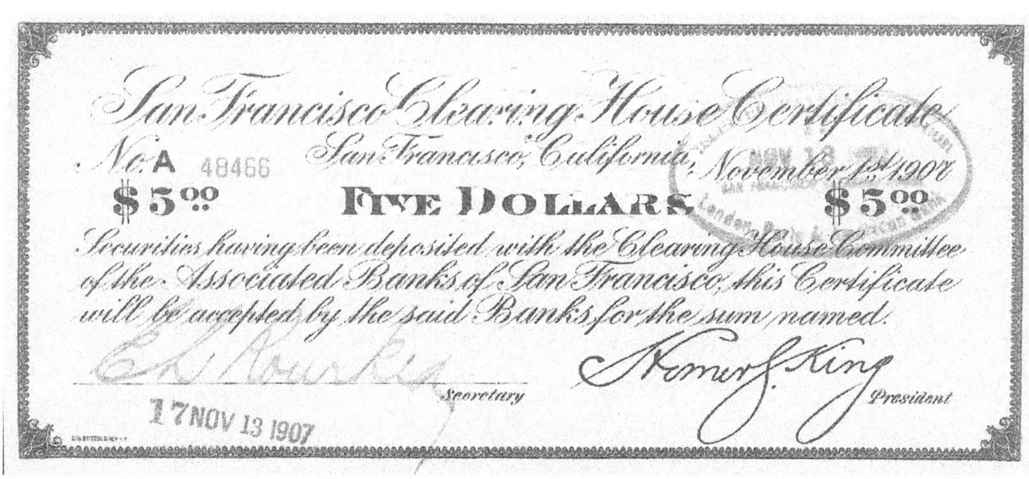

CA730-5. 5 Dollars Nov. 1, 1907. Black on light gray underprint. Imprint: Lith. Britton & Rey, S.F. (shown at 71%)
b. Issued, cancelled. **VG, 20. VF, 40.**
c. Unissued, cancelled. **Fine, 20. EF, 40.**

CA730-10. 10 Dollars Nov. 1, 1907. Black on light blue underprint. As above.
b. Issued, cancelled. **VG, 20. VF, 40.**
c. Unissued, cancelled. **Fine, 20. EF, 40.**

CA730-20. 20 Dollars Nov. 1, 1907. Black on light blue underprint. As above.
- b. Issued, cancelled. **VG, 20. VF, 40.**
- c. Unissued, cancelled. **Fine, 20. EF, 40.**

B. Two-sided Issue

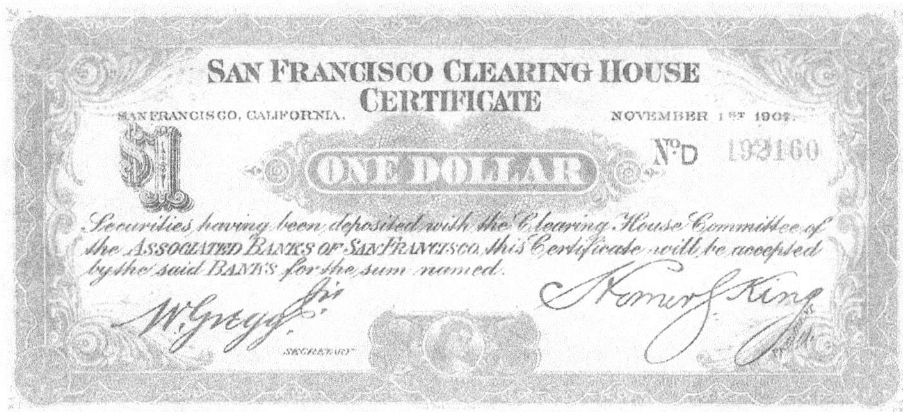

CA750-1. 1 Dollar Nov. 1, 1907. Black text on red-brown frame and value at center. Small Liberty head at lower center. Back brown. Imprint: Lith. Britton & Rey, S.F. (shown at 64%)
- a. Issued, not cancelled. **VG, 25. VF, 60.**
- b. Issued, cancelled. **VG, 20. VF, 40.**
- c. Unissued, cancelled. **Fine, 20. EF, 40.**

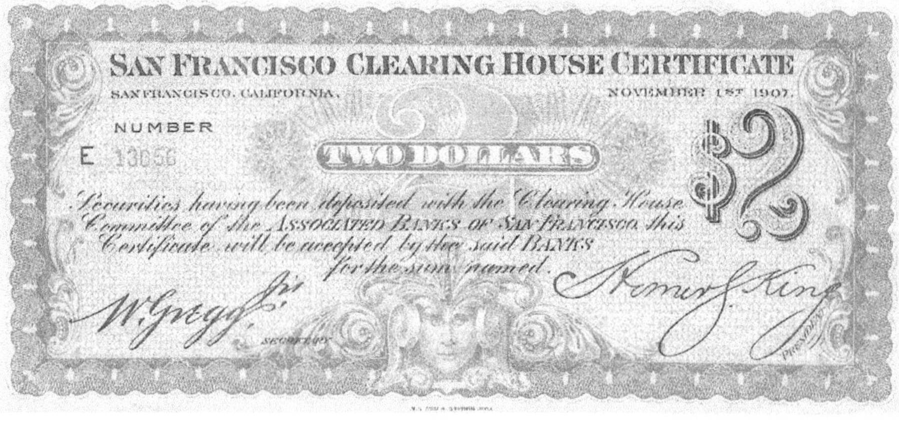

CA750-2. 2 Dollars Nov. 1, 1907. Black text on lighter or darker blue frame. Allegorical head at lower center. Back blue or grayish purple. Printer as above. (shown at 65%)

a. Issued, not cancelled. **VG, 110. VF, 225.**
b. Issued, cancelled. **VG, 25. VF, 55.**
c. Unissued, cancelled. **Fine, 20. EF, 40.**

NOTE: Printer's bug on CA750-2. at bottom center is backwards.

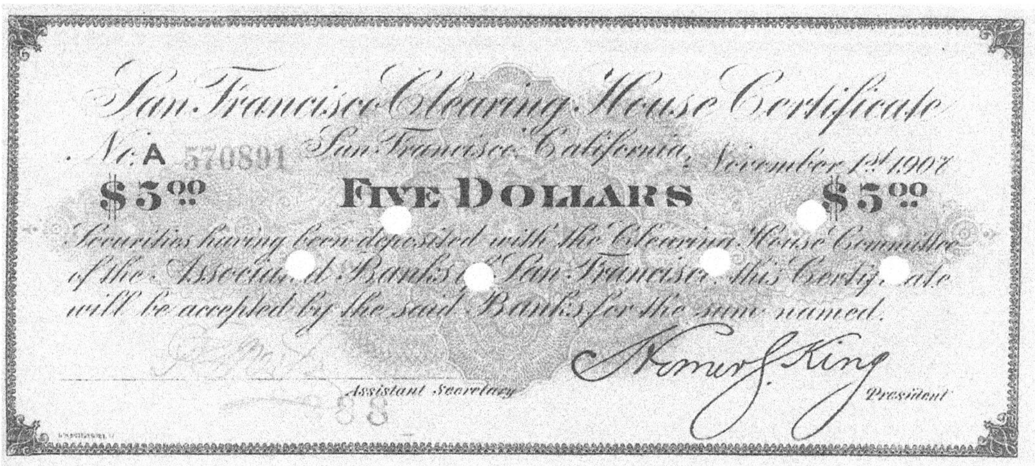

CA750-5. 5 Dollars Nov. 1, 1907. Black text on large blue guilloche, light blue paper. Back blue. Printer as above. (shown at 72%)

b. Issued, cancelled. **VG, 20. VF, 40.**

c. Unissued, cancelled. **Fine, 20. EF, 40.**

CA750-10. 10 Dollars Nov. 1, 1907. Black text on large green guilloche, light green paper. Back green. Printer as above.

b. Issued, cancelled. **VG, 20. VF, 40.**

c. Unissued, cancelled. **Fine, 20. EF, 40.**

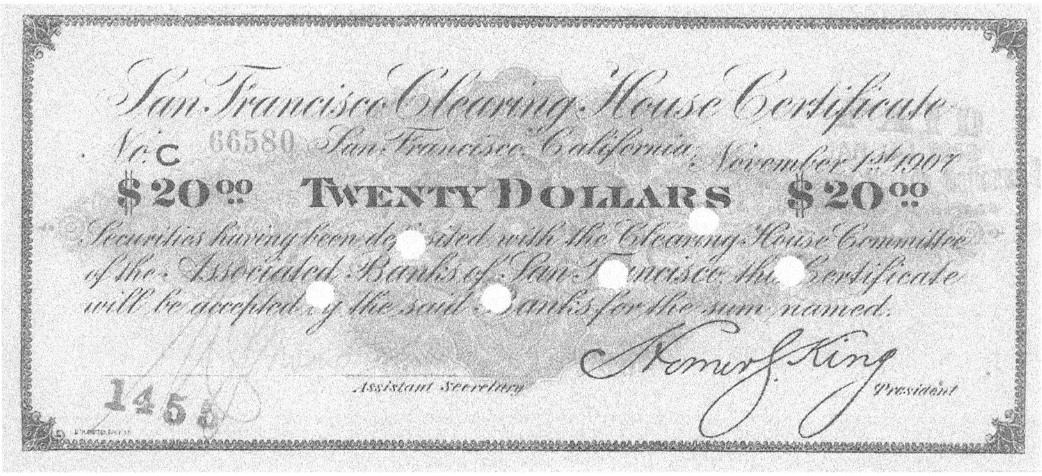

CA750-20. 20 Dollars Nov. 1, 1907. Black text on large orange guilloche, light blue paper. Back orange. Printer as above. (shown at 71%)

b. Issued, cancelled. **VG, 20. VF, 40.**

c. Unissued, cancelled. **Fine, 20. EF, 40.**

NOTE: There are two serial number styles used for San Francisco issues. The first is a smaller size with squarish numerals; the second has larger and more rounded numerals.

Loan Committee of the San Francisco Clearing House Association

CA770-1000. 1000 Dollars Oct. 28, 1907. (list)

c. Unissued, cancelled. **R5**

CA770-2000. 2000 Dollars 1907. (list)

d. Unissued, remainder. **R5**

CA770-5000. 5000 Dollars 1907. (list)
d. Unissued, remainder. R5

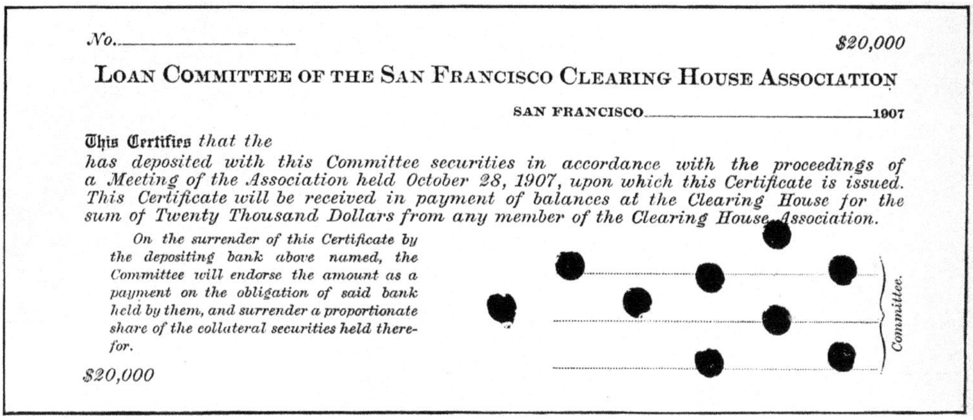
No.______ $20,000

LOAN COMMITTEE OF THE SAN FRANCISCO CLEARING HOUSE ASSOCIATION

SAN FRANCISCO______1907

This Certifies that the
has deposited with this Committee securities in accordance with the proceedings of a Meeting of the Association held October 28, 1907, upon which this Certificate is issued. This Certificate will be received in payment of balances at the Clearing House for the sum of Twenty Thousand Dollars from any member of the Clearing House Association.

On the surrender of this Certificate by the depositing bank above named, the Committee will endorse the amount as a payment on the obligation of said bank held by them, and surrender a proportionate share of the collateral securities held therefor.

$20,000

Committee.

CA770-20000. 20,000 Dollars 1907. (b/w) (shown at 70%)
c. Unissued, cancelled. R5
d. Unissued, remainder. R5

NORTHERN ELECTRIC COMPANY

CA800-1. 1 Dollar (pay roll check) Nov. 15, 1907. Black text on red-brown frame, with company symbol at center. Embossed seal at left. Back red-brown. Series D. Imprint: Lith. Britton & Rey, S.F. (shown at 67%)

a. Issued, not cancelled.	**R4**
b. Issued, cancelled.	**R2**
d. Unissued, remainder.	**EF, 200. Unc., 450.**

CA800-5. 5 Dollars Nov. 15, 1907. Black text on aqua blue frame, with symbol at center. Uniface. Printer as above. Series A.

c. Unissued, cancelled.	**R2**
d. Unissued, remainder.	**EF, 200. Unc., 450.**

Series B
No.
San Francisco, California, November 15th 1907. $10.00
On January 15, 1908 Northern Electric Company
will pay to the bearer hereof the sum of
$10.00 TEN DOLLARS $10.00
WITNESS the name and seal of Northern Electric Company, the engraved fac-simile signature of its President, and the signature of its Secretary or Assistant Secretary.
NORTHERN ELECTRIC COMPANY,
By President.
By Secretary

CA800-10. 10 Dollars Nov. 15, 1907. Black text on blue frame, with symbol at center. Uniface. Printer as above. Series B. (shown at 71%)

b. Issued, cancelled.	**R2**
c. Unissued, cancelled.	**EF, 200. Unc., 450.**

CA800-20. 20 Dollars Nov. 15, 1907. Black text on light blue frame, with symbol at center. Uniface. Printer as above. Series C.

c. Unissued, cancelled.	**R2**
d. Unissued, remainder.	**EF, 200. Unc., 450.**

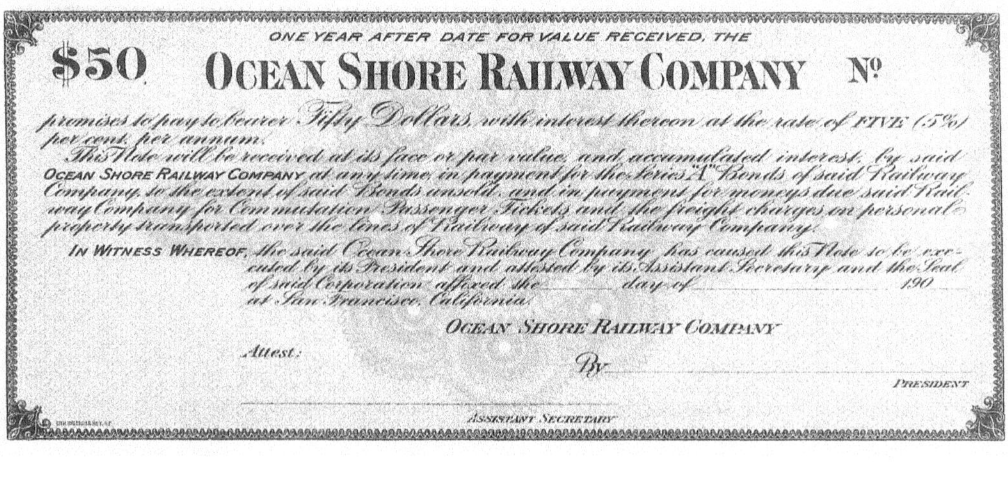
ONE YEAR AFTER DATE FOR VALUE RECEIVED, THE
$50 OCEAN SHORE RAILWAY COMPANY No
promises to pay to bearer Fifty Dollars, with interest thereon at the rate of FIVE (5%) per cent. per annum.
This Note will be received at its face or par value, and accumulated interest, by said OCEAN SHORE RAILWAY COMPANY, at any time, in payment for the Series "A" Bonds of said Railway Company, to the extent of said Bonds unsold, and in payment for moneys due said Railway Company for Commutation Passenger Tickets and the freight charges on personal property transported over the lines of Railway of said Railway Company.
IN WITNESS WHEREOF, the said Ocean Shore Railway Company has caused this Note to be executed by its President and attested by its Assistant Secretary and the Seal of said Corporation affixed the day of 190 at San Francisco, California.
OCEAN SHORE RAILWAY COMPANY
Attest: By
PRESIDENT
ASSISTANT SECRETARY

OCEAN SHORE RAILWAY COMPANY

CA820-50. 50 Dollars (bond) 190_ (1907). Black text on light blue underprint. Back blue, with large denomination at center. 5 percent interest-bearing note. Imprint: Lith. Britton & Rey, S.F. (shown at 71%)
d. Unissued, remainder. **R4**

CA820-100. 100 Dollars 190_ (1907). Black text on light orange underprint. Back light orange. As above.
d. Unissued, remainder. **R5**

San Luis Obispo

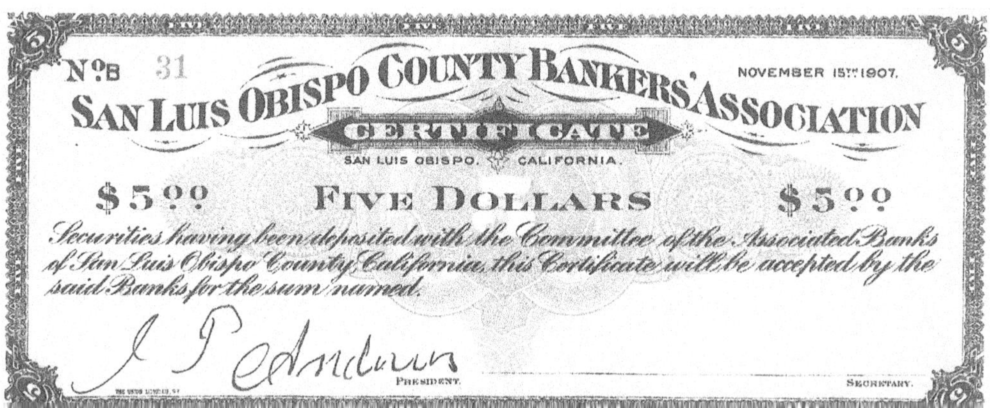

San Luis Obispo County Bankers' Association Certificate

CA840-5. 5 Dollars Nov. 1, 1907. Black on green underprint. Back green. Imprint: The Union Litho. Co. S.F. (shown at 68%)

c. Unissued, cancelled. **R4**
d. Unissued, remainder. **R3**

Santa Rosa

Sonoma County Clearing House Certificate

CA860-1. 1 Dollar Nov. 6, 1907. Black on orange underprint, yellow paper. Back orange with ornate design. Imprint: Lith. Britton & Rey, S.F. (shown at 73%)

a. Issued, not cancelled. **VG, 400. VF, 750.**
b. Issued, cancelled. **VG, 250. VF, 450.**
c. Unissued, cancelled. **Unc., 350.**
d. Unissued, remainder. **Unc., 350.**

CA860-5. 5 Dollars Nov. 6, 1907. Face as above. Uniface. Printer as above.

a. Issued, not cancelled. **R5**
b. Issued, cancelled. **R5**

CA860-10. 10 Dollars Nov. 6, 1907. As CA860-5.

a. Issued, not cancelled. **R5**
b. Issued, cancelled. **R5**

CA860-20. 20 Dollars Nov. 6, 1907. As above.
  a. Issued, not cancelled. R5
  b. Issued, cancelled. R5

CA860-1000. 1000 Dollars Nov. 6, 1907. Black on aqua blue underprint, yellow paper. As above. (shown at 65%)
  b. Issued, cancelled. R5

Stockton

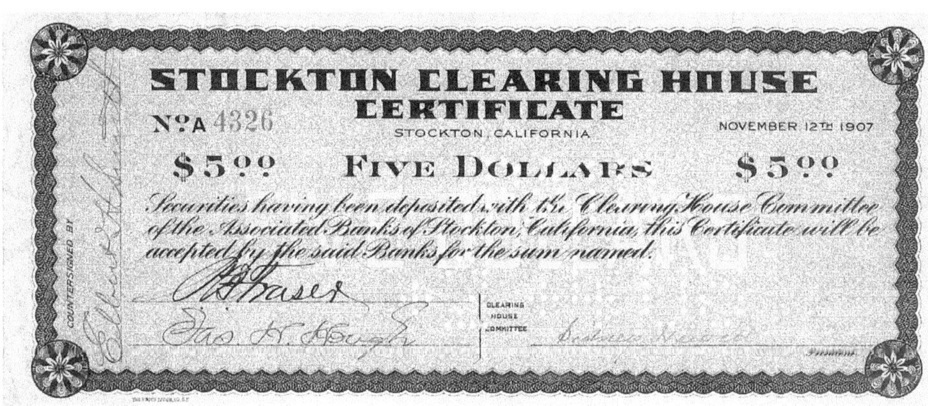

Stockton Clearing House Certificate

CA880-5. 5 Dollars Nov. 12, 1907. Black on brown underprint, white value in words across center. Back red-brown. Imprint: The Union Litho. Co., S.F. (shown at 62%)
- b. Issued, cancelled. **R3**
- u. Unissued. **SENC**

CA880-10. 10 Dollars Nov. 12, 1907. (list)
- b. Issued, cancelled. **R5**

CA880-20. 20 Dollars Nov. 12, 1907. (list)
- b. Issued, cancelled. **R5**

CA880-500. 500 Dollars Nov. 12, 1907. Black on tan underprint. As above.
- b. Issued, cancelled. **R4**

CA880-1000. 1000 Dollars Nov. 12, 1907. (list)
- b. Issued, cancelled. **R5**

Ventura

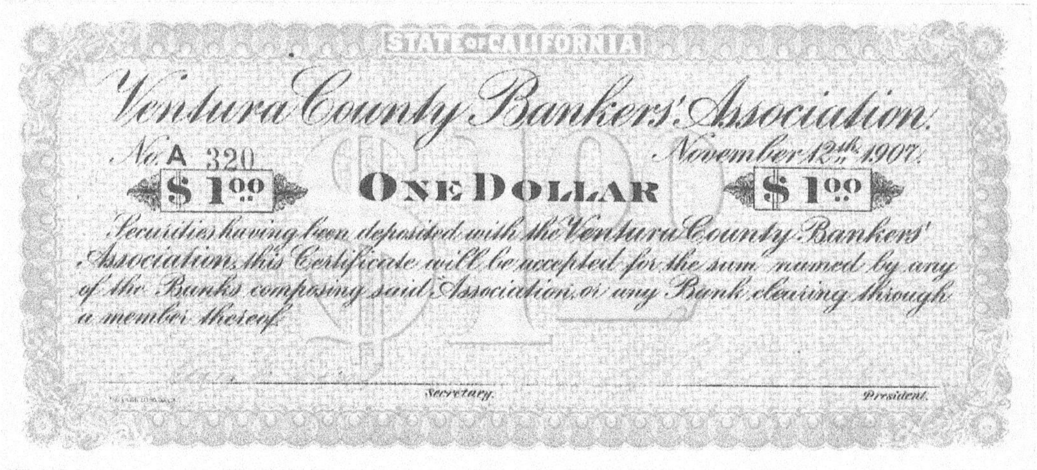

Ventura County Bankers Association

CA900-1. 1 Dollar Nov. 12, 1907. Dark blue and deep orange, with large denomination numerals at center. Uniface. Imprint: The Union Litho. Co. L.A. (shown at 69%)
- a. Issued, not cancelled. **R5**
- c. Unissued, cancelled. **R3**

CA900-2. 2 Dollars Nov. 12, 1907. Dark blue and light orange. As above.
- c. Unissued, cancelled. **R5**

CA900-5. 5 Dollars Nov. 12, 1907. Dark blue and deep orange. As above.
- c. Unissued, cancelled. **R5**

CA900-10. 10 Dollars Nov. 12, 1907. Dark blue and light orange. As above.
- c. Unissued, cancelled. **R5**

CA900-20. 20 Dollars Nov. 12, 1907. Dark blue and light orange. As above.
- c. Unissued, cancelled. **R4**

Colorado

Boulder

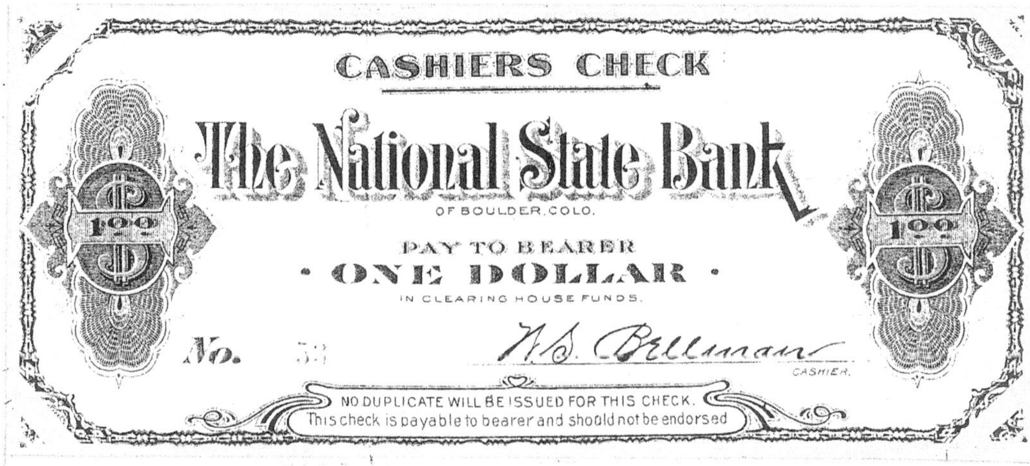

The National State Bank

CO500-1. 1 Dollar Cashiers Check ND (1907). (b/w) (shown at 74%)
  a. Issued, not cancelled. **R5**

Denver

The Big Five Company

CO520-2. 2 Dollars Draft to Mercantile National Bank of New York. ND (1907). Black with pink guilloche at center. Uniface. Imprint: Rocky Mountain Bank Note Co. Denver. (shown at 70%)
  d. Unissued, remainder. **R5**

The Capitol National Bank

A. Uniface Issue

CO540-5. 5 Dollars Cashiers Check Nov. 5, 1907. Black.
  d. Unissued, remainder. **R5**

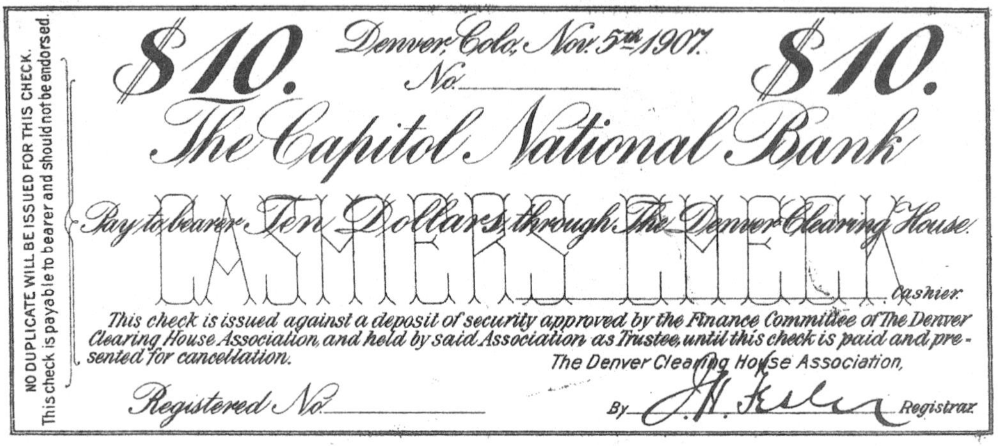

CO540-10. 10 Dollars Nov. 5, 1907. As above. (shown at 76%)
d. Unissued, remainder. R5
CO540-20. 20 Dollars Nov. 5, 1907. As above.
d. Unissued, remainder. R5
e. Sample. R5

B. Two-sided Issue
CO560-5. 5 Dollars Cashiers Check Nov. 5, 1907. Black. Back blue; state capitol building in guilloche. Imprint: The Rocky Mountain Bank Note Co., Denver.
d. Unissued, remainder. R5
CO560-10. 10 Dollars Nov. 5, 1907. As above. (b/w)
d. Unissued, remainder. R5

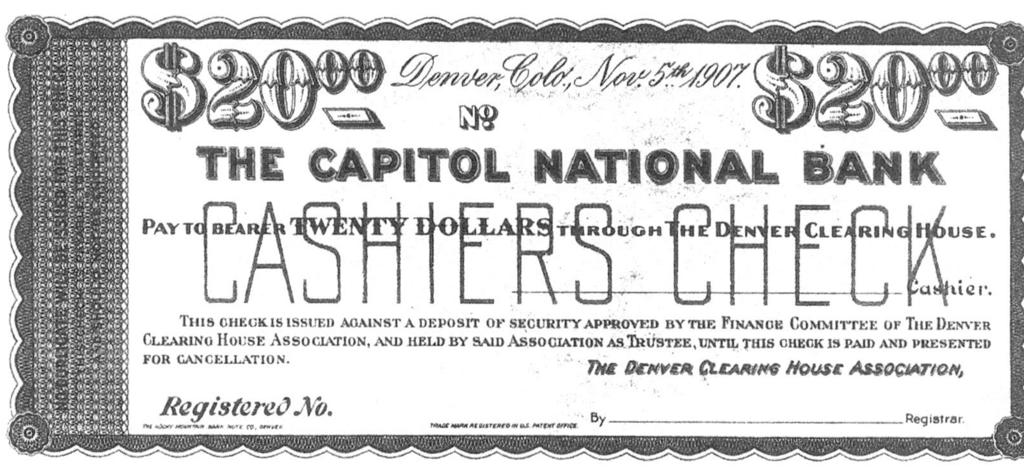

CO560-20. 20 Dollars Nov. 5, 1907. As above. (shown at 74%)
e. Sample. R5

The Central National Bank

A. Uniface Issue
CO580-5. 5 Dollars Cashiers Check Nov. 5, 1907. Black. (b/w)
d. Unissued, remainder. R5
CO580-10. 10 Dollars Nov. 5, 1907. (b/w)
d. Unissued, remainder. R5
B. Two-sided Issue

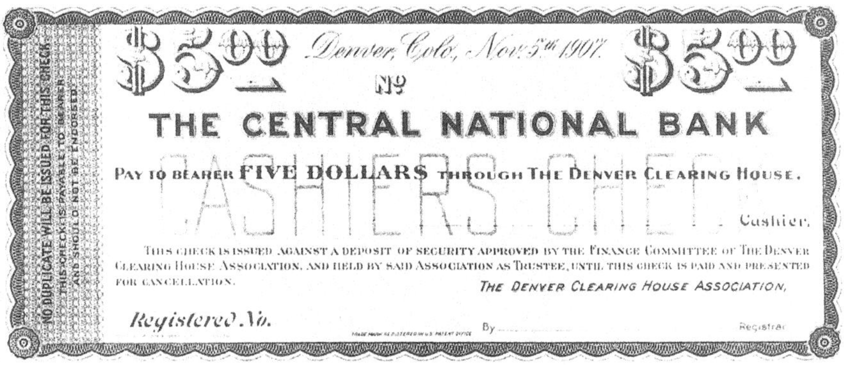

CO600-5. 5 Dollars Cashiers Check Nov. 5, 1907. Black. Back blue. As CO560-5. (shown at 60%)
d. Unissued, remainder. R5

The Colorado National Bank

CO620-5. 5 Dollars Cashiers Check Nov. 5, 1907. Black. Back blue; state capitol building in guilloche at center. Imprint: The Rocky Mountain Bank Note Co., Denver (as CO560-5.). (shown at 60%)
c. Unissued, cancelled. R4
d. Unissued, remainder. R4
e. Sample. R3

CO620-10. 10 Dollars Nov. 5, 1907. Black on deep orange paper, face and back. As above.
c. Unissued, cancelled. R4
d. Unissued, remainder. R4
e. Sample. R3

The Denver National Bank

A. Uniface Issue

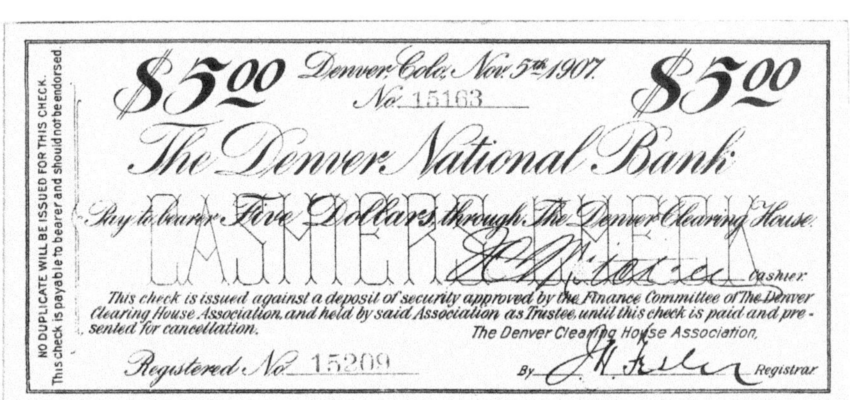

CO640-5. 5 Dollars Nov. 5, 1907. Black. (shown at 60%)
c. Unissued, cancelled. R4
u. Issued. SENC
CO640-10. 10 Dollars Nov. 5, 1907. Black on orange paper.
d. Unissued, remainder. R5
CO640-20. 20 Dollars Nov. 5, 1907. Yellow paper.
d. Unissued, remainder. R5

B. Two-sided Issue
CO660-5. 5 Dollars Nov. 5, 1907. As CO620-5. (shown at 73%)
c. Unissued, cancelled. R4
d. Unissued, remainder. R4
CO660-10. 10 Dollars Nov. 5, 1907. As CO620-10.
d. Unissued, remainder. R4
CO660-20. 20 Dollars Nov. 5, 1907. Dark blue on yellow paper. Back dark blue. Design as above.
d. Unissued, remainder. R5

The First National Bank

A. Uniface Issue

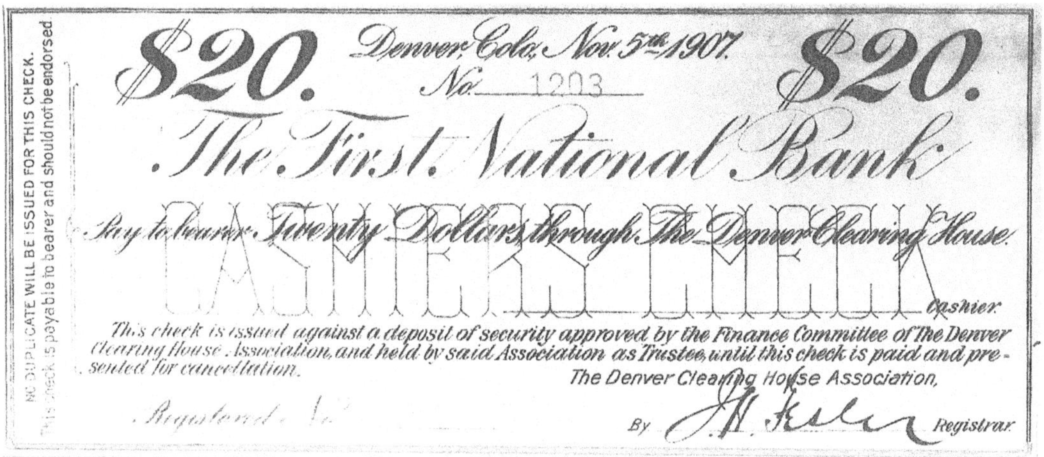

CO680-20. 20 Dollars Nov. 5, 1907. Black. (shown at 75%)
d. Unissued, remainder. **R5**

B. Two-sided Issue
CO700-10. 10 Dollars Nov. 5, 1907. As CO620-10.
d. Unissued, remainder. **R5**

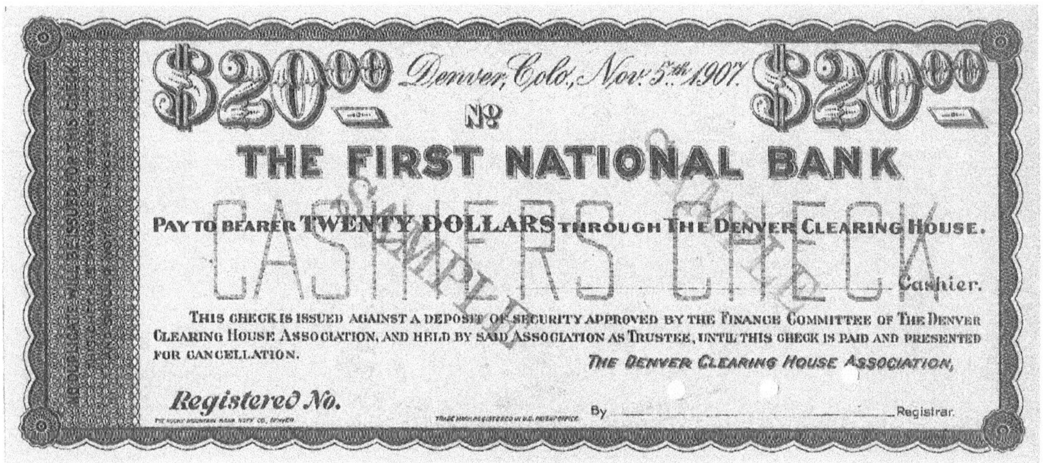

CO700-20. 20 Dollars Nov. 5, 1907. As CO660-20. (shown at 72%)
  c. Unissued, cancelled. **R5**
  e. Sample. **R5**

The National Bank of Commerce

A. Uniface Issue

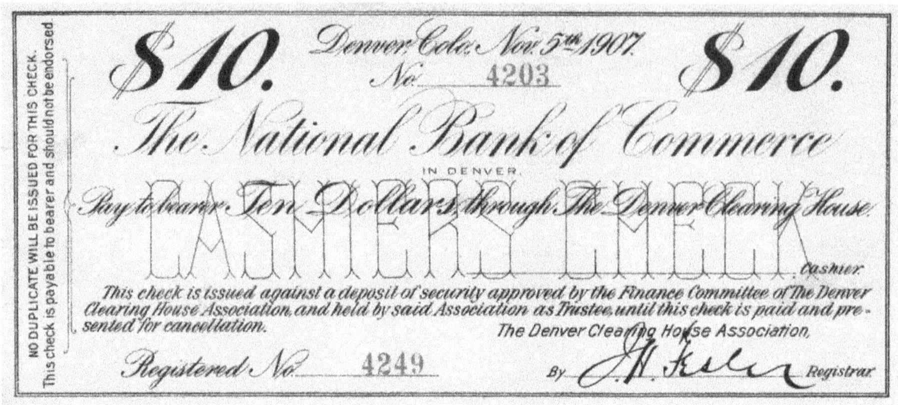

CO720-10. 10 Dollars Nov. 5, 1907. Black. (shown at 65%)
  d. Unissued, remainder. **R4**
CO720-20. 20 Dollars Nov. 5, 1907. As above.
  d. Unissued, remainder. **R4**

B. Two-sided Issue

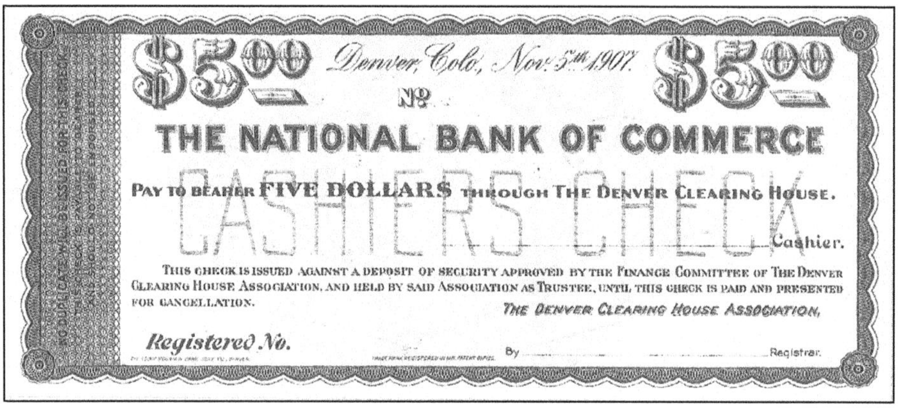

CO740-5. 5 Dollars Nov. 5, 1907. As CO620-5. (shown at 62%)
- d. Unissued, remainder. R4

CO740-10. 10 Dollars Nov. 5, 1907. As CO620-10.
- c. Unissued, cancelled. R4
- d. Unissued, remainder. R4

CO740-20. 20 Dollars Nov. 5, 1907. As CO660-20.
- c. Unissued, cancelled. R4
- d. Unissued, remainder. R4

The United States National Bank

A. Uniface Issue

CO760-5. 5 Dollars Cashiers Check Nov. 5, 1907. Black.
- d. Unissued, remainder. R5

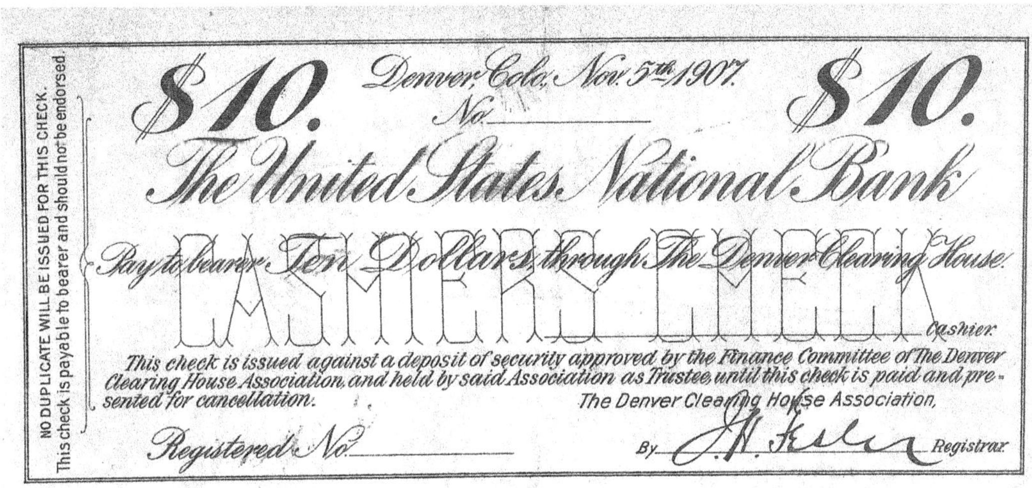

CO760-10. 10 Dollars Nov. 5, 1907. As above. (shown at 75%)
- d. Unissued, remainder. R5

B. Two-sided Issue

CO780-5. 5 Dollars Cashiers Check Nov. 5, 1907. Imprint as CO620-5.
- c. Unissued, cancelled. R4
- e. Sample. R4

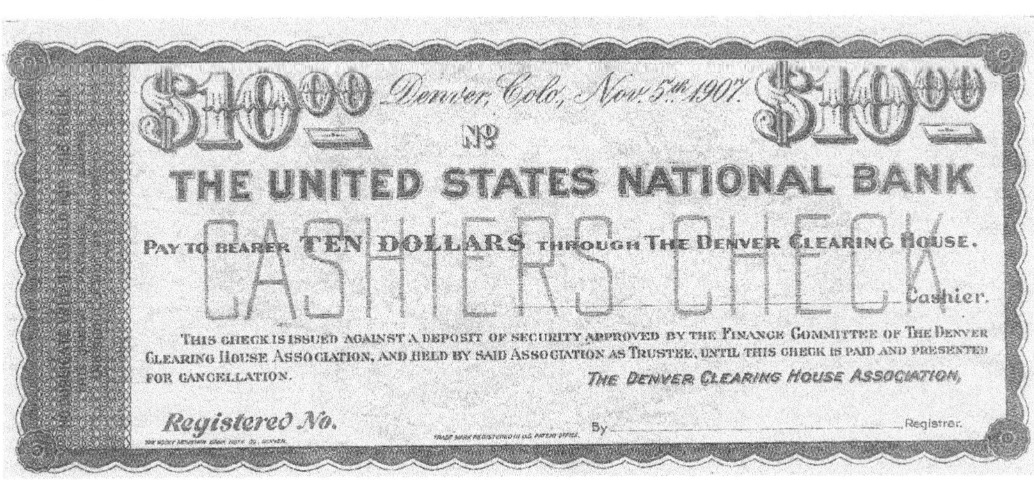

CO780-10. 10 Dollars Nov. 5, 1907. As CO620-10. (shown at 73%)
- d. Unissued, remainder. **R3**
- e. Sample. **R4**

Fort Collins

Fort Collins Clearing House/ Commercial Bank & Trust Co.

CO800-2. 2 Dollars Nov. 20, 1907. Black and brown on yellow paper. Back brown. (shown at 73%)
- b. Issued, cancelled. **VF, 60. Unc., 100.**
- d. Unissued, remainder. **EF, 30. Unc., 60.**

CO800-5. 5 Dollars November, 1907. Blue on light blue paper. Back black.
- b. Nov. 5. Issued, cancelled. **VF, 60. Unc., 100.**
- d1. Nov. 5. Unissued, remainder. **EF, 30. Unc., 60.**
- d2. Nov. 12. Unissued, remainder. **EF, 30. Unc., 60.**

CO800-10. 10 Dollars November, 1907. Green on light green paper. Back black.
- b. Nov. 5. Issued, cancelled. **VF, 80. Unc., 120.**
- d. Nov. 12. Unissued, remainder. **EF, 40. Unc., 70.**

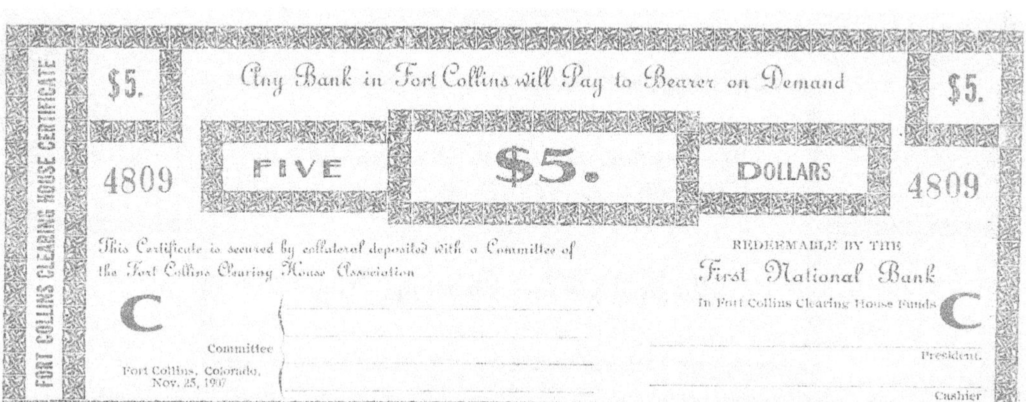

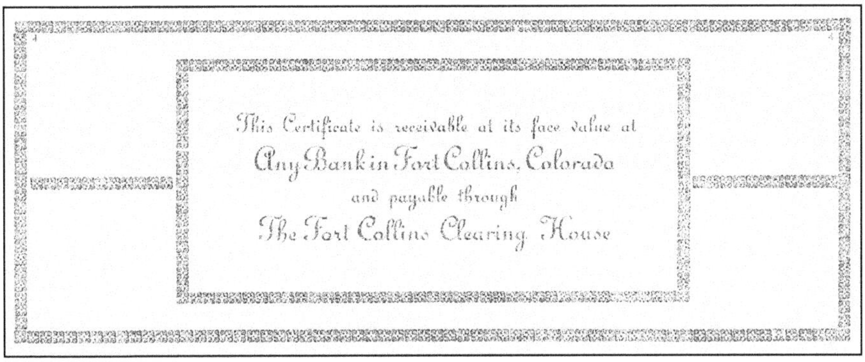

Fort Collins Clearing House/First National Bank

CO820-5. 5 Dollars Nov. 25, 1907. As CO800-5. (shown at 60%)
d. Unissued, remainder. **EF, 30. Unc., 60.**
CO820-10. 10 Dollars Nov. 25, 1907. As CO800-10.
d. Unissued, remainder. **EF, 30. Unc., 60.**

Fort Collins Clearing House/ Poudre Valley National Bank

CO840-5. 5 Dollars Nov. 25, 1907. As CO800-5.
d. Unissued, remainder. **EF, 50. Unc, 85.**
CO840-10. 10 Dollars Nov. 25, 1907. As CO800-10.
d. Unissued, remainder. **EF, 40. Unc., 90.**

Loveland

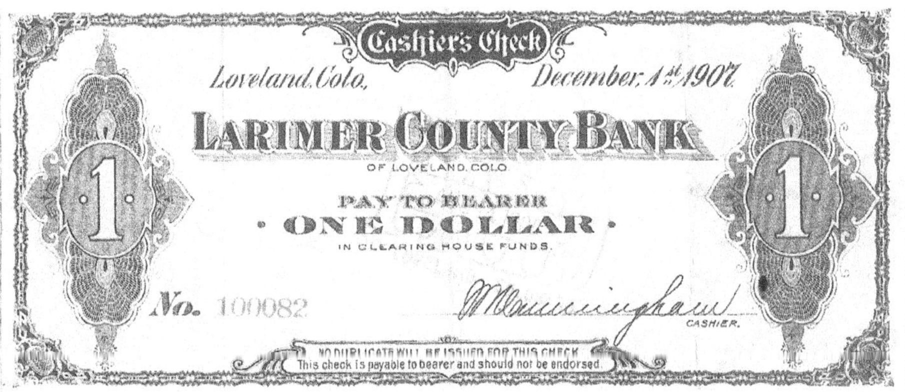

Larimer County Bank

CO870-1. 1 Dollar Cashier's Check Dec. 1, 1907. Black and blue. Back brown; Indians observing train at center. (shown at 65%)
a. Issued, not cancelled. R4
b. Issued, cancelled. R4

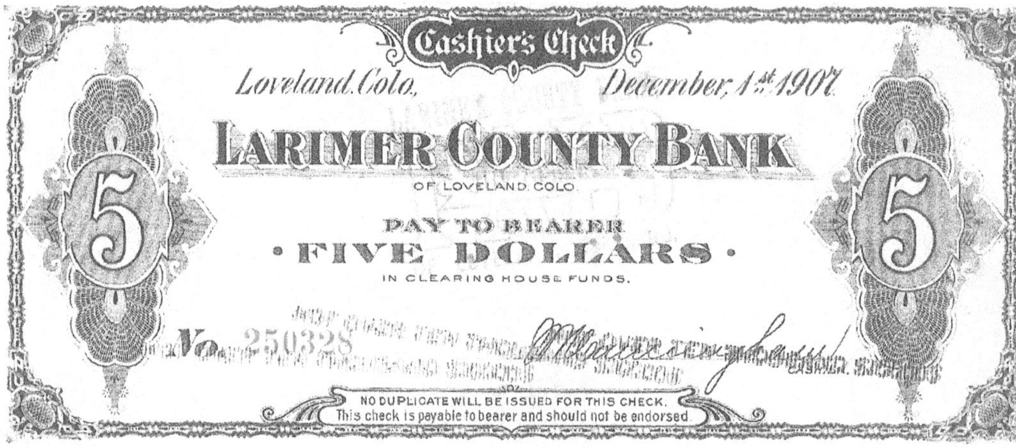

CO870-5. 5 Dollars Dec. 1, 1907. As above, but with three blue checkwriter lines at lower center. Back orange. (shown at 75%)
b. Issued, cancelled. R4

Loveland National Bank

CO900-1. 1 Dollar Cashiers Check Nov. 5, 1907. Black on brown paper. Bank monogram at lower left. Back blue; Colorado arms at center.
a. Issued, not cancelled. R5
b. Issued, cancelled. R4

CO900-5. 5 Dollars Nov. 5, 1907. Black on white paper. Back orange. As above.
b. Issued, cancelled. R4

CO900-10. 10 Dollars Nov. 5, 1907. Black on yellow paper. As above.
b. Issued, cancelled. R4

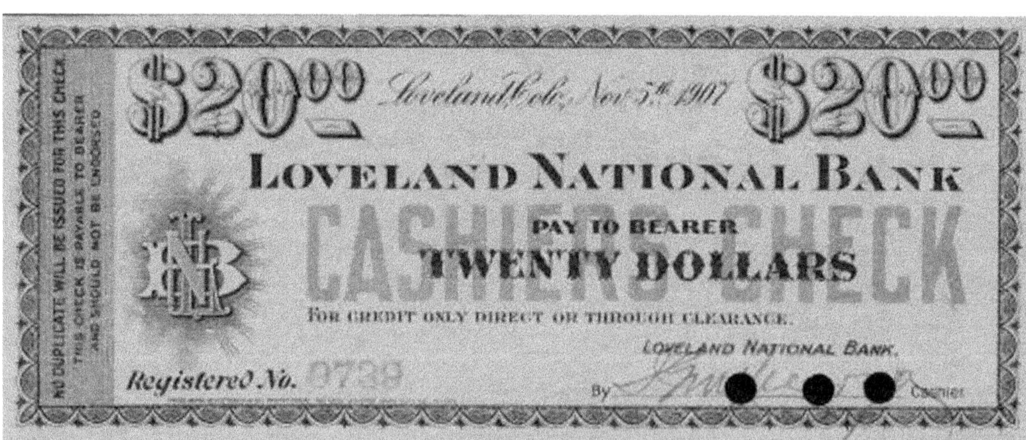

CO900-20. 20 Dollars Nov. 5, 1907. Black on orange paper. As above. (shown at 75%)
b. Issued, cancelled. R4

Rocky Ford

THE STATE BANK OF ROCKY FORD

CO920-1. 1 Dollar Cashier's Check Nov. 20, 1907 (stamped date). Black on gray paper. Altered check form; "Payable in Clearing House Funds" stamped at top. Uniface. Imprint: The Franklin Press Co., Pueblo, Colo.
b. Issued, cancelled. **Fine, 175. VF, 300.**

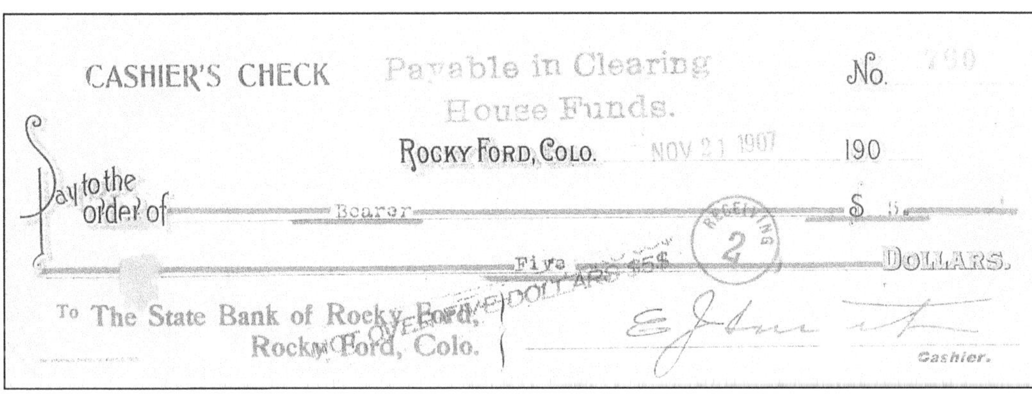

CO920-5. 5 Dollars Nov. 9, 20, 21, 1907. Black on yellow paper. As above. (shown at 66%)
b. Issued, cancelled. **Fine, 140. VF, 250.**
CO920-10. 10 Dollars Nov. 9, 20, 1907. Black on gray paper. As above.
b. Issued, cancelled. **Fine, 175. VF, 300.**
CO920-20. 20 Dollars Nov. 20, Dec. 14, 1907. Black on dark pink paper. As above.
b. Issued, cancelled. **Fine, 225. VF, 375.**

CONNECTICUT

Hartford

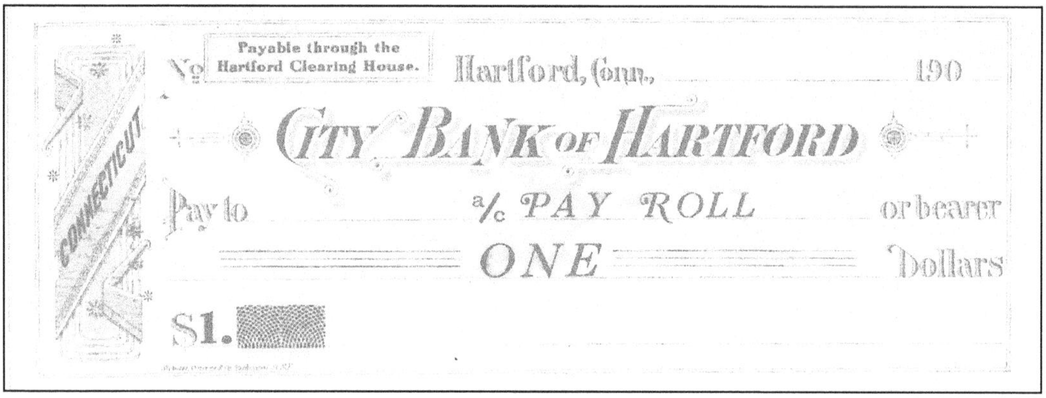

CITY BANK OF HARTFORD

CT500-1. 1 Dollar Pay Roll Check 190_ (1907). Brown and red. Uniface. Imprint: Stewart, Warren & Co. 29 Howard St. N.Y. (shown at 68%)
d. Unissued, remainder. R5

HARTFORD CLEARING HOUSE ASSOCIATION

CT525-1. 1 Dollar Payroll check 190_ (1907). As CT525-5.
u. Unissued? SENC
CT525-2. 2 Dollars 190_ (1907). As above.
u. Unissued? SENC

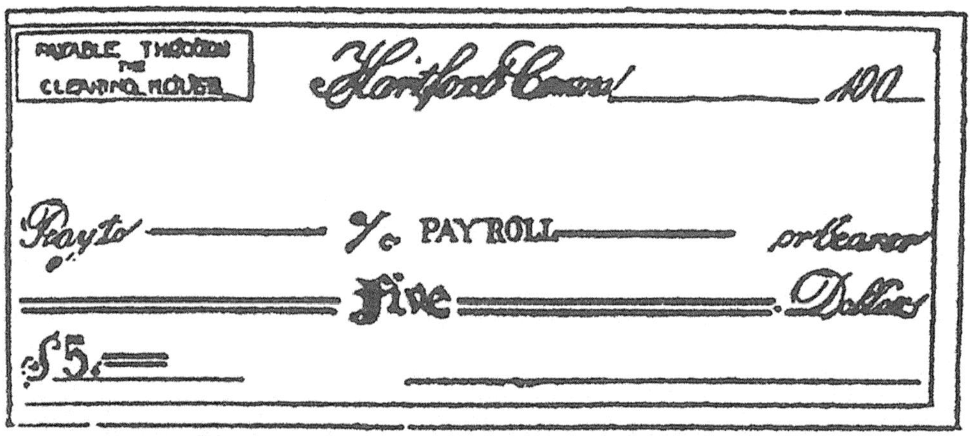

FACSIMILE OF CLEARING HOUSE CHECK.

This is only two-thirds the actual size—Under the date line in the blank space the name of the bank is printed.

CT525-5. 5 Dollars 190_ (1907). As above. (b/w) (shown at 74%)
u. Unissued? SENC
CT525-10. 10 Dollars 190_ (1907). As above.
u. Unissued?. SENC
CT525-20. 20 Dollars 190_ (1907). As above.
u. Unissued? SENC
NOTE: In an article appearing in a local *Hartford Courant* newspaper Nov. 6, 1907, it described efforts of local businessmen to alleviate the shortage of currency by accepting special forms of checks payable to bearer.

These pieces were authorized by the clearing house association two days previously, on the 4th, and were prepared in denominations as listed above. They were distributed to banks but most likely none were issued. The prototype five-dollar check was illustrated in the same newspaper of Nov. 15 (see CT525-5. above).

Hartford National Bank

CT550-1. 1 Dollar 190_ (1907). Altered check form payable through clearing house. Black with red text line. Uniface. Imprint: The Dodd Lith. Co. Hartford, CT.
  b. Unissued, remainder. **R5**

CT550-2. 2 Dollars 190_. As above. (shown at 62%)
  d. Unissued, remainder. **R5**
CT550-5. 5 Dollars 190_. As above.
  d. Unissued, remainder. **R5**
CT550-10. 10 Dollars 190_. As above.
  d. Unissued, remainder. **R5**

Delaware

Wilmington

A cashier's check issue is reported to have been issued in Wilmington. No details are known at present.

Florida

Jacksonville

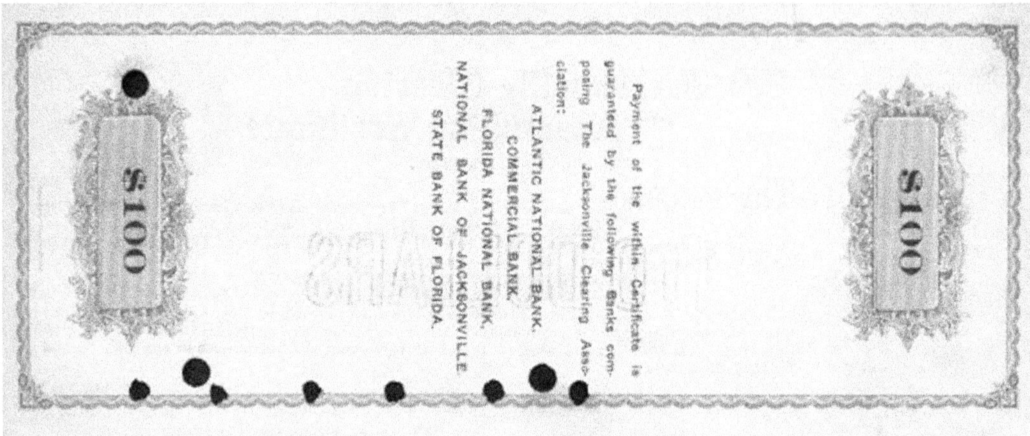

THE JACKSONVILLE CLEARING ASSOCIATION CERTIFICATE

FL500-100. 100 Dollars Nov. 4, 1907. Black with brown border; large red value across center in outline. Man carrying sheaf at left. Back brown; vertical listing in black of the five member banks of the clearing house. Imprint: Foote & Davies Co. Atlanta. (shown at 75%)
c. Unissued, cancelled. R4

Key West

KEY WEST CLEARING HOUSE ASSOCIATION CERTIFICATE

FL520-2. 2 Dollars Nov. 25, 1907. Black on green underprint. Hope standing at left. Imprint: Foote & Davies Co., Atlanta.
c. Unissued, cancelled. R4

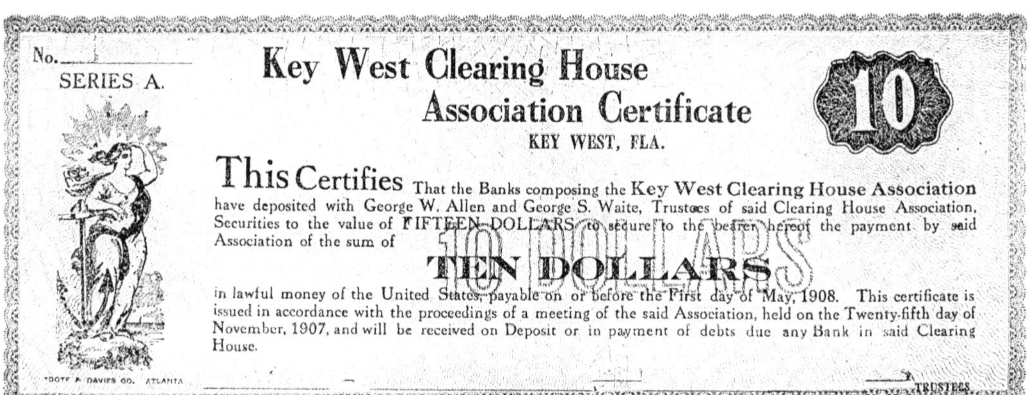

FL520-10. 10 Dollars Nov. 25, 1907. As above. Series A. (b/w) (shown at 77%)
c. Unissued, cancelled. R5

Pensacola

THE CITIZENS NATIONAL BANK OF PENSACOLA

FL550-5. 5 Dollars Cashiers Check Nov. 20, 1907. Black on green underprint. Large red value across center.
c. Unissued, cancelled. R4

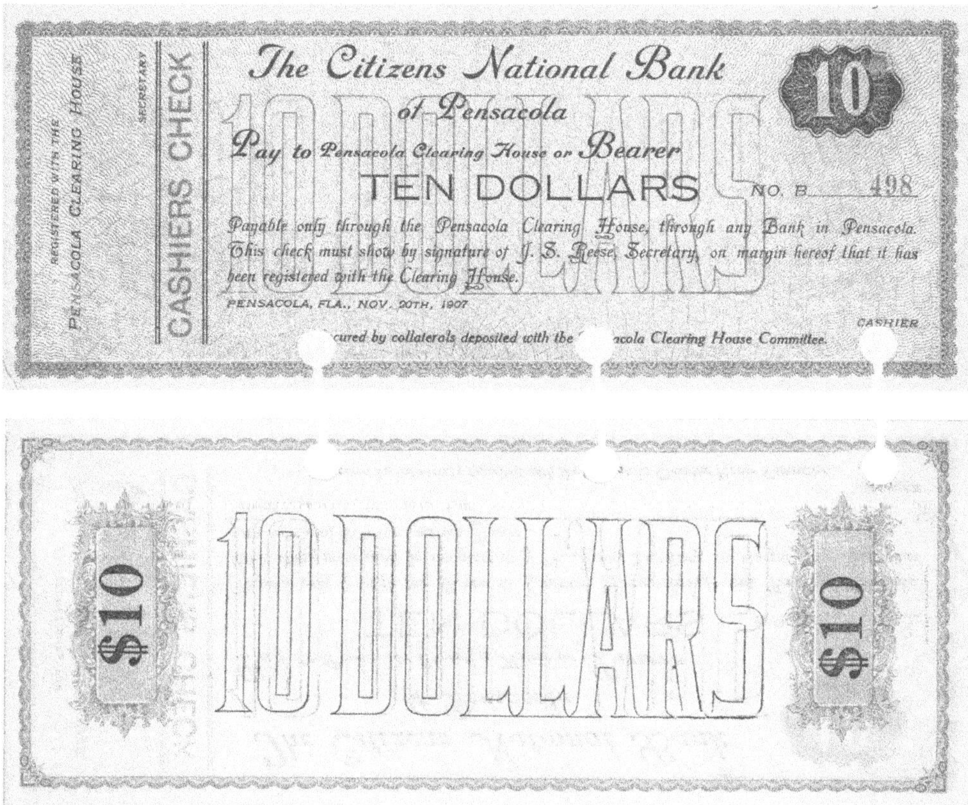

FL550-10. 10 Dollars Nov. 20, 1907. As above. (shown at 60%)
c. Unissued, cancelled. R4

The First National Bank of Pensacola

FL570-1. 1 Dollar Cashiers Check Nov. 20, 1907. Black on green underprint. Large red outline value across center. Back green ends, large red outline value across center.
c. Unissued, cancelled. R5

FL570-2. 2 Dollars Nov. 20, 1907. As above.
c. Unissued, cancelled. R5

FL570-5. 5 Dollars Nov. 20, 1907. As above.
c. Unissued, cancelled. R5

FL570-10. 10 Dollars Nov. 20, 1907. As above.
c. Unissued, cancelled. R5

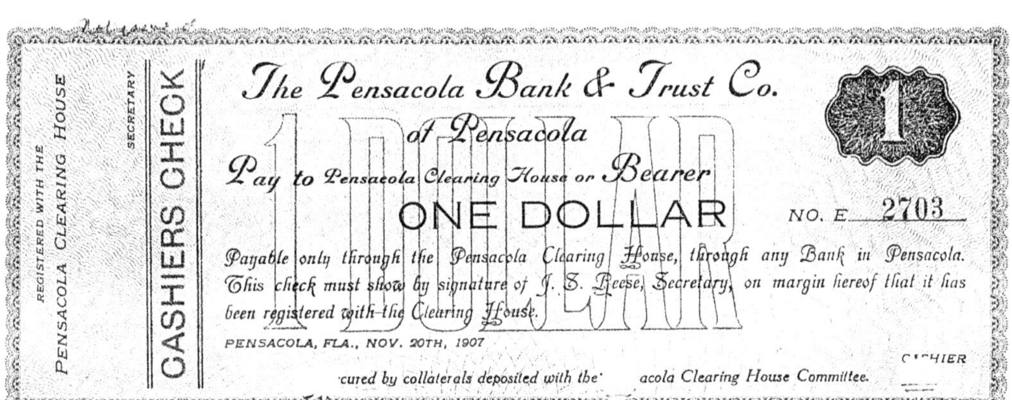

The Pensacola Bank & Trust Co. of Pensacola

FL590-1. 1 Dollar Cashiers Check Nov. 20, 1907. Black on green underprint. Large red outline value across center on face and back. (shown at 76%)
c. Unissued, cancelled. R4

St. Augustine

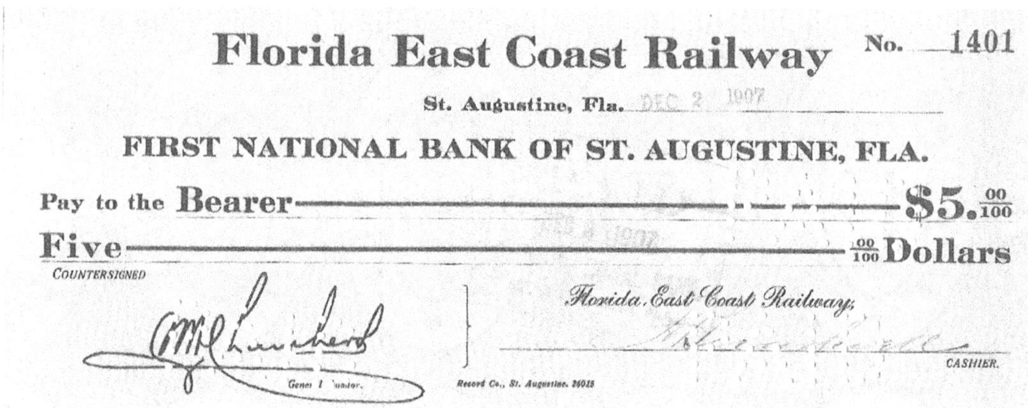

Florida East Coast Railway No. 1401
St. Augustine, Fla. DEC 2 1907
FIRST NATIONAL BANK OF ST. AUGUSTINE, FLA.
Pay to the Bearer $5.00/100
Five 00/100 Dollars
COUNTERSIGNED
General Auditor.
Florida East Coast Railway,
CASHIER.
Record Co., St. Augustine. 26015

Florida East Coast Railway/ First National Bank of St. Augustine, Fla.

FL610-5. 5 Dollars (payroll check) Dec. 2, 1907 (stamped date). Black on blue safety paper. Uniface. Imprint: Record Co., St. Augustine. 26015. (shown at 66%)
b. Issued, cancelled. R5

FL610-10. 10 Dollars Nov. 15, 1907 (stamped date). Black on gray safety paper. As above.
b. Issued, cancelled. R5

FL610-20. 20 Dollars Dec. 2, 1907 (stamped date). Black on cream safety paper. As above.
b. Issued, cancelled. R5

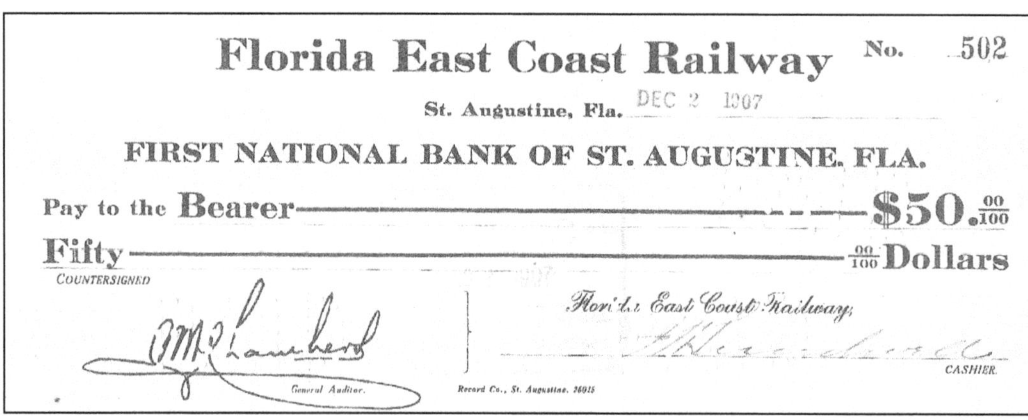

Florida East Coast Railway No. 502
St. Augustine, Fla. DEC 2 1907
FIRST NATIONAL BANK OF ST. AUGUSTINE, FLA.
Pay to the Bearer $50.00/100
Fifty 00/100 Dollars
COUNTERSIGNED
General Auditor.
Florida East Coast Railway,
CASHIER.
Record Co., St. Augustine. 26015

FL610-50. 50 Dollars Dec. 2, 1907 (stamped date). Black on gold safety paper. As above. (shown at 66%)
b. Issued, cancelled. R5

Tampa

Tampa Clearing House Association Certificate

FL630-100. 100 Dollars Nov. 6, 1907. Black and green. Large red outline value across center. Man and woman at left. Vertical list of member banks on back. Imprint: Foote & Davies Co., Atlanta. (shown at 64%)

c. Unissued, cancelled. **R4**

Georgia

Atlanta

Atlanta Clearing House Association Certificate

Series B Issue

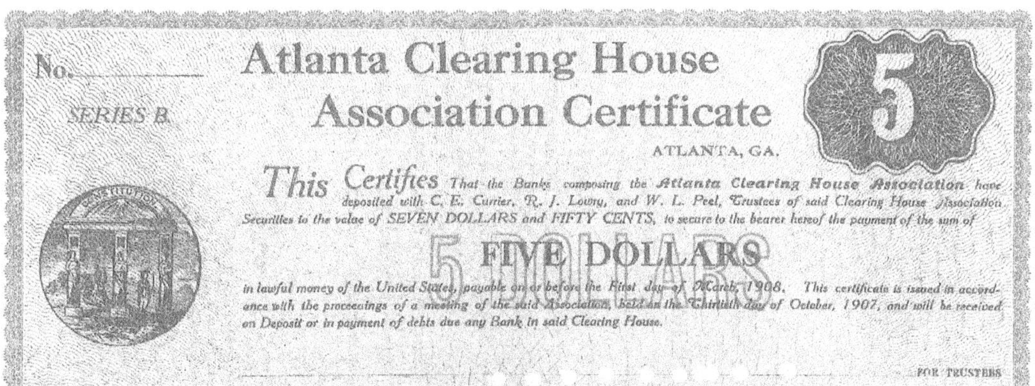

GA500-5. 5 Dollars Oct. 30, 1907. Black and green. Value in red outline across lower center. Georgia seal at left. Vertical list of member banks on back. Printer as GA500-100. but without imprint. (shown at 66%)

c. Unissued, cancelled. **VF, 100. EF, 175.**

GA500-10. 10 Dollars Oct. 30, 1907. As above.

b. Issued, cancelled. **VF, 100. EF, 175.**

GA500-20. 20 Dollars Oct. 30, 1907. As above.

b. Issued, cancelled. **VF, 100. EF, 175.**

GA500-50. 50 Dollars Oct. 30, 1907. As above.
c. Unissued, cancelled. R1

GA500-100. 100 Dollars Oct. 30, 1907. As above. Imprint: Foote & Davies Co. Atlanta. (shown at 66%)
c. Unissued, cancelled. R2

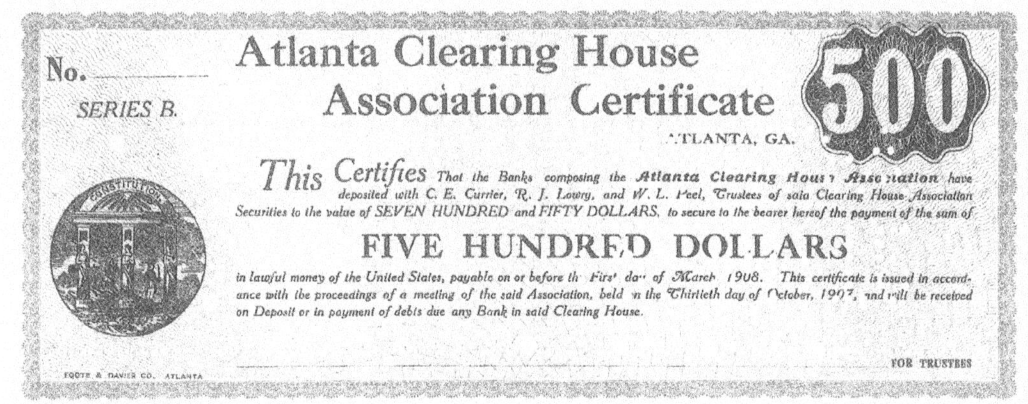

GA500-500. 500 Dollars Oct. 30, 1907. As above, with imprint. (shown at 64%)
c. Unissued, cancelled. R2

Various Series C-F

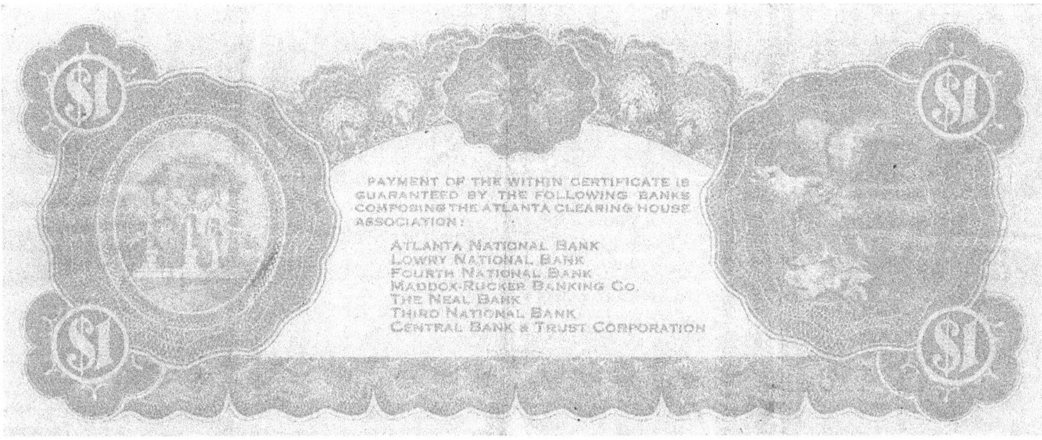

GA520-1. 1 Dollar Oct. 30, 1907. Deep green. Eagle at top center. Back orange; state seal at left, eagle at right. Series C. Imprint: Brandon, Nashville. (shown at 73%)

a. Issued, not cancelled. R3

b. Issued, cancelled. R3

GA520-5. 5 Dollars Oct. 30, 1907. As above. Series D.

b. Issued, cancelled. R3

GA520-10. 10 Dollars Oct. 30, 1907. As above. Series E.

b. Issued, cancelled. R3

GA520-20. 20 Dollars Oct. 30, 1907. As above. Series F.

b. Issued, cancelled. R3

NOTE: An amount of $1,500,000 was issued in Atlanta beginning Oct. 31, 1907.

Augusta

Augusta Clearing House Association Certificate

GA540-1. 1 Dollar Nov. 2, 1907. Black and green. Value in red outline across lower center. Crusader on horseback at left. Vertical list of member banks on back. Series D. Imprint: Foote & Davies Co. Atlanta.

a. Issued, not cancelled. R4

c. Unissued, cancelled. R3

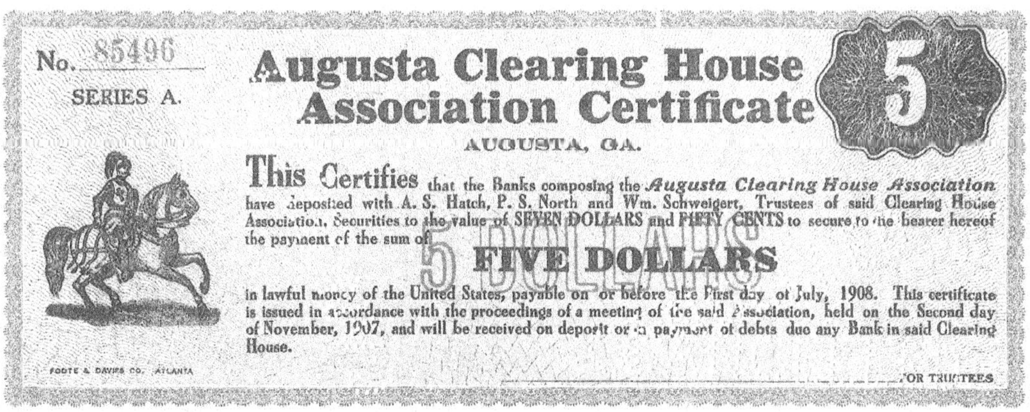

GA540-5. 5 Dollars Nov. 2, 1907. As above. Series A. (shown at 66%)

d. Unissued, remainder. **VF, 50. EF, 75.**

GA540-10.A 10 Dollars Nov. 2, 1907. As above. Series B. Denomination in guilloche at left and right on back.

d. Unissued, remainder. **VF, 35. EF, 60.**

GA540-10.B 10 Dollars Nov. 2, 1907. Face as above. Denomination at left and right on back without guilloche.

d. Unissued, remainder. VF, 40. EF, 75.

NOTE: An amount of $370,000 was issued beginning Nov. 4, 1907. Some unissued $10 notes have an unreadable scribble in the signature area.

ERROR NOTE: An example of GA540-10.d is known with all face printing on the green back design, and all printing usually found on the back over the plain green underprint of the face.

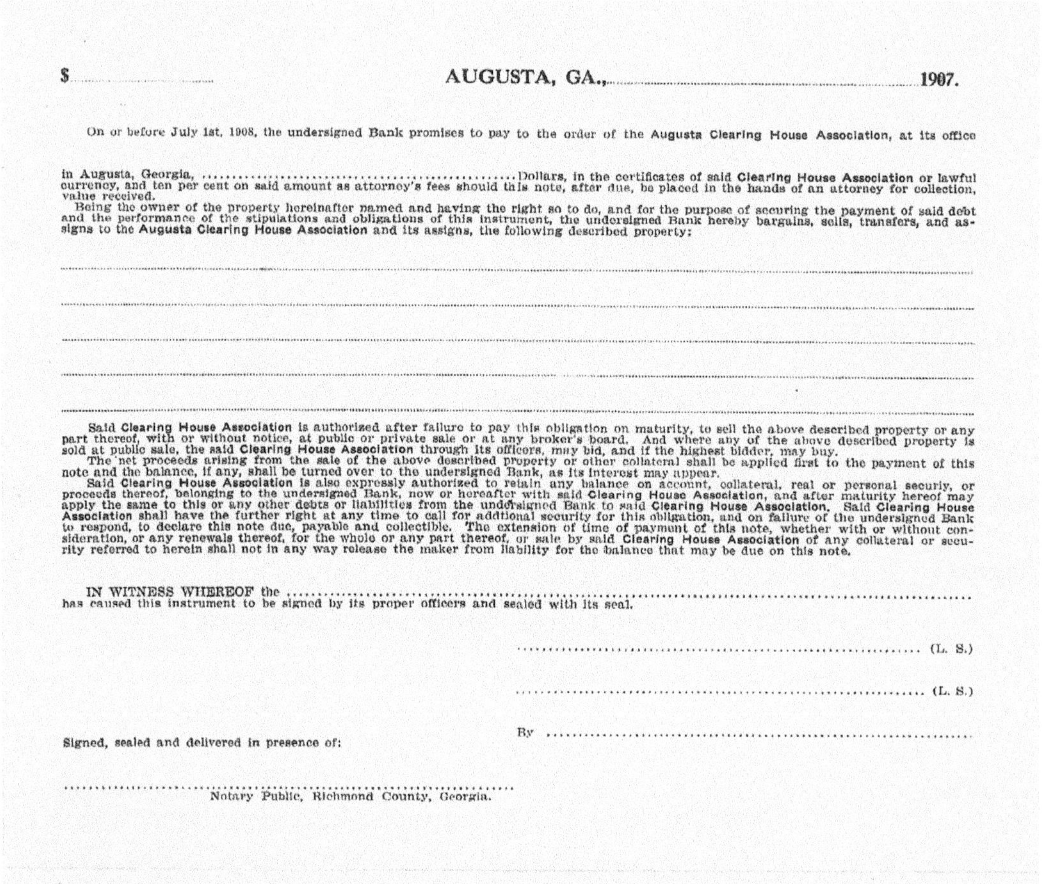

$........ AUGUSTA, GA.,........ 1907.

On or before July 1st, 1908, the undersigned Bank promises to pay to the order of the Augusta Clearing House Association, at its office in Augusta, Georgia, ...Dollars, in the certificates of said Clearing House Association or lawful currency, and ten per cent on said amount as attorney's fees should this note, after due, be placed in the hands of an attorney for collection, value received.

Being the owner of the property hereinafter named and having the right so to do, and for the purpose of securing the payment of said debt and the performance of the stipulations and obligations of this instrument, the undersigned Bank hereby bargains, sells, transfers, and assigns to the Augusta Clearing House Association and its assigns, the following described property:

Said Clearing House Association is authorized after failure to pay this obligation on maturity, to sell the above described property or any part thereof, with or without notice, at public or private sale or at any broker's board. And where any of the above described property is sold at public sale, the said Clearing House Association through its officers, may bid, and if the highest bidder, may buy.

The net proceeds arising from the sale of the above described property or other collateral shall be applied first to the payment of this note and the balance, if any, shall be turned over to the undersigned Bank, as its interest may appear.

Said Clearing House Association is also expressly authorized to retain any balance on account, collateral, real or personal securiy, or proceeds thereof, belonging to the undersigned Bank, now or hereafter with said Clearing House Association, and after maturity hereof may apply the same to this or any other debts or liabilities from the undersigned Bank to said Clearing House Association. Said Clearing House Association shall have the further right at any time to call for addtional security for this obligation, and on failure of the undersigned Bank to respond, to declare this note due, payable and collectible. The extension of time of payment of this note, whether with or without consideration, or any renewals thereof, for the whole or any part thereof, or sale by said Clearing House Association of any collateral or security referred to herein shall not in any way release the maker from liability for the balance that may be due on this note.

IN WITNESS WHEREOF the ....
has caused this instrument to be signed by its proper officers and sealed with its seal.

.... (L. S.)

.... (L. S.)

By ....

Signed, sealed and delivered in presence of:

....
Notary Public, Richmond County, Georgia.

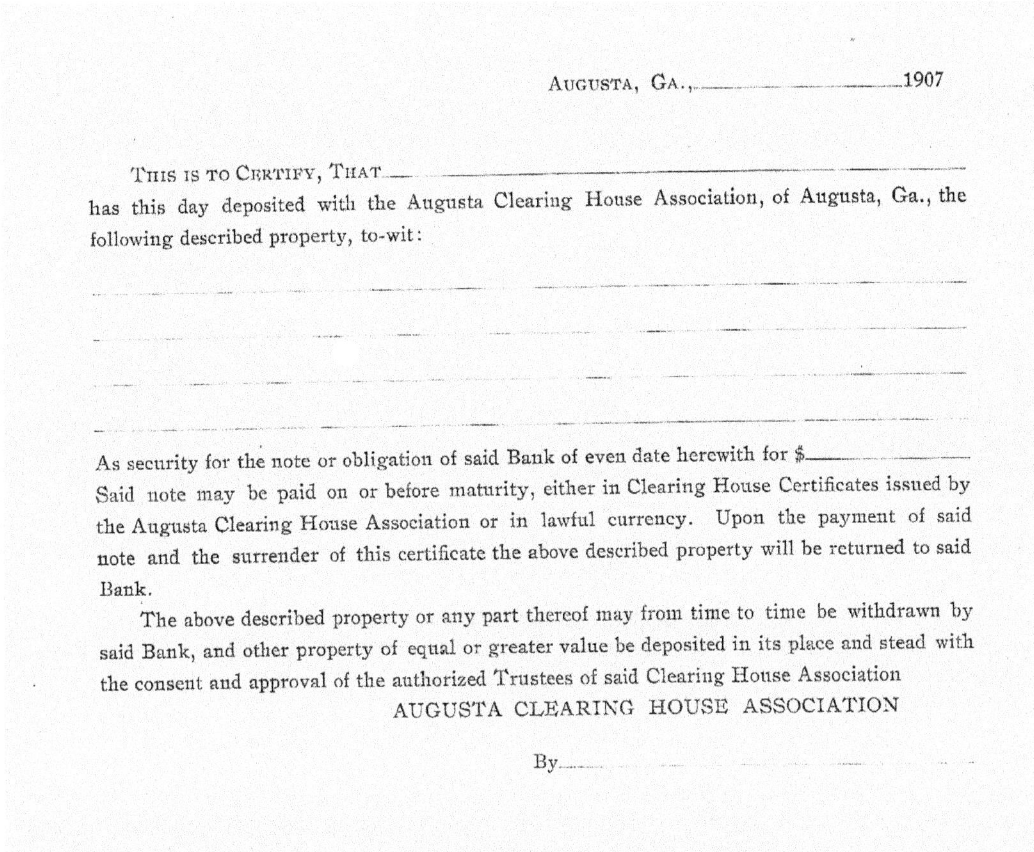

AUGUSTA, GA., ________________1907

THIS IS TO CERTIFY, THAT ____
has this day deposited with the Augusta Clearing House Association, of Augusta, Ga., the following described property, to-wit:

As security for the note or obligation of said Bank of even date herewith for $____________
Said note may be paid on or before maturity, either in Clearing House Certificates issued by the Augusta Clearing House Association or in lawful currency. Upon the payment of said note and the surrender of this certificate the above described property will be returned to said Bank.

The above described property or any part thereof may from time to time be withdrawn by said Bank, and other property of equal or greater value be deposited in its place and stead with the consent and approval of the authorized Trustees of said Clearing House Association

AUGUSTA CLEARING HOUSE ASSOCIATION

By________________________

BANK PROMISSORY NOTE TO CLEARING HOUSE

GA560-Var. Various Amounts 1907. Black text. Promise to pay clearing house whatever amount is required at time of encashment. 214 × 178mm. (shown at 65%)
d. Unissued, remainder. **R5**

Bainbridge

BAINBRIDGE CLEARING HOUSE ASSOCIATION CERTIFICATE

GA580-1. 1 Dollar Nov. 6, 1907. Black and orange on blue paper. Large red outline value across lower center. Indian at left. Vertical list of member banks on back. Series B. Imprint: Foote & Davies Co. Atlanta.
c. Unissued, cancelled (handwritten "Specimen"). **R5**

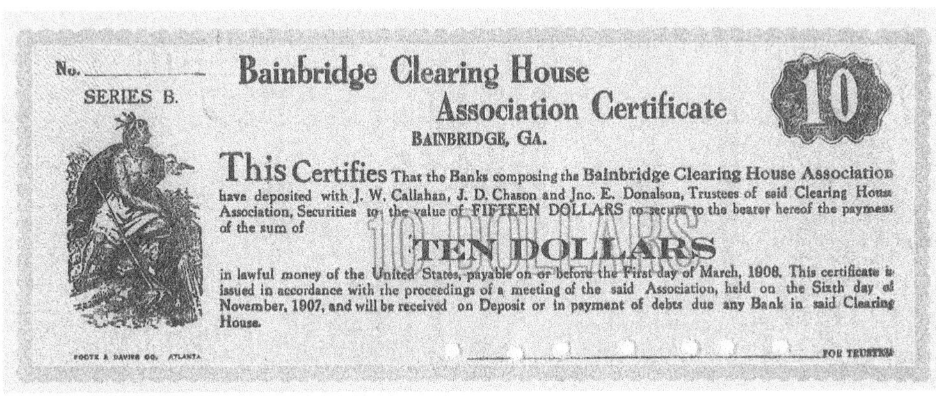

GA580-10. 10 Dollars Nov. 6, 1907. As above. (shown at 59%)
c. Unissued, cancelled. R3

Bishop

Bishop Banking Company Certificate

GA600-20. 20 Dollars Dec. 11, 1907. Design and imprint as GA580. Single bank name on back. Series A. (shown at 66%)
c. Unissued, cancelled. R5

Blakely

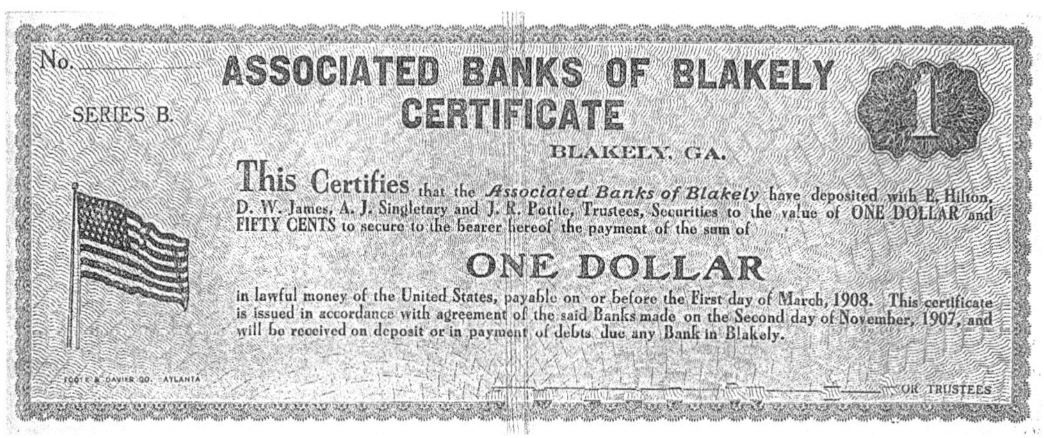

Associated Banks of Blakely Certificate

GA620-1. 1 Dollar Nov. 2, 1907. Black and brown. American flag at left. Single bank name on back. Imprint as GA580. (shown at 66%)
c. Unissued, cancelled. R4

Brunswick

It is reported that $109,000 in certificates was issued in Brunswick, but no details about any specific notes are known at present.

Columbia

COLUMBIA CLEARING HOUSE ASSOCIATION CERTIFICATE

GA630-20. 20 Dollars Nov. 4, 1907. Farmer with sheaf at left. Series B. Imprint as GA580.
c. Unissued, cancelled. R5

Columbus

COLUMBUS CLEARING HOUSE ASSOCIATION CERTIFICATE

GA640-1. 1 Dollar Oct. 31, 1907. Orange and black. Large red outline value across center. American eagle with ribbon and motto at left. List of banks on back. Imprint as GA580.
c. Unissued, cancelled. R4

GA640-2. 2 Dollars Oct. 31, 1907. As above. (b/w) (shown at 58%)
c. Unissued, cancelled. R5

GA640-100. 100 Dollars Oct. 31, 1907. As above.
c. Unissued, cancelled. R5

Cordele

CORDELE CLEARING HOUSE ASSOCIATION CERTIFICATE

GA660-1. 1 Dollar Nov. 2, 1907. (list)
u. Cancelled. SENC

Dawson

DAWSON CLEARING HOUSE ASSOCIATION CERTIFICATE

GA680-1. 1 Dollar Nov. 6, 1907. Black and green. Value in red outline across lower center. Lion at left. Vertical list of member banks on back. Series A. Imprint as GA580.
c. Unissued, cancelled. R5

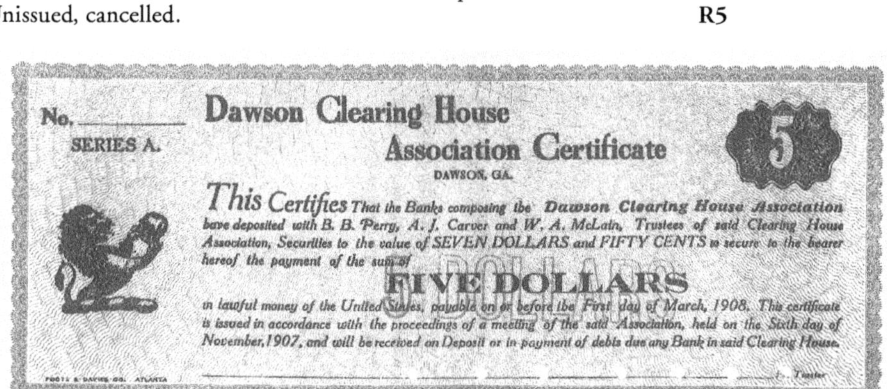

GA680-5. 5 Dollars Nov. 6, 1907. As above. (shown at 56%)
c. Unissued, cancelled. R3

Dothan

DOTHAN CLEARING HOUSE ASSOCIATION CERTIFICATE

GA690-1. 1 Dollar Nov. 18, 1907. Eagle with outstretched wings on mountaintop at left, sunrise behind. Series A. Imprint as GA580.
c. Unissued, cancelled. R5

Douglas

DOUGLAS CLEARING HOUSE ASSOCIATION CERTIFICATE

GA700-2. 2 Dollars Nov. 7, 1907. Black and green. Large red outline value across center. Farmer with horse and dog at left. Vertical list of member banks on back. Series A. Imprint as GA580. (shown at 65%)
c. Unissued, cancelled. R4
GA700-20. 20 Dollars Nov. 7, 1907. As above.
d. Unissued, remainder. R5

Fitzgerald

FITZGERALD CLEARING HOUSE ASSOCIATION CERTIFICATE

GA720-5. 5 Dollars Nov. 1, 1907. (list)
u. Cancelled. SENC

Gadsden

GADSDEN CLEARING HOUSE ASSOCIATION CERTIFICATE

GA730-10. 10 Dollars Nov. 2, 1907. Eagle with spread wings and ribbon in circle at left. Series B.
c. Unissued, cancelled. R5
GA730-20. 20 Dollars Nov. 2, 1907. As above.
c. Unissued, cancelled. R5

Griffin

GRIFFIN CLEARING HOUSE ASSOCIATION CERTIFICATE

GA740-10. 10 Dollars Nov. 1, 1907. Green and orange. Value in red outline across lower center. State seal at left. Vertical list of member banks on back. Series B. Imprint: Foote & Davies Co. Atlanta.
d. Unissued, remainder. R4

GA740-20. 20 Dollars Nov. 1, 1907. As above. (shown at 76%)
d. Unissued, remainder. **R4**

Jackson

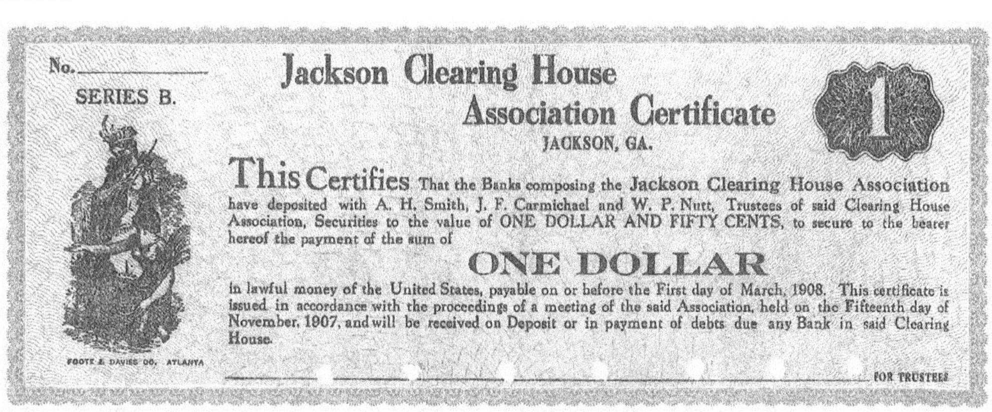

JACKSON CLEARING HOUSE ASSOCIATION CERTIFICATE

GA760-1. 1 Dollar Nov. 15, 1907. Black and brown. Man and birds at left. Vertical list of member banks on back. Series B. Imprint: Foote & Davies Co. Atlanta. (shown at 63%)
c. Unissued, cancelled. **R3**

Macon

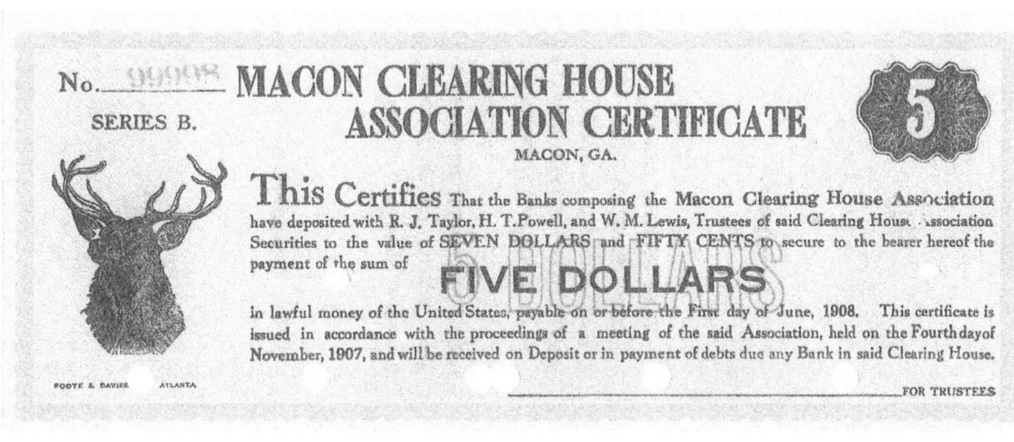

MACON CLEARING HOUSE ASSOCIATION CERTIFICATE

GA780-5. 5 Dollars Nov. 4, 1907. Black and orange. Large red outline value in red across center. Elk head at left. Vertical list of member banks on back. Series B. Imprint: Foote & Davies Co. Atlanta. (shown at 65%)
c. Unissued, cancelled. **R2**
u. Cancelled. **SENC**
GA780-10. 10 Dollars Nov. 4, 1907. As above.
c. Unissued, cancelled. **R5**
GA780-20. 20 Dollars Nov. 4, 1907. As above.
c. Unissued, cancelled. **R5**
NOTE: An amount of $325,000 was issued beginning on Nov. 4, 1907.

Milledgeville

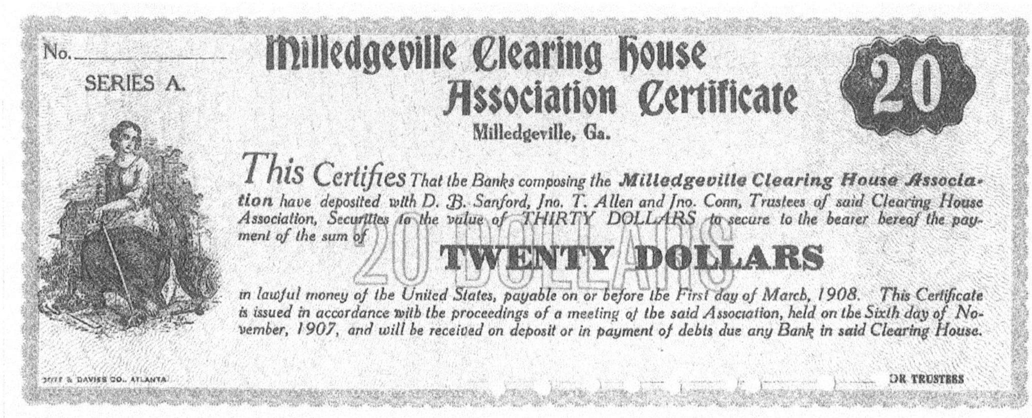

MILLEDGEVILLE CLEARING HOUSE ASSOCIATION CERTIFICATE

GA800-20. 20 Dollars Nov. 6, 1907. Black and brown. Value in red outline across lower center. Seated woman with implements at left. Vertical list of member banks on back. Series A. Imprint: Foote & Davies Co. Atlanta. (shown at 65%)
c. Unissued, cancelled. **R3**

Newnan

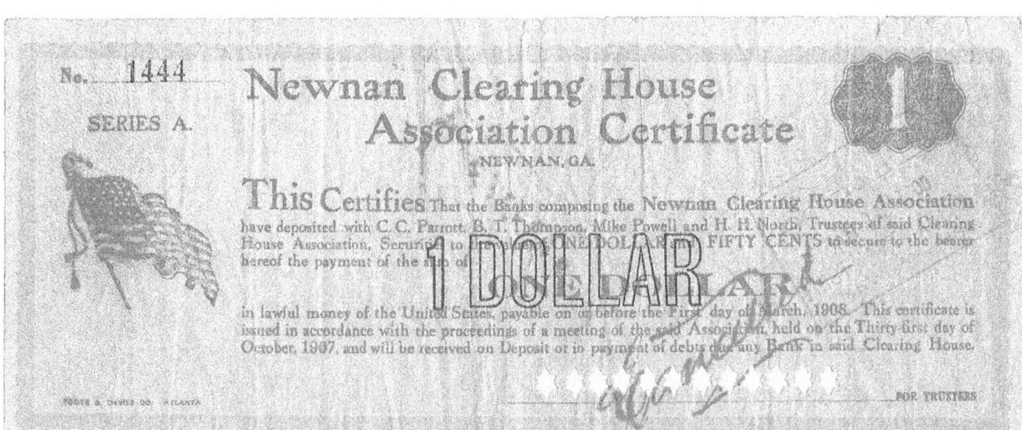

NEWNAN CLEARING HOUSE ASSOCIATION CERTIFICATE

GA820-1. 1 Dollar Oct. 31, 1907. Red and orange on blue paper. Black outline value across lower center. American flag at left. Vertical list of member banks on back. Series A. Imprint: Foote & Davies Co. Atlanta. (shown at 65%)
c. Unissued, cancelled. **R5**

GA820-5.A 5 Dollars Oct. 31, 1907. As above.
 b. Issued, cancelled. R4

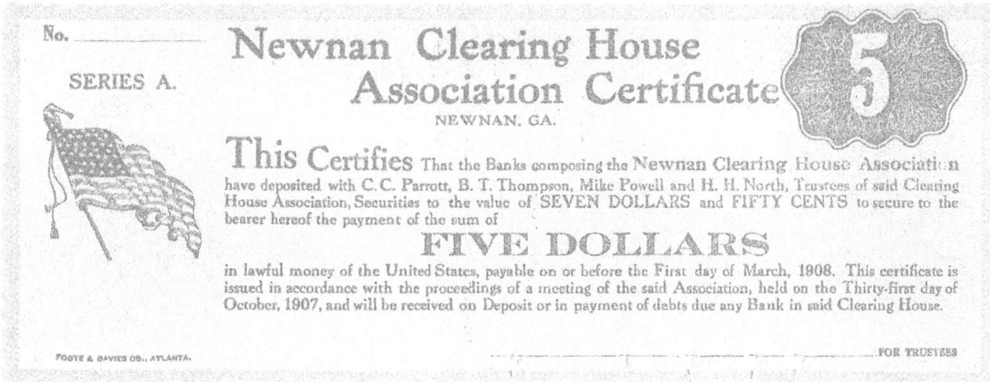

GA820-5.B 5 Dollars Oct. 31, 1907. As above, but without black outline value across lower center. (shown at 64%)
 c. Unissued, cancelled. R4
GA820-10. 10 Dollars Oct. 31, 1907. As above, with black outline value.
 b. Issued, cancelled. R5
GA820-20. 20 Dollars Oct. 31, 1907. As above.
 b. Issued, cancelled. R5

Rome

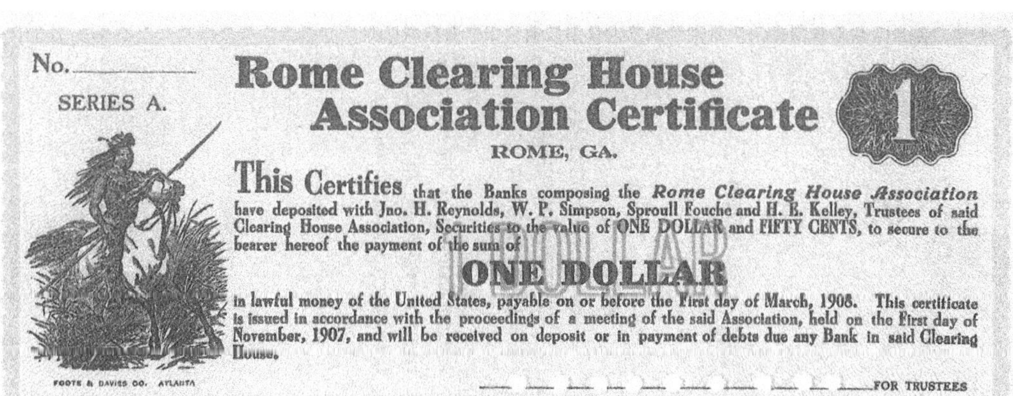

ROME CLEARING HOUSE ASSOCIATION CERTIFICATE

GA840-1. 1 Dollar Nov. 1, 1907. Black and orange. Value in red outline across lower center. Indian on horseback at left. Vertical list of member banks on back. Series A. Imprint: Foote & Davies Co. Atlanta. (shown at 65%)
 b. Issued, cancelled. R4
 c. Unissued, cancelled. R4
GA840-50. 50 Dollars Nov. 1, 1907. As above.
 c. Unissued, cancelled. R5

Savannah

SAVANNAH CLEARING ASSOCIATION

A. Series with Numeral and A—No State Seal

GA860-1. 1 Dollar Nov. 4, 1907. Black on apple green underprint. Red circular guilloche at center, and red numeral at upper right. Vertical list of member banks on back. Series 1 A.
c. Unissued, cancelled. R4

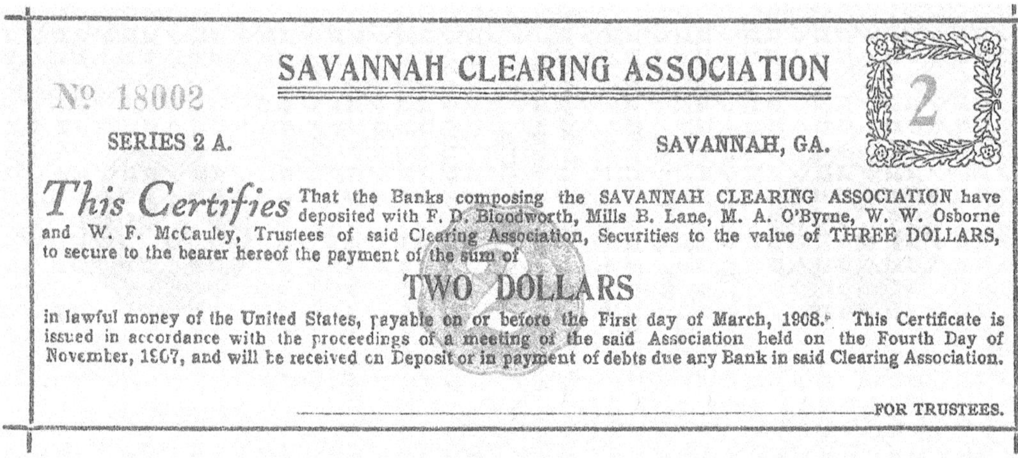

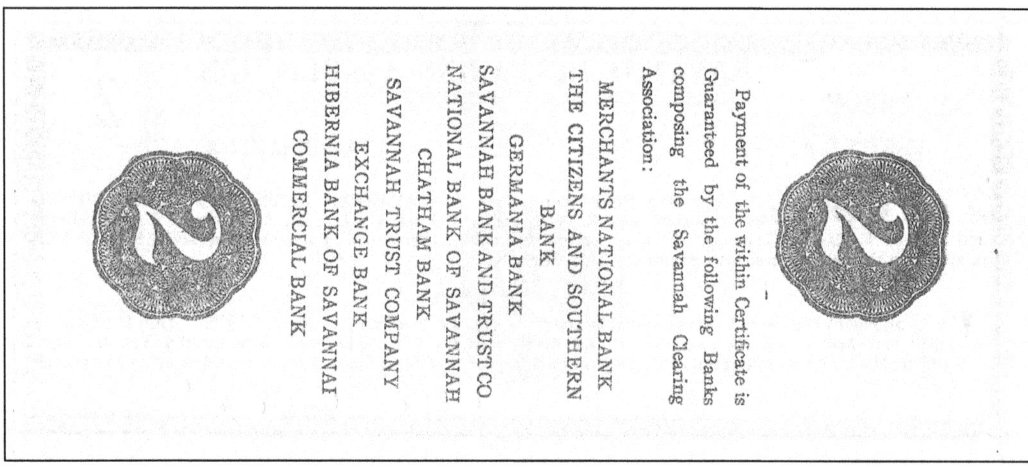

GA860-2. 2 Dollars Nov. 4, 1907. As above. Series 2 A. (shown at 72%)
c. Unissued, cancelled. R5

B. Letter Series Without Numeral — State Seal Series

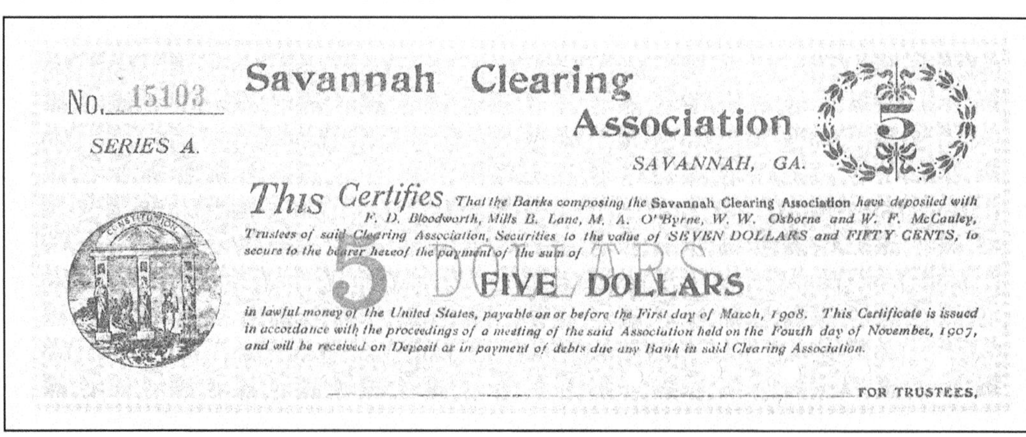

GA880-5. 5 Dollars Nov. 4, 1907. Black on green underprint. Red value in numeral and words at lower center. State seal at left. Vertical list of member banks on back. Series A. (shown at 64%)
c. Unissued, cancelled. **R5**

GA880-10. 10 Dollars Nov. 4, 1907. As above. Series B.
c. Unissued, cancelled. **R4**

GA880-20. 20 Dollars Nov. 4, 1907. As above. Series C.
c. Unissued, cancelled. **R4**

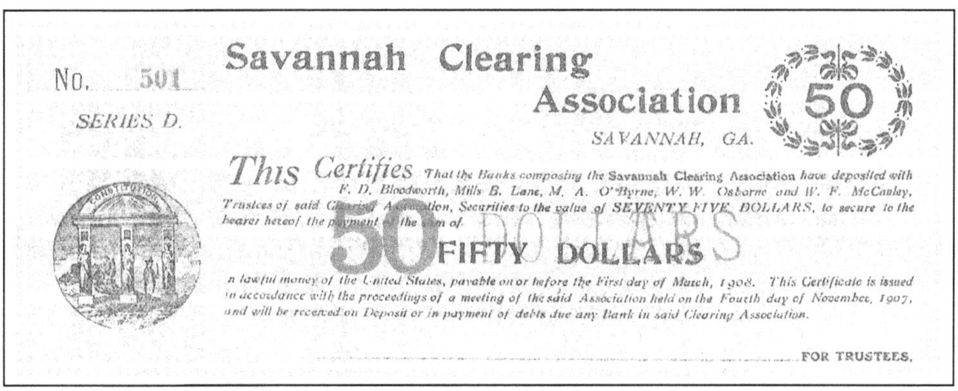

GA880-50. 50 Dollars Nov. 4, 1907. As above. Series D. (shown at 60%)
c. Unissued, cancelled. **R5**

Sparta

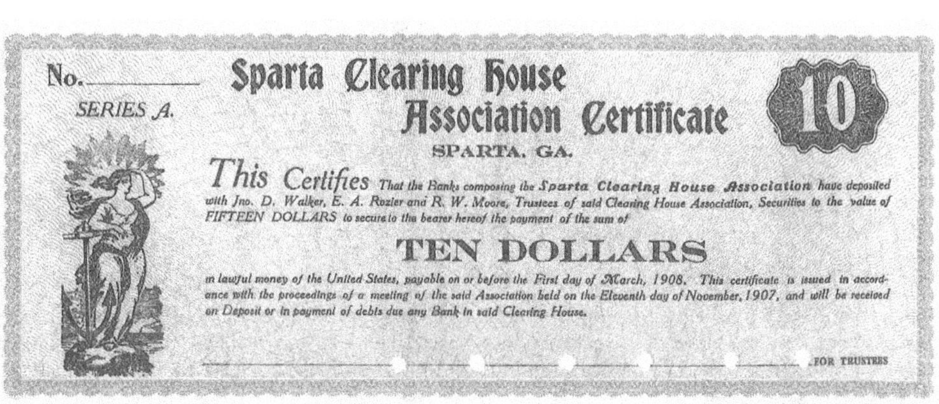

Sparta Clearing House Association Certificate

GA900-10. 10 Dollars Nov. 11, 1907. Black and brown. Allegory of Hope at the Seashore (woman with anchor) at left. Vertical list of member banks on back. Series A. Printer: Foote & Davies Co. Atlanta (without imprint). (shown at 60%)
c. Unissued, cancelled. **R4**

Sylvester

The Sylvester Clearing House Association Certificate

GA920-10. 10 Dollars Nov. 9, 1907. Black and brown. Value in red outline across lower center. Eagle on shield at left. Vertical list of member banks on back. Series A. Imprint: Foote & Davies Co. Atlanta. (shown at 65%)
c. Unissued, cancelled. **R4**

Thomaston

Thomaston Clearing House Association Certificate

GA940-1. 1 Dollar 1907. Series A. (list)
u. Unissued. **SENC**

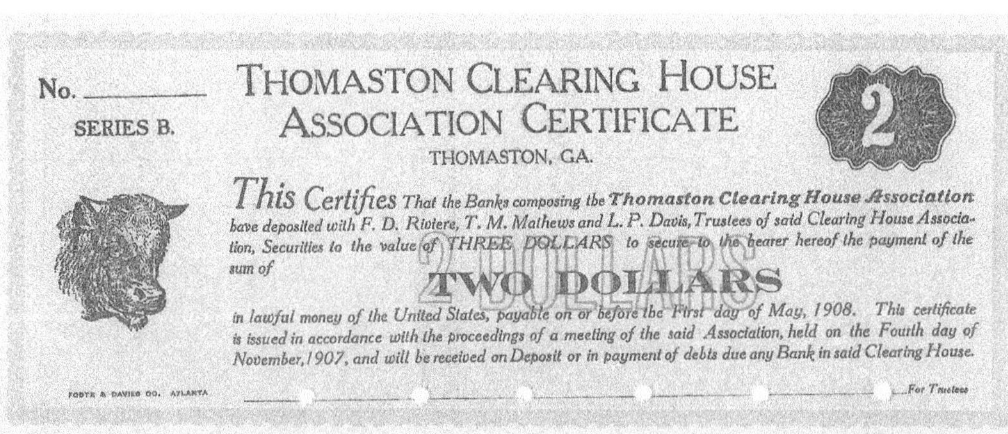

GA940-2. 2 Dollars Nov. 4, 1907. Black and orange on blue paper. Value in red outline across lower center. Cow's head at left. Vertical list of member banks on back. Series B. Imprint: Foote & Davies Co. Atlanta. (shown at 65%)
c. Unissued, cancelled. **R4**

GA940-20. 20 Dollars Nov. 4, 1907. Series E. As above.
c. Unissued, cancelled. R5

Thomasville

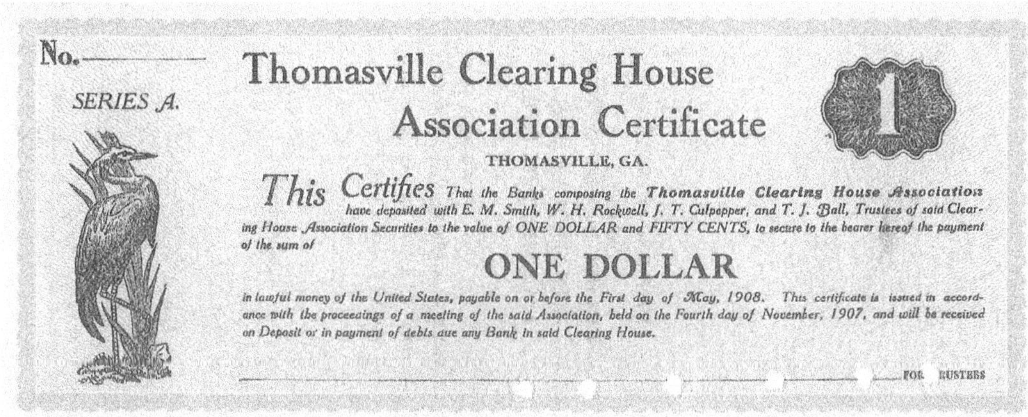

THOMASVILLE CLEARING HOUSE ASSOCIATION CERTIFICATE

GA960-1. 1 Dollar Nov. 4, 1907. Black and orange on blue paper. Stork at left. Vertical list of member banks on back. Series A. Printer: Foote & Davies Co. Atlanta (without imprint). (shown at 65%)
c. Unissued, cancelled. R4

Tifton

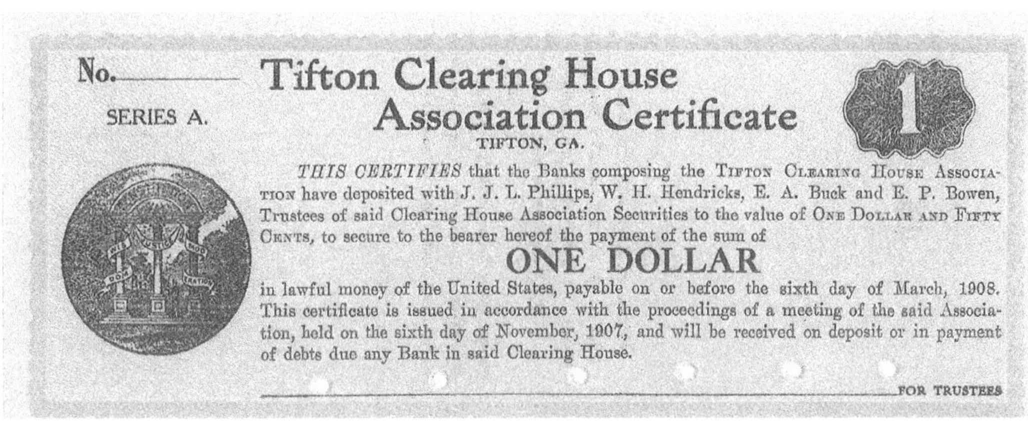

TIFTON CLEARING HOUSE ASSOCIATION CERTIFICATE

GA980-1. 1 Dollar Nov. 6, 1907. Black and orange on blue paper. State seal at left. Vertical list of member banks on back. Series A. Printer: Foote & Davies Co. Atlanta (without imprint). (shown at 64%)
c. Unissued, cancelled. R4
u. Issued. SENC

Valdosta

VALDOSTA CLEARING HOUSE ASSOCIATION CERTIFICATE

GA1000-10. 10 Dollars Nov. 5, 1907. Black and green. Value in red outline across lower center. Farmer with animals at left. Red value across center. Vertical list of member banks on back. Series A. Imprint: Foote & Davies Co. Atlanta. (shown at 66%)

c. Unissued, cancelled. R4

Waycross

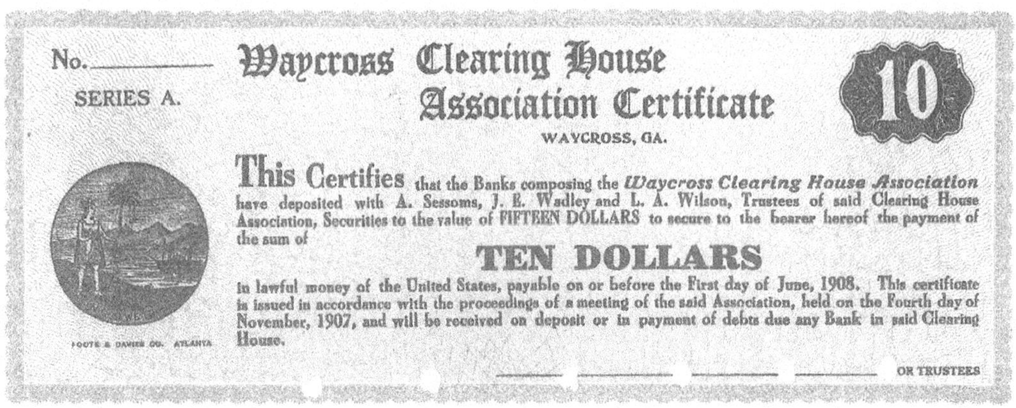

WAYCROSS CLEARING HOUSE ASSOCIATION CERTIFICATE

GA1020-10. 10 Dollars Nov. 4, 1907. Black and brown. Indian viewing river scene at left. Vertical list of member banks on back. Series A. Imprint: Foote & Davies Co. Atlanta. (shown at 65%)

c. Unissued, cancelled. R4

GA1020-20. 20 Dollars Nov. 4, 1907. As above.

c. Unissued, cancelled. R5

Willacoochee

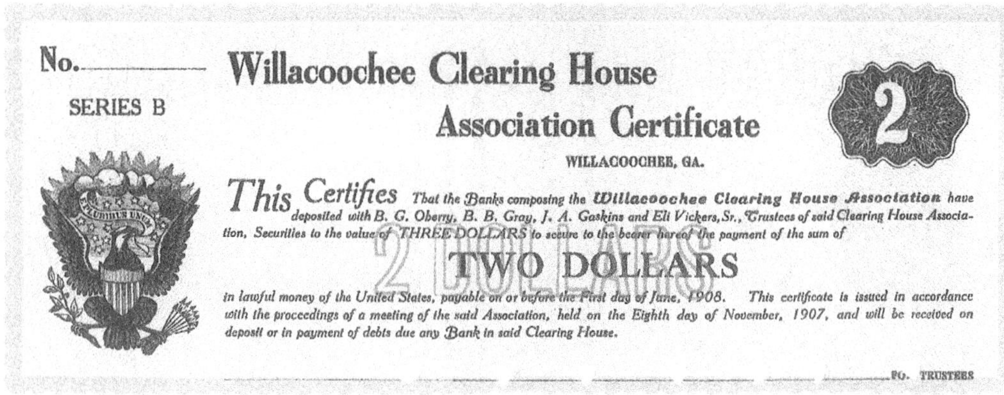

WILLACOOCHEE CLEARING HOUSE ASSOCIATION CERTIFICATE

GA1040-2. 2 Dollars Nov. 8, 1907. Black and orange. Value in red outline across lower center. American eagle with ribbon at left. Vertical list of member banks on back. Series B. Printer: Foote & Davies Co. Atlanta (without imprint). (shown at 65%)
c. Unissued, cancelled. R4

GA1040-5. 5 Dollars Nov. 8, 1907. As above. Series C.
c. Unissued, cancelled. R4

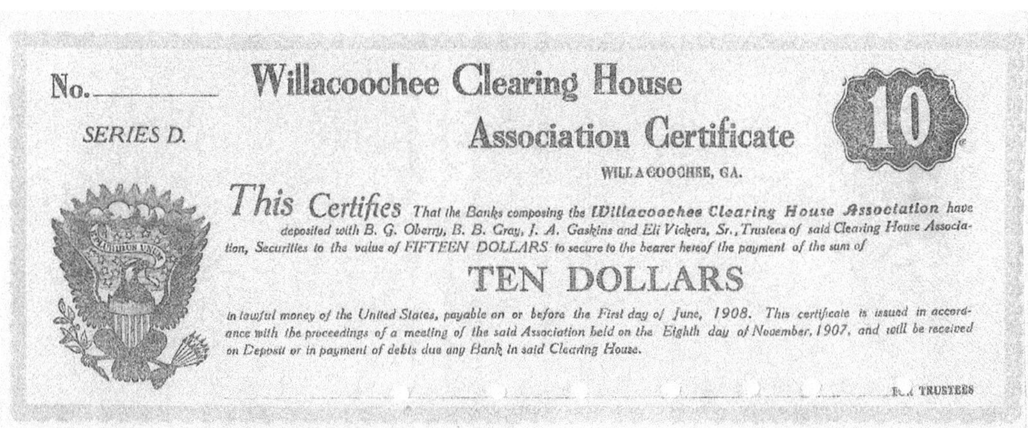

GA1040-10. 10 Dollars Nov. 8, 1907. Blue paper, otherwise as above. Without red outline value. Series D. (shown at 65%)
c. Unissued, cancelled. R4

IDAHO

Boise

THE FIRST NATIONAL BANK OF IDAHO

ID500-1. 1 Dollar Cashier's Check Nov. 5, 1907. Black on green paper. Large red value and dollar signs outline at center. Embossed seal at left. Uniface.
b. Issued, cancelled. R5

ID500-2. 2 Dollars Nov. 5, 1907. Black on blue paper. As above.
b. Issued, cancelled. R5

ID500-10. 10 Dollars Nov. 5, 1907. Black on light lavender paper. As above. (shown at 75%)
b. Issued, cancelled. **R5**

Coeur d'Alene

American Trust Company/ Coeur d'Alene Clearinghouse Association

ID520-5. 5 Dollars (cashier's check) Dec. 24, 1907 (handwritten date). Black on cream paper. Eagle at left, blue value above to right. Uniface. Imprint: Bankers Supply Co. Litho. Denver.
b. Issued, cancelled. **R5**

ID520-10. 10 Dollars Dec. 28, 1907. As above. (shown at 63%)
b. Issued, cancelled. **R5**
ID520-20. 20 Dollars Dec. 23, 1907. As above.
b. Issued, cancelled. **R5**

ID520-50. 50 Dollars Jan. 11, 1908. As above. (shown at 66%)
 b. Issued, cancelled. R5

Milner

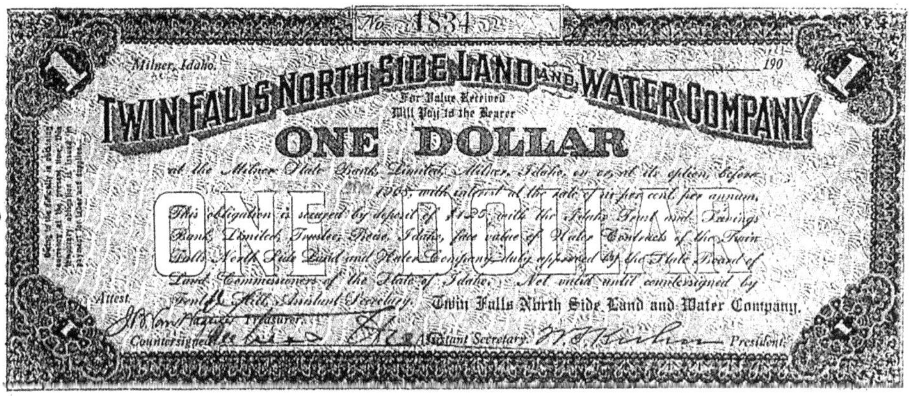

Twin Falls North Side Land and Water Company

ID540-1. 1 Dollar (pay roll check). 190_ (1907). Black on light purple underprint. Value in white wording across center. Value on green back. (shown at 68%)
 a. Issued, not cancelled. R5

Illinois

Chicago

Chicago Clearing House Association

Only four of the clearing house member banks are known to have issued panic scrip in 1907: Nos. 1, 3, 5 and 11. All colors were the same for each denomination.

A. No. 1: The First National Bank of Chicago

IL500-1. 1 Dollar Nov. 11, 1907. Black and blue. One line of text at top, bank number at upper right and issuing bank's name at lower left in red. Darker area vertically at right center (anti-counterfeiting device). One line of text on back. Imprint: Western Bank Note and Engraving Company Chicago.
 a. Issued, not cancelled. **VG, 25. VF, 60.**
 b. Issued, cancelled. **VG, 20. VF, 45.**
 c. Unissued, cancelled. **VF, 25. EF, 60.**
 f. Specimen. **Unc., 250.**

IL500-2. 2 Dollars Nov. 11, 1907. Black and light gold. Red components as above. Darker area at left center. Imprint as above.
 a. Issued, not cancelled. **VG, 75. VF, 150.**
 b. Issued, cancelled. **VG, 25. VF, 50.**

IL500-5. 5 Dollars Nov. 11, 1907. Black and green. As above. (shown at 55%)
- c. Unissued, cancelled. **VG, 50. VF, 100.**

IL500-10. 10 Dollars Nov. 11, 1907. Black and blue. As above.
- b. Issued, cancelled. **VG, 35. VF, 85.**
- c. Unissued, cancelled. **VF, 30. EF, 70.**
- f. Specimen. **Unc., 250.**

NOTE: One example of IL500-10. was redeemed at Temple City, CA, on Oct. 30, 1964!

What became of the $15,000,000 Issue of Chicago Clearing House Certificates.

COMPLIMENTS OF THE

Chicago Coated Board Co.

CHICAGO, ILLS.

Manufacturers of

Patent Coated, Folding Box Boards, Jute, Pulp, News, Clip and Special Box Boards

DAILY CAPACITY 220,000 POUNDS

THIS piece of paper board was made from certificates issued by the Chicago Clearing House Association during the money panic of November, 1907. The run from which this sample was taken consisted of three tons, $6,842,000 of certificates being used. The total amount of certificates destroyed was $14,432,000. They were put into our beaters by Clearing House representatives, and the photograph shows them in the act of filling a beater.

The run was made on our No. 3 machine, which trims eighty-one inches. The finish was all given on the machine which has three stacks of calenders. A sheet thirteen points thick, tested (Mullen tester used), one hundred and sixty-four pounds per square inch.

You don't often see souvenirs from the Panic of 1907. This piece of thick cardboard, made by the Chicago Coated Board Co., is composed of local Clearing House certificates used as indicated in the text. Almost the entire $15 million was destroyed and apparently used to produce these souvenir cardboards, yet the Chicago Clearing House certificates are among the more easily available of the entire series. On the back at bottom is text, "Souvenir of Panic/of 1907." (shown at 60%)

B. No. 3: The Commercial National Bank of Chicago

IL510-1. 1 Dollar Nov. 11, 1907. As 500-1. (shown at 63%)
- a. Issued, not cancelled. **VG, 25. VF, 55.**
- c. Unissued, cancelled. **VG, 20. VF, 50.**

IL510-2. 2 Dollars Nov. 11, 1907. As 500-2.
- a. Issued, not cancelled. **VG, 75. VF, 150.**
- c. Unissued, cancelled. **VG, 20. VF, 50.**
- f. Specimen. **Unc., 250.**

IL510-5. 5 Dollars Nov. 11, 1907. As 500-5.
- a. Issued, not cancelled. **R3**
- b. Issued, cancelled. **VG, 30. VF, 75.**
- f. Specimen. **Unc., 250.**

IL510-10. 10 Dollars Nov. 11, 1907. As 500-10.
- c. Unissued, cancelled. **R3**

C. No. 5: The Corn Exchange National Bank of Chicago

IL520-1. 1 Dollar Nov. 11, 1907. As 500-1.
- a. Issued, not cancelled. **VG, 25. VF, 55.**
- b. Issued, cancelled. **VG, 20. VF, 50.**
- f. Specimen. **Unc., 250.**

IL520-2. 2 Dollars Nov. 11, 1907. As 500-2.
- a. Issued, not cancelled. **VG, 75. VF, 150.**
- b. Issued, cancelled. **VG, 35. VF, 75.**
- f. Specimen. **Unc., 250.**

IL520-5. 5 Dollars Nov. 11, 1907. As 500-5.
- f. Specimen. **Unc., 250.**

IL520-10. 10 Dollars Nov. 11, 1907. As 500-10.
- f. Specimen. **Unc., 250.**

D. No. 11: The Continental National Bank of Chicago

IL530-1. 1 Dollar Nov. 11, 1907. As 500-1.
- a. Issued, not cancelled. **VG, 25. VF, 60.**
- f. Specimen. **Unc., 250.**

IL530-2. 2 Dollars Nov. 11, 1907. As 500-2. (shown at 64%)
- a. Issued, not cancelled. **VG, 75. VF, 150.**
- b. Issued, cancelled. **VG, 55. VF, 110.**
- f. Specimen. **Unc., 250.**

IL530-5. 5 Dollars Nov. 11, 1907. As 500-5.
- f. Specimen. **Unc., 250.**

Illinois Central Railroad Company

IL550-2. 2 Dollars Nov. 1, 1907. To Corn Exchange National Bank. Black. Company symbol at upper left. Uniface. Imprint: Western Bank Note & Eng. Co. Chicago.
- b. Issued, cancelled. **R2**

IL550-5. 5 Dollars Nov. 1, 1907. As above. To Corn Exchange National Bank.
- b. Issued, cancelled. **R3**

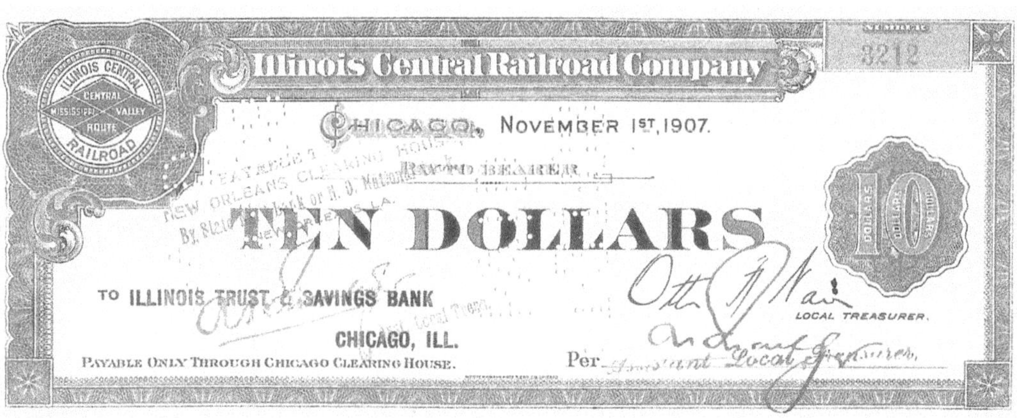

IL550-10. 10 Dollars Nov. 1, 1907. To Illinois Trust and Savings Bank, otherwise as above. (shown at 63%)
- b. Issued, cancelled. **VF, 25. AU, 55.**
- c. Unissued, cancelled. **VF, 35. AU, 65.**

IL550-20. 20 Dollars Nov. 1, 1907. To The Merchants Loan & Trust Co., otherwise as above.
- b. Issued, cancelled. **VF, 40. AU, 75.**

N. R. ALLEN'S SONS COMPANY

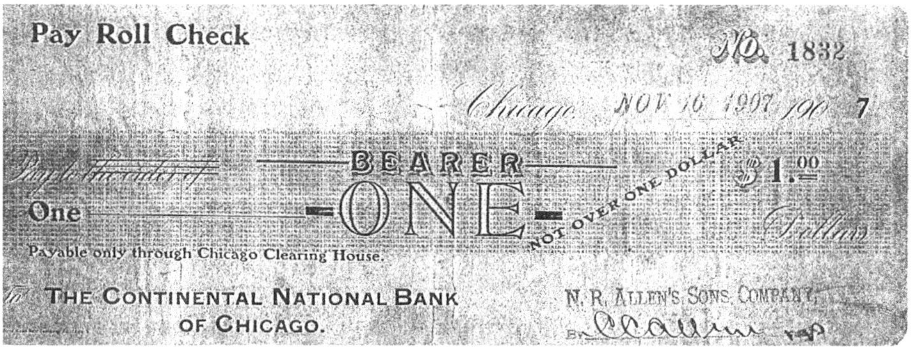

IL570-1. 1 Dollar Pay Roll Check Nov. 16, 1907. Black on light blue paper. Purple stripe across center. To The Continental National Bank of Chicago. (shown at 65%)
a. Issued, not cancelled. R5

PENN IRON MINING COMPANY/
THE FIRST NATIONAL BANK OF CHICAGO

IL580-5. 5 Dollars (payroll check) Nov. 20, 1907. Imprint: P.P. Parsons & Co. Chicago. (b/w) (shown at 65%)
u. Issued. SENC

Erie

A Certificate of Deposit dated 1907 was offered in the NASCA auction of October, 1986. No further details are known at present.

Harrisburg

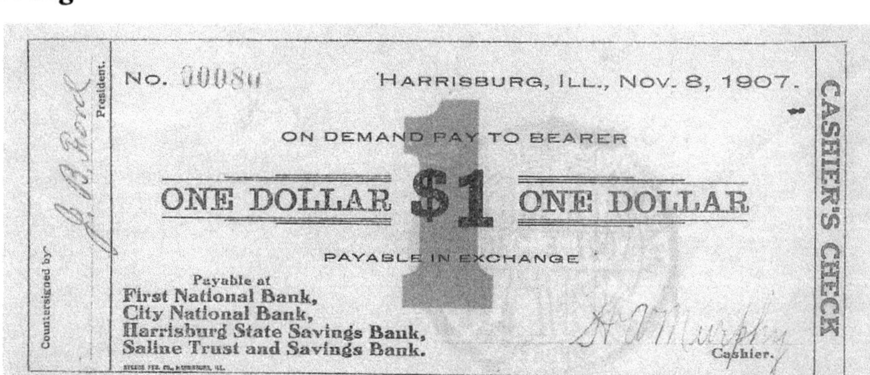

Various Banks

IL600-1. 1 Dollar Cashier's Check Nov. 8, 1907. Black on light yellow paper. Large denomination numeral in red at center. Payable at the four listed banks at lower left. Uniface. Imprint: Steele Ptg. Co., Harrisburg, Ill. (shown at 65%)

b. Issued, cancelled. **R5**

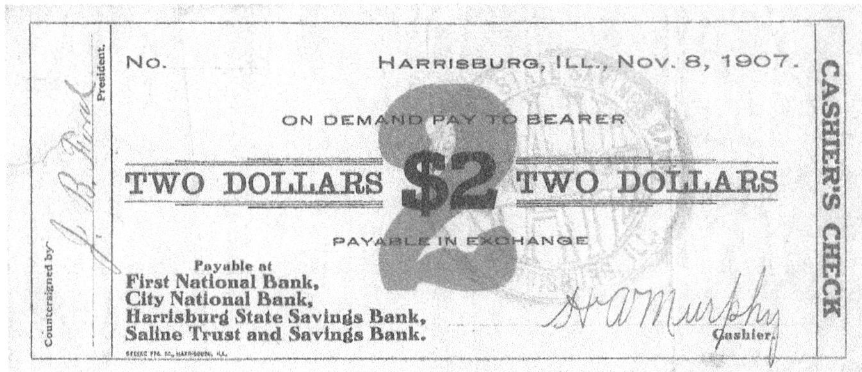

IL600-2. 2 Dollars Nov. 8, 1907. As above. (shown at 65%)

b. Issued, cancelled. **R5**

Joliet

Citizens National Bank

IL620-1. 1 Dollar Cashier's Check ND (1907). Green. Names of four banks at right, eagle at center on back.

a. Issued, not cancelled. **R5**

b. Issued, cancelled. **VG, 95. VF, 185.**

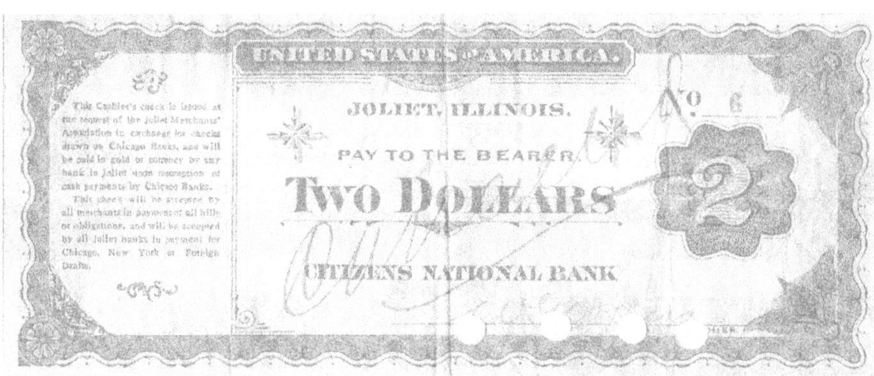

IL620-2. 2 Dollars ND. As above. (shown at 62%)
b. Issued, cancelled. R3
IL620-5. 5 Dollars ND. As above.
b. Issued, cancelled. R3
IL620-10. 10 Dollars ND. As above.
b. Issued, cancelled. R3

First National Bank of Joliet

IL630-1. 1 Dollar ND (1907). Similar to IL620-1.
b. Issued, cancelled. R4

Joliet National Bank

IL640-1. 1 Dollar ND (1907). Similar to IL620-1. (shown at 63%)
a. Issued, not cancelled. R4

Will County National Bank

IL660-1. 1 Dollar ND (1907). Similar to IL620-1. (shown at 63%)
- a. Issued, not cancelled. VG, 175. VF, 300.
- b. Issued, cancelled. VG, 95. VF, 175.

Moline

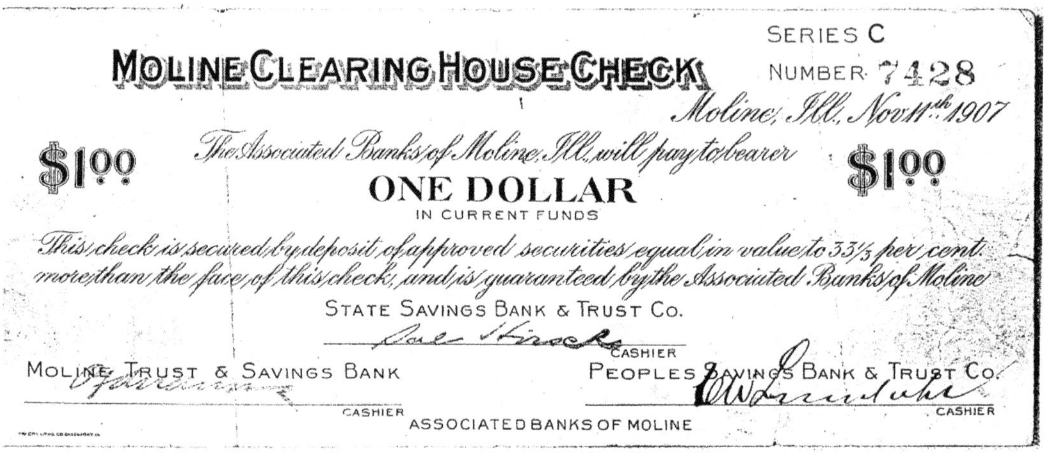

Associated Banks of Moline/ Moline Clearing House Check

IL680-1. 1 Dollar Nov. 11, 1907. Three banks named. (b/w) (shown at 75%)
- a. Issued, not cancelled. **R5**

IL680-5. 5 Dollars Nov. 11, 1907. (list)
- b. Issued, cancelled. **R5**

Peoria

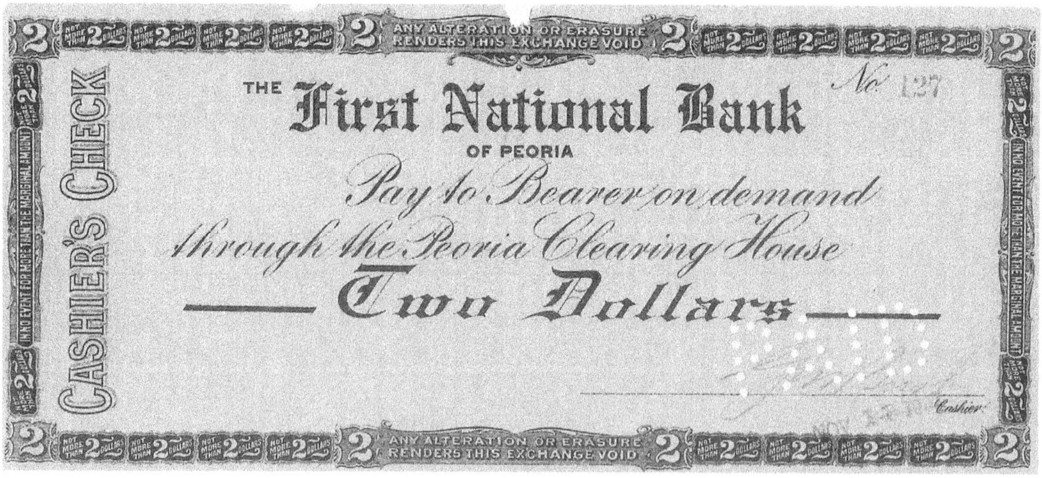

The First National Bank of Peoria

IL700-2. 2 Dollars Cashier's Check Nov. 19, 1907 (stamped date). Black on blue paper. Text line at upper center. Uniface. (shown at 66%)
- b. Issued, cancelled. **R4**
- d. Unissued, remainder. **R3**

IL700-5. 5 Dollars Nov. 19, 1907 (stamped date). Black on yellow paper. Without text line at upper center. Uniface. (shown at 65%)

b. Issued, cancelled. R3

IL700-10. 10 Dollars ND (1907). Black on light pink paper. Uniface.

d. Unissued, remainder. R3

IL700-20. 20 Dollars ND (1907). (b/w)

b. Issued, cancelled. R4

Peoria Clearing House Association

A. Home Savings & State Bank of Peoria, Illinois

IL720-2. 2 Dollars Nov. 25, 1907. Black and blue. Text line at top, and issuing bank's name at lower left in red. Vertical text line and box in black on back. Imprint: Columbian Bank Note Co. Chicago. (shown at 67%)

c. Unissued, cancelled. R4

B. First National Bank

IL730-2. 2 Dollars Cashier's Check Nov. 11, 1907. Black on blue paper. As IL720-2.

b. Issued, cancelled. R3

d. Unissued, remainder. R3

IL730-5. 5 Dollars Nov. 19, 1907. Black on cream paper. As above.

b. Issued, cancelled. R3

IL730-10. 10 Dollars 1907. Black on light pink paper. As above. Uniface.

d. Unissued, remainder. R3

IL730-20. 20 Dollars 1907. Black on gold paper. Uniface.

b. Issued, cancelled. R3

Pulaski County

The Pulaski County Clearing House Association

IL750-1. 1 Dollar Nov. 4, 1907. Black on light tan paper. List of participating banks at left. Checkwriter line below value at right.
a. Issued, not cancelled. **R5**

IL750-5. 5 Dollars Nov. 4, 1907. As above. (shown at 75%)
b. Issued, cancelled. **R5**

IL750-10. 10 Dollars Nov. 4, 1907. As above.
a. Issued, not cancelled. **R5**

Springfield

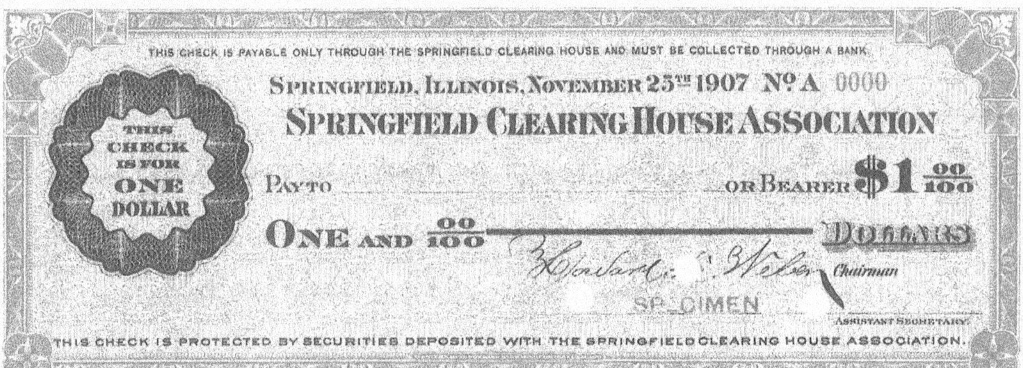

Springfield Clearing House Association

IL775-1. 1 Dollar Nov. 25, 1907. Black and green. One line of text on back. Imprint: Western Bank Note and Engraving Company Chicago. (shown at 64%)
f. Specimen. **Unc., 250.**

IL775-2. 2 Dollars Nov. 25, 1907. Black and pale red. As above.
f. Specimen. **Unc., 250.**

IL775-5. 5 Dollars Nov. 25, 1907. Black and brown. As above.
f. Specimen. **Unc., 250.**

IL775-10. 10 Dollars Nov. 25, 1907. Black and light orange. As above.
f. Specimen. **Unc., 250.**

INDIANA

Fort Wayne

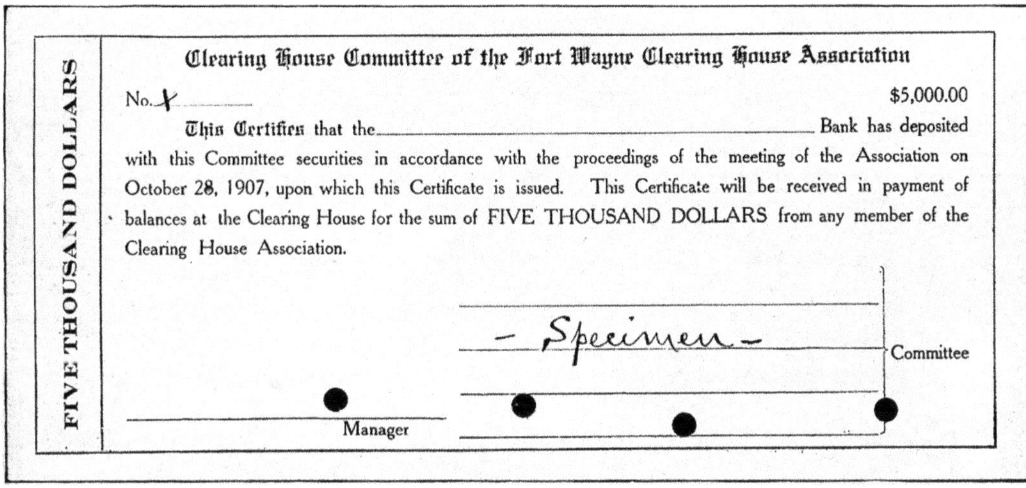

FIVE THOUSAND DOLLARS

Clearing House Committee of the Fort Wayne Clearing House Association

No. X $5,000.00

This Certifies that the ______ Bank has deposited with this Committee securities in accordance with the proceedings of the meeting of the Association on October 28, 1907, upon which this Certificate is issued. This Certificate will be received in payment of balances at the Clearing House for the sum of FIVE THOUSAND DOLLARS from any member of the Clearing House Association.

– Specimen – Committee

Manager

CLEARING HOUSE COMMITTEE OF THE FORT WAYNE CLEARING HOUSE ASSOCIATION

IN500-5000. 5,000 Dollars Oct. 28, 1907. Clearing House Loan Certificate. (b/w) (shown at 76%)
f. Specimen. **R5**

GERMAN-AMERICAN NATIONAL BANK/ FORT WAYNE CLEARING HOUSE ASSOCIATION

IN520-5. 5 Dollars Clearing House Check Nov. 1907. Black on brown frame.
f. Specimen. **R5**

HAMILTON NATIONAL BANK/ FORT WAYNE CLEARING HOUSE ASSOCIATION

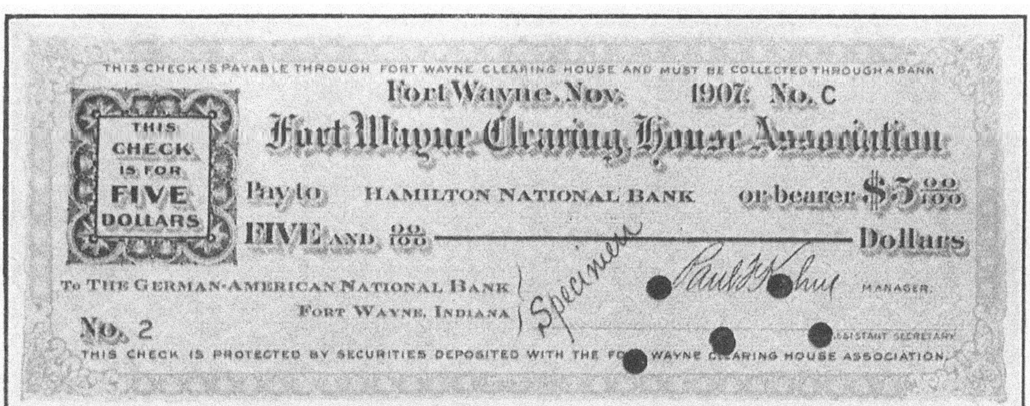

THIS CHECK IS PAYABLE THROUGH FORT WAYNE CLEARING HOUSE AND MUST BE COLLECTED THROUGH A BANK

Fort Wayne, Nov. 1907. No. C

Fort Wayne Clearing House Association

THIS CHECK IS FOR FIVE DOLLARS

Pay to HAMILTON NATIONAL BANK or bearer $5 00/100

FIVE AND 00/100 Dollars

To THE GERMAN-AMERICAN NATIONAL BANK FORT WAYNE, INDIANA

Specimen

Paul F. Kuhn MANAGER

No. 2

ASSISTANT SECRETARY

THIS CHECK IS PROTECTED BY SECURITIES DEPOSITED WITH THE FORT WAYNE CLEARING HOUSE ASSOCIATION.

IN530-5. 5 Dollars Clearing House Check Nov. 1907. Black on brown frame. (shown at 75%)
f. Specimen. **R5**

Greentown

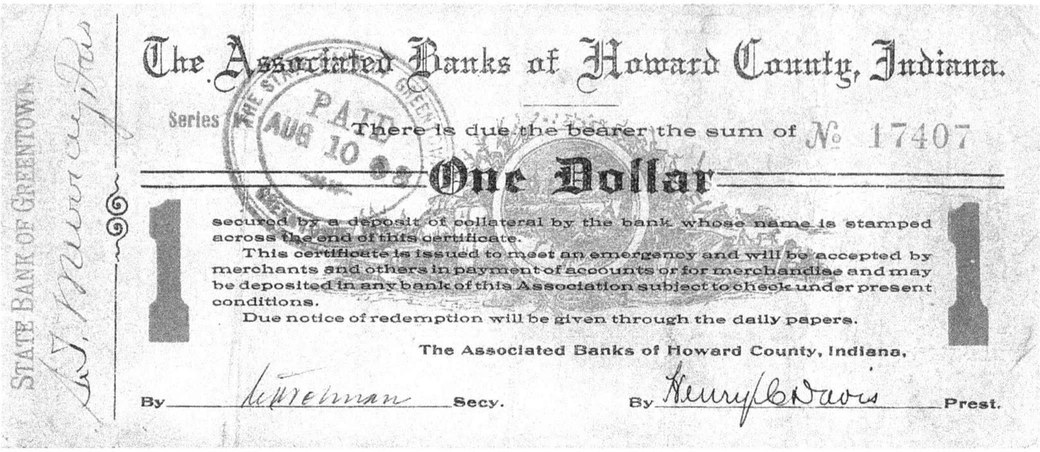

The Associated Banks of Howard County, Indiana/ State Bank of Greentown

IN540-1. 1 Dollar ND (1907). Black on green center of seal and farm implements, red numeral at left and right. State Bank of Greentown bank name stamped along left margin. Uniface. (shown at 75%)

b. Issued, cancelled. R3

d. Unissued, remainder. No bank name at left. R3

IN540-2. 2 Dollars ND. Design as above. No bank name at left. (b/w)

d. Unissued, remainder. R5

IN540-10. 10 Dollars ND. Design as above. No bank name at left. (b/w)

d. Unissued, remainder. R5

Indianapolis

The American National Bank

IN580-1. 1 Dollar Cashiers Check 1907. Black. Bank shield at left, value in guilloche at right. Uniface. (shown at 73%)

d. Unissued, remainder. R5

IN580-2. 2 Dollars 1907. Light brown. Design as above.

d. Unissued, remainder. R5

IN580-5. 5 Dollars 1907. Red. Design as above.

d. Unissued, remainder. R5

IN580-10. 10 Dollars 1907. Dark green. Design as above. (shown at 63%)
  d. Unissued, remainder. R5
IN580-20. 20 Dollars 1907. Orange. Design as above.
  d. Unissued, remainder. R5

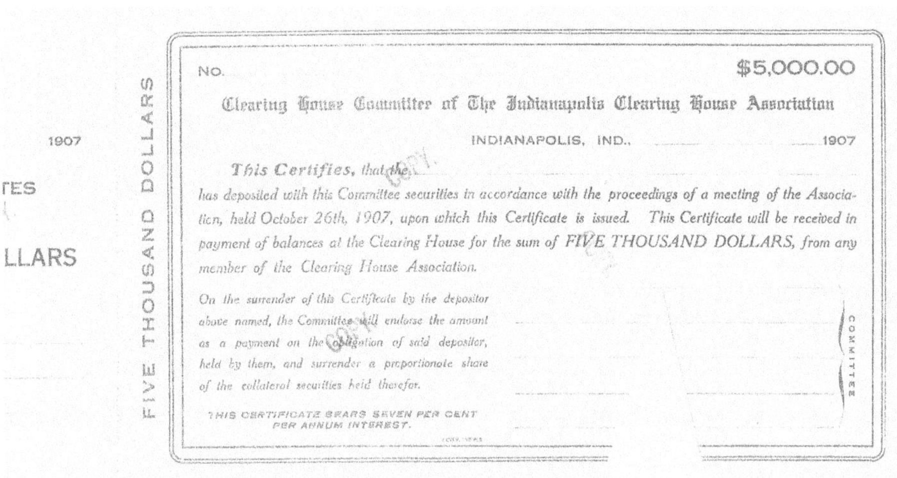

Clearing House Committee of the Indianapolis Clearing House Association

IN600-5000. 5,000 Dollars Loan Certificate Oct. 26, 1907. Black on off-white paper. Uniface. Size: ca. 212 × 131mm. without stub. Imprint: Levey, Ind'pls. (shown at 50%)
  c. Unissued, cancelled.

New Carlisle

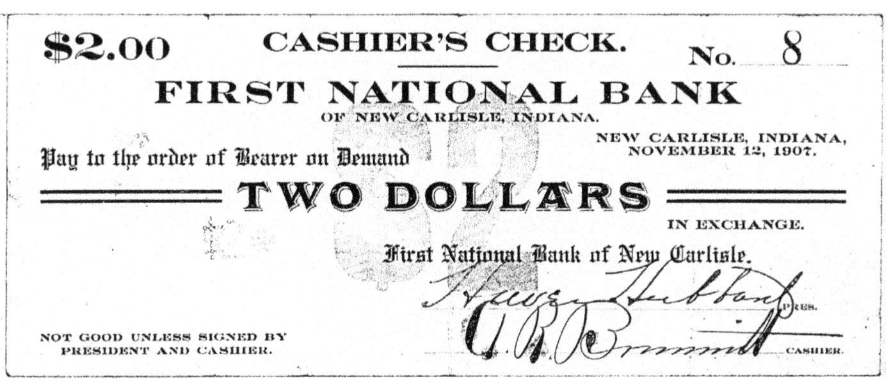

First National Bank

IN620-2. 2 Dollars Cashier's Check Nov. 12, 1907. Large denomination in underprint at center. (b/w) (shown at 64%)
  a. Issued, not cancelled. R5

South Bend

South Bend Clearing House Association

IN640-1.A 1 Dollar Nov. 20, 30, 1907. Black on brown underprint. Account with American Trust Company. Uniface. (shown at 68%)
  a. Issued, not cancelled. R5
  c. Unissued, cancelled. R5
IN640-1.B 1 Dollar Nov. 20, 1907. As above but account with Citizens National Bank.
  a. Issued, not cancelled. R5
IN640-1.C 1 Dollar Dec. 30, 1907. As above but account name blank. Payable to "Any Associated Bank."
  u. Unissued. R5
IN640-5. 5 Dollars Nov. 20, 1907. Account with Citizens National Bank. Imprint: Goes Litho. Co. Chicago. (b/w)
  a. Issued, not cancelled. R5

Iowa

Cedar Rapids

The American Trust and Savings Bank

A. First Issue
IA500-1. 1 Dollar Cashier's Check Oct. 29, 1907. Black on yellow paper.
  b. Issued, cancelled. R5
IA500-2. 2 Dollars Oct. 29, 1907. Black on light blue paper. As above.
  b. Issued, cancelled. R5
IA500-5. 5 Dollars Nov. 1, 1907. Black on yellow paper. As above.
  b. Issued, cancelled. R5

IA500-10. 10 Dollars Oct. 29, 1907. Black on pinkish paper. As above. (shown at 60%)
b. Issued, cancelled. R5

B. Second Issue

IA510-5. 5 Dollars Cashiers Check Nov. 1, 1907. Design similar to IA540-2. (shown at 60%)
b. Issued, cancelled. R5

The Cedar Rapids National Bank

IA520-1. 1 Dollar Cashier's Check Oct. 28, 1907. Black on off-white paper. Blue checkwriter line diagonally. Uniface.
b. Issued, cancelled. R5

IA520-2. 2 Dollars Oct. 28, 1907. As above.
b. Issued, cancelled. R5

IA520-5. 5 Dollars Oct. 28, 1907. As above.
b. Issued, cancelled. R5

IA520-10. 10 Dollars Oct. 28, 1907. As above.
b. Issued, cancelled. R5

IA520-20. 20 Dollars Oct. 28, 1907. As above.(shown at 55%)
b. Issued, cancelled. R5

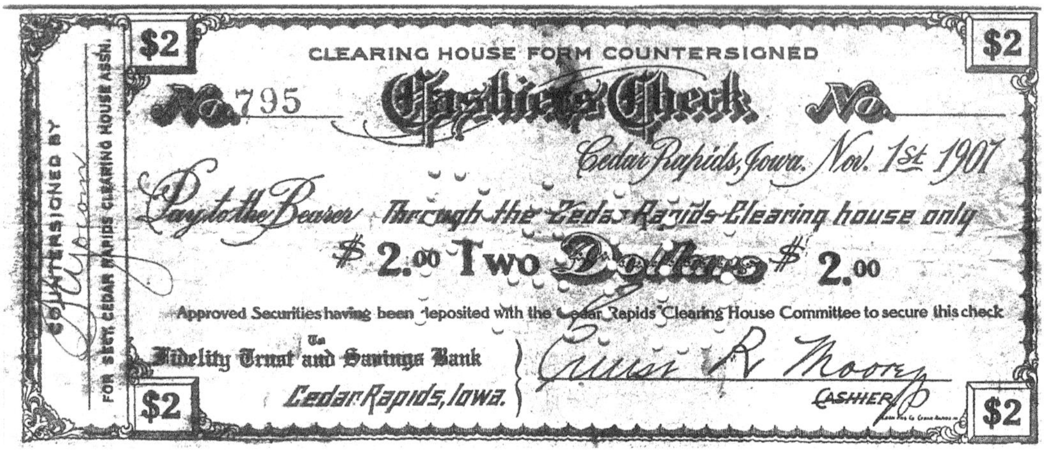

Fidelity Trust and Savings Bank

IA540-1. 1 Dollar Cashiers Check Nov. 1, 1907. Black on light tan paper. Uniface. Imprint: Alden Eng. Co. Cedar Rapids IA.
b. Issued, cancelled. R5

IA540-2. 2 Dollars Nov. 1, 1907. Black on blue paper. As above. (shown at 73%)
b. Issued, cancelled. R5

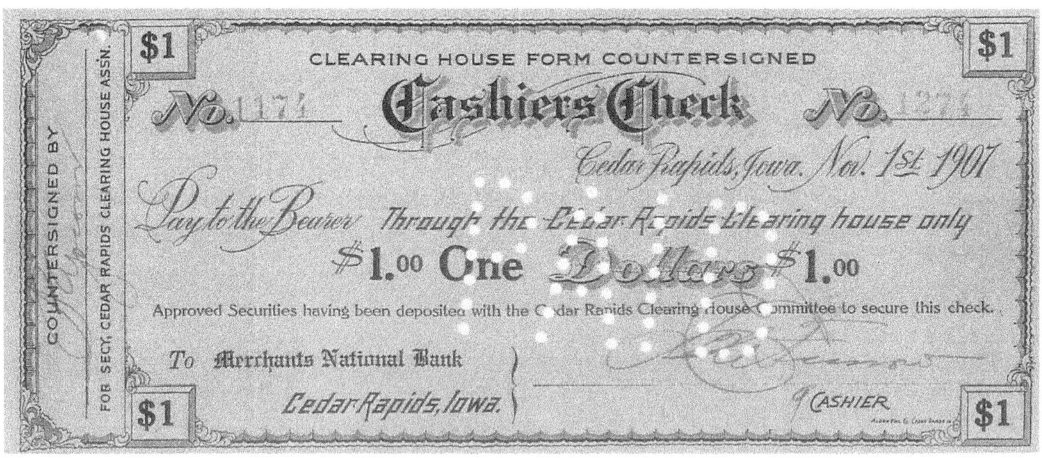

Merchants National Bank

IA550-1. 1 Dollar Cashiers Check Nov. 1, 1907. Black on light tan paper. Uniface. Design, format and imprint as IA540. (shown at 73%)
b. Issued, cancelled. R5

Security Savings Bank

IA560-1. 1 Dollar Cashiers Check Nov. 1, 1907. Black on light tan paper. Design, format and imprint as IA540.
b. Issued, cancelled. R5

IA560-2. 2 Dollars Nov. 1, 1907. Black on blue paper. As above.
b. Issued, cancelled. R5

$5 CLEARING HOUSE FORM COUNTERSIGNED $5

Cashiers Check No. 1288

Cedar Rapids, Iowa. Nov. 1st 1907

Pay to the Bearer Through the Cedar Rapids Clearing house only

$ 5.00 Five Dollars $ 5.00

Approved Securities having been deposited with the Cedar Rapids Clearing House Committee to secure this check

To Security Savings Bank Cedar Rapids, Iowa.

CASHIER

COUNTERSIGNED BY FOR SECY. CEDAR RAPIDS CLEARING HOUSE ASSN.

$5 $5

IA560-5. 5 Dollars Nov. 1, 1907. Black on yellow paper. As above. (shown at 63%)
  b. Issued, cancelled. R5
IA560-10. 10 Dollars Nov. 1, 1907. Black on gold paper. As above.
  b. Issued, cancelled. R5

Council Bluffs

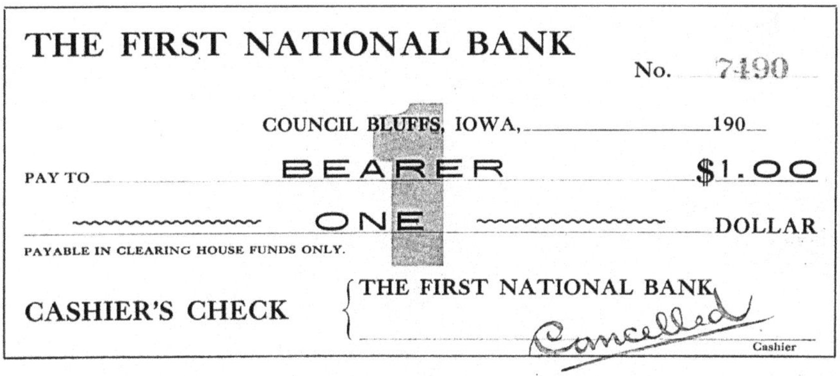
THE FIRST NATIONAL BANK No. 7490

COUNCIL BLUFFS, IOWA, 190__

PAY TO BEARER $1.00

ONE DOLLAR

PAYABLE IN CLEARING HOUSE FUNDS ONLY.

CASHIER'S CHECK THE FIRST NATIONAL BANK

Cancelled

Cashier

THE FIRST NATIONAL BANK

IA580-1. 1 Dollar Cashier's Check 190__ (1907). Large numeral at center. (b/w) (shown at 65%)
  c. Unissued, cancelled. R5
IA580-2. 2 Dollars 190__. As above. (b/w)
  c. Unissued, cancelled. R5
IA580-5. 5 Dollars 190__. As above. (b/w)
  c. Unissued, cancelled. R5

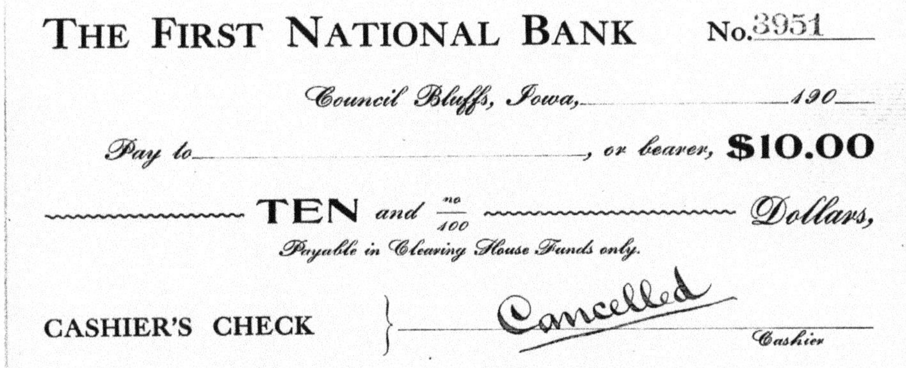
THE FIRST NATIONAL BANK No. 3951

Council Bluffs, Iowa, 190__

Pay to ______, or bearer, $10.00

TEN and no/100 Dollars,

Payable in Clearing House Funds only.

CASHIER'S CHECK Cancelled

Cashier

IA580-10. 10 Dollars 190__. Generally similar to above, but no large numeral at center. (b/w) (shown at 65%)

c. Unissued, cancelled. R5

IA580-20. 20 Dollars 190__. As IA580-10. (b/w)

c. Unissued, cancelled. R5

NOTE: An issue of clearing house loan certificates is reported to have been issued in Council Bluffs, but no specifics are known at present.

Davenport

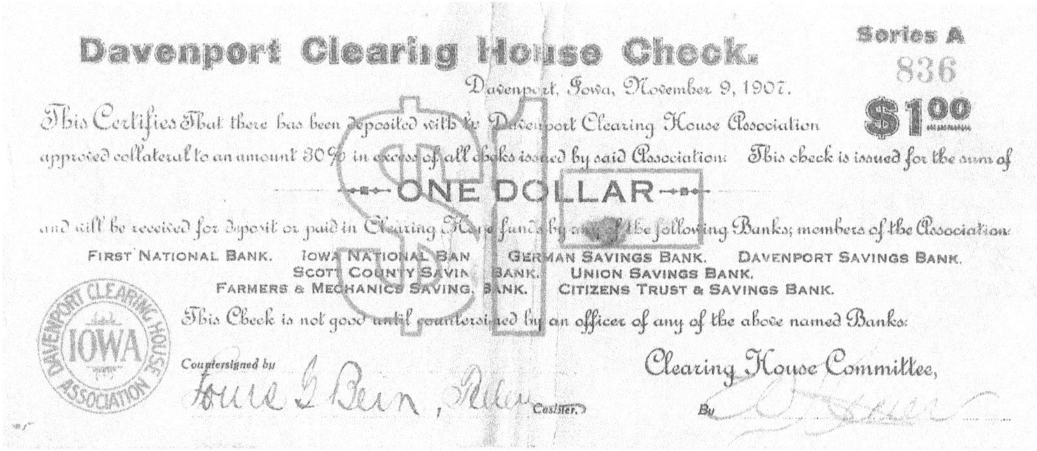

DAVENPORT CLEARING HOUSE CHECK

IA600-1. 1 Dollar Nov. 9, 1907. Black on yellow paper. Red outline denomination at center, clearing house emblem at lower left. Names of clearing house member banks across lower center. Series A. Back green with one line of red text across center. (shown at 74%)

a. Issued, not cancelled. R4

Des Moines

THE DES MOINES CLEARING HOUSE ASSOCIATION

IA620-1.A 1 Dollar Oct. 28, 1907. Black on blue underprint. Uniface. Imprint: Iowa Litho. Co. Des Moines.

a. Issued, not cancelled. **Fine, 175. EF, 325.**

b. Issued, cancelled. **Fine, 80. EF, 150.**

c. Unissued, cancelled. **VF, 70. EF, 130.**

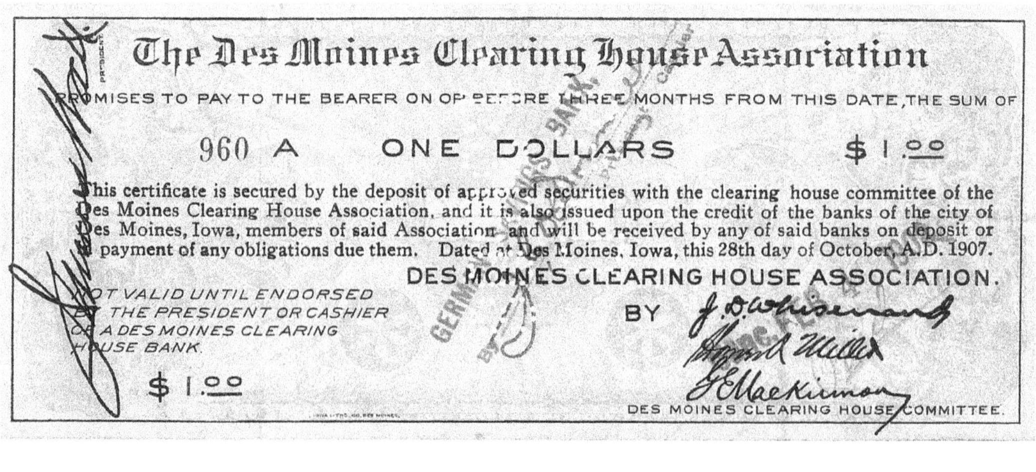

IA620-1.B 1 Dollars (error) Oct. 28, 1907. As above except for denomination error. (shown at 73%)
b. Issued, cancelled. **VF, 100. EF, 200.**
IA620-2. 2 Dollars Oct. 28, 1907. Black on light brown underprint. As above.
b. Issued, cancelled. Fine, 175. EF, 325.
c. Unissued, cancelled. **VF, 100. EF, 200.**
IA620-5. 5 Dollars Oct. 28, 1907. Black on yellow underprint. As above.
b. Issued, cancelled. **Fine, 175. EF, 325.**
c. Unissued, cancelled. **VF, 125. EF, 250.**
IA620-10. 10 Dollars Oct. 28, 1907. Black on brown underprint. As above.
b. Issued, cancelled. **Fine, 200. EF, 400.**
c. Unissued, cancelled. **VF, 150. EF, 300.**
IA620-20. 20 Dollars Oct. 28, 1907. Black on green underprint. As above.
b. Issued, cancelled. **Fine, 250. EF, 500.**
c. Unissued, cancelled. **VF, 200. EF, 400.**
IA620-50. 50 Dollars Oct. 28, 1907. Black on yellow underprint. As above.
c. Unissued, cancelled. **R5**
IA620-500. 500 Dollars Oct. 28, 1907. Black on light yellow paper. Vertical list of member banks on back.
b. Issued, cancelled. **R4**

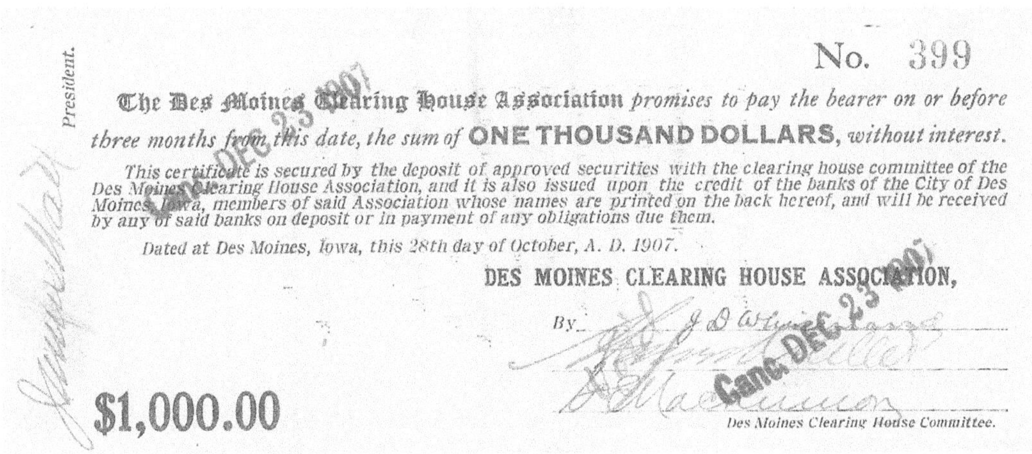

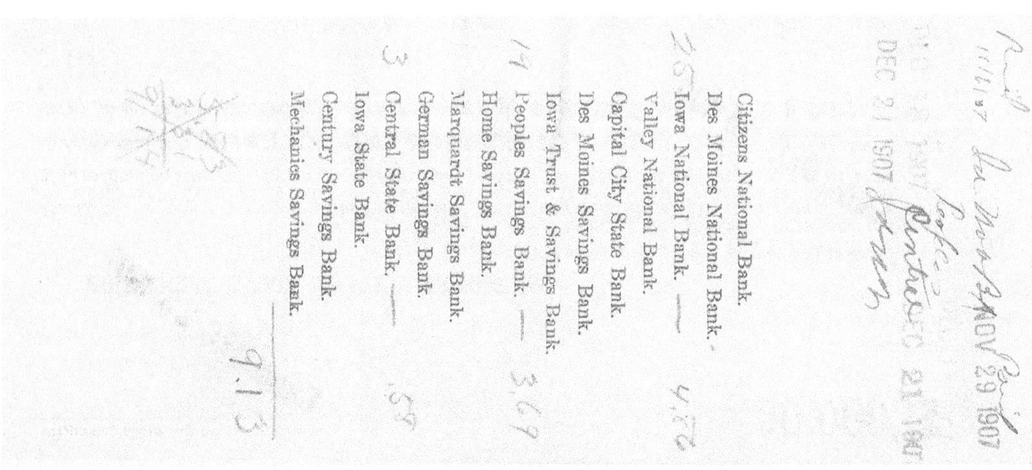

IA620-1000. 1000 Dollars Oct. 28, 1907. Black on yellow paper. As above. (shown at 75%)
b. Issued, cancelled. **R4**

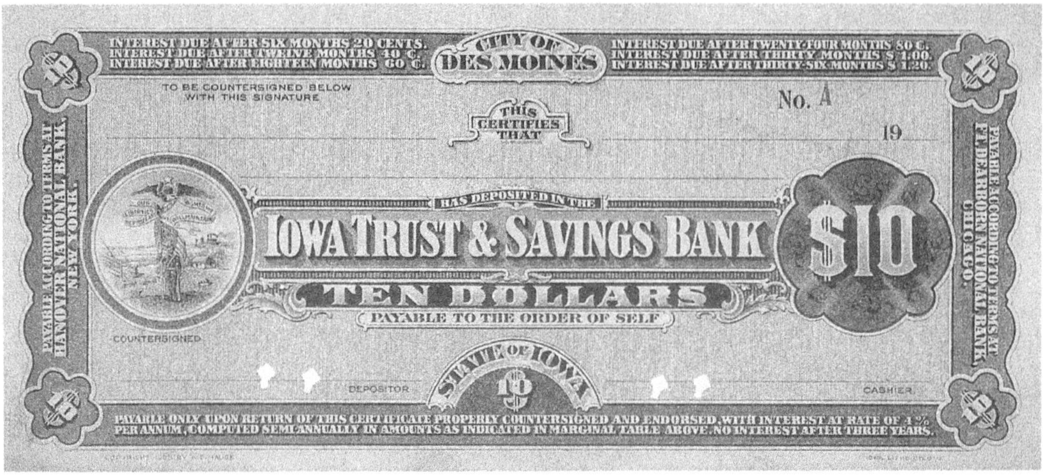

Iowa Trust & Savings Bank

IA640-10. 10 Dollars Certificate of Deposit ND (1907). Brown. State seal at left. Uniface. Imprint: Copyright 1906 by A. O. Hauge. (shown at 73%)

c. Unissued, cancelled. R5

Muscatine

Associated Banks Certificate/
Cook, Musser & Co. State Bank & Trust Co.

A. Uniface Issue

IA660-5. 5 Dollars Clearing House Check Oct. 31, Nov. 1, 1907. Embossed seal at right. Five banks named at center. (shown at 74%)

b. Issued, cancelled. R5

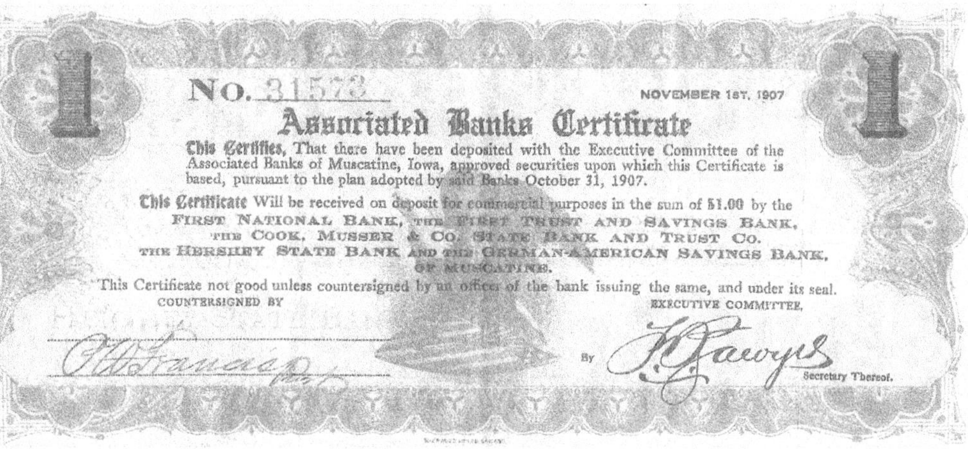

B. Two-sided Issue

IA680-1. 1 Dollar Nov. 1, 1907. Green. Eagle and shield at center facing left on face. Imprint: Sherwood Lith. Co. Chicago. (shown at 71%)

a. Issued, not cancelled. R5

b. Issued, cancelled. R5

IA680-2. 2 Dollars Nov. 1, 1907. (list)

b. Issued, cancelled. R5

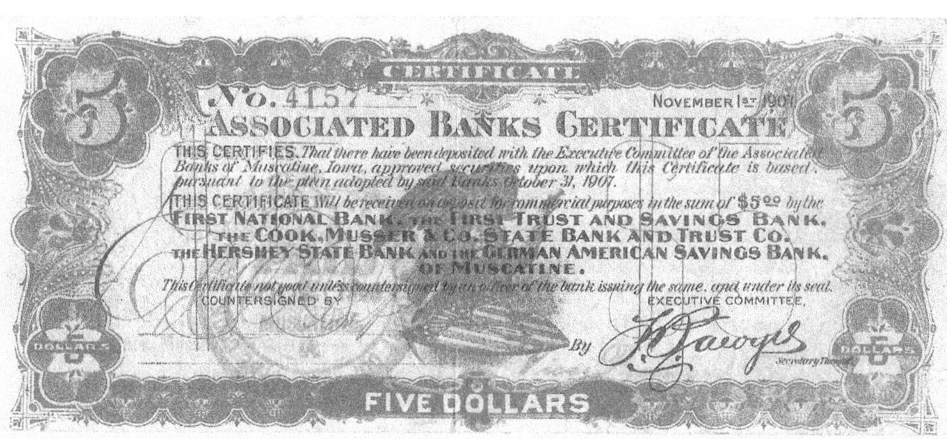

IA680-5. 5 Dollars Nov. 1, 1907. Blue. Eagle and shield at center facing right. (shown at 66%)
  b. Issued, cancelled. R4
IA680-10. 10 Dollars Nov. 1, 1907. (b/w)
  b. Issued, cancelled. R5
NOTE: IA680 was backed by six banks named on each certificate.

Sioux City

The First National Bank

IA720-5. 5 Dollars Cashier's Check ND (1907). Black on green underprint. Bank name in red at upper center. Back green; allegory with standing woman, eagle on open safe, capitol building at left, farm animals at lower center. Cornucopias at upper left and right. Imprint: Perkins Bros. Co. Sioux City. (shown at 75%)
  b. Issued, cancelled. R3
  d. Unissued, remainder. R3
IA720-10. 10 Dollars (1907). As above.
  b. Issued, cancelled. R4
IA720-20. 20 Dollars (1907). As above.
  b. Issued, cancelled. R4

The Iowa State Savings Bank

IA740-2. 2 Dollars Cashier's Check ND (1907). Similar to IA720. (shown at 69%)
  d. Unissued, remainder. R4
IA740-5. 5 Dollars ND (1907). As above.
  d. Unissued, remainder. R4

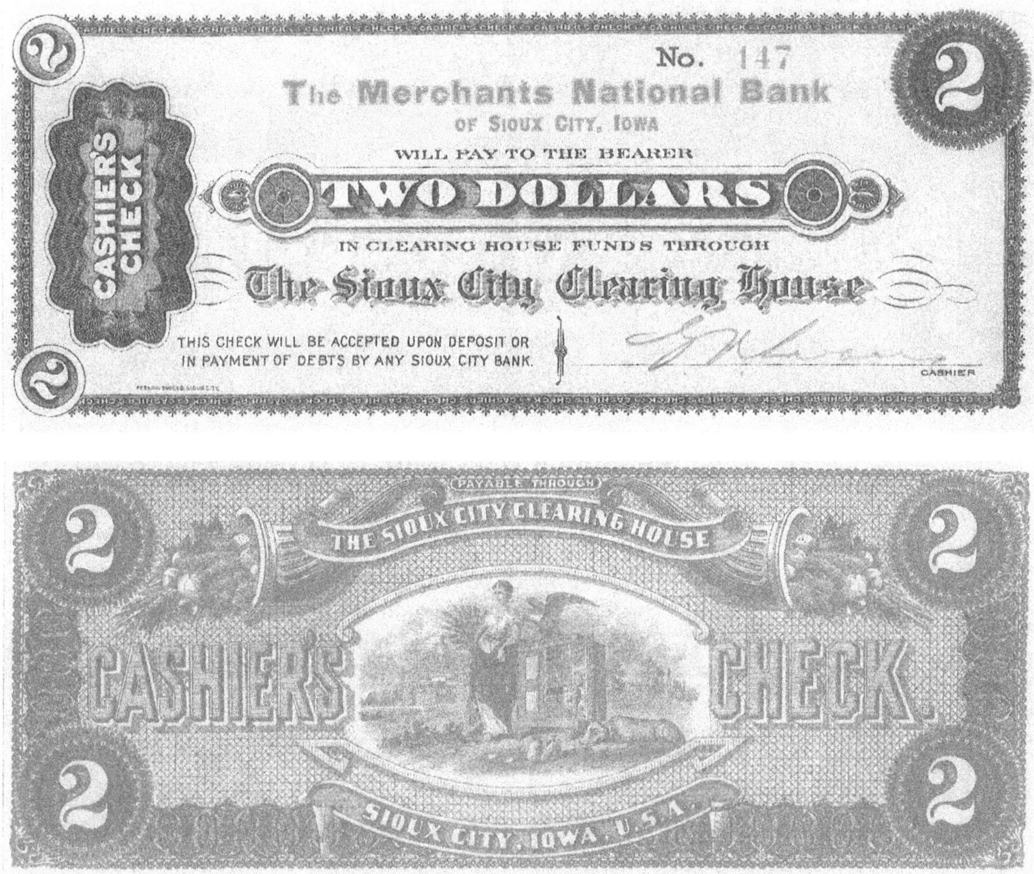

The Merchants National Bank

IA760-2. 2 Dollars Cashier's Check ND (1907). Similar to IA740-2. (shown at 68%)

a. Issued, not cancelled. **R4**

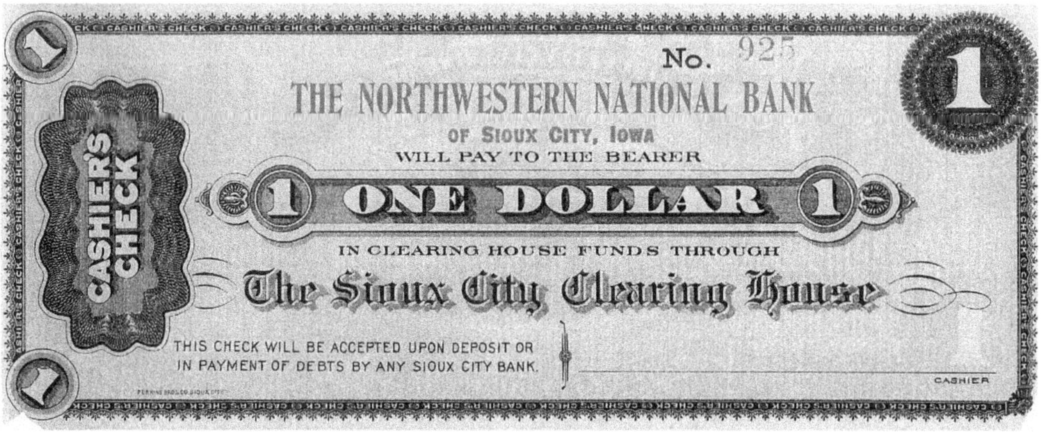

The Northwestern National Bank

IA780-1. 1 Dollar Cashier's Check ND (1907). Design similar to IA760-2. (shown at 69%)

d. Unissued, remainder. **R4**

The Security National Bank

A. Ornate Design

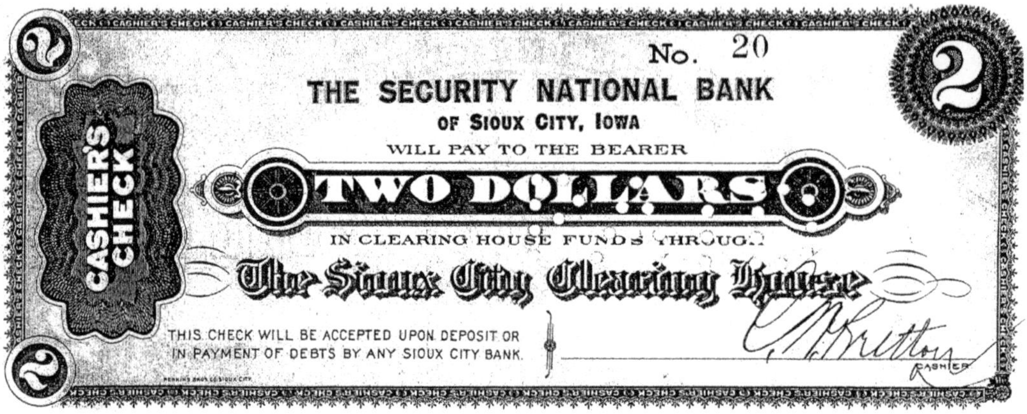

IA800-2. 2 Dollars Cashier's Check ND (1907). As IA740-2. (shown at 71%)
  b. Issued, cancelled. R3
IA800-5. 5 Dollars ND (1907). As above.
  b. Issued, cancelled. R3
IA800-10. 10 Dollars ND (1907). As above.
  b. Issued, cancelled. R4
  c. Unissued, cancelled. R4
IA800-20. 20 Dollars ND (1907). As above.
  b. Issued, cancelled. R4

B. Plain Design

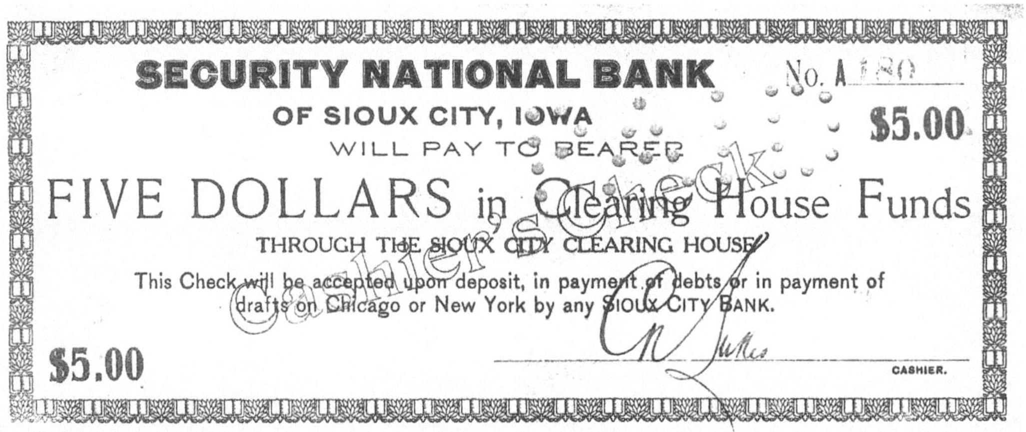

IA820-5. 5 Dollars Cashier's Check ND (1907). Black and olive green, with red denomination lower left and upper right. Text only. (shown at 74%)
  b. Issued, cancelled. R5
IA820-10. 10 Dollars ND (1907). As above.
  b. Issued, cancelled. R5
IA820-20. 20 Dollars ND (1907). As above.
  b. Issued, cancelled. R5

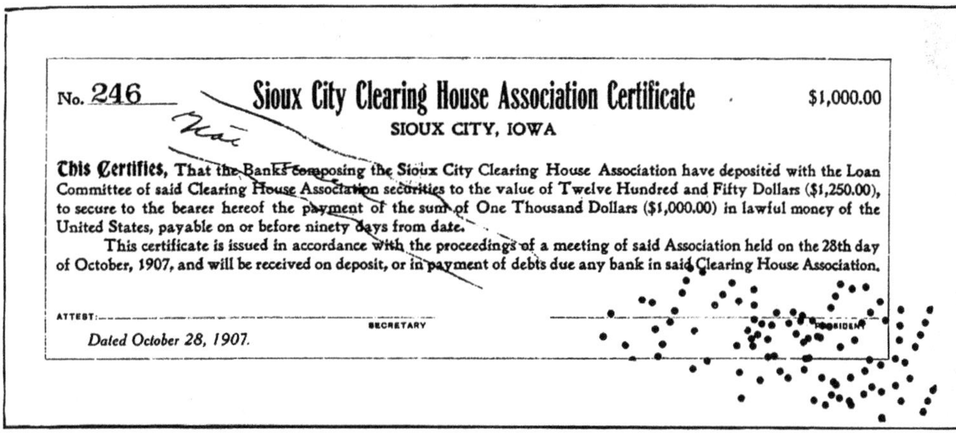
No. 246 Sioux City Clearing House Association Certificate $1,000.00

SIOUX CITY, IOWA

This Certifies, That the Banks composing the Sioux City Clearing House Association have deposited with the Loan Committee of said Clearing House Association securities to the value of Twelve Hundred and Fifty Dollars ($1,250.00), to secure to the bearer hereof the payment of the sum of One Thousand Dollars ($1,000.00) in lawful money of the United States, payable on or before ninety days from date.

This certificate is issued in accordance with the proceedings of a meeting of said Association held on the 28th day of October, 1907, and will be received on deposit, or in payment of debts due any bank in said Clearing House Association.

ATTEST: SECRETARY PRESIDENT

Dated October 28, 1907.

Sioux City Clearing House Association Certificate

IA840-1000. 1000 Dollars Oct. 28, 1907. (b/w) (shown at 70%)

c. Unissued, cancelled. R5

Kansas

Atchison

Atchison Savings Bank

KS500-1. 1 Dollar Cashier's Check ND (1907). Black.

u. Issued. SENC

KS500-5. 5 Dollars. As above. (list)

u. Issued. SENC

KS500-10. 10 Dollars. As above. (list)

u. Issued, SENC

NOTE: Reported dates of issue range from Nov. 19 to Dec. 12, 1907. States of existence have not been verified.

Exchange National Bank

KS520-1. 1 Dollar Cashier's Check Nov. 1, 1907. Blue on gray underprint. Portrait of William Hetherington at left. Uniface. Imprint: Union Bank Note Co. K.C. Mo.

b. Issued, cancelled. R2

c. Unissued, cancelled. R2

d. Unissued, remainder. R2

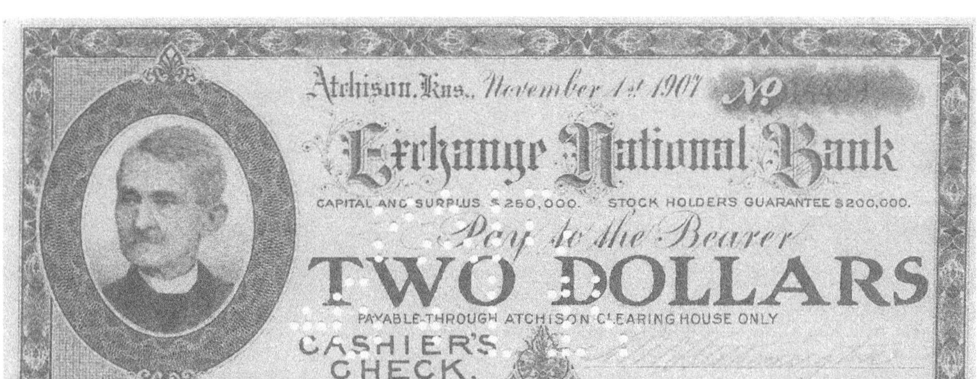
Atchison, Kas., November 1st 1907 No.

Exchange National Bank

CAPITAL AND SURPLUS $250,000. STOCK HOLDERS GUARANTEE $200,000.

Pay to the Bearer

TWO DOLLARS

PAYABLE THROUGH ATCHISON CLEARING HOUSE ONLY

CASHIER'S CHECK.

CASHIER.

KS520-2. 2 Dollars Nov. 1, 1907. As above. (shown at 70%)
b. Issued, cancelled. R4
c. Unissued, cancelled. R4

KS520-5. 5 Dollars Nov. 1, 1907. As above. (shown at 75%)
f. Printer's Specimen (punched UBNCo.) R4

First National Bank

KS540-1. 1 Dollar Cashier's Check Nov. 8, 1907. Black on off-white paper. Bank emblem at left, two quail at bottom center. Uniface. Imprint: Union Bank Note Co. K.C. Mo. (shown at 74%)
a. Issued, not cancelled. R4
b. Issued, cancelled. R4

KS540-2. 2 Dollars Nov. 8, 1907. As above.
a. Issued, not cancelled. R4
u. Unissued? SENC

KS540-5. 5 Dollars Nov. 8, 1907. As above.
a. Issued, not cancelled. R4
b. Issued, cancelled. R4

KS540-10. 10 Dollars Nov. 8, 1907. As above.
a. Issued, not cancelled. R4
u. Unissued? SENC

Garden City

The United States Sugar and Land Company

KS560-10. 10 Dollars (promissory note) 190__ (1907). Black on rose paper.
c. Unissued, cancelled. R5

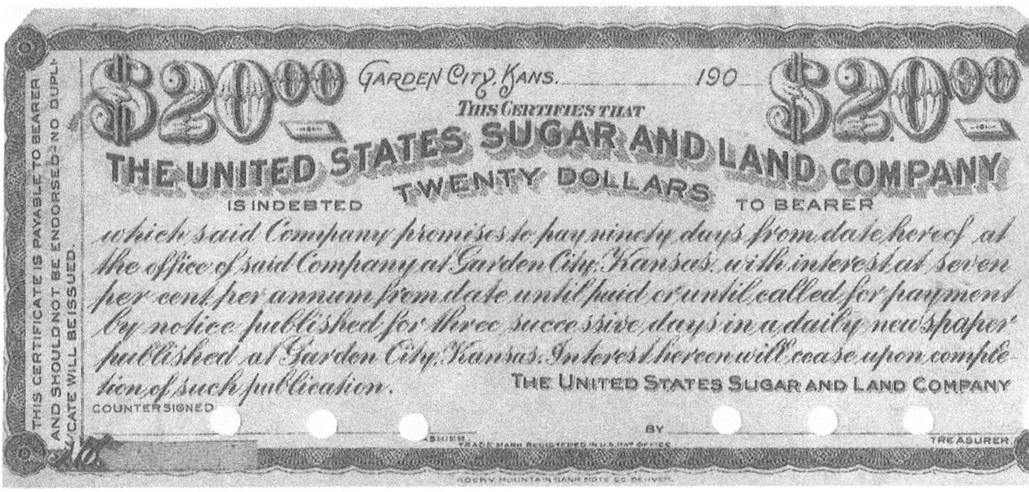

KS560-20. 20 Dollars 190__. Black on tan underprint. Uniface. Imprint: Rocky Mountain Bank Note Co. Denver. (shown at 77%)
c. Unissued, cancelled. R5

Independence

Citizens National Bank

KS580-5. 5 Dollars Cashiers Check ND (1907). Black on off-white paper. Washington at left. Uniface. Imprint: Combe Litho—St. Joseph, Mo.
c. Unissued, cancelled. R5

KS580-20. 20 Dollars ND (1907). As above.
f. Specimen. R5

The Commercial National Bank

KS600-10. 10 Dollars Cashiers Check ND (1907). Black on orange underprint. Design and imprint as KS580. Specimen marking in red.
f. Specimen. R5

KS600-20. 20 Dollars ND (1907). Black on yellow paper. As above.
f. Printer's Specimen (Combe Printing Co. St. Joseph, MO.). R5

The First National Bank

KS620-1. 1 Dollar Cashiers Check ND (1907). Design and imprint as KS580.
f. Specimen. R5

KS620-2. 2 Dollars ND (1907). Black on gray underprint. As above.
c. Unissued, cancelled. R4

KS620-5. 5 Dollars ND (1907). Black on yellow paper. As above.
f. Printer's Specimen (Combe Printing Co.). R5

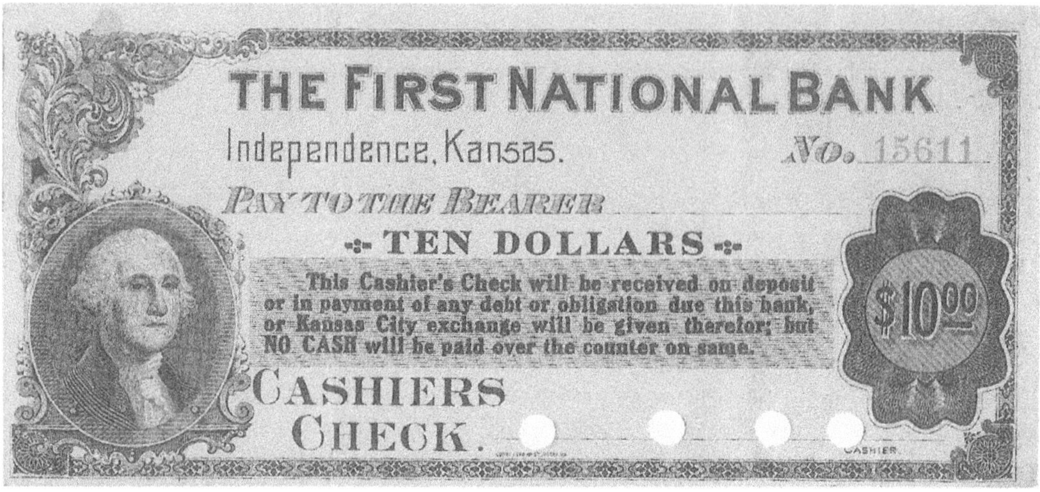

KS620-10. 10 Dollars ND (1907). Black on gold paper. As above. (shown at 77%)

- c. Unissued, cancelled. R4
- f. Specimen. R5

KS620-20. 20 Dollars ND (1907). As above.

- f. Specimen. R5

Iola

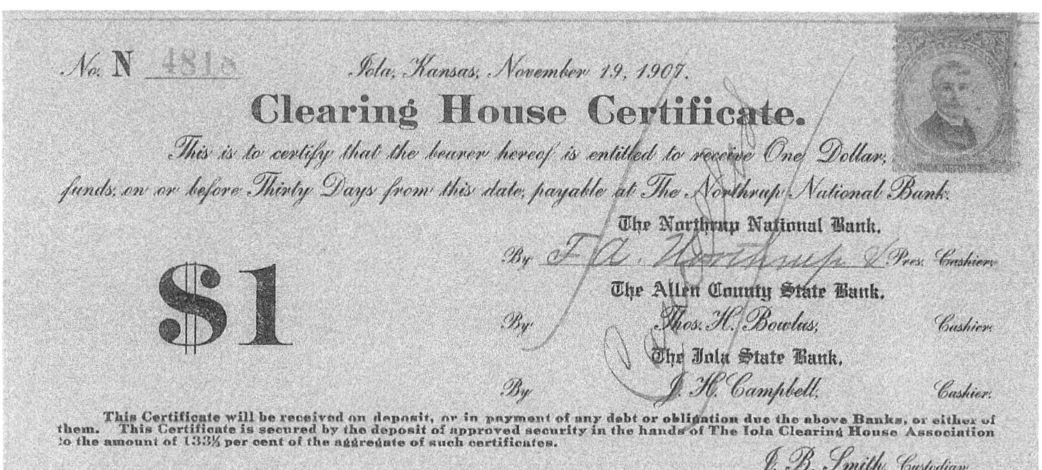

IOLA CLEARING HOUSE

KS630-1. 1 Dollar Nov. 12, 19, 1907. Black on blue-gray paper. Payable at the Northrup National Bank. Brown adhesive stamp with Northrup portrait at upper right. (shown at 77%)

- b. Issued, cancelled. R5

Parsons

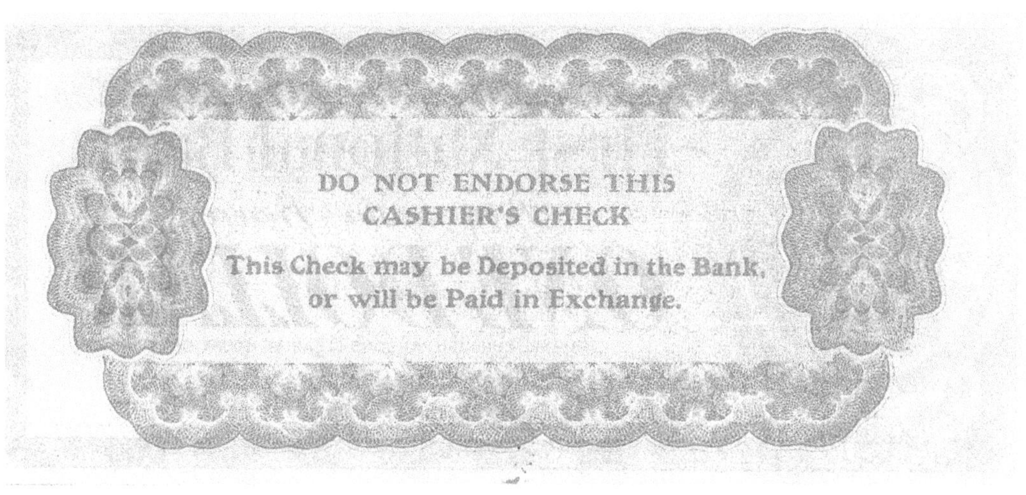

The First National Bank

KS640-1. 1 Dollar Cashier's Check Nov. 12, 1907. Black. State seal at left. Back green. Imprint: Union Bank Note Co. K.C. Mo. (shown at 76%)

a. Issued, not cancelled.	R3
b. Issued, cancelled.	**Fine, 125. EF, 250.**
d. Unissued, remainder.	R3

KS640-5. 5 Dollars Nov. 12, 1907. As above.

b. Issued, cancelled.	R3
d. Unissued, remainder.	R3

KS640-10. 10 Dollars Nov. 12, 1907. As above.

b. Issued, cancelled.	R4

Parsons Commercial Bank

KS660-5. 5 Dollars Cashier's Check Nov. 12, 1907. As KS640-5.

d. Unissued, remainder.	R3

KS660-10. 10 Dollars Nov. 12, 1907. As KS640-10.

u. Unissued?	SENC

Pittsburg

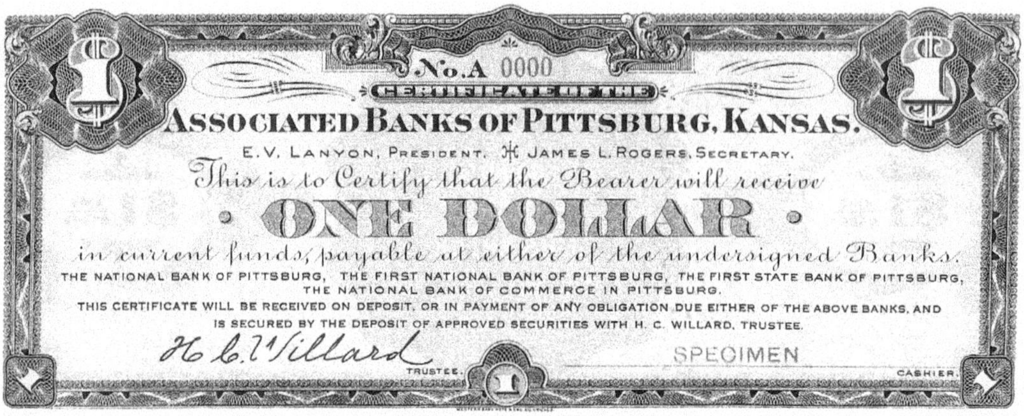

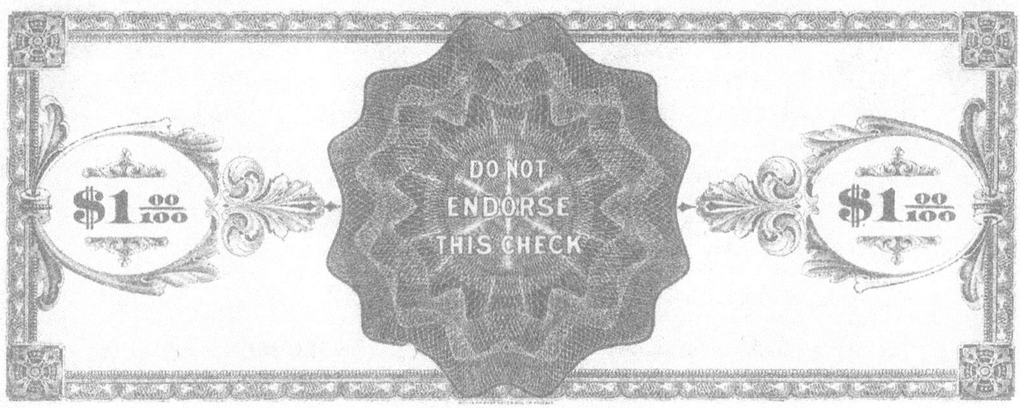

Associated Banks of Pittsburg, Kansas

KS680-1. 1 Dollar ND (1907). Black on blue underprint. Back blue. Imprint: Western Bank Note & Eng. Co. Chicago. (shown at 64%)
- d. Unissued, remainder. **R1**
- f. Specimen. **R3**

KS680-2. 2 Dollars ND (1907). Black on green underprint. Back green. Imprint as above.
- d. Unissued, remainder. **R1**
- f. Specimen. **R3**

KS680-5. 5 Dollars ND (1907). Black on brown underprint. Back brown. Imprint as above.
- f. Specimen. **R3**

KS680-10. 10 Dollars ND (1907). Black on gold underprint. Back brownish orange. Imprint as above.
- d. Unissued, remainder. **R1**
- f. Specimen. **R3**

Topeka

The Associated Banks of the City of Topeka

KS700-1. 1 Dollar (1907). Black on cream paper. Uniface. Imprint: Hall Litho. Co. Topeka 07.
- c. Unissued, cancelled. **R5**

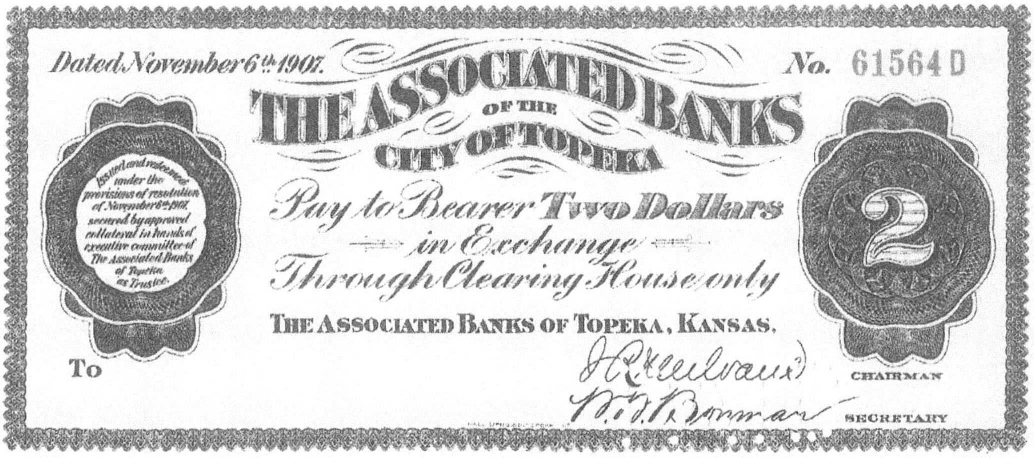

KS700-2. 2 Dollars Nov. 6, 1907. Black. As above. (shown at 75%)
c. Unissued, cancelled. R4
KS700-5. 5 Dollars Nov. 6, 1907. Black on light blue paper. As above.
c. Unissued, cancelled. R4
KS700-10. 10 Dollars Nov. 6, 1907. As above.
c. Unissued, cancelled. R4
NOTE: Banks of Topeka put up $25,000 each in commercial paper against which scrip could be issued to an amount of 75% of its value. A total of only $44,000.00 was issued, and all was retired by Jan. 1, 1908.

Wichita

CITIZENS STATE BANK

KS720-1. 1 Dollar Cashier's Check 190__ (1907). (Chase Bank Money Museum, 1941)
d. Unissued, remainder. R5

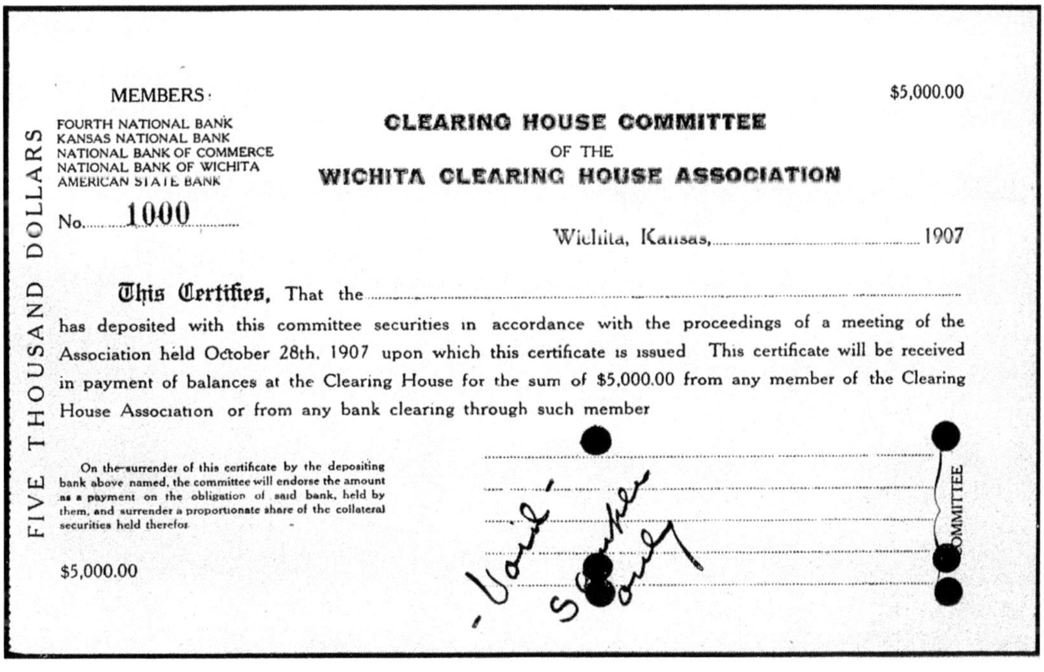

Clearing House Committee of the Wichita Clearing House Association

KS740-5000. 5000 Dollars Oct. 28, 1907. Larger size. (b/w) (shown at 75%)
e. Sample. R5

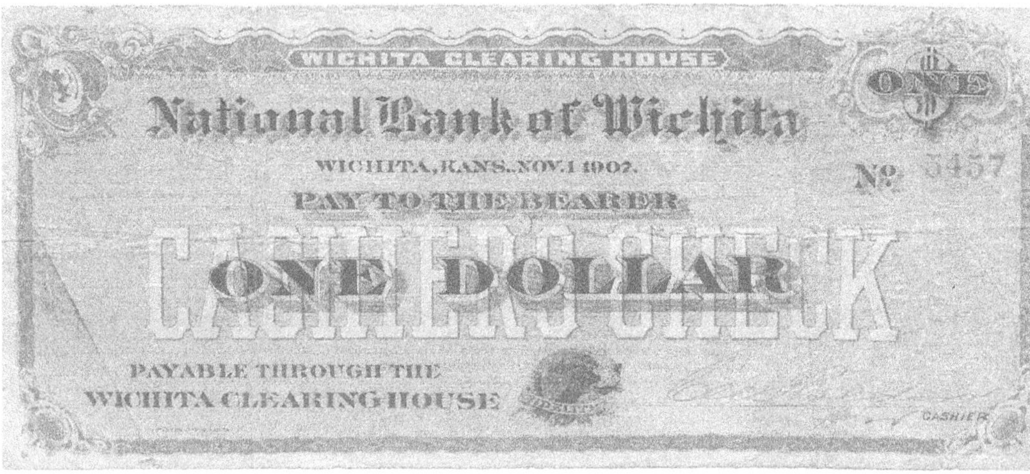

National Bank of Wichita/Wichita Clearing House

KS760-1. 1 Dollar Cashier's Check Nov. 1, 1907. Black and green. Dog's head at lower center. Uniface. Imprint: Western Litho. Co. Wichita. (shown at 76%)
a. Issued, not cancelled. R3
b. Issued, cancelled. R3
d. Unissued, remainder. R3

KS760-2. 2 Dollars Nov. 1, 1907. Black and light brown. As above.
d. Unissued, remainder. R4

KS760-5. 5 Dollars Nov. 1, 1907. Black and gold. As above.
d. Unissued, remainder. R4

KS760-10. 10 Dollars Nov. 1, 1907. Black and brown. As above.
d. Unissued, remainder. R5

KS760-25. 25 Dollars Nov. 1, 1907. Black and red on dull tan paper. No vignettes. Imprint: Claude O. Funk Printing Co., Wichita.
d. Unissued, remainder. R5

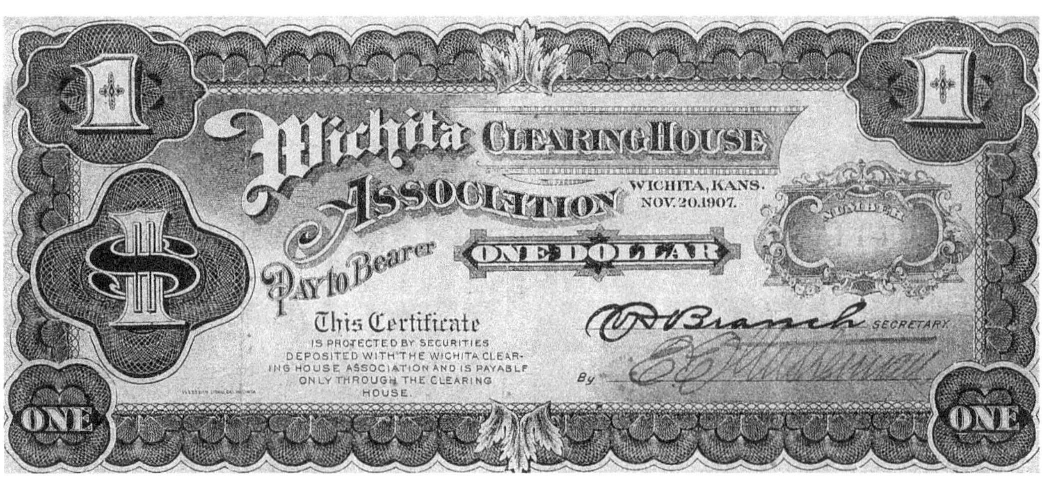

Wichita Clearing House Association

KS780-1. 1 Dollar Nov. 20, 1907. Black. Back green; eagle and shield at center, griffins below. Imprint: Western Litho. Co. Wichita. (shown at 76%)
a. Issued, not cancelled. **VG, 175. VF, 350.**

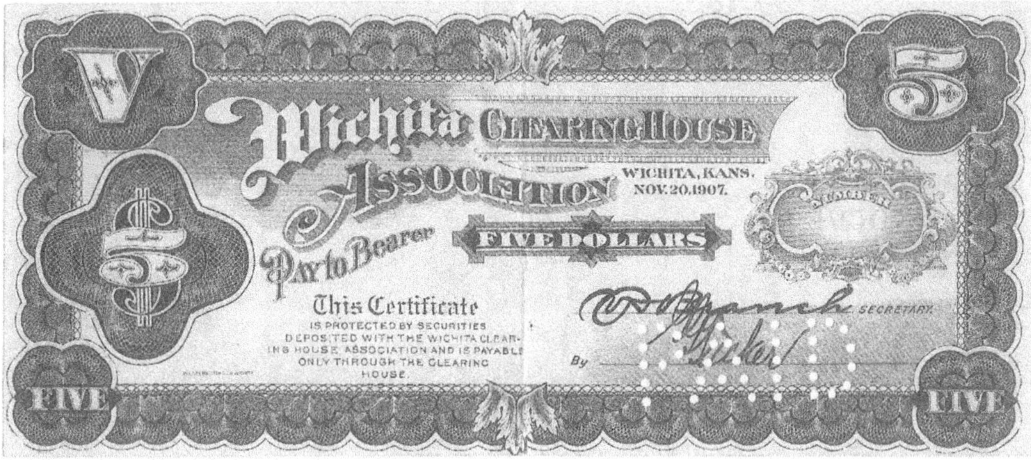

KS780-5. 5 Dollars Nov. 20, 1907. Face as above. Back gold; girl at center, griffins below. (shown at 74%)
b. Issued, cancelled. **VG, 200. VF, 425.**
KS780-10. 10 Dollars Nov. 20, 1907. As above. (list)
u. Issued? **SENC**

Kentucky

Henderson

Henderson Clearing House Association

A. Henderson National Bank

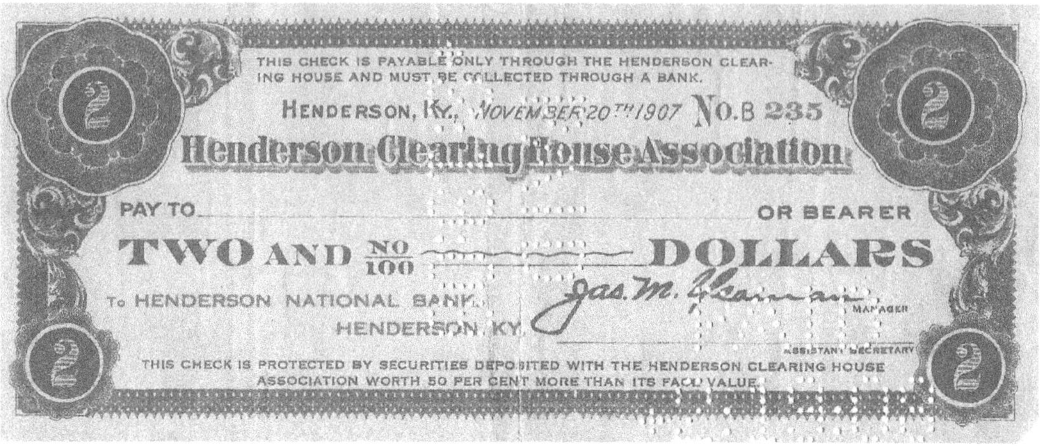

KY500-2. 2 Dollars Clearing House Check Nov. 20, 1907. Blue on gray paper. Bank name in red at lower left. List of member banks on back. Imprint: Brandon-Nashville. (shown at 73%)
c. Unissued, cancelled. **R4**
KY500-5. 5 Dollars Nov. 20, 1907. As above.
c. Unissued, cancelled. **R4**
KY500-10. 10 Dollars Nov. 20, 1907. As above.
c. Unissued, cancelled. **R4**

B. Ohio Valley Banking & Trust Co.

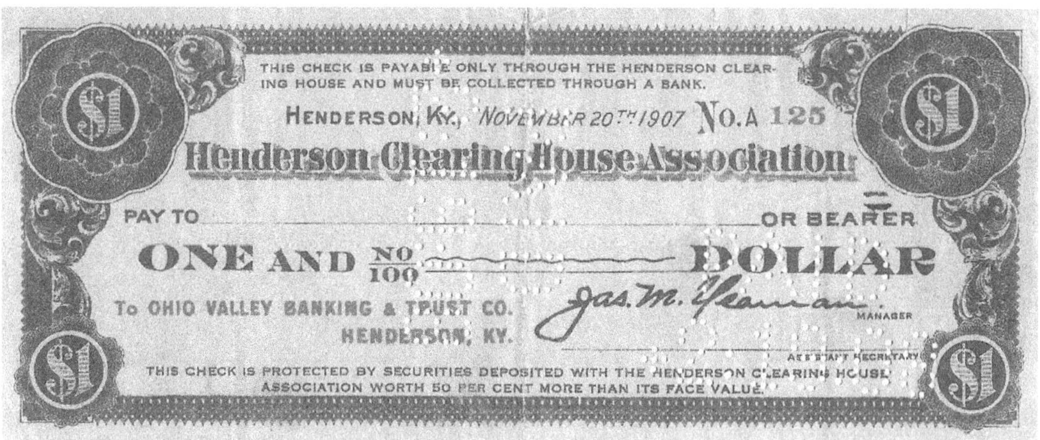

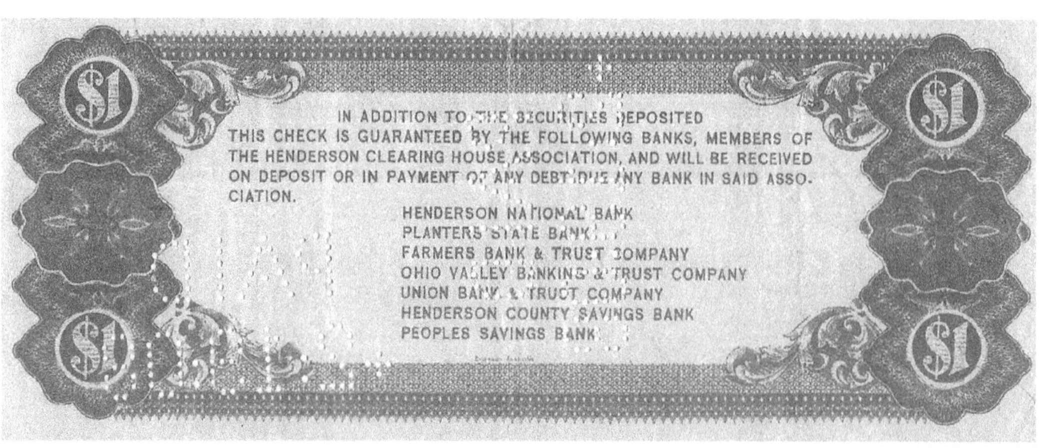

KY510-1. 1 Dollar Clearing House Check Nov. 20, 1907. As KY-500. (shown at 73%)
  a. Issued, not cancelled. **R4**
  c. Unissued, cancelled. **R4**

Lexington

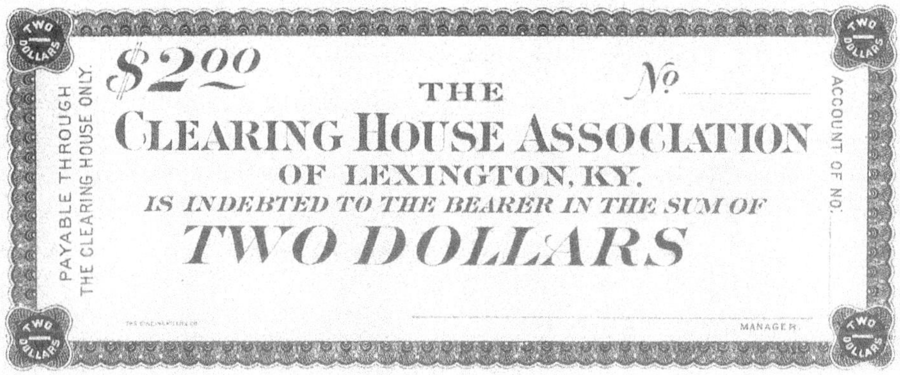

THE CLEARING HOUSE ASSOCIATION OF LEXINGTON, KY.

KY540-2. 2 Dollars ND (1907). Black on green underprint. Uniface. Imprint: The Cincinnati Lith. Co. (shown at 64%)
  d. Unissued, remainder. **VF, 45. AU, 95.**
  f. Specimen. **EF, 35. Unc., 70.**

KY540-5. 5 Dollars ND. Black on blue underprint. As above.
  c. Unissued, cancelled. **VF, 45. AU, 95.**
  d. Unissued, remainder. **VF, 45. AU, 95.**
  f. Specimen. **EF, 35. Unc., 70.**

KY540-10. 10 Dollars ND. Black on green underprint. As above.
  d. Unissued, remainder. **VF, 45. AU, 95.**
  f. Specimen. **EF, 35. Unc., 70.**

NOTE: An issue of clearing house loan certificates is reported to have been issued in Lexington. No further details are presently known.

Louisville

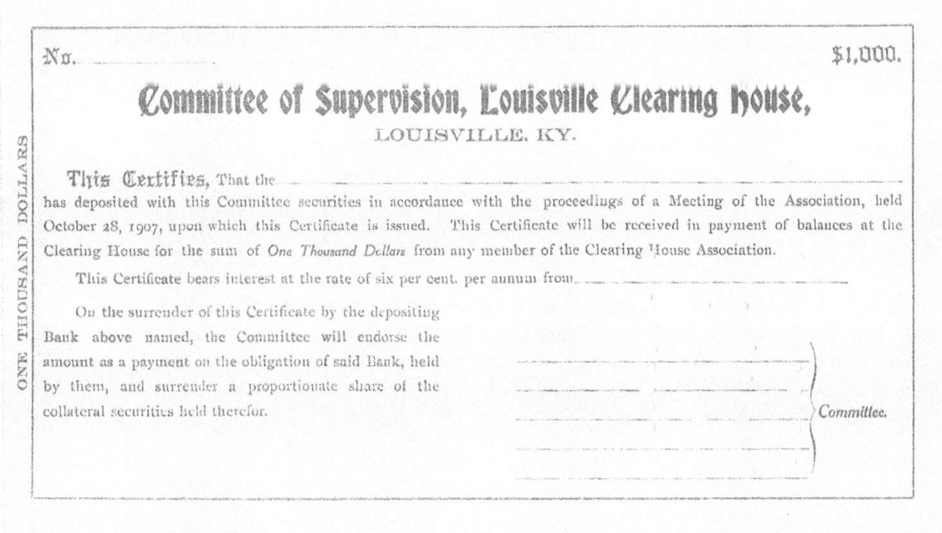

No. $1,000.

Committee of Supervision, Louisville Clearing House,

LOUISVILLE, KY.

ONE THOUSAND DOLLARS

This Certifies, That the ______ has deposited with this Committee securities in accordance with the proceedings of a Meeting of the Association, held October 28, 1907, upon which this Certificate is issued. This Certificate will be received in payment of balances at the Clearing House for the sum of *One Thousand Dollars* from any member of the Clearing House Association.

This Certificate bears interest at the rate of six per cent. per annum from ______

On the surrender of this Certificate by the depositing Bank above named, the Committee will endorse the amount as a payment on the obligation of said Bank, held by them, and surrender a proportionate share of the collateral securities held therefor.

Committee.

Committee of Supervision, Louisville Clearing House

KY570-1000. 1,000 Dollars Loan Certificate Oct. 28, 1907. Black. 6% interest-bearing certificate. Large size, with stub at left. (shown at 54%)

c. Unissued, cancelled. R5

KY570-5000. 5,000 Dollars Oct. 28, 1907. Dark blue. As above.

d. Unissued, remainder. R5

KY570-10,000. 10,000 Dollars Oct. 28, 1907. Dark brown on light beige paper. As above.

d. Unissued, remainder. R5

KY570-20,000. 20,000 Dollars Oct. 28, 1907. Red. As above.

c. Unissued, cancelled. R5

NOTE: A cashier's check backed by various banks is reported to have been issued in Louisville. No further details are presently known.

Madisonville

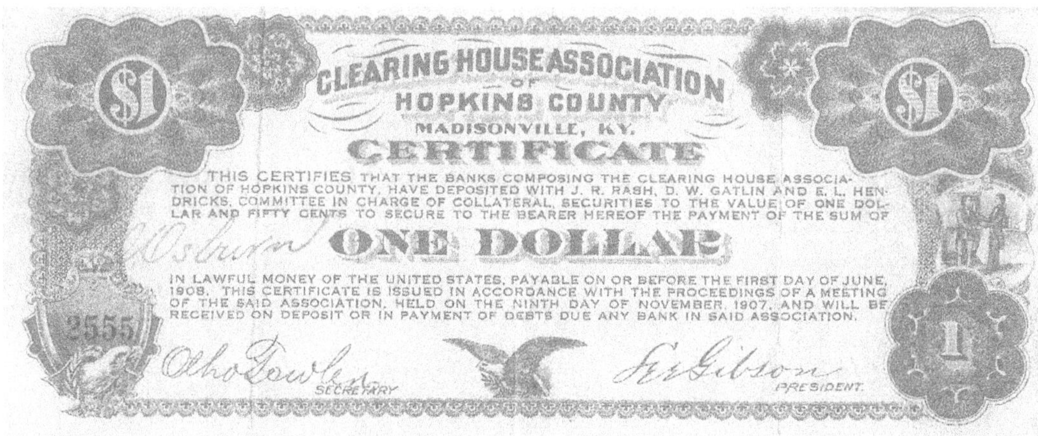

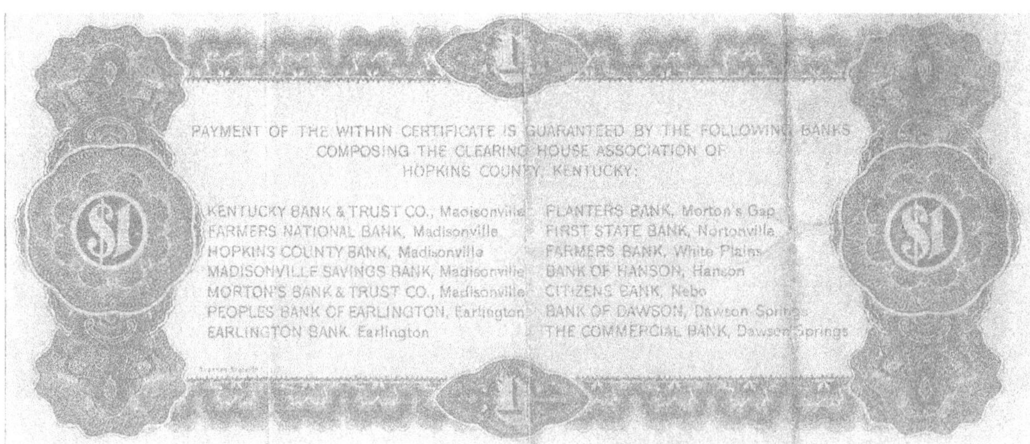

Clearing House Association of Hopkins County

KY590-1. 1 Dollar Clearing House Certificate Nov. 9, 1907. Green on beige paper. Eagle's head at lower left, eagle at lower center, state seal at right. List of member banks on back. Imprint: Brandon-Nashville. (shown at 73%)

a. Issued, not cancelled. R5

Paducah

PADUCAH CLEARING HOUSE ASSOCIATION

KY620-1. 1 Dollar Clearing House Check Dec. 2, 1907. Black and red. Indian head at lower center. List of member banks on back. Imprint: Western Bank Note & Engr. Co. Chicago.
f. Specimen. R2
KY620-2. 2 Dollars Dec. 2, 1907. Black and green. As above.
f. Specimen. R2
KY620-5. 5 Dollars Dec. 2, 1907. Black and orange.
f. Specimen. R2
KY620-10. 10 Dollars Dec. 2, 1907. Black and brown. As above.
f. Specimen. R2

LOUISIANA

New Orleans

NEW ORLEANS CLEARING HOUSE ASSOCIATION CERTIFICATE

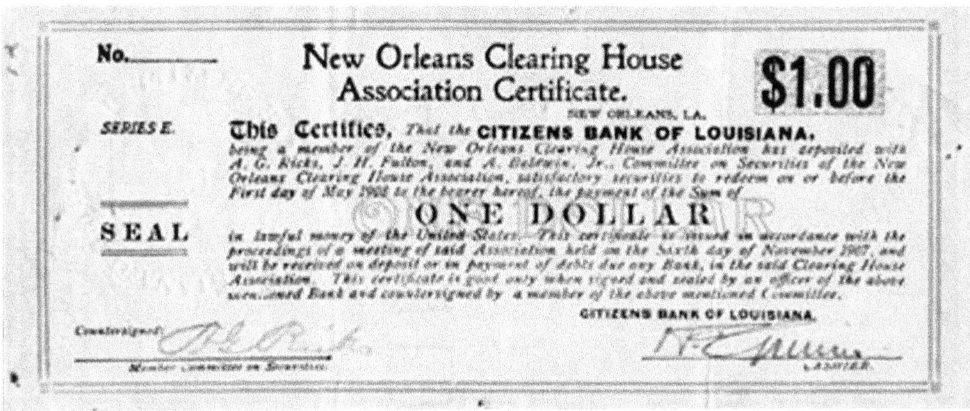

A. Citizens Bank of Louisiana
LA500-1. 1 Dollar Nov. 6, 1907. Black and brown. Embossed seal at left. Uniface. (shown at 70%)
a. Issued, not cancelled. R5

B. Commercial-Germania Trust & Savings Bank
LA525-1. 1 Dollar Nov. 6, 1907. Black and red. Generally as above.
a. Issued, not cancelled. R5

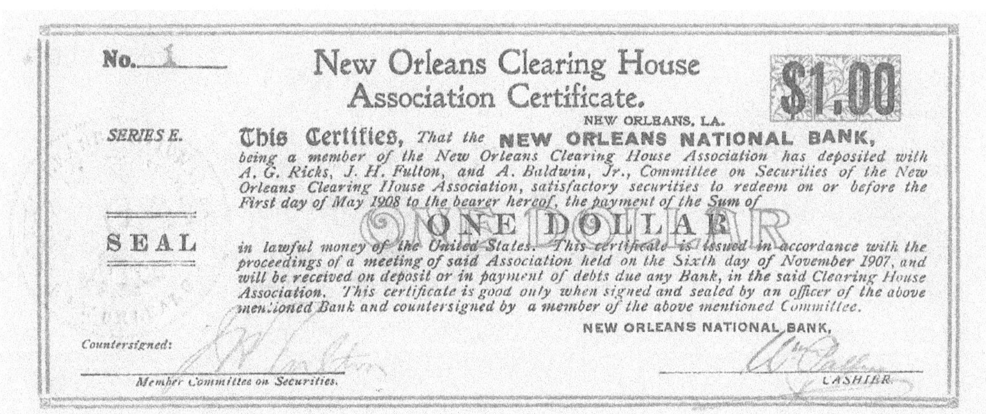

C. New Orleans National Bank
LA550-1. 1 Dollar Nov. 6, 1907. Black and red on yellow safety paper. Generally as above. (shown at 70%)
a. Issued, not cancelled. **R5**
LA550-2. 2 Dollars Nov. 6, 1907. As above.
a. Issued, not cancelled. **R5**
LA550-5. 5 Dollars Nov. 4, 1907. As above except for date.
a. Issued, not cancelled. **R5**

MARYLAND

Baltimore

BALTIMORE CLEARING HOUSE

MD500-1000. 1,000 Dollars Loan Certificate 190_ (1907). Orange. Uniface. Larger size.
c. Unissued, cancelled. **R5**

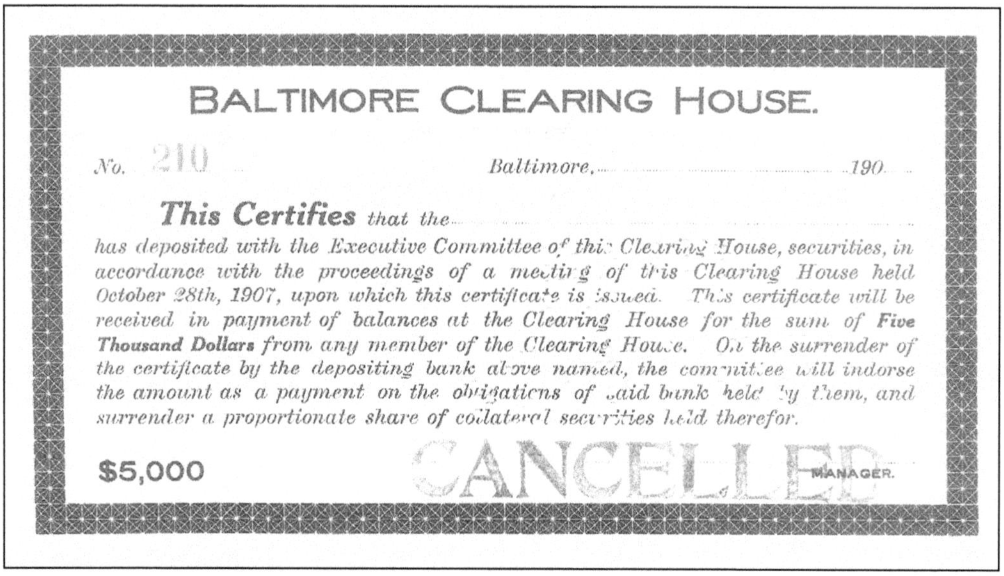

BALTIMORE CLEARING HOUSE.

No. 210 Baltimore, 190

This Certifies that the

has deposited with the Executive Committee of this Clearing House, securities, in accordance with the proceedings of a meeting of this Clearing House held October 28th, 1907, upon which this certificate is issued. This certificate will be received in payment of balances at the Clearing House for the sum of **Five Thousand Dollars** from any member of the Clearing House. On the surrender of the certificate by the depositing bank above named, the committee will indorse the amount as a payment on the obligations of said bank held by them, and surrender a proportionate share of collateral securities held therefor.

$5,000 CANCELLED MANAGER.

MD500-5000. 5,000 Dollars 190_. Black. As above. (shown at 65%)
c. Unissued, cancelled. **R5**
MD500-10,000. 10,000 Dollars 190_. Green. As above.
c. Unissued, cancelled. **R5**

Massachusetts

Boston

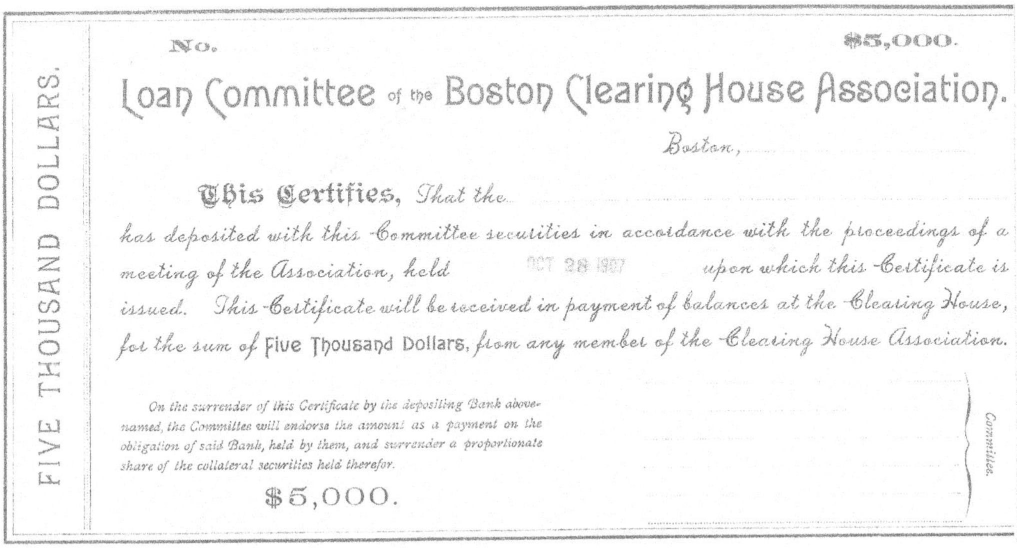

Loan Committee of the Boston Clearing House Association

MA500-5000. 5,000 Dollars Loan Certificate Oct. 28, 1907 (stamped date). Black. Uniface. Large size. (shown at 52%)

e. Sample. R5

MA500-10,000. 10,000 Dollars Oct. 28, 1907. As above.

e. Sample. R5

MA500-20,000. 20,000 Dollars Oct. 28, 1907. As above.

e. Sample. R5

MA500-25,000. 25,000 Dollars Oct. 28, 1907. As above.

e. Sample. R5

The Boston Clearing House Association

MA525-2000. 2,000 Dollars 1907. (list)

f. Specimen. R5

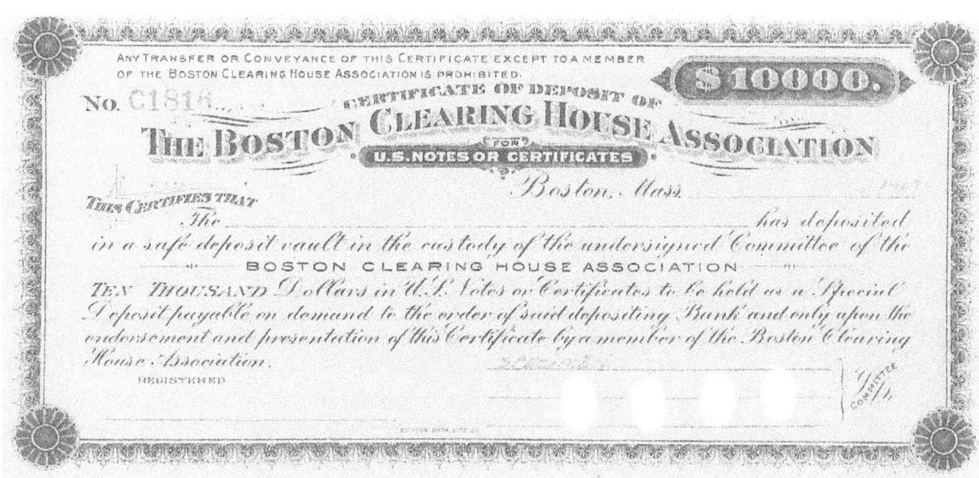

MA525-10,000. 10,000 Dollars Certificate of Deposit ND (1907). Black on blue paper. Imprint: Boston Bank Note Co.
c. Unissued, cancelled. **R5**

C. F. King/Atlantic National Bank

MA575-5. 5 Dollars Personal Check ND (1907). Blue. Portrait of C.F. King at center, small portraits of family members in all four corners. Uniface. Imprint: Boston Bank Note Co. (shown at 72%)
d. Unissued, remainder. **R5**
f. Specimen. **R5**

MA575-10. 10 Dollars ND. Brown. As above.
f. Specimen. **R5**

Lynn

Various Banks

A cashier's check is reported to have been issued in Lynn. No details are known at present.

Taunton

Various Banks

A cashier's check is reported to have been issued in Taunton. No details are known at present.

Michigan

Detroit

American Car and Foundry Co./ The People's State Bank

MI500-10. 10 Dollars Pay Check Nov. 23, 1907. Black on blue paper. Bank building at upper left. Uniface. Imprint: Artcraft Litho. Co. Detroit. (shown at 53%)

c. Unissued, cancelled. R5

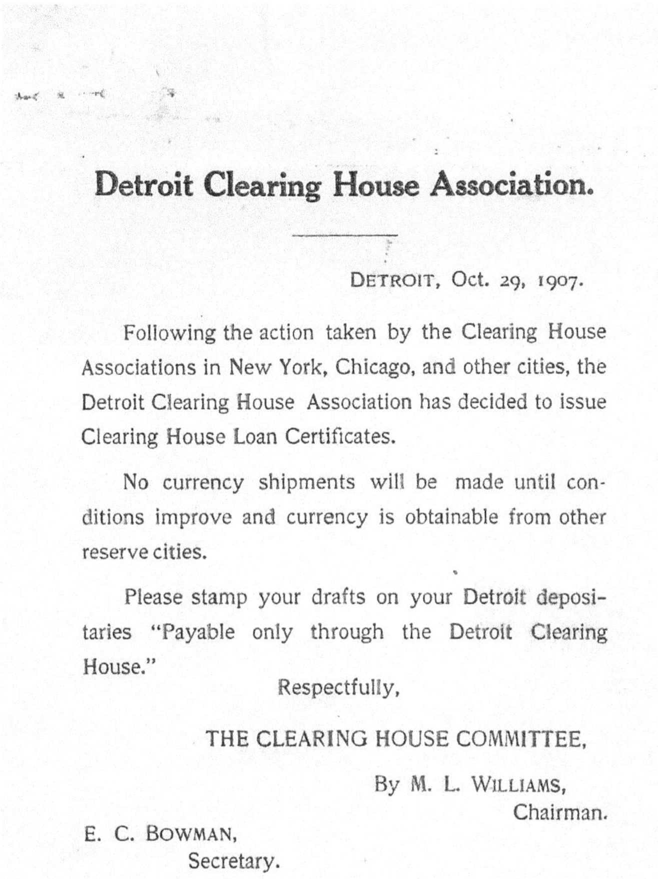

Detroit Clearing House Association.

DETROIT, Oct. 29, 1907.

Following the action taken by the Clearing House Associations in New York, Chicago, and other cities, the Detroit Clearing House Association has decided to issue Clearing House Loan Certificates.

No currency shipments will be made until conditions improve and currency is obtainable from other reserve cities.

Please stamp your drafts on your Detroit depositaries "Payable only through the Detroit Clearing House."

Respectfully,

THE CLEARING HOUSE COMMITTEE,

By M. L. WILLIAMS,
Chairman.

E. C. BOWMAN,
Secretary.

Detroit Clearing House Association

According to the illustrated flyer, the Detroit Clearing House Association issued Clearing House Loan Certificates. As of the publication of this catalog, no example has been verified. (shown at 65%)

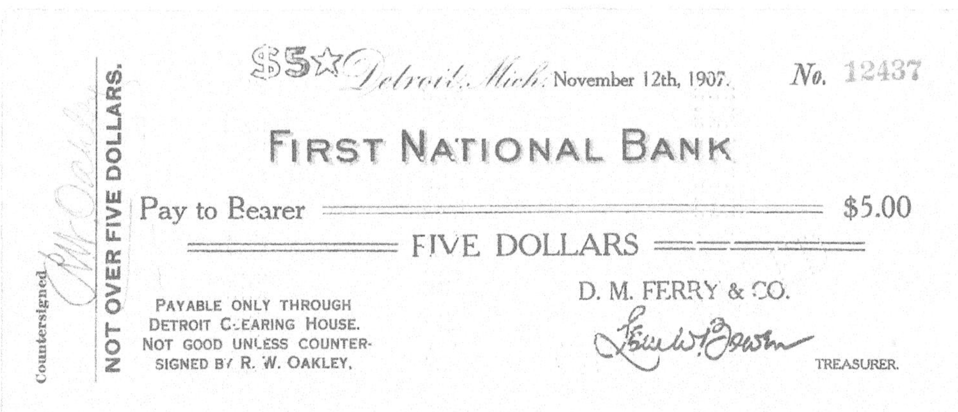

$5☆ Detroit, Mich. November 12th, 1907. No. 12437

FIRST NATIONAL BANK

Pay to Bearer $5.00

FIVE DOLLARS

D. M. FERRY & CO.

TREASURER.

PAYABLE ONLY THROUGH DETROIT CLEARING HOUSE. NOT GOOD UNLESS COUNTERSIGNED BY R. W. OAKLEY.

Countersigned

NOT OVER FIVE DOLLARS.

D. M. Ferry & Co./First National Bank

MI550-5. 5 Dollars (payroll check) Nov. 12, 1907. Black. Uniface. (shown at 60%)
b. Issued, cancelled. **R5**

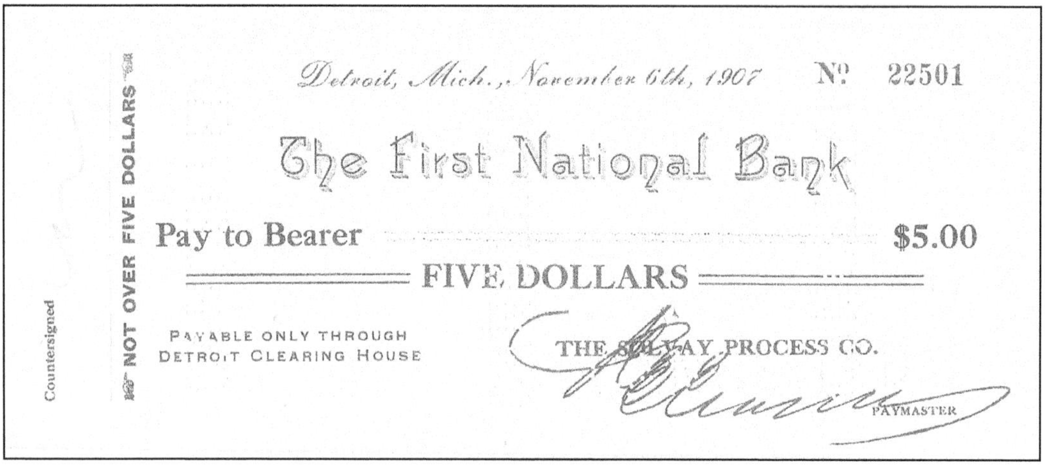

The Solvay Process Co./The First National Bank

MI600-5. 5 Dollars (payroll check) Nov. 6, 1907. Black on light pink paper. Uniface. (shown at 64%)
b. Issued, cancelled. **R5**

Grand Rapids

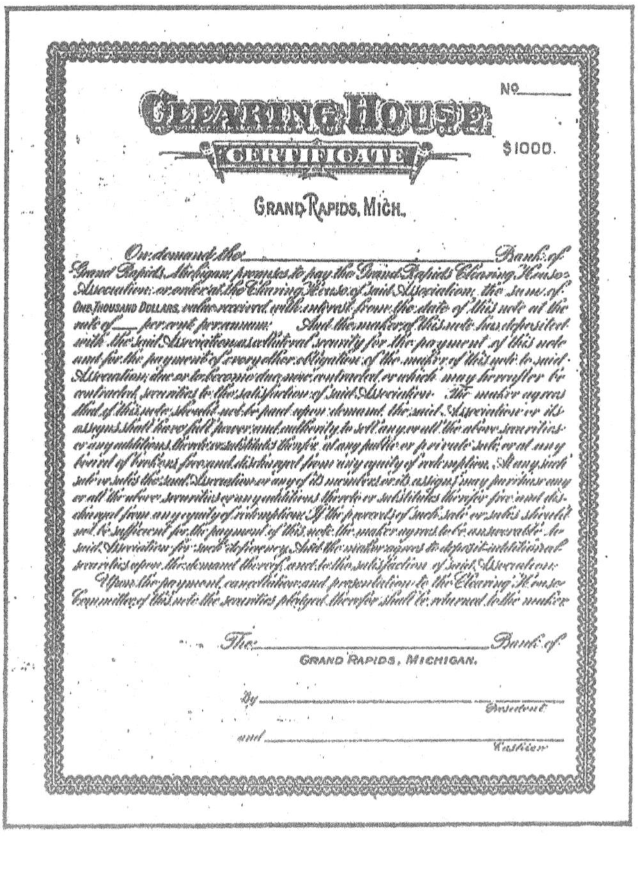

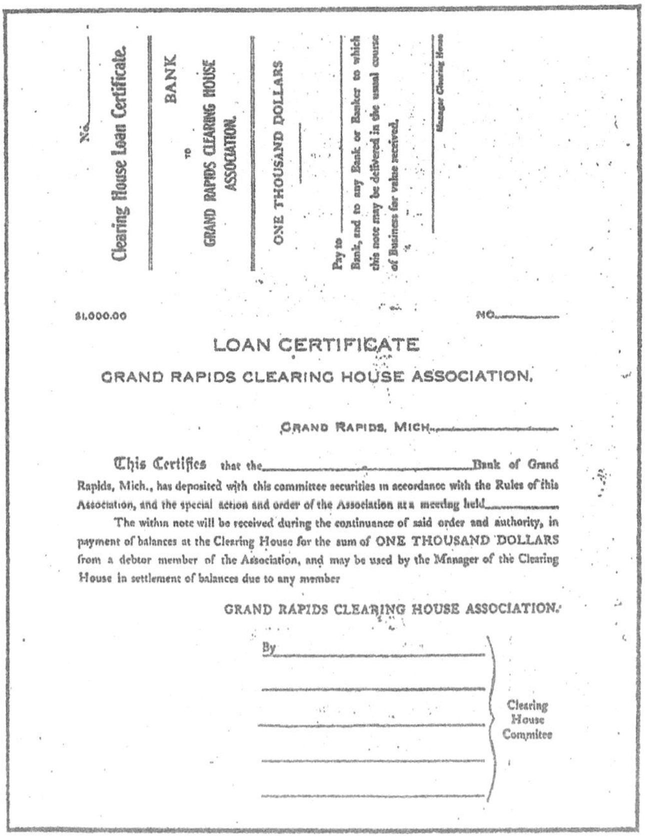
No.____
Clearing House Loan Certificate.
____ BANK
to
GRAND RAPIDS CLEARING HOUSE ASSOCIATION.
ONE THOUSAND DOLLARS
Pay to ____
Bank, and to any Bank or Banker to which this note may be delivered in the usual course of Business for value received.
Manager Clearing House

$1,000.00 NO.____

LOAN CERTIFICATE

GRAND RAPIDS CLEARING HOUSE ASSOCIATION.

GRAND RAPIDS, MICH.____

This Certifies that the____Bank of Grand Rapids, Mich., has deposited with this committee securities in accordance with the Rules of this Association, and the special action and order of the Association at a meeting held____

The within note will be received during the continuance of said order and authority, in payment of balances at the Clearing House for the sum of ONE THOUSAND DOLLARS from a debtor member of the Association, and may be used by the Manager of the Clearing House in settlement of balances due to any member

GRAND RAPIDS CLEARING HOUSE ASSOCIATION.

By____

Clearing House Committee

CLEARING HOUSE CERTIFICATE

MI620-1000. 1,000 Dollars Loan Certificate ND (1907). (b/w) (shown at 71%)
d. Unissued, remainder. **R5**

GRAND RAPIDS CLEARING HOUSE ASSOCIATION

Three of the clearing house member banks are known to have issued panic scrip in 1907: Nos. 1, 3 and 4. All colors and designs were the same for each denomination.

A. No. 1: The Old National Bank

MI630-1. 1 Dollar Nov. 25, 1907. Black and blue. Bank name at lower left. One line of text on back. Imprint: Western Bank Note and Engraving Company Chicago.
f. Specimen. **R5**

MI630-2. 2 Dollars Nov. 25, 1907. Black and brown. As above.
f. Specimen. **R5**

B. No. 3: The Grand Rapids National Bank

MI645-1. 1 Dollar Nov. 25, 1907. Black and blue. As MI630-1.
f. Specimen. **R5**

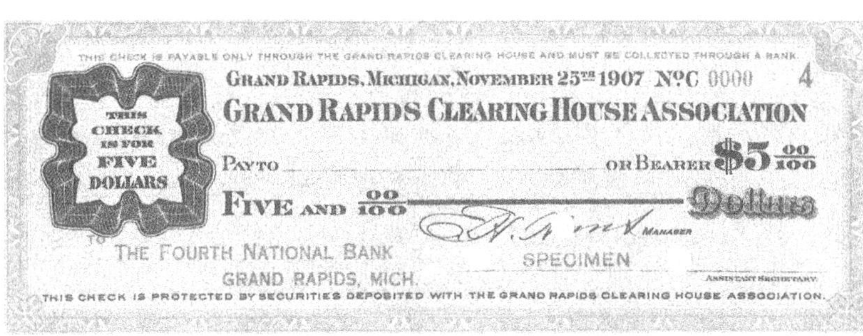

C. No. 4: The Fourth National Bank
MI660-2. 2 Dollars Nov. 25, 1907. Black and brown. As above.
f. Specimen. R5
MI660-5. 5 Dollars Nov. 25, 1907. Black and green. As above. (shown at 50%)
f. Specimen. R5
MI660-10. 10 Dollars Nov. 25, 1907. Black and blue. As above.
f. Specimen. R5

Iron Mountain

Pewabic Company

MI675-20.A 20 Dollars Pay Roll Check Dec. 14, 1907. Black on green safety paper. "Payable only through Milwaukee Clearing House." Uniface.
c. Unissued, cancelled. R5

PAY ROLL CHECK.
PAYABLE ONLY THROUGH MILWAUKEE CLEARING HOUSE.
No.
No.
PEWABIC COMPANY
$20
IRON MOUNTAIN, MICH. DECEMBER 14, 1907.
PAY TO BEARER
TWENTY DOLLARS
PEWABIC COMPANY
by
CASHIER

MI675-20.B 20 Dollars Dec. 14, 1907. Black on yellow paper, otherwise as above. (shown at 80%)
d. Unissued, remainder. R5

Iron River

Various Banks

A cashier's check is reported to have been issued. No specifics are known at present.

Ironwood

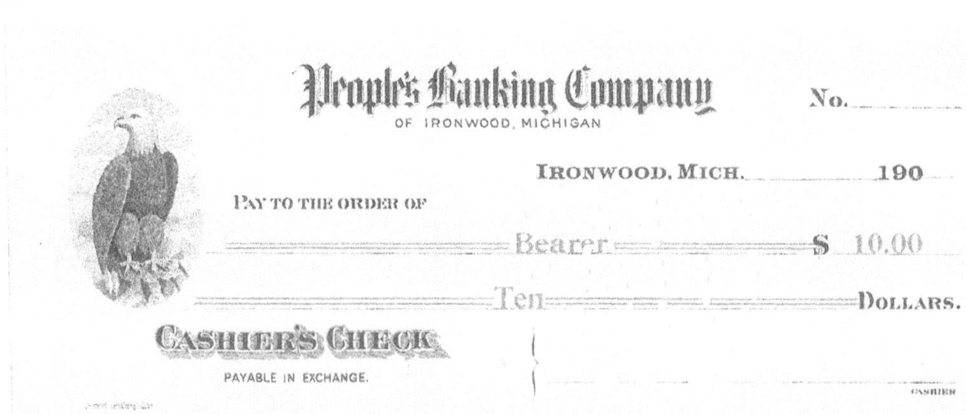
People's Banking Company
OF IRONWOOD, MICHIGAN
No.
IRONWOOD, MICH. 190
PAY TO THE ORDER OF
Bearer $ 10.00
Ten DOLLARS.
CASHIER'S CHECK
PAYABLE IN EXCHANGE.
CASHIER

People's Banking Company

MI700-10. 10 Dollars Cashier's Check 190_ (1907). Black and red on light green safety paper. Eagle on mountaintop at left. Uniface. Imprint: Christie Lithograph & Printing Co. Duluth. (shown at 60%)
c. Unissued, cancelled. **R5**

Kalamazoo

A cashier's check is reported to have been issued in Kalamazoo. No details are known at present.

Lansing

Olds Motor Works/Manufacturers' Pay Check

MI725-1. 1 Dollar Nov. 20, 26, 1907 (stamped date). Black on light green paper. Embossed seal at upper left. Uniface. (shown at 65%)
a. Issued, not cancelled. **R5**
b. Issued, cancelled. **R5**

Manufacturers' Pay Check

MI735-1. 1 Dollar ND (1907). Black on blue paper. Uniface.
d. Unissued, remainder. **EF, 30. Unc., 50.**
MI735-2. 2 Dollars ND (1907). Black on pink paper. As above.
d. Unissued, remainder. **EF, 30., Unc., 50.**
MI735-5. 5 Dollars ND (1907). Black on yellow paper. As above.
d. Unissued, remainder. **EF, 30. Unc., 50.**

MI735-10. 10 Dollars ND (1907). Black on pink paper. As above. (shown at 65%)
d. Unissued, remainder. **EF, 30. Unc., 50.**

MINNESOTA

Austin

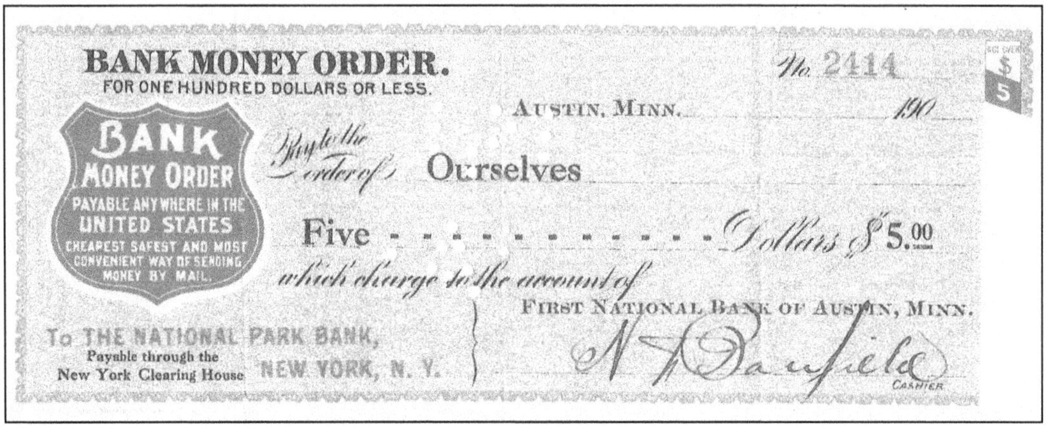

FIRST NATIONAL BANK OF AUSTIN, MINN.

MN500-5. 5 Dollars Bank Money Order 190_ (1907). Black and red with green border on green underprint. Shield with white lettering on red background at left. Value indicated with tab at upper right. Black text lines vertically on back. Imprint: McGill-Warner Co., St. Paul, Minn. (shown at 68%)
b. Issued, cancelled. **R4**
d. Unissued, remainder. **R4**
MN500-10. 10 Dollars Nov. 27, 1907. As above.
b. Issued, cancelled. **R4**
MN500-20. 20 Dollars Nov. 14, 1907 (stamped date). As above.
b. Issued, cancelled. **R4**
NOTE: Total issue is reported to have been $100,000; all was redeemed in two years except a single $5 not turned in until 1927.

MERCHANTS BANK

MN525-1. 1 Dollar Cashier's Check Oct. 31, 1907. (list)
b. Issued, cancelled. **R5**
MN525-2. 2 Dollars Oct. 31, 1907. (list)
b. Issued, cancelled. **R5**
MN525-5. 5 Dollars Nov. 20, 1907. (list)
b. Issued, cancelled. **R5**
MN525-10. 10 Dollars Nov. 20, 1907. (list)
b. Issued, cancelled. **R5**

Duluth

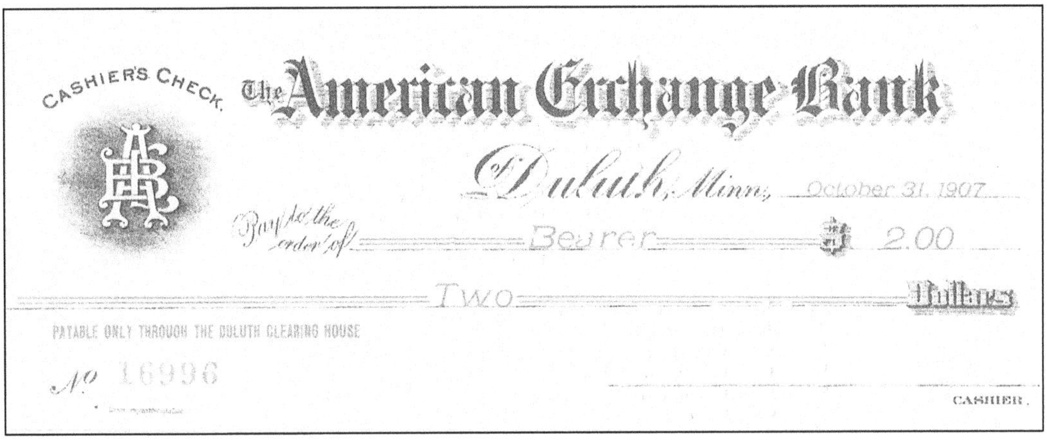

THE AMERICAN EXCHANGE BANK

MN550-2. 2 Dollars Cashier's Check Oct. 31, 1907. Black and red. Bank monogram at upper left. Uniface. Imprint: Christie Lithograph & Printing Co. Duluth. (shown at 64%)
c. Unissued, cancelled. R4

THE CITY NATIONAL BANK

MN575-1. 1 Dollar Cashier's Check Oct. 31, 1907. Uniface. Imprint: Duluth Lithograph & Printing Co. (b/w)
b. Issued, cancelled. R5
MN575-2. 2 Dollars Oct. 31, 1907. As above.
b. Issued, cancelled. R5

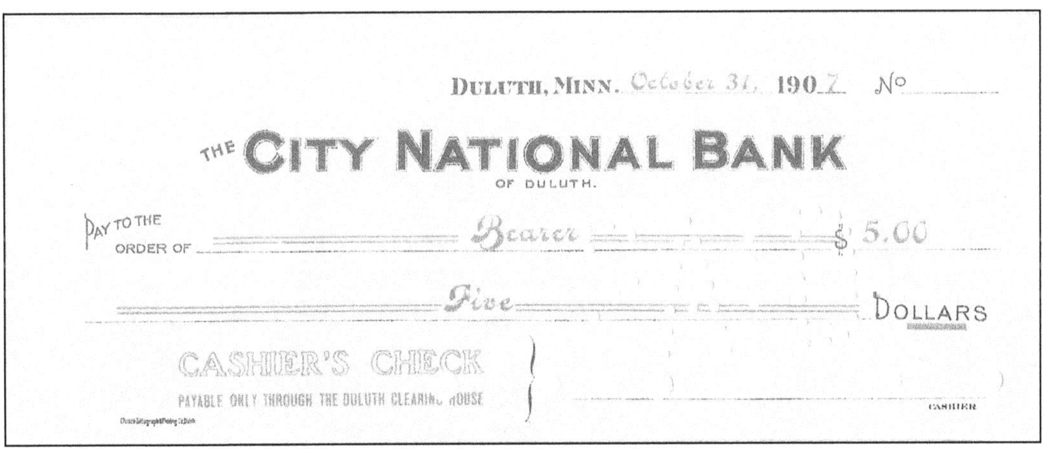

MN575-5. 5 Dollars Oct. 31, 1907. Black and red on light pink paper. Uniface. Imprint as MN550-2. (shown at 64%)
c. Unissued, cancelled. R5
MN575-10. 10 Dollars Oct. 31, 1907. As MN575-2.
b. Issued, cancelled. R5

DULUTH & IRON RANGE RAILROAD COMPANY

MN600-1. 1 Dollar Pay Roll Check Dec. 1, 1907. Black on blue paper. Initials of company vertically at center in monogram. Two lines of text on back. Imprint as MN550-2.
b. Issued, cancelled. R3
c. Unissued, cancelled. R3

MN600-2. 2 Dollars Nov. 1, 1907. Black on white paper. As above.
c. Unissued, cancelled. R3
MN600-5. 5 Dollars Nov. 1, 1907. As above.
c. Unissued, cancelled. R3
MN600-10. 10 Dollars Nov. 1, 1907. As above.
c. Unissued, cancelled. R3

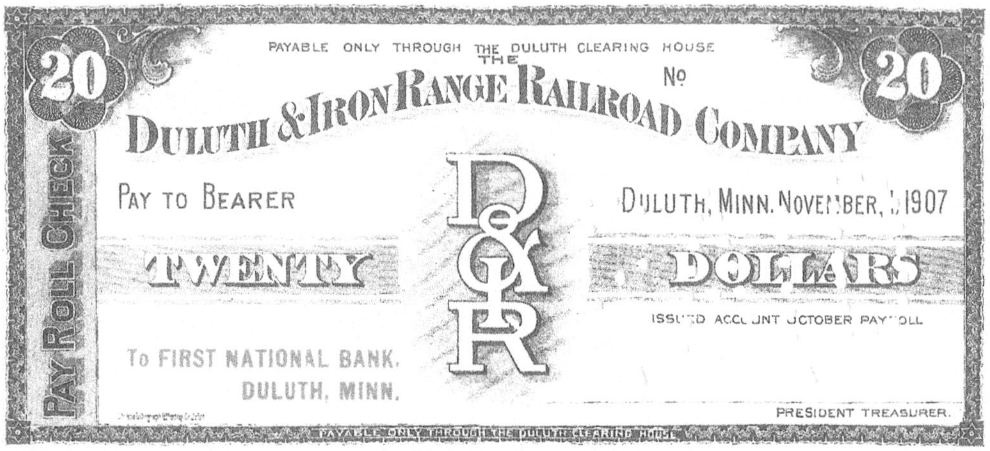

MN600-20. 20 Dollars Nov. 1, 1907. As above. (shown at 75%)
c. Unissued, cancelled. R4
MN600-50. 50 Dollars Nov. 1, 1907. As above. (list)
u. Unissued? SENC

Duluth, Missabe & Northern Railway Company

MN625-2. 2 Dollars Pay Roll Check Dec. 1, 1907. Black on cream paper. Imprint as MN550-2.
c. Unissued, cancelled. R4
MN625-5. 5 Dollars Dec. 1, 1907. As above.
c. Unissued, cancelled. R4

MN625-10. 10 Dollars Nov. 1, Dec. 1, 1907. As above. (shown at 76%)
b. Nov. 1. Issued, cancelled. R2
c. Dec. 1. Unissued, cancelled. R3

MN625-20. 20 Dollars Nov. 1, 1907. As above.
b. Issued, cancelled. R5
MN625-50. 50 Dollars Dec. 1, 1907. As above.
c. Unissued, cancelled. R5

First National Bank of Duluth

A. First Issue

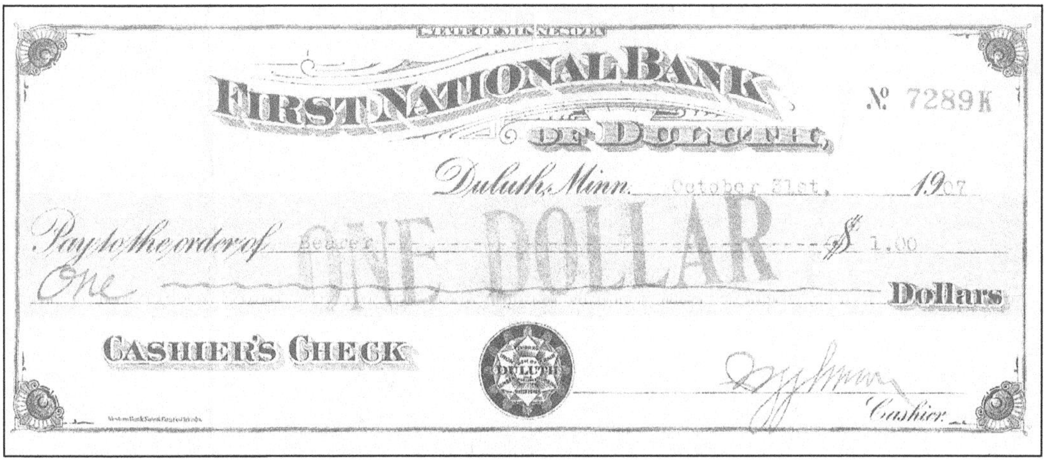

MN650-1. 1 Dollar Cashier's Check Oct. 31, 1907 (typed date). Black on light red underprint strip across center. Red value in large letters stamped at center. Duluth emblem at lower center. Uniface. Imprint: Western Bank Note & Eng. Co. Chicago. (shown at 64%)
a. Issued, not cancelled. R5
c. Unissued, cancelled. R5

B. Second Issue

MN675-1. 1 Dollar Cashier's Check Nov. 1, 1907. Similar to MN650 but with significant differences including printed denomination. Imprint as MN550-2. (shown at 64%)
a. Issued, not cancelled. R5
c. Unissued, cancelled. R5
MN675-2. 2 Dollars Nov. 1, 1907. As above.
a. Issued, not cancelled. R5
MN675-10. 10 Dollars Nov. 1, 1907. As above.
c. Unissued, cancelled. R5

Oliver Iron Mining Company

A. Nov. 1 issue with vignette

MN700-1. 1 Dollar (payroll check) Nov. 1, 1907. Black. Two miners working at center. Known District: Menominee. Imprint as MN550-2.

a. Issued, not cancelled. **R5**

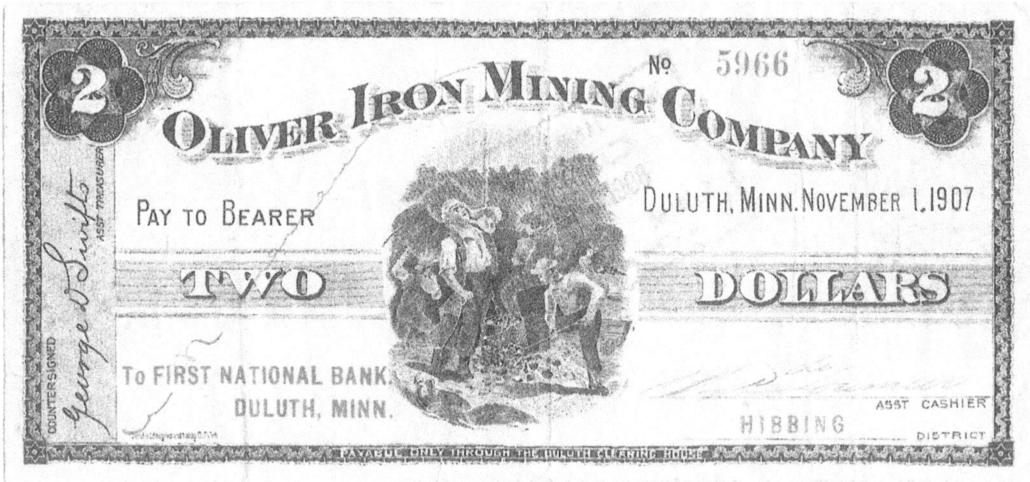

MN700-2. 2 Dollars Nov. 1, 1907. Black. Known Districts: Fayai and Hibbing. Design and imprint as above. (shown at 76%)

a. Issued, not cancelled. **R4**

b. Issued, cancelled. **R4**

B. Dec. 1 issue without vignette

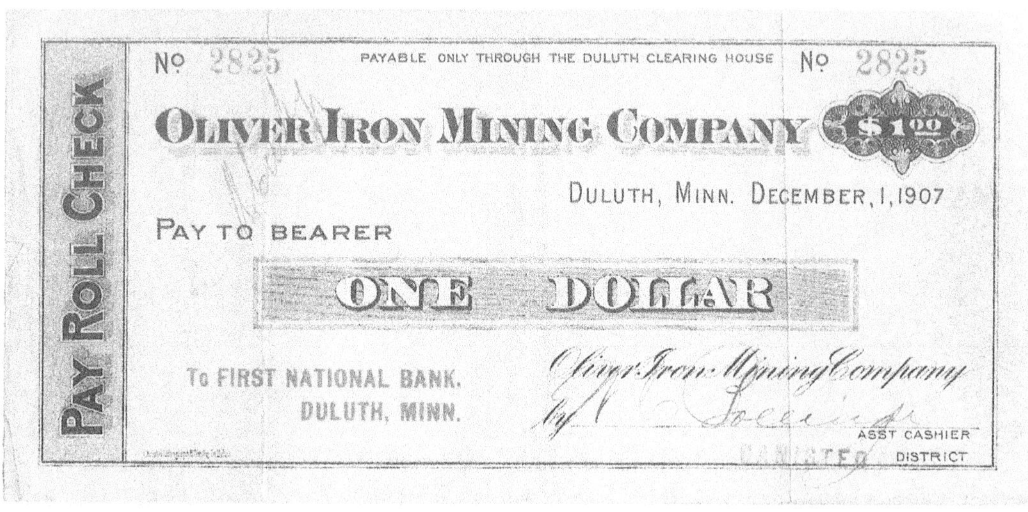

MN705-1. 1 Dollar Pay Roll Check Dec. 1, 1907. Black on light tan paper. Uniface. Known Districts: Menominee and Canisteo. Imprint as MN550-2. (shown at 76%)

a. Issued, not cancelled. **R4**

Pickands, Mather & Co.

A. Nov. 1 issue, green safety paper with vignette

MN725-1. 1 Dollar (payroll check) Nov. 1, 1907. Black on green underprint. Several miners working at center (vignette different from MN700-1). Imprint as MN550-2.

c. Unissued, cancelled. **R4**

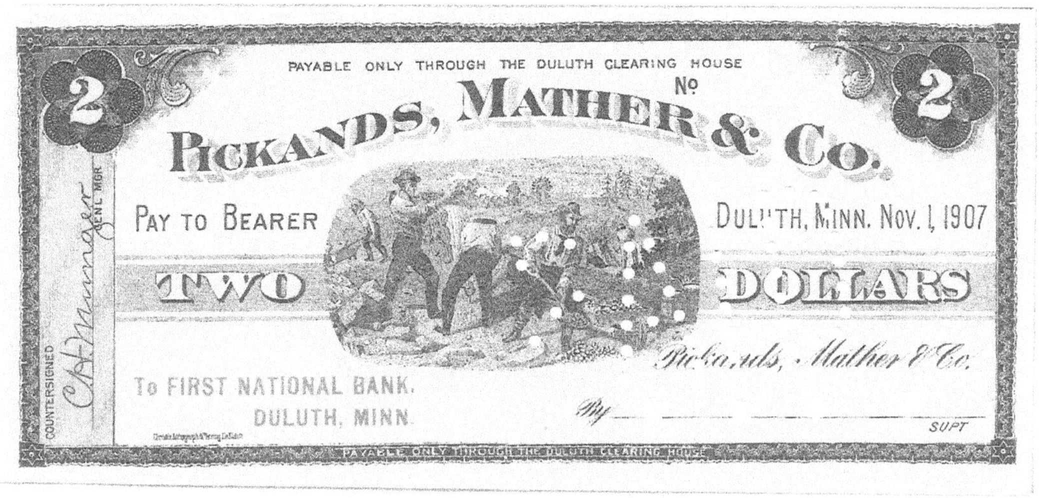

MN725-2. 2 Dollars Nov. 1, 1907. As above. (shown at 76%)
c. Unissued, cancelled. **R4**
MN725-5. 5 Dollars Nov. 1, 1907. As above.
c. Unissued, cancelled. **R4**
MN725-10. 10 Dollars Nov. 1, 1907. As above.
c. Unissued, cancelled. **R4**
MN725-20. 20 Dollars Nov. 1, 1907. As above.
c. Unissued, cancelled. **R4**

B. Dec. 1 issue, plain blue paper without vignette.

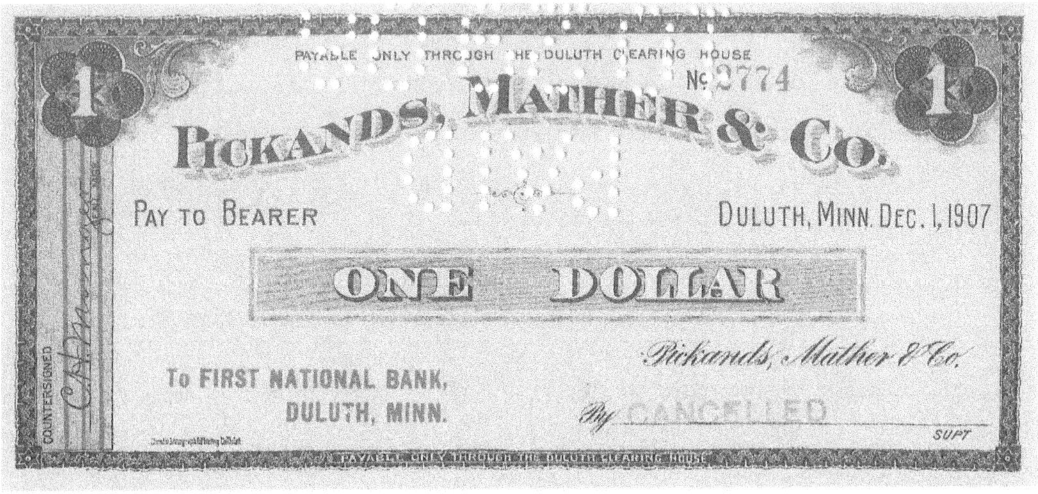

MN750-1. 1 Dollar Dec. 1, 1907. Black. Imprint as MN550-2. (shown at 77%)
c. Unissued, cancelled. **R4**
MN750-2. 2 Dollars Dec. 1, 1907. As above.
c. Unissued, cancelled. **R4**
MN750-5. 5 Dollars Dec. 1, 1907. As above.
c. Unissued, cancelled. **R4**
MN750-10. 10 Dollars Dec. 1, 1907. As above.
c. Unissued, cancelled. **R4**
MN750-20. 20 Dollars Dec. 1, 1907. As above.
c. Unissued, cancelled. **R4**

Republic Iron & Steel Company

MN775-1. 1 Dollar Pay Roll Check Nov. 1, 1907. Black on light gray underprint, light pink paper. Miners working at center in same vignette as MN725. Imprint as MN550-2.
- a. Issued, not cancelled. R5
- c. Unissued, cancelled. R5

MN775-2. 2 Dollars Nov. 1, 1907. Cream paper. As above.
- c. Unissued, cancelled. R5

MN775-5. 5 Dollars Nov. 1, 1907. As above. (b/w)
- c. Unissued, cancelled. R5

MN775-10. 10 Dollars Nov. 1, 1907. As above. (shown at 77%)
- c. Unissued, cancelled. R5

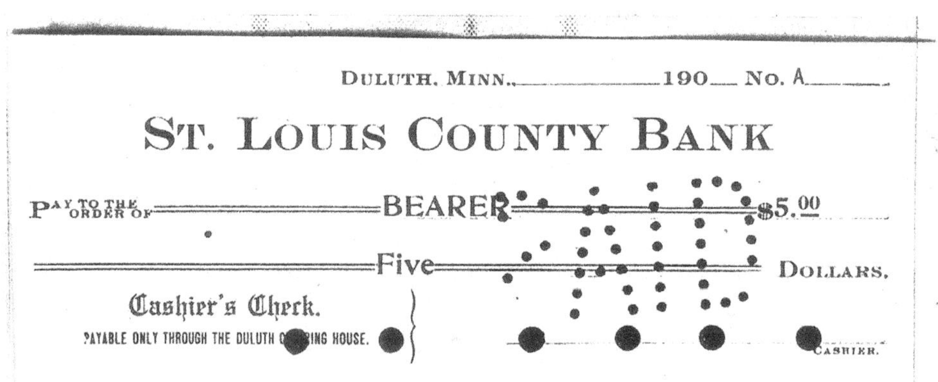

St. Louis County Bank

MN800-1. 1 Dollar Cashier's Check 190_ (1907). Black on off-white paper. Uniface.
- c. Unissued, cancelled. R5

MN800-5. 5 Dollars 190_ (1907). As above. (shown at 60%)
- c. Unissued, cancelled. R5

Hibbing

Croxton Mining Company

MN825-1. 1 Dollar Pay Roll Check Nov. 1, 1907. Miners working in same vignette as MN725. Imprint as MN550-2.
- c. Unissued, cancelled. R5

MN825-2. 2 Dollars Nov. 1, 1907. As above. (list)
c. Unissued, cancelled. R5

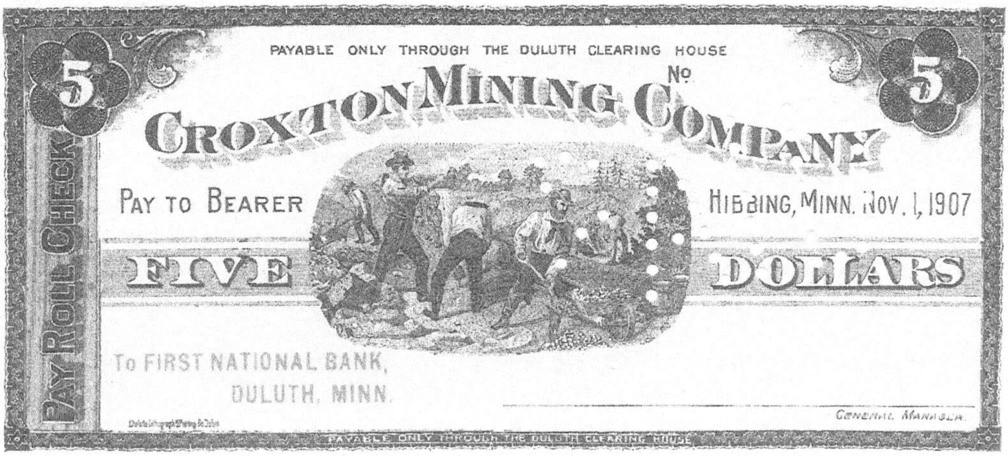

MN825-5. 5 Dollars Nov. 1, 1907. Black on cream safety paper. As above. (shown at 76%)
c. Unissued, cancelled. R5
MN825-10. 10 Dollars Nov. 1, 1907. As above.
c. Unissued, cancelled. R5

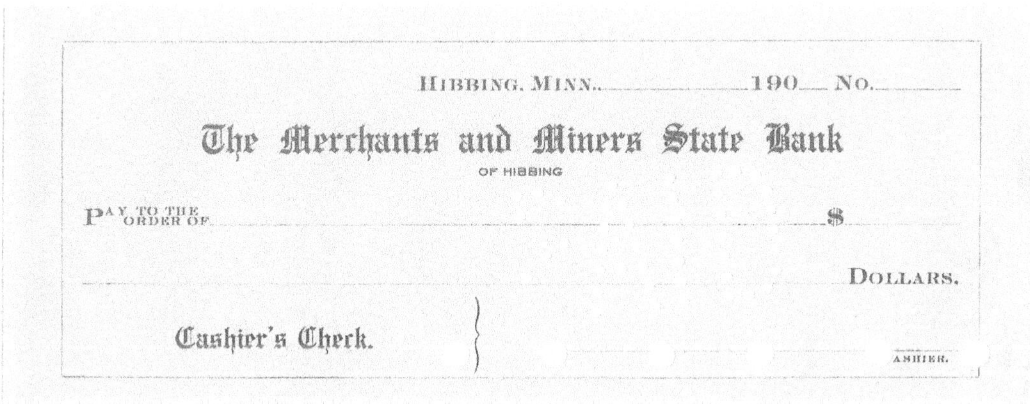

The Merchants and Miners State Bank

MN850-Var. Various Amounts Cashier's Check 190_ (1907). Black on blue safety paper. Uniface. (shown at 61%)
c. Unissued, cancelled. R5

Nassau Ore Company

MN875-1. 1 Dollar Pay Roll Check Nov. 1, 1907. As MN-825. (b/w)
c. Unissued, cancelled. R5
MN875-2. 2 Dollars Nov. 1, 1907. As above. (b/w)
c. Unissued, cancelled. R5
MN875-5. 5 Dollars Nov. 1, 1907. As above. (b/w)
c. Unissued, cancelled. R5

MN875-10. 10 Dollars Nov. 1, 1907. Black on green safety paper. As above. (shown at 76%)
c. Unissued, cancelled. **R5**

Pittsburg Iron Ore Company

A. Brunt Mine

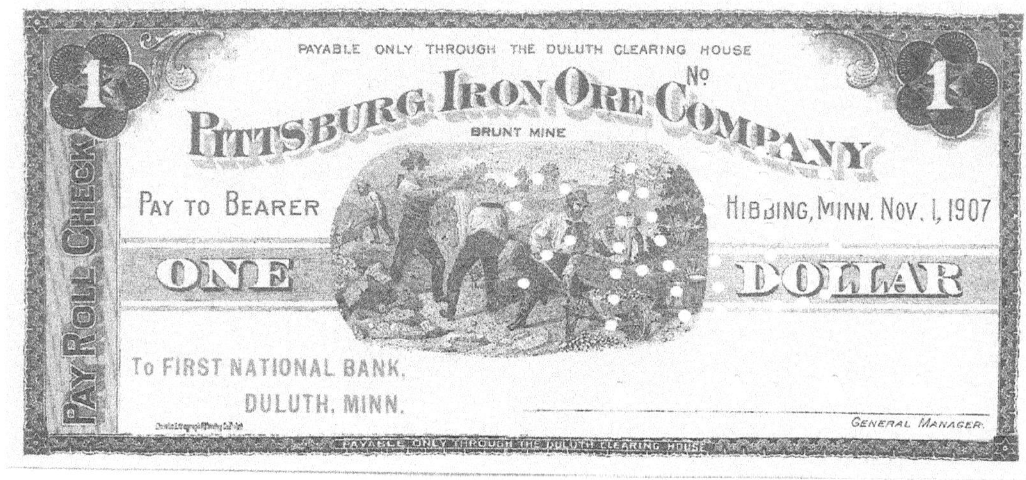

MN900-1. 1 Dollar Pay Roll Check Nov. 1, 1907. Black on green safety paper. Miner vignette as MN825. Imprint as MN550-2. (shown at 76%)
c. Unissued, cancelled. **R4**
MN900-2. 2 Dollars Nov. 1, 1907. Design as above. (b/w)
c. Unissued, cancelled. **R4**
MN900-5. 5 Dollars Nov. 1, 1907. As above. (b/w)
c. Unissued, cancelled. **R4**
MN900-10. 10 Dollars Nov. 1, 1907. As above.
c. Unissued, cancelled. **R4**

B. Hobart Mine
MN915-1. 1 Dollar Nov. 1, 1907. Black on white paper. As MN900.
c. Unissued, cancelled. **R4**
MN915- 2. 2 Dollars Nov. 1, 1907. As above.
c. Unissued, cancelled. **R4**

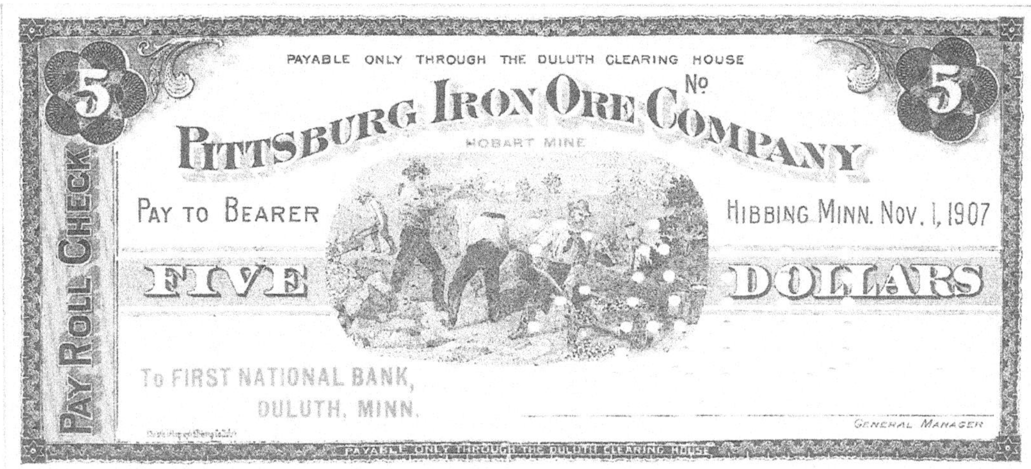

MN915-5. 5 Dollars Nov. 1, 1907. As above. (shown at 76%)
c. Unissued, cancelled. **R4**
MN915-10. 10 Dollars Nov. 1, 1907. As above.
c. Unissued, cancelled. **R4**
MN915-20. 20 Dollars Nov. 1, 1907. As above.
c. Unissued, cancelled. **R4**

The Shenango Furnace Company

MN950-1. 1 Dollar (payroll check) Nov. 1, 1907. Black on white paper. Vignette as MN900. Imprint as MN550-2.
c. Unissued, cancelled. **R5**
MN950-2. 2 Dollars Nov. 1, 1907. Black. As above.
c. Unissued, cancelled. **R5**

MN950-5. 5 Dollars Nov. 1, 1907. As above. (shown at 76%)
c. Unissued, cancelled. **R5**
MN950-10. 10 Dollars Nov. 1, 1907. As above.
c. Unissued, cancelled. **R5**
MN950-20. 20 Dollars Nov. 1, 1907. As above.
c. Unissued, cancelled. **R5**

Minneapolis

Loan Committee of the Minneapolis Clearing House Association

MN975-5000. 5,000 Dollars Loan Certificate Nov. 5, 1907. (list)
c. Unissued, cancelled. R5

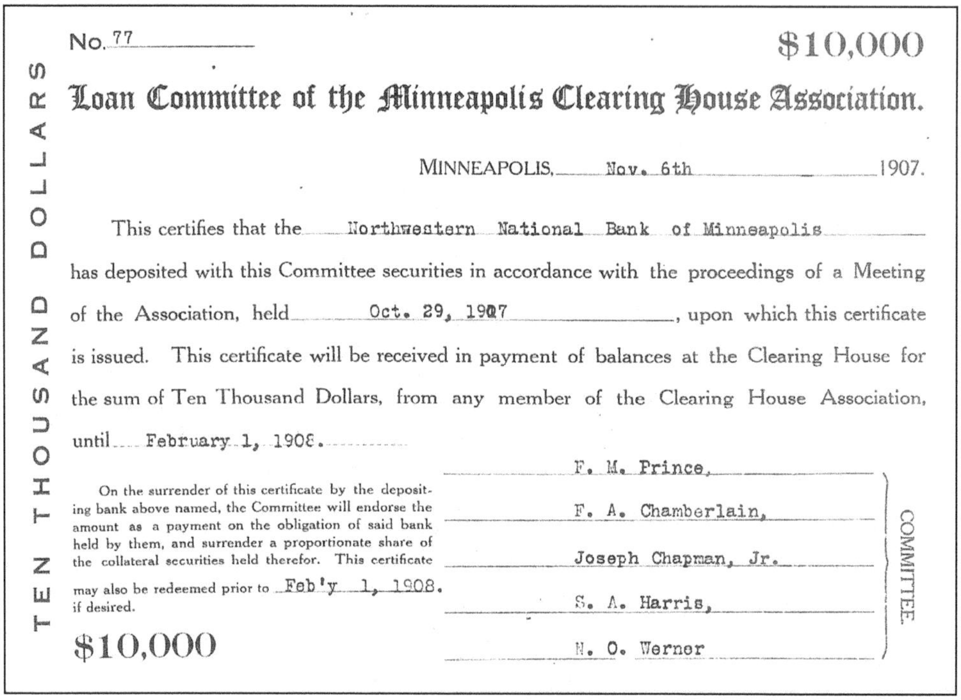
No. 77 $10,000

Loan Committee of the Minneapolis Clearing House Association.

MINNEAPOLIS, Nov. 6th 1907.

This certifies that the Northwestern National Bank of Minneapolis has deposited with this Committee securities in accordance with the proceedings of a Meeting of the Association, held Oct. 29, 1907, upon which this certificate is issued. This certificate will be received in payment of balances at the Clearing House for the sum of Ten Thousand Dollars, from any member of the Clearing House Association, until February 1, 1908.

On the surrender of this certificate by the depositing bank above named, the Committee will endorse the amount as a payment on the obligation of said bank held by them, and surrender a proportionate share of the collateral securities held therefor. This certificate may also be redeemed prior to Feb'y 1, 1908. if desired.

F. M. Prince,
F. A. Chamberlain,
Joseph Chapman, Jr.
S. A. Harris,
N. O. Werner
COMMITTEE.

$10,000

TEN THOUSAND DOLLARS

MN975-10,000. 10,000 Dollars Nov. 6, 1907. (b/w photocopy) All dates and names typed in. Large size. (shown at 66%)
e. Sample. R5
MN975-25,000. 25,000 Dollars Dec. 4, 1907. (list)
c. Unissued, cancelled. R5

St. Paul

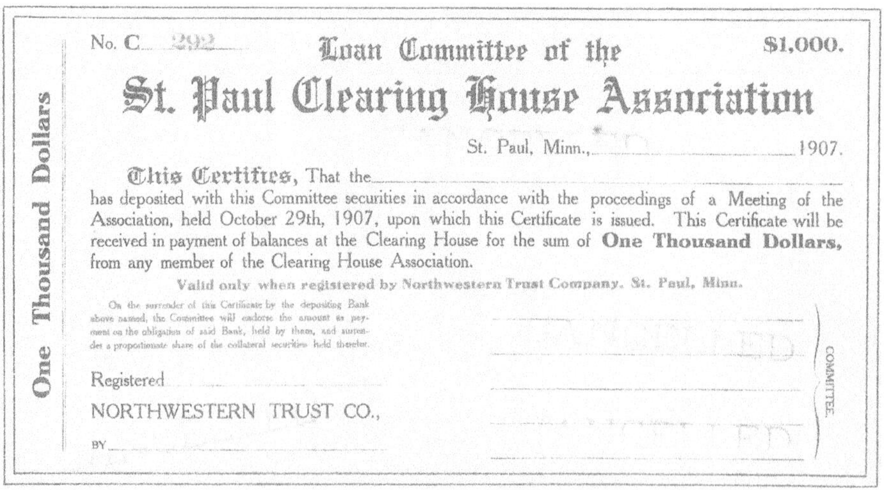
No. C 292 $1,000.

Loan Committee of the
St. Paul Clearing House Association

St. Paul, Minn., 1907.

This Certifies, That the
has deposited with this Committee securities in accordance with the proceedings of a Meeting of the Association, held October 29th, 1907, upon which this Certificate is issued. This Certificate will be received in payment of balances at the Clearing House for the sum of **One Thousand Dollars,** from any member of the Clearing House Association.

Valid only when registered by Northwestern Trust Company. St. Paul, Minn.

On the surrender of this Certificate by the depositing Bank above named, the Committee will endorse the amount as payment on the obligation of said Bank, held by them, and surrender a proportionate share of the collateral securities held therefor.

Registered
NORTHWESTERN TRUST CO.,
BY

COMMITTEE.

One Thousand Dollars

Loan Committee of the St. Paul Clearing House Association

MN1000-1000. 1,000 Dollars Loan Certificate Oct. 29, 1907. Black and red on blue paper. One text line on back, with lines for signatures beneath. Large size. (shown at 49%)
c. Unissued, cancelled. R5

MN1000-5000. 5,000 Dollars 1907. As above, on yellow paper.
b. Issued, cancelled. R5
e. Sample. R5

MN1000-10,000. 10,000 Dollars 1907. (list)
e. Sample. R5

MN1000-20,000. 20,000 Dollars 1907. Black and red on white paper. As above.
b. Issued, cancelled. R5

MN1000-50,000. 50,000 Dollars 19__ (1907). Black and red. As above.
c. Unissued, cancelled. R5

Virginia

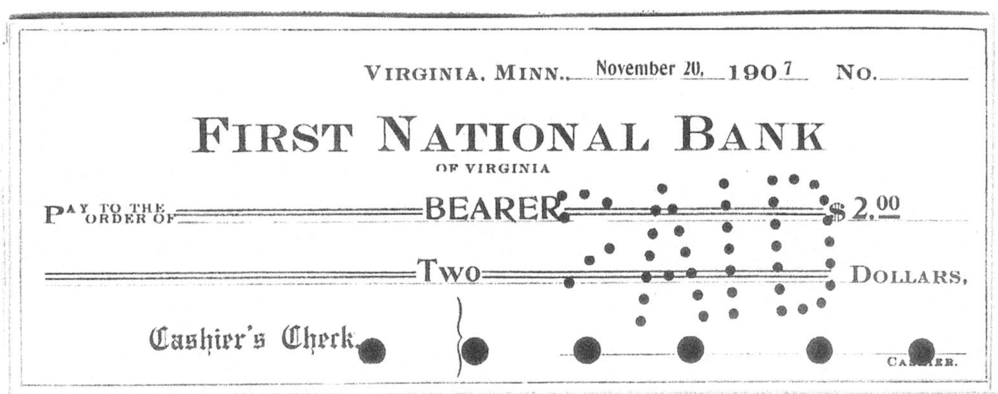

First National Bank of Virginia

MN1025-2. 2 Dollars Cashier's Check Nov. 20, 1907. Black. (shown at 65%)
c. Unissued, cancelled. R5

Mississippi

Hattiesburg

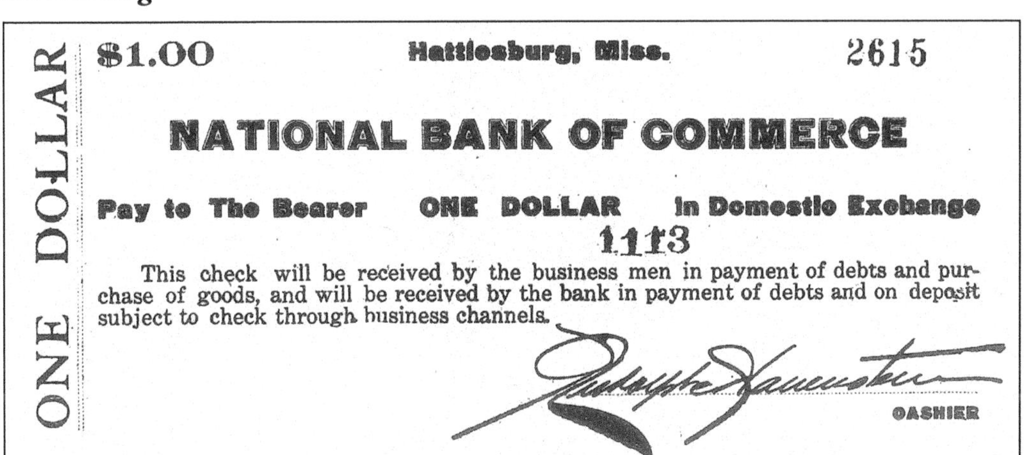

National Bank of Commerce

MS500-1. 1 Dollar (cashier's check) ND (1907). Black. (b/w) (shown at 82%)
a. Issued, not cancelled. R5

Vicksburg

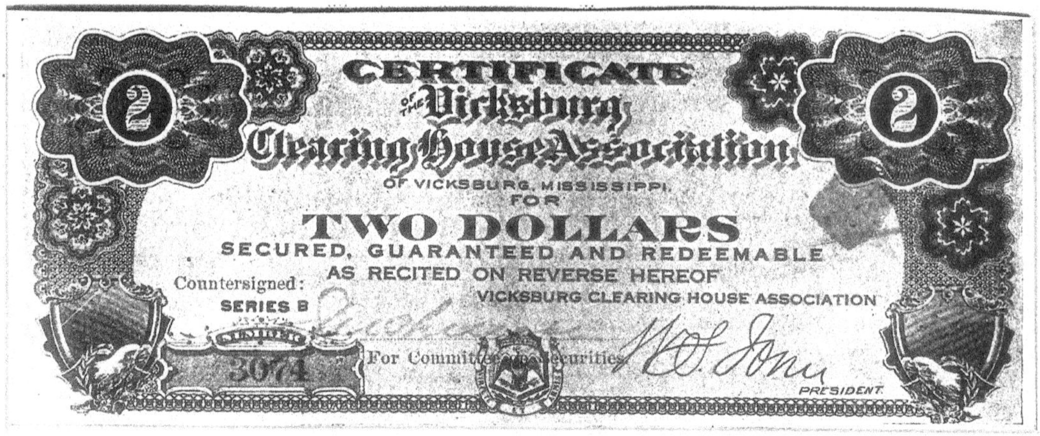

Vicksburg Clearing House Association

MS550-1. 1 Dollar Clearing House Certificate ND (1907). Green on off-white paper. Shield with eagle's head at each lower corner. Series A. Imprint (on back): Brandon — Nashville.
a. Issued, not cancelled. R5

MS550-2. 2 Dollars ND (1907). As above. Series B. (b/w) (shown at 71%)
a. Issued, not cancelled. R5

MS550-5. 5 Dollars ND (1907). As above. Series C. (b/w)
a. Issued, not cancelled. R5

MS550-10. 10 Dollars ND (1907). As above. Series D. (b/w)
a. Issued, not cancelled. R5

Missouri

Aurora

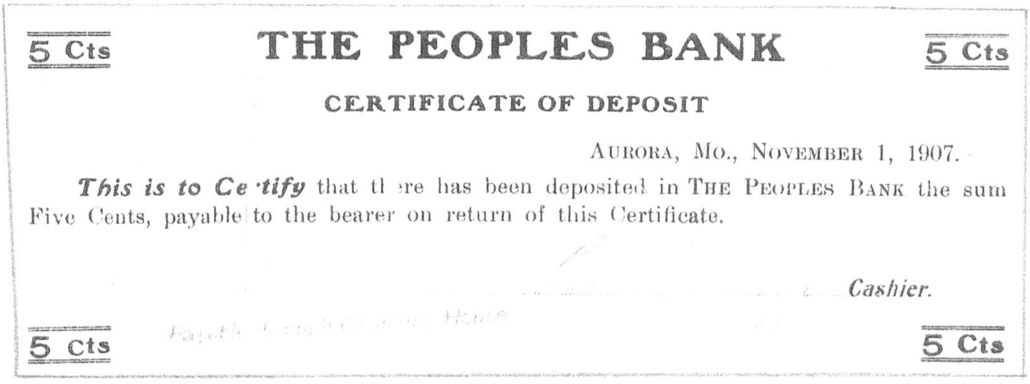

The Peoples Bank

MO500-.05 5 Cents Certificate of Deposit Nov. 1, 1907. (b/w) (shown at 75%)
a. Issued, not cancelled. R5

Bonne Terre

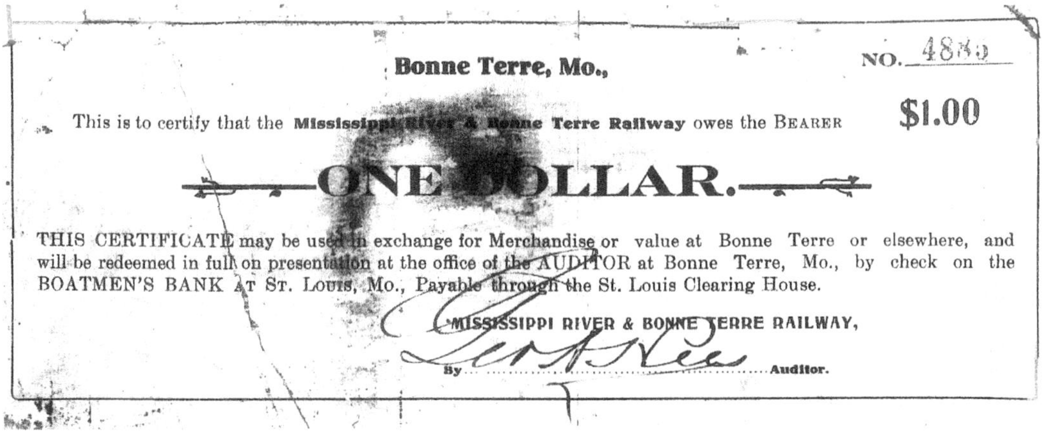
Bonne Terre, Mo., NO. 4880

This is to certify that the Mississippi River & Bonne Terre Railway owes the BEARER $1.00

ONE DOLLAR.

THIS CERTIFICATE may be used in exchange for Merchandise or value at Bonne Terre or elsewhere, and will be redeemed in full on presentation at the office of the AUDITOR at Bonne Terre, Mo., by check on the BOATMEN'S BANK AT ST. LOUIS, Mo., Payable through the St. Louis Clearing House.

MISSISSIPPI RIVER & BONNE TERRE RAILWAY,

By .... Auditor.

Mississippi River & Bonne Terre Railway

MO525-1. 1 Dollar (payroll check) ND (1907). (b/w) (shown at 69%)
a. Issued, not cancelled. **R5**

Doe Run

Doe Run Lead Company

MO550-1. 1 Dollar (payroll certificate) ND (1907). Black on light yellow paper. Uniface.
b. Issued, cancelled. **VG, 25. VF, 60.**
MO550-2. 2 Dollars ND (1907). Black on light orange paper. As above.
b. Issued, cancelled. **VG, 30. VF, 65.**

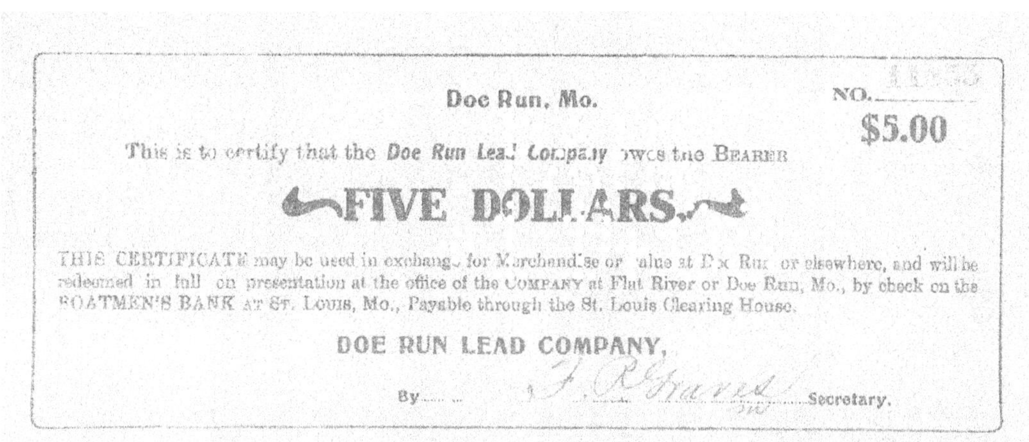
Doe Run, Mo. NO.

$5.00

This is to certify that the Doe Run Lead Company owes the BEARER

FIVE DOLLARS.

THIS CERTIFICATE may be used in exchange for Merchandise or value at Doe Run or elsewhere, and will be redeemed in full on presentation at the office of the COMPANY at Flat River or Doe Run, Mo., by check on the BOATMEN'S BANK AT ST. LOUIS, Mo., Payable through the St. Louis Clearing House.

DOE RUN LEAD COMPANY,

By .... Secretary.

MO550-5. 5 Dollars ND (1907). Black on light blue paper. As above. (shown at 67%)
b. Issued, cancelled. **VG, 30. VF, 65.**

Joplin

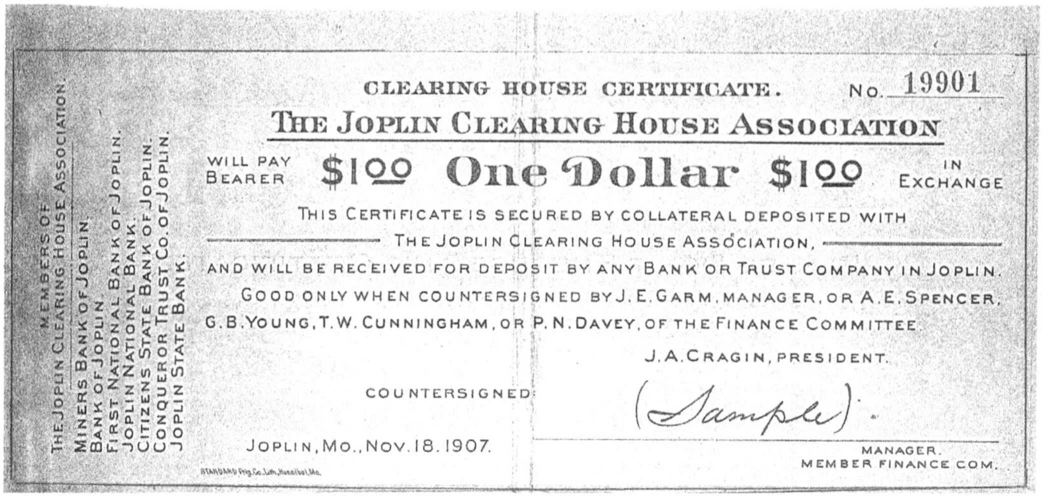

THE JOPLIN CLEARING HOUSE ASSOCIATION

MO575-1. 1 Dollar Nov. 18, 1907. Imprint: STANDARD Prtg. Co., Lith, Hannibal, Mo. (b/w) (shown at 63%)
e. Sample. **R5**

JOPLIN STATE BANK

MO600-1. 1 Dollar Cashier's Check Nov. 7, 9, 11, 12, 16, 1907 (stamped dates). Black on yellow paper. Uniface. (shown at 76%)
b. Issued, cancelled. **VG, 30. VF, 75.**

MO600-2. 2 Dollars Nov. 9, 11, 14, 1907. Black on gray paper. As above.
b. Issued, cancelled. **VG, 40. VF, 85.**

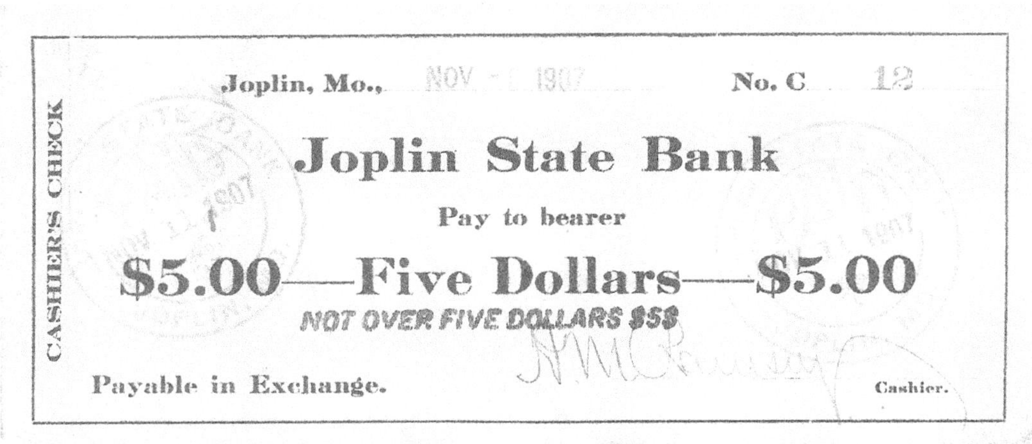

MO600-5.A 5 Dollars Nov. 8, 9, 1907. Black on light beige paper. Checkwriter line *NOT OVER FIVE DOLLARS 5* under printed value in words at center, otherwise as above. (shown at 75%)
b. Issued, cancelled. R3
MO600-5.B 5 Dollars Nov. 9, 10, 11, 16, 1907. Without checkwriter line, otherwise as MO600-5.A.
b. Issued, cancelled. **VG, 40. VF, 85.**

Miners Bank of Joplin

MO625-1. 1 Dollar Cashier's Check ND (1907). Black on yellow paper. Uniface.
d. Unissued, remainder. R4

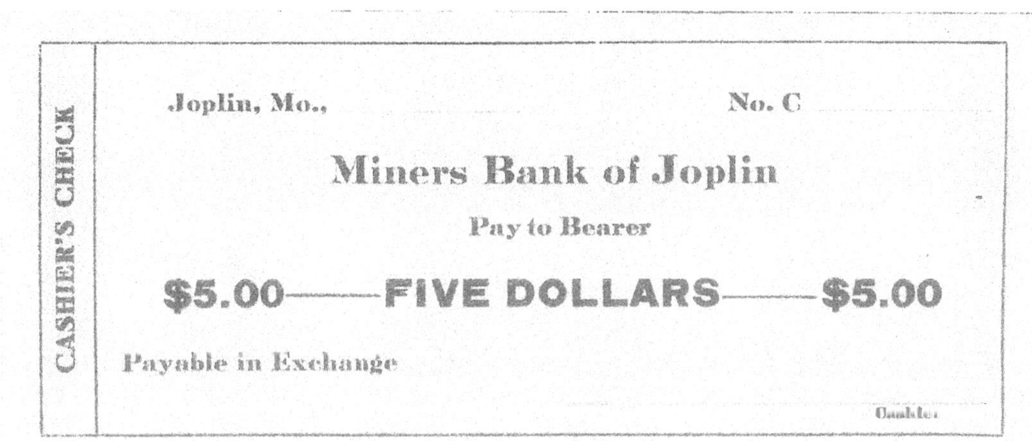

MO625-5. 5 Dollars ND (1907). Black on light beige paper. As above. (shown at 75%)
d. Unissued, remainder. R4

Kansas City

Commerce Trust Company

MO650-1. 1 Dollar Treasurer's Check Nov. 12, 1907. Black. Eagle on globe at left, wheat sheaf at lower center. Uniface. Imprint: Union Bank Note Co. K.C. Mo.
a. Issued, not cancelled. R2
b. Issued, cancelled. R2
c. Unissued, cancelled. R2
MO650-2. 2 Dollars Nov. 12, 1907. As above.
d. Unissued, remainder. R2

MO650-5. 5 Dollars Nov. 12, 1907. As above. (shown at 75%)
d. Unissued, remainder. **R2**
MO650-10. 10 Dollars Nov. 12, 1907. As above.
d. Unissued, remainder. **EF, 120. Unc., 200.**

Kansas City Clearing House Association

MO675-2. 2 Dollars Nov. 12, 1907. Black. Imprint: Union Bank Note Co. K.C. Mo.
a. Issued, not cancelled. **Fine, 100. EF, 200.**
b. Issued, cancelled. **Fine, 80. EF, 160.**
c. Unissued, cancelled. **EF, 90. Unc., 175.**

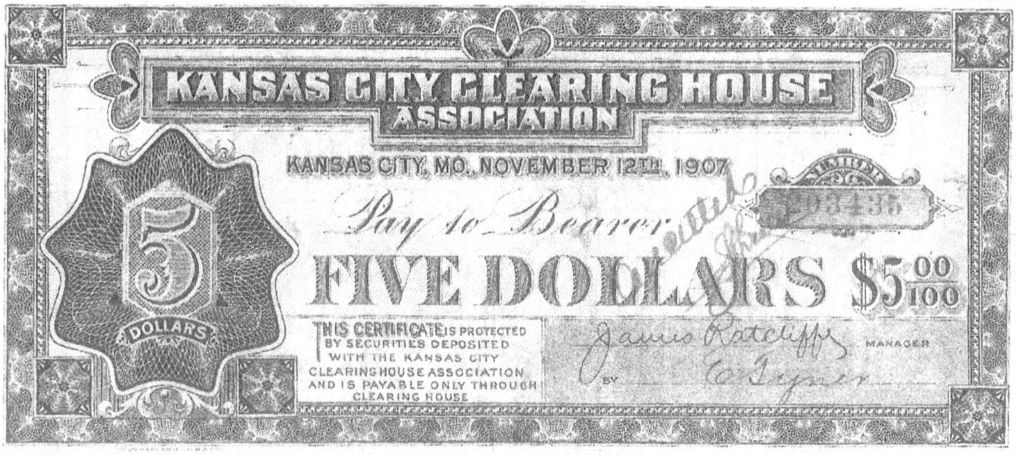

MO675-5. 5 Dollars Nov. 12, 1907. As above. (shown at 74%)
b. Issued, cancelled. **EF, 120. Unc., 225.**
MO675-10. 10 Dollars Nov. 12, 1907. As above.
b. Issued, cancelled. **EF, 90. Unc., 175.**

Missouri Savings Bank

MO700-5. 5 Dollars Cashier's Check Nov. 5, 1907. Black. State seal at upper center. Uniface. Imprint as MO675. (shown at 62%)

a. Issued, not cancelled. **R5**

b. Issued, cancelled. **R5**

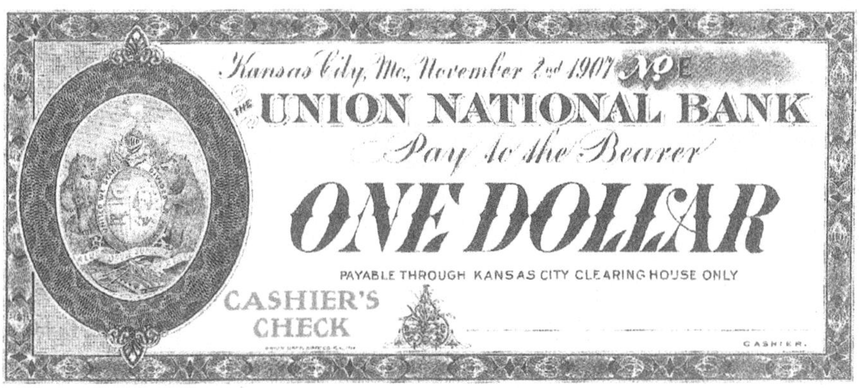

Union National Bank

MO725-1. 1 Dollar Cashier's Check Nov. 2, 1907. Black. State seal in oval at left. Uniface. Imprint as MO675. (shown at 63%)

a. Issued, not cancelled. **R4**

c. Unissued, cancelled. **R4**

St. Joseph

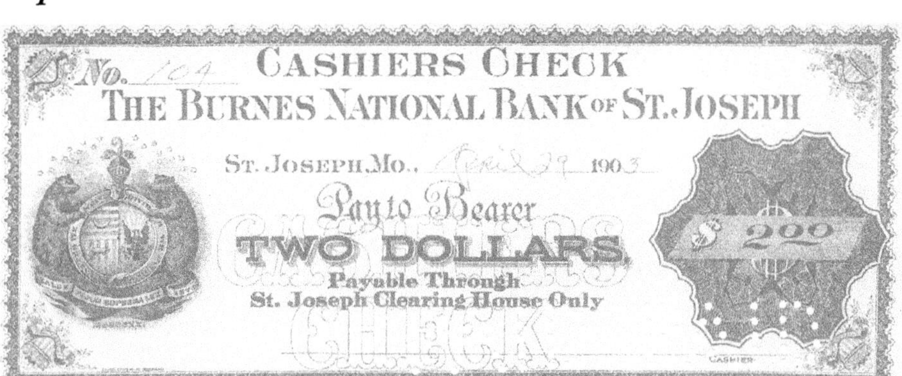

The Burnes National Bank of St. Joseph

MO750-2. 2 Dollars Cashiers Check April 29, 1903 (handwritten fictitious date). Black. Design of state seal at left. Uniface. Imprint: Combe Litho-St. Joseph, Mo. (shown at 63%)
c. Unissued, cancelled. R5

MO750-5. 5 Dollars May 16, 1904; Jan. 8, 1907 (handwritten fictitious dates). As above.
c. Unissued, cancelled. R5

Clearing House Committee of the St. Joseph Clearing House Association

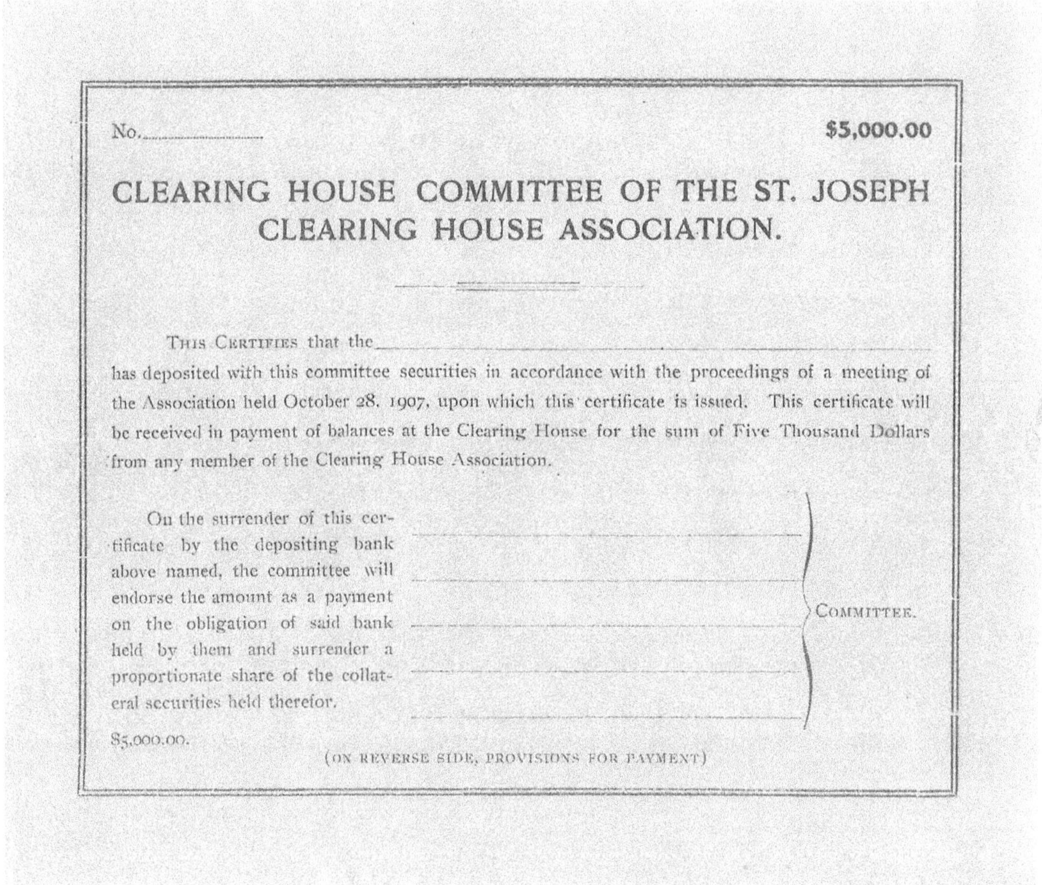
No.............. $5,000.00

CLEARING HOUSE COMMITTEE OF THE ST. JOSEPH CLEARING HOUSE ASSOCIATION.

This Certifies that the ____________

has deposited with this committee securities in accordance with the proceedings of a meeting of the Association held October 28, 1907, upon which this certificate is issued. This certificate will be received in payment of balances at the Clearing House for the sum of Five Thousand Dollars from any member of the Clearing House Association.

On the surrender of this certificate by the depositing bank above named, the committee will endorse the amount as a payment on the obligation of said bank held by them and surrender a proportionate share of the collateral securities held therefor.

Committee.

$5,000.00.

(On reverse side, provisions for payment)

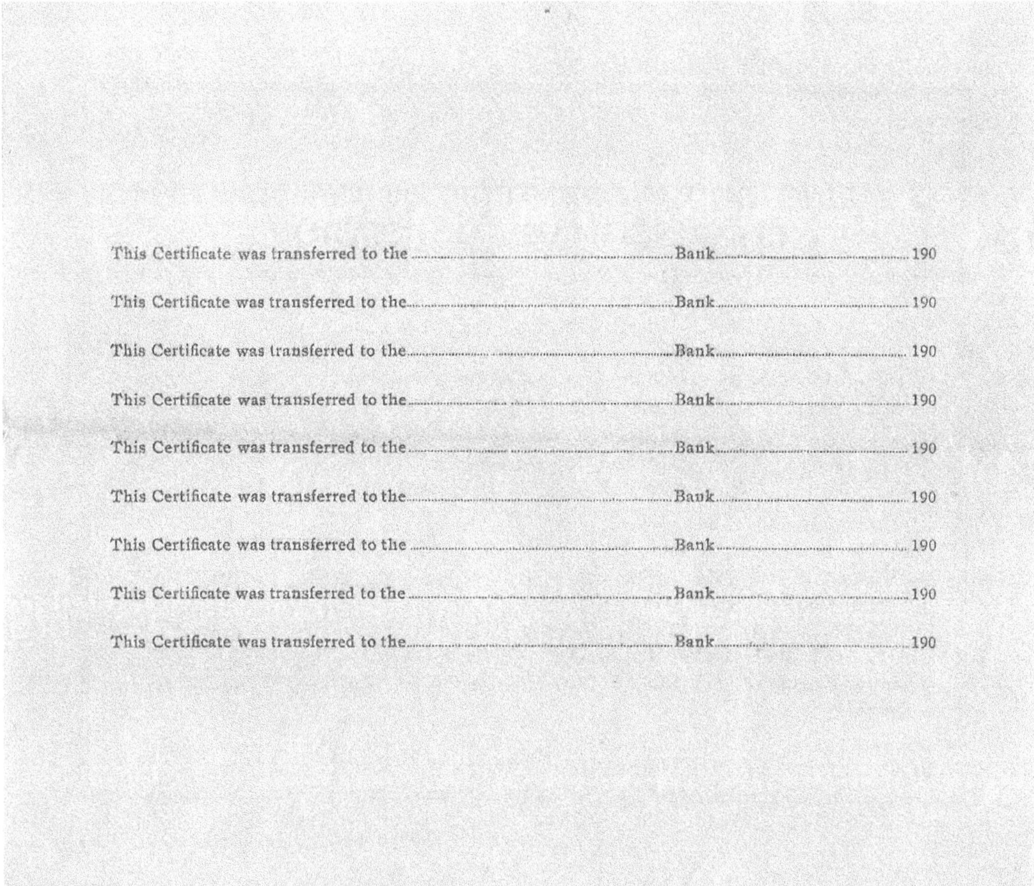

MO775-5000. 5,000 Dollars Oct. 28, 1907. Black on light blue paper. Large size. (shown at 64%)
d. Unissued, remainder. R5
MO775-10,000. 10,000 Dollars Oct. 28, 1907. Black on white paper. As above.
d. Unissued, remainder. R5

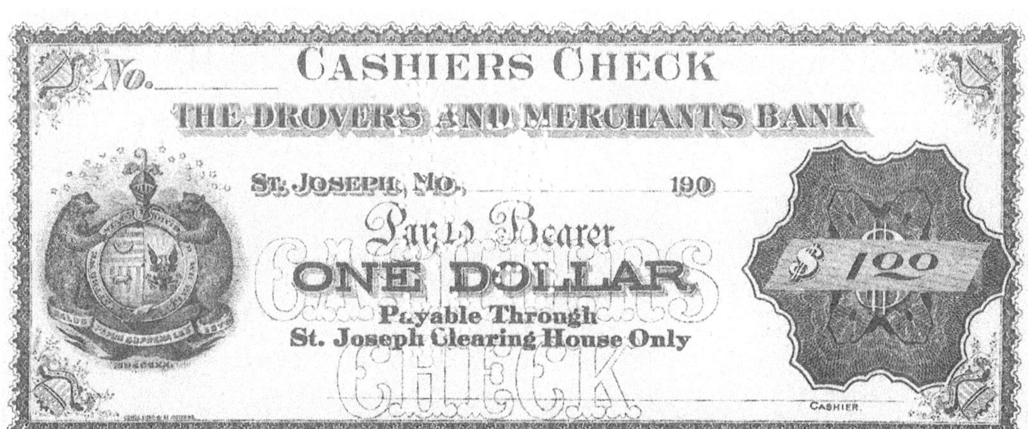

The Drovers and Merchants Bank

MO800-1. 1 Dollar Cashiers Check 190- (1907). Black on light blue safety paper. Design of state seal at left. Uniface. Imprint as MO750. (shown at 72%)

c. Unissued, cancelled. R4
f. Specimen. R5

MO800-5. 5 Dollars 190_ (1907). Black on white paper. As above.
c. Unissued, cancelled. R4
f. Specimen. R5

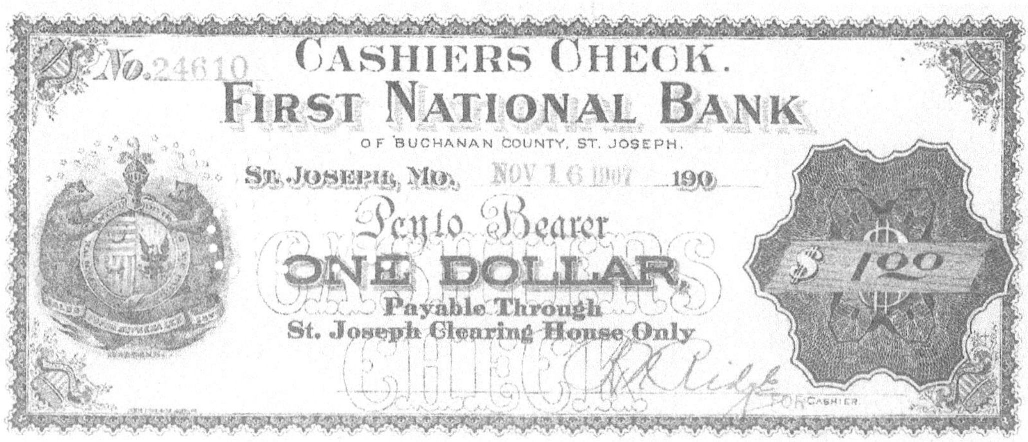

FIRST NATIONAL BANK (OF BUCHANAN COUNTY)

MO825-1. 1 Dollar Cashiers Check Nov. 16, 1907 (stamped date). Similar to MO800-1. (shown at 72%)
b. Issued, cancelled. R5

MERCHANTS BANK

MO850-1. 1 Dollar Cashier's Check Oct. 31, 1907 (stamped date). Black on light blue paper. State seal at left. Uniface. Imprint: Combe Printing Co., St. Joseph, Mo. (shown at 69%)
b. Issued, cancelled. R5

MO850-2. 2 Dollars Oct. 31, 1907 (stamped date). Black on pink paper. As above.
b. Issued, cancelled. R5

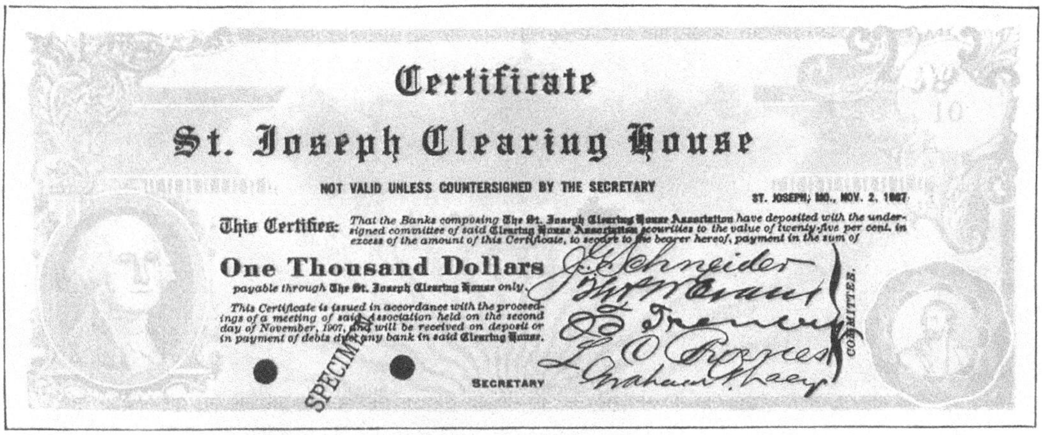

St. Joseph Clearing House/Certificate

MO868-1000. 1000 Dollars Nov. 2, 1907. Black text on light brown underprint. Washington at left, man at right. List of six member banks on back. (shown at 76%)
f. Specimen. **R5**

The St. Joseph Clearing House Association

MO875-1. 1 Dollar Dec. 2, 1907. Black on light brown underprint. Association monogram at upper left. Imprint: Western Bank Note & Eng. Co. Chicago.
b. Issued, cancelled. **R2**
f. Specimen. **Unc., 325.**

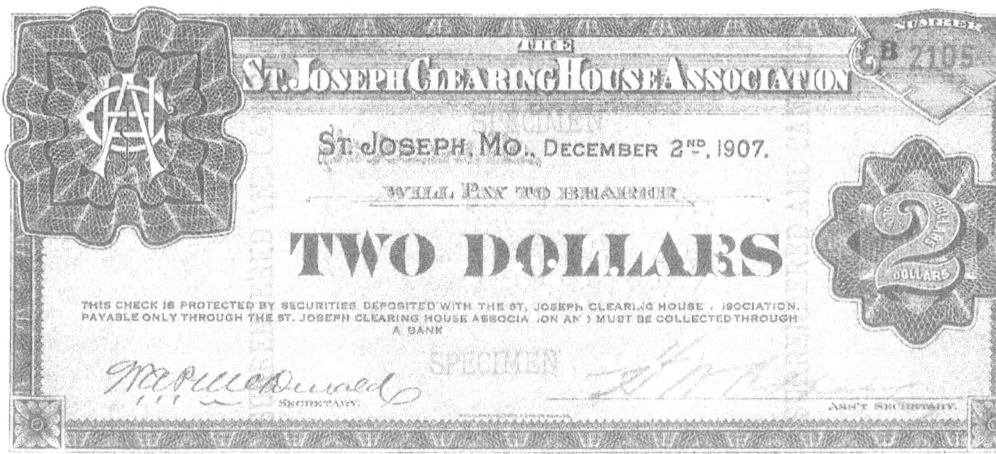

MO875-2. 2 Dollars Dec. 2, 1907. Black on red underprint. As above. (shown at 75%)
b. Issued, cancelled. **R2**
f. Specimen. **Unc., 325.**
MO875-5. 5 Dollars Dec. 2, 1907. Black on green underprint. As above.
f. Specimen. **Unc., 325.**
MO875-10. 10 Dollars Dec. 2, 1907. Black on blue underprint. As above.
b. Issued, cancelled. **R2**
f. Specimen. **Unc., 325.**

St. Louis

Central National Bank

MO900-1. 1 Dollar (cashier's check) Nov. 1, 1907. (list)
u. Unissued. **SENC**

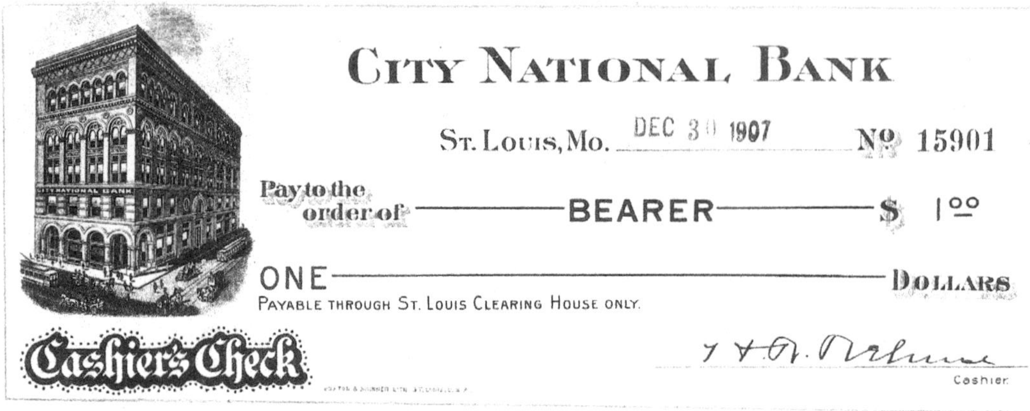

City National Bank

MO925-1. 1 Dollar Cashier's Check Dec. 30, 1907 (stamped date). Bank building at left. Imprint: Buxton & Skinner Lith. St. Louis, U.S.A. (b/w) (shown at 65%)

a. Issued, not cancelled. R5

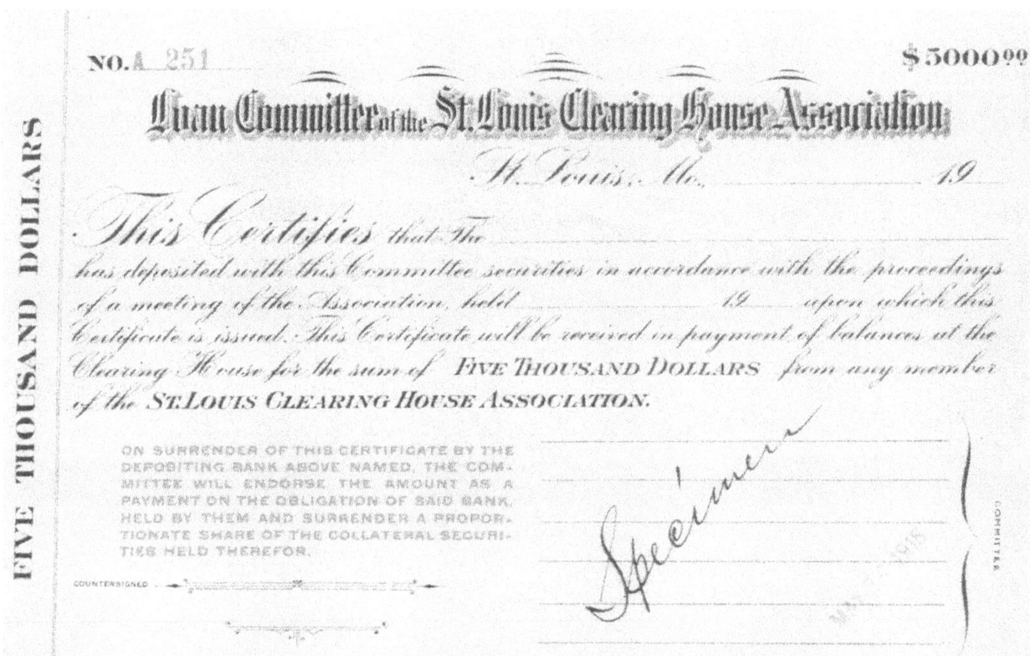

Loan Committee of the St. Louis Clearing House Association

MO940-5000. Five Thousand Dollars 19_ (1907). Black. Large size. (shown at 65%)

c. Unissued, cancelled. R5

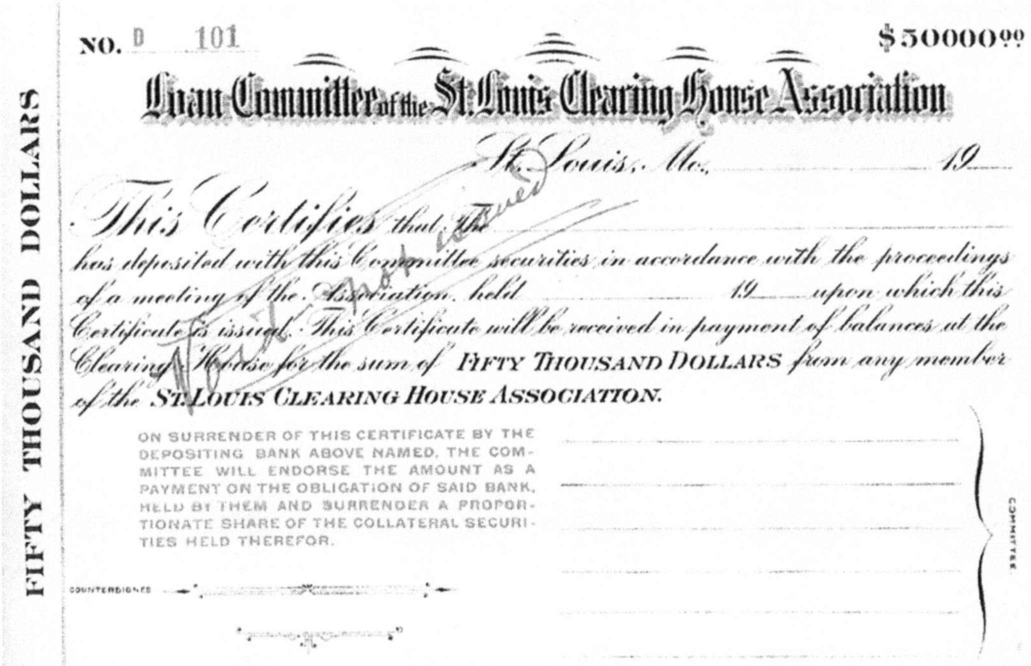

MO940-50,000. 50 Thousand Dollars. As above. (shown at 64%)
c. Unissued, cancelled. R5

Mechanics-American National Bank

MO950-1. 1 Dollar Cashiers Check Nov. 1, 1907. Bank emblem (U.S. shield with arm and hammer superimposed) at upper left. (b/w) (shown at 65%)
a. Issued, not cancelled. R4
b. Issued, cancelled. R4

MO950-5. 5 Dollars Nov. 1, 1907. (list)
b. Issued, cancelled. R5

MO950-10. 10 Dollars Nov. 1, 1907. (list)
b. Issued, cancelled. R5

MO950-20. 20 Dollars Nov. 1, 1907. (list)
b. Issued, cancelled. R5

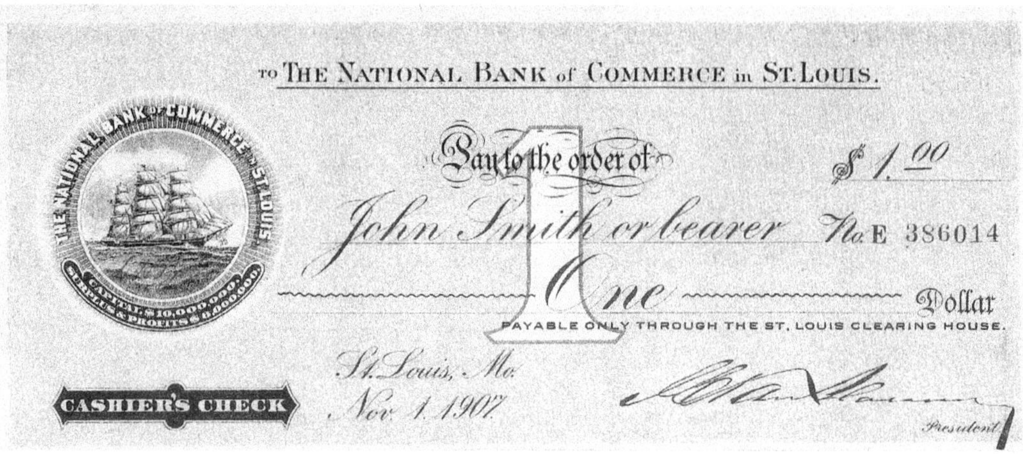

The National Bank of Commerce in St. Louis

MO975-1. 1 Dollar Cashier's Check Nov. 1, 1907. Black on gray underprint. Bank emblem with sailing ship at left. Uniface. (shown at 65%)

a. Issued, not cancelled. **EF, 200. Unc., 450.**
b. Issued, cancelled. **EF, 175. Unc., 400.**

MO975-5. 5 Dollars Nov. 1, 1907. Design as above. (b/w)

b. Issued, cancelled. **R4**

MO975-10. 10 Dollars Nov. 1, 1907. Design as above. (b/w)

b. Issued, cancelled. **R4**

Third National Bank of St. Louis

MO1000-1.A 1 Dollar Cashier's Check Nov. 1, 1907. Black and red on light red underprint, white paper. Uniface. (shown at 63%)

a. Issued, not cancelled. **R2**
b. Issued, cancelled. **R2**

MO1000-1.B 1 Dollar Nov. 1, 1907. As above but on pink paper.

a. Issued, not cancelled. **R3**

MO1000-5. 5 Dollars Nov. 1, 1907. Black on green underprint, gray safety paper. Large perforated 3 at center. Back blue; official writing on back.

b. Issued, cancelled. **R3**

MO1000-10. 10 Dollars Nov. 1, 1907. Black on orange underprint, gray safety paper. Large numeral 3 as above. Back gray; inscription as above.

b. Issued, cancelled. **R4**

THE WASHINGTON NATIONAL BANK

MO1025-1. 1 Dollar Cashier's Check Nov. 1, 1907. Washington portrait at left. (b/w) (shown at 63%)
  a. Issued, not cancelled. R5

Sedalia

CITIZENS NATIONAL BANK

MO1050-1. 1 Dollar Cashier's Check Nov. 12, 1907. Dark green on yellow paper, with red numeral at center. Uniface. Imprint: Union Bank Note Co. K.C. Mo.
  b. Issued, cancelled. R5

MO1050-2. 2 Dollars Nov. 12, 1907. As above.
  b. Issued, cancelled. R5

MO1050-5. 5 Dollars Nov. 12, 1907. As above.
  b. Issued, cancelled. R5

MO1050-10. 10 Dollars Nov. 12, 1907. As above. (shown at 73%)
  b. Issued, cancelled. R5

SEDALIA TRUST COMPANY

MO1075-1. 1 Dollar Cashier's Check Nov. 12, 1907. Black on light green paper. Red denomination at center. Imprint as MO1050. (shown at 74%)

b. Issued, cancelled. R4

MO1075-2. 2 Dollars Nov. 12, 1907. As above.

b. Issued, cancelled. R4

MO1075-5. 5 Dollars Nov. 12, 1907. As above.

b. Issued, cancelled. R4

MO1075-10. 10 Dollars Nov. 12, 1907. As above.

b. Issued, cancelled. R4

NEBRASKA

Bradshaw

FIRST NATIONAL BANK

NE500-Var. Various Amounts Cashier's Check 1907 (various stamped or handwritten dates in October and November). Black. Value entered by hand as well as by check protector line. Embossed bank seal at center. Uniface. (shown at 72%)

a. Issued, not cancelled. **VF, 85. EF, 135.**

b. Issued, cancelled. **VF, 35. EF, 60.**

NOTE: Checks were usually prepared for fixed amounts, but sometimes they were made out for exact amounts as needed. Most of the known pieces are for $5, $10 and $20; other values include $4.86, $9.30, $9.50, $10.35, $14.70, $25, $35, $39.32, $45 and $65.

Hastings

Clearing House

Clearing house certificates and certificates of deposit are reported to have been issued in Hastings to a total of $7,713.00. No further details are known at present.

Various Banks

A cashier's check is believed to have been issued for banks in Hastings. No details are known at present.

Lincoln

City National Bank

NE575-1. 1 Dollar Cashier's Check Nov. 4, 1907. (b/w)
a. Issued, not cancelled. **R5**
NE575-2. 2 Dollars Nov. 4, 1907. (b/w)
a. Issued, not cancelled. **R5**
NE575-5. 5 Dollars Oct. 30, 1907. (b/w)
a. Issued, not cancelled. **R5**

NE575-10. 10 Dollars Nov. 4, 1907. (b/w) (shown at 75%)
a. Issued, not cancelled. **R5**

Clearing House

A loan certificate is believed to have been issued in Lincoln. No details are known at present.

Farmers and Merchants Bank

NE625-1. 1 Dollar Cashier Check Nov. 6, 1907. Bank building in small circle at left. (b/w)
a. Issued, not cancelled. **R5**
NE625-2. 2 Dollars Oct. 29, 1907. As above. (b/w)
a. Issued, not cancelled. **R5**

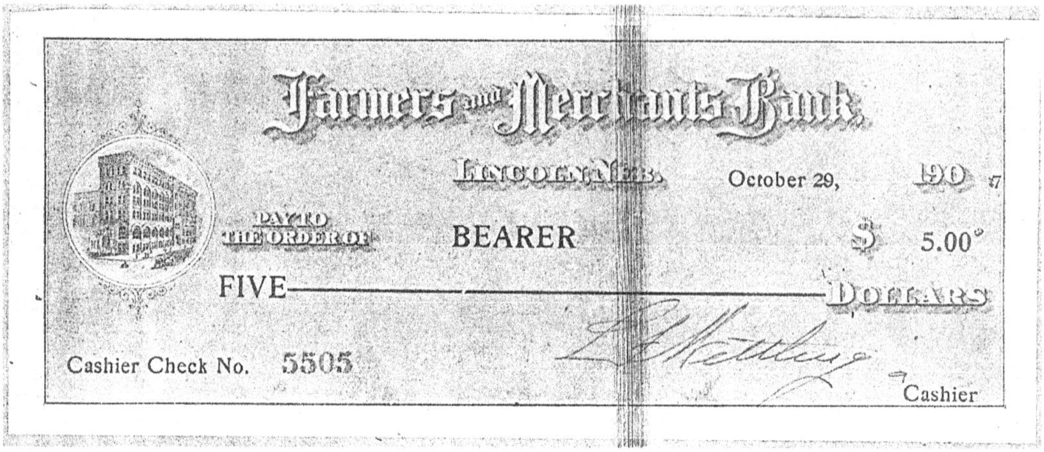

NE625-5. 5 Dollars Oct. 29, 1907. As above. (b/w) (shown at 76%)
  a. Issued, not cancelled. **R5**
NE625-10. 10 Dollars Oct. 29, 1907. As above. (b/w)
  a. Issued, not cancelled. **R5**

The First National Bank of Lincoln, Nebraska

NE650-1. 1 Dollar (cashier's check) ND (1907). Black on pale blue safety paper. Uniface.
  b. Issued, cancelled. **R5**

NE650-2. 2 Dollars ND (1907). Black on pale green safety paper. As above. (shown at 70%)
  b. Issued, cancelled. **R5**
NE650-5. 5 Dollars ND (1907). Black on light gray safety paper. As above.
  b. Issued, cancelled. **R5**
NE650-10. 10 Dollars ND (1907). Black on pale gre en safety paper with blue underprint. As above.
  b. Issued, cancelled. **R5**
NE650-20. 20 Dollars ND (1907). Black on light beige safety paper. As above.
  b. Issued, cancelled. **R5**
NOTE: Small or large headings are seen on NE650-2, 5, and 10.

National Bank of Commerce

NE675-1. 1 Dollar Cashier's Check ND (1907). Large denomination wording at center. (b/w)
  a. Issued, not cancelled. **R5**
NE675-2. 2 Dollars ND (1907). As above. (b/w)
  d. Unissued, remainder. **R5**

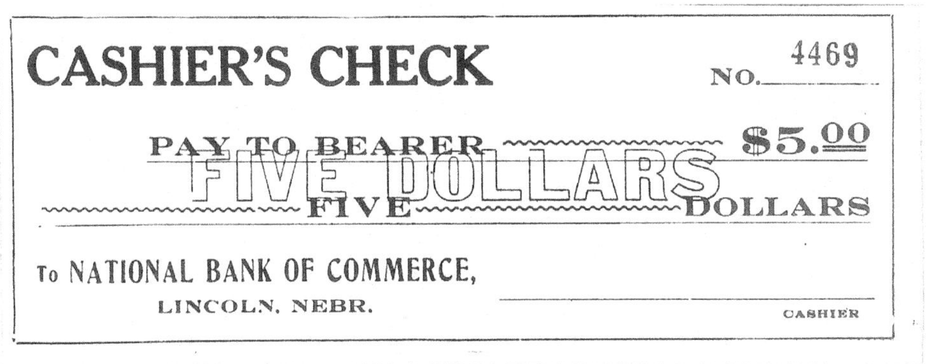

NE675-5. 5 Dollars ND (1907). As above. (b/w) (shown at 68%)
d. Unissued, remainder. R5

NE675-10. 10 Dollars ND (1907). As above, except without large denomination wording at center. (b/w)
d. Unissued, remainder. R5

Omaha

NOTE: Omaha banks were allowed to issue their own cashier's checks in amounts of $1, $2, $5, $10 and $20 after they had deposited collateral with the manager of the clearing house.

The First National Bank of Omaha

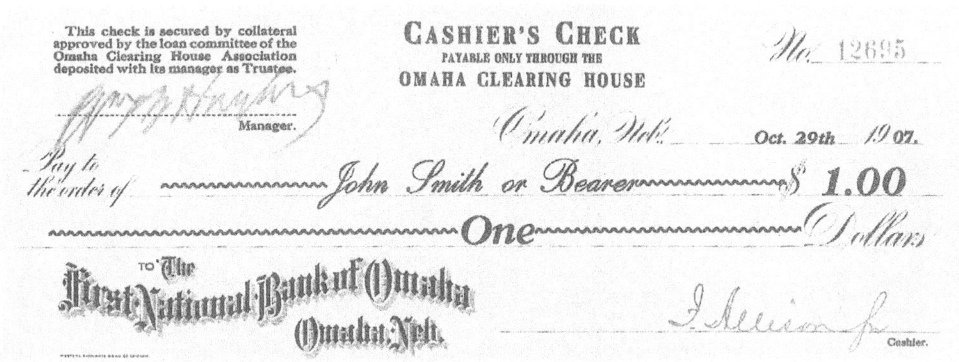

NE700-1. 1 Dollar Cashier's Check Oct. 29, 1907. Black on light pink safety paper. One text line on back. Imprint: Western Bank Note & Eng. Co. Chicago. (shown at 58%)
a. Issued, not cancelled. R4

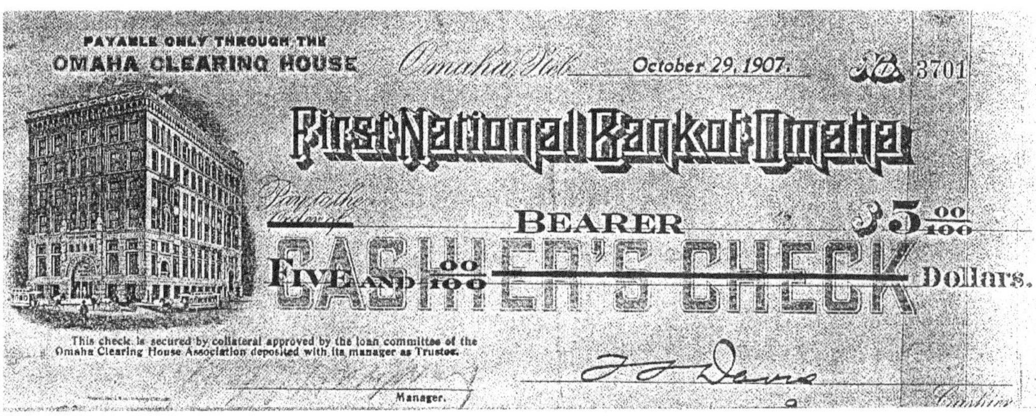

NE700-5. 5 Dollars Oct. 29, 1907. Bank building at left. Imprint: Western Bank Note Company, Chicago. (b/w) (shown at 75%)

a. Issued, not cancelled. **R5**

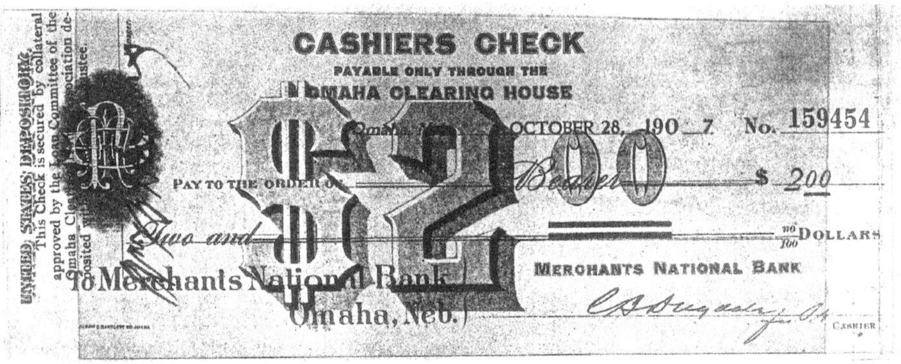

MERCHANTS NATIONAL BANK

NE725-2. 2 Dollars Cashiers Check Oct. 28, 1907. Large denomination at center. Vertical text and signature at left, partly over bank monogram. Imprint: Klopp & Bartlett Co. Omaha. (shown at 55%)

a. Issued, not cancelled. **R5**

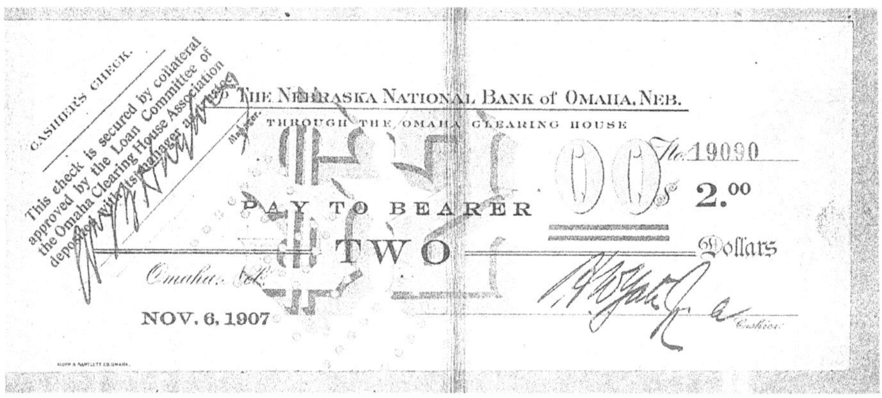

THE NEBRASKA NATIONAL BANK OF OMAHA, NEB.

NE760-2. 2 Dollars Cashier's Check Nov. 6, 1907. Large denomination at center. Diagonal text and signature at upper left. Imprint as NE725-2. (shown at 55%)

b. Issued, cancelled. **R5**

NE760-10. 10 Dollars Nov. 6, 1907. As above. (b/w)

b. Issued, cancelled. **R5**

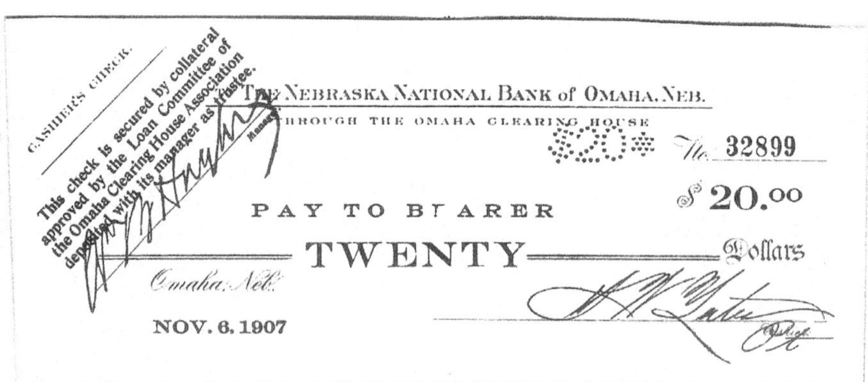

NE760-20. 20 Dollars Nov. 6, 1907. As above. Without large denomination at center or imprint. (b/w) (shown at 58%)
a. Issued, not cancelled. R5

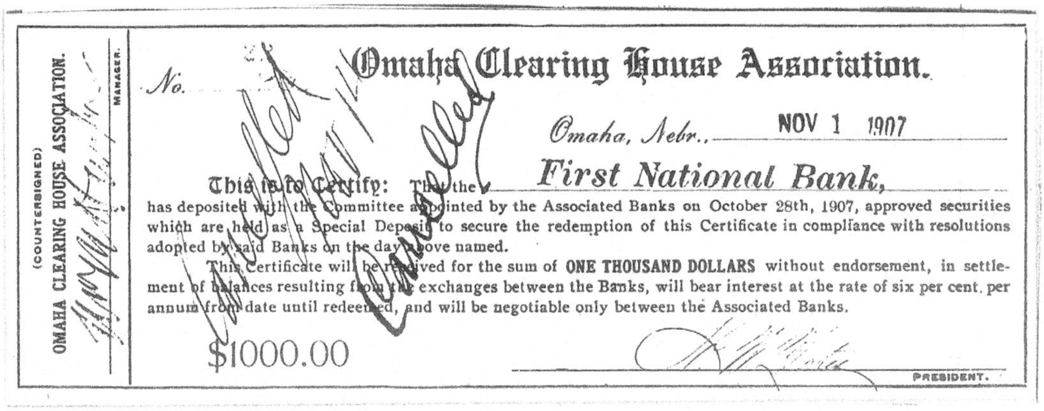

Omaha Clearing House Association/First National Bank

NE800-1000. 1,000 Dollars (loan certificate) Nov. 1, 1907. Black. (shown at 63%)
b. Issued, cancelled. R5

NE800-5000. 5,000 Dollars Nov. 6, 1907. As above.
b. Issued, cancelled. R5
c. Unissued, cancelled. R5

NE800-10,000. 10,000 Dollars Oct. 30, 1907. As above.
b. Issued, cancelled. R5
c. Unissued, cancelled. R5

The Omaha National Bank

NE825-10. 10 Dollars Cashier's Check Oct. 30, 1907. Bank building at left. Imprint: Rees Printing Co. Omaha. (b/w)
a. Issued, not cancelled. R5

United States National Bank of Omaha

NE850-1. 1 Dollar (clearing house check) Nov. 1, 1907. Woman at left, large denomination at center. Imprint: Western Bank Note & Eng. Co. Chicago. (b/w) (shown at 63%)
a. Issued, not cancelled. R5

South Omaha

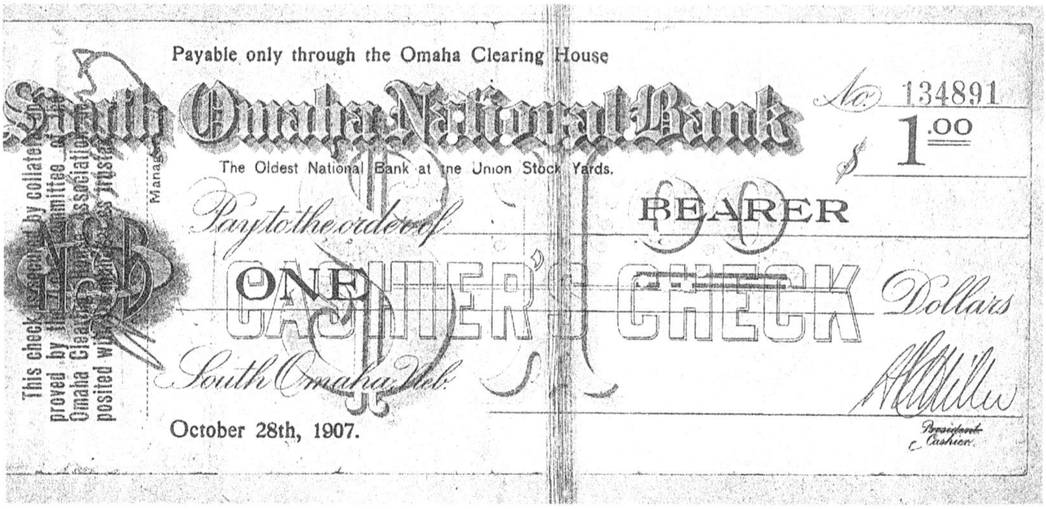

South Omaha National Bank

NE875-1. 1 Dollar Cashier's Check Oct. 28, 1907. Vertical text overprinted at left. (b/w) (shown at 67%)
b. Issued, cancelled. **R4**
NE875-2. 2 Dollars Oct. 28, 1907. (list)
u. Issued. **SENC**

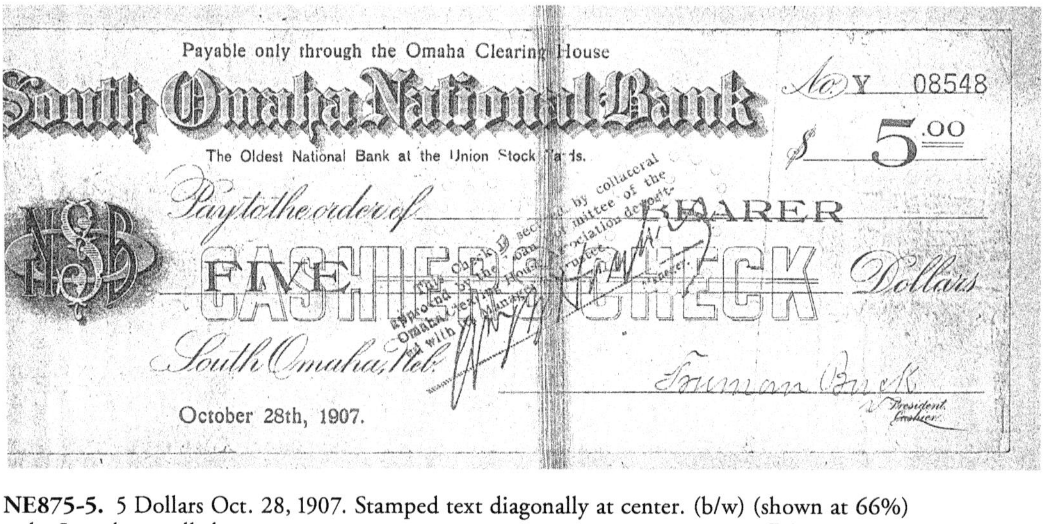

NE875-5. 5 Dollars Oct. 28, 1907. Stamped text diagonally at center. (b/w) (shown at 66%)
b. Issued, cancelled. **R5**
NE875-10. 10 Dollars Oct. 28, 1907. (list)
u. Unissued. **SENC**

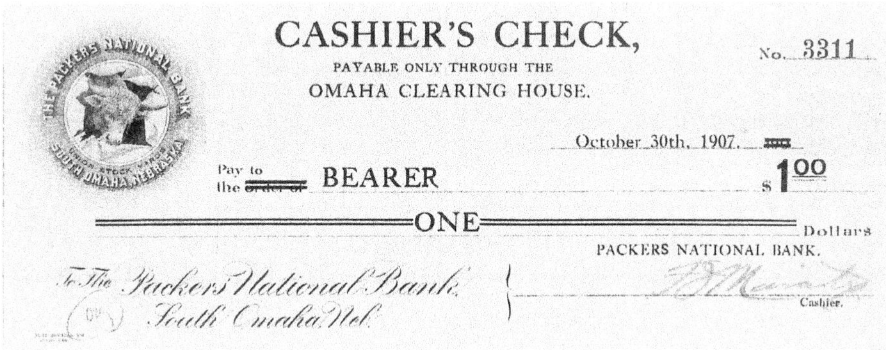

THE PACKERS NATIONAL BANK

NE900-1. 1 Dollar Cashier's Check Oct. 30, 1907. Black on pink paper. Bank emblem with bull's head at upper left. Uniface. Imprint: State Journal Co. Lincoln, Neb. (shown at 55%)
a. Issued, not cancelled. **R5**

UNION STOCK YARDS NATIONAL BANK

NE925-1. 1 Dollar Cashier's Check ND (1907). Black on cream paper. Bank emblem with bull's head at left. Uniface. Imprint: Rees Printing Co. Omaha.
b. Issued, cancelled (lower right corner cut off). **R3**

NE925-5. 5 Dollars ND (1907). Black. As above.
b. Issued, cancelled. **R3**

NE925-10. 10 Dollars ND (1907). Black. As above.
b. Issued, cancelled. **R3**

NE925-20. 20 Dollars ND (1907). Black on tan paper. As above. (shown at 55%)
b. Issued, cancelled. **R3**

Wausa

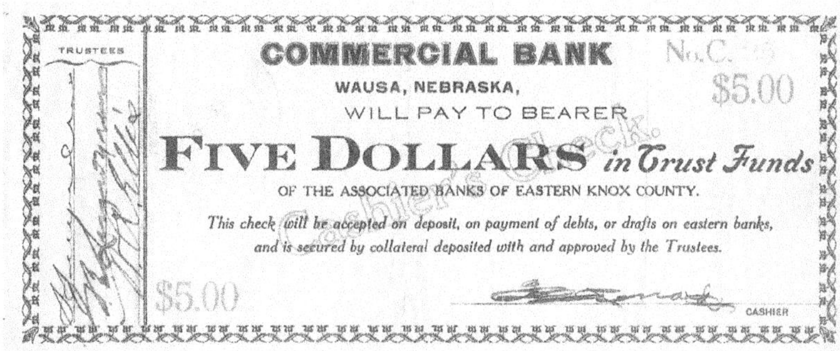

Commercial Bank

NE950-5. 5 Dollars Cashier's Check ND (1907). Black. Orange "Cashier's Check" across center, also denomination numerals at lower left and upper right. Three signatures at left. Uniface. (shown at 56%)
b. Issued, cancelled. **Fine, 35. EF, 65.**

NE950-10. 10 Dollars ND (1907). As above.
b. Issued, cancelled. **Fine, 45. EF, 75.**

Nevada

Goldfield

Goldfield Consolidated Mines Company

NV525-.10 10 Cents ND (1907). Small size. (shown at 100%)
b. Issued, cancelled. **R5**

NV525-.25 25 Cents ND (1907). Fragment known. (shown at 100%)
b. Issued, cancelled. **R5**

NV525-1. 1 Dollar ND (1907). (shown at 100%)
b. Issued, cancelled. R5

NOTE: As listed in the Lyn Knight Currency Auctions Memphis sale of June, 1999 (lot 42), this scrip was issued by order of mine owner George Wingfield. Miners were forced to accept half their pay in this scrip usable only in the company store. They rebelled and a general strike was called. Violence broke out, and Nevada's Governor John Sparks asked Pres. Theodore Roosevelt for U.S. Army intervention. It turned out that the need for such action had been greatly exaggerated. Roosevelt was furious, Sparks was embarrassed, and Wingfield had won a major victory against the miners' union. Practically all the scrip was destroyed.

NOTE: A satirical 5-dollar note was prepared by the miners decrying the scrip system imposed by the Consolidated Mines Company. This note is described under the Parody Issues on page 374 as P2000.

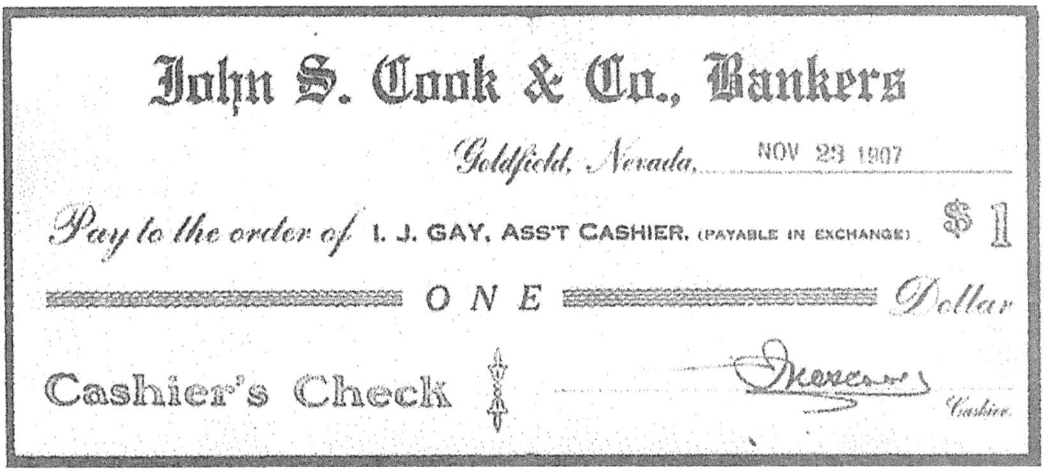

John S. Cook & Co., Bankers

NV550-1. 1 Dollar Cashier's Check Nov. 23, 1907. Black on gray underprint. Red text at lower left. One vertical text line and place for signature on back. (shown at 84%)
a. Issued, not cancelled. R5

NOTE: This bank was owned by George Wingfield who also ran the Consolidated Mines Company.

Rawhide

An issue of clearing house scrip is reported but no details are presently known.

Reno

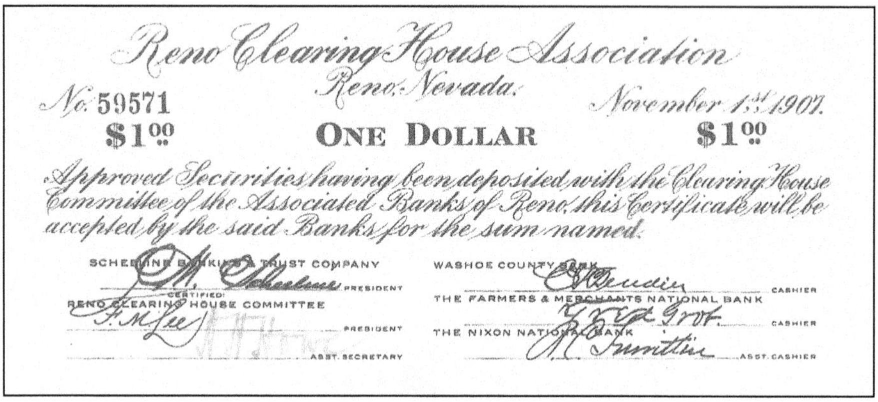

RENO CLEARING HOUSE ASSOCIATION

NV600-1.A 1 Dollar Nov. 1, 1907. Black on light blue-gray paper. Lines for six signatures at bottom. Without additional value numeral at upper left. Uniface. (shown at 61%)

a. Issued, not cancelled. **R2**
b. Issued, cancelled. **R2**

NV600-1.B 1 Dollar Nov. 1, 1907. As above, but with additional value numeral with dollar signs in blue at upper left. (shown at 60%)

b. Issued, cancelled. **R4**

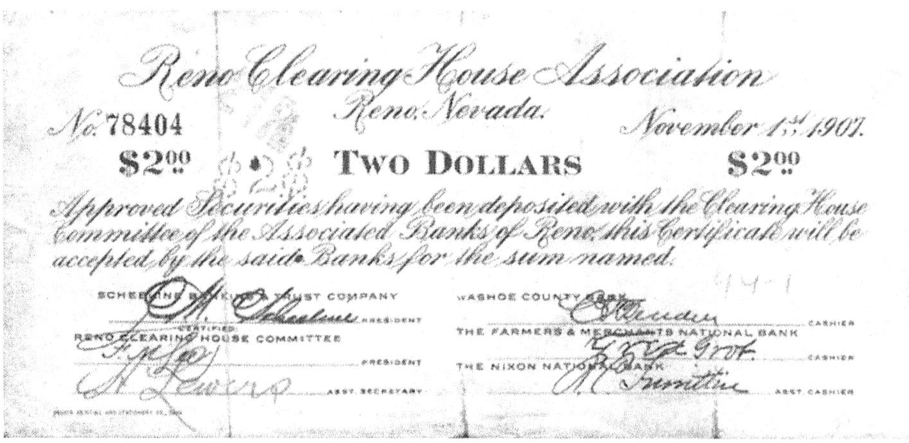

NV600-2. 2 Dollars Nov. 1, 1907. Black on gray paper. (shown at 64%)
b. Issued, cancelled. R4

Rhyolite

RHYOLITE CLEARING HOUSE CERTIFICATE

NV625-1. 1 Dollar Nov. 30, 1907. Black on brown underprint. Ornate back design. Imprint: Lith. Britton & Rey, S. F. (shown at 74%)
a. Issued, not cancelled. **VG, 1200. VF, 2000.**
d. Unissued, remainder. **EF, 400. Unc., 700.**
f. Specimen. **R5**

NV625-5. 5 Dollars Nov. 30, 1907. Black on light red underprint. As above. (shown at 63%)
d. Unissued, remainder. **EF, 400. Unc., 700.**
NV625-10. 10 Dollars Nov. 30, 1907. Black on blue underprint, blue paper. As above.
d. Unissued, remainder. **EF, 400. Unc., 700.**
NV625-20. 20 Dollars Nov. 30, 1907. Black on orange underprint, light orange paper. As above.
d. Unissued, remainder. **EF, 400. Unc., 700.**

NEW HAMPSHIRE

Berlin

VARIOUS BANKS

A cashier's check is reported to have been issued in Berlin. No details are known at present.

NEW JERSEY

Bayonne

VARIOUS BANKS

A clearing house certificate is reported to have been issued in Bayonne. No details are known at present.

NEW MEXICO

Las Vegas

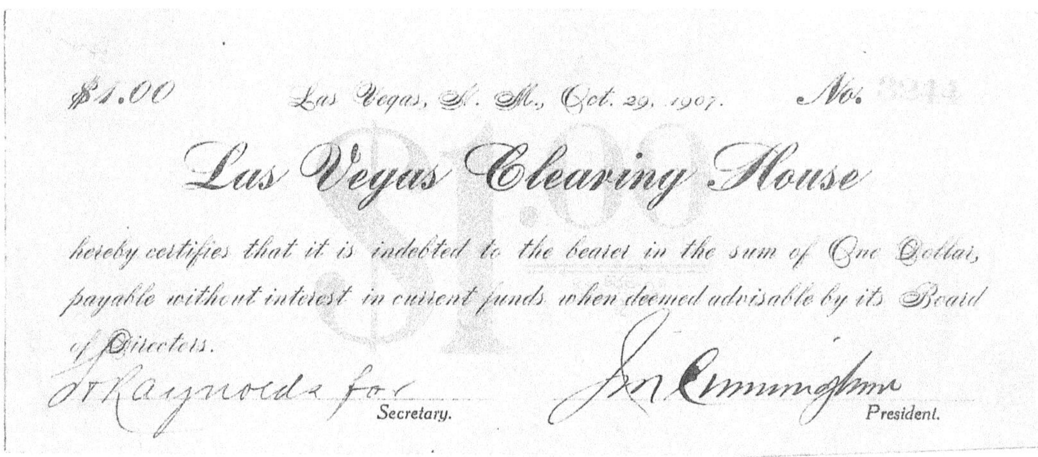

LAS VEGAS CLEARING HOUSE

NM500-1. 1 Dollar Oct. 29, 1907. Black text. Large denomination numerals in underprint at center in blue. Uniface. (shown at 73%)
a. Issued, not cancelled. **R5**

$5.00 Las Vegas, N. M., Oct. 29, 1907. No. 4500
Las Vegas Clearing House
hereby certifies that it is indebted to the bearer in the sum of Five Dollars, payable without interest in current funds when deemed advisable by its Board of Directors.
NOT OVER FIVE DOLLARS 5
Secretary. President.

NM500-5. 5 Dollars Oct. 29, 1907. As above, but *NOT OVER FIVE DOLLARS 5* line added at lower center. (shown at 60%)
b. Issued, cancelled. R5

NM500-10. 10 Dollars Oct. 29, 1907. As above. Without added line of text.
b. Issued, cancelled. R5

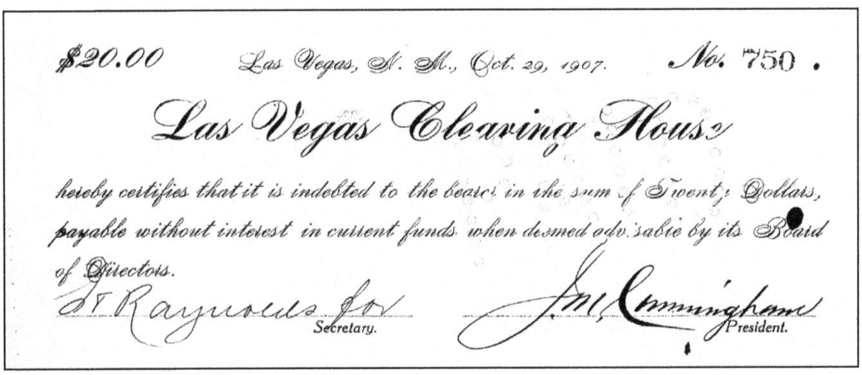
$20.00 Las Vegas, N. M., Oct. 29, 1907. No. 750
Las Vegas Clearing House
hereby certifies that it is indebted to the bearer in the sum of Twenty Dollars, payable without interest in current funds when deemed advisable by its Board of Directors.
Secretary. President.

NM500-20. 20 Dollars Oct. 29, 1907. Without large denomination in underprint. (shown at 60%)
b. Issued, cancelled. R5

New York

Buffalo

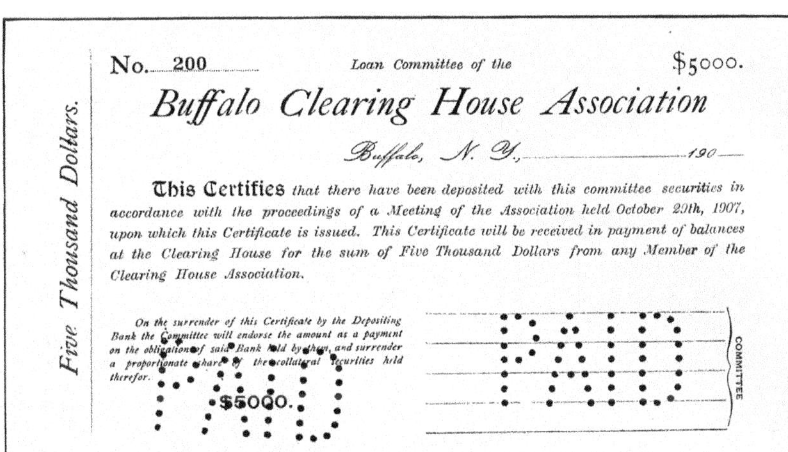
Five Thousand Dollars.
No. 200 Loan Committee of the $5000.
Buffalo Clearing House Association
Buffalo, N. Y., 190
This Certifies that there have been deposited with this committee securities in accordance with the proceedings of a Meeting of the Association held October 29th, 1907, upon which this Certificate is issued. This Certificate will be received in payment of balances at the Clearing House for the sum of Five Thousand Dollars from any Member of the Clearing House Association.
On the surrender of this Certificate by the Depositing Bank the Committee will endorse the amount as a payment on the obligation of said Bank held by them, and surrender a proportionate share of the collateral securities held therefor.
$5000.
PAID
COMMITTEE

Buffalo Clearing House Association

NY500-5000. 5,000 Dollars Loan Certificate Oct. 29, 1907 (handwritten date). Lines at lower right for five signatures. Larger size. (b/w) (shown at 58%)

c. Unissued, cancelled. **R3**

New York City

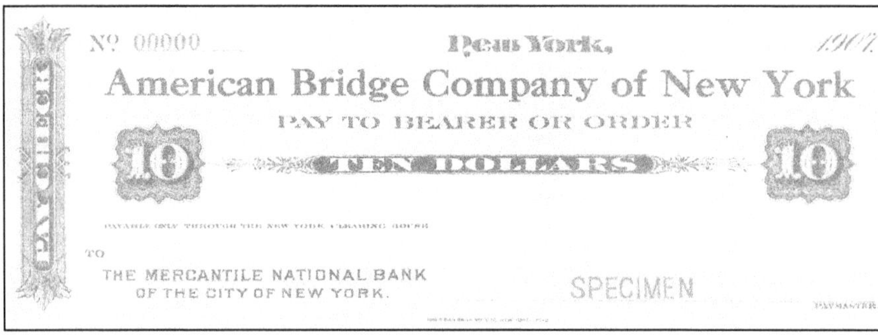

American Bridge Company of New York/ Mercantile National Bank

NY550-10. 10 Dollars Pay Check 1907. Black on gray underprint. Uniface. Imprint: American Bank Note Co. New York. Litho. (shown at 56%)

f. Specimen. **R4**

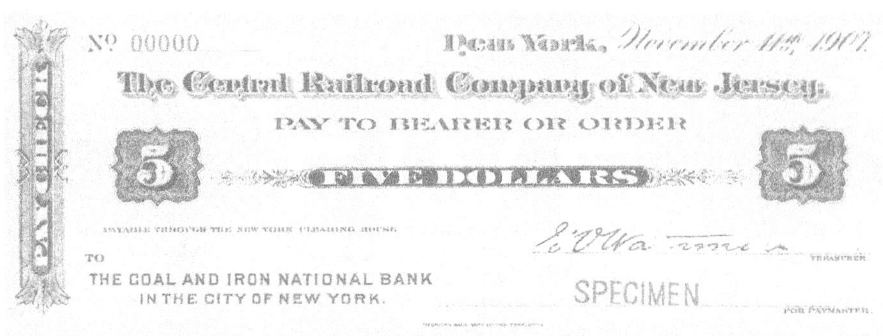

The Central Railroad Company of New Jersey/ The Coal and Iron National Bank

NY575-5. 5 Dollars Pay Check Nov. 11, 1907. Black on green pattern underprint. Uniface. Imprint: American Bank Note Co. New York Litho. (shown at 58%)

f. Specimen. **R4**

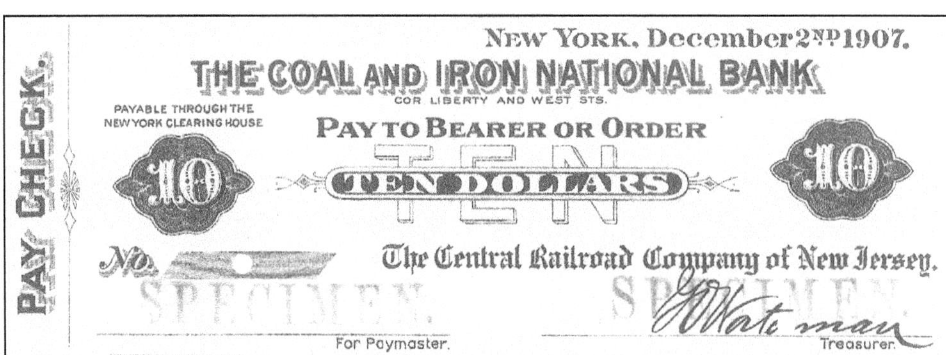

The Coal and Iron National Bank/ The Central Railroad Company of New Jersey

NY585-10. 10 Dollars Dec. 2, 1907. Black on cream paper. Uniface. Imprint: New York Bank Note Co. Litho. (shown at 62%)
b. Issued, cancelled. R5
f. Specimen. R4

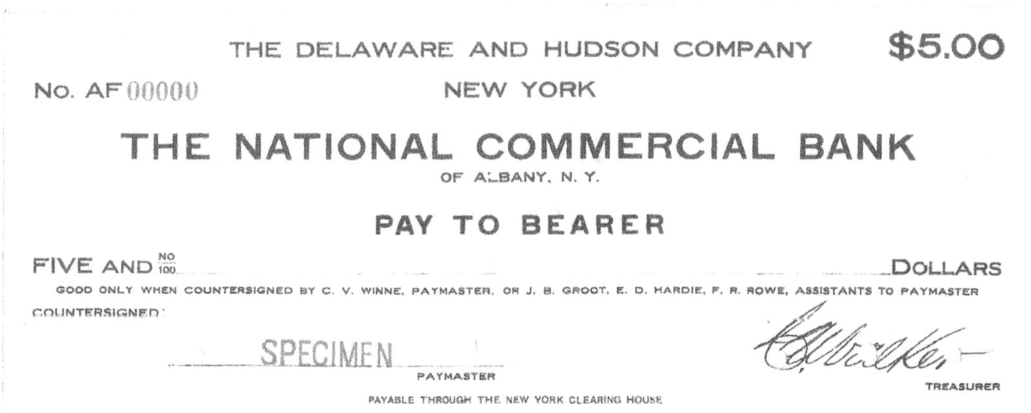

The Delaware and Hudson Company/ National Commercial Bank of Albany, NY

NY600-5. 5 Dollars (payroll check) ND (1907). Black. Uniface. (shown at 63%)
f. Specimen. R5
NY600-10. 10 Dollars ND (1907). As above.
f. Specimen. R5

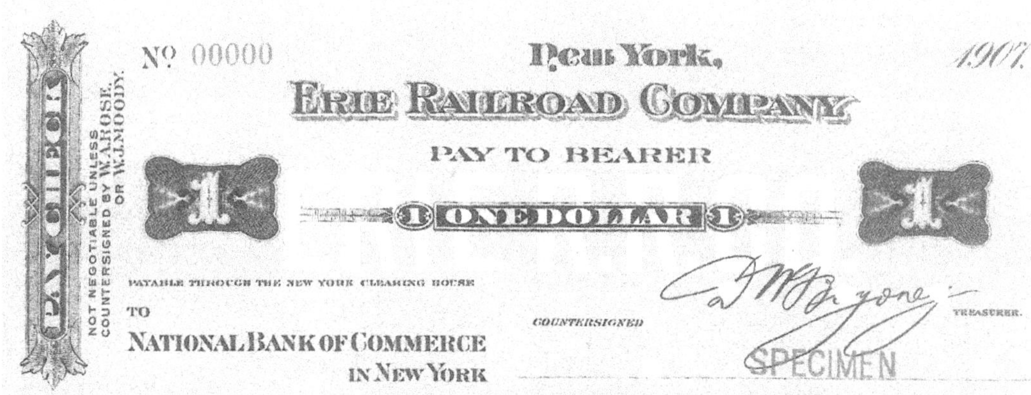

Erie Railroad Company

NY625-1. 1 Dollar Pay Check 1907. Black on green underprint. Uniface. Imprint as NY575-5. (shown at 70%)
f. Specimen. R5
NY625-2. 2 Dollars 1907. As above.
f. Specimen. R5
NY625-5. 5 Dollars 1907. As above.
f. Specimen. R5
NY625-10. 10 Dollars 1907. As above.
f. Specimen. R5
NY625-20. 20 Dollars 1907. As above.
f. Specimen. R5

Loan Committee of the New York Clearing House Association

NY650-5000. 5,000 Dollars Loan Certificate Oct. 26, 1907. Black on gold paper. Large size.
c. Unissued, cancelled. R5

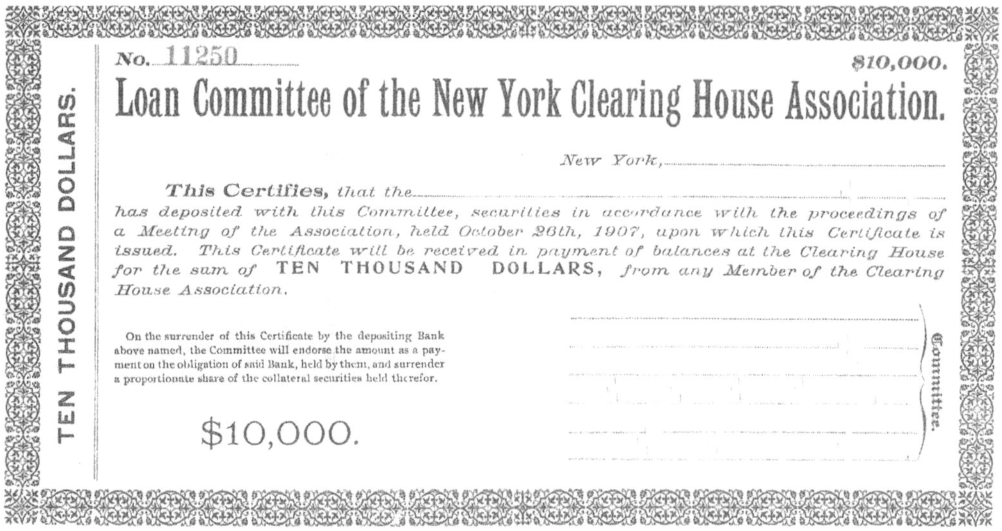

NY650-10,000. 10,000 Dollars Oct. 26, 1907. Black on white paper. As above. (shown at 52%)
c. Unissued, cancelled. R5
NY650-20,000. 20,000 Dollars Oct. 26, 1907. Black on lilac paper. As above.
c. Unissued, cancelled. R5
NY650-50,000. 50,000 Dollars Oct. 26, 1907. Black on light blue paper. As above.
c. Unissued, cancelled. R5
NY650-100,000. 100,000 Dollars Oct. 26, 1907. Black on blue paper. As above.
c. Unissued, cancelled. R5

New York Clearing House Association

A. Deposit in Gold Certificates

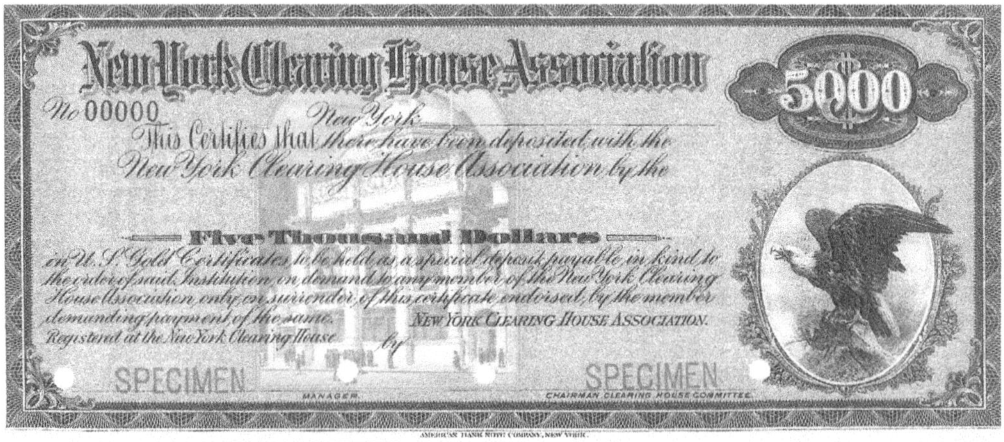

NY675-5000. 5000 Dollars (certificate of deposit) ND (1907). Black on reddish orange underprint containing bank building at center. Eagle at right. Back green with various text lines. Printer: ABNC. (shown at 64%)
f. Specimen. R5
NY675-10,000. 10,000 Dollars ND (1907). As above.
f. Specimen. R5

B. Deposit in Silver Certificates

NY685-5000.A 5000 Dollars (certificate of deposit) Feb. 5, 1908 (stamped date). Black on gray-blue underprint with bank as NY675. Liberty with cap at right. Back gray-blue. Printer: ABNC.
  f. Specimen. **R5**

NY685-5000.B 5000 Dollars ND (1907). Black on purple underprint. Design as above. Back purple.
  f. Specimen. **R5**

NY685-10,000. 10,000 Dollars ND (1907). As above. (shown at 66%)
  f. Specimen. **R5**

C. Deposit in U.S. Legal Tender Notes

NY700-5000. 5000 Dollars (certificate of deposit) ND (1907). Black on green underprint with bank as NY675. George Washington at right. Back red. Printer: ABNC. (shown at 63%)
  f. Specimen. **R5**

NY700-10,000. 10,000 Dollars ND (1907). As above.
  f. Specimen. **R5**

NOTE: All the above have text on back: "Resolution Adopted October 2, 1860." It is possible these were used before the Panics of 1893 or 1907, but no issued examples of any of them are known. The Stack's Rich Uhrich Collection auction of Feb. 26–27, 2008, offered four different pieces, all Specimens. One had a 1908 date stamped (see NY680-5000.), giving some credence to their usage during the 1907 Panic.

New York Central & Hudson River Rail Road Co.

NY725-10. 10 Dollars Pay Check 1907. Black on blue underprint. Uniface. Imprint as NY575.
  f. Specimen. **R5**

NY725-20. 20 Dollars 1907. As above.
f. Specimen. R5

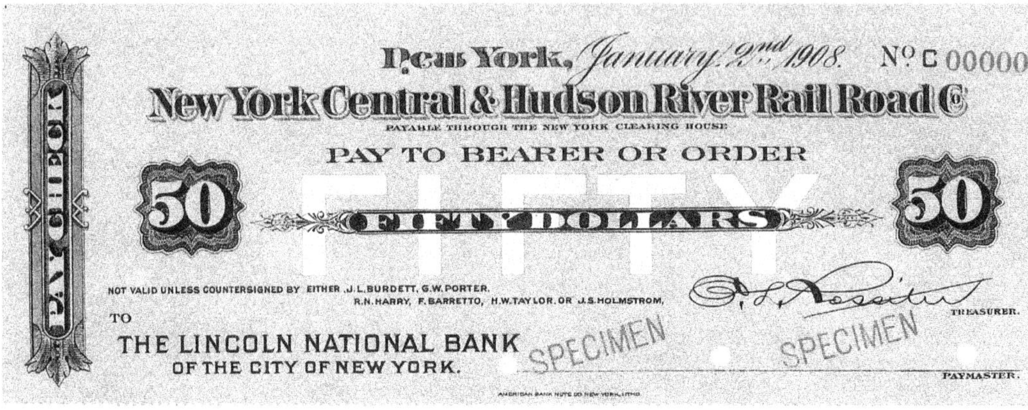

NY725-50. 50 Dollars 1907. As above. (shown at 67%)
f. Specimen. R5

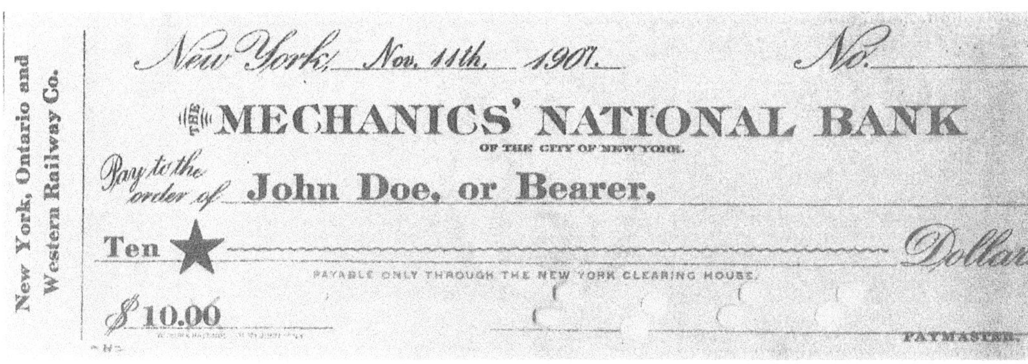

New York, Ontario and Western Railway Co./ Mechanics' National Bank

NY750-10. 10 Dollars (payroll check) Nov. 1, 11, 1907. Black. Arm and hammer at center. Uniface. Imprint: Wilbur & Hastings Lith. 57 Fulton St. N.Y. (b/w) (shown at 70%)
c. Unissued, cancelled. R5
d. Unissued, remainder. R5

Southern Pacific Rail Road/National City Bank

NY775-5. 5 Dollars (payroll check) ND (1907). Black. Imprint as NY575.
f. Specimen. R5

Standard Oil Company of New York/ The National City Bank

A. Notes with red face print, name Standard Oil Company only

NY800-1. 1 Dollar Pay Roll Account ND (1907). Red on gray safety paper. Uniface. Imprint: The Hepner Press, N.Y.
c. Unissued, cancelled. R5

PAY ROLL ACCOUNT

No. C. New York.

The National City Bank

OF NEW YORK.

Pay to the Order of BEARER — PAYABLE ONLY THROUGH NEW YORK CLEARING HOUSE

Two 00/100 Dollars.

STANDARD OIL COMPANY

$2 00/100

The Hepner Press, N. Y. — ATTORNEY.

NY800-2. 2 Dollars Nov. 29, 1907. Red on light blue safety paper. As above. (shown at 73%)
- a. Issued, not cancelled. **R5**
- c. Unissued, cancelled. **R5**

NY800-5. 5 Dollars ND (1907). Red on light blue safety paper. As above.
- c. Unissued, cancelled. **R5**

NY800-10. 10 Dollars ND (1907). Red on white safety paper. As above.
- c. Unissued, cancelled. **R5**

B. Notes with blue face print, company name with "of New York"

PAY ROLL ACCOUNT

No. D. New York,

The National City Bank

OF NEW YORK.

Pay to the Order of BEARER — PAYABLE ONLY THROUGH NEW YORK CLEARING HOUSE

One 00/100 Dollar.

Standard Oil Co. of New York

$1 00/100

The Hepner Press, N. Y. — Attorney.

NY825-1. 1 Dollar ND (1907). Blue on cream safety paper. Similar to NY800-1. (shown at 75%)
- c. Unissued, cancelled. **R4**

NY825-2. 2 Dollars Dec. 20, 1907. Dark blue on green safety paper. As above.
- a. Issued, not cancelled. **R5**
- c. Unissued, cancelled (ND). **R4**

NY825-5. 5 Dollars ND (1907). Dark blue on light blue safety paper. As above.
- c. Unissued, cancelled. **R4**

NY825-10. 10 Dollars ND (1907). Blue on white safety paper. As above.
- c. Unissued, cancelled. **R4**

Staten Island Rapid Transit Railway/ Coal and Iron National Bank of New Jersey

NY850-5. 5 Dollars Pay Roll Check Nov. 15, 1907. Black on peach underprint.
- f. Specimen. **R5**

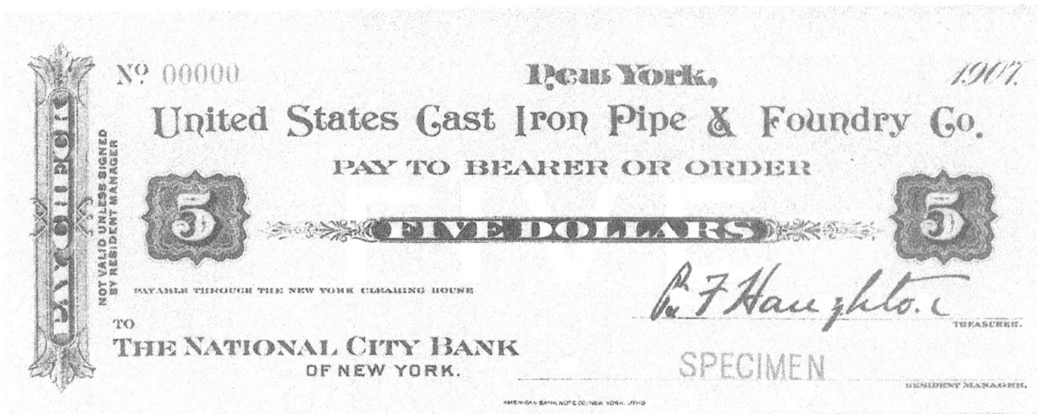

**UNITED STATES CAST IRON PIPE & FOUNDRY CO./
NATIONAL CITY BANK**

NY875-5. 5 Dollars Pay Check 1907. Black on green underprint. Uniface. Imprint as NY575-5. (shown at 68%)
f. Specimen. **R5**

NORTH CAROLINA

Alamance

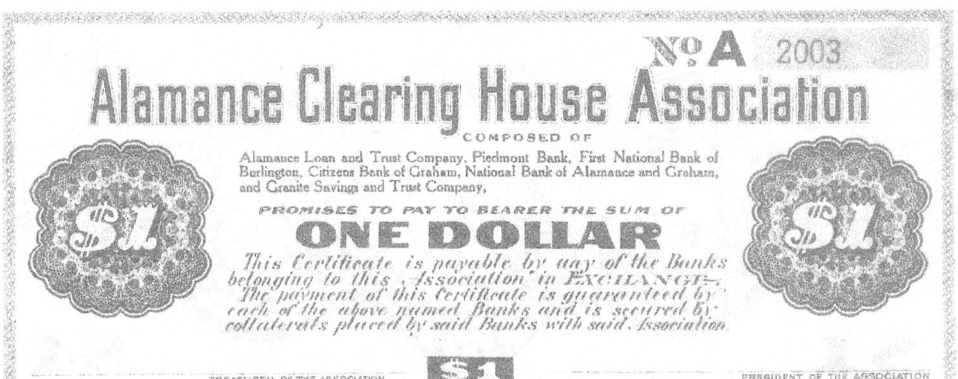

Alamance Clearing House Association

NC500-1. 1 Dollar ND (1907). Black. Back orange; state seal at center. (shown at 70%)
  d. Unissued, remainder. R4

Asheville

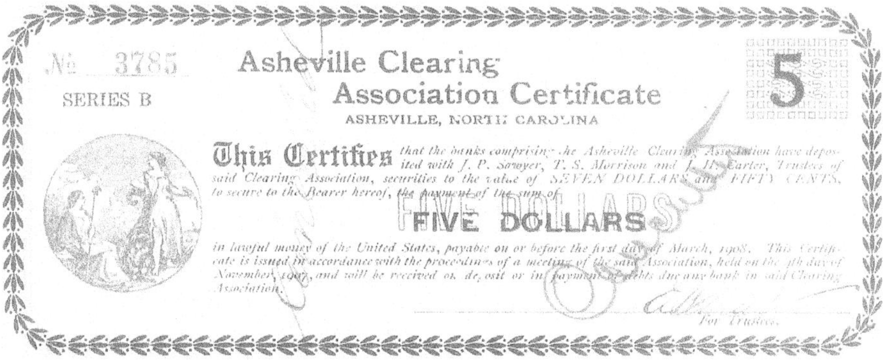

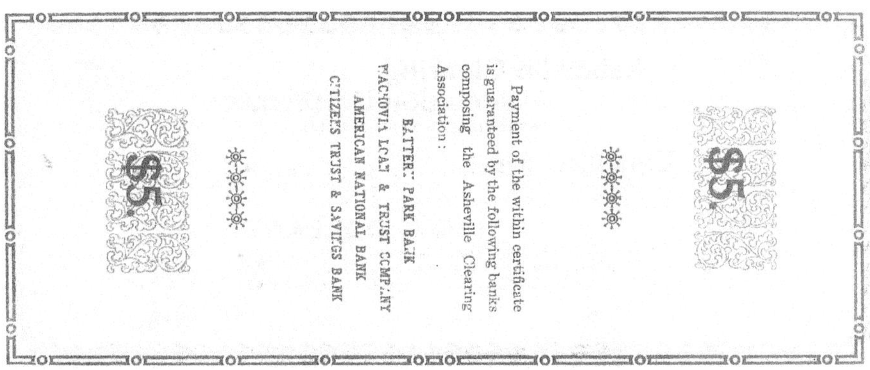

Asheville Clearing Association Certificate

NC525-1. 1 Dollar Nov. 4, 1907. Black and brown on gold paper. State seal at left. List of member banks on back. Series A. (shown at 65%)
  a. Issued, not cancelled. R5
  b. Issued, cancelled. R5

NC525-5. 5 Dollars Nov. 4, 1907. Black and brown on light blue paper. As above. Series B.
  b. Issued, cancelled. R5

Greensboro

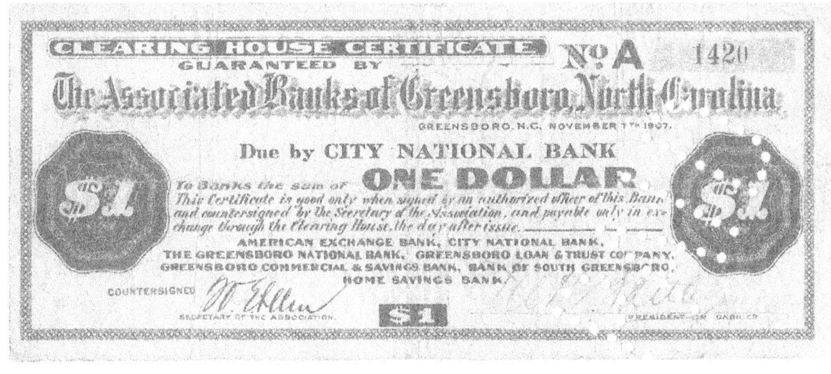

City National Bank/ Associated Banks of Greensboro, North Carolina

NC550-1. 1 Dollar Clearing House Certificate Nov. 7, 1907. Black. Text, "Guaranteed by the Associated Banks of Greensboro, North Carolina." Back brown; ornate design. (shown at 60%)
- a. Issued, not cancelled. **R5**
- b. Issued, cancelled. **VG, 150. VF, 300.**

NC550-2. 2 Dollars Nov. 7, 1907. As above.
- b. Issued, cancelled. **VG, 150. VF, 300.**

NC550-5. 5 Dollars Nov. 7, 1907. As above.
- b. Issued, cancelled. **VG, 150. VF, 300.**

NC550-10. 10 Dollars Nov. 7, 1907. As above.
- b. Issued, cancelled. **VG, 150. VF, 300.**

Greensboro Loan & Trust Company

A. Plain Design — Uniface

NC575-1. 1 Dollar Clearing House Certificate Nov. 3, 1907. Black on green paper. Embossed seal at right. "Guaranteed by all the banks of Greensboro." (shown at 60%)
- a. Issued, not cancelled. **R5**

B. Ornate Design — Two-sided

NC600-1. 1 Dollar Nov. 7, 1907. Black. Back brown; design and text as NC550.
  a. Issued, not cancelled. **R5**
  b. Issued, cancelled. **VG, 150. VF, 300.**
NC600-2. 2 Dollars Nov. 7, 1907. As above.
  b. Issued, cancelled. **VG, 150. VF, 300.**
NC600-5. 5 Dollars Nov. 7, 1907. As above.
  b. Issued, cancelled. **R3**
NC600-10. 10 Dollars Nov. 7, 1907. As above.
  b. Issued, cancelled. **R4**
NC600-20. 20 Dollars Nov. 7, 1907. As above.
  b. Issued, cancelled. **R5**

Winston-Salem

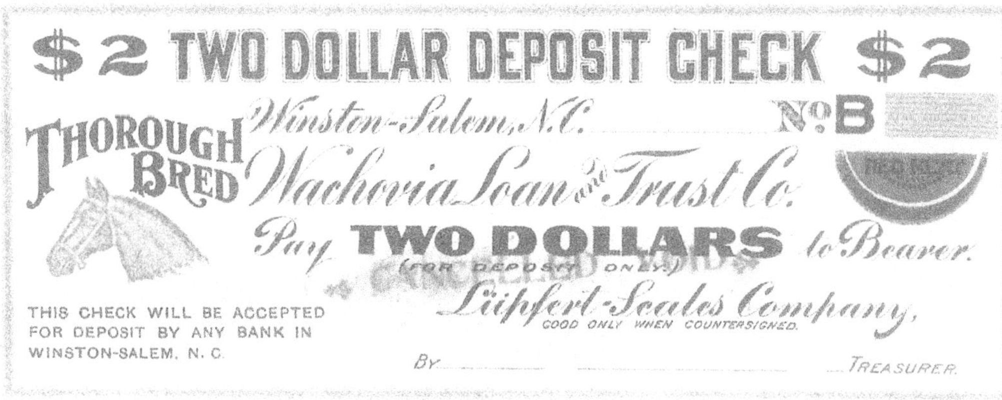

Lupfert Scales Company/Wachovia Loan and Trust Co.

NC625-2. 2 Dollars Deposit Check ND (1907). Black text, green border, red horse's head at left, symbol at right. Uniface. (shown at 75%)
  c. Unissued, cancelled. **R5**

Peoples National Bank

A. Cashier's Check
NC650-10. 10 Dollars Nov. 2, 12, 1907. (list)
  b. Issued, cancelled. **R5**
  d. Unissued, remainder. **R5**

B. Certificate of Deposit

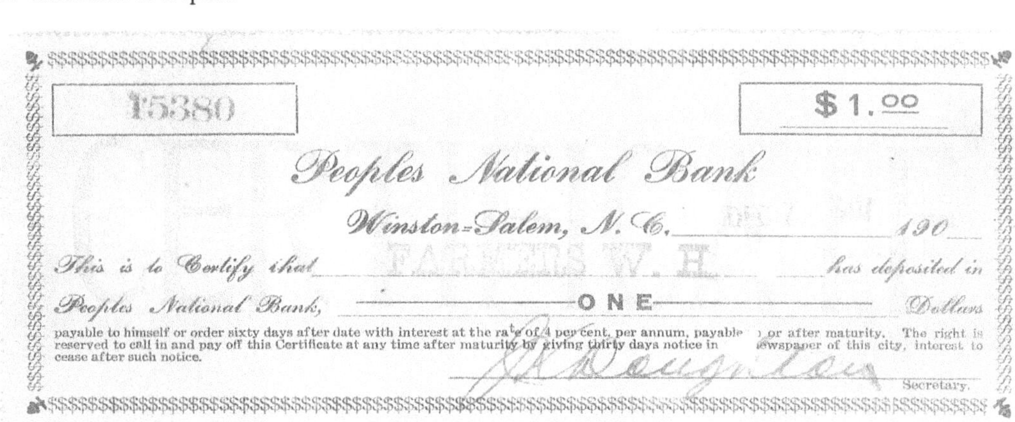

NC675-1. 1 Dollar Dec. 7, 12, 1907 (stamped date). Black. Large word CERTIFICATE across center in yellow-green. Back yellow-green. (shown at 76%)
- b. Issued, cancelled. R5
- c. Unissued, cancelled. R3

NC675-2. 2 Dollars 190_ (1907). As above.
- c. Unissued, cancelled. R5

NC675-5. 5 Dollars 190_ (1907). As above.
- c. Unissued, cancelled. R5

NC675-10. 10 Dollars Dec. 12, 1907 (stamped date). As above.
- b. Issued, cancelled. R5
- c. Unissued, cancelled. R5

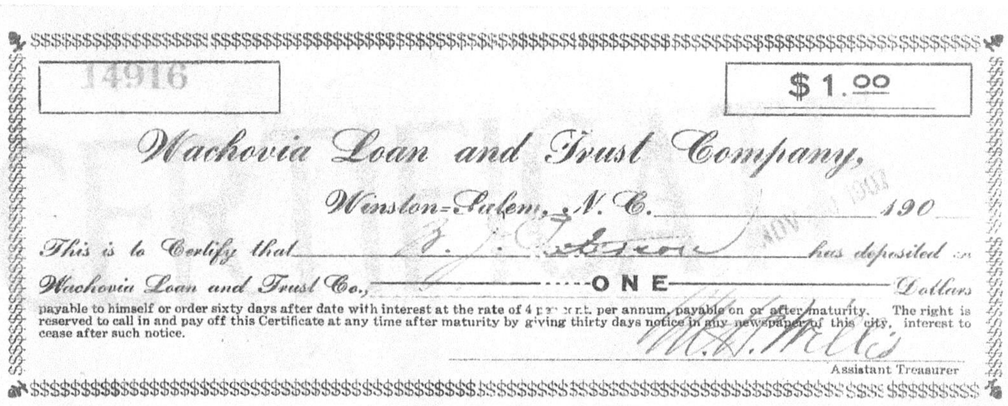

Wachovia Loan and Trust Company

NC700-1. 1 Dollar (certificate of deposit) Nov. 20, 1907 (stamped date). Black. Large word CERTIFICATE across center in light brown. Back brown. (shown at 76%)
- b. Issued, cancelled. R5

NC700-2. 2 Dollars Nov. 7, 30, 1907 (stamped dates). As above.
- b. Issued, cancelled. R5

NC700-5. 5 Dollars (1907). (list)
- c. Unissued, cancelled. R5

NC700-10. 10 Dollars (1907). (list)
- c. Unissued, cancelled. R5

North Dakota

Fargo

Clearing House Association of the City of Fargo

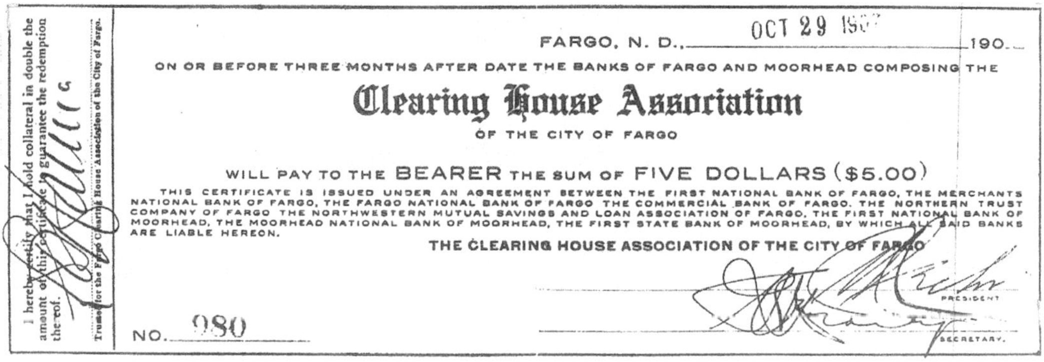
I hereby certify that I hold collateral in double the amount of this certificate to guarantee the redemption thereof.
Trustee for the Fargo Clearing House Association of the City of Fargo.
FARGO, N. D., OCT 29 1907 190_
ON OR BEFORE THREE MONTHS AFTER DATE THE BANKS OF FARGO AND MOORHEAD COMPOSING THE
Clearing House Association
OF THE CITY OF FARGO
WILL PAY TO THE BEARER THE SUM OF FIVE DOLLARS ($5.00)
THIS CERTIFICATE IS ISSUED UNDER AN AGREEMENT BETWEEN THE FIRST NATIONAL BANK OF FARGO, THE MERCHANTS NATIONAL BANK OF FARGO, THE FARGO NATIONAL BANK OF FARGO THE COMMERCIAL BANK OF FARGO. THE NORTHERN TRUST COMPANY OF FARGO THE NORTHWESTERN MUTUAL SAVINGS AND LOAN ASSOCIATION OF FARGO, THE FIRST NATIONAL BANK OF MOORHEAD, THE MOORHEAD NATIONAL BANK OF MOORHEAD, THE FIRST STATE BANK OF MOORHEAD, BY WHICH ALL SAID BANKS ARE LIABLE HEREON.
THE CLEARING HOUSE ASSOCIATION OF THE CITY OF FARGO
PRESIDENT
NO. 980
SECRETARY

ND500-5. 5 Dollars Oct. 29, 1907 (stamped date). (b/w) (shown at 63%)
b. Issued, cancelled. R5

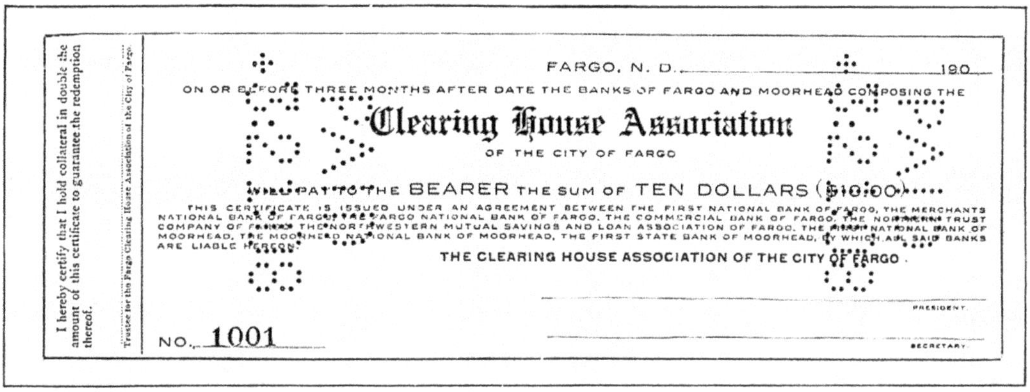
I hereby certify that I hold collateral in double the amount of this certificate to guarantee the redemption thereof.
Trustee for the Fargo Clearing House Association of the City of Fargo.
FARGO, N. D. 190_
ON OR BEFORE THREE MONTHS AFTER DATE THE BANKS OF FARGO AND MOORHEAD COMPOSING THE
Clearing House Association
OF THE CITY OF FARGO
WILL PAY TO THE BEARER THE SUM OF TEN DOLLARS ($10.00)
THIS CERTIFICATE IS ISSUED UNDER AN AGREEMENT BETWEEN THE FIRST NATIONAL BANK OF FARGO, THE MERCHANTS NATIONAL BANK OF FARGO, THE FARGO NATIONAL BANK OF FARGO, THE COMMERCIAL BANK OF FARGO. THE NORTHERN TRUST COMPANY OF FARGO THE NORTHWESTERN MUTUAL SAVINGS AND LOAN ASSOCIATION OF FARGO, THE FIRST NATIONAL BANK OF MOORHEAD, THE MOORHEAD NATIONAL BANK OF MOORHEAD, THE FIRST STATE BANK OF MOORHEAD, BY WHICH ALL SAID BANKS ARE LIABLE HEREON.
THE CLEARING HOUSE ASSOCIATION OF THE CITY OF FARGO.
PRESIDENT
NO. 1001
SECRETARY

ND500-10. 10 Dollars 190_ (1907). Black on yellow paper. (shown at 62%)
c. Unissued, cancelled. R5
d. Unissued, remainder. R5

ND500-20. 20 Dollars 190_ (1907). (list)
u. Unissued. SENC

ND500-100. 100 Dollars 190_ (1907). (b/w)
c. Unissued, cancelled. R5

Ohio

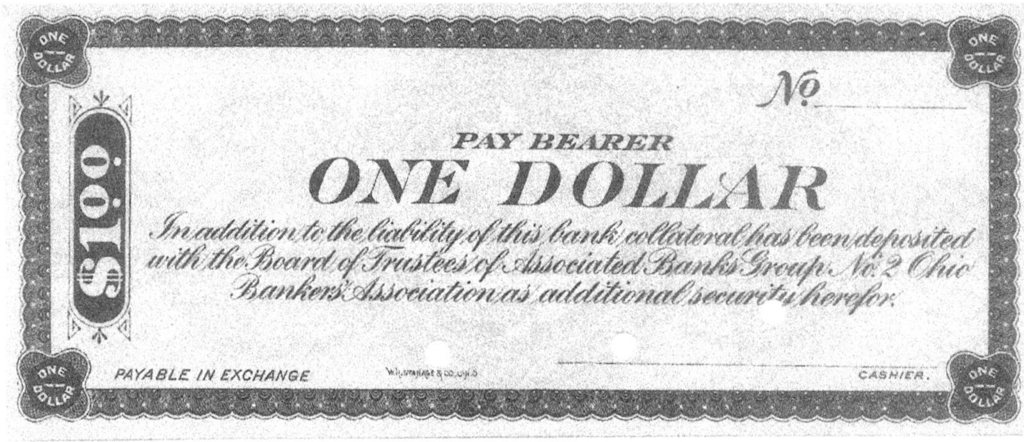

Associated Banks Group No. 2 Ohio Bankers Association

OH500-1. 1 Dollar (exchange certificate) ND (1907). Black on green underprint. Back orange; eagle's head at center, small beehive at left and cornucopia at right. Imprint: W.H. Stanage & Co. Cin.O. (shown at 72%)

c. Unissued, cancelled. VF, 20. AU, 45.
d. Unissued, remainder. VF, 20. AU, 45.

OH500-2. 2 Dollars ND (1907). As above.

d. Unissued, remainder. VF, 20. AU, 45.

OH500-5. 5 Dollars ND (1907). As above.

c. Unissued, cancelled. VF, 20. AU, 45.
d. Unissued, remainder. VF, 20. AU, 45.

OH500-10. 10 Dollars ND (1907). As above.

c. Unissued, cancelled. VF, 20. AU, 45.
f. Specimen. R4

Canton

The City National Bank

A. Cashier's Check

OH525-2. 2 Dollars (cashier's check) Nov. 11, 1907. (b/w)

c. Unissued, cancelled. R4
d. Unissued, remainder. R4

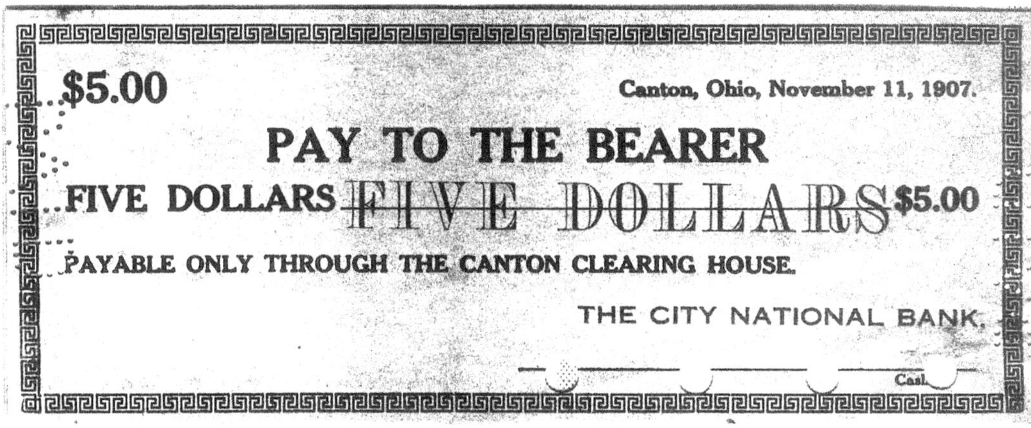

OH525-5. 5 Dollars Nov. 11, 1907. (b/w) (shown at 71%)
c. Unissued, cancelled. R4
OH525-10. 10 Dollars Nov. 11, 1907. (list)
c. Unissued, cancelled. R4

B. Payroll Check
OH530-5. 5 Dollars (1907). Black on pink paper. Uniface. Similar to OH600-5.
c. Unissued, cancelled. R4

The First National Bank

OH550-1. 1 Dollar (cashier's check) Nov. 11, 1907. Black and red on pink paper. Uniface.
c. Unissued, cancelled. **EF, 20. Unc., 50.**
d. Unissued, remainder. **EF, 20. Unc., 50.**
OH550-2. 2 Dollars Nov. 11, 1907. Black and orange on light tan paper. As above.
c. Unissued, cancelled. **EF, 20. Unc., 50.**
d. Unissued, remainder. **EF, 20. Unc., 50.**
OH550-5. 5 Dollars Nov. 11, 1907. Black and red on yellow paper. As above.
c. Unissued, cancelled. **EF, 20. Unc., 50.**
d. Unissued, remainder. **EF, 20. Unc., 50.**

OH550-10.A 10 Dollars Nov. 11, 1907. Black and red on blue paper. As above. (shown at 73%)
c. Unissued, cancelled. **EF, 20. Unc., 50.**
d. Unissued, remainder. **EF, 20. Unc., 50.**
OH550-10.B 10 Dollars Nov. 11, 1907. As above but yellow paper.
d. Unissued, remainder. **EF, 20. Unc., 50.**

THE GEORGE D. HARTER BANK

OH575-1. 1 Dollar (cashier's check) Nov. 11, 1907. Black and red on pink paper. As OH550-1. (shown at 71%)
d. Unissued, remainder. **EF, 25. Unc., 55.**
OH575-2. 2 Dollars Nov. 11. 1907. Black and orange on light tan paper. As above.
d. Unissued, remainder. **R3**
OH575-5. 5 Dollars Nov. 11, 1907. Black and red on yellow paper. As above.
d. Unissued, remainder. **R3**
OH575-10. 10 Dollars Nov. 11, 1907. Black and red on blue paper. As above.
b. Issued, cancelled. **R2**

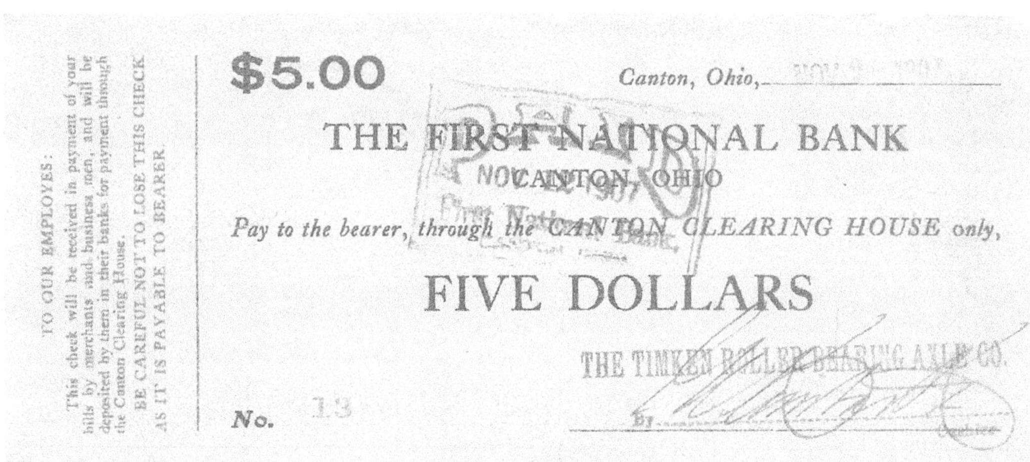

THE TIMKEN ROLLER BEARING AXLE CO./ FIRST NATIONAL BANK

OH600-5. 5 Dollars (payroll check) Nov. 9, 1907 (stamped date). Black on pink paper. Red text vertically at left. Uniface. (shown at 74%)
b. Issued, cancelled. **R1**

Cincinnati

AMERICAN NATIONAL BANK

OH625-2. 2 Dollars (cashier's check) Nov. 4, 1907. Black on blue underprint. Uniface. Imprint: The Strobridge Litho. Co. Cin. O.
a. Issued, not cancelled. **R3**

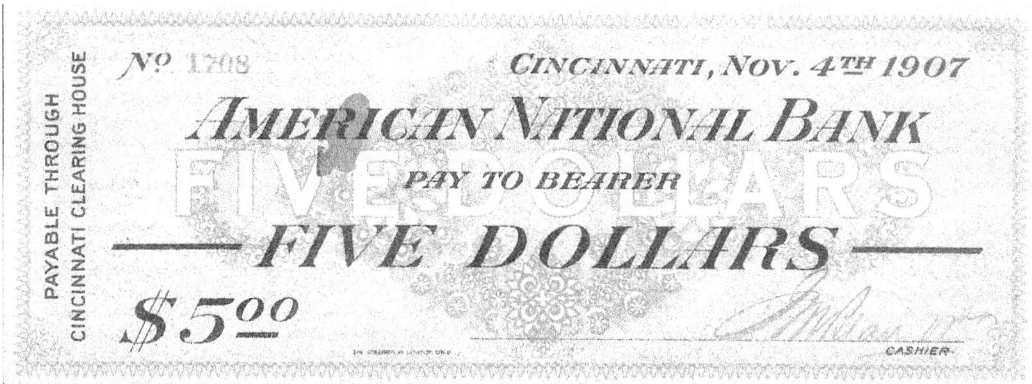

OH625-5. 5 Dollars Nov. 4, 1907. Black on green underprint. As above. (shown at 67%)
a. Issued, not cancelled. R3

Atlas National Bank

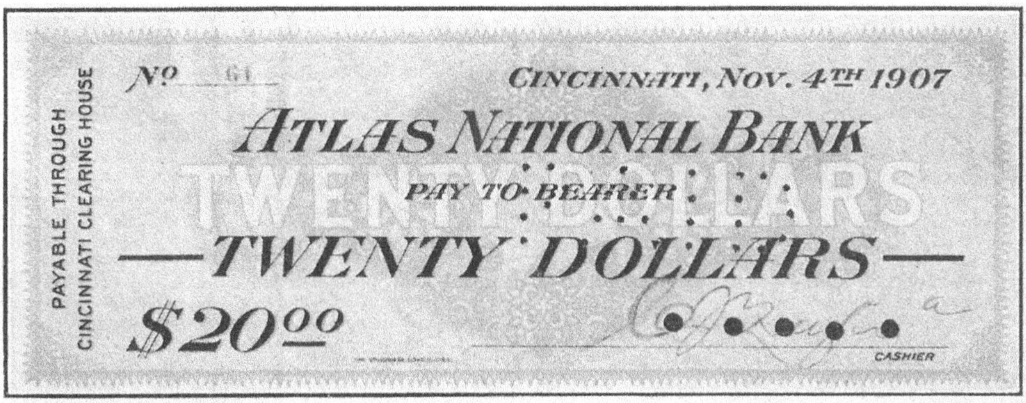

OH650-20. 20 Dollars (cashier's check) Nov. 4, 1907. Black on brown underprint. Design and imprint as above. (shown at 75%)
b. Issued, cancelled. R5

Citizens National Bank

OH675-2. 2 Dollars (cashier's check) Nov. 4, 1907. Black on blue underprint. Uniface. Imprint as OH625.
b. Issued, cancelled. R4
OH675-5. 5 Dollars Nov. 4, 1907. Black on green underprint. As above.
b. Issued, cancelled. R4

OH675-10. 10 Dollars Nov. 4, 1907. Black on light brown underprint. As above. (shown at 63%)
b. Issued, cancelled. R4
OH675-20. 20 Dollars Nov. 4, 1907. Black on gold underprint. As above.
b. Issued, cancelled. R4

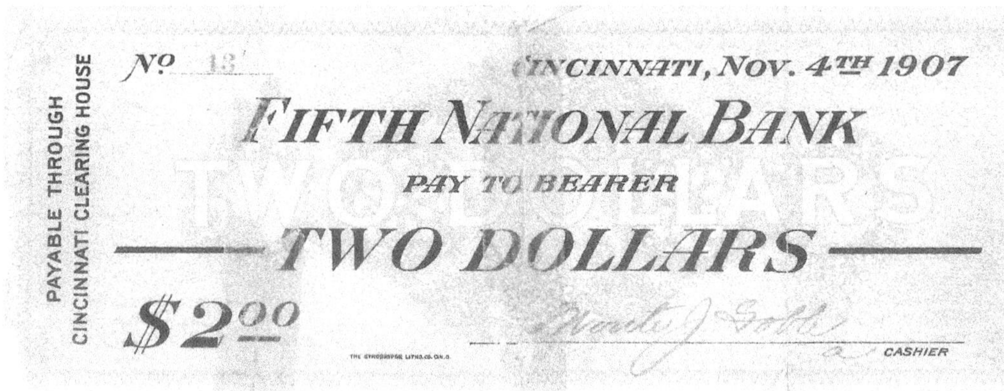

Fifth National Bank

OH700-2. 2 Dollars (cashier's check) Nov. 4, 1907. Black on blue underprint. Uniface. Imprint as OH625. (shown at 67%)
a. Issued, not cancelled. R4
b. Issued, cancelled. R4
OH700-5. 5 Dollars Nov. 4, 1907. Black on green underprint. As above.
b. Issued, cancelled. R4
OH700-10. 10 Dollars Nov. 4, 1907. Black on brown underprint, otherwise as above.
b. Issued, cancelled. R4
OH700-20. 20 Dollars Nov. 4, 1907. Black on orange underprint, otherwise as above.
b. Issued, cancelled. R4

First National Bank

OH725-2. 2 Dollars (cashier's check) Nov. 4, 1907. Black on light blue underprint. Imprint similar to OH625.
a. Issued, not cancelled. **VG, 100. VF, 250.**
b. Issued, cancelled. **VG, 50. VF, 90.**

OH725-5. 5 Dollars Nov. 4, 1907. Black on green underprint. As above. (shown at 68%)
b. Issued, cancelled. **VG, 50. VF, 90.**
OH725-10. 10 Dollars Nov. 4, 1907. Black on light brown underprint. As above.
b. Issued, cancelled. **VG, 60. VF, 100.**
OH725-20. 20 Dollars Nov. 4, 1907. Black on gold underprint. As above.
b. Issued, cancelled. **VG, 75. VF, 150.**

Fourth National Bank

OH735-2. 2 Dollars (cashier's check) Nov. 4, 1907. Black on light blue underprint. Uniface. Imprint as OH625. (shown at 75%)

a. Issued, not cancelled. R4

German National Bank

OH750-2. 2 Dollars (cashier's check) Nov. 4, 1907. Black on light green underprint. Uniface. Imprint as OH625.

b. Issued, cancelled. R4

OH750-5. 5 Dollars Nov. 4, 1907. Black on green underprint, otherwise as above. (shown at 68%)

b. Issued, cancelled. R4

OH750-20. 20 Dollars Nov. 4, 1907. Black on orange underprint, otherwise as above.

b. Issued, cancelled. R4

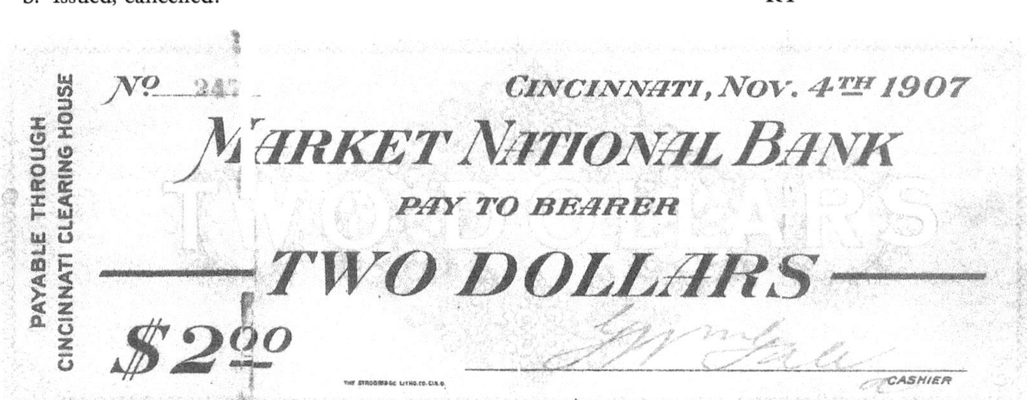

Market National Bank

OH775-2. 2 Dollars (cashier's check) Nov. 4, 1907. Black on light blue underprint. Imprint as OH625. (shown at 69%)
a. Issued, not cancelled. R4

OH775-5. 5 Dollars Nov. 4, 1907. Black on green underprint, otherwise as above.
b. Issued, cancelled. R4

Merchants National Bank

OH800-2. 2 Dollars (cashier's check) Nov. 4, 1907. Black on blue underprint. Uniface. Imprint as OH625.
a. Issued, not cancelled. R2
b. Issued, cancelled. R2

OH800-5. 5 Dollars Nov. 4, 1907. Black on green underprint, otherwise as above.
a. Issued, not cancelled. R2
b. Issued, cancelled. R2

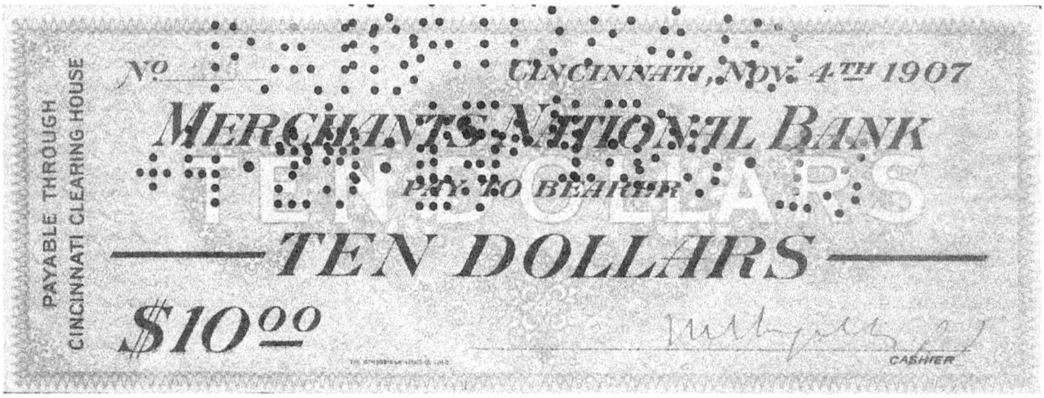

OH800-10. 10 Dollars Nov. 4, 1907. Black on light brown underprint, otherwise as above. (shown at 68%)
a. Issued, not cancelled. R3
b. Issued, cancelled. R3

OH800-20. 20 Dollars Nov. 4, 1907. Black on orange underprint, otherwise as above.
a. Issued, not cancelled. R4
b. Issued, cancelled. R4

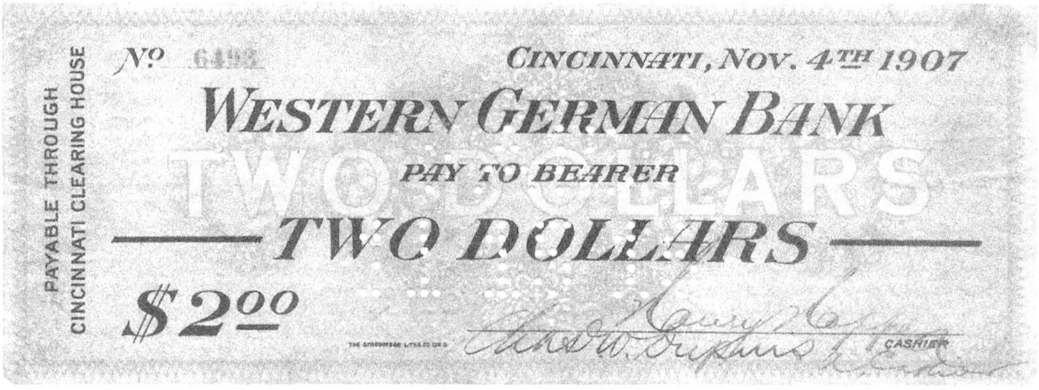

Western German Bank

OH825-2. 2 Dollars (cashier's check) Nov. 4, 1907. Black on light green underprint. Uniface. Imprint as OH625. (shown at 67%)
b. Issued, cancelled. R4

Cleveland

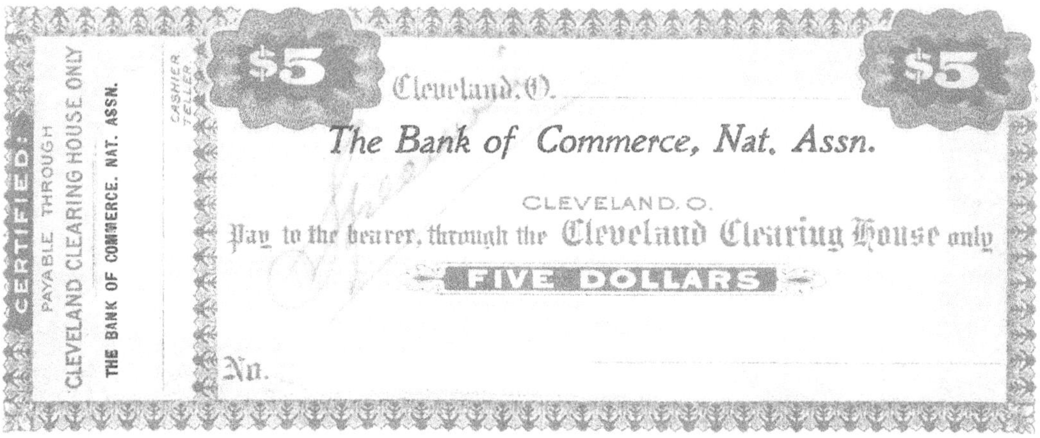

THE BANK OF COMMERCE, NAT. ASSN.

OH850-5. 5 Dollars Certified Check ND (1907). Red. Back text about negotiability and loss of check in six languages (English, German, Italian, Czech, Polish, Hungarian). Imprint: The Morgan Litho. Co. Cleveland, O. (shown at 78%)
c. Unissued, cancelled (handwritten "Specimen" across face). **R5**
OH850-10. 10 Dollars ND (1907). Green. As above.
c. Unissued, cancelled as above. **R5**

CLEVELAND CLEARING HOUSE ASSOCIATION

Five of the clearing house member banks are known to have produced panic scrip in 1907: Nos. 3, 4, 8, 10 and 15. All colors were the same for each denomination.

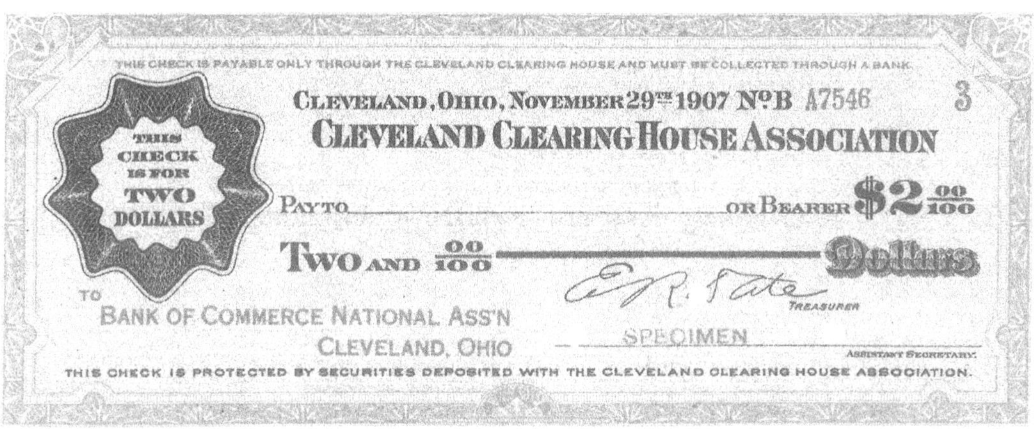

A. No. 3: Bank of Commerce National Ass'n
OH875-2. 2 Dollars Nov. 29, 1907. Black and blue. One line of text at top, bank number at upper right and issuing bank's name at lower left in red. One line of text on back. Imprint: Western Bank Note and Engraving Company Chicago. (shown at 64%)
f. Specimen. **Unc., 250.**
OH875-5. 5 Dollars Nov. 29, 1907. Black and brown. As above.
f. Specimen. **Unc., 250.**
OH875-10. 10 Dollars Nov. 29, 1907. Black and orange. As above.
f. Specimen. **Unc., 250.**

B. No. 4: Central National Bank
OH890-1. 1 Dollar Nov. 29, 1907. Black and green. As above.
a. Issued, not cancelled. Pay to The Citizens Savings & Trust Co. **R3**
f. Specimen. **Unc., 250.**

OH890-2. 2 Dollars Nov. 29, 1907. Black and blue. As above.
f. Specimen. **Unc., 250.**

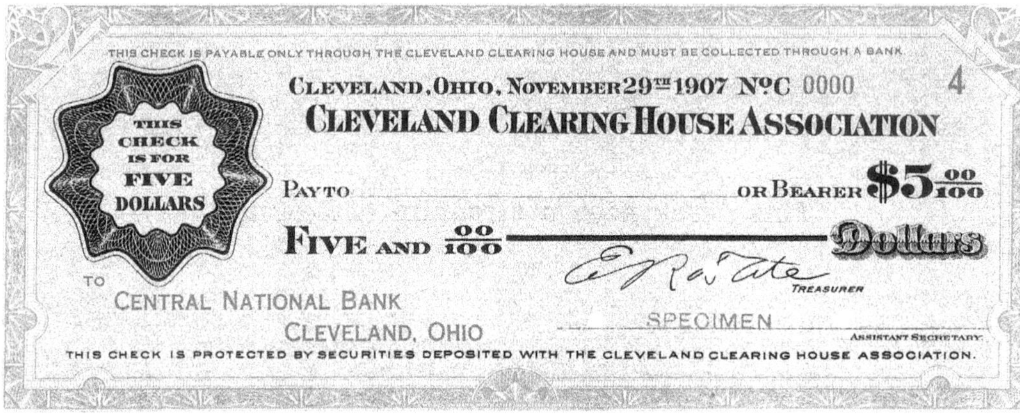

OH890-5. 5 Dollars Nov. 29, 1907. Black and brown. As above. (shown at 64%)
f. Specimen. **Unc., 250.**
OH890-10. 10 Dollars Nov. 29, 1907. Black and orange. As above.
f. Specimen. **Unc., 250.**
u. Issued. **SENC**

C. No. 8: National Commercial Bank
OH900-1. 1 Dollar Nov. 29, 1907. Black and green. As above.
a. Issued, not cancelled. **R4**
f. Specimen. **Unc., 250.**
OH900-2. 2 Dollars Nov. 29, 1907. Black and blue. As above.
f. Specimen. **Unc., 250.**
OH900-5. 5 Dollars Nov. 29, 1907. Black and brown. As above.
f. Specimen. **Unc., 250.**

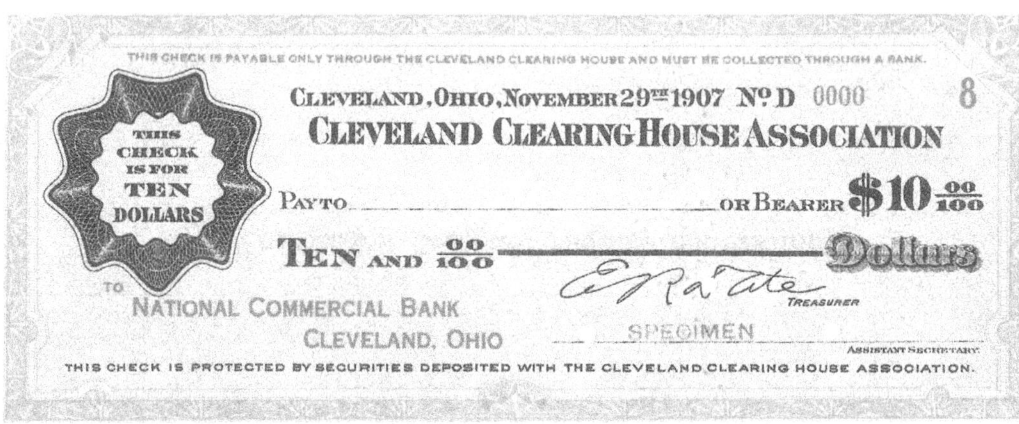

OH900-10. 10 Dollars Nov. 29, 1907. Black and orange. As above. (shown at 64%)
f. Specimen. **Unc., 250.**

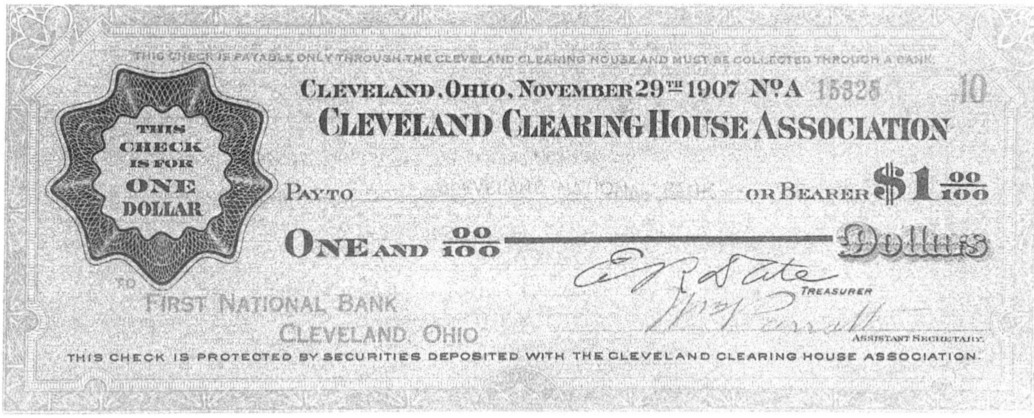

D. No. 10: First National Bank
OH925-1. 1 Dollar Nov. 29, 1907. Black and green. As above. (shown at 64%)
a. Issued, not cancelled. **R5**
OH925-2. 2 Dollars Nov. 29, 1907. Black and blue. As above.
f. Specimen. **Unc., 250.**
OH925-5. 5 Dollars Nov. 29, 1907. Black and brown. As above.
f. Specimen. **Unc., 250.**
OH925-10. 10 Dollars Nov. 29, 1907. Black and orange. As above.
f. Specimen. **Unc., 250.**

E. No. 15: Union National Bank
OH950-1. 1 Dollar Nov. 29, 1907. Black and green. As above.
f. Specimen. **Unc., 250.**
OH950-2. 2 Dollars Nov. 29, 1907. Black and blue. As above.
a. Issued, not cancelled. **R5**
OH950-5. 5 Dollars Nov. 29, 1907. Black and brown. As above.
a. Issued, not cancelled. Pay to Guardian Savings & Trust Co. **R5**
f. Specimen. **Unc., 250.**
OH950-10. 10 Dollars Nov. 29, 1907. Black and orange. As above.
f. Specimen. **Unc., 250.**

The Cleveland Trust Company

OH975-1. 1 Dollar Certified Check ND (1907). Black and red on blue paper. Uniface. (shown at 62%)
c. Unissued, cancelled. **R4**

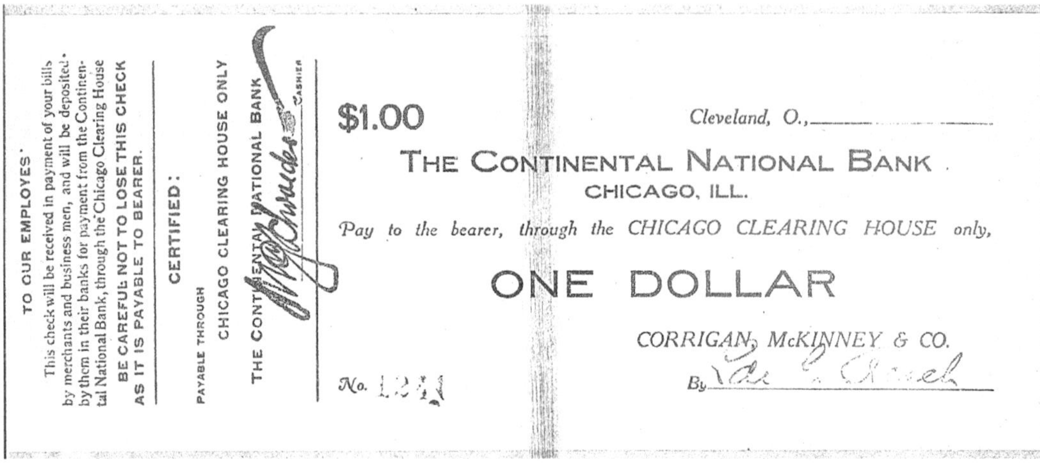

Corrigan, McKinney & Co./The Continental National Bank

OH1000-1. 1 Dollar Certified Check ND (1907). (b/w) (shown at 64%)
a. Issued, not cancelled. R5

Depositors Savings and Trust

OH1010-1. 1 Dollar Money Order Nov. 8, 1907. Black on blue underprint. Uniface.
a. Issued, not cancelled. R5
OH1010-1000. 1,000 Dollars ND (1907). As above.
f. Specimen. R5

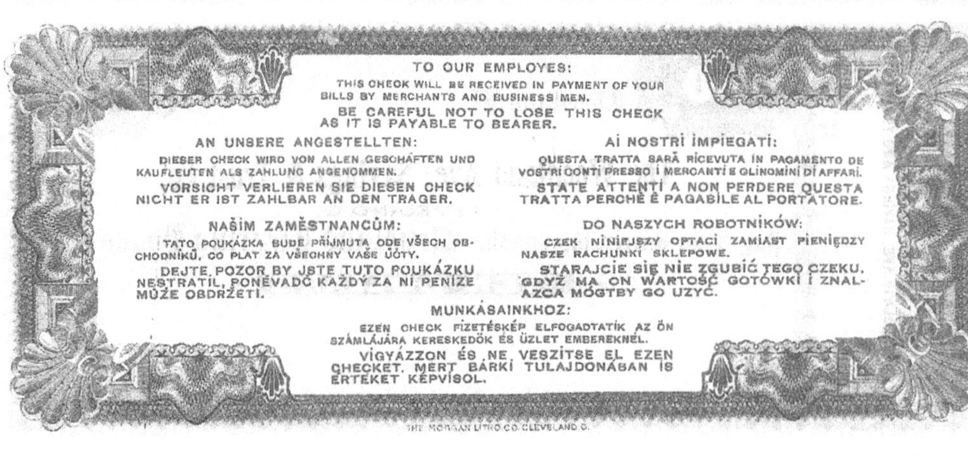

The Dime Savings & Banking Co.

OH1025-1. 1 Dollar Certified Check ND (1907). Black. Text on back similar to OH850. Imprint: The Morgan Litho. Co. Cleveland, O. (shown at 75%)
c. Unissued, cancelled. **R5**
OH1025-2. 2 Dollars ND (1907). Blue, with black bank name. As above.
c. Unissued, cancelled. **R5**
OH1025-5. 5 Dollars ND (1907). Red, with black bank name. As above.
c. Unissued, cancelled. **R5**
OH1025-10. 10 Dollars ND (1907). Green, with black bank name. Back as above.
c. Unissued, cancelled. **R5**

The First National Bank

A. Plain Design

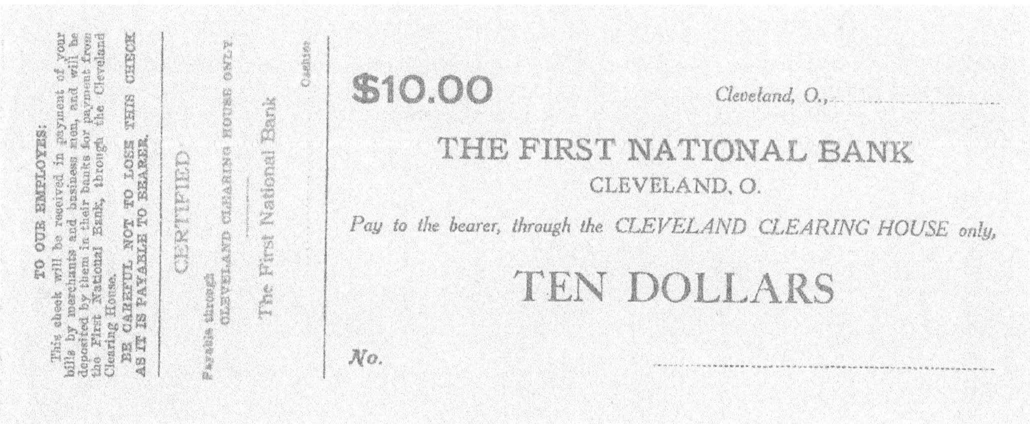

OH1050-10. 10 Dollars Certified Check ND (1907). Black on green paper. Uniface. (shown at 63%)
d. Unissued, remainder. **R4**

B. Design with Corner Guilloches

OH1075-2. 2 Dollars Certified Check ND (1907). Blue, with black bank name. Design and imprint similar to OH850. (shown at 75%)
d. Unissued, remainder. **R5**
OH1075-5. 5 Dollars ND (Dec. 8, 1907, unofficial date). Red, with black bank name. As above.
d. Unissued, remainder. **R5**
OH1075-10. 10 Dollars ND (unofficial date as above). Green, with black bank name. As above.
d. Unissued, remainder. **R5**

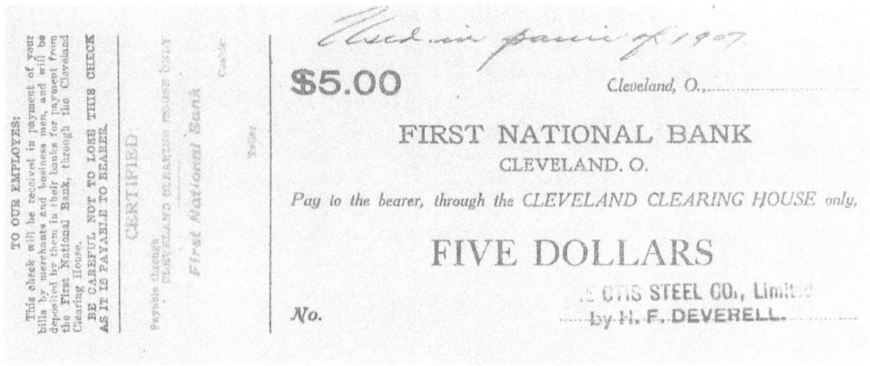

THE OTIS STEEL CO., LIMITED/FIRST NATIONAL BANK

OH1100-5. 5 Dollars Certified Check ND (1907). Black on pink paper. Uniface. (shown at 55%)
d. Unissued, remainder. R5

OH1100-10. 10 Dollars ND (1907). Black on blue paper. As above.
d. Unissued, remainder. R5

THE UNION NATIONAL BANK

A. Plain Design

OH1112-5. 5 Dollars Certified Check ND (1907). Similar to OH1100. (b/w) (shown at 55%)
c. Unissued, cancelled. R5

OH1112-10. 10 Dollars ND (1907). As above. (b/w)
c. Unissued, cancelled. R5

B. Design with Corner Guilloches

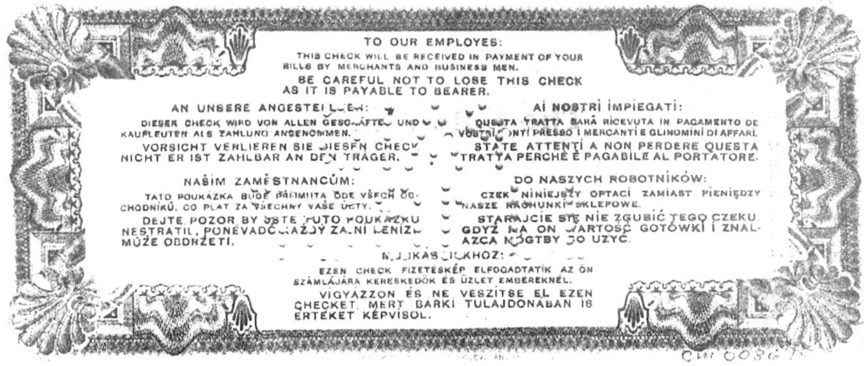

OH1115-5. 5 Dollars ND (1907). Similar to OH850. (b/w) (shown at 66%)
c. Unissued, cancelled. **R5**

THE WOODLAND AVE. SAVINGS & TRUST CO.

OH1125-5. 5 Dollars Certified Check ND (1907). Red, with black bank name. Similar to OH850. (shown at 68%)
c. Unissued, cancelled. **R5**
OH1125-10. 10 Dollars ND (1907). Green, with black bank name. As above.
d. Unissued, remainder. **R5**

Columbus

A clearing house loan certificate is believed to have been issued. No specifics are known at present.

East Liverpool

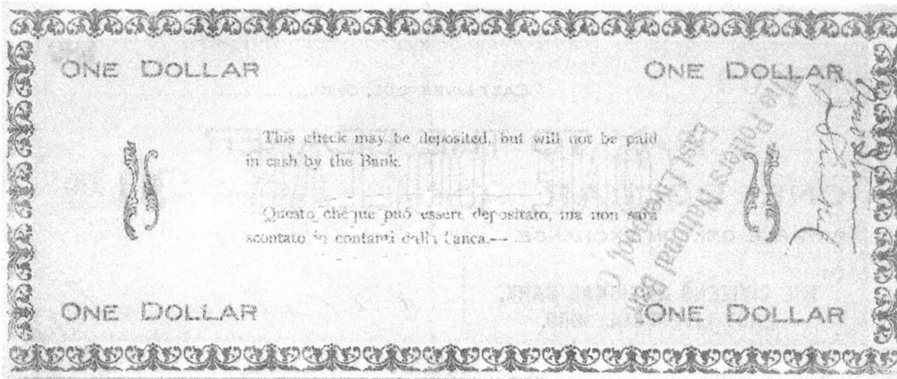

The Citizens National Bank

OH1175-1. 1 Dollar (pay check) ND (1907). Black on light tan underprint. Text on back about negotiability in two languages, English and Italian. (shown at 63%)
c. Unissued, cancelled. **R4**
OH1175-2. 2 Dollars ND (1907). Black on green underprint. As above.
c. Unissued, cancelled. **R4**
OH1175-5. 5 Dollars ND (1907). Black on gray underprint. As above.
c. Unissued, cancelled. **R4**

OH1175-10. 10 Dollars Nov. 30, 1907 (stamped date). Black on blue underprint. (shown at 63%)
b. Issued, cancelled. **R4**
OH1175-20. 20 Dollars ND (1907). Black on orange underprint.
c. Unissued, cancelled. **R4**

Dollar Savings Bank

OH1200-1. 1 Dollar (payroll check) ND (1907). (list)
u. Unissued. **SENC**
OH1200-5. 5 Dollars ND (1907). (list)
u. Unissued. **SENC**

First National Bank

OH1225-1. 1 Dollar (payroll check) ND (1907). (list)
u. Unissued. **SENC**
OH1225-2. 2 Dollars ND (1907). (list)
u. Unissued. **SENC**
OH1225-5. 5 Dollars ND (1907). (list)
u. Unissued. **SENC**

OH1225-10. 10 Dollars ND (1907). (list)
u. Unissued. SENC
OH1225-20. 20 Dollars ND (1907). (list)
u. Unissued. SENC

Elyria

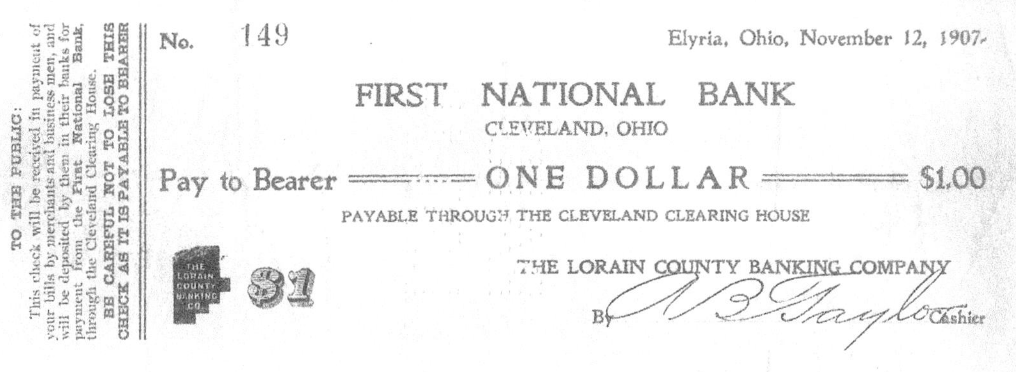
TO THE PUBLIC: This check will be received in payment of your bills by merchants and business men, and will be deposited by them in their banks for payment from the First National Bank, through the Cleveland Clearing House. BE CAREFUL NOT TO LOSE THIS CHECK AS IT IS PAYABLE TO BEARER

No. 149 Elyria, Ohio, November 12, 1907

FIRST NATIONAL BANK
CLEVELAND, OHIO

Pay to Bearer ONE DOLLAR $1.00

PAYABLE THROUGH THE CLEVELAND CLEARING HOUSE

THE LORAIN COUNTY BANKING CO. $1

THE LORAIN COUNTY BANKING COMPANY
By A B Gaylord Cashier

The Lorain County Banking Company/ First National Bank

OH1250-1. 1 Dollar (cashier's check) Nov. 12, 1907. Blue and black. Uniface. (shown at 66%)
b. Issued, cancelled. R5

The Savings Deposit Bank & Trust Company/ Union National Bank

OH1275-1. 1 Dollar (cashier's check) Nov. 11, 1907. Black on blue paper. Embossed seal at left. Uniface.
a. Issued, not cancelled. R3
OH1275-2. 2 Dollars Nov. 11, 1907. As above.
b. Issued, cancelled. R2
OH1275-3.A 3 Dollars Nov. 11, 1907. As above.
a. Issued, not cancelled. R4
b. Issued, cancelled. R4

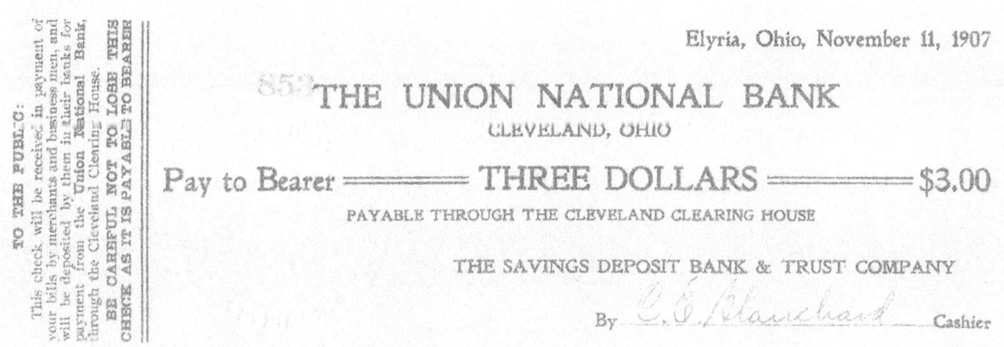
TO THE PUBLIC: This check will be received in payment of your bills by merchants and business men, and will be deposited by them in their banks for payment from the Union National Bank, through the Cleveland Clearing House. BE CAREFUL NOT TO LOSE THIS CHECK AS IT IS PAYABLE TO BEARER

Elyria, Ohio, November 11, 1907

THE UNION NATIONAL BANK
CLEVELAND, OHIO

Pay to Bearer THREE DOLLARS $3.00

PAYABLE THROUGH THE CLEVELAND CLEARING HOUSE

THE SAVINGS DEPOSIT BANK & TRUST COMPANY
By C. E. Blanchard Cashier

OH1275-3.B 3 Dollars Nov. 11, 1907. As above, but on green paper. (shown at 66%)
a. Issued, not cancelled. R4
OH1275-5. 5 Dollars Nov. 11, 1907. As above, blue paper.
b. Issued, cancelled. R4

Hamilton

Miami Valley National Bank

OH1300-1. 1 Dollar (cashier's check) Nov. 9, 1907. Black on blue underprint. Uniface. Imprint: The Strobridge Litho. Co. Cin. O.
b. Issued, cancelled. **R5**
OH1300-2. 2 Dollars Nov. 9, 1907. Black on olive green underprint. As above.
b. Issued, cancelled. **R5**
OH1300-5. 5 Dollars Nov. 9, 1907. Black on green underprint. As above.
b. Issued, cancelled. **R5**
OH1300-10. 10 Dollars Nov. 9. 1907. Black on brown underprint. As above.
b. Issued, cancelled. **R5**

Second National Bank

OH1325-1. 1 Dollar (cashier's check) Nov. 9, 1907. Design and imprint similar to OH1300. (shown at 57%)
a. Issued, not cancelled. **R5**

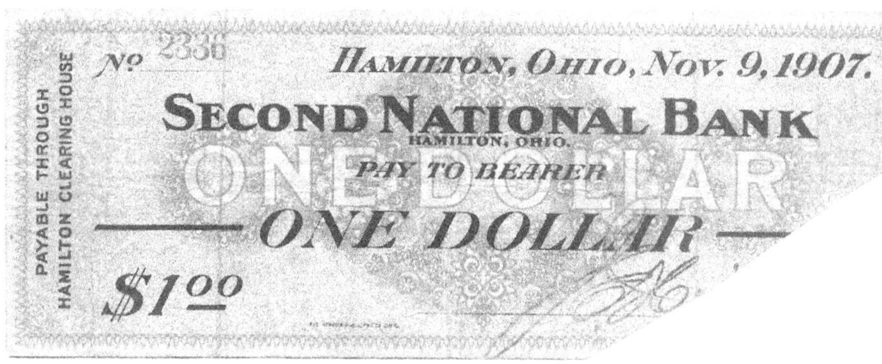

b1. Issued, cancelled (most by lower right corner removal). (shown at 60%) **VG, 25. VF, 45.**

b2. Issued, cancelled, with perforations. (shown at 64%) **VG, 25. VF, 45.**
OH1325-2. 2 Dollars Nov. 9, 1907. Black on olive green underprint. As above.
b. Issued, cancelled by corner removal. **VG, 25. VF, 45.**
OH1325-5. 5 Dollars Nov. 9, 1907. Black on green underprint. As above.
b. Issued, cancelled as above. **VG, 25. VF, 45.**
OH1325-10. 10 Dollars Nov. 9, 1907. Black on brown underprint. As above.
b. Issued, cancelled as above. **VG, 25. VF, 45.**
NOTE: Sets Nos. 1 and 2 are cancelled but without removal of lower right corner. (See OH1325-1. b1 above.)

Lewisburg

Moore's Cheery Study

OH1350-.15 15 Cents Dec. 1, 1907 (hand dated). Black on pale blue guilloche, brown paper. Uniface. Smaller size.
a. Issued, not cancelled. **EF, 15. Unc., 20.**

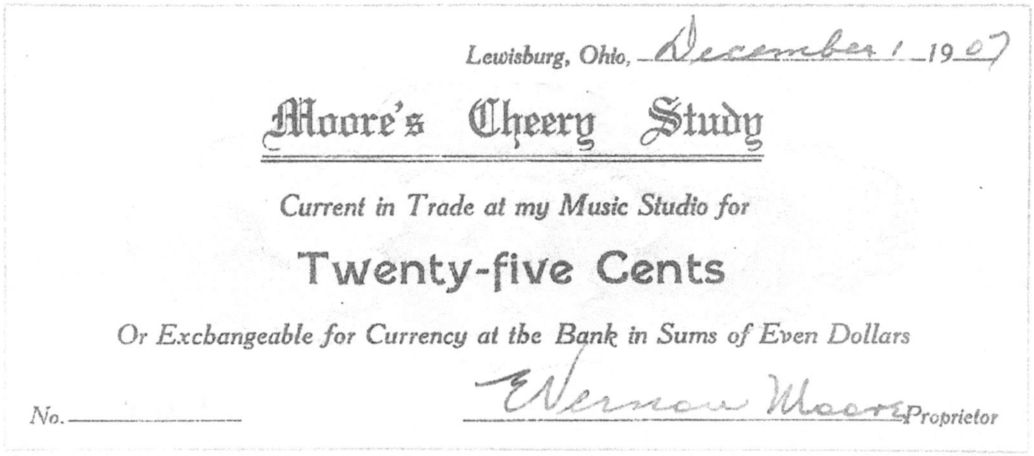

OH1350-.25 25 Cents Dec. 1, 1907 (hand dated). As above, but green underprint and white paper. (shown at 90%)
a. Issued, not cancelled. **EF, 20. Unc., 25.**

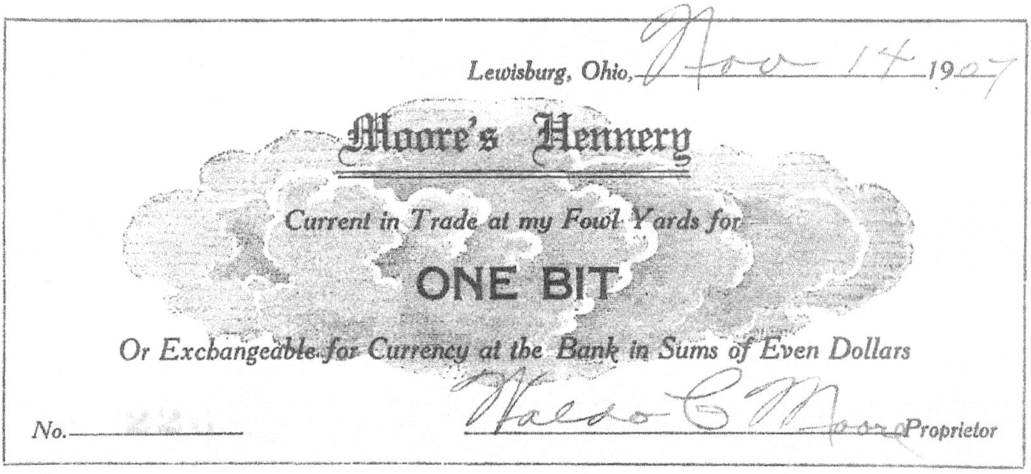

Moore's Hennery

OH1375-1.A 1 Bit Nov. 14, 1907 (hand dated). Black on purple guilloche. Uniface. Smaller size. (shown at 90%)
a. Issued, not cancelled. **EF, 20. Unc., 25.**

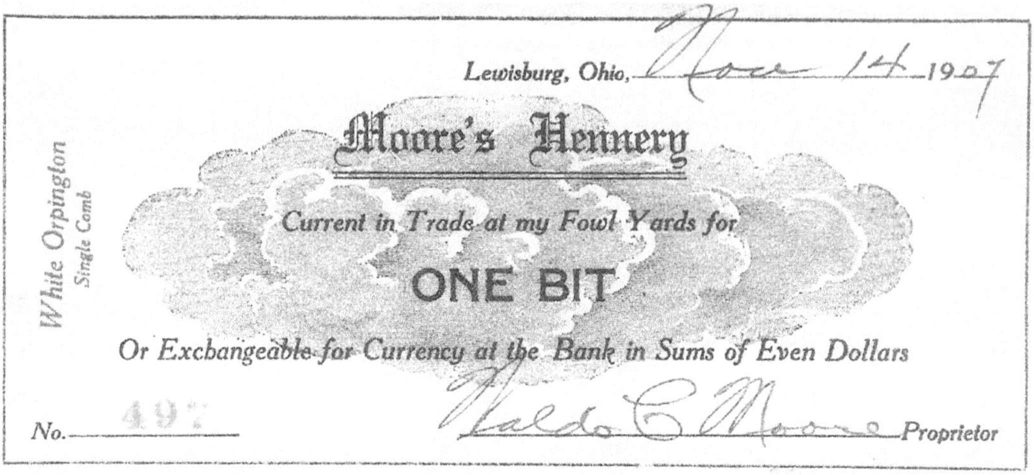

OH1375-1.B 1 Bit Nov. 14, 1907. As above, but with two lines of vertical red text at left. (shown at 90%)
a. Issued, not cancelled. **EF, 20. Unc., 25.**

NOTE: Waldo C. Moore, signer of some of the above notes, went on to become president of the American Numismatic Association in 1919. He also issued two sets of Lewisburg depression scrip in 1933.

Lorain

Lorain Clearing House Association

Three of the clearing house member banks are known to have issued panic scrip in 1907: Nos. 2, 3 and 5. All colors are the same for each denomination.

A. No. 2: The City Bank Company

OH1400-1. 1 Dollar Dec. 20, 1907. Black and purple. One line of text at top, bank number at upper right and issuing bank's name at lower left in red. One line of text on back. Imprint: Western Bank Note & Eng. Co. Chicago.
f. Specimen. **R5**

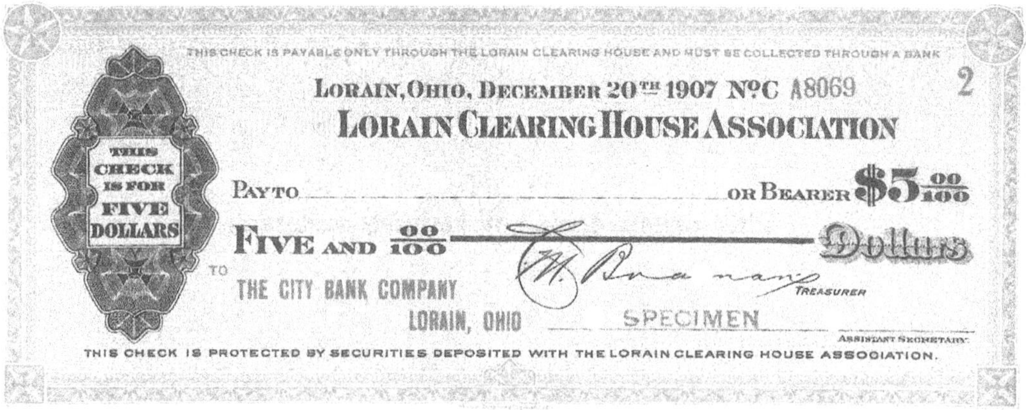

OH1400-5. 5 Dollars Dec. 20, 1907. Black and green. As above. (shown at 63%)
f. Specimen. **R5**

OH1400-10. 10 Dollars Dec. 20, 1907. Black and blue. As above.
f. Specimen. **R5**

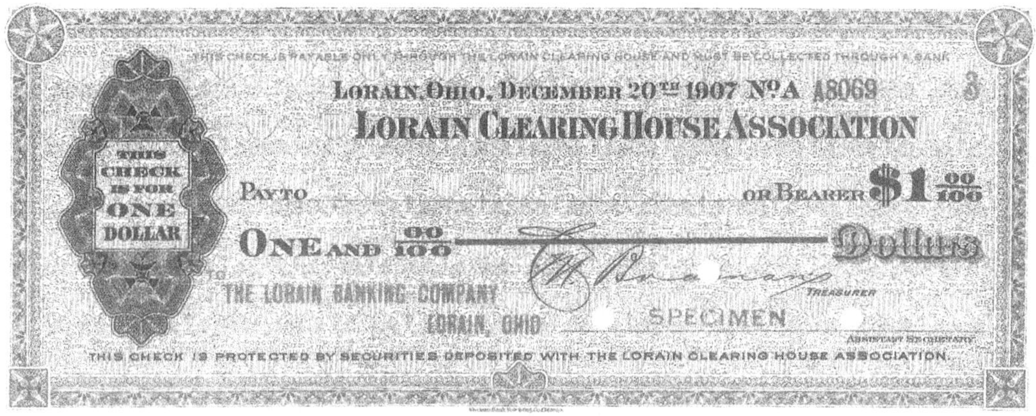

B. No. 3: The Lorain Banking Company
OH1425-1. 1 Dollar Dec. 20, 1907. Black and purple. As above. (shown at 63%)
f. Specimen. R5
OH1425-2. 2 Dollars Dec. 20, 1907. Black and red. As above.
f. Specimen. R5
OH1425-5. 5 Dollars Dec. 20, 1907. Black and green. As above.
f. Specimen. R5

C. No. 5: The Pennfield Bank
OH1450-1. 1 Dollar Dec. 20, 1907. Black and purple. As above.
f. Specimen. R5
OH1450-2. 2 Dollars Dec. 20, 1907. Black and red. As above.
f. Specimen. R5
OH1450-10. 10 Dollars Dec. 20, 1907. Black and blue. As above.
f. Specimen. R5

Portsmouth

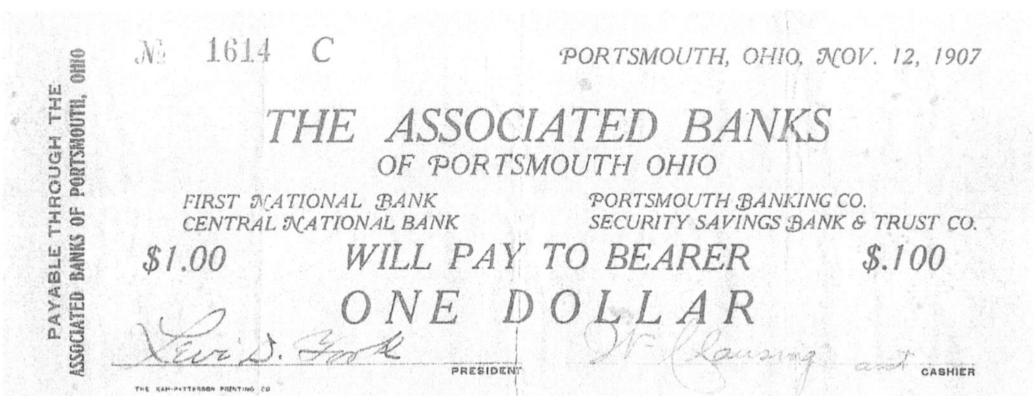

The Associated Banks of Portsmouth Ohio

OH1475-1. 1 Dollar Clearing House Certificate Nov. 12, 1907. Black on light green paper. Four banks named at center. Imprint: The Kan-Patterson Printing Co. (shown at 68%)
a. Issued, not cancelled. R5

NOTE: This piece contains a printing error showing the denomination as $1.00 at left, and $.100 with misplaced decimal point at right.

Youngstown

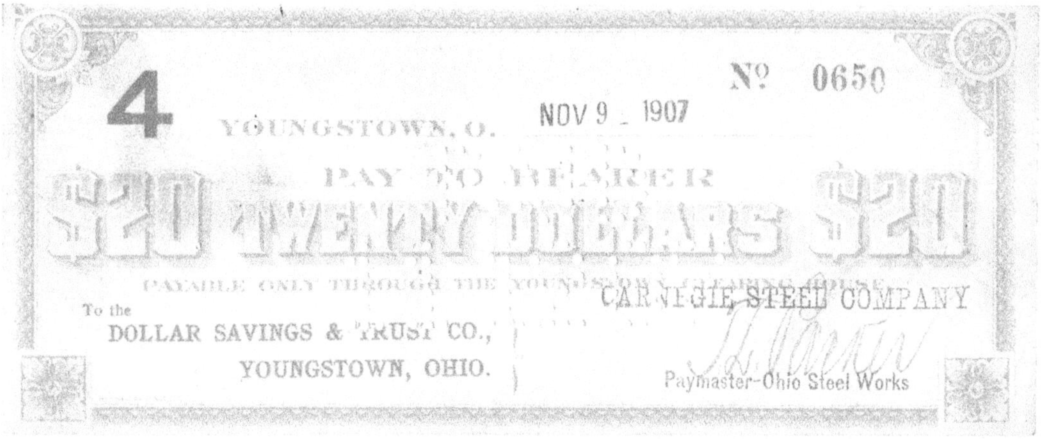

Carnegie Steel Company/Dollar Savings & Trust Co.

OH1500-20. 20 Dollars (clearing house check) Nov. 9, 1907 (stamped date). Brown. Small area of text on back in four languages. Imprint: Republic Bank Note Co. (shown at 75%)
b. Issued, cancelled. **R4**

Dollar Savings & Trust Co.

OH1525-1. 1 Dollar (clearing house check) Nov. 18, 1907. Black and green. Like OH1500 except for lack of specific issuer's name.
a. Issued, not cancelled. **R4**
b. Issued, cancelled. **R4**
u. Unissued. **SENC**
OH1525-2. 2 Dollars Nov. 18, 1907. (list)
b. Issued, cancelled. **R5**

OH1525-5. 5 Dollars Nov. 9, 1907. Blue. (shown at 75%)
b. Issued, cancelled. **R5**
u. Unissued. **SENC**
OH1525-10. 10 Dollars Nov. 18, 1907. (list)
b. Issued, cancelled. **R5**
u. Unissued. **SENC**
OH1525-20. 20 Dollars Nov. 18, 1907. (list)
b. Issued, cancelled. **R5**

The Youngstown Clearing House Association

OH1550-1. 1 Dollar Nov. 18, 1907. Black and green. Imprint: Western Bank Note & Eng. Co. Chicago.
- a. Issued, not cancelled (pay to First National Bank). **R5**
- b. Issued, cancelled. **R5**
- f. Specimen. **Unc., 250.**

OH1550-2. 2 Dollars Nov. 18, 1907. Black and blue. As above.
- b. Issued, cancelled. **R5**
- f. Specimen. **Unc., 250.**

OH1550-5. 5 Dollars Nov. 18, 1907. Black and reddish-brown. As above.
- b. Issued, cancelled. **R5**
- f. Specimen. **Unc., 250.**

OH1550-10. 10 Dollars Nov. 18, 1907. Black and brown. As above. (shown at 65%)
- b. Issued, cancelled. **R5**
- f. Specimen. **Unc., 250.**

OH1550-20. 20 Dollars Nov. 18, 1907. Black and orange. As above.
- b. Issued, cancelled. **R5**
- f. Specimen. **Unc., 250.**

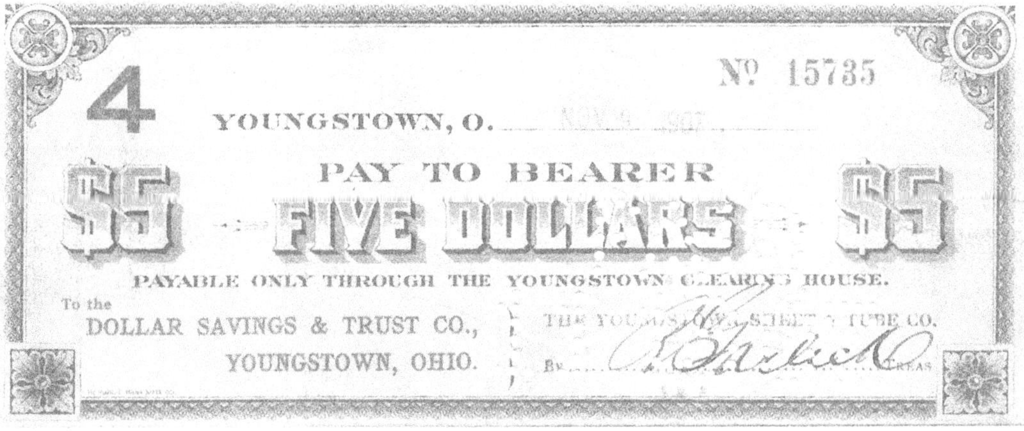

The Youngstown Sheet & Tube Co./ Dollar Savings & Trust Co.

OH1575-5. 5 Dollars (payroll check) Nov. 9, 1907 (stamped date). Blue. Similar to OH1500. (shown at 75%)
- b. Issued, cancelled. **VG, 100. VF, 200.**

OH1575-10. 10 Dollars Nov. 9, 1907. Green. As above.
- b. Issued, cancelled. **VG, 100. VF, 200.**

OKLAHOMA

Bartlesville

BARTLESVILLE CLEARING HOUSE ASSOCIATION

OK500-5. 5 Dollars Dec. 16, 1907. Black. Back orange. Imprint: Union Bank Note Co. K.C. Mo. (shown at 75%)

c. Unissued, cancelled. **R5**

Beggs

FIRST NATIONAL BANK

OK525-1. 1 Dollar Cashier's Check Nov. 9, 1907. Black. Large purple denomination numeral stamped at right center. Imprint: Dorsey Printing Co., Dallas 627.

b. Issued, cancelled. **R3**

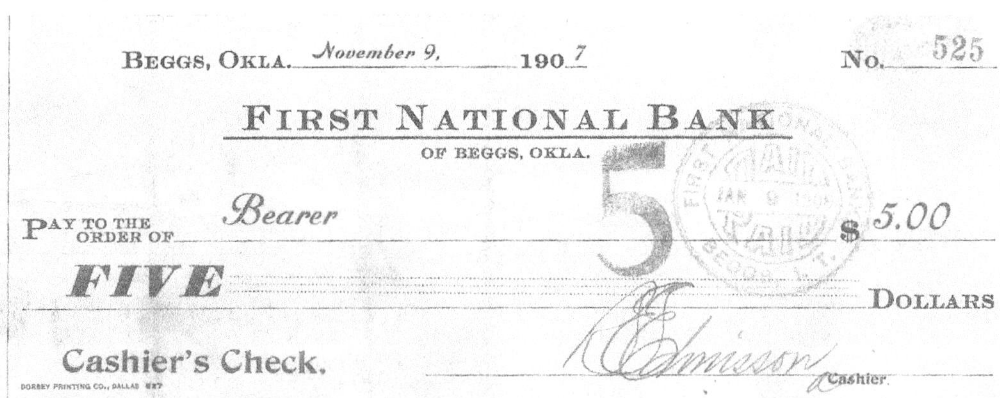

OK525-5. 5 Dollars Nov. 9, 1907. Black. As above. (shown at 70%)

b. Issued, cancelled. **R4**

Carney

$5.00 $5.00
CARNEY STATE BANK
Carney, Oklahoma, ______ 190__
This Certifies that ______ has deposited
in this bank FIVE DOLLARS payable to bearer
on ______ 190__, without interest, on return of this certificate.
No. 824
CASHIER PRESIDENT

Carney State Bank

OK550-5. 5 Dollars (certificate of deposit) 190_ (1907). Black on pale blue safety paper. Uniface. Imprint: The State Capital Co. Guthrie, Oklahoma. (shown at 68%)
d. Unissued, remainder. R2
OK550-10. 10 Dollars 190_ (1907). Black on pale gray safety paper. As above.
d. Unissued, remainder. R2
OK550-20. 20 Dollars 190_ (1907). Black on light green safety paper. As above.
d. Unissued, remainder. R2

Guthrie

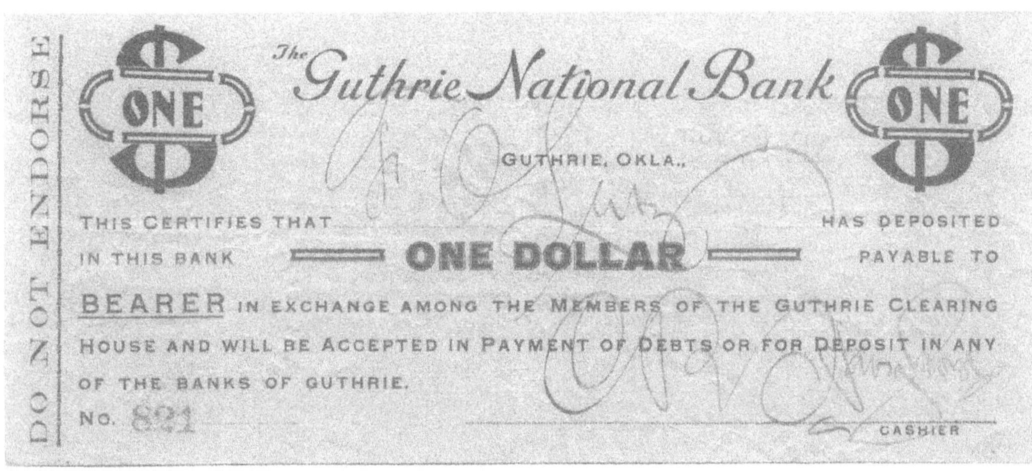
DO NOT ENDORSE
ONE ONE
The Guthrie National Bank
GUTHRIE, OKLA.,
THIS CERTIFIES THAT ______ HAS DEPOSITED
IN THIS BANK ONE DOLLAR PAYABLE TO
BEARER IN EXCHANGE AMONG THE MEMBERS OF THE GUTHRIE CLEARING HOUSE AND WILL BE ACCEPTED IN PAYMENT OF DEBTS OR FOR DEPOSIT IN ANY OF THE BANKS OF GUTHRIE.
No. 821
CASHIER

The Guthrie National Bank

OK575-1. 1 Dollar (certificate of deposit) Nov. 30, 1907 (stamped date). Red on brown paper. Embossed seal at lower left. Uniface. No imprint. (shown at 75%)
b. Issued, cancelled. **Fine, 80. VF, 150.**
OK575-2. 2 Dollars Nov. 5, 1907 (stamped date). As above.
b. Issued, cancelled. **Fine, 80. VF, 150.**
OK575-5. 5 Dollars Nov. 25, Dec. 7, 1907 (stamped dates). As above.
b. Issued, cancelled. **R1**

Guthrie Savings Bank

A. Design with smaller value at upper corners and with imprint

OK600-1. 1 Dollar Nov. 2, 1907 (stamped date). Black. Embossed seal at lower left center. Much different text than OK610, including redemption date and no mention of clearing house involvement. Imprint: The State Capital Co. Guthrie, Oklahoma.
Issued, cancelled. **R5**

OK600-5. 5 Dollars Nov. 2, 1907 (stamped date). Black on light blue underprint. As above. (shown at 67%)
b. Issued, cancelled. **R5**

B. Design like OK575 with large dollar sign and value word at upper corners
OK610-1. 1 Dollar (certificate of deposit) Nov. 2–Dec. 24, 1907 (stamped dates). Red on brown paper. No imprint.
b. Issued, cancelled. **VG, 45. VF, 100.**
NOTE: An example is known with penned date of Oct. 1, 1907 inserted where the stamped date is normally seen. This date is believed to be spurious. (The note itself was cancelled on Dec. 5, 1907.)
OK610-2. 2 Dollars Nov. 4–Dec. 23, 1907 (stamped dates). As above.
b. Issued, cancelled. **VG, 45. VF, 100.**

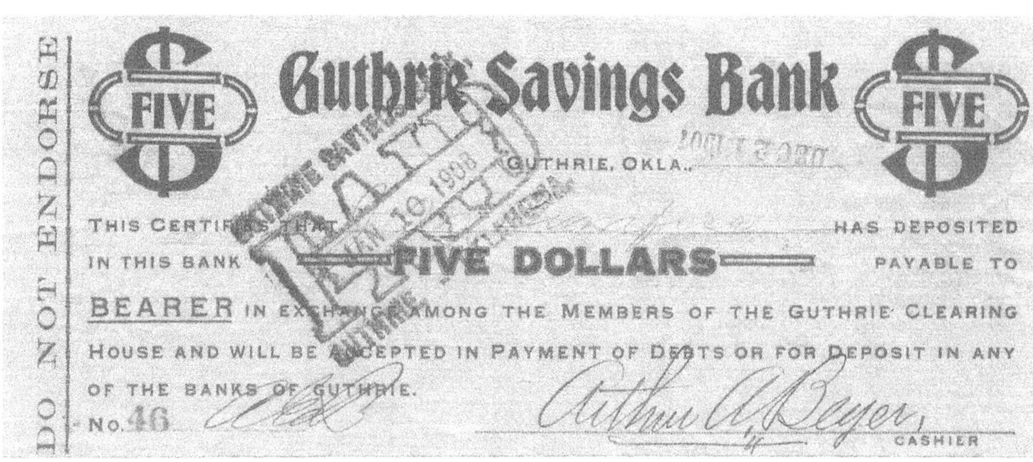

OK610-5. 5 Dollars Nov. 6–Dec. 23, 1907 (stamped dates). As above. (shown at 76%)
b. Issued, cancelled. **VG, 45. VF, 100.**
OK610-10. 10 Dollars Nov. 25–Dec. 24, 1907 (stamped dates). As above.
b. Issued, cancelled. **VG, 45. VF, 100.**

McAlester

McAlester Clearing House Association

OK625-1. 1 Dollar ND (1907). Black on light brown paper. Back green. Imprint: Union Bank Note Co. K.C. Mo. (shown at 70%)

d. Unissued, remainder. **R5**

Muskogee

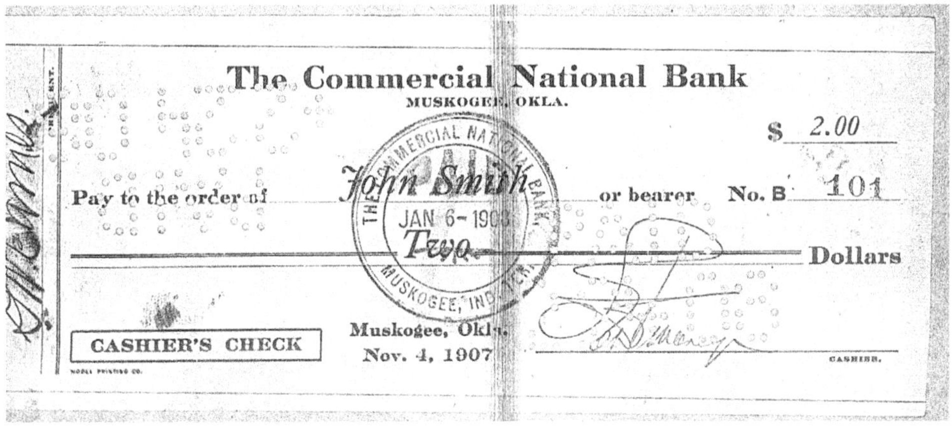

The Commercial National Bank

OK650-2. 2 Dollars Cashier's Check Nov. 4, 1907. Payable to John Smith. Imprint: Model Printing Co. (b/w) (shown at 60%)
b. Issued, cancelled. R5

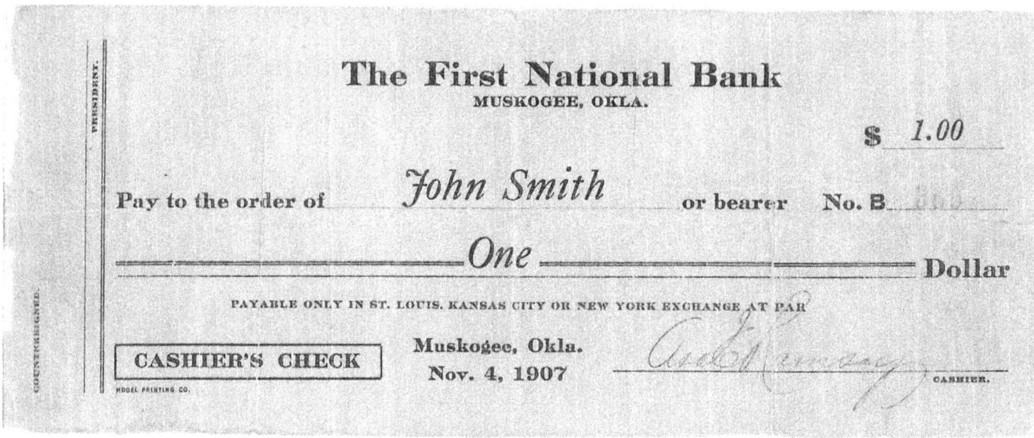

The First National Bank

OK675-1. 1 Dollar Cashier's Check Nov. 4, 1907. Black on light brown paper. Payable to John Smith. Uniface. Imprint as OK650. (shown at 65%)
a. Issued, not cancelled. R5

Oklahoma City

The American National Bank

OK700-2. 2 Dollars Cashiers Check Nov. 14, 1907 (stamped date). Large ornate denomination at center. Imprint: Oklahoma Engraving & Printing Co. Oklahoma City, Okla. (b/w)
b. Issued, cancelled. R5

OK700-5. 5 Dollars Nov. 14, 1907. As above. (b/w)
b. Issued, cancelled. R5

OK700-10. 10 Dollars Nov. 29, 1907. As above. (b/w) (shown at 65%)
b. Issued, cancelled. R5

The Columbia Bank and Trust Co.

OK715-Var. Various amounts Certificate of Deposit Nov. 5, 1907 (handwritten date). Black on cream background. Uniface. (shown at 74%)

b. Issued, cancelled. R5

Oklahoma City Clearing House

A clearing house loan certificate is believed to have been issued. No specifics are known at present.

The Oklahoma City National Bank

OK750-5. 5 Dollars Cashiers Check ND (1907). Large ornate denomination at center. Imprint as OK700. (b/w) (shown at 59%)

b. Issued, cancelled. R5

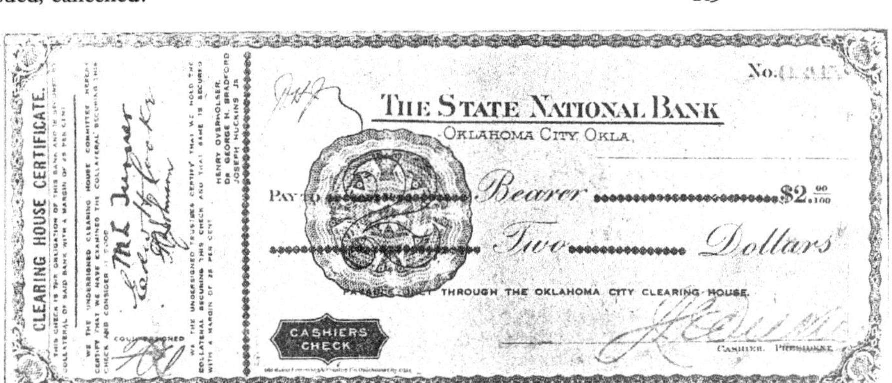

The State National Bank

OK775-2. 2 Dollars Cashiers Check ND (1907). Large ornate denomination at center. Imprint as OK700. (b/w) (shown at 56%)
b. Issued, cancelled. **R5**

Spiro

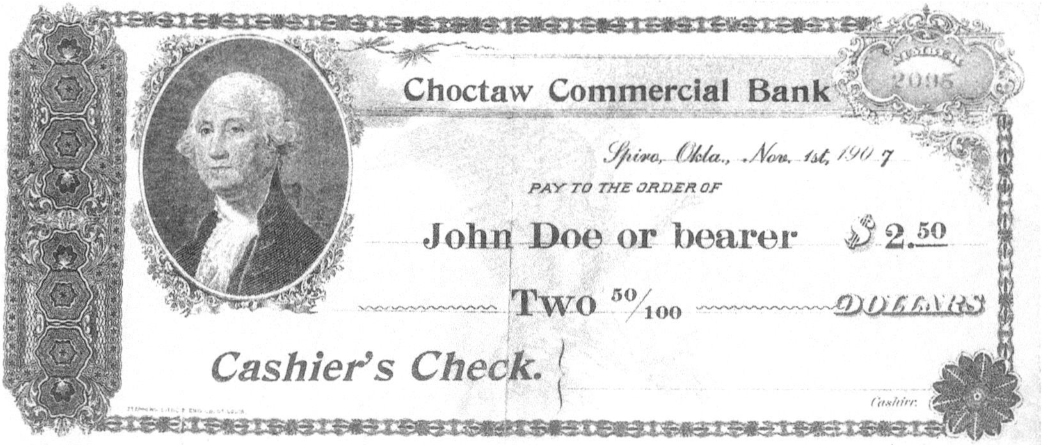

Choctaw Commercial Bank

OK800-2.50 2.50 Dollars Cashier's Check Nov. 1, 1907. Black. George Washington portrait at left, eagle underprint in green at center. Uniface. Imprint: Stephens Litho & Eng. Co. St. Louis. (shown at 66%)
d. Unissued, remainder. **R5**

Woodward

The Gerlach Bank

OK825-1. 1 Dollar Cashiers Check Nov. 3, 12, 1907. Vertical text of 13 lines indicating conditions of circulation at right on back. (b/w) (shown at 76%)
b. Issued, cancelled. **R5**

Oregon

Clatskanie

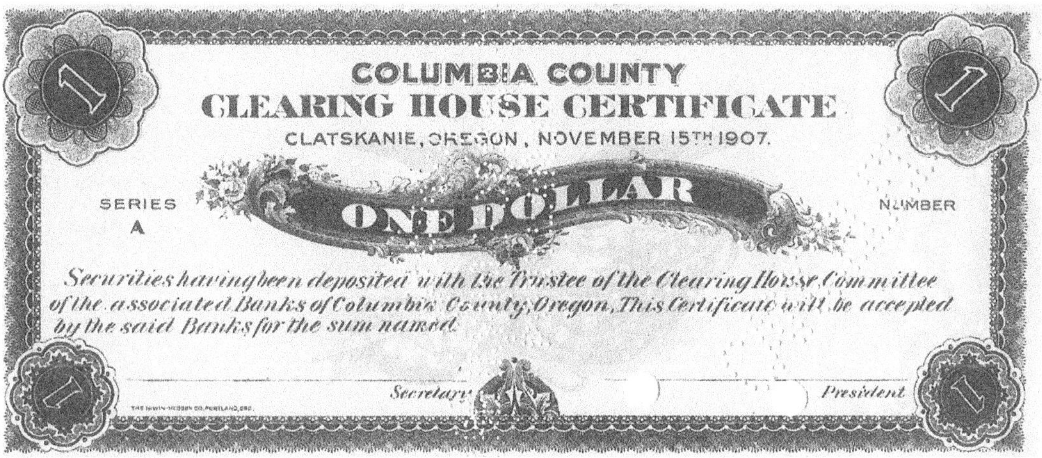

Columbia County Clearing House Certificate

OR500-1. 1 Dollar Nov. 15, 1907. Black on yellow-gold paper, eagle and flag in gold at center as underprint. Uniface. Imprint: The Irwin-Hodson Co. Portland, Ore. (shown at 72%)
c. Unissued, cancelled. R5
OR500-2. 2 Dollars Nov. 15, 1907. As above.
c. Unissued, cancelled. R5

Eugene

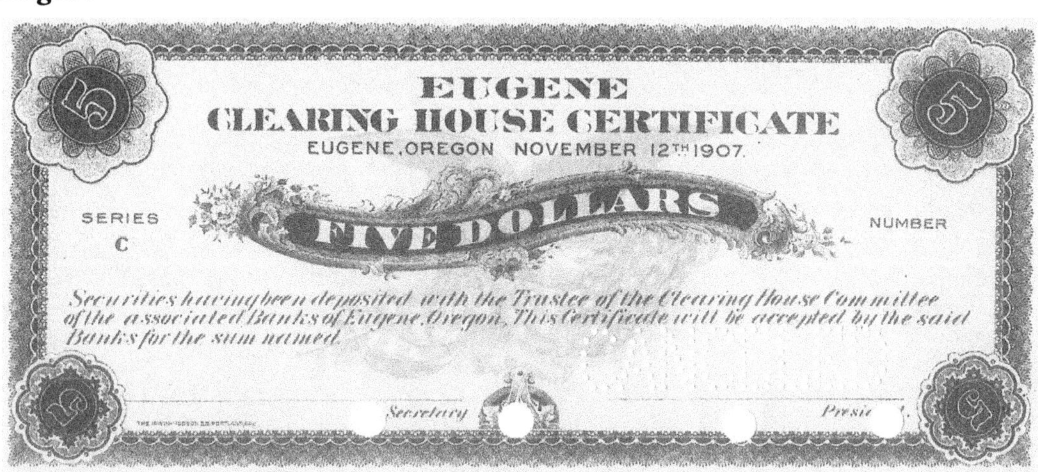

Eugene Clearing House Certificate

OR525-1. 1 Dollar Nov. 12, 1907. Similar to OR500 in design and imprint. (shown at 72%)
a. Issued, not cancelled. R5
c. Unissued, cancelled. R4
OR525-2. 2 Dollars Nov. 12, 1907. As above.
c. Unissued, cancelled. R4
OR525-5. 5 Dollars Nov. 12, 1907. As above.
c. Unissued, cancelled. R4
OR525-10. 10 Dollars Nov. 12, 1907. As above.
c. Unissued, cancelled. R4

Portland

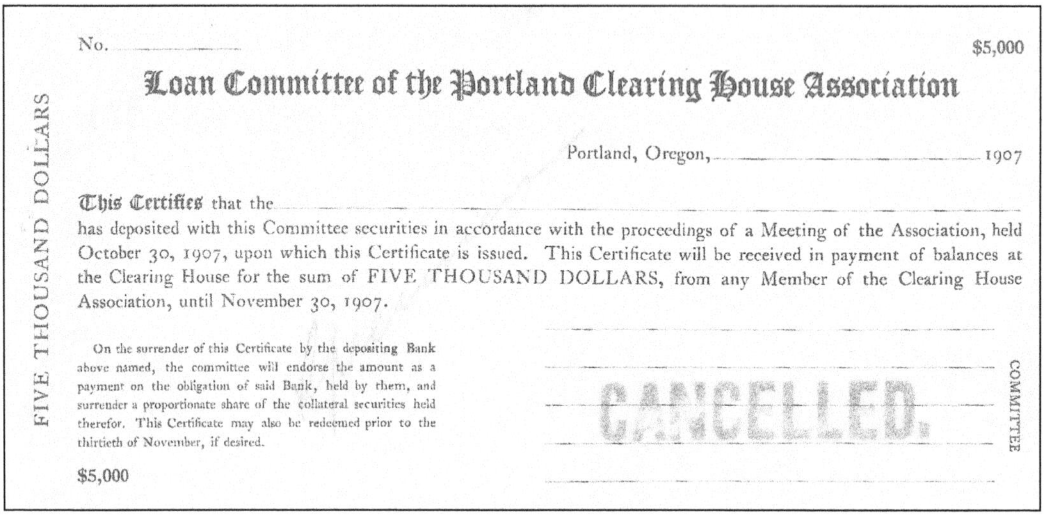
No. $5,000

Loan Committee of the Portland Clearing House Association

Portland, Oregon, 1907

This Certifies that the
has deposited with this Committee securities in accordance with the proceedings of a Meeting of the Association, held October 30, 1907, upon which this Certificate is issued. This Certificate will be received in payment of balances at the Clearing House for the sum of FIVE THOUSAND DOLLARS, from any Member of the Clearing House Association, until November 30, 1907.

On the surrender of this Certificate by the depositing Bank above named, the committee will endorse the amount as a payment on the obligation of said Bank, held by them, and surrender a proportionate share of the collateral securities held therefor. This Certificate may also be redeemed prior to the thirtieth of November, if desired.

$5,000

FIVE THOUSAND DOLLARS

CANCELLED.

COMMITTEE

Loan Committee of the Portland Clearing House Association

OR550-5000. 5,000 Dollars Oct. 30, 1907. Black on cream paper. Uniface. (shown at 70%)
c. Unissued, cancelled (also with handwritten "Specimen" across face). **R5**

Portland Clearing House Association

A. Uniface larger size notes, 204 × 108mm.

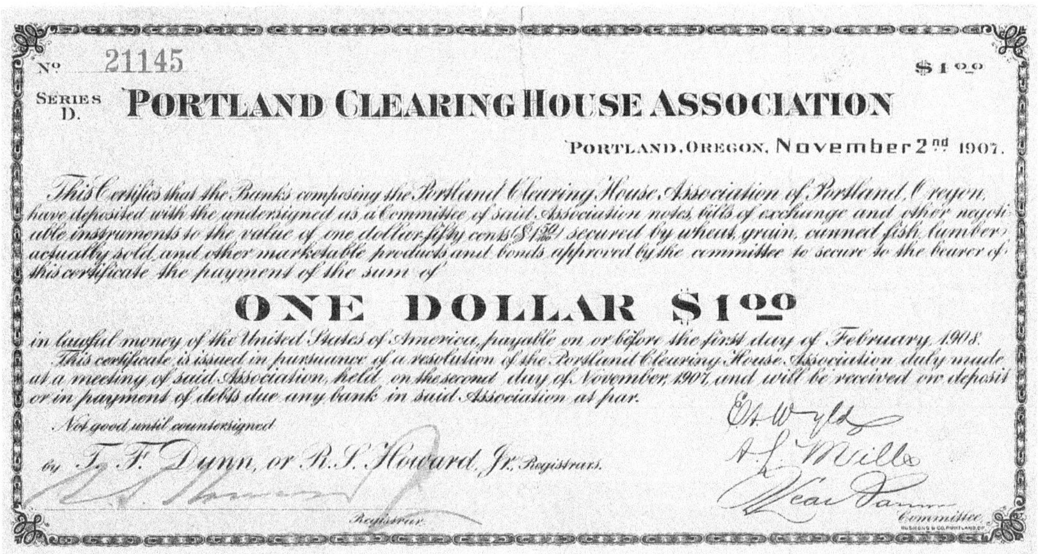
No. 21145 $1.00

Series D. PORTLAND CLEARING HOUSE ASSOCIATION

Portland, Oregon, November 2nd 1907.

This Certifies that the Banks composing the Portland Clearing House Association of Portland, Oregon, have deposited with the undersigned as a Committee of said Association notes, bills of exchange and other negotiable instruments to the value of one dollar fifty cents ($1.50) secured by wheat, grain, canned fish, lumber actually sold and other marketable products and bonds approved by the committee to secure to the bearer of this certificate the payment of the sum of

ONE DOLLAR $1.00

in lawful money of the United States of America, payable on or before the first day of February, 1908. This certificate is issued in pursuance of a resolution of the Portland Clearing House Association duly made at a meeting of said Association, held on the second day of November, 1907, and will be received on deposit or in payment of debts due any bank in said Association at par.

Not good until countersigned by T. F. Dunn, or R. S. Howard, Jr. Registrars.

Registrar. Committee.

OR575-1. 1 Dollar Nov. 2, 1907. Black on light beige paper. Imprint: Bushong & Co. Portland, Or. (shown at 68%)
a. Issued, not cancelled. **R3**
OR575-5 5 Dollars Nov. 2, 1907. As above. (list)
e. Sample. **R5**

B. Notes printed on both sides, smaller size, 160 × 83mm.

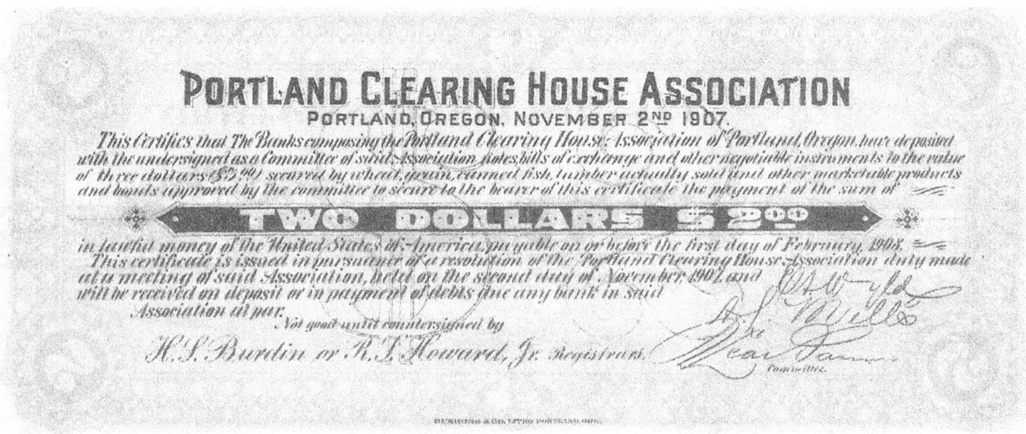

OR600-1. 1 Dollar Nov. 2, 1907. Face: black on gold underprint of ornate shield at center. Lion head at left. Imprint: The Irwin-Hodson Co. Portland, Ore. Back: black text on gold underprint. Imprint: Bushong & Co. Litho. Portland, Ore. (shown at 72%)

a. Issued, not cancelled.	**VG, 100. VF, 225.**
b. Issued, cancelled.	**VG, 90. VF, 200.**
c. Unissued, cancelled.	**EF, 175. Unc., 300.**

OR600-2. 2 Dollars Nov. 2, 1907. As above.

a. Issued, not cancelled.	**VG, 200. VF, 400.**
b. Issued, cancelled.	**VG, 100. VF, 225.**
c. Unissued, cancelled.	**EF, 175. Unc., 300.**

OR600-5. 5 Dollars Nov. 2, 1907. As above.

c. Unissued, cancelled.	**R4**

OR600-10. 10 Dollars Nov. 2, 1907. As above.

b. Issued, cancelled.	**R5**
c. Unissued, cancelled.	**R4**

OR600-20. 20 Dollars Nov. 2, 1907. As above.

c. Unissued, cancelled.	**R5**

NOTE: Composition of the three known sheets from this issue is as follows: 16-subject (four $1, four $2, four $5, two each of $10 and $20); four-subject (two each $5 and $10); four-subject (two each $5 and $20).

Pennsylvania

Allegheny

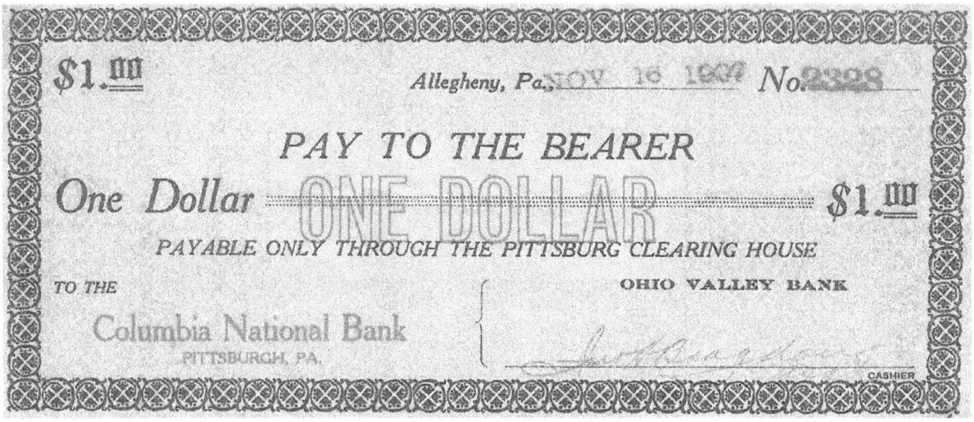

Ohio Valley Bank/Columbia National Bank

PA500-1. 1 Dollar (cashier's check) Nov. 16, 1907 (stamped date). Black on green underprint, brown paper. Text in English and Czech on back about depositing and cashing the check. (shown at 70%)

a. Issued, not cancelled. **R4**

b. Issued, cancelled. **VG, 50. VF, 100.**

Altoona

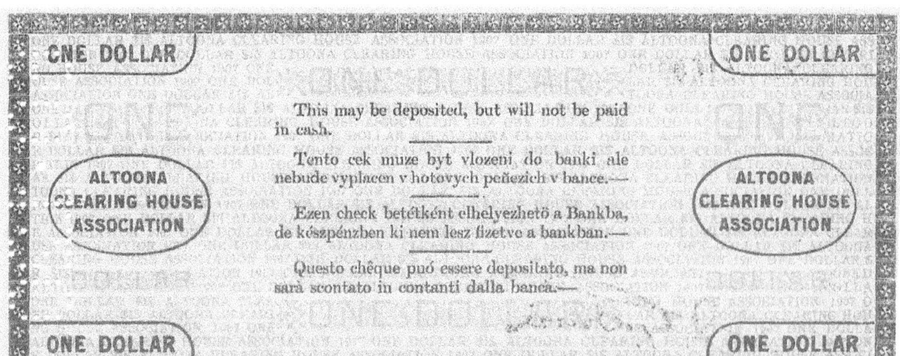

Altoona Clearing House Association

PA550-1. 1 Dollar 1907. Blue on light green text lines that include 1907 year date. Dull gold paper. Back text in four languages: English, Czech, Hungarian and Italian. (shown at 64%)
c. Unissued, cancelled. **AU, 25. Unc., 50.**
PA550-2. 2 Dollars 1907. Blue on blue-green underprint. Blue paper. As above.
c. Unissued, cancelled. **AU, 25. Unc., 50.**
PA550-5. 5 Dollars 1907. Blue on light brown underprint. As above.
c. Unissued, cancelled. **AU, 25. Unc., 50.**
PA550-10. 10 Dollars 1907. Blue on red underprint. Pink paper. As above.
c. Unissued, cancelled. **AU, 25. Unc., 50.**
PA550-20. 20 Dollars 1907. Blue on light orange underprint. As above.
c. Unissued, cancelled. **AU, 25. Unc., 50.**
NOTE: A significant group of punch cancelled examples in all denominations is known, all fully signed and numbered but without specific date. They were sold during 2007 in three-subject (partial) sheets of each value, and are cataloged as having been unissued. Also, a single four-subject sheet of 1 Dollar notes is known.

Bangor

Slate Belt Clearing House Association

PA575-5. 5 Dollars ND (1907). Brown on green safety paper. Uniface. Imprint: American Bank Note Co. New York, Litho.
f. Specimen. **R5**

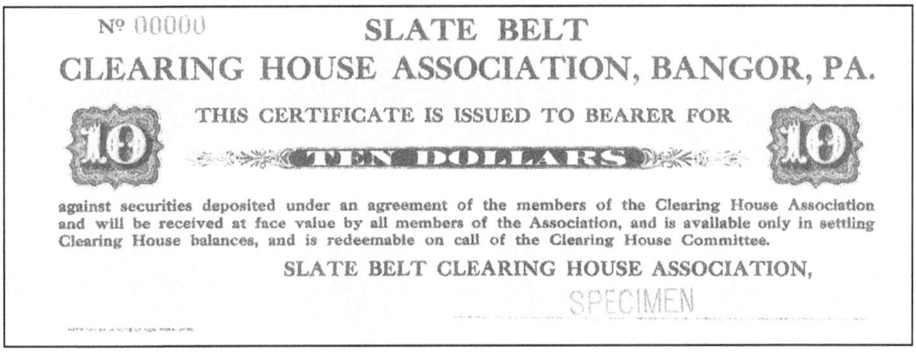

PA575-10. 10 Dollars ND (1907). Blue on green safety paper. As above. (shown at 60%)
f. Specimen. **R5**
PA575-20. 20 Dollars ND (1907). Black on green safety paper. As above.
f. Specimen. **R5**

Easton

Easton Clearing House Association

A. Loan Certificate Issue
A clearing house loan certificate is believed to have been issued in Easton. No specifics are known at present.

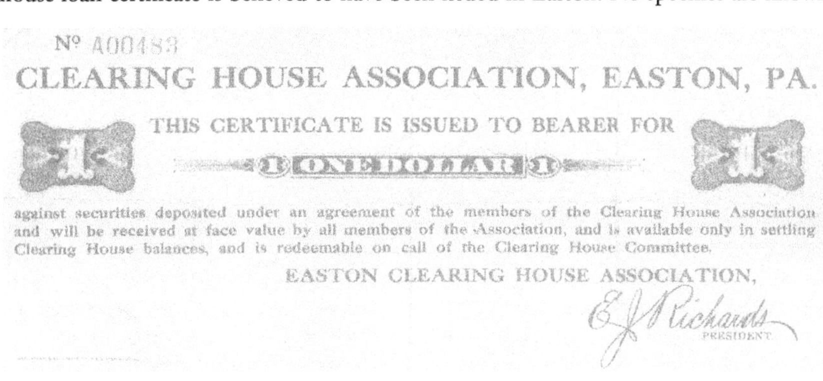

B. Clearing House Certificate Issue

PA625-1. 1 Dollar ND, Nov. 18, 1907 (stamped date). Brown on light green safety paper. Uniface. Imprint: American Bank Note Co. New York, Litho. (shown at 59%)
- a. Issued, not cancelled (not dated). **R5**
- f. Specimen (dated). **R5**

PA625-2. 2 Dollars ND, Nov. 19, 1907. Blue on same paper as the $1. As above.
- a. Issued, not cancelled (not dated). **R5**
- f. Specimen (dated). **R5**

PA625-5. 5 Dollars ND (1907). Dark green. As above.
- f. Specimen. **R5**

PA625-10. 10 Dollars Nov. 18, 1907. Black. As above.
- f. Specimen. **R5**

PA625-20. 20 Dollars Nov. 19, 1907 (stamped date). Red-orange. As above.
- f. Specimen. **R5**

PA625-500. 500 Dollars Nov. 19, 1907. Orange. As above.
- f. Specimen. **R5**

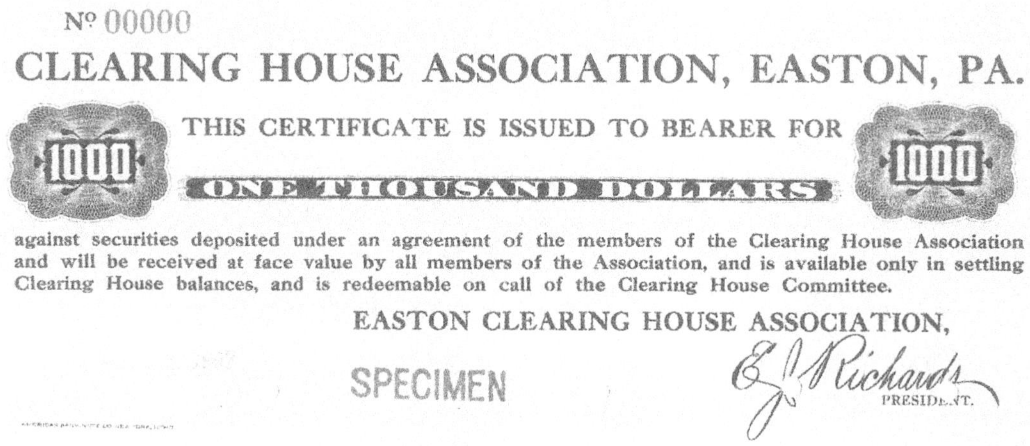

PA625-1000. 1000 Dollars Nov. 19, 1907. Deep purple. As above. (shown at 75%)
- f. Specimen. **R5**

Ford City

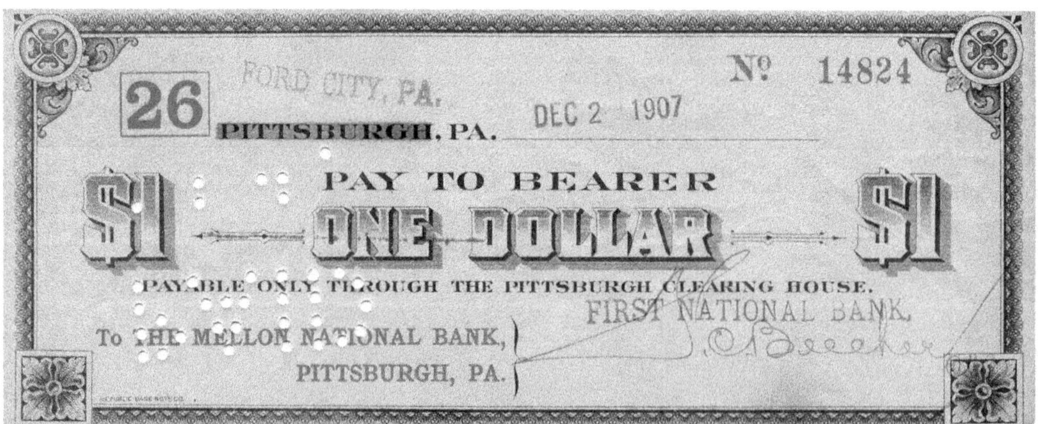

First National Bank/Mellon National Bank

PA635-1. 1 Dollar (payroll check) Dec. 2, 1907 (stamped date). City name *Pittsburgh* lined out. Black on light blue paper. Pittsburgh scrip Type I, bank no. 26. (See Pittsburgh) (shown at 75%)
- b. Issued, cancelled. **R4**

PA635-2. 2 Dollars Dec. 2, 1907. Black on gold paper, otherwise as above.
b. Issued, cancelled. R4

Harrisburg

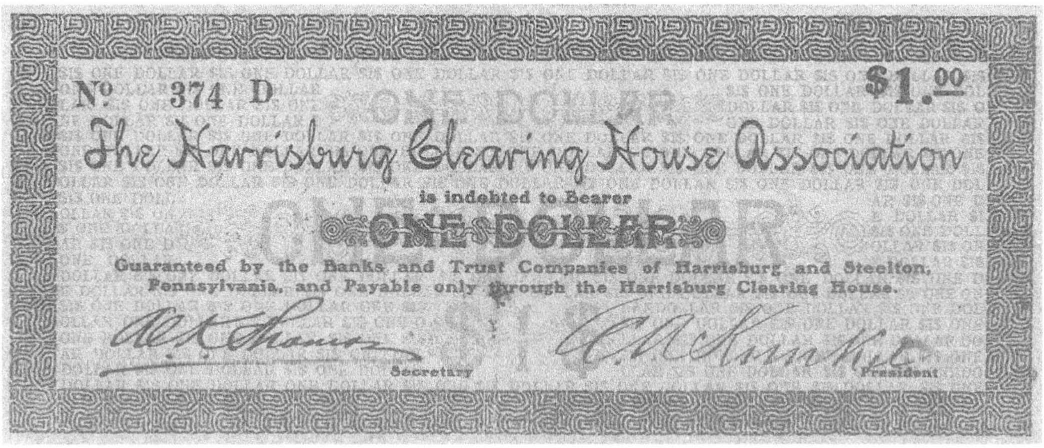

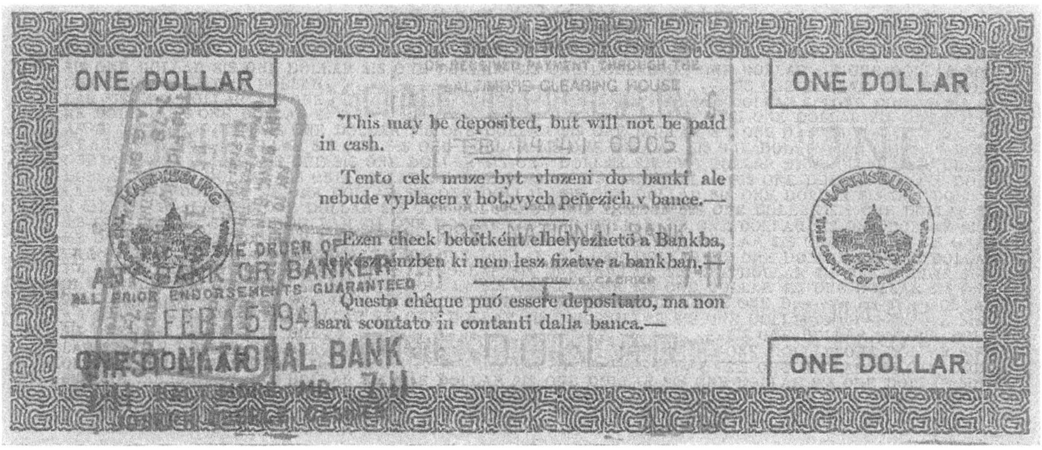

THE HARRISBURG CLEARING HOUSE ASSOCIATION

PA650-1. 1 Dollar ND (1907). Black on light brown underprint. Dark pink paper. Back text in four languages, similar to PA550. (shown at 73%)
a. Issued, not cancelled. **VG, 50. VF, 125.**
b. Issued, cancelled. **VG, 40. VF, 110.**

PA650-5. 5 Dollars ND (1907). (list)
u. Unissued? SENC

PA650-10. 10 Dollars ND (1907). (list)
b. Issued, cancelled. R4

PA650-20. 20 Dollars ND (1907).
b. Issued, cancelled. R4

HARRISBURG NATIONAL BANK

PA675-5.A 5 Dollars ND (1907). Black on brown paper. Red denomination words in outline across center. Back text in five languages (German added).
d. Unissued, remainder. R3

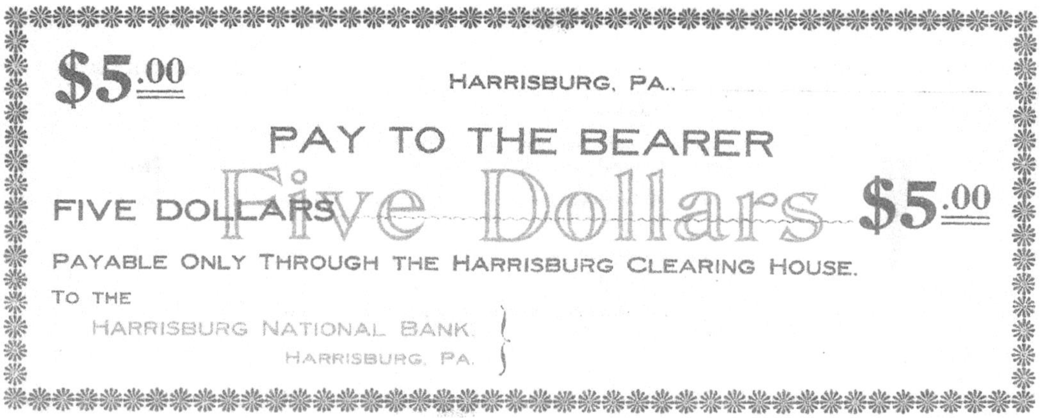

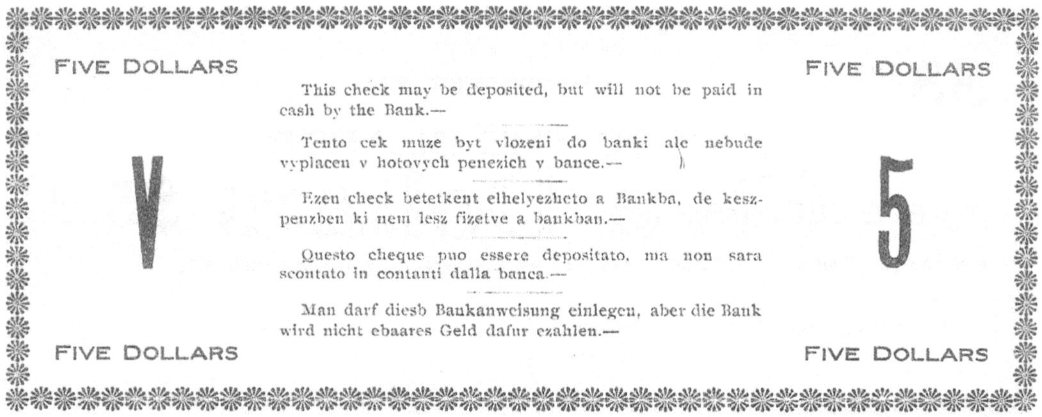

PA675-5.B 5 Dollars ND (1907). As above but white paper. (shown at 74%)
- d. Unissued, remainder. R3

PA675-5.C 5 Dollars ND (1907). As above but blue paper.
- d. Unissued, remainder. R3

Harrisburg Trust Company

PA680-5. 5 Dollars ND (1907). As PA675-5.B. Light pink paper. (shown at 74%)
- d. Unissued, remainder. R4

Middletown Car Works/Harrisburg Trust Company

PA700-5. 5 Dollars (payroll check) Nov. 11, 1907 (stamped date). Similar to PA675-5.B.
b. Issued, cancelled. **R5**

Mount Pleasant

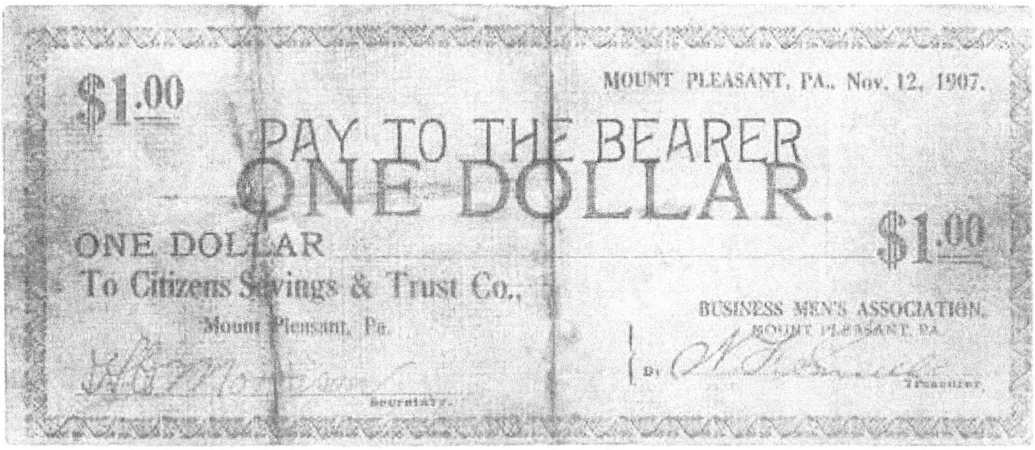

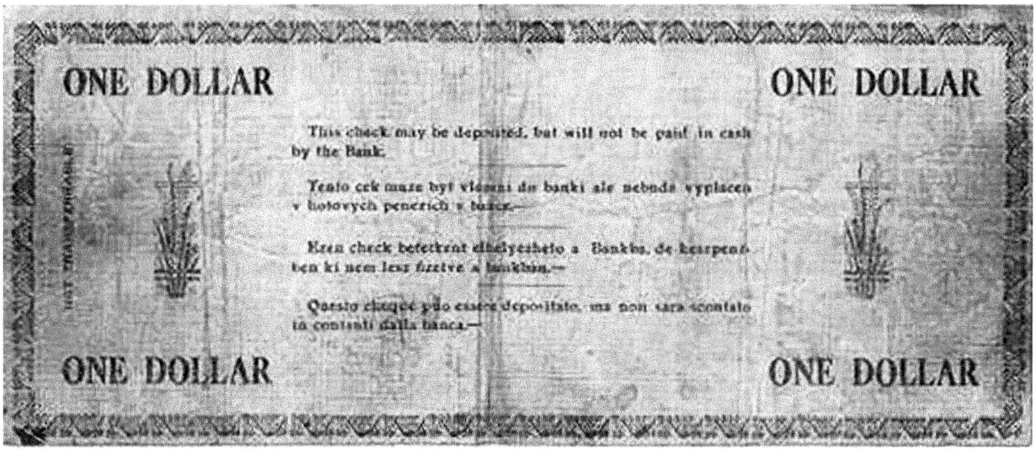

Mount Pleasant Business Men's Association/ Citizens Savings & Trust Co.

PA725-1. 1 Dollar (treasurer's check) Nov. 12, 1907. Black on blue paper. Red denomination words across center. Back text in four languages. (shown at 62%)
a. Issued, not cancelled. **R5**

Philadelphia

American Bridge Co./Philadelphia National Bank

PA750-1. 1 Dollar Pay Check Nov. 21, 1907. Black and red text on light blue underprint. Uniface. Imprint: American Bank Note Co., Phila.
f. Specimen. **R5**

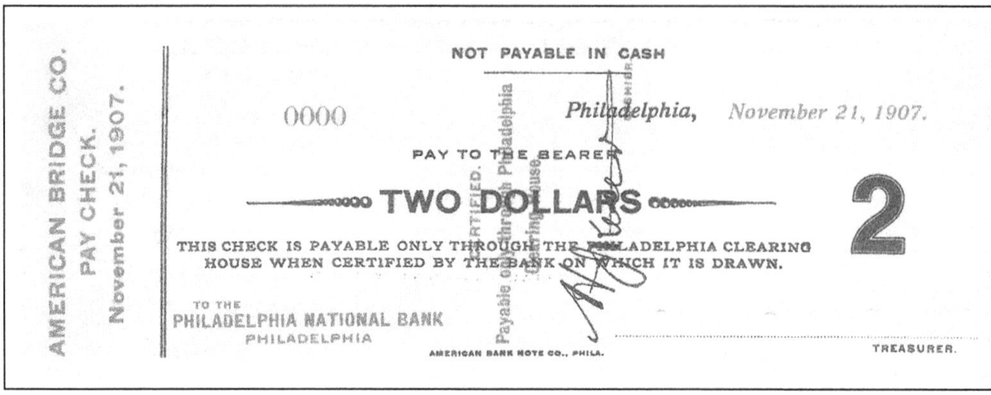

PA750-2. 2 Dollars Nov. 21, 1907. Black and red text on light orange underprint. As above. (shown at 66%)
f. Specimen. **R5**

City National Bank/Clearing House Due Bill

PA775-Var. Various Amounts 190_ (1907). Black on dark mustard yellow paper. Uniface. (shown at 71%)
d. Unissued, remainder. **R5**

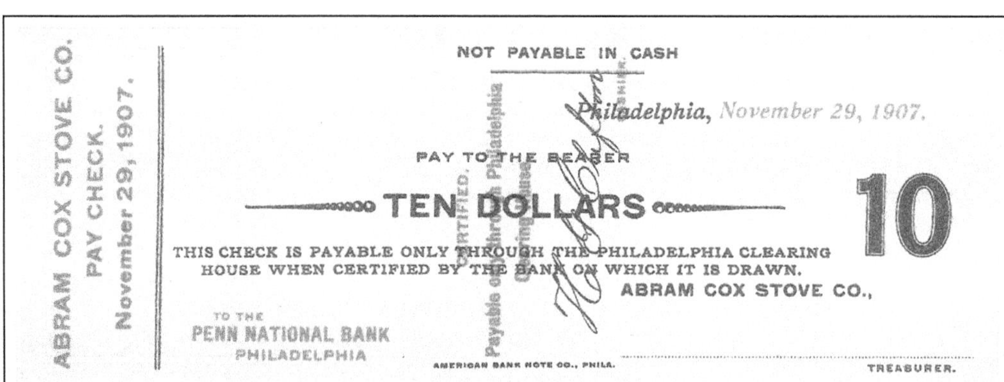

Abram Cox Stove Co./Penn National Bank

PA800-10. 10 Dollars Pay Check Nov. 29, 1907. Black and red text on gold underprint. Similar to PA750. (shown at 69%)
f. Specimen. **R5**

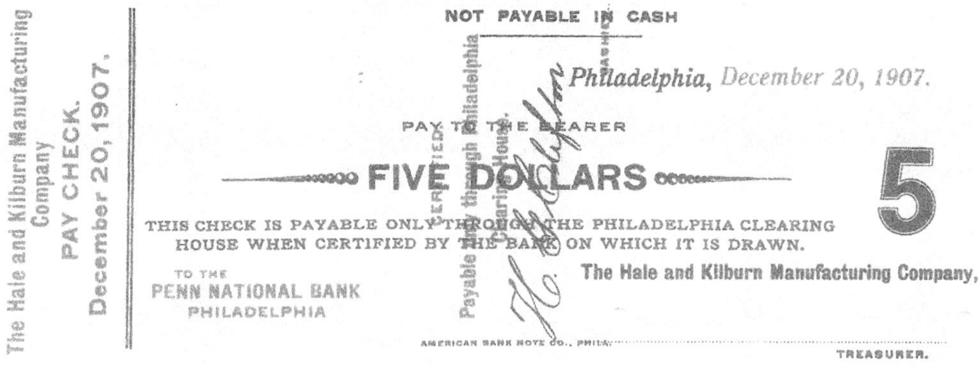

The Hale and Kilburn Manufacturing Company/ Penn National Bank

PA825-5. 5 Dollars Pay Check Dec. 20, 1907. Black and red text on light green underprint. Similar to PA750. (shown at 72%)
c. Unissued, cancelled. R5

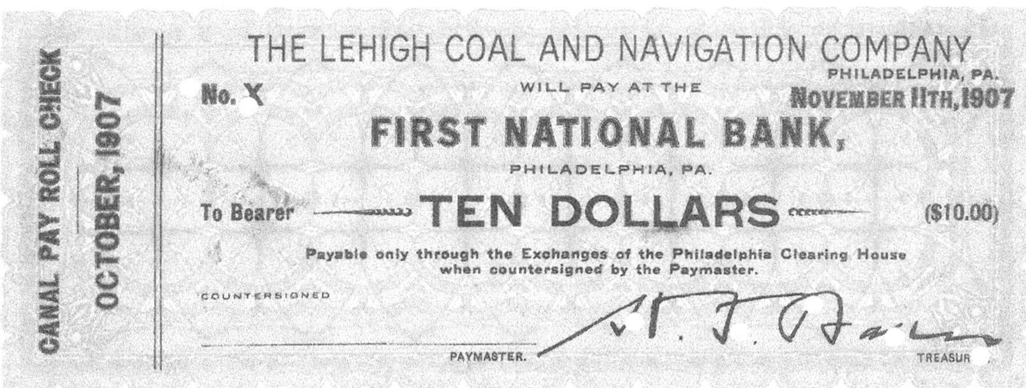

The Lehigh Coal and Navigation Company/ First National Bank

PA850-10. 10 Dollars Pay Roll Check Nov. 11, 1907. Black on salmon underprint. Uniface. (shown at 70%)
c. Unissued, cancelled. R5

Philadelphia and Reading Railway Company/ Market Street National Bank

PA875-5. 5 Dollars (payroll check) Nov. 15, 1907. Black on gold underprint. Uniface. Imprint (crude): American Bank Note Compy. (shown at 72%)
c. Unissued, cancelled. **R5**

PA875-10. 10 Dollars Nov. 15, 1907. Black on green underprint. As above.
b. Issued, cancelled. **R5**

Stiffel & Freeman/Quaker National Bank

PA890-1. 1 Dollar Pay Check Nov. 22 1907. Black. Uniface. Vertical red overprint words at center, "Payable only through Philadelphia Clearing House." Printer: ABN, Phila.
b. Issued, cancelled. **R5**

Pittsburgh

Most payroll scrip issues from Pittsburgh fall into one of two basic types: Type I with red bank number (or letters) and imprint; Type II without special designation or imprint. Listings will include reference to these types as necessary. Additionally, most dates are stamped.

Type I: Red bank number (or letters) at upper left, usually within a box. Red bank name at lower left. Four-language text on back (English, Czech, Hungarian and Italian) is vertical. Some with imprinted red oval logo stating "Design of this Check Registered, Nov. 18, 1907." Imprint: Republic Bank Note Co.

Type II: No bank number. Orange bank name at lower left. Background underprint design on face consists of small swastikas. Large orange denomination words in outline across center. Four-language text on back is horizontal. No imprint.

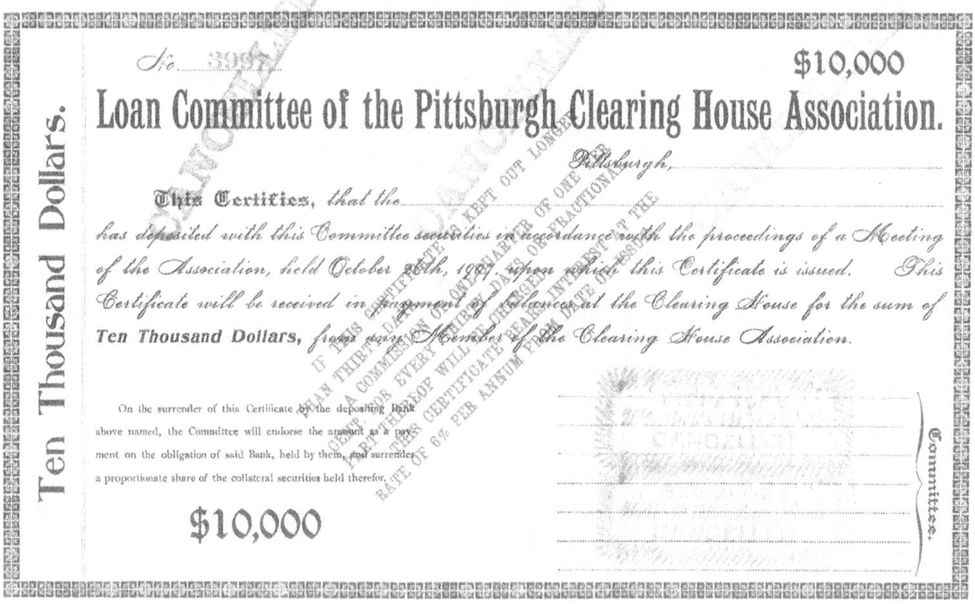
$10,000
Loan Committee of the Pittsburgh Clearing House Association.
Pittsburgh,
This Certifies, that the
has deposited with this Committee securities in accordance with the proceedings of a Meeting of the Association, held October 26th, 1907, upon which this Certificate is issued. This Certificate will be received in payment of balances at the Clearing House for the sum of Ten Thousand Dollars, from any Member of the Clearing House Association.
On the surrender of this Certificate by the depositing Bank above named, the Committee will endorse the amount as a payment on the obligation of said Bank, held by them, and surrender a proportionate share of the collateral securities held therefor.
$10,000
Committee.
Ten Thousand Dollars.

Loan Committee of the Pittsburgh Clearing House Association

PA900-10,000. 10,000 Dollars Oct. 26, 1907. Black text with red overprint. One line of text on back. Large size. (shown at 53%)
c. Unissued, cancelled. **R5**

The Pittsburgh Clearing House Association

PA905-5000. 5000 Dollars (certificate of deposit) Aug. 14, 1908 (stamped date). Payable in United States Gold Coin. Black on orange underprint. Inner factory scene at right. Back orange, with vertical format. Different factory scene at bottom. Printer: ABNC. (shown at 74%)

f. Specimen. **R5**

NOTE: The stamped date on PA905 is an indication that it could possibly have been used during the Panic of 1907. No issued example is presently reported.

American Steel and Wire Company

A. Scrip Type I

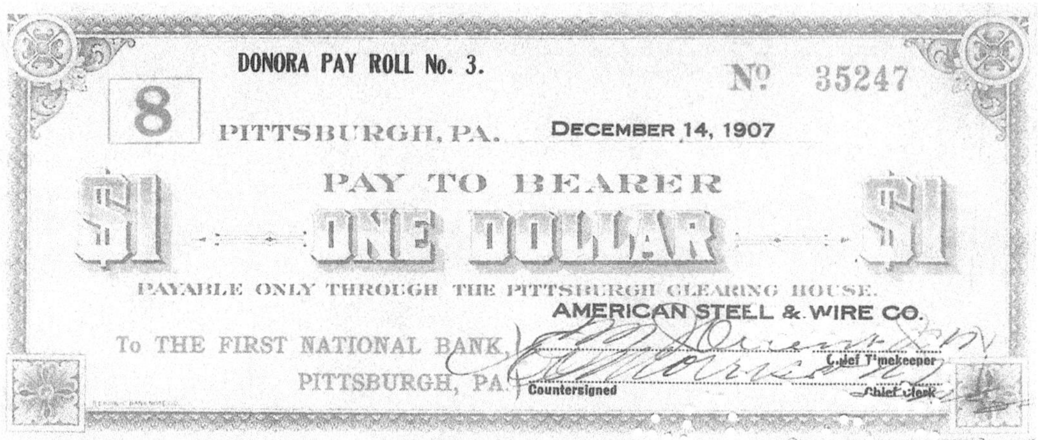

PA910-1. 1 Dollar Dec. 14, 1907 (printed date). Black on blue paper. Bank no. 8, bank name in red. The First National Bank as depository bank. *Donora Pay Roll No. 3* text line added at top. (shown at 76%)
b. Issued, cancelled. R3
PA910-2. 2 Dollars Dec. 14, 1907. Black on gold paper. As above.
b. Issued, cancelled. R3
PA910-5. 5 Dollars Dec. 14, 1907. Blue on gray paper. As above.
b. Issued, cancelled. R3
PA910-10. 10 Dollars Dec. 14, 1907. Green on white paper. As above. Design registry logo added at top in red.
b. Issued, cancelled. R3

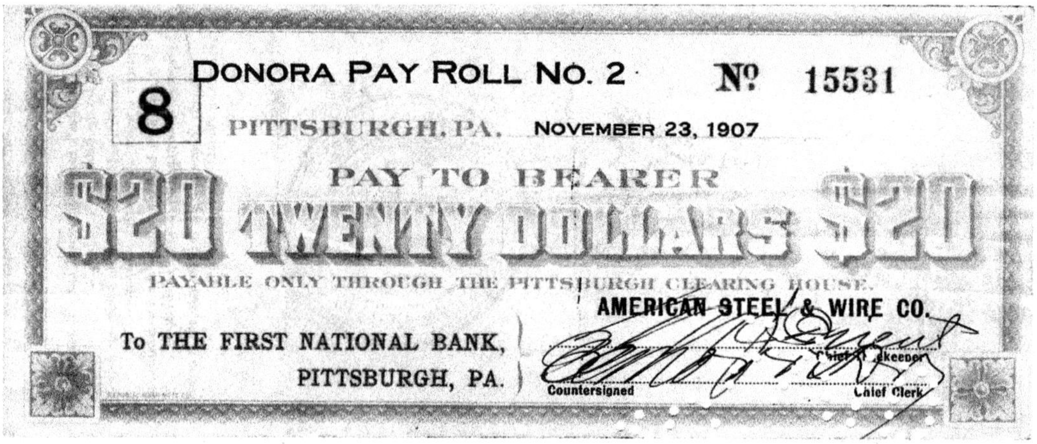

PA910-20. 20 Dollars Nov. 23, 1907 (printed date). As above. *Donora Pay Roll No. 2* text line added at top. (shown at 85%)
b. Issued, cancelled. R4

B. Scrip Type II
PA912-5. 5 Dollars Nov. 9, 1907 (stamped date). Black on light blue underprint. First National Bank as depository bank. Issuer's name stamped.
b. Issued, cancelled. R3

PA912-10. 10 Dollars Nov. 9, 1907. Black on light green underprint. As above. (shown at 61%)
b. Issued, cancelled. R3

PA912-20. 20 Dollars Nov. 9, 1907. Black on pale gold underprint. As above.
b. Issued, cancelled. R3

C. Scrip Type III

PA913-1. 1 Dollar Dec. 15, 1907 (stamped date). Black on light grey underprint. First National Bank as depository bank. Issuer's name stamped.
u. Issued. **SENC**

ATLANTIC CRUSHED COKE CO.

PA918-5. 5 Dollars Nov. 16, 1907. Blue on gray paper. Scrip Type I. As PA910-5. (shown at 63%)
b. Issued, cancelled. R5

BOOTH-FLYNN COMPANY

PA925-1. 1 Dollar Nov. 15, 1907. Black on blue paper. Bank name in red. Scrip Type I, bank no. 23. The National Bank of Western Pennsylvania as depository bank.
a. Issued, not cancelled. R4

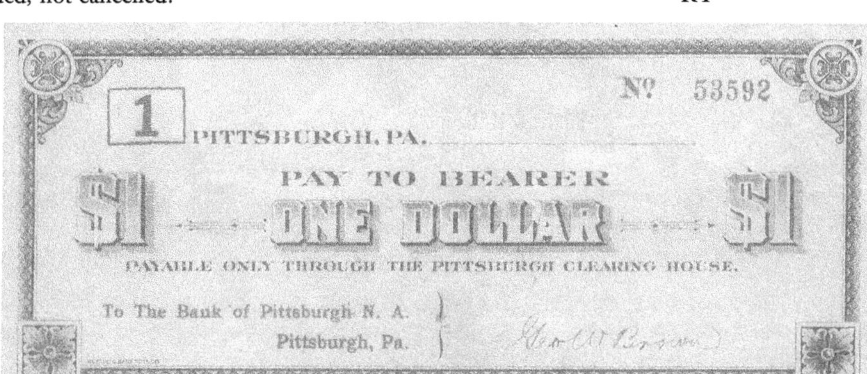

Geo. W. Brown

PA950-1. 1 Dollar Jan. 8, 1908. Black on light blue paper. Scrip Type I, bank no. 1. The Bank of Pittsburgh N. A. as depository bank. Account (issuer) name handwritten. (shown at 63%)
a. Issued, not cancelled. R3

Carnegie Steel Co.

PA970-20. 20 Dollars ND (1907). Black on brown paper. Scrip Type 1, bank no. 26. Mellon National Bank as depository bank.
c. Unissued, cancelled. R4

Ellsworth Collieries Co.

PA1000-5. 5 Dollars Dec. 28, 1907. Blue. Scrip Type I, bank letters UT straight up. The Union Trust Company as depository bank. (shown at 75%)
b. Issued, cancelled. R4

PA1000-10. 10 Dollars Dec. 7, 1907. Green. Scrip Type I, bank letters UT in italics. As above.
b. Issued, cancelled. R4

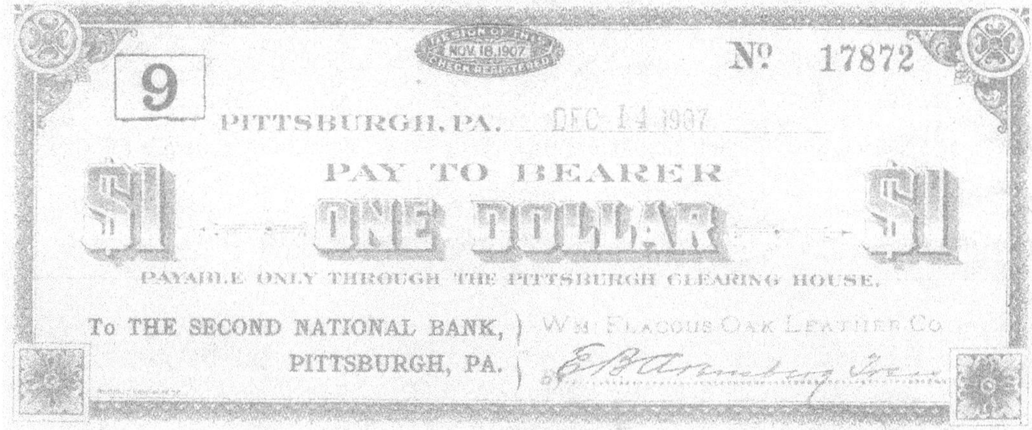

Wm. Flaccus Oak Leather Co.

PA1050-1. 1 Dollar Dec. 14, 1907. Green on light green paper. Scrip Type I, bank no. 9. The Second National Bank as depository bank. Check registry logo for design in red oval at upper center. (shown at 76%)
a. Issued, not cancelled. R4

Franklin Savings and Trust Co.

A. First Issue- notes with bank number

PA1060-1. 1 Dollar ND (1907). Scrip Type I, bank no. 26.
e. Sample. R4

PA1060-2. 2 Dollars ND (1907). As above. (shown at 72%)
e. Sample. R4
PA1060-5. 5 Dollars ND (1907). As above.
e. Sample. R4
PA1060-10. 10 Dollars ND (1907). As above.
e. Sample. R4

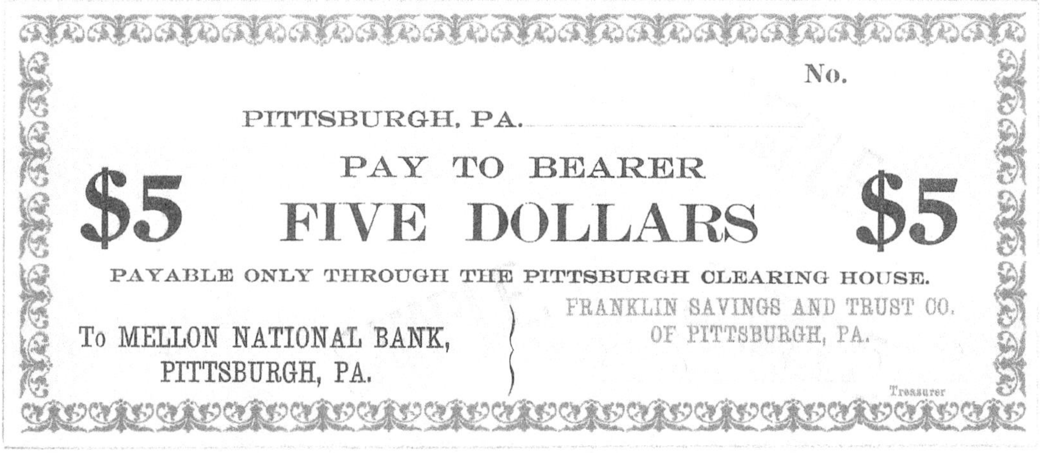

B. Second Issue—notes with Mellon National Bank as depository bank with borders in color and no bank number. Back style of scrip Type I. No imprint. (shown at 72%)
PA1061-1. 1 Dollar ND (1907). Green border.
e. Sample (stamped). R4
PA1061-2. 2 Dollars ND (1907). As above but with blue border.
e. Sample as above. R4
PA1061-5. 5 Dollars ND (1907). As above but with red border.
e. Sample as above. R4
PA1061-10. 10 Dollars ND (1907). As above but with brown border.
e. Sample as above. R4

H. C. Frick Coke Company

PA1068-10. 10 Dollars Nov. 5, 1907. Green. Scrip Type I, bank no. 26. Mellon National Bank as depository bank.
c. Unissued, cancelled. R5

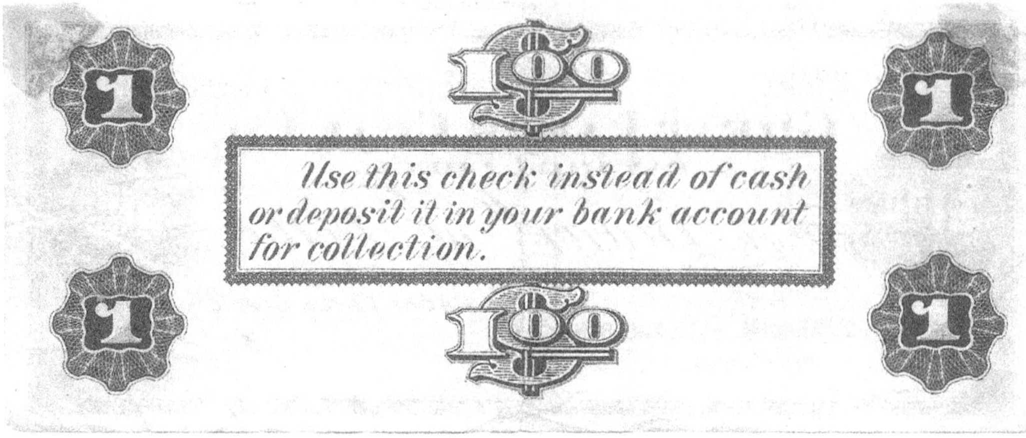

Great Lakes Coal Co.

PA1075-1. 1 Dollar Pay Roll Check Nov. 16, 1907; Jan. 11, 1908 (stamped dates). Black on green underprint including large numeral 1 at center. Commercial National Bank as depository bank. Back black. Imprint: Western Bank Note Co. Pgh. (shown at 71%)

a. Issued, not cancelled. **R4**
b. Issued, cancelled. **R3**

PA1075-2. 2 Dollars Dec. 14, 1907 (stamped date). Black on pink underprint, otherwise as above.

b. Issued, cancelled. **R4**

PA1075-5. 5 Dollars Nov. 16, 1907 (stamped date). Black on light orange underprint, otherwise as above.

b. Issued, cancelled. **R4**

PA1075-10. 10 Dollars Nov. 30, 1907 (stamped date). Black on blue underprint, otherwise as above.

b. Issued, cancelled. **R4**

Martin Grogan

PA1100-5. 5 Dollars Nov. 12, 1907. Black on blue-gray underprint. Scrip Type II, Marine National Bank as depository bank. Account (issuer) name handwritten. (shown at 73%)

b. Issued, cancelled. **R4**

Jones & Laughlin

PA1125-1. 1 Dollar Nov. 22, 1907. Scrip Type I, bank no. 13.

b. Issued, cancelled. **R4**

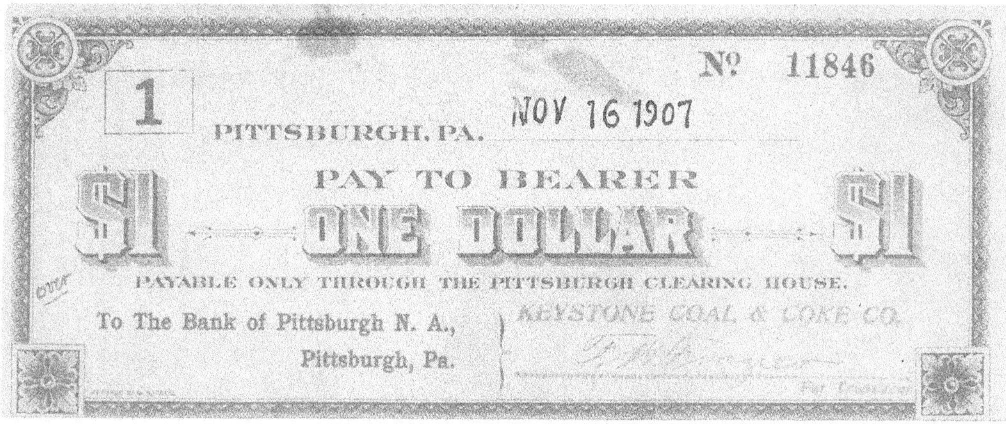

KEYSTONE COAL & COKE CO.

PA1150-1. 1 Dollar Nov. 16, 1907. Black on blue paper. Scrip Type I, bank no. 1. The Bank of Pittsburgh N. A. as depository bank. (shown at 73%)

a. Issued, not cancelled. **R4**

b. Issued, cancelled. **R4**

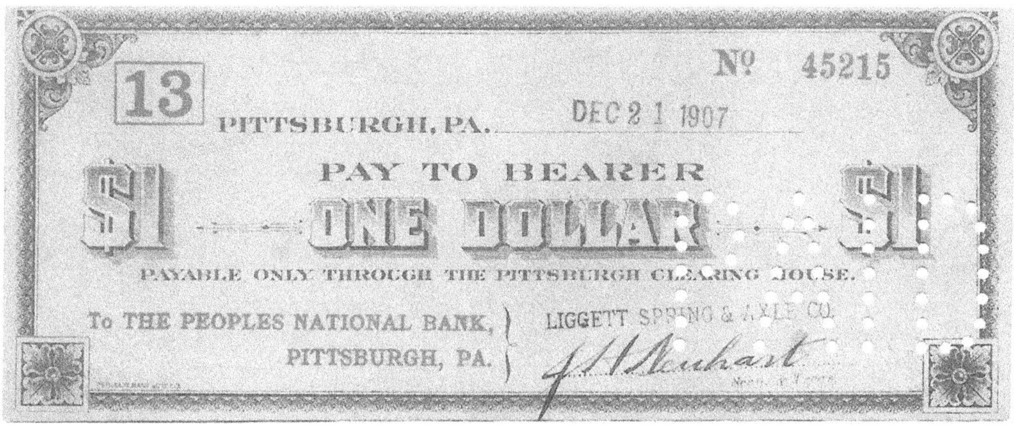

LIGGETT SPRING & AXLE CO.

PA1175-1.A 1 Dollar Dec. 21, 1907. Green on light green paper. Scrip Type I, bank no. 13. The Peoples National Bank as depository bank. (shown at 73%)

b. Issued, cancelled. **R3**

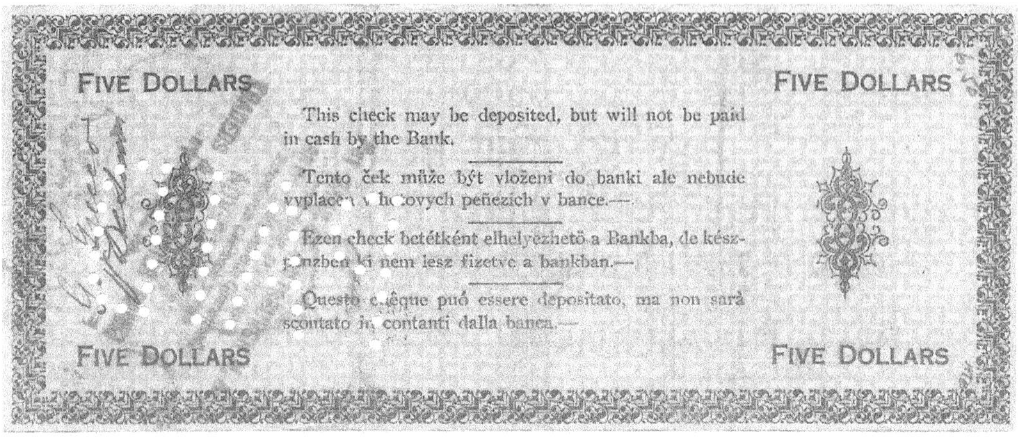

PA1175-5.B 5 Dollars Nov. 9, 1907. Black on blue-gray underprint. Scrip Type II, Peoples National Bank as depository bank. (shown at 71%)

b. Issued, cancelled. R4

PA1175-10.A 10 Dollars Dec. 7, 1907. Green on cream paper. Scrip Type I, bank no. 13. The Peoples National Bank as depository bank.

b. Issued, cancelled. R4

Lutz & Schramm Co.

PA1200-5. 5 Dollars Dec. 21, 1907. Black on blue-gray underprint. Scrip Type II, German National Bank as depository bank. (shown at 73%)

b. Issued, cancelled. R4

B. F. McCann

PA1225-5. 5 Dollars Nov. 19, 1907. (list) Scrip Type II, Federal National Bank as depository bank.

b. Issued, cancelled. R4

PA1225-10. 10 Dollars Nov. 19, 1907. (list) Scrip Type II, bank as above.

b. Issued, cancelled. R4

PA1225-20. 20 Dollars Nov. 19, 1907. (list) Scrip Type II, bank as above.

b. Issued, cancelled. R4

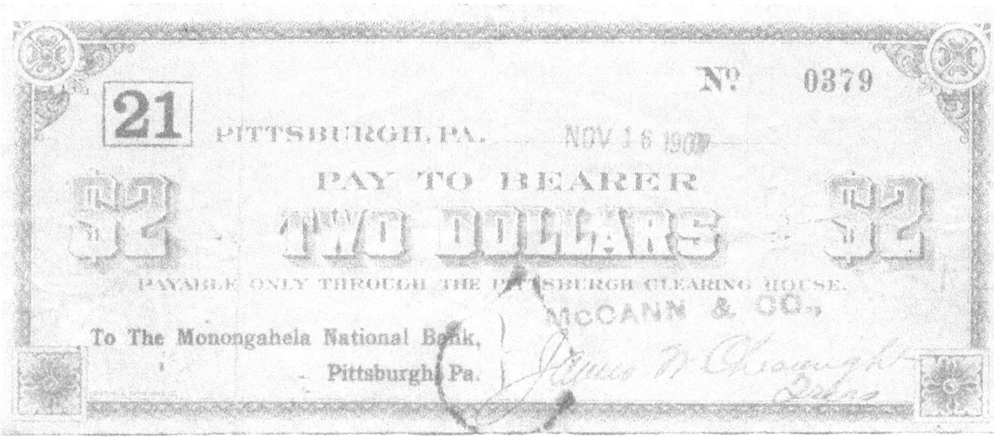

McCann & Co.

PA1250-2. 2 Dollars Nov. 16, 1907. Black on gold paper. Scrip Type I, bank no. 21. The Monongahela National Bank as depository bank. (shown at 73%)

b. Issued, cancelled. **R4**

M. J. Moroney

PA1275-1. 1 Dollar Nov. 15, 1907. Black on light greenish blue paper. Scrip Type I, bank no. 13. The Peoples National Bank as depository bank. Account (issuer) name handwritten. (shown at 73%)

a. Issued, not cancelled. **R4**

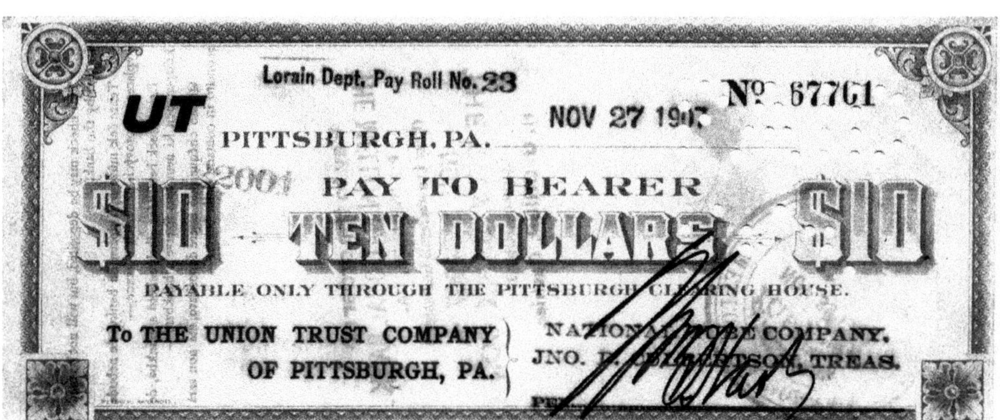

National Tube Company

PA1300-10. 10 Dollars Nov. 27, 1907. Green on white paper. Scrip Type I, bank letters italicized red UT. The Union Trust Company as depository bank. *Lorain Dept. Pay Roll No. 23* text line stamped at top. (shown at 73%)

b. Issued, cancelled. **R4**

New York & Cleveland Gas Coal Company

PA1325-1. 1 Dollar Nov. 15, 1907. (list) Scrip Type I, bank no. 1. The Bank of Pittsburgh N. A. as depository bank.

b. Issued, cancelled. **R4**

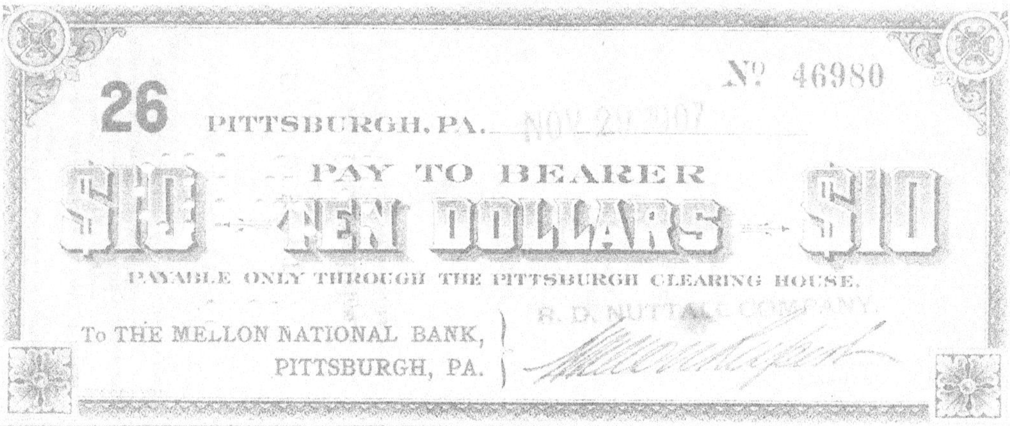

R. D. Nuttall Company

PA1350-10.A 10 Dollars Nov. 29, 1907. Green on white paper. Scrip Type I, bank no. 26 (without box). The Mellon National Bank as depository bank. (shown at 75%)

b. Issued, cancelled. **R4**

PA1350-20.B 20 Dollars Nov. 15, 23, 1907. Black on gold underprint. Scrip Type II, Mellon National Bank as depository bank. (shown at 73%)

b. Issued, cancelled. **R4**

Pittsburgh Printing Company

PA1375-5. 5 Dollars Nov. 11, 1907 (handwritten date). Black on blue-gray underprint. Scrip Type II, Federal National Bank as depository bank. (shown at 73%)

b. Issued, cancelled. R4

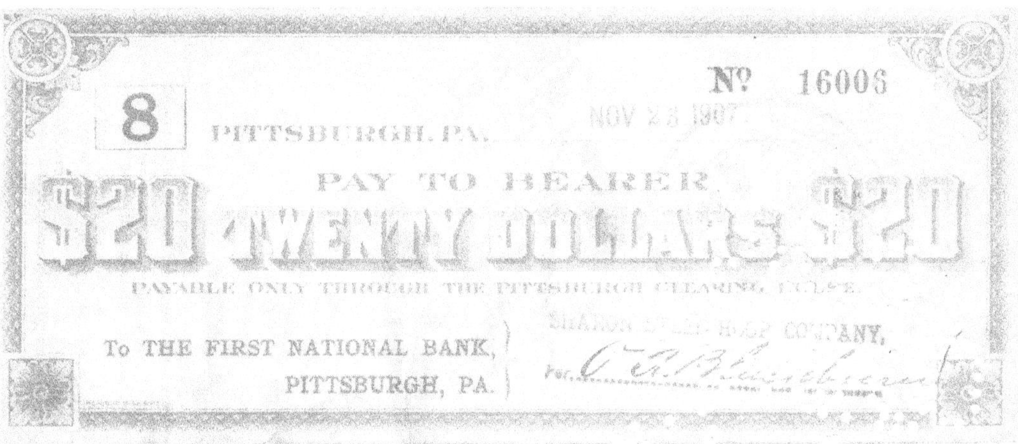

Sharon Steel Hoop Company

PA1400-20. 20 Dollars Nov. 23, 1907. Brown on cream paper. Scrip Type I, bank no. 8. The First National Bank as depository bank. (shown at 75%)

b. Issued, cancelled. R4

L. C. Smith & Bros. Typewriter Co.

PA1425-1. 1 Dollar Nov. 16, 1907 (handwritten date). Blue on light blue paper. Scrip Type I, bank no. 21. The Monongahela National Bank as depository bank. (shown at 75%)
a. Issued, not cancelled. R4

Spang, Chalfant & Co., Inc.

PA1450-1. 1 Dollar Nov. 23, 1907. Green on light green paper. Scrip Type I, bank no. 13. The Peoples National Bank as depository bank. (shown at 76%)
b. Issued, cancelled. R3
PA1450-2. 2 Dollars Dec. 14, 1907. Blue-black on gold paper. As above.
b. Issued, cancelled. R3
PA1450-5. 5 Dollars Nov. 23, 1907. Blue on white paper. As above.
b. Issued, cancelled. R4
PA1450-10. 10 Dollars Nov. 23, 1907. Green on white paper. As above.
b. Issued, cancelled. R4
PA1450-20. 20 Dollars Nov. 23, 1907. Brown on cream paper. As above.
b. Issued, cancelled. R4

Standard Engineering Co.

PA1475-1. 1 Dollar Dec. 7, 1907. Black-green on light green paper. Scrip Type I, bank no. 22. The Columbia National Bank as depository bank. (shown at 78%)
a. Issued, not cancelled. R4

Standard Steel Car Co.

PA1500-10. 10 Dollars Jan. 11, 1908. Green. Scrip Type I, bank no. 26. Check registry for design in red oval logo at upper center. The Mellon National Bank as depository bank. (shown at 69%)

b. Issued, cancelled. R4

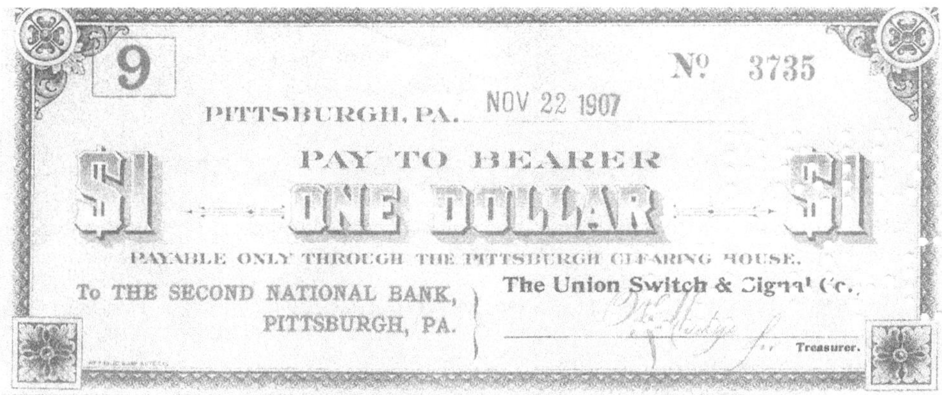

The Union Switch & Signal Co.

PA1525-1.A 1 Dollar Nov. 22, 1907. Blue on light blue paper. Scrip Type I, bank no. 9. The Second National Bank as depository bank. (shown at 70%)

b. Issued, cancelled. R4

PA1525-5.B 5 Dollars Nov. 8, 1907. Black on gray-blue underprint. Scrip Type II, Second National Bank as depository bank.

b. Issued, cancelled. R4

PA1525-20.B 20 Dollars Nov. 8, 1907. Black on gold underprint. Scrip Type II, Second National Bank as depository bank. (shown at 66%)
b. Issued, cancelled. **R4**

UNITED ENGINEERING & FOUNDRY CO.

PA1550-1.A 1 Dollar Nov. 20, 1907. Scrip Type I, bank no. 23; The National Bank of Western Pennsylvania as depository bank.
a. Issued, not cancelled. **R4**

PA1550-5.B 5 Dollars Nov. 8, 1907. Black on gray-blue underprint. Scrip Type II; The Bank of Pittsburgh, N. A. as depository bank.
b. Issued, cancelled. **R4**

PA1550-10.A 10 Dollars Nov. 8, Dec. 6, 1907. Green on light green paper. Scrip Type I, bank no. 1; The Bank of Pittsburgh N. A. as depository bank.
b. Issued, cancelled. **R4**

PA1550-10.B 10 Dollars Dec. 9, 1907. Scrip Type II; The Bank of Pittsburgh, N. A. as depository bank. (shown at 63%)
b. Issued, cancelled. **R4**

PA1550-10.C 10 Dollars Nov. 8, 1907. (list) Scrip Type II; Union Trust Company as depository bank.
b. Issued, cancelled. **R4**

PA1550-20.A 20 Dollars Nov. 8, 1907. (list) Scrip Type I; bank number and name as above.
b. Issued, cancelled. **R4**

PA1550-20.B 20 Dollars Nov. 8, 1907. Black and red on light orange underprint. Scrip Type II; The Bank of Pittsburgh, N. A. as depository bank.
b. Issued, cancelled. **R4**

Scrip with Depository Bank Name, Without Issuer's Name or Date

A. The Allegheny National Bank

PA1575-1. 1 Dollar ND (1907). Scrip Type I, bank no. 7.
c. Unissued, cancelled. **EF, 20. Unc., 35.**

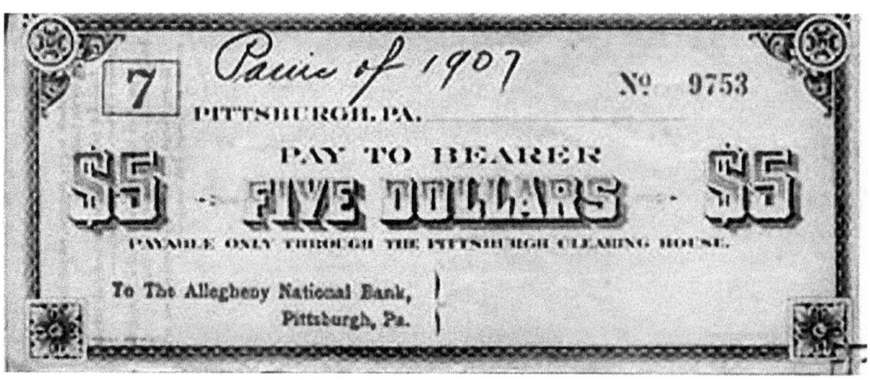

PA1575-5. 5 Dollars ND (1907). Scrip Type I, bank no. 7. (shown at 63%)
c. Unissued, cancelled. **EF, 20. Unc., 35.**
PA1575-10. 10 Dollars ND (1907). Scrip Type I, bank no. 7. (list)
c. Unissued, cancelled. **EF, 20. Unc., 35.**

B. The Bank of Pittsburgh N. A.
PA1600-1.A 1 Dollar ND (1907). Green on light green paper. Scrip Type I, bank no. 1.
c. Unissued, cancelled. **EF, 20. Unc., 35.**

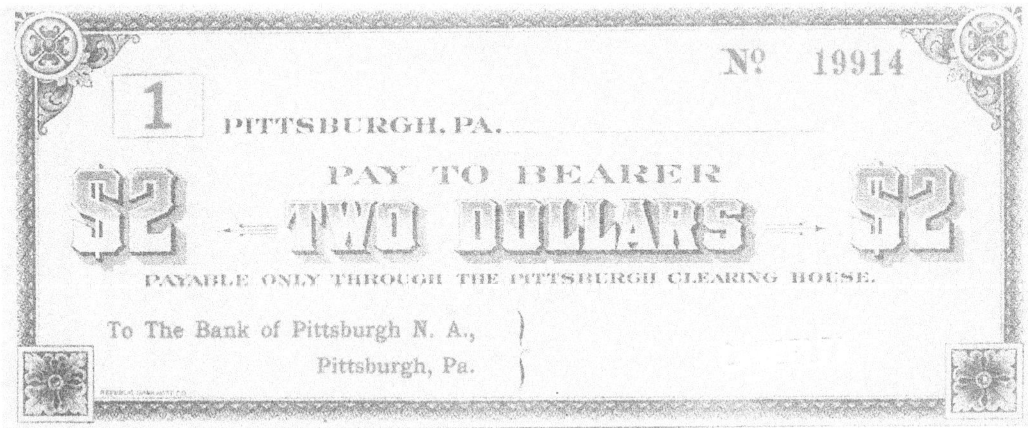

PA1600-2.A 2 Dollars ND (1907). Brown on gold paper. Scrip Type I, bank no. 1. (shown at 75%)
c. Unissued, cancelled. **EF, 20. Unc., 35.**
PA1600-5.A 5 Dollars ND (1907). Blue. Scrip Type I, bank no. 1.
c. Unissued, cancelled. **EF, 20. Unc., 35.**
PA1600-5.B 5 Dollars ND (1907). Black on gray underprint. Scrip Type II.
c. Unissued, cancelled. **EF, 20. Unc., 35.**

PA1600-10.A 10 Dollars ND (1907). Green. Design registry logo in red oval at upper center. Scrip Type I, bank no. 1. (shown at 78%)
c. Unissued, cancelled. **EF, 30. Unc., 50.**

PA1600-10.B 10 Dollars ND (1907). Black on light green underprint. Scrip Type II. (shown at 73%)
c. Unissued, cancelled. **EF, 20. Unc., 35.**

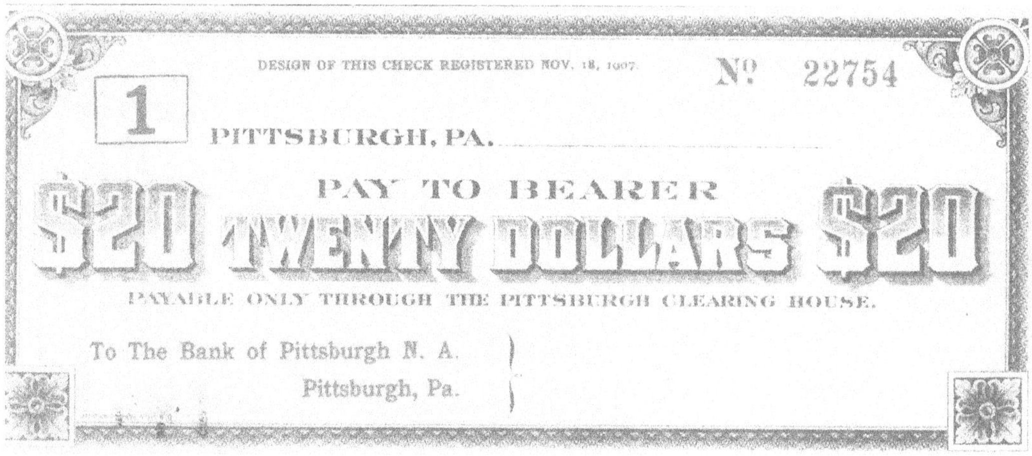

PA1600-20.A 20 Dollars ND (1907). Brown. Scrip Type I, bank no. 1. Added text line in red about design registry Nov. 18, 1907 at upper center. (shown at 78%)
c. Unissued, cancelled. **EF, 20. Unc., 35.**

C. The Columbia National Bank
PA1625-1. 1 Dollar ND (1907). Green on light green paper. Scrip Type I, bank no. 22. (shown at 78%)
d. Unissued, remainder. **EF, 20. Unc., 35.**
PA1625-2. 2 Dollars ND (1907). Brown on gold paper. Scrip Type I, bank no. 22.
d. Unissued, remainder. **EF, 20. Unc., 35.**

D. The Diamond National Bank
PA1650-1. 1 Dollar ND (1907). Green on light green paper. Scrip Type I, bank no. 19 (in box).
c. Unissued, cancelled. **EF, 30. Unc., 50.**
PA1650-5. 5 Dollars ND (1907). Blue. Scrip Type I, bank no. 19 (without box).
c. Unissued, cancelled. **EF, 30. Unc., 50.**

PA1650-10. 10 Dollars ND (1907). Green. Scrip Type I, bank no. 19 as above. (shown at 77%)
c. Unissued, cancelled. **EF, 30. Unc., 50.**
PA1650-20. 20 Dollars ND (1907). Brown. Scrip Type I, bank no. 19 as above.
c. Unissued, cancelled. **EF, 30. Unc., 50.**

E. The Farmers Deposit National Bank
PA1675-1. 1 Dollar ND (1907). Blue on light blue paper. Scrip Type I, bank no. 11. (shown at 76%)
f. Specimen. **EF, 20. Unc., 35.**
PA1675-2. 2 Dollars ND (1907). Brown on gold paper. Scrip Type I, bank no. 11.
f. Specimen. **EF, 20. Unc., 35.**
PA1675-5.A 5 Dollars ND (1907). Blue. Scrip Type I, bank no. 11.
f. Specimen. **EF, 20. Unc., 35.**

PA1675-5.B 5 Dollars ND (1907). Black on gray underprint. Scrip Type II. (shown at 74%)
f. Specimen. **EF, 20. Unc., 35.**
PA1675-10.A 10 Dollars ND (1907). Green. Scrip Type I, bank no 11. Check registry for design in red oval logo at upper center.
f. Specimen. **EF, 20. Unc., 35.**
PA1675-10.B 10 Dollars ND (1907). Black on light green underprint. Scrip Type II.
f. Specimen. **EF, 20. Unc., 35.**
PA1675-20. 20 Dollars ND (1907). Brown. Scrip Type I, bank no. 11.
f. Specimen. **EF, 20. Unc., 35.**

F. The First National Bank
PA1700-1. 1 Dollar ND (1907). (list) Scrip Type I, bank no. 8.
c. Unissued, cancelled. **EF, 20. Unc., 35.**
PA1700-2. 2 Dollars ND (1907). (list) Scrip Type I, bank no. 8.
c. Unissued, cancelled. **EF, 20. Unc., 35.**

PA1700-5. 5 Dollars ND (1907). Blue. Scrip Type I, bank no. 8. (shown at 79%)
c. Unissued, cancelled. **EF, 20. Unc., 35.**
e. Sample. **EF, 20. Unc., 35.**
PA1700-10. 10 Dollars ND (1907). Green. Design registry logo in red oval at upper center. Scrip Type I, bank no. 8.
c. Unissued, cancelled. **EF, 20. Unc., 35.**

PA1700-20.A 20 Dollars ND (1907). Brown. Design registry logo in red oval at upper center. Scrip Type I, bank no. 8. (shown at 78%)
c. Unissued, cancelled. **EF, 20. Unc., 35.**
PA1700-20.B 20 Dollars ND (1907). Black on light brown underprint. Scrip Type II.
c. Unissued, cancelled. **EF, 20. Unc., 35.**

G. German Savings & Deposit Bank
PA1750-1. 1 Dollar Pay Check ND (1907). Black on green pattern underprint. Uniface. Imprint: American Bank Note Co. New York, Litho. (shown at 68%)
f. Specimen. **R4**

H. Germania Savings Bank
PA1775-5. 5 Dollars ND (1907). Black on gray underprint. Scrip Type II. (shown at 72%)
d. Unissued, remainder. **EF, 20. Unc., 35.**
PA1775-10. 10 Dollars ND (1907). Black on yellow underprint. Scrip Type II.
d. Unissued, remainder. **EF, 20. Unc., 35.**
PA1775-20. 20 Dollars ND (1907). Black on gold underprint. Scrip Type II.
d. Unissued, remainder. **EF, 20. Unc., 35.**

I. The National Bank of Western Pennsylvania
PA1800-1. 1 Dollar ND (1907). (list) Scrip Type I, bank no. 23.
f. Specimen. **EF, 30. Unc., 50.**
PA1800-2. 2 Dollars ND (1907). (list) Scrip Type I, bank no. 23.
f. Specimen. **EF, 30. Unc., 50.**
PA1800-5. 5 Dollars ND (1907). (list) Scrip Type I, bank no. 23.
f. Specimen. **EF, 30. Unc., 50.**
PA1800-10. 10 Dollars ND (1907). (list) Scrip Type I, bank no. 23.
f. Specimen. **EF, 30. Unc., 50.**
PA1800-20. 20 Dollars ND (1907). (list) Scrip Type I, bank no. 23.
f. Specimen. **EF, 30. Unc., 50.**

J. The Peoples National Bank
PA1825-1. 1 Dollar ND (1907). Black on light blue paper. Scrip Type I, bank no. 13.
c. Unissued, cancelled. **EF, 20. Unc., 35.**
PA1825-2. 2 Dollars ND (1907). Brown on gold paper. Scrip Type I, bank no. 13.
c. Unissued, cancelled. **EF, 20. Unc., 35.**
PA1825-5. 5 Dollars ND (1907). Blue. Scrip Type I, bank no. 13. Check registry for design in red oval at upper center.
c. Unissued, cancelled. **EF, 20. Unc., 35.**
PA1825-10. 10 Dollars ND (1907). Green. Scrip Type I, bank no. 13. Check registry in oval as above.
c. Unissued, cancelled. **EF, 20. Unc., 35.**
PA1825-20.A 20 Dollars ND (1907). Brown. Scrip Type I, bank no. 13.
c. Unissued, cancelled. **EF, 20. Unc., 35.**

PA1825-20.B 20 Dollars ND (1907). Black on gold underprint. Scrip Type II. (shown at 58%)
c. Unissued, cancelled. **EF, 20. Unc., 35.**

K. Second National Bank
PA1850-10. 10 Dollars ND (1907). Black on light green underprint. Scrip Type II. (shown at 58%)
d. Unissued, remainder. **EF, 20. Unc., 35.**

Scrip Without Bank or Issuer Name

PA1875-5. 5 Dollars ND (1907). Black on gray underprint. Scrip Type II. (shown at 60%)
e. Sample. **EF, 20. Unc., 35.**

PA1875-10. 10 Dollars ND (1907). Black on gold underprint. Scrip Type II. (shown at 60%)
c. Unissued, cancelled. **EF, 20. Unc., 35.**
e. Sample. **EF, 20. Unc., 35.**
PA1875-20. 20 Dollars ND (1907). Black on gold underprint. Scrip Type II.
e. Sample. **EF, 20. Unc., 35.**
f. Specimen. **EF, 20. Unc., 35.**

Wilkes-Barre

Wilkes-Barre Clearing House Association

PA1900-5. 5 Dollars ND (1907). Dark green on light green pattern underprint. Uniface. Imprint: American Bank Note Co. New York, Litho. (shown at 64%)
f. Specimen. **R5**
PA1900-10. 10 Dollars ND (1907). As above.
f. Specimen. **R5**
PA1900-20. 20 Dollars ND (1907). As above.
f. Specimen. **R5**

Wilkinsburg

J.M. Taylor

PA1925-10. 10 Dollars Nov. 8, 1907. Black on gray underprint. Scrip Type II (see Pittsburgh). Wilkinsburg Trust Company as depository bank. Account (issuer) name handwritten.
b. Issued, cancelled. **R4**

Scrip with Depository Bank Name, Without Issuer's Name or Date

A. First National Bank of Wilkinsburg
PA1950-5.B1 5 Dollars ND (1907). Black on gray underprint. Scrip Type II. (shown at 73%)
c. Unissued, cancelled. **EF, 30. Unc., 50.**
PA1950-5.B2 5 Dollars ND (1907). As above but greenish paper.
c. Unissued, cancelled. **EF, 30. Unc., 50.**

B. Wilkinsburg Trust Company
PA1975-10. 10 Dollars Nov. 8, 1907. Black on light tan underprint. Scrip Type II. (shown at 73%)
c. Unissued, cancelled. **R5**

Rhode Island

Providence

Grosvenor-Dale Co./ The Rhode Island Hospital Trust Co.

RI600-5. 5 Dollars (payroll check) Nov. 18, 1907. Black on light yellow underprint. Uniface. (shown at 81%)
c. Unissued, cancelled. **R5**
RI600-10. 10 Dollars Nov. 18, 1907. As above.
c. Unissued, cancelled. **R5**

South Carolina

Charleston

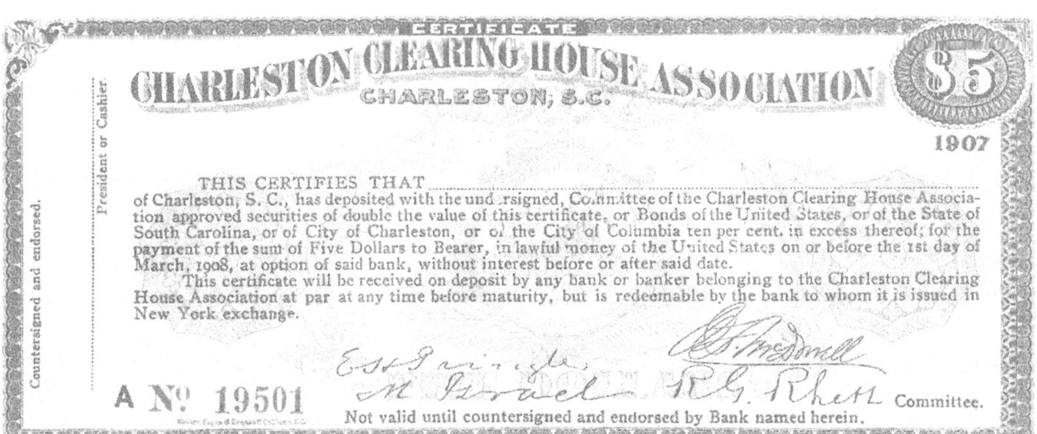

Charleston Clearing House Association

SC500-5. 5 Dollars 1907. Red-brown on ornate green underprint. Back green; U.S. shield at left and right, circular design with state emblems at center. Imprint (on both sides): Walker, Evans & Cogswell Co. Chas'n, S.C. (shown at 63%)

c. Unissued, cancelled.	R4
d. Unissued, remainder.	R4

SC500-10. 10 Dollars 1907. Green on ornate orange underprint. As above.

c. Unissued, cancelled.	R4

Columbia

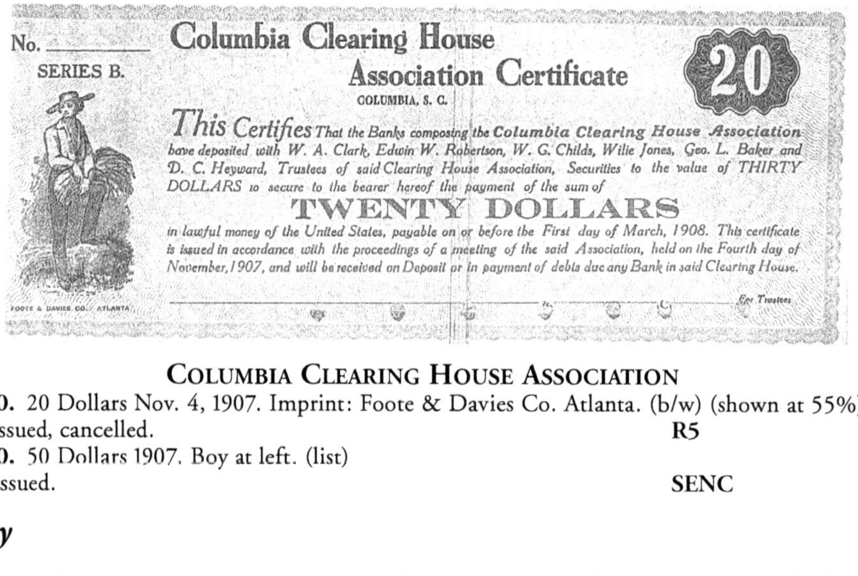

Columbia Clearing House Association

SC525-20. 20 Dollars Nov. 4, 1907. Imprint: Foote & Davies Co. Atlanta. (b/w) (shown at 55%)

c. Unissued, cancelled.	R5

SC525-50. 50 Dollars 1907. Boy at left. (list)

u. Unissued.	SENC

Gaffney

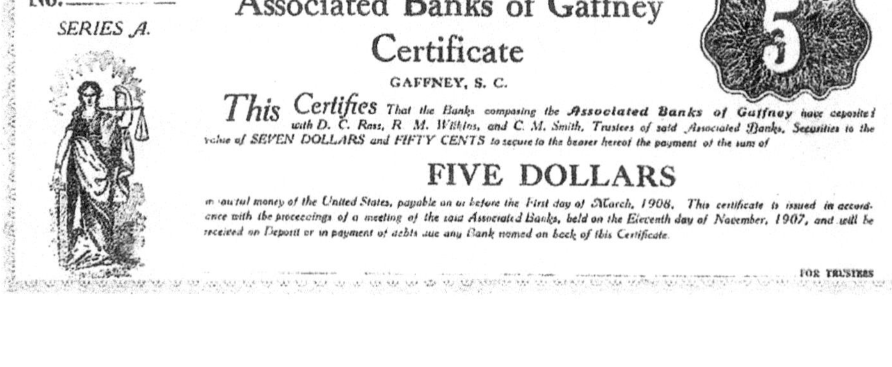

Associated Banks of Gaffney

SC550-5. 5 Dollars (certificate of deposit) Nov. 11, 1907. Black and green. Justice and scales at left. List of member banks on back. Series A. (shown at 55%)
c. Unissued, cancelled. R5

SC550-10. 10 Dollars Nov. 11, 1907. Similar to above.
c. Unissued, cancelled. R5

Greenville

Greenville Clearing House Association Certificate

SC575-1. 1 Dollar (certificate of deposit) Nov. 12, 1907. Black and green, with red denomination at center. Woman at left. List of member banks on back. Imprint: Foote & Davies Co. Atlanta.
c. Unissued, cancelled. R5

SC575-2. 2 Dollars Nov. 12, 1907. Black and orange. As above.
c. Unissued, cancelled. R5

SC575-5. 5 Dollars Nov. 12, 1907. Light tan and black. As above.
c. Unissued, cancelled. R5

SC575-10. 10 Dollars Nov. 12, 1907. Green and light tan. As above.
c. Unissued, cancelled. R5

Greenwood

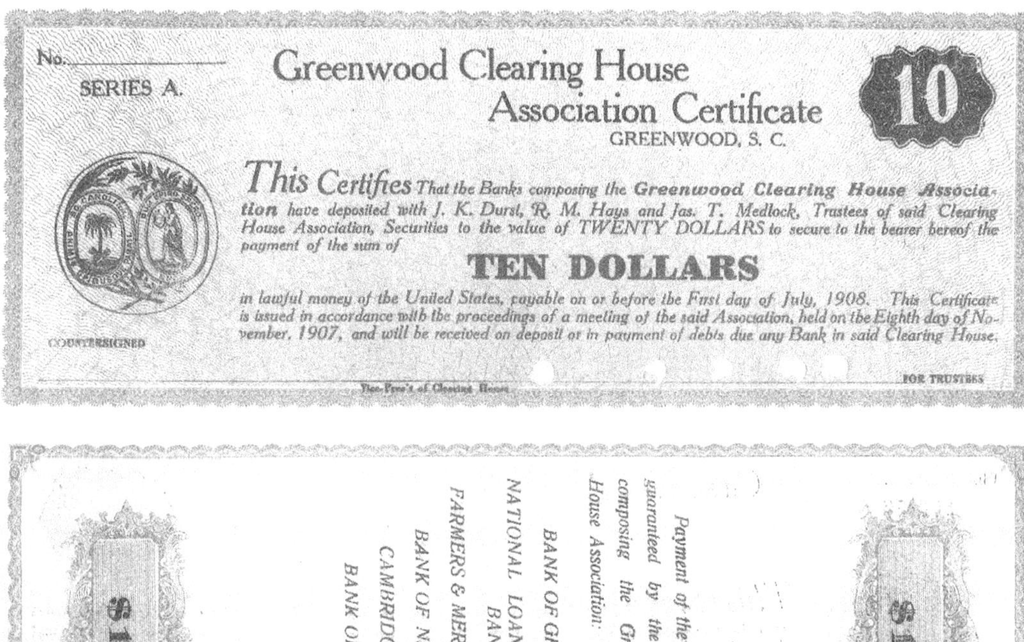

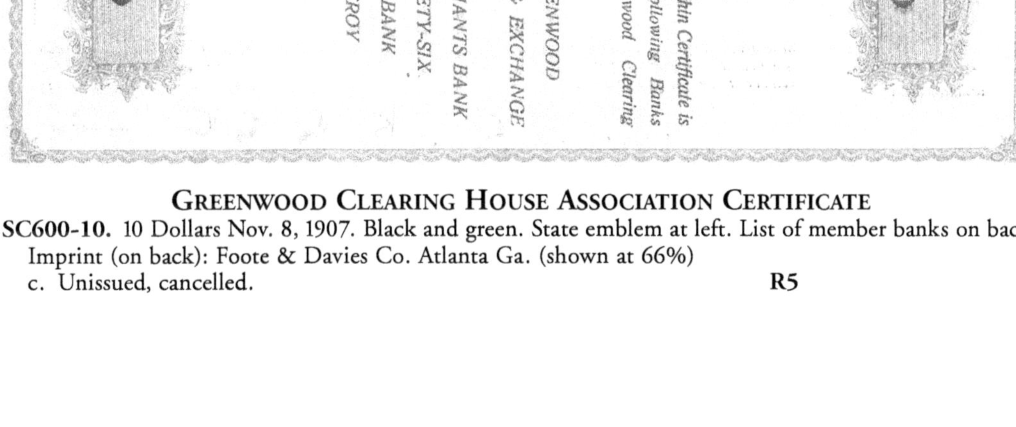

Greenwood Clearing House Association Certificate

SC600-10. 10 Dollars Nov. 8, 1907. Black and green. State emblem at left. List of member banks on back. Imprint (on back): Foote & Davies Co. Atlanta Ga. (shown at 66%)
c. Unissued, cancelled. R5

Rock Hill

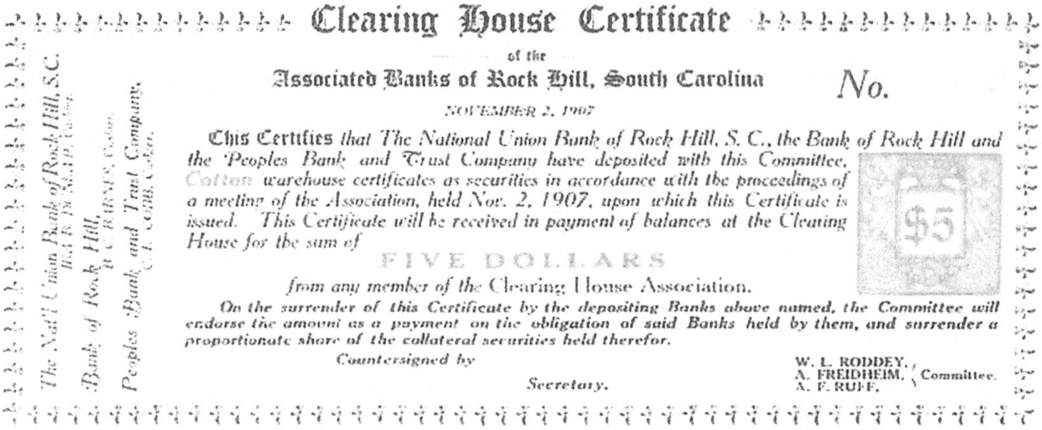

Associated Banks of Rock Hill, South Carolina

SC625-5. 5 Dollars Nov. 2, 1907. Black and red. Value in red square at right. Uniface. (shown at 72%)

d. Unissued, remainder. **R5**

Spartanburg

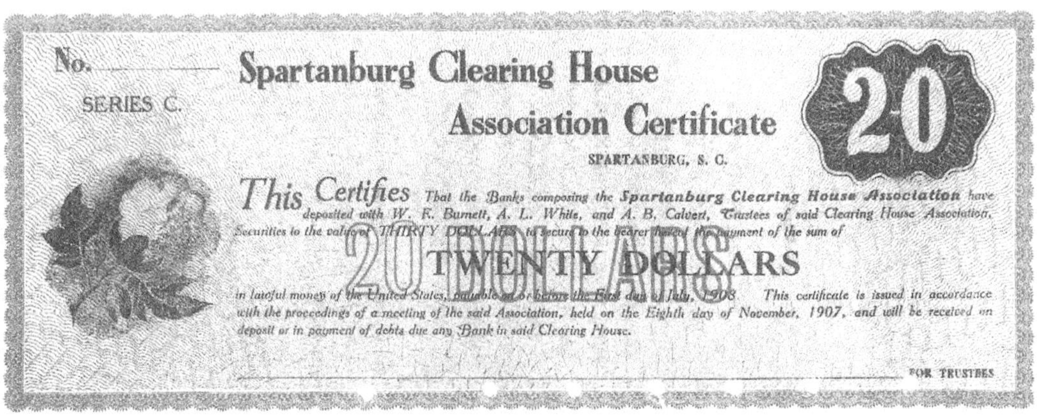

Spartanburg Clearing House Association Certificate

SC650-5. 5 Dollars Nov. 8, 1907. Black and green. Cotton boll at left. Red denomination at center. List of member banks on back. Imprint as SC600. (shown at 66%)

b. Issued, cancelled. **R4**

SC650-10. 10 Dollars Nov. 8, 1907. As above.
c. Unissued, cancelled. R4
SC650-20. 20 Dollars Nov. 8, 1907. As above.
c. Unissued, cancelled. R4

Yorkville

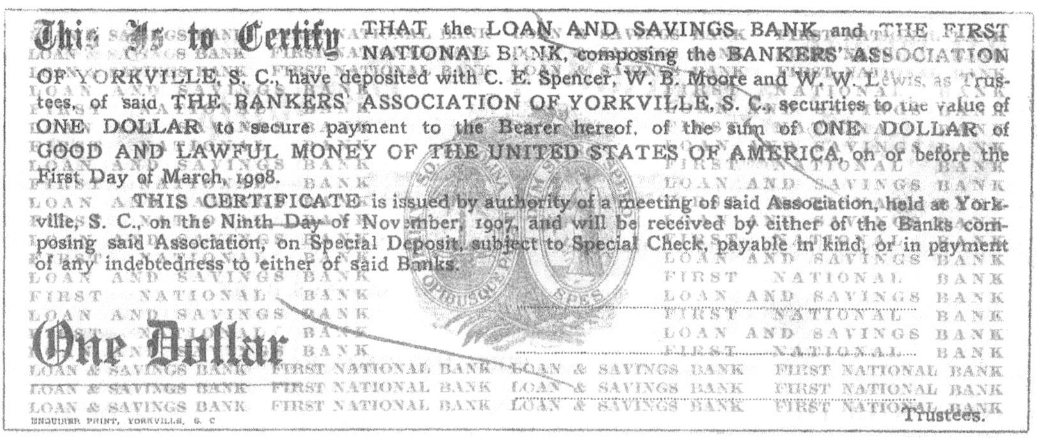

Bankers' Association of Yorkville, S. C.

SC675-1. 1 Dollar Nov. 9, 1907. Black text on brown underprint of bank names, with eagle at center. State seal in brown at center in brown underprint on back. Imprint: Enquirer Print, Yorkville, S. C. (shown at 76%)
a. Issued, not cancelled. R5
d. Unissued, remainder. R5

Tennessee

Bristol

Bristol Clearing House Association (Va., Tenn.)

TN500-1. 1 Dollar Nov. 1, 1907. (list)
b. Issued, cancelled. R5

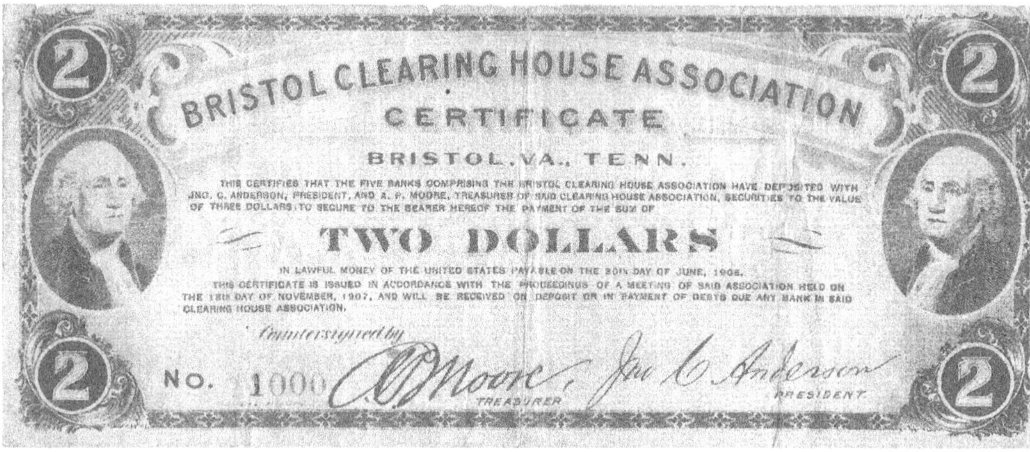

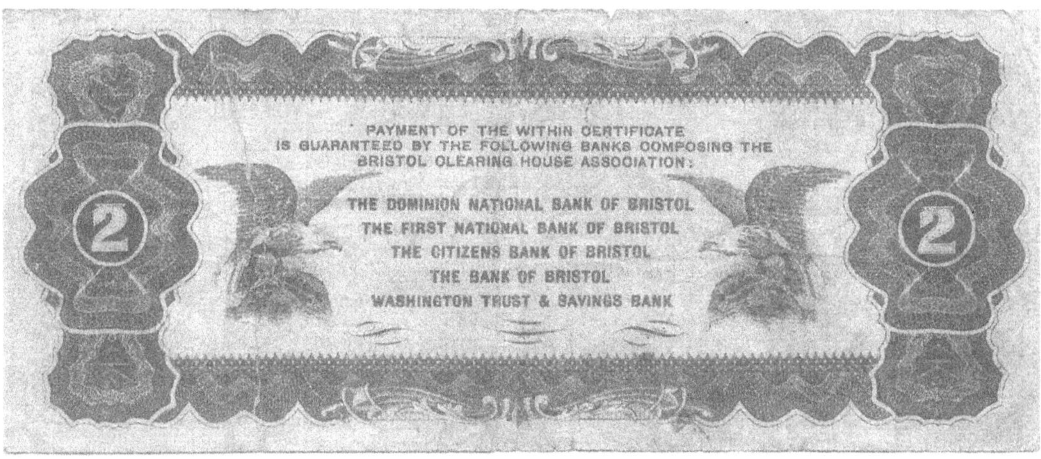

TN500-2. 2 Dollars Nov. 18, 1907. Green. Washington portrait at left and right. Eagle at left and right on back. Imprint: Foster Webb & Parkes Nashville. (shown at 73%)

a. Issued, not cancelled.	**R5**
b. Issued, cancelled.	**VG, 125. VF 300.**

Clifton

PEOPLES BANK

TN525-1. 1 Dollar Nov. 25, 1907. Brown on light blue pattern underprint. Back green; large eagle at center. Imprint and perforation: Foster Webb & Parkes Nashville. (shown at 72%)

e. Printer's sample. **R5**

Dyersburg

DYERSBURG CLEARING HOUSE CERTIFICATE

TN550-1. 1 Dollar Nov. 4, 1907. Olive green on pale greenish gray paper. Large denomination at center on back. (shown at 63%)

a. Issued, not cancelled. **R5**

Knoxville

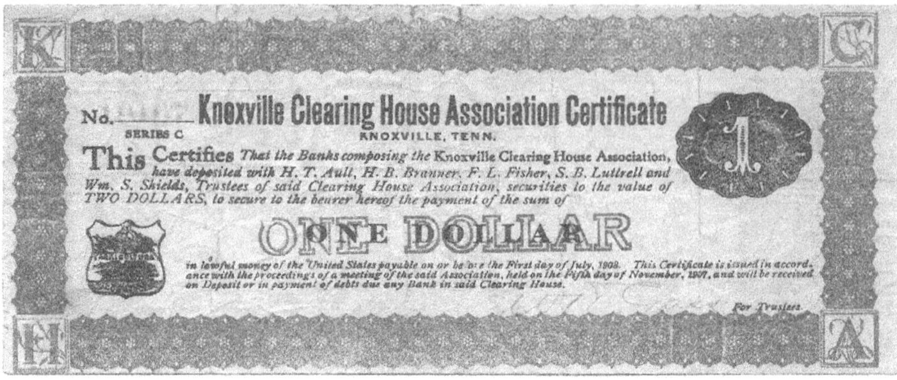

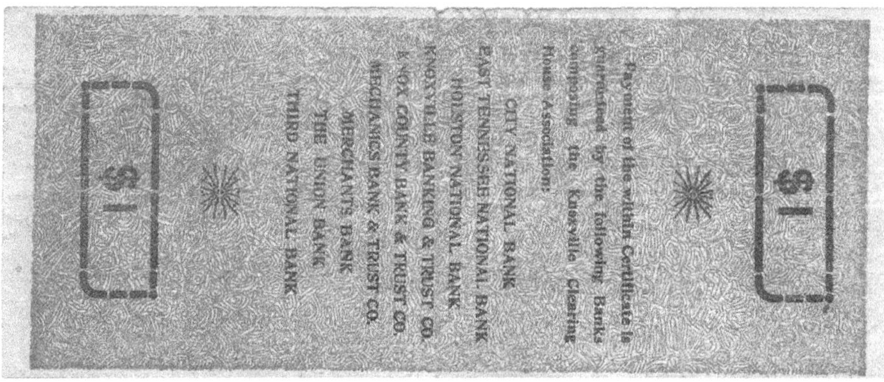

KNOXVILLE CLEARING HOUSE ASSOCIATION CERTIFICATE

TN575-1. 1 Dollar Nov. 5, 1907. Red-brown and black on gray paper. State shield at lower left. List of member banks on back. (shown at 63%)

a. Issued, not cancelled.	R5
b. Issued, cancelled.	R4

TN575-5. 5 Dollars Nov. 5, 1907. Design as above.

b. Issued, cancelled.	R5

TN575-10. 10 Dollars Nov. 5, 1907. (list)

b. Issued, cancelled.	R5

NOTE: An amount of $282,500 was issued beginning Nov. 7, 1907.

Memphis

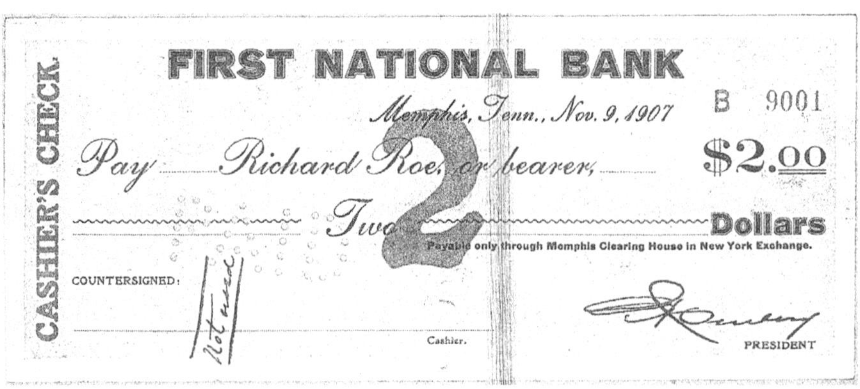

First National Bank

TN600-2. 2 Dollars Cashier's Check Nov. 9, 1907. Large denomination numeral at center. (b/w) (shown at 60%)

c. Unissued, cancelled. R5

State National Bank

TN625-1. 1 Dollar Cashier's Check Nov. 9, 1907. Black on green underprint. Large red denomination numeral at center. Green pattern on back. (shown at 77%)

a. Issued, not cancelled. R5

b. Issued, cancelled. R5

TN625-2. 2 Dollars Nov. 9, 1907. Black and red on light blue underprint. As above. Back light blue.

b. Issued, cancelled. R5

TN625-5. 5 Dollars Nov. 9, 1907. Black and red on light brown underprint. As above. Back brown.

b. Issued, cancelled. R5

TN625-10. 10 Dollars Nov. 9, 1907. Black and red on gold underprint. As above. Back yellow.

b. Issued, cancelled. R5

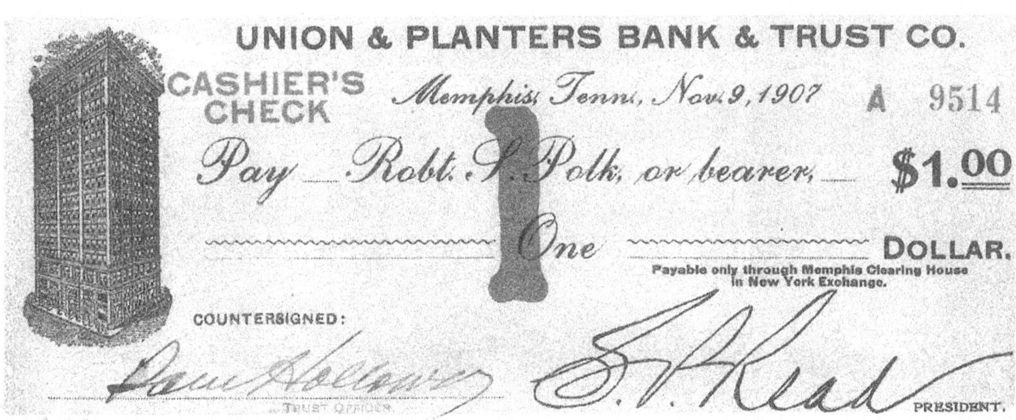

Union & Planters Bank & Trust Co.

TN650-1. 1 Dollar Cashier's Check Nov. 9, 1907. Black and red on green underprint. Bank building at left, large red denomination numeral at center. Back green. (shown at 75%)

a. Issued, not cancelled. R4

Nashville

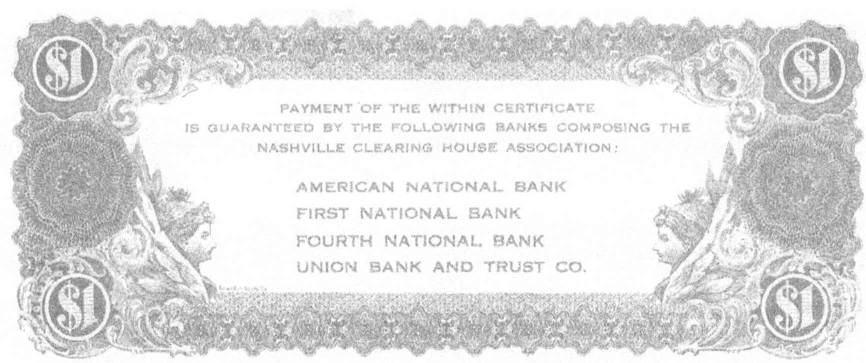

NASHVILLE CLEARING HOUSE ASSOCIATION CERTIFICATE

TN675-1. 1 Dollar Nov. 1, 1907. Green on light green underprint. List of member banks on back. Imprint: Brandon-Nashville. (shown at 62%)

a. Issued, not cancelled. **R5**

b. Issued, cancelled. **VG, 150. VF, 325.**

TN675-2. 2 Dollars Nov. 1, 1907. (b/w)

a. Issued, not cancelled. **R5**

TN675-5. 5 Dollars Nov. 1, 1907. Dark green, otherwise similar to above.

b. Issued, cancelled. **R4**

NOTE: An amount of $468,700 was issued beginning Nov. 2, 1907.

Union City

Obion County Association of Banks

TN700-1. 1 Dollar Nov. 4, 1907. Black on red underprint. List of member banks with signature representing each on back, with state emblem below. Left and right sections clipped as cancellation. (shown at 68%)

b. Issued, cancelled. R3

TN700-5. 5 Dollars Nov. 4, 1907. Black on green underprint, otherwise as above.

b. Issued, cancelled. R3

Weakley County

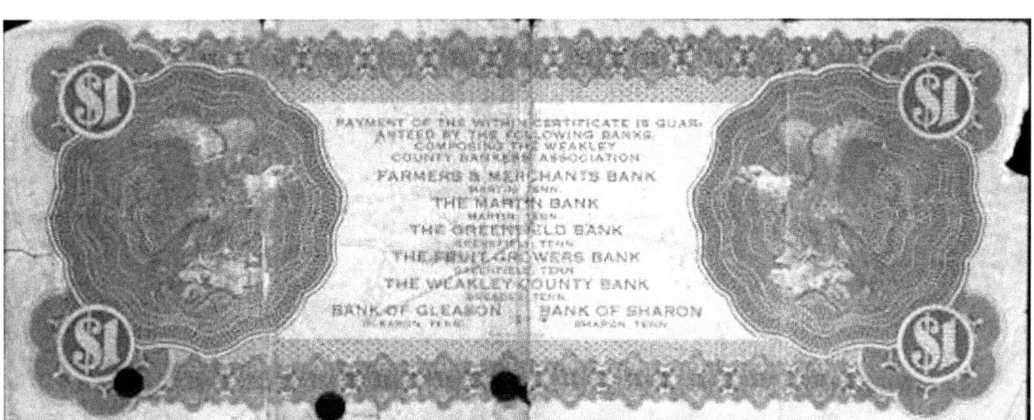

Weakley County Bankers' Association

TN725-1. 1 Dollar Nov. 18, 1907. Green. List of member banks at center on back, condor at left and right. (shown at 74%)
b. Issued, cancelled. R5

Texas

Belton

Belton State Bank

An issue of $1 scrip is believed to have been issued in Belton, but no details are presently known.

Dallas

A clearing house loan certificate is believed to have been issued. No specifics are known at present.

Grandview

First National Bank

A. First Issue

TX550-10. 10 Dollars Cashier's Check Nov. 7, 1907. Blue. Large eagle at center on back. Imprint: X — Co. Dallas. (shown at 73%)

b. Issued, cancelled. R5

B. Second Issue

TX560-1. 1 Dollar Cashier's Check Nov. 12, 1907. Black and blue. Red outline denomination at center. Back blue-green without text; ornate border with small shields at upper and lower center. Imprint as above. (shown at 66%)

a. Issued, not cancelled. R5

b. Issued, cancelled. R5

Houston

A cashier's check issue is believed to have been issued in Houston, but no details are presently known.

Hubbard

The First National Bank of Hubbard

TX575-5. 5 Dollars Cashier's Check Nov. 19, 1907 (handwritten date). Black and blue, as TX560. Red outline denomination at center. Back also as TX560.

b. Issued, cancelled. R5

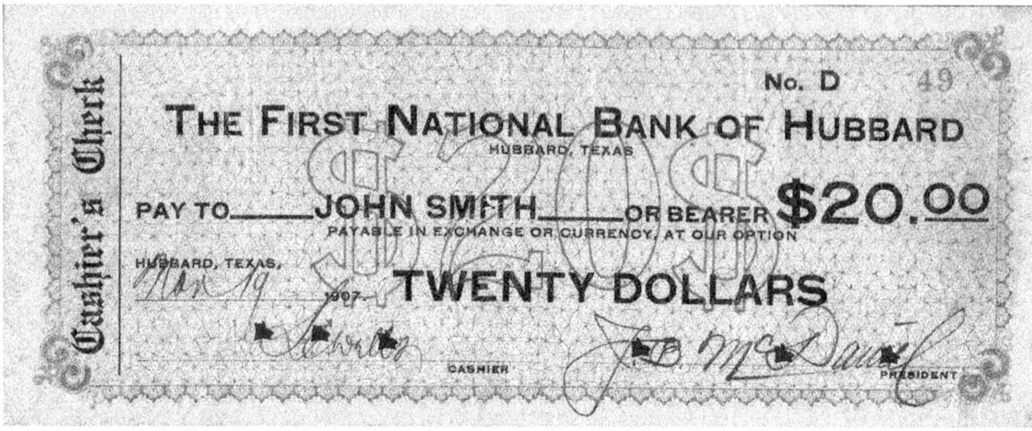

TX575-20. 20 Dollars Nov. 19, 1907. As above. (shown at 67%)
b. Issued, cancelled. **R5**

Prosper

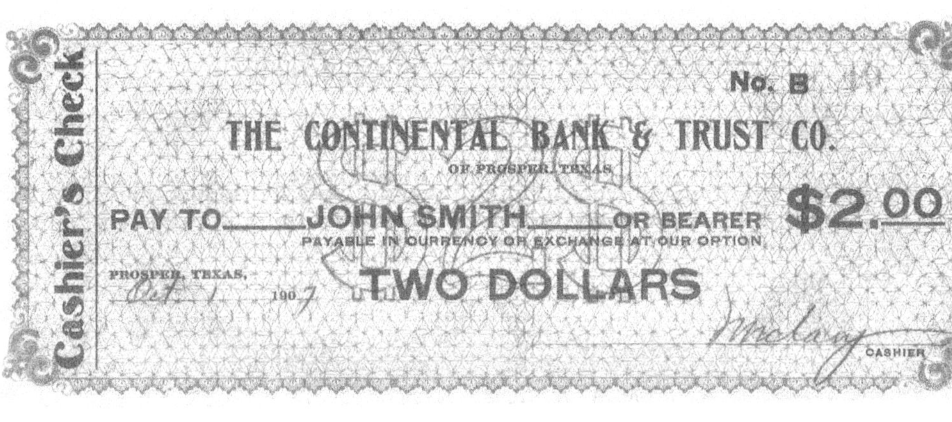

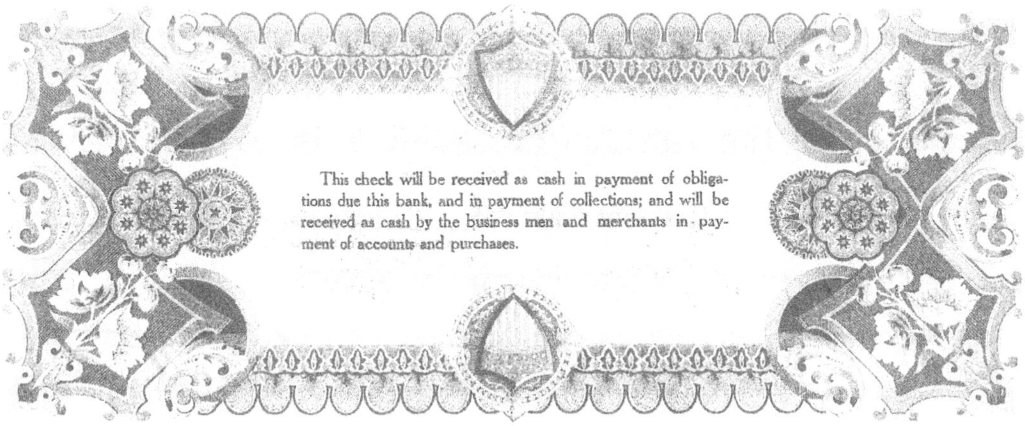

THE CONTINENTAL BANK & TRUST CO.

TX600-2. 2 Dollars Cashier's Check (Oct. 1, 7, 1907—spurious handwritten dates and signature). Black and blue. Red outline denomination at center. Back blue; ornate border with small shields at upper and lower center. Four lines of black text at center. (shown at 66%)

c. Unissued, cancelled. **R2**

San Antonio

ALAMO NATIONAL BANK

TX625-1. 1 Dollar Cashier's Check Nov. 11, 1907. Black and green on aqua safety paper. Eagle and shield at upper left, large green denomination at center. Embossed clearing house association seal at left. Small dog head labeled Fidelity at lower center on back.

a. Issued, not cancelled. **R5**

Frost National Bank

TX650-1. 1 Dollar Cashier's Check Nov. 11, 1907. Darker paper, otherwise as TX625. (shown at 61%)
a. Issued, not cancelled. R5

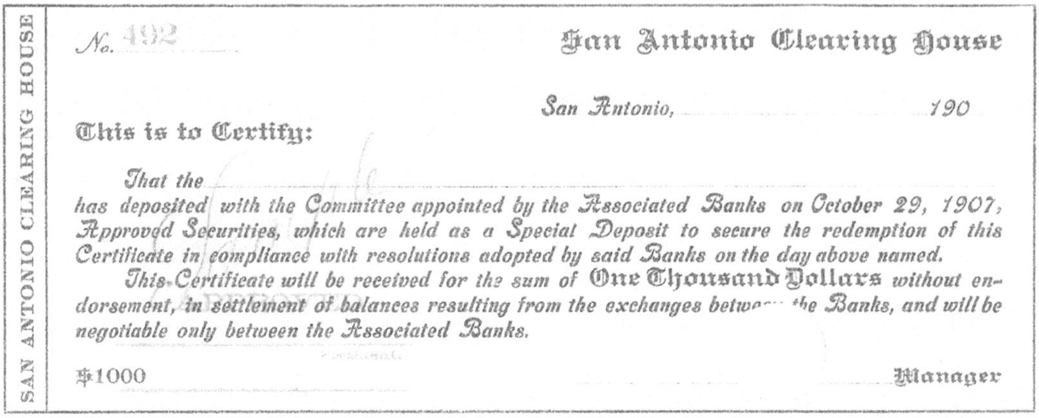

San Antonio Clearing House

TX700-1000. 1,000 Dollars (loan certificate) Oct. 29, 1907. Black. Larger size. (shown at 66%)
c. Unissued, cancelled (with or without handwritten "Sample" at left). R5

San Antonio Clearing House, notes without name

TX725-1. 1 Dollar Cashier's Check Nov. 11, 1907. As TX625. (shown at 70%)
c. Unissued, cancelled. R4

TX725-5. 5 Dollars Nov. 11, 1907. Black and green on light green safety paper, otherwise as above.
c. Unissued, cancelled. R4

TX725-10. 10 Dollars Nov. 11, 1907. Black and green on cream safety paper, otherwise as above.
c. Unissued, cancelled (handwritten "Sample" at center). R4

Sweetwater

The First National Bank

TX750-1. 1 Dollar (cashier's check) Nov. 20, 1907. Black on textured light yellowish blue paper. Uniface. Small size, 138 × 74mm.
b. Issued, cancelled. R5

TX750-5. 5 Dollars Nov. 20, 1907. Black on textured light green paper, otherwise as above.
b. Issued, cancelled. R5

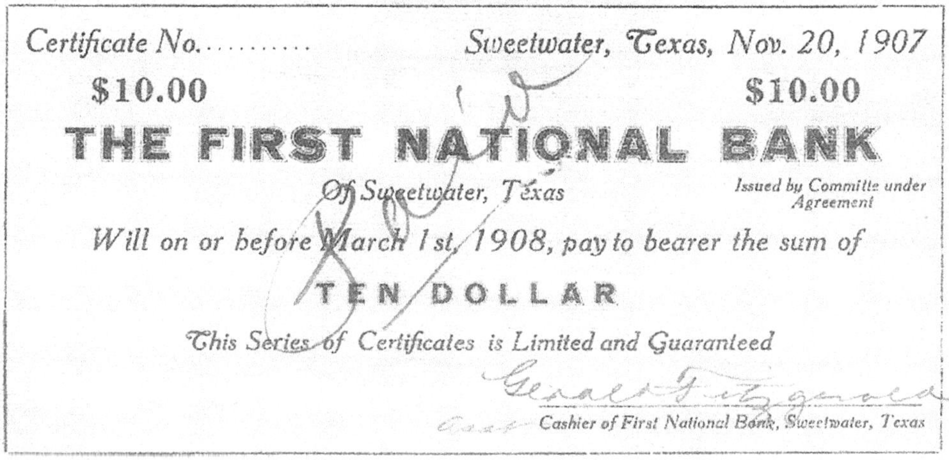

TX750-10. 10 Dollars Nov. 20, 1907. Black on textured light blue paper, otherwise as above. Value stated as "Ten Dollar." (shown at 66%)
b. Issued, cancelled. R5

Temple

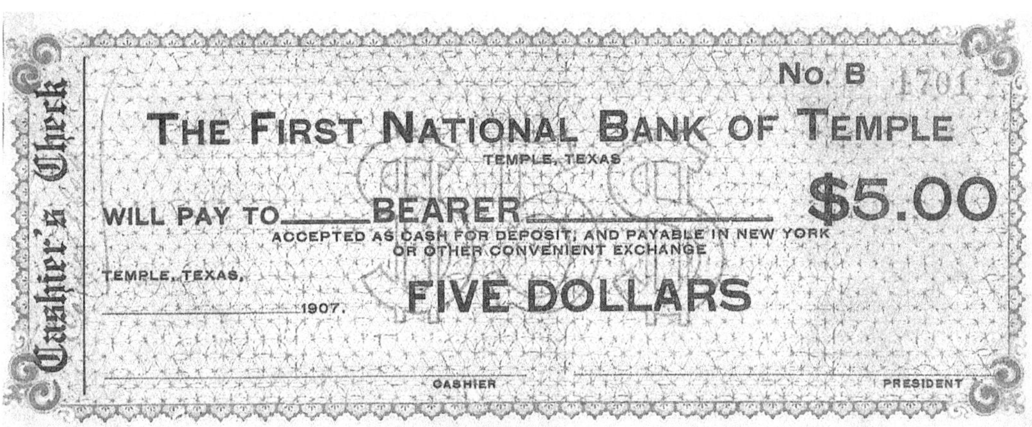

THE FIRST NATIONAL BANK OF TEMPLE

TX775-1. 1 Dollar Cashier's Check Nov. 23, 1907 (stamped date). Blue-green on white paper. Large red outline denomination at center. Back blue; ornate border with shield at upper and lower center. No text at center. Imprint: X—Co. Dallas. (shown at 70%)
b. Issued, cancelled. R5

TX775-5. 5 Dollars Nov. 23, 1907. As above.
c. Unissued, cancelled. R5

TX775-10. 10 Dollars Nov. 23, 1907. As above.
c. Unissued, cancelled. R5

THE TEMPLE STATE BANK OF TEMPLE

TX800-1. 1 Dollar Cashier's Check ND (1907). Black and blue. Red outline denomination at center. Back blue; small shield at upper and lower center. (shown at 68%)

d. Unissued, remainder. R5

UTAH

Ogden

FIRST NATIONAL BANK OF OGDEN

UT500-1. 1 Dollar Cashier's Check Nov. 27, 1907. Black on large green denomination underprint at center. Uniface. Imprint: Utah Litho. Co. S.L.C.

b. Issued, cancelled. R5
c. Unissued, cancelled. R5

UT500-2. 2 Dollars Nov. 27, 1907. As above.

b. Issued, cancelled. R5
c. Unissued, cancelled. R5

UT500-5. 5 Dollars Nov. 27, 1907. As above.

b. Issued, cancelled. R5
c. Unissued, cancelled. R5

UT500-10. 10 Dollars Nov. 27, 1907. As above.

b. Issued, cancelled. R5
c. Unissued, cancelled. R5

UT500-20. 20 Dollars Nov. 27, 1907. As above.

b. Issued, cancelled. R5

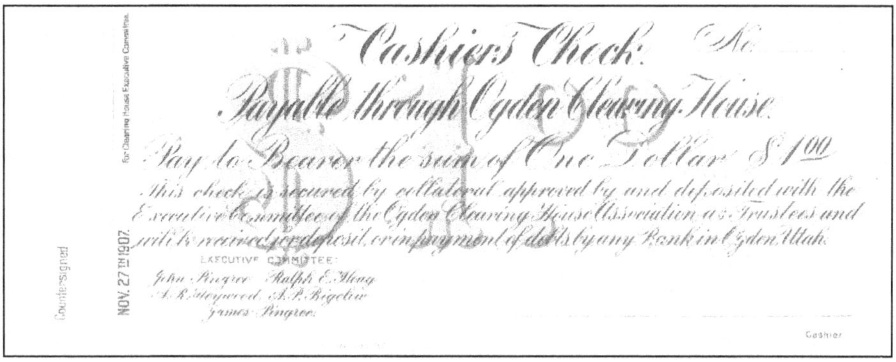

OGDEN CLEARING HOUSE (NO ISSUER NAMED)

UT525-1. 1 Dollar Cashiers Check Nov. 27, 1907. As UT500. (shown at 57%)
c. Unissued, cancelled. **R3**

UT525-2. 2 Dollars Nov. 27, 1907. As above.
c. Unissued, cancelled. **R3**

UT525-5. 5 Dollars Nov. 27, 1907. As above.
c. Unissued, cancelled. **R3**

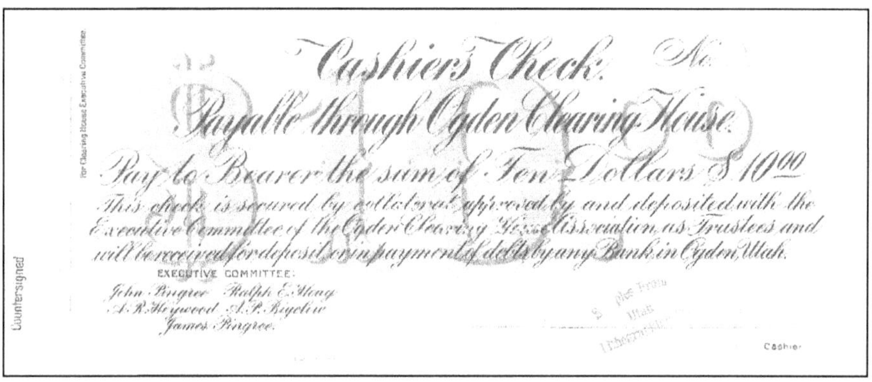

UT525-10. 10 Dollars Nov. 27, 1907. As above. (shown at 57%)
c. Unissued, cancelled. **R3**
e. Printer's sample. **R5**

Richfield

GOLD MOUNTAIN CONSOLIDATED MINING CO.

UT550-1. 1 Dollar (pay check) ND (1907). Payable in 1908. Black on pale blue paper. Large red denomination at center. Richfield Commercial & Savings Bank as depositor bank. Uniface.
a. Issued, not cancelled. **EF, 175. Unc., 300.**

UT550-2. 2 Dollars ND (1907). As above. (shown at 59%)
a. Issued, not cancelled. **EF, 175. Unc., 300.**
UT550-5. 5 Dollars ND (1907). As above.
a. Issued, not cancelled. **EF, 175. Unc., 300.**
UT550-10. 10 Dollars ND (1907). As above.
a. Issued, not cancelled. **EF, 175. Unc., 300.**

Salt Lake City

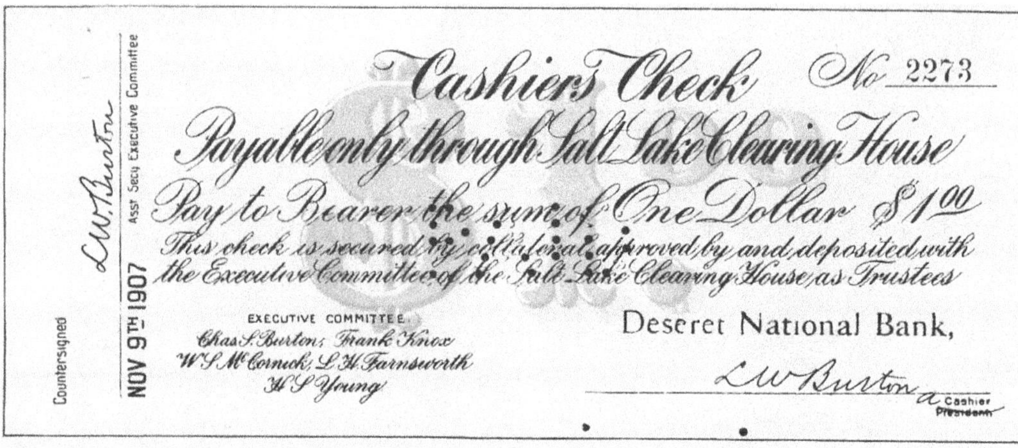

Deseret National Bank

UT575-1. 1 Dollar Cashiers Check Nov. 9, 1907. Design and color as UT625. (shown at 75%)
b. Issued, cancelled. **R5**

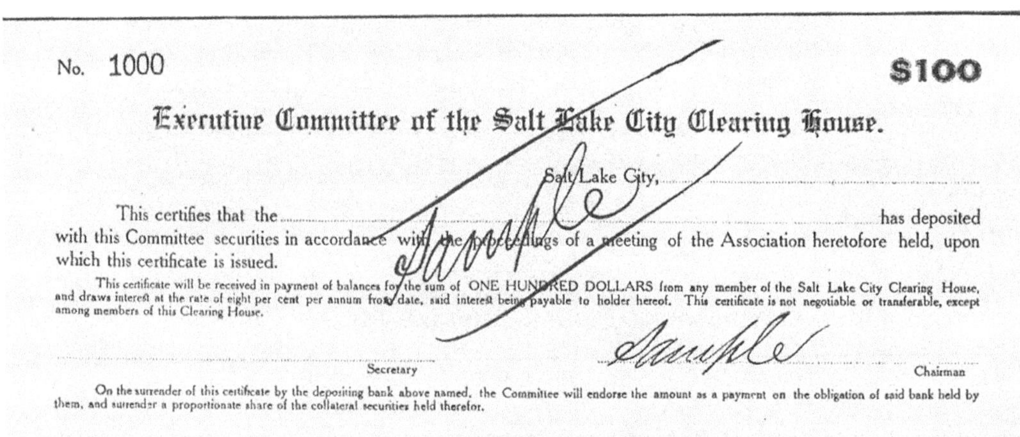

Executive Committee of the Salt Lake City Clearing House

UT600-100. 100 Dollars ND (1907). 8% interest-bearing certificate. (b/w) (shown at 76%)
e. Sample. **R5**

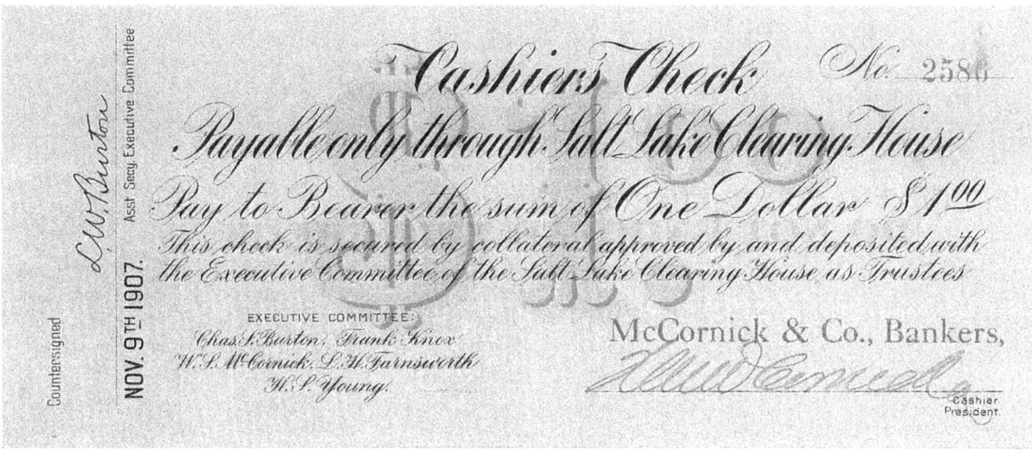

McCornick & Co., Bankers

UT625-1. 1 Dollar Cashiers Check Nov. 9, 1907. Black on gray paper. Large orange denomination at center. One red text line across center on back. Imprint as UT500. (shown at 69%)

a. Issued, not cancelled. R5

Salt Lake Clearing House (no issuer named)

UT650-1. 1 Dollar Cashiers Check Nov. 9, 1907. As UT625.

c. Unissued, cancelled. R3

e. Sample. R3

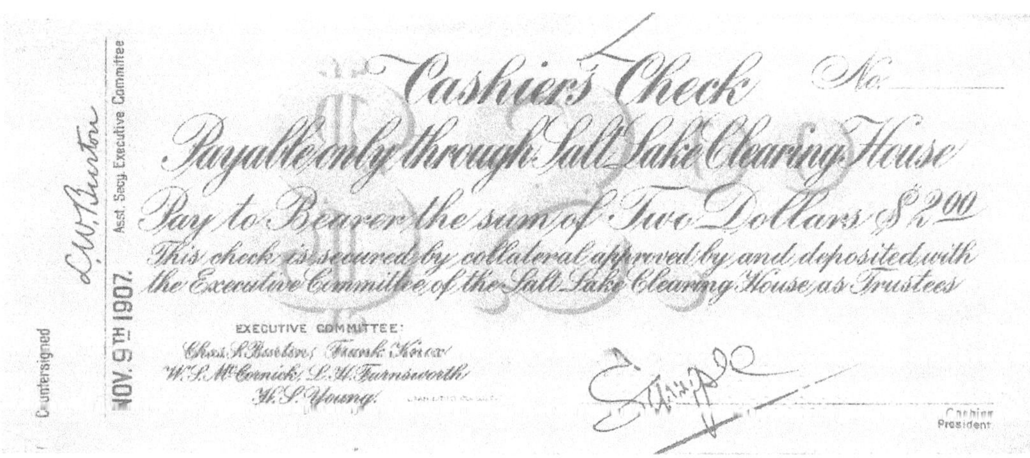

UT650-2. 2 Dollars Nov. 9, 1907. Blue paper, otherwise as above. (shown at 69%)

c. Unissued, cancelled. R3

e. Sample. R3

Utah-Idaho Sugar Co./ The National City Bank, New York

UT675-1. 1 Dollar (payroll check) Nov. 9, 1907. Black on tan paper. Uniface. "Not More than One Dollar" diagonally in red line across face.

a. Issued, not cancelled. R5

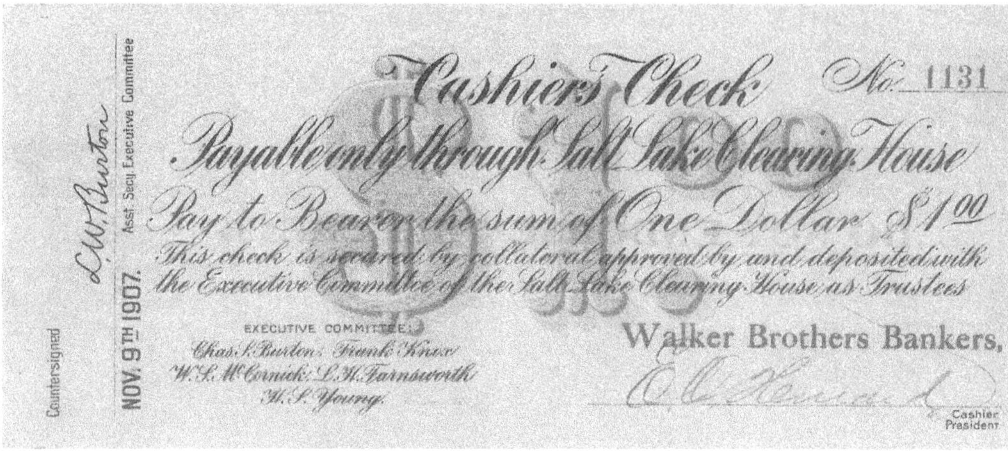

Walker Brothers Bankers

UT700-1. 1 Dollar Cashiers Check Nov. 9, 1907. As UT625. (shown at 69%)
a. Issued, not cancelled. **R5**

UT700-10. 10 Dollars ND (1907). As above. Yellow paper. Imprint: Utah Litho. Co. S.L.C.
b. Issued, cancelled. **R5**
c. Unissued, cancelled. **R5**

Virginia

Blackstone

Bank of Lunenburg

An issue of scrip is reported to have been issued by this bank. No details are known at present.

Bristol

Bristol Clearing House

VA525-1. 1 Dollar Nov. 1, 1907. (list)
b. Issued, cancelled. **R5**

VA525-2. 2 Dollars Nov. 1, 1907. (list)
b. Issued, cancelled. **R5**

Chase City

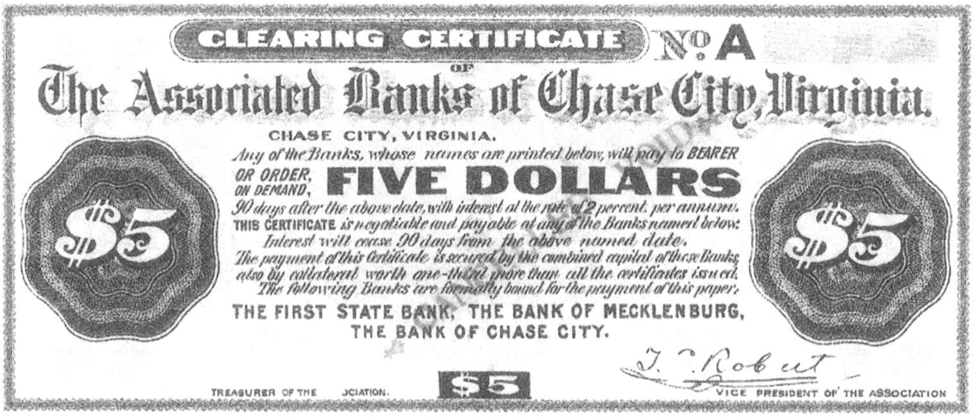

THE ASSOCIATED BANKS OF CHASE CITY, VIRGINIA

VA550-5. 5 Dollars Clearing Certificate ND (1907). Black. Back green. (shown at 71%)
  c. Unissued, cancelled. **R5**

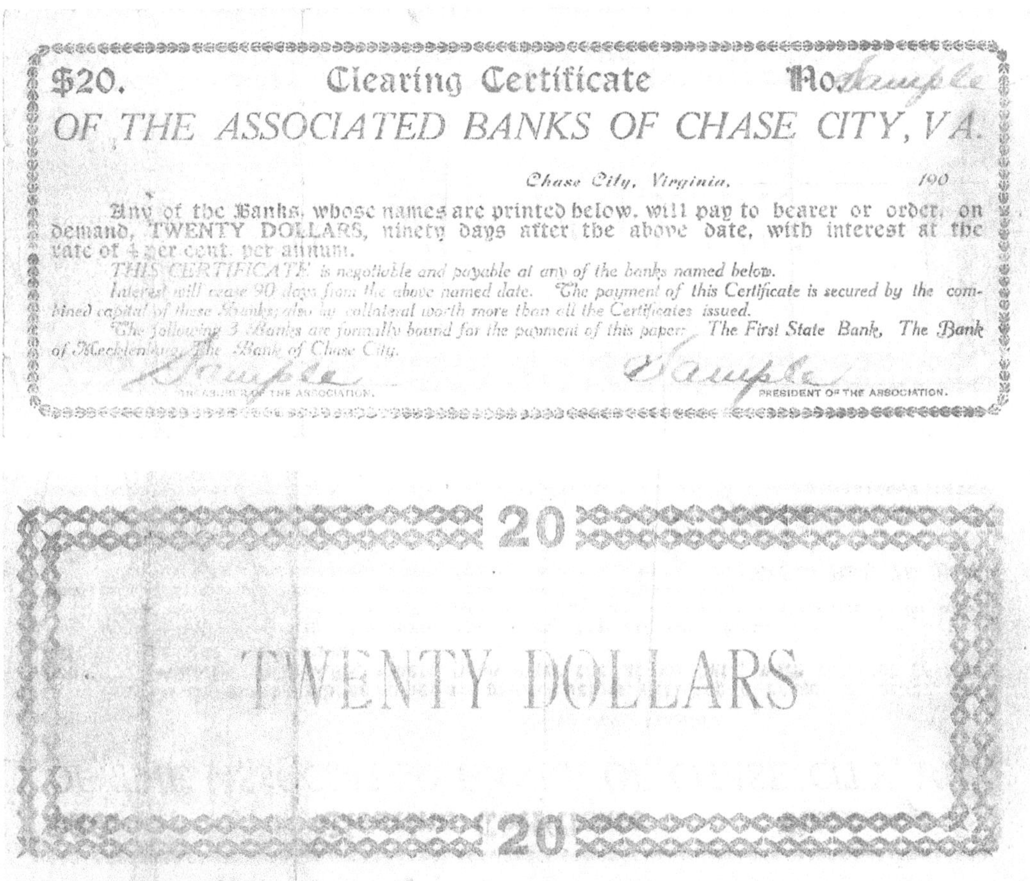

VA550-20. 20 Dollars 190_ (1907). Blue-green. Back in inverted position. (shown at 73%)
  e. Sample. **R5**

Danville

The Associated Banks of Danville, Virginia

VA575-1. 1 Dollar Clearing Certificate Dec. 2, 1907. (b/w)
- b. Issued, cancelled (stamped SPECIMEN/NOT NEGOTIABLE). **R5**
- u. Unissued. **SENC**

VA575-2. 2 Dollars Dec. 2, 1907. (list)
- b. Issued, cancelled as above. **R5**

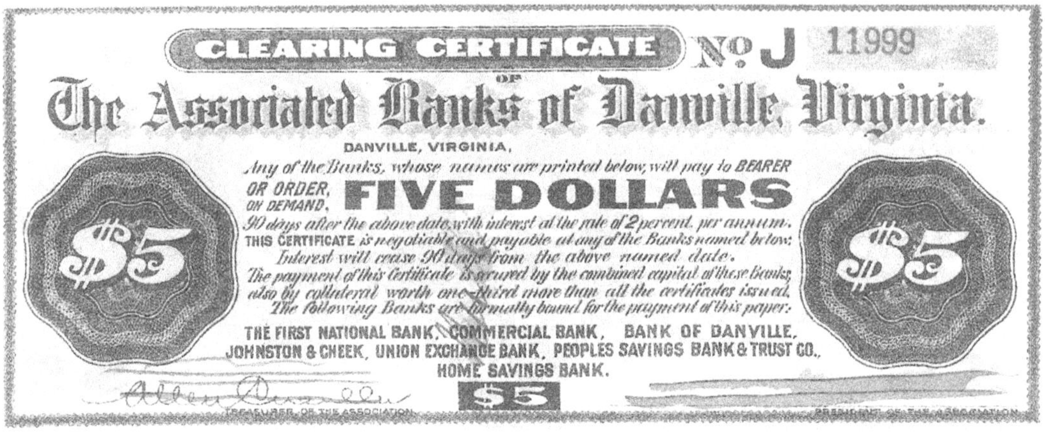

VA575-5. 5 Dollars ND (1907). Black and blue. Back blue. Design as VA550-5. (shown at 76%)
- c. Unissued, cancelled. **R2**

VA575-10. 10 Dollars Dec. 2, 1907. As above.
- b. Issued, cancelled as the $1. **R5**
- c. Unissued, cancelled. **R2**

VA575-20. 20 Dollars ND (1907). As above.
- b. Issued, cancelled as the $1. **R5**
- c. Unissued, cancelled. **R2**

Lynchburg

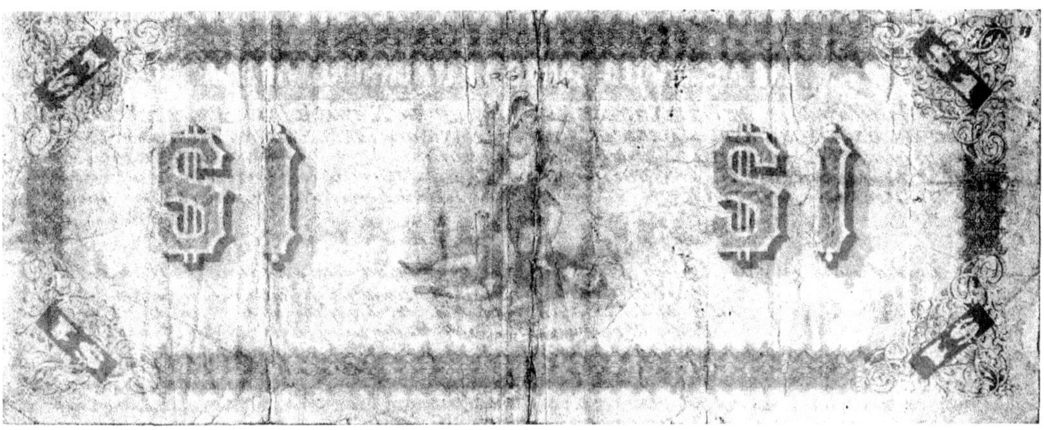

THE ASSOCIATED BANKS OF LYNCHBURG, VIRGINIA

VA600-1. 1 Dollar Clearing House Certificate Nov. 12, 1907. Black. Back gold; helmeted allegory of Virginia at center, value at left and right. (shown at 76%)

a. Issued, not cancelled.	**VG, 250. VF, 500.**
u. Cancelled.	SENC

VA600-2. 2 Dollars ND (1907). (list)

u. Cancelled	SENC

VA600-5. 5 Dollars ND (1907). (list)

u. Cancelled.	SENC

VA600-10. 10 Dollars ND (1907). (list)

u. Cancelled.	SENC

Martinsville

THE ASSOCIATED BANKS OF MARTINSVILLE, VIRGINIA

VA625-1. 1 Dollar Clearing Certificate ND (1907). (list)

u. Unissued.	SENC

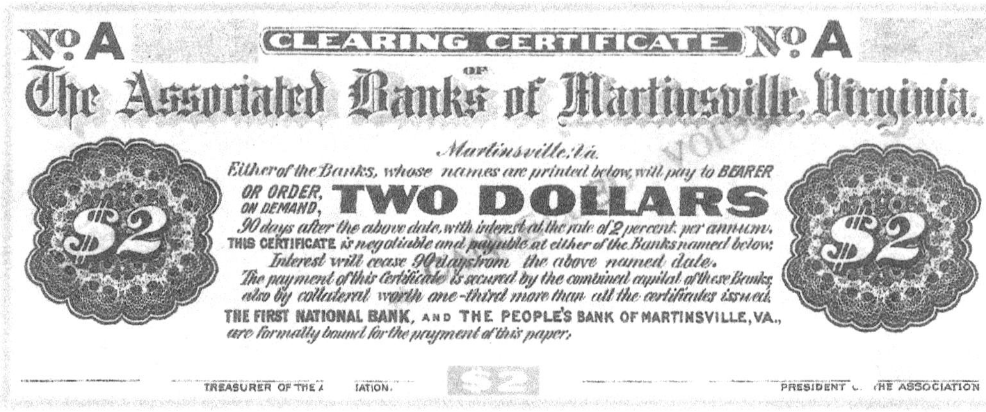

VA625-2. 2 Dollars ND (1907). Black and orange. Back orange; helmeted allegory of Virginia at center. (shown at 74%)
c. Unissued, cancelled. **R5**

Richmond

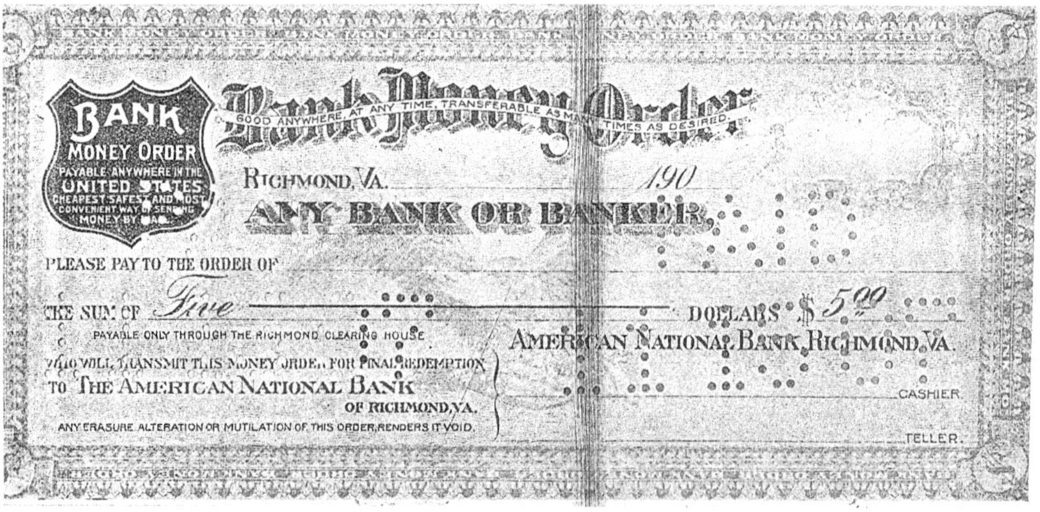

American National Bank, Richmond, Va.

VA650-5. 5 Dollars Bank Money Order 190_ (1907). Eagle and shield in underprint at center. Shield with inscription at upper left. (b/w) (shown at 71%)

c. Unissued, cancelled. R5

f. Specimen. R5

South Boston

The Associated Banks of South Boston & Houston, Virginia

VA675-1. 1 Dollar Clearing Certificate ND (1907). Black. Back green. (shown at 76%)

c. Unissued, cancelled. R5

VA675-2. 2 Dollars ND (1907). As above.

c. Unissued, cancelled. R5

VA675-5. 5 Dollars ND (1907). As above.

c. Unissued, cancelled. R5

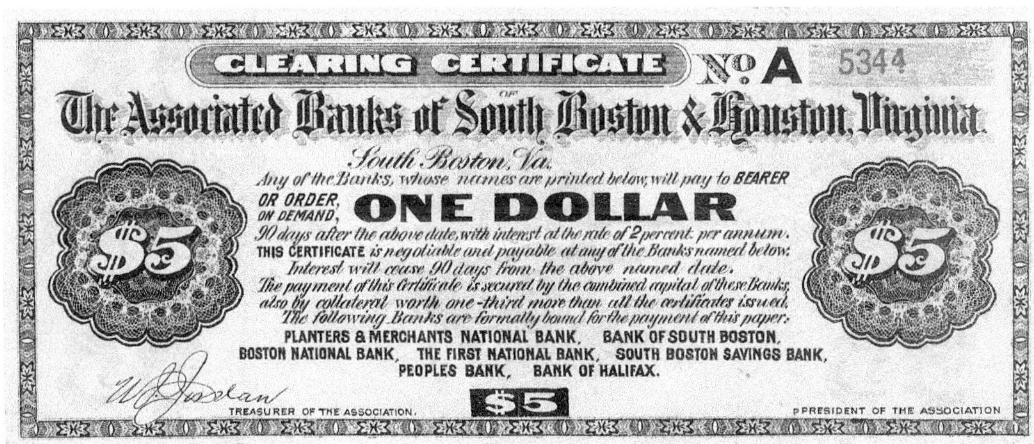

Error Note: An unissued but not cancelled $5 note, VA675-5, with wrong value of ONE DOLLAR across center. There is no hand signature at right. (shown at 74%)

Washington

Anacortes

Bank of Commerce of Anacortes

WA500-1. 1 Dollar (cashier's check) Nov. 18, 1907. Black on gray paper. Uniface. (shown at 70%)
b. Issued, cancelled. **R5**

Bank of Commerce of Anacortes/ Skagit County Clearing House Certificate

WA525-1. 1 Dollar Nov. 15, 1907. Black on green underprint of large eagle on rock at center. Back green. (shown at 70%)

b. Issued, cancelled. R5

Bellingham

Bellingham Clearing House Association

A. Wider notes, uniface. 179 × 86mm.

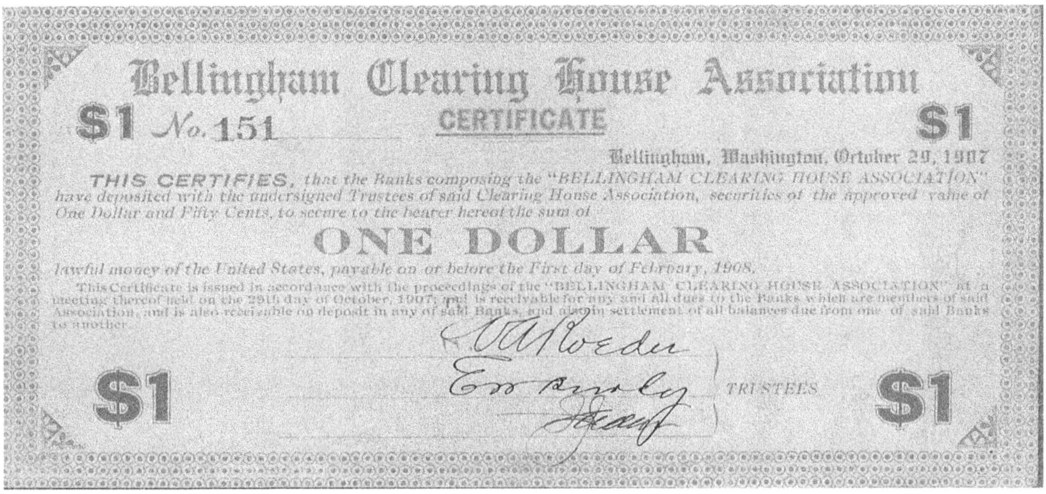

WA550-1. 1 Dollar Oct. 29, 1907. Brown on gold paper. Three hand signatures below. Red denomination at corners. (shown at 75%)

a. Issued, not cancelled. R5

b. Issued, cancelled (triangular piece removed at right). R4

WA550-2. 2 Dollars Oct. 29, 1907. Black on white paper. As above.

b. Issued, cancelled as above. R4

WA550-5. 5 Dollars Oct. 29, 1907. Black on green paper. As above. (shown at 77%)

b. Issued, cancelled as above. R4

WA550-10. 10 Dollars Oct. 29, 1907. Black on blue paper. As above.
b. Issued, cancelled as above. **R4**
WA550-20. 20 Dollars Oct. 29, 1907. Black on light yellow paper. As above.
b. Issued, cancelled as above. **R5**

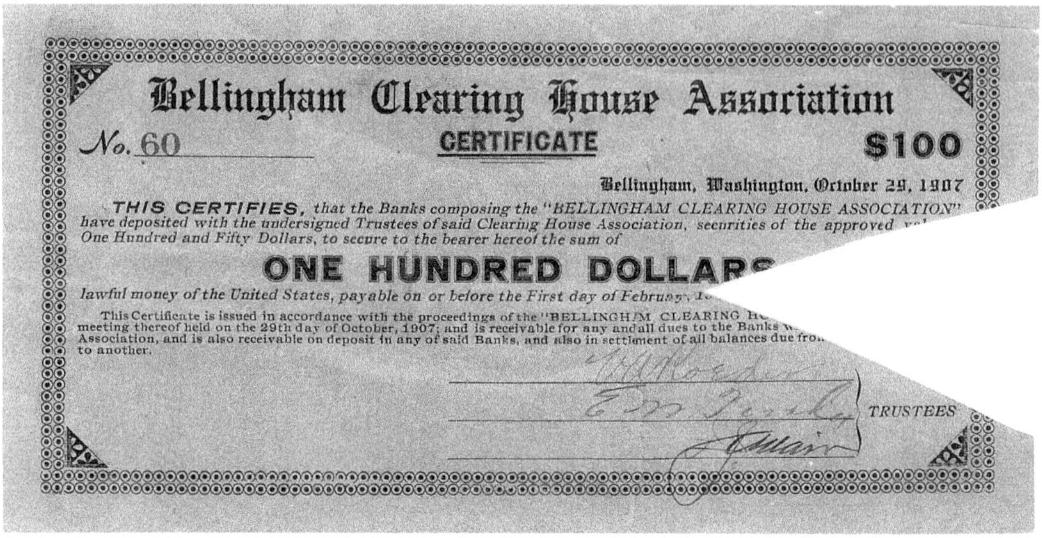

WA550-100. 100 Dollars Oct. 29, 1907. Black on gray paper. As above except for larger size, 192 × 100mm. (shown at 71%)
b. Issued, cancelled as above. **R5**

B. Narrower notes, two-sided. 183 × 81mm.

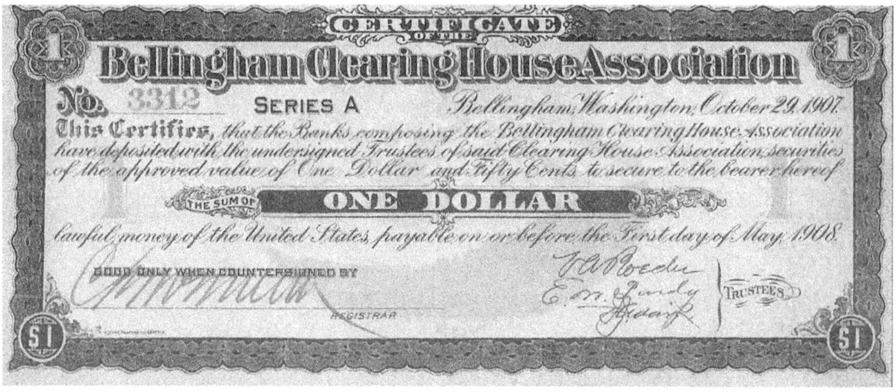

WA575-1. 1 Dollar Oct. 29, 1907. Black on orange underprint of Mt. Baker at center, value in orange at left and right. Imprint: Tucker Hanford Co. Seattle. (shown at 65%)
a. Issued, not cancelled. **R5**
b. Issued, cancelled. **VG, 75. VF, 180.**
WA575-2. 2 Dollars Oct. 29, 1907. As above.
b. Issued, cancelled. **VG, 75. VF, 180.**
WA575-5. 5 Dollars Oct. 29, 1907. As above.
b. Issued, cancelled. **VG, 75. VF, 180.**

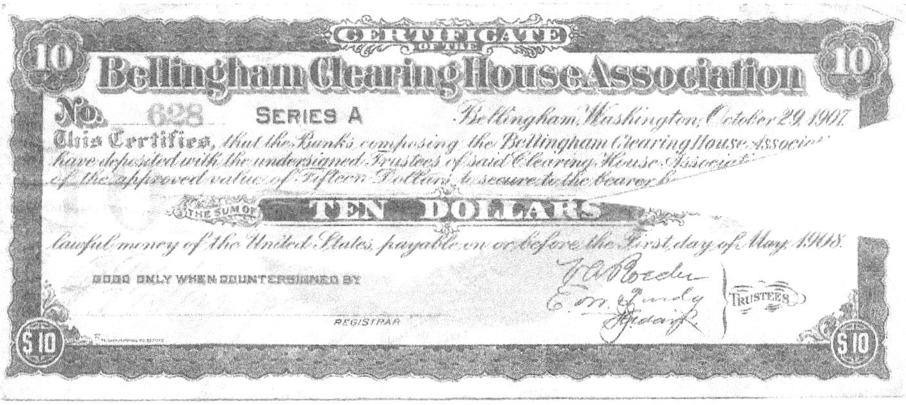

WA575-10. 10 Dollars Oct. 29, 1907. As above. (shown at 65%)
 b. Issued, cancelled. **VG, 75. VF, 180.**
WA575-20. 20 Dollars Oct. 29, 1907. As above.
 b. Issued, cancelled. **VG, 75. VF, 180.**
NOTE: Most examples of WA575 have a long triangular piece cut out of the right side for cancellation. At least one set is known with cancellation that does not remove this section.

Chehalis County

CERTIFICATE OF THE ASSOCIATED BANKS OF CHEHALIS COUNTY

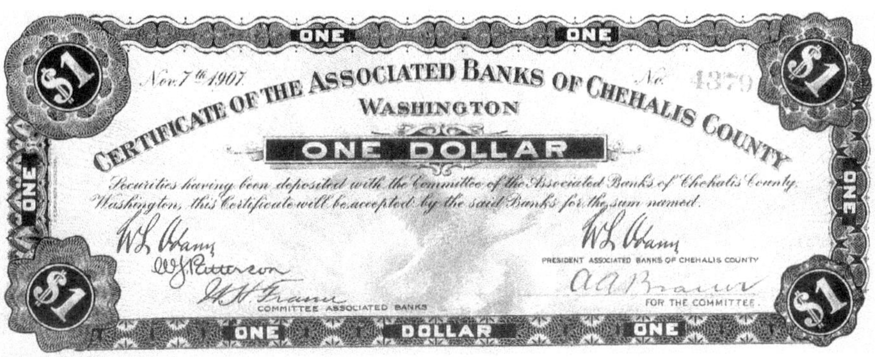

WA600-1. 1 Dollar Nov. 7, 1907. Black on tan underprint of eagle on rock at lower center. Uniface. Imprint: N.P. Bank Note Co. Tacoma. (shown at 55%)
 a. Issued, not cancelled. **R2**

Ellensburg

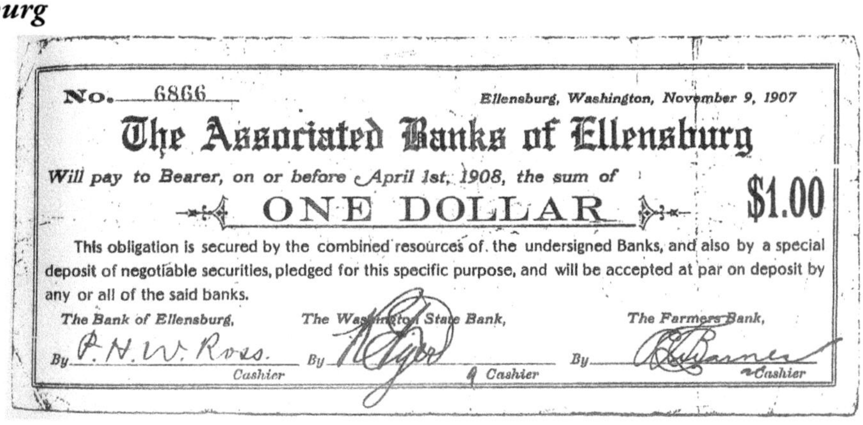

The Associated Banks of Ellensburg

WA625-1. 1 Dollar (certificate of deposit) Nov. 9, 1907. (b/w) (shown at 55%)
- a. Issued, not cancelled. **R5**

Olympia

Associated Banks of Olympia

WA650-1.A 1 Dollar Nov. 4, 1907. Black on orange paper. Three handwritten signatures. Uniface.
- a. Issued, not cancelled. **R5**
- u. Unissued. **SENC**

WA650-1.B 1 Dollar Nov. 4, 1907. More ornate type. Black on green underprint including eagle at center. Back green. Three printed signatures. Imprint: N.P. Bank Note Co. Tacoma.
- a. Issued, not cancelled. **R5**
- u. Unissued. **SENC**

Seattle

No.______ $10,000.00

LOAN COMMITTEE
OF THE
SEATTLE CLEARING HOUSE ASSOCIATION

Seattle,______1907

THIS CERTIFIES that the______
has deposited with this Committee securities in accordance with the proceedings of a meeting of the Association held November 4, 1907, upon which this certificate is issued. This Certificate will be received in payment of balances at the Clearing House for the sum of ______TEN THOUSAND______Dollars from any member of the Clearing House Association.

On the surrender of this certificate by the depositing bank above named, the committee will endorse the amount as a payment on the obligation of said bank held by them, and surrender a proportionate share of the collateral securities held therefor.

COMMITTEE

$10,000.00

$10,000.00

Loan Committee of the Seattle Clearing House Association

WA675-10,000. 10,000 Dollars Nov. 4, 1907. Black. Uniface. Larger size. (shown at 68%)
- c. Unissued, cancelled. **R5**

Seattle Clearing House Association

A. *Clearing House* title straight at top, numerals at upper corners

WA700-1. 1 Dollar Nov. 4, 1907 (date on back). Black on blue paper. Back green. Series B, C, E, F, G, I. Imprint (small): Tucker, Hanford Co. Seattle.
- a. Issued, not cancelled. **VG, 200. VF, 400.**
- b. Issued, cancelled. **VG, 175. VF, 325.**

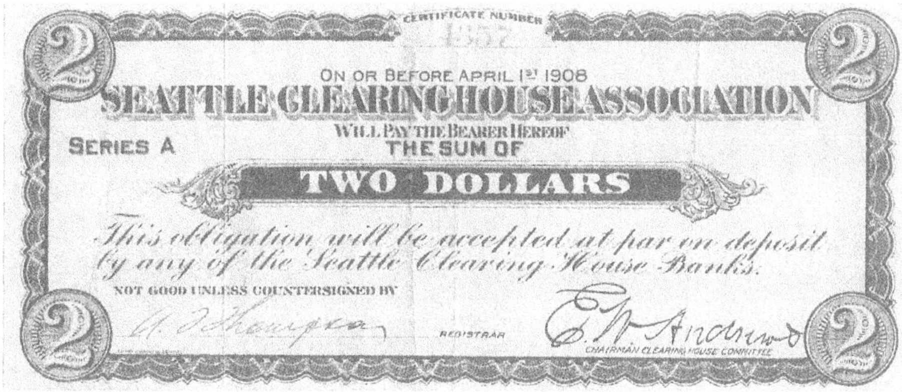

WA700-2. 2 Dollars Nov. 4, 1907. Black on pink paper. As above. Series A, C, G. (shown at 64%)
   a. Issued, not cancelled. **R4**
   b. Issued, cancelled. **VG, 175. VF, 375.**

B. *Clearing House* title straight at top, without numerals at upper corners

WA715-10. 10 Dollars Nov. 4, 1907. Black on light yellow underprint. Large denomination in gray at lower center. Back green. Series A. No imprint.
   b. Issued, cancelled. **R4**

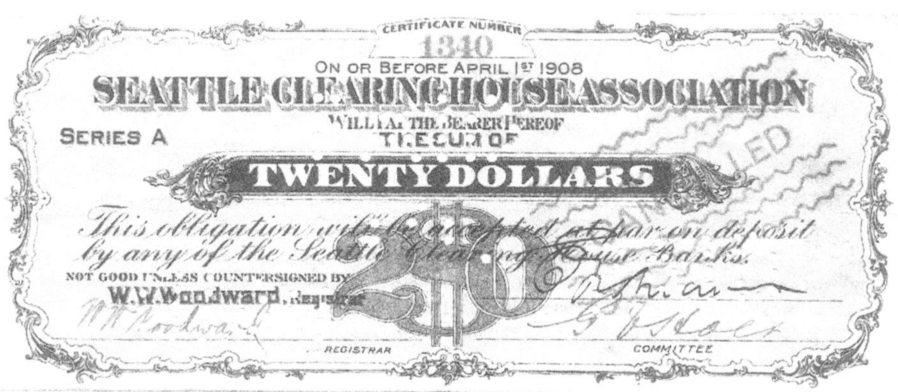

WA715-20. 20 Dollars Nov. 4, 1907. Black on light brown underprint. As above. (shown at 64%)
   b. Issued, cancelled. **R4**

C. *Clearing House* title curved at top, without border

WA730-5. 5 Dollars Nov. 4, 1907. Black on light orange paper. Back green. No imprint. Series B.
   d. Unissued, remainder. **R4**

WA730-10. 10 Dollars Nov. 4, 1907. Black on light yellow underprint. Design similar to above. Series B. (shown at 68%)

b. Issued, cancelled. **R4**

D. *Clearing House* title curved towards bottom at center, and with border

WA745-5. 5 Dollars Nov. 4, 1907. Black on light yellow paper. Different face design than above. Back green. Series C. Imprint (large): Tucker Hanford Co. Seattle. (shown at 65%)

b. Issued, cancelled. **R4**

Skagit County

Skagit County Clearing House

WA775-1. 1 Dollar Nov. 15, 1907. Similar to WA650-1.B but smaller size.

a. Issued, not cancelled. **R5**

b. Issued, cancelled. **R5**

NOTE: See also WA525 for Skagit County issue under Anacortes.

Snohomish County

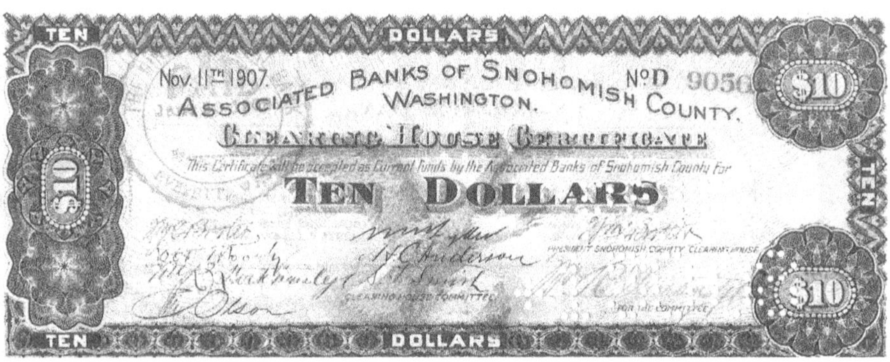

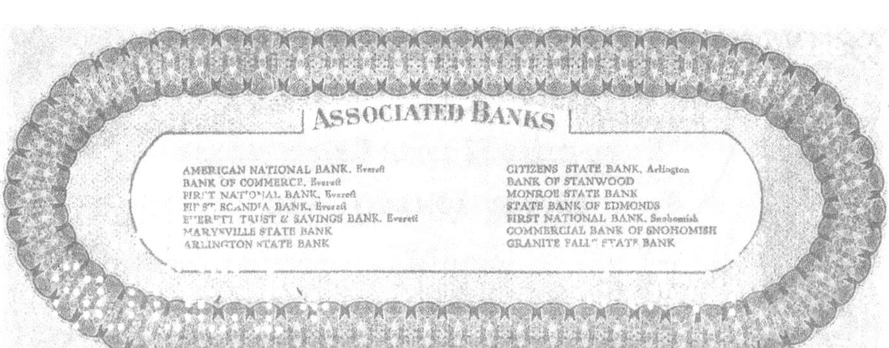

Associated Banks of Snohomish County

WA800-1.A 1 Dollar Clearing House Certificate Nov. 11, 1907. Black on yellow underprint of large eagle on rock at lower center. Back green; list of member banks at center area. Imprint: N.P. Bank Note Co. Tacoma. (shown at 57%)
a. Issued, not cancelled. **VG, 200. VF, 450.**
b. Issued, cancelled. **R4**

WA800-1.B 1 Dollar Nov. 11, 1907. As above except for green underprint.
b. Issued, cancelled. **R4**

WA800-2. 2 Dollars Nov. 11, 1907. As above.
b. Issued, cancelled. **R5**

WA800-5. 5 Dollars Nov. 11, 1907. Green eagle underprint, otherwise as above.
b. Issued, cancelled. **R5**

WA800-10. 10 Dollars Nov. 11, 1907. As above.
b. Issued, cancelled. **R4**

WA800-20. 20 Dollars Nov. 11, 1907. As above.
b. Issued, cancelled. **R5**

South Bend

Associated Banks of South Bend

WA825-1. 1 Dollar Nov. 11, 1907. Black and blue. Washington at right on back. For the Willapa Harbor Clearing House Committee.
a. Issued, not cancelled. **R5**

NOTE: The town name of Willapa is misspelled "Willipa" on this issue.

Spokane

Spokane Clearing House Association Check

WA850-1. 1 Dollar Nov. 1, 1907. Green and black. Washington portrait at left, small Liberty head at lower center. Back orange. Imprint: Spokane Litho. Co.
a. Issued, not cancelled. **VG, 90. VF, 200.**
b. Issued, cancelled. **R3**

WA850-2. 2 Dollars Nov. 1, 1907. As above.
a. Issued, not cancelled. **R3**
b. Issued, cancelled. **R3**

WA850-5. 5 Dollars Nov. 1, 1907. Orange and black. Back green. Design as above.
b. Issued, cancelled. **R3**

WA850-10. 10 Dollars Nov. 1, 1907. As above.
b. Issued, cancelled. **R4**

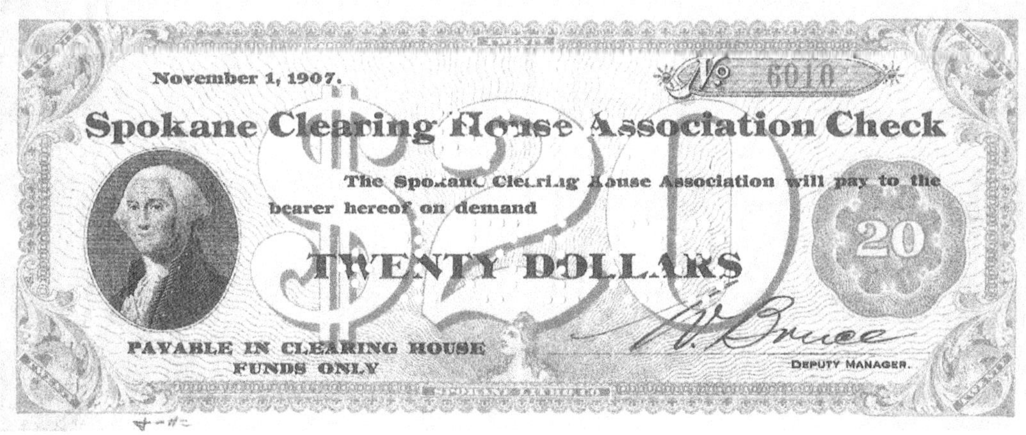

WA850-20. 20 Dollars Nov. 1, 1907. Light brown and black. Back orange. Design as above. (shown at 70%)
b. Issued, cancelled. **R4**

NOTE: By resolution an amount of $2,200,000 in these checks was issued at Spokane, apportioned to the various clearing house banks in proportion to their deposits.

Tacoma

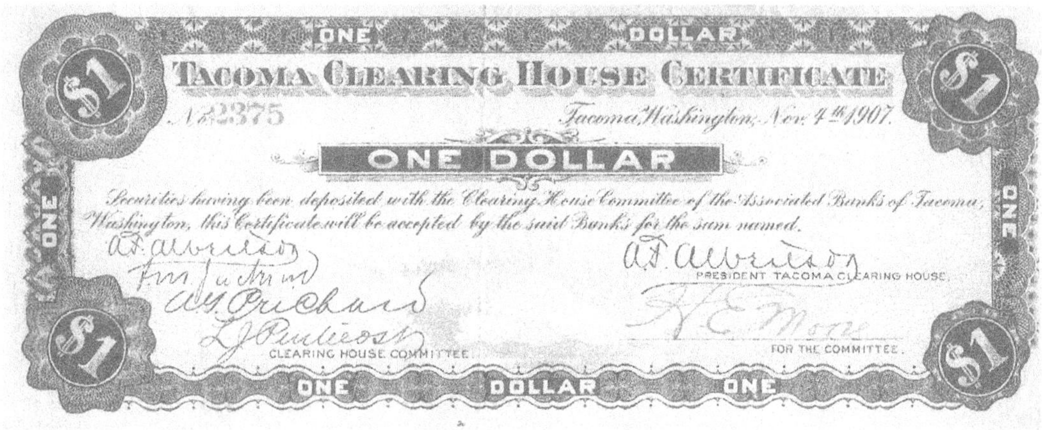

Tacoma Clearing House Certificate

WA875-1. 1 Dollar Nov. 4, 1907. Black on green mountain scene at lower center. Uniface. No imprint. (shown at 65%)
- a. Issued, not cancelled. **VG, 200. VF, 450.**
- b. Issued, cancelled. **VG, 150. VF, 325.**

WA875-2. 2 Dollars Nov. 4, 1907. As above.
- b. Issued, cancelled. **R4**

WA875-5. 5 Dollars Nov. 4, 1907. Black on orange mountain scene at lower center. Uniface. Imprint: N.P. Bank Note Co. Tacoma.
- b. Issued, cancelled. **R4**

WA875-10. 10 Dollars Nov. 4, 1907. As above.
- b. Issued, cancelled. **R5**

WA875-20. 20 Dollars Nov. 4, 1907. As above.
- b. Issued, cancelled. **R4**

Willapa Harbor

Willapa Harbor Clearing House Association

WA900-1. 1 Dollar Nov. 1907. Green. Washington at left and right.
- a. Issued, not cancelled. **R5**

West Virginia

Wheeling

Wheeling Clearing House

A loan certificate issue is reported to have been issued in Wheeling. No details are known at present.

WISCONSIN

Hurley

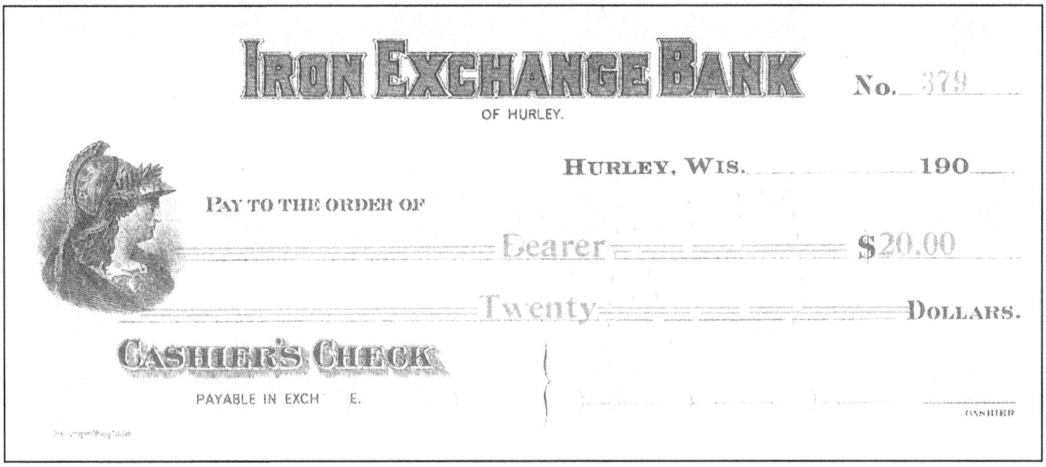

IRON EXCHANGE BANK

WI500-20. 20 Dollars Cashier's Check 190_ (1907). Black and red on green safety paper. Helmeted Minerva at left. Uniface. Imprint: Christie Lithograph & Printing Co. Duluth. (shown at 67%)

c. Unissued, cancelled. R5

Janesville

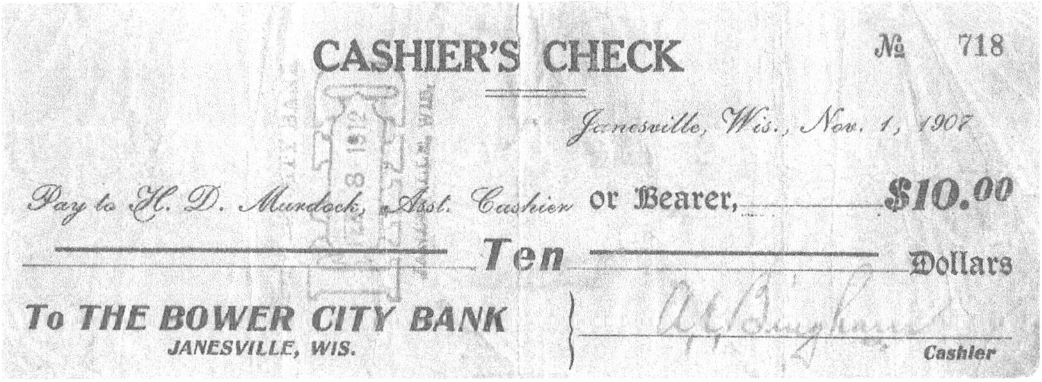

THE BOWER CITY BANK

WI525-10. 10 Dollars Cashier's Check Nov. 1, 1907. Black on green paper. Uniface. (shown at 65%)

b. Issued, cancelled. R5

Merrill

German American State Bank

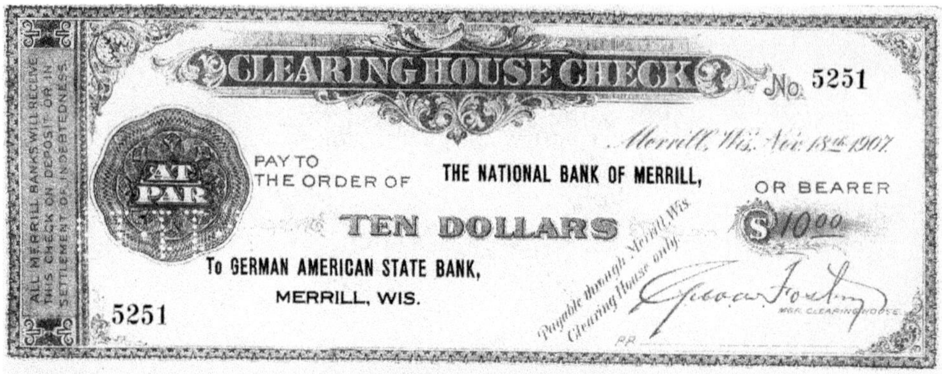

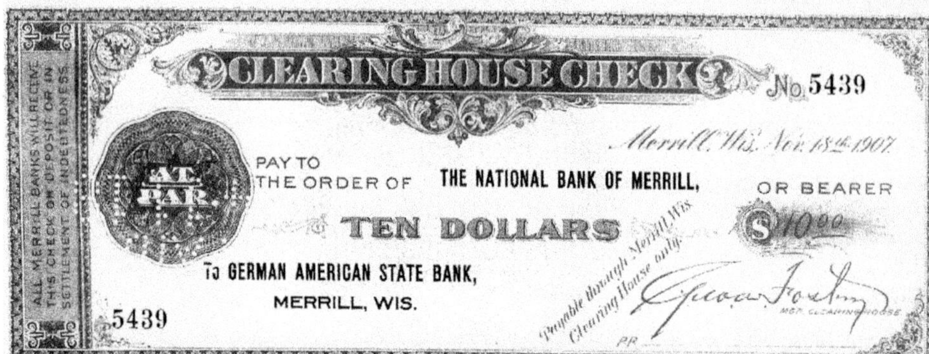

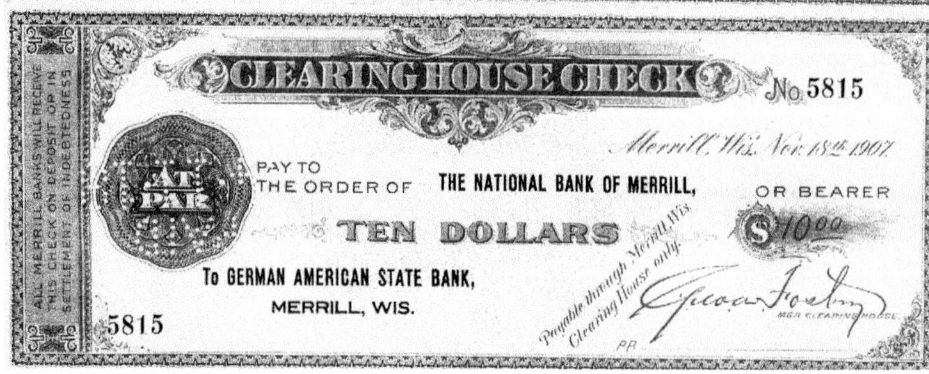

NO ENDORSEMENT NECESSARY.
THIS CHECK IS PROTECTED BY SECURITIES DEPOSITED WITH THE MERRILL, WIS. CLEARING HOUSE ASSOCIATION.
NO ENDORSEMENT NECESSARY.
NO ENDORSEMENT NECESSARY.
THIS CHECK IS PROTECTED BY SECURITIES DEPOSITED WITH THE MERRILL, WIS. CLEARING HOUSE ASSOCIATION.
NO ENDORSEMENT NECESSARY.
NO ENDORSEMENT NECESSARY.
THIS CHECK IS PROTECTED BY SECURITIES DEPOSITED WITH THE MERRILL, WIS. CLEARING HOUSE ASSOCIATION.
NO ENDORSEMENT NECESSARY.

NO ENDORSEMENT NECESSARY.
THIS CHECK IS PROTECTED BY SECURITIES DEPOSITED WITH THE MERRILL, WIS. CLEARING HOUSE ASSOCIATION
NO ENDORSEMENT NECESSARY.

WI550-10. 10 Dollars Clearing House Check Nov. 18, 1907. Green and black face, blue back. (shown at 65%)
c. Unissued, cancelled. R5

NOTE: This issue is known in sheet form only (four-subject). One sheet is presently recorded as part of the Chet Krause Collection.

Milwaukee

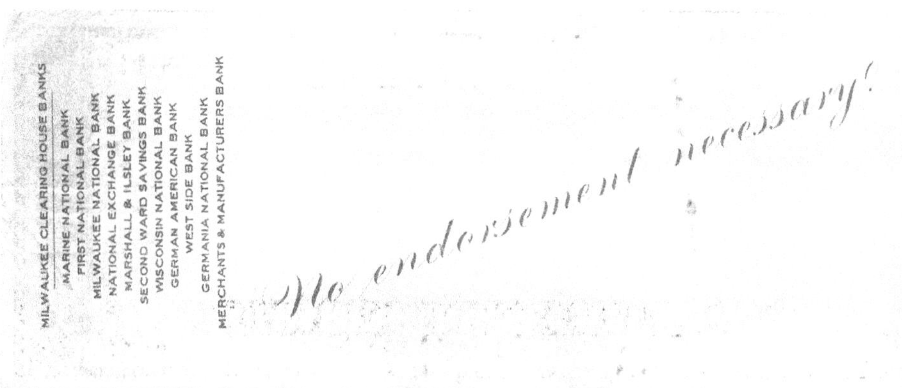

First National Bank

WI575-1. 1 Dollar Nov. 6, 1907. Black face and back. Payable to Milwaukee National Bank. List of member banks at left on back; diagonal text line on back "No endorsement necessary" is large and in script lettering. (shown at 58%)
a. Issued, not cancelled. R3

WI575-5. 5 Dollars Nov. 6, 1907. (list)
b. Issued, cancelled. R5

Marine National Bank

WI600-1. 1 Dollar Clearing House Check Nov. 6, 1907. Black on green safety paper. Design as above. Payable to Wisconsin National Bank. Diagonal text line on back in small capital lettering. (shown at 61%)

a. Issued, not cancelled. **R5**

b. Issued, cancelled. **R4**

WI600-5. 5 Dollars Nov. 6, 1907. As above. Payable to Wisconsin National Bank.

b. Issued, cancelled. **R5**

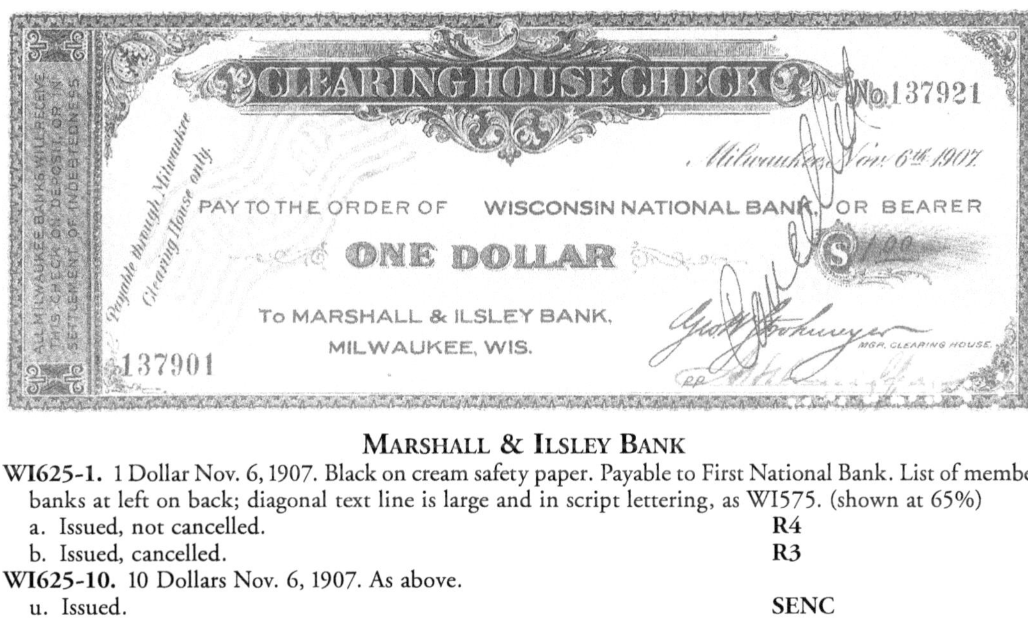

Marshall & Ilsley Bank

WI625-1. 1 Dollar Nov. 6, 1907. Black on cream safety paper. Payable to First National Bank. List of member banks at left on back; diagonal text line is large and in script lettering, as WI575. (shown at 65%)

a. Issued, not cancelled. **R4**

b. Issued, cancelled. **R3**

WI625-10. 10 Dollars Nov. 6, 1907. As above.

u. Issued. **SENC**

National Exchange Bank

WI650-1.A 1 Dollar Nov. 6, 1907. Black on cream safety paper. Payable to Marshall & Ilsley Bank. Diagonal text line on back as WI575.

a. Issued, not cancelled. **R4**

WI650-1.B 1 Dollar Nov. 6, 1907. As above, but payable to Wisconsin National Bank.

a. Issued, not cancelled. **R4**

WI650-10. 10 Dollars Nov. 6, 1907. Green and black on green safety paper. Payable to Marshall & Ilsley Bank. Diagonal line as WI575-1. (shown at 64%)

b. Issued, cancelled. **R5**

SECOND WARD SAVINGS BANK

WI675-1. 1 Dollar Nov. 6, 1907. (list)

u. Issued. **SENC**

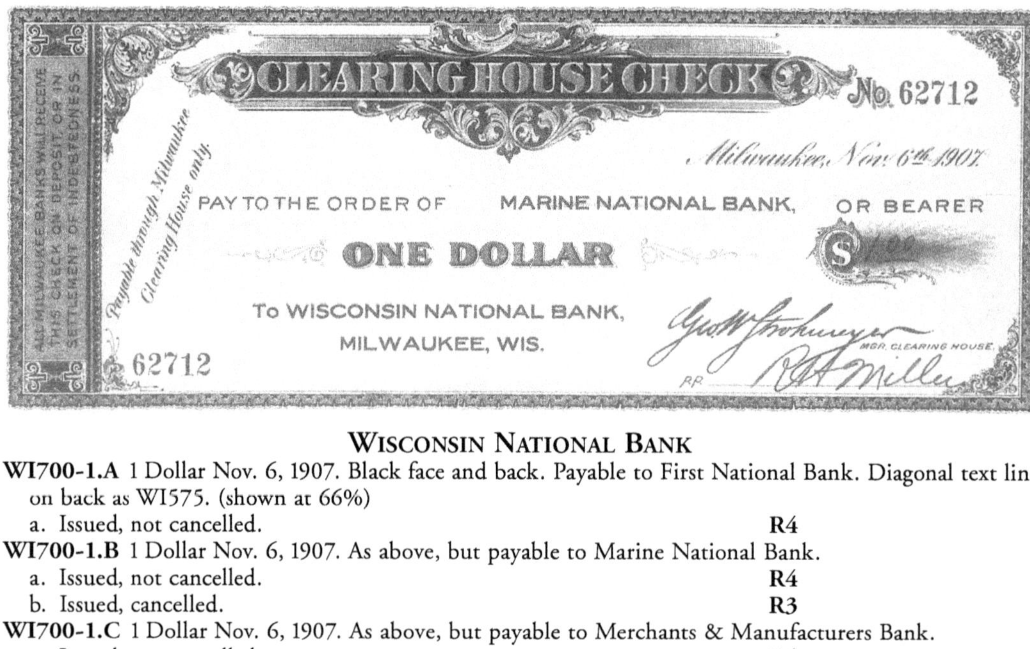

WISCONSIN NATIONAL BANK

WI700-1.A 1 Dollar Nov. 6, 1907. Black face and back. Payable to First National Bank. Diagonal text line on back as WI575. (shown at 66%)

a. Issued, not cancelled. **R4**

WI700-1.B 1 Dollar Nov. 6, 1907. As above, but payable to Marine National Bank.

a. Issued, not cancelled. **R4**

b. Issued, cancelled. **R3**

WI700-1.C 1 Dollar Nov. 6, 1907. As above, but payable to Merchants & Manufacturers Bank.

a. Issued, not cancelled. **R4**

WI700-1.D 1 Dollar Nov. 6, 1907. As above, but payable to Second Ward Savings Bank.

a. Issued, not cancelled. **R4**

WI700-10. 10 Dollars Nov. 6, 1907. As above. Payable to Germania National Bank. (b/w)

b. Issued, cancelled. **R5**

Racine

A cashier's check issue is reported to have been issued in Racine. No details are known at present.

Superior

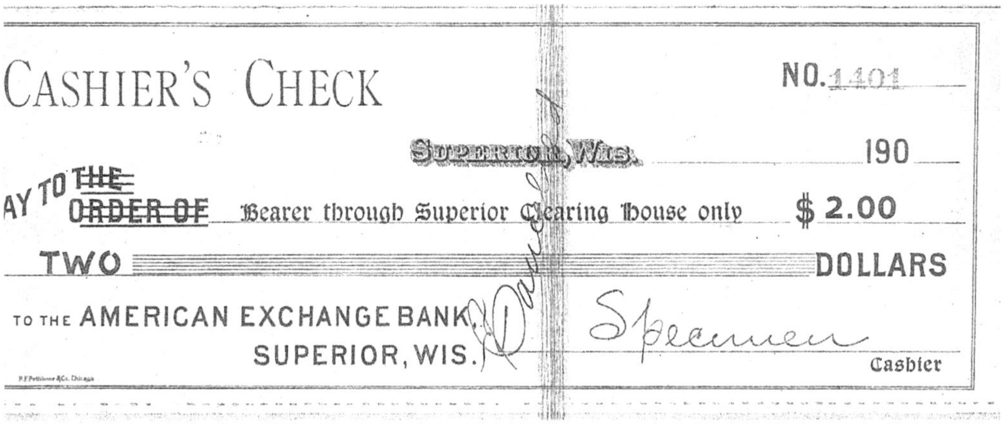

American Exchange Bank

WI750-2. 2 Dollars Cashier's Check 190_ (1907). Imprint: P.F. Pettibone & Co. Chicago. (b/w) (shown at 66%)

c. Unissued, cancelled (handwritten "Specimen"). **R5**

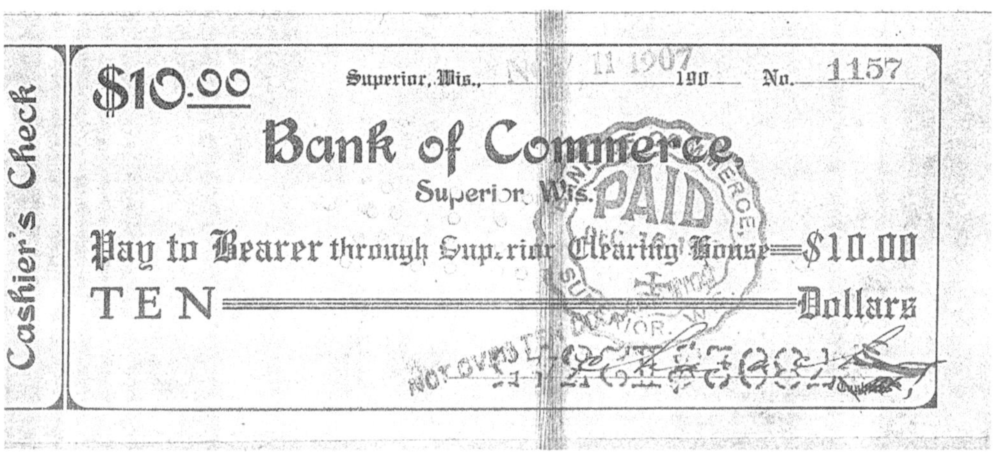

Bank of Commerce

WI800-10. 10 Dollars Cashier's Check Nov. 11, 1907 (stamped date). (b/w) (shown at 66%)

b. Issued, cancelled. **R5**

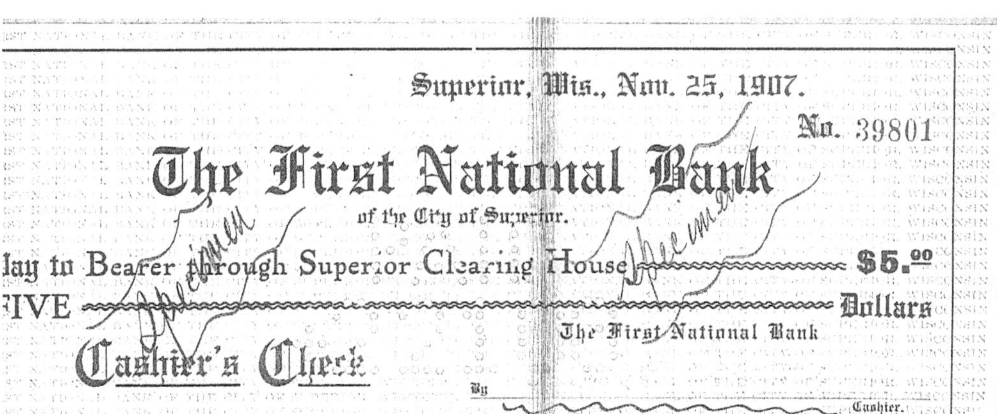

The First National Bank

WI850-5. 5 Dollars Cashier's Check Nov. 25, 1907. (b/w) (shown at 65%)
  c. Unissued, cancelled (handwritten "Specimen" twice). R5

Wyoming

Cheyenne

The Citizens' National Bank

WY500-1. 1 Dollar Cashier's Check Nov. 15, 1907. (list)
  c. Unissued, cancelled. R5

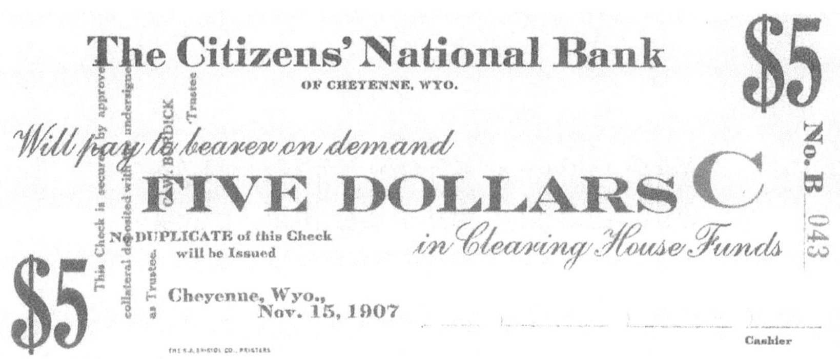

WY500-5. 5 Dollars Nov. 15, 1907. Black on light brown paper. Red text vertically at left. Uniface. Imprint: The S.A. Bristol Co., Printers. (shown at 60%)
  c. Unissued, cancelled. R5
WY500-10. 10 Dollars Nov. 15, 1907. Yellow paper, otherwise as above.
  c. Unissued, cancelled. R5
WY500-20. 20 Dollars Nov. 15, 1907. Pink paper, otherwise as above.
  c. Unissued, cancelled. R5

First National Bank

WY525-1. 1 Dollar Cashier's Check Nov. 15, 1907. Black on green underprint. Red overprint text at left and letter F at right. Uniface. Imprint: The S.A. Bristol Co., Printers.
  a. Issued, not cancelled. R5
WY525-5. 5 Dollars Nov. 15, 1907. Black on cream paper. As above but letter S at right.
  c. Unissued, cancelled. R5
WY525-10. 10 Dollars Nov. 15, 1907. (list)
  c. Unissued, cancelled. R5
WY525-20. 20 Dollars Nov. 15, 1907. (list)
  c. Unissued, cancelled. R5

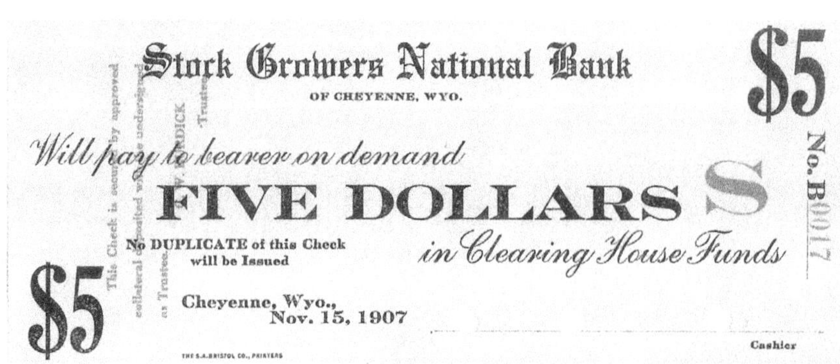

Stock Growers National Bank

WY550-5. 5 Dollars Cashier's Check Nov. 15, 1907. Black on buff paper. Format and imprint similar to WY525. Large red S at right. (shown at 60%)
c. Unissued, cancelled. R5

WY550-10. 10 Dollars Nov. 15, 1907. Yellow paper. As above.
c. Unissued, cancelled. R5

WY550-20. 20 Dollars Nov. 15, 1907. Pink paper. As above.
c. Unissued, cancelled. R5

Evanston

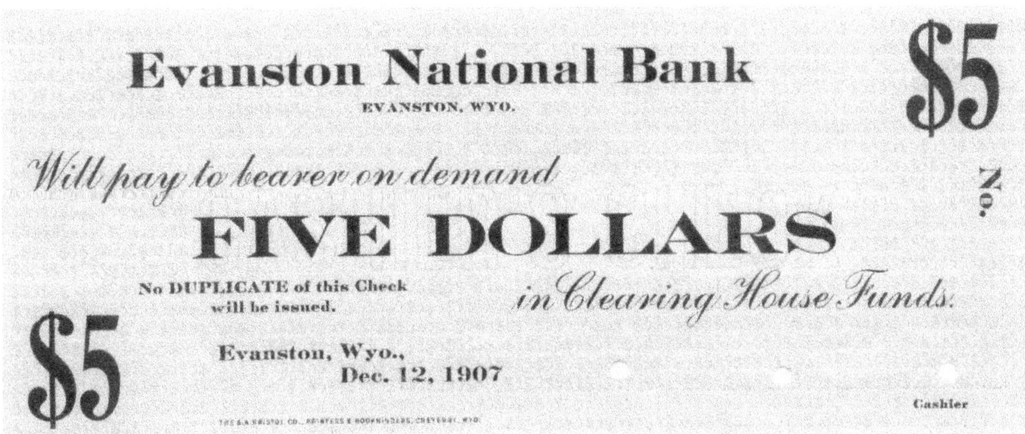

Evanston National Bank

WY575-5. 5 Dollars Dec. 12, 1907. Black on off-white paper with pinkish tint. No red text at left. Uniface. Imprint: The S.A. Bristol Co. Printers & Bookbinders, Cheyenne, Wyo. (shown at 74%)
c. Unissued, cancelled. R5

Rock River

Cosgriff & Rumsey, Bankers

WY600-5. 5 Dollars Nov. 22, 1907. Pink paper. Format as WY500. Imprint as WY575.
c. Unissued, cancelled. R5

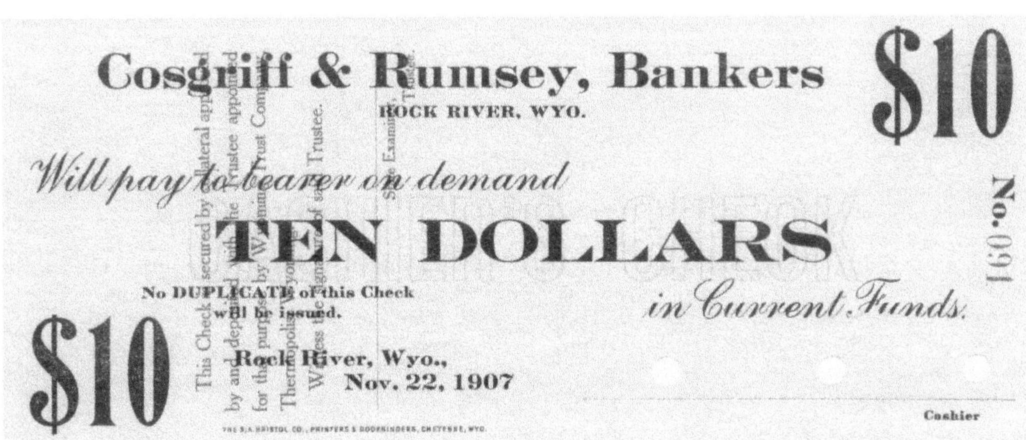

WY600-10. 10 Dollars Nov. 22, 1907. Yellow paper. As above. (shown at 75%)
c. Unissued, cancelled. R5

Thermopolis

Wyoming Trust Company

WY625-1. 1 Dollar Nov. 25, 1907. Blue paper. Format as WY500.
 d. Unissued, remainder. **R5**
WY625-10. 10 Dollars Nov. 25, 1907. Yellow paper. As above.
 c. Unissued, cancelled. **R5**

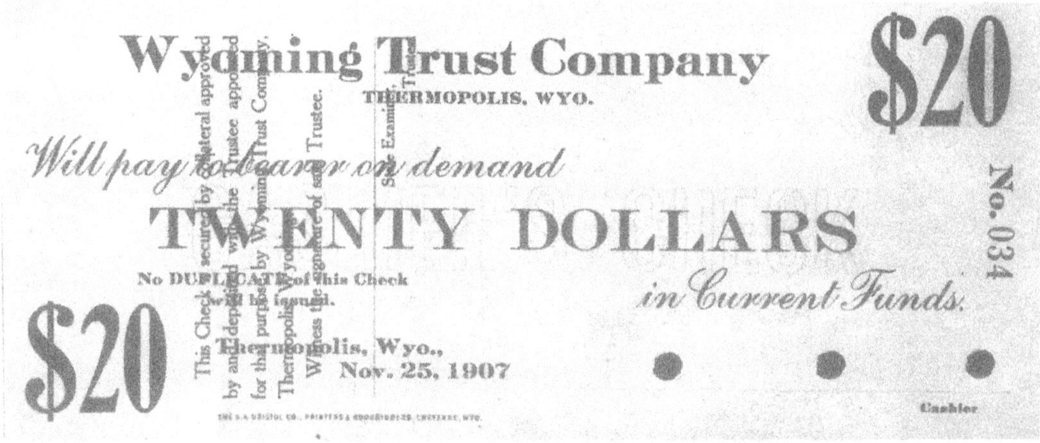

WY625-20. 20 Dollars Nov. 25, 1907. Pink paper. As above. Imprint as WY575. (shown at 75%)
 c. Unissued, cancelled. **R5**

SPECIMEN BOOK—Western Bank Note Company

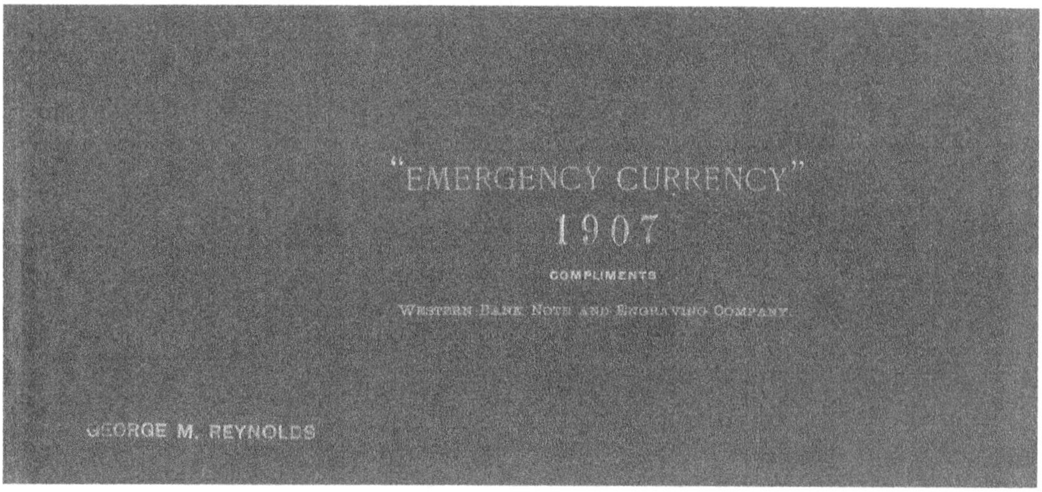

A book titled EMERGENCY CURRENCY 1907 produced by Western Bank Note Company of Chicago contains the following pieces, all with word SPECIMEN on each note and all with serial number of zeros except for the Cleveland issue: Chicago—$1 Bank no. 1, $2 Bank no. 3, $5 Bank no. 11, $10 Bank no. 5; Youngstown—$1, $2, $5, $10, $20; Grand Rapids—$1 Bank no. 3, $2 Bank no. 1, $5 Bank no. 4; Paducah—$1, $2, $5, $10; Cleveland—$1 Bank no. 5, serial number A7546. This book was in the Lyn Knight auction sale of June 2004 at Memphis, Tennessee. (shown at 53%)

III. Scrip from the Financial Crisis of 1914

Historical Background

A monetary crisis at the outbreak of World War I arose that threatened the United States with financial disaster. The biggest gold outflow in a generation imperiled America's ability to repay its debts abroad. Fear that the United States would abandon the gold standard sent the dollar plummeting on world markets. Without a central bank in the summer of 1914, the United States resembled a headless financial giant. William Gibbs McAdoo stepped in with courageous action by shutting down the New York Stock Exchange for more than four months to prevent Europeans from selling their American securities and demanding gold in return. He brought about the issuance of a great deal of "emergency currency" by the federal government throughout the country to prevent a replay of the bank runs that swept America in 1907. And he launched the United States as a world monetary power by maintaining America's commitment to the gold standard. His actions provide a blueprint for crisis control that merits attention today. All these fiscal achievements removed most of the need for local scrip, accounting for the very few issues found in this section of the catalog. In fact, what had been feared as the start of a business downturn because of World War I had turned into the very opposite during the years America was not directly involved in the war.

McAdoo's recipe emphasizes an exit strategy that allows policymakers to throttle a crisis while minimizing collateral damage. His accomplishments place him in the company of such individuals as Paul Volcker and Alan Greenspan as great financial leaders. McAdoo, in fact, brought the Federal Reserve into existence as the 1914 crisis waned. He served as the first chairman of the Federal Reserve Board.

Catalog Listing

District of Columbia

Securities Committee of the Washington, D.C. Clearing House Association

DC2500-1000. 1,000 Dollars Aug. 3, 1914. Black with green numerals in underprint across center. Uniface. Size: 210 × 195mm.

c. Unissued, cancelled. **R5**

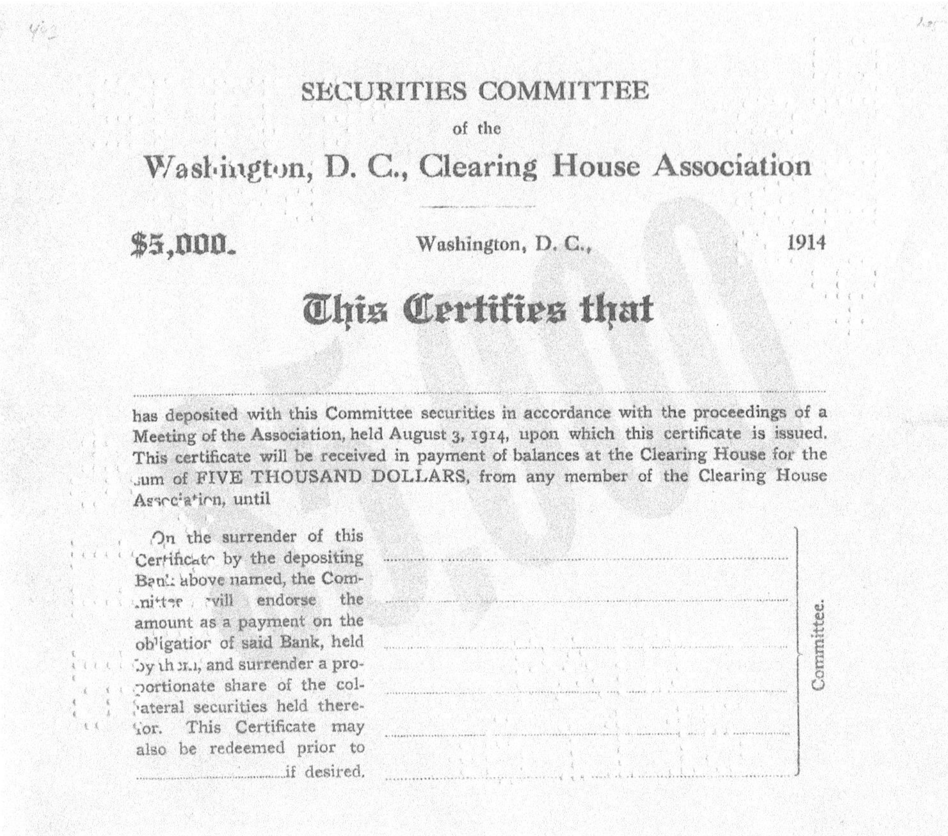
SECURITIES COMMITTEE
of the
Washington, D. C., Clearing House Association

$5,000. Washington, D. C., 1914

This Certifies that

has deposited with this Committee securities in accordance with the proceedings of a Meeting of the Association, held August 3, 1914, upon which this certificate is issued. This certificate will be received in payment of balances at the Clearing House for the sum of FIVE THOUSAND DOLLARS, from any member of the Clearing House Association, until

On the surrender of this Certificate by the depositing Bank above named, the Committee will endorse the amount as a payment on the obligation of said Bank, held by them, and surrender a proportionate share of the collateral securities held therefor. This Certificate may also be redeemed prior to ....if desired.

Committee.

DC2500-5000. 5,000 Dollars Aug. 3, 1914. Black with blue-green numerals on gray paper. As above. (shown at 66%)
c. Unissued, cancelled. **R5**
DC2500-10000. 10,000 Dollars Aug. 3, 1914. Black with yellow numerals. As above.
c. Unissued, cancelled. **R5**

GEORGIA

Cordele

CRISP COUNTY COTTON ASSOCIATION
CORDELE, GEORGIA.
CERTIFICATE
AGREE TO PAY BEARER
ONE DOLLAR
At CORDELE, GEORGIA, on or before November 1st, 1915, subject to the conditions as printed on back of this certificate.
CRISP COUNTY COTTON ASSOCIATION.
by............ FOR TRUSTEES.
SERIES A
16532

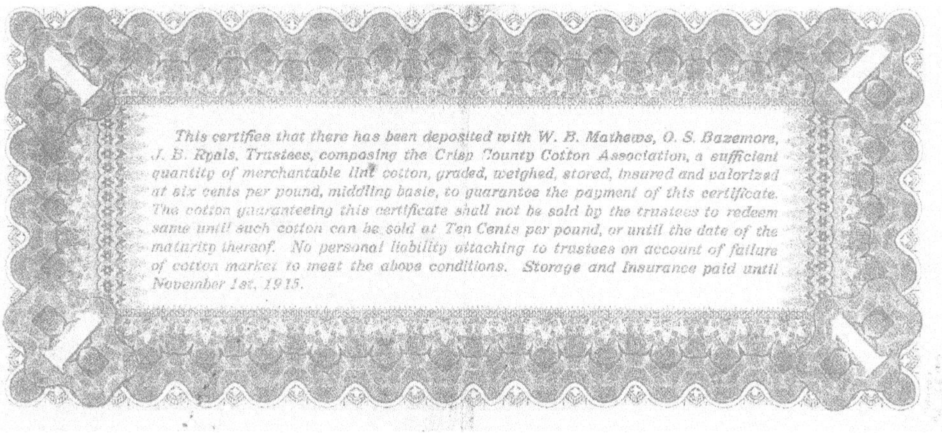

CRISP COUNTY COTTON ASSOCIATION

GA2600-1. 1 Dollar ND. Payable on or before Nov. 1, 1915. Blue-black. Cotton bales at upper left. Back green; text indicating backing with cotton. Imprint: Foote & Davies Co. Atlanta, Ga. (shown at 68%)

d. Unissued, remainder. R5

Pinehurst

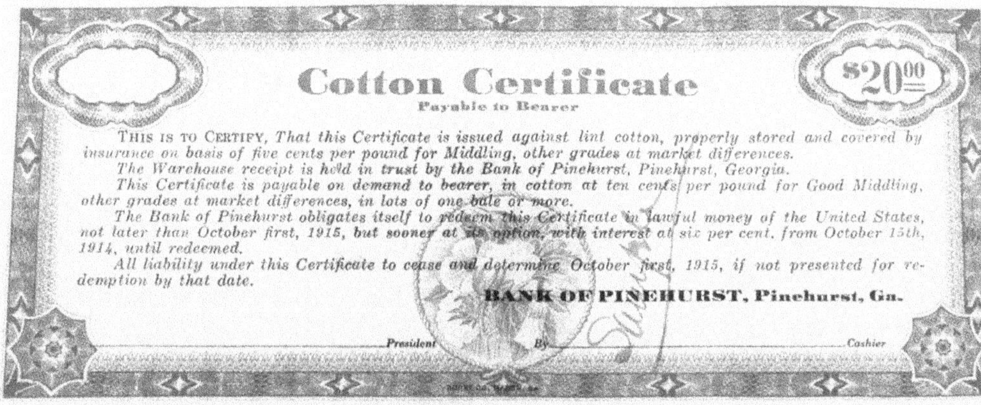

Bank of Pinehurst

GA2660-20. 20 Dollars Cotton Certificate Oct. 15, 1914. Black text on blue paper with main heading and value at upper right corner in red. Cotton bale in circle at lower center. (shown at 78%)
e. Sample (handwritten on face). R5

Sylvania

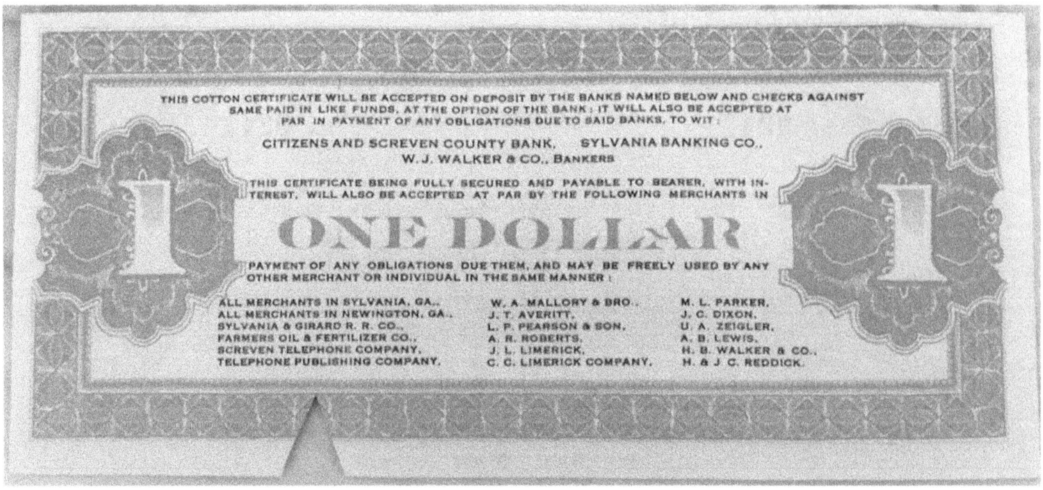

Consolidated Warehouse Company

GA2700-1. 1 Dollar Cotton Certificate of Deposit October 1, 1914. Black text on gray paper. Green design of shields at upper corners, cotton bale at center. Two red serial numbers. Imprint: Braid & Button, Inc., Lithographers, Savannah, Ga. (shown at 75%)
c. Unissued, cancelled. R5

GA2700-5. 5 Dollars 1914. Design as the $1.00. (b/w)
a. Issued, not cancelled. R5

NOTE: Officials in the county of Screven drew up a plan to ease distress caused by World War I. Summarizing an explanatory letter to the *Atlanta Constitution* of September 21, 1914, by Citizens and Screven County Bank President W. J. Walker: The plan was based on bonded and insured cotton warehouse receipts, against which cotton certificates valued at $1.00 and $5.00 are issued. These pieces were accepted for deposit and debt, being in all respects as valid and fluid as currency of the national government.

It worked like this: the farmer deposits his cotton in a duly accredited and bonded warehouse. Each bale is insured against fire to the amount of $45. Based on that cotton or its warehouse receipt, the certificates are issued on a basis of seven cents per pound. They mature six months from October 1, 1914, are redeemable in federal legal tender, and bear interest at 6% per annum. The recognized soundness of these certificates, and the relief they provided led to their wide circulation not only in Screven but in surrounding communities as well.

Text on the back of the certificates includes the following: "This cotton certificate will be accepted on deposit by the banks named below and checks against same paid in like funds, at the option of the bank; it will also be accepted at par in payment of any obligations due to said banks, to wit:

Citizens and Screven County Bank
Sylvania Banking Company
W. J. Walker & Co., Bankers

This certificate, being fully secured and payable to bearer, with interest, will also be accepted at par by the following merchants (there follows a list of many places that participated in this plan)."

Apparently there was a good bit of discussion regarding the workings of this plan, and how the proposed monetary certificates would look both in appearance and text. In a number of files Jamie Yakes had access to there are some word copies as well as a model $5 certificate from a nonexistent Eureka Warehouse Company from the ephemeral Doeville, Blank County, Georgia; it is shown following. At present this piece is most likely unique.

Amount, Five Dollars ($5.00) Due 1 April, 1915

No.______ No.______

EUREKA WAREHOUSE COMPANY

OF DOEVILLE, BLANK COUNTY, GEORGIA

Chartered and Bonded Under the Laws of Georgia

INTEREST RATE 6%

This Certifies that there has been deposited with the Union Trust Company of Doeville, Georgia, as trustee for the holders of this instrument and others of like tenor, approved warehouse receipts of the above-named warehouse company attached to farmers' notes on the basis of seven cents (7c) per pound for middling upland cotton, to secure to the bearer hereof payment by the said Eureka Warehouse Company of the sum of

FIVE DOLLARS

in lawful money of United States of America six months after October 1st, 1914, with interest from October 1st, 1914, at the rate of six per cent (6%) per annum. The cotton securing this certificate is insured against fire at the rate of $45 per bale, against which certificates may be issued to not exceed $35 a bale. This certificate is payable, principal and interest, on presentation at First National Bank of Johnsville, Georgia, any time during April, 1915

ACCEPTED AT PAR

OVER

Treasurer Eureka Warehouse Company

Treasurer Doeville Trust Company, Trustee

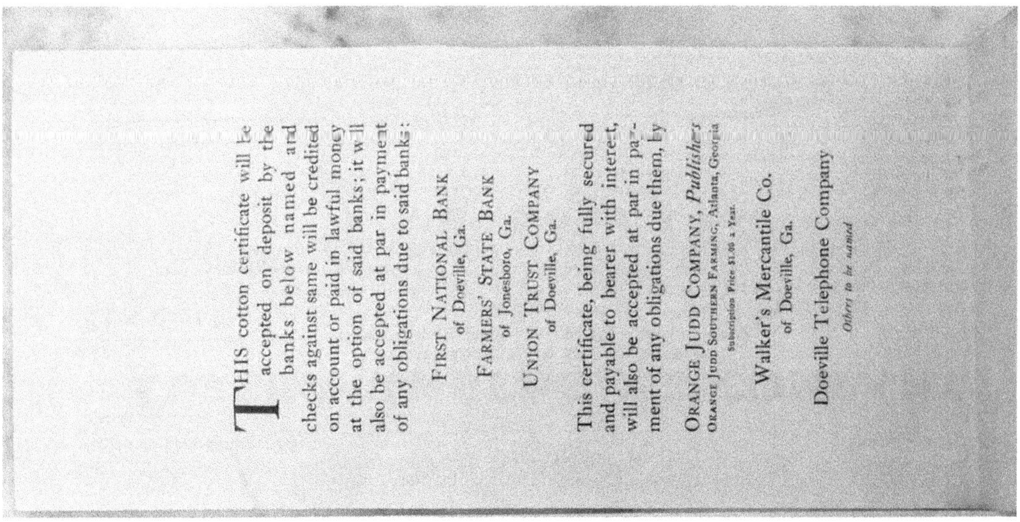

THIS cotton certificate will be accepted on deposit by the banks below named and checks against same will be credited on account or paid in lawful money at the option of said banks; it will also be accepted at par in payment of any obligations due to said banks:

FIRST NATIONAL BANK
of Doeville, Ga.

FARMERS' STATE BANK
of Jonesboro, Ga.

UNION TRUST COMPANY
of Doeville, Ga.

This certificate, being fully secured and payable to bearer with interest, will also be accepted at par in payment of any obligations due them, by

ORANGE JUDD COMPANY, *Publishers*
ORANGE JUDD SOUTHERN FARMING, Atlanta, Georgia
Subscription Price $1.00 a Year.

Walker's Mercantile Co.
of Doeville, Ga.

Doeville Telephone Company
Others to be named

This is the model $5 certificate from the nonexistent Eureka Warehouse Company. (shown at 75%)

ILLINOIS

Chicago

CHICAGO CLEARING HOUSE ASSOCIATION

IL2500-Var. Various Amounts 191_. Black. Allegorical woman at upper left. Uniface. Imprint: Western Bank Note & Eng. Co. Chicago Branch American Bank Note Company. (shown at 64%)
p. Proof. **R5**
IL2500-10,000.A 10,000 Dollars 191_. Word copy indicating United States Notes held in a special deposit, payable on demand to association members when properly endorsed. **R5**
IL2500-10,000.B 10,000 Dollars 191_. As above, but special deposit of Gold Certificates is indicated. **R5**
IL2500-20,000. 20,000 Dollars 191_. As above. **R5**

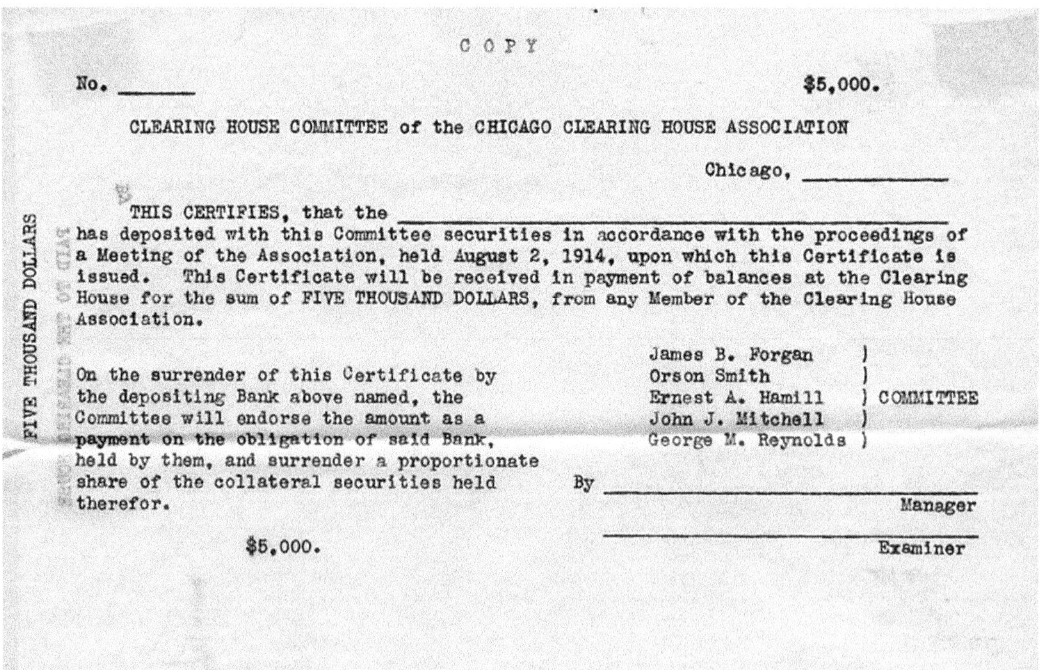

COPY

No. ______ $5,000.

CLEARING HOUSE COMMITTEE of the CHICAGO CLEARING HOUSE ASSOCIATION

Chicago, __________

THIS CERTIFIES, that the ______________________________
has deposited with this Committee securities in accordance with the proceedings of a Meeting of the Association, held August 2, 1914, upon which this Certificate is issued. This Certificate will be received in payment of balances at the Clearing House for the sum of FIVE THOUSAND DOLLARS, from any Member of the Clearing House Association.

FIVE THOUSAND DOLLARS

On the surrender of this Certificate by the depositing Bank above named, the Committee will endorse the amount as a payment on the obligation of said Bank, held by them, and surrender a proportionate share of the collateral securities held therefor.

James B. Forgan
Orson Smith
Ernest A. Hamill
John J. Mitchell
George M. Reynolds
COMMITTEE

By ______________________
Manager

____
Examiner

$5,000.

Clearing House Committee of the Chicago Clearing House Association

IL2550-5,000. 5000 Dollars Aug. 2, 1914. Word copy of proposed Certificate to be used by any member bank. (shown at 69%) R5

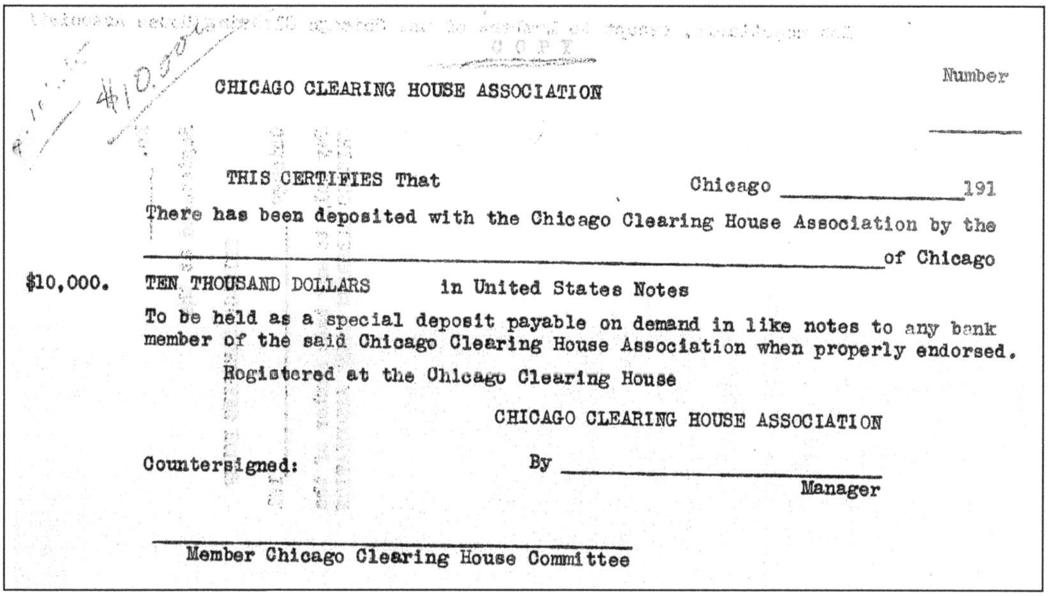
COPY

Number

CHICAGO CLEARING HOUSE ASSOCIATION

THIS CERTIFIES That Chicago ______ 191

There has been deposited with the Chicago Clearing House Association by the

______ of Chicago

$10,000. TEN THOUSAND DOLLARS in United States Notes

To be held as a special deposit payable on demand in like notes to any bank member of the said Chicago Clearing House Association when properly endorsed.

Registered at the Chicago Clearing House

CHICAGO CLEARING HOUSE ASSOCIATION

Countersigned: By ______ Manager

______ Member Chicago Clearing House Committee

IL2550-10,000. 10,000 Dollars Aug. 2, 1914. Word copy similar to above. (shown at 70%) R5

IL2550-50,000. 50,000 Dollars Aug. 2, 1914. As above. R5

Indiana

Ambia

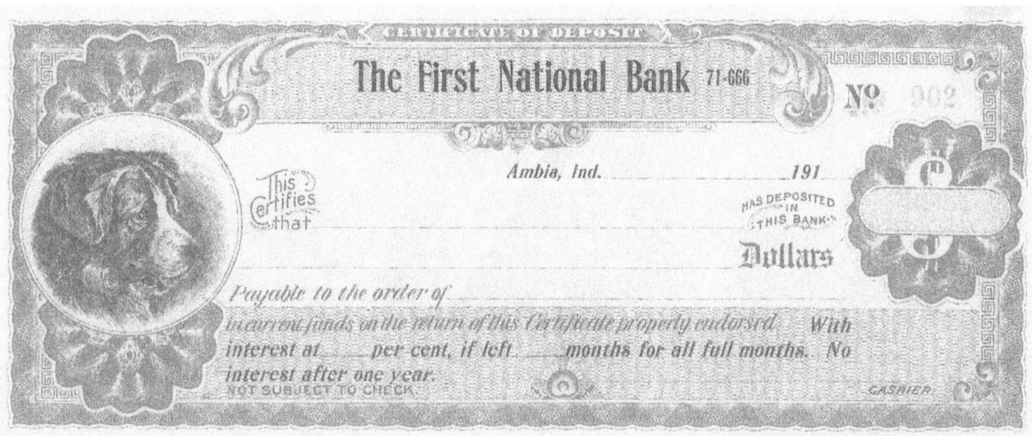

The First National Bank

IN2500-Var. Various Amounts 191_. Certificate of Deposit. Black and green. Dog's head at left. Back green. (shown at 65%)

d. Unissued, remainder. R5

Kansas

Newton

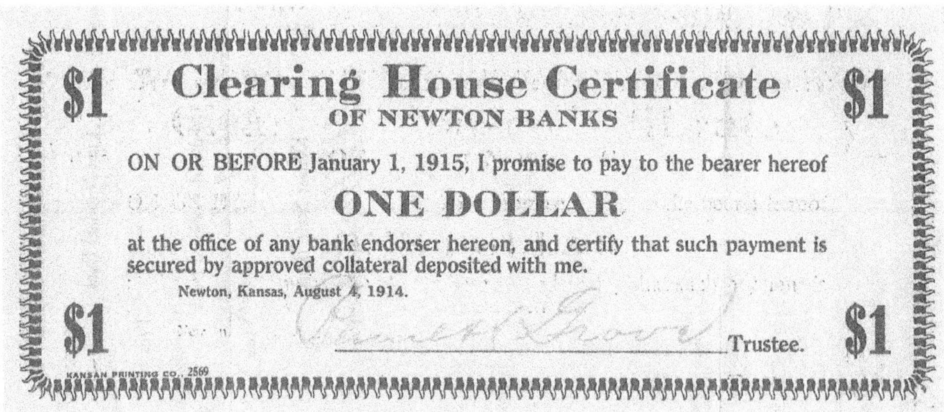

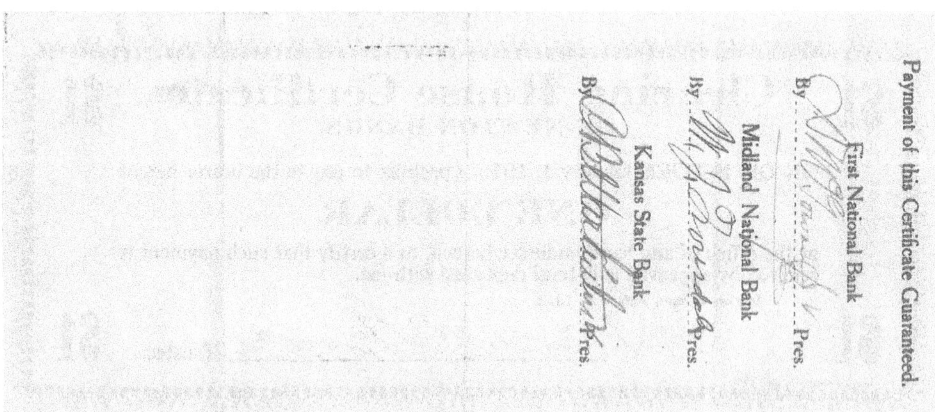

Clearing House Certificate of Newton Banks

KS2600-1. 1 Dollar Aug. 4, 1914. Black on yellowish paper. Redemption guarantees on back by signatures from three different bank presidents. Imprint: Kansas Printing Co., 2569. (shown at 68%)
a. Issued, not cancelled. **R5**

Wichita

Wichita Clearing House Association

KS2700-1. 1 Dollar Clearing House Certificate Aug. 3, 1914. Black. Back gold; design of KS780-5. Imprint: Western Litho. Co. Wichita. (shown at 75%)
a. Issued, not cancelled. **R3**

KS2700-5. 5 Dollars Aug. 3, 1914. As above.
u. Issued. **SENC**

KS2700-10. 10 Dollars Aug. 3, 1914. As above.
c. Unissued, cancelled. **R5**

MINNESOTA

St. Paul

LOAN COMMITTEE OF THE ST. PAUL CLEARING HOUSE ASSOCIATION

MN2500-1000. 1000 Dollars 1914. Black.
c. Unissued, cancelled. R5

MN2500-5000. 5,000 Dollars 1914. (list)
u. Unissued. SENC

NOTE: Higher denominations are reported but not confirmed.

MISSOURI

St. Louis

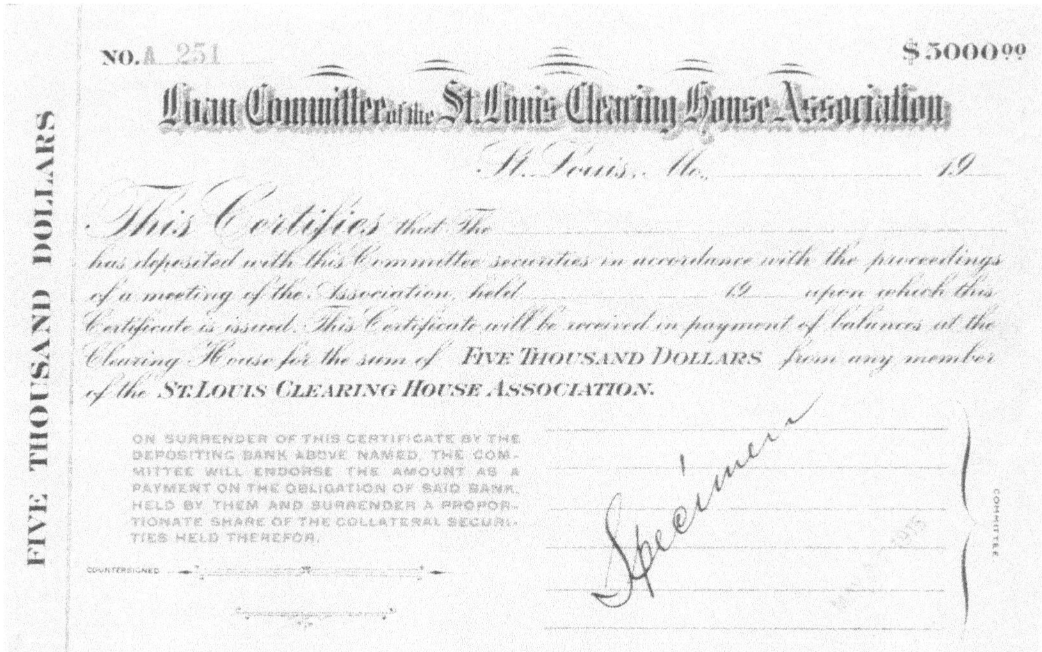
NO. A 251 $5000.00

Loan Committee of the St. Louis Clearing House Association

St. Louis, Mo., 19

This Certifies that The has deposited with this Committee securities in accordance with the proceedings of a meeting of the Association, held 19 upon which this Certificate is issued. This Certificate will be received in payment of balances at the Clearing House for the sum of FIVE THOUSAND DOLLARS from any member of the ST. LOUIS CLEARING HOUSE ASSOCIATION.

ON SURRENDER OF THIS CERTIFICATE BY THE DEPOSITING BANK ABOVE NAMED, THE COMMITTEE WILL ENDORSE THE AMOUNT AS A PAYMENT ON THE OBLIGATION OF SAID BANK, HELD BY THEM AND SURRENDER A PROPORTIONATE SHARE OF THE COLLATERAL SECURITIES HELD THEREFOR.

COUNTERSIGNED

Specimen

COMMITTEE

FIVE THOUSAND DOLLARS

LOAN COMMITTEE OF THE ST. LOUIS CLEARING HOUSE ASSOCIATION

MO2500-5000. 5,000 Dollars Loan Certificate May 27, 1915 (stamped date). Black. Some text in red at lower left. Uniface. Large size. (shown at 64%)
f. Specimen. R5

MO2500-50,000. 50,000 Dollars Loan Certificate 19__ (1914). As above.
c. Unissued, cancelled. R5

NEVADA

Ely

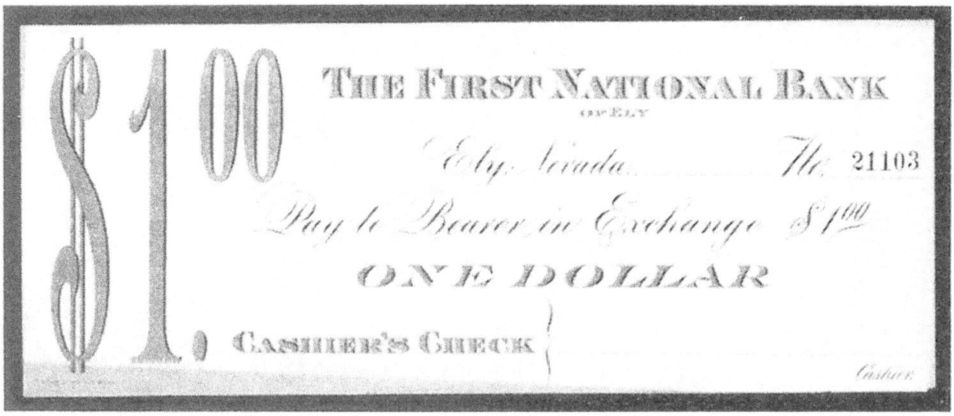

THE FIRST NATIONAL BANK

NV2500-1. 1 Dollar Cashier's Check ND (1914). Large denomination at left. Uniface. Imprint: Utah Litho. Co. S.L.C. (shown at 75%)
d. Unissued, remainder. **R5**

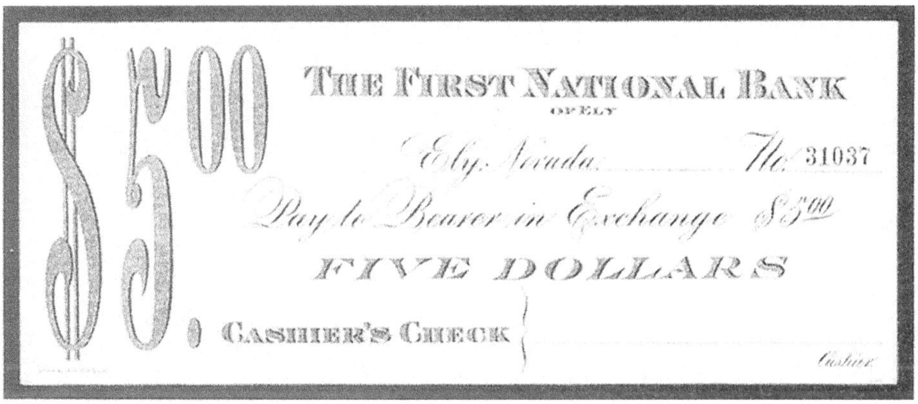

NV2500-5. 5 Dollars ND (1914). As above. (shown at 66%)
d. Unissued, remainder. **R5**

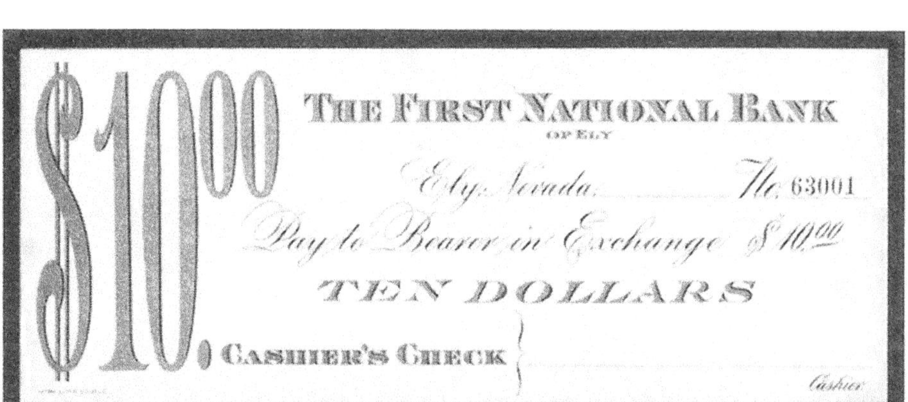

NV2500-10. 10 Dollars ND (1914). As above. (shown at 65%)
d. Unissued, remainder. **R5**

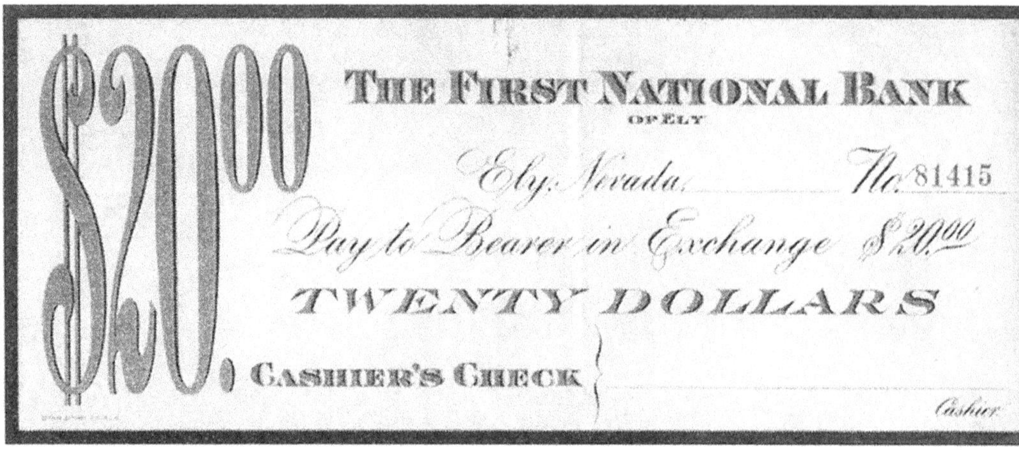

NV2500-20. 20 Dollars ND (1914). As above. (shown at 75%)
d. Unissued, remainder. **R5**

NOTE: This set was included in the Lyn Knight Currency Auctions Memphis sale of June 1999 (lots 25–28). The story is told that during the minor financial pinch of 1914, the president of this bank ordered a four-denomination scrip issue from the Utah Litho. Co. of Salt Lake City. They were to be called Cashier's Checks as a way of evading the ban against the use of private currency. All the scrip arrived at the bank after the need for it had subsided and none was ever issued. Instead, the bank president went into the alley behind the bank and burned every piece except one of each value that he saved for himself. The four pieces in the sale were from his estate and are thus the only surviving examples of this printing. It is not known where they are located at this time.

New York

Rochester

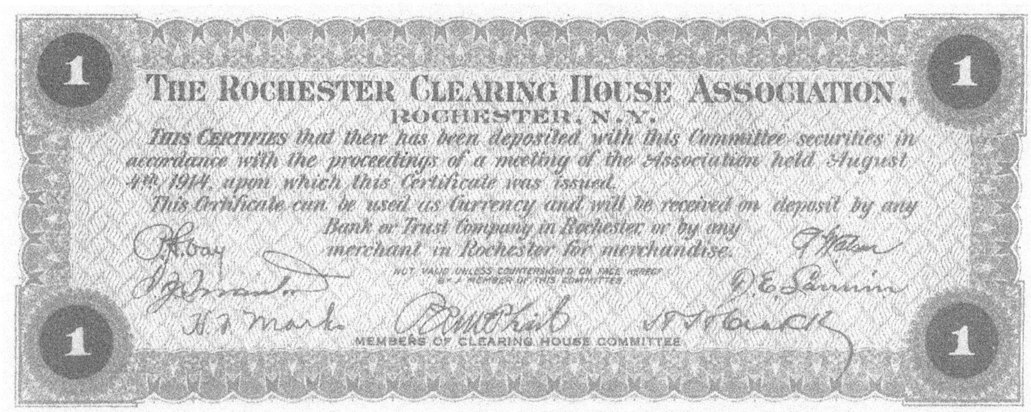

THE ROCHESTER CLEARING HOUSE ASSOCIATION

NY2500-1. 1 Dollar Aug. 4, 1914. Black. New York state seal at left. Back green with black text. (shown at 71%)
d. Unissued, remainder. R5
NY2500-5. 5 Dollars Aug. 4, 1914. Face as above. Back blue with black text.
d. Unissued, remainder. R5
NY2500-10. 10 Dollars Aug. 4, 1914. Face as above. Back red with black text.
d. Unissued, remainder. R5
NY2500-20. 20 Dollars Aug. 4, 1914. Face as above. Back purple with black text.
d. Unissued, remainder. R5
NOTE: All values of this Rochester issue are known only as uncut strips of two subjects.

OHIO

Cincinnati

No.
Date
Issued to
or order.
Amount

CLEARING HOUSE CERTIFICATE.
Cincinnati, Ohio. ____ 1914
This Certificate is issued to ____ or order, for
FIVE THOUSAND DOLLARS,
against security deposited under an agreement of the members of the CINCINNATI CLEARING HOUSE ASSOCIATION of August 3, 1914, and is available only in settling Clearing House balances.
Committee.
$5,000.00

CINCINNATI CLEARING HOUSE ASSOCIATION

OH2500-5000. 5000 Dollar Clearing House Certificate __ 1914. Black text on white paper with stub. (shown at 66%)
d. Unissued, remainder. R5

No.
Date
Issued to
or order.
Amount

CLEARING HOUSE CERTIFICATE.
Cincinnati, Ohio. 1914
This Certificate is issued to or order, for
TWENTY THOUSAND DOLLARS,
against security deposited under an agreement of the members of the CINCINNATI CLEARING HOUSE ASSOCIATION of August 3, 1914, and is available only in settling Clearing House balances.
Committee.
$20,000.00

OH2500-20,000. 20,000 Dollar Clearing House Certificate __ 1914. As previous. (shown at 66%)
d. Unissued, remainder. **R5**

Tennessee

Nashville

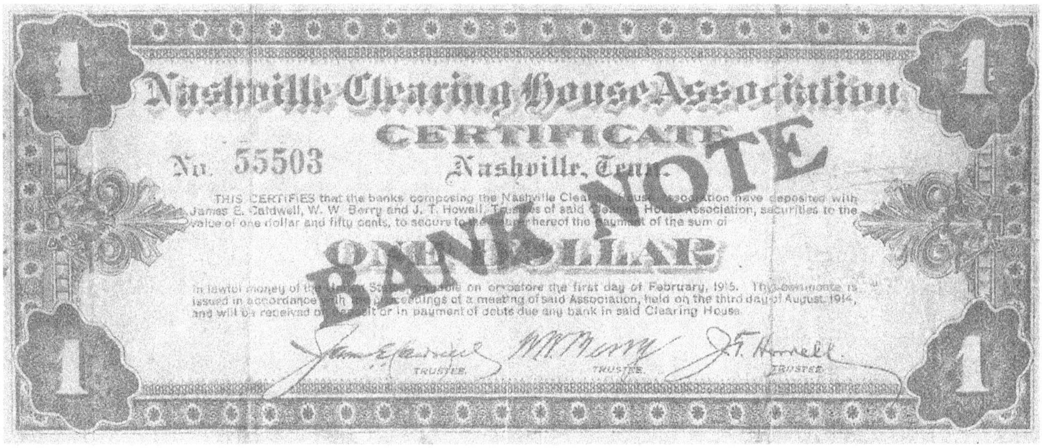

Nashville Clearing House Association

TN2500-1.A 1 Dollar (certificate of deposit) Aug. 3, 1914. Green. Diagonal red BANK NOTE overprint across center. Back light orange; list of member banks at center. Imprint: Brandon Nashville/Trade Mark Registered. (shown at 73%)
a. Issued, not cancelled. **R3**
b. Issued, cancelled. **R4**

TN2500-1.B 1 Dollar Aug. 3, 1914. Deep green face, dark orange back. Much different style and border on both sides than above. Also without red BANK NOTE overprint across center. (shown at 73%)

b. Issued, cancelled. R4

APPENDICES

Appendix A. 1907 Pseudo or Parody Scrip

This section contains pieces that superficially resemble notes but are in reality a form of propaganda. Makers of these kinds of pseudo-notes used designs more or less resembling currency and distributed them in various ways so that they may have been picked up by the public. Of course they were immediately recognized as spurious, but their messages were at least looked at by the finders, and when that happened their makers had won the day.

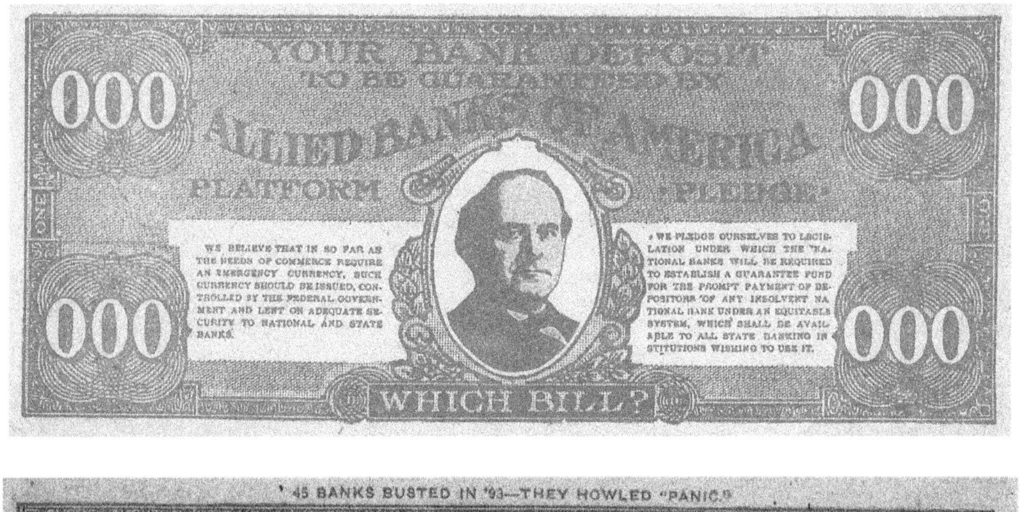

Allied Banks of America

P1000 000 (Dollars). Green face; William Jennings Bryan at center. Platform pledge: *We believe that in so far as the needs of commerce require an emergency currency, such currency should be issued, controlled by the federal government and left on adequate security to national and state banks.* More text at right: *we pledge ourselves to legislation under which the national banks will be required to establish a guarantee fund for the prompt payment of depositors of any insolvent national bank under an equitable system, which shall be available to all state banking institutions wishing to use it.* (shown at 71%)
Back yellow-brown; William Howard Taft at center. *Republican Clearing Script,* etc. (shown at 71%)
No imprint. **Fine, 30. ExF, 50.**
P1100 000 (Dollars). Yellow-brown face with design and text as above. Back green with design and text also as above. **Fine, 30. ExF, 50.**
NOTE: P1000 and 1100 are both printed on a very low grade of paper.

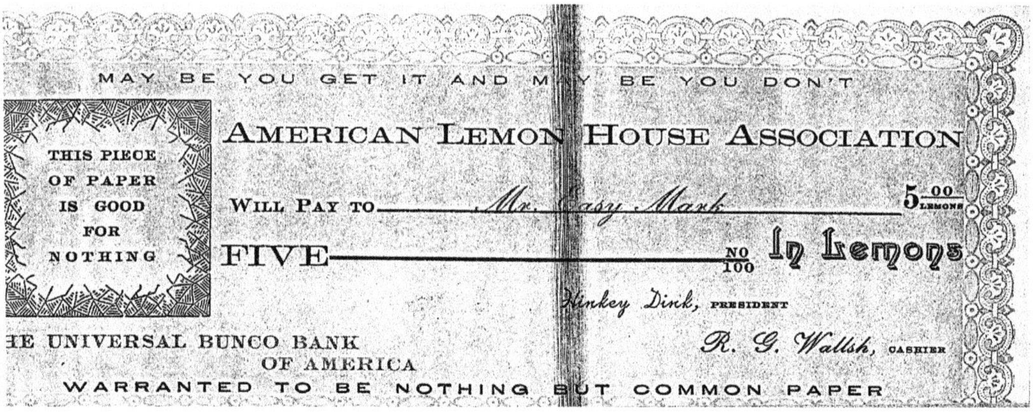

American Lemon House Association

P1200 5 Lemons ND (1907). Payable at The Universal Bunco Bank of America (b/w) (shown at 68%) **R5**

NOTE: This and P1700 are part of the A. Piatt Andrew Collection now at the American Numismatic Society.

Any Old Bank/Republican Clearing Script

P1500 000 (cashier's check) ND (1907). (list) **R5**
NOTE: P1500 could be an additional report of the pieces now listed under P1000 and P1100.

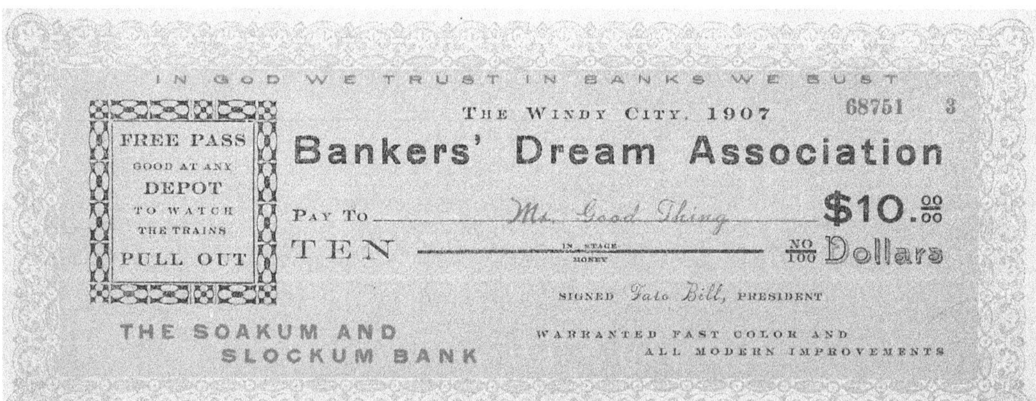

BANKERS' DREAM ASSOCIATION

P1700 10 Dollars 1907. Black on blue underprint, orange bank name at lower left. Orange text line across upper area, "In God We Trust, In Banks We Bust." Issued at "The Windy City" (Chicago). Text in box at left about Free Pass at any depot to watch trains pull out. Payable at the "Soakum and Slockum Bank." (shown at 64%)

Uniface. **R5**

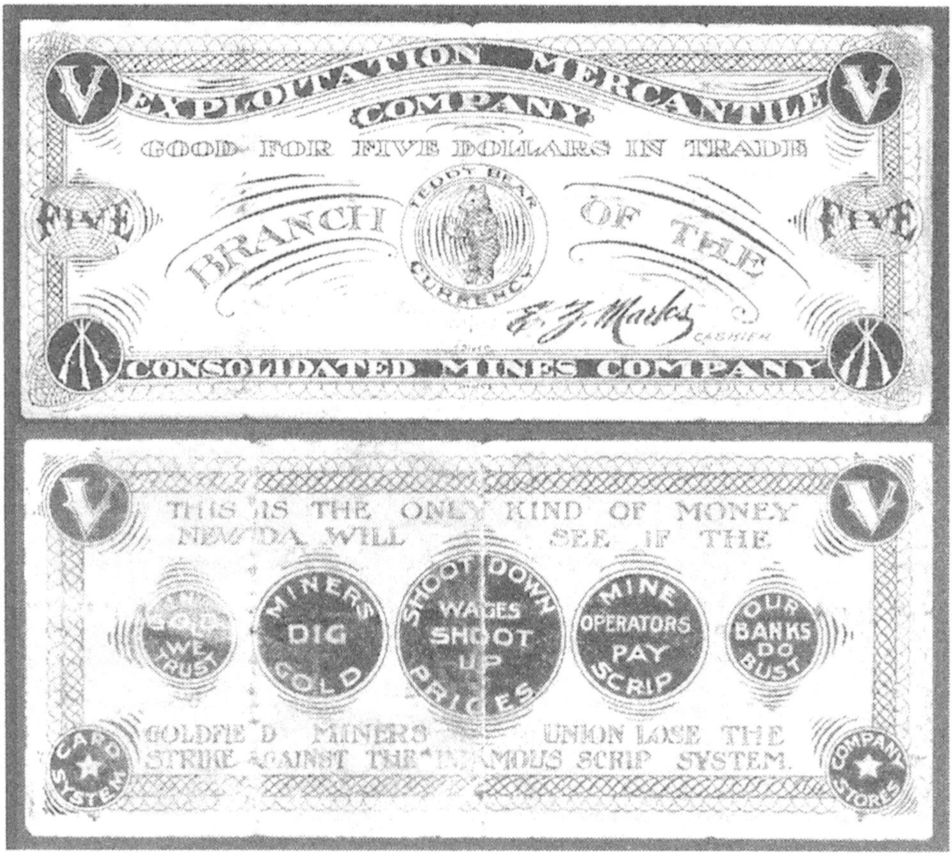

EXPLOITATION MERCANTILE COMPANY

P2000 Satirical Note for 5 Dollars in trade ND (1907) (shown at 100%). Listed in the Lyn Knight auction sale of Memphis 1999. Note produced by the miners' union of the Nevada company Goldfield Consolidated Mines, made to discredit Wingfield and the other owners for their actions in forcing scrip upon the miners. Known today as "Teddy Bear" scrip because of the image on the face symbolizing TR's decision to send troops to quell the strike. Only a few examples are known today. See NV525 in the 1907 catalog section, pages 210–11, for illustrations of the notes. **R5**

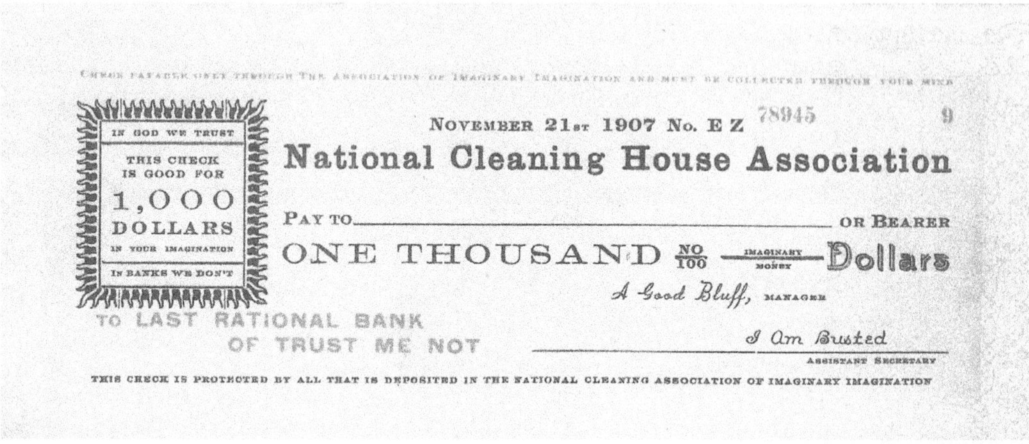

NATIONAL CLEANING HOUSE ASSOCIATION

P2500 $1000 Nov. 21.1907. Black on blue underprint, orange bank name at lower left, orange text line across upper area, "Check payable only through the association of imaginary imagination and must be collected through your mind." Payable at the Last Rational Bank of Trust Me Not. Uniface. (shown at 65%)

Fine, 45. EF, 85.

THE UNIVERSAL BUNKO BANK OF AMERICA

P3500 5 Dollars (cashier's check) ND (1907). (list) **R5**

NOTE: P3500 could be an additional report of the piece now listed as P1200.

Appendix B. Miscellaneous Scrip

The items included here were called to our attention by individuals who knew of our strong interest in scrip of all kinds. Some were also found in various auctions. At first we gave them no particular notice, but then it occurred to us that these pieces really did not fit into any established period or circumstance, so why not create a special section here devoted to just such "lost" notes. They will never be listed anywhere else, and they are as interesting in their own right as many in the regular sections of this book.

ARKANSAS

Amity/Glenwood

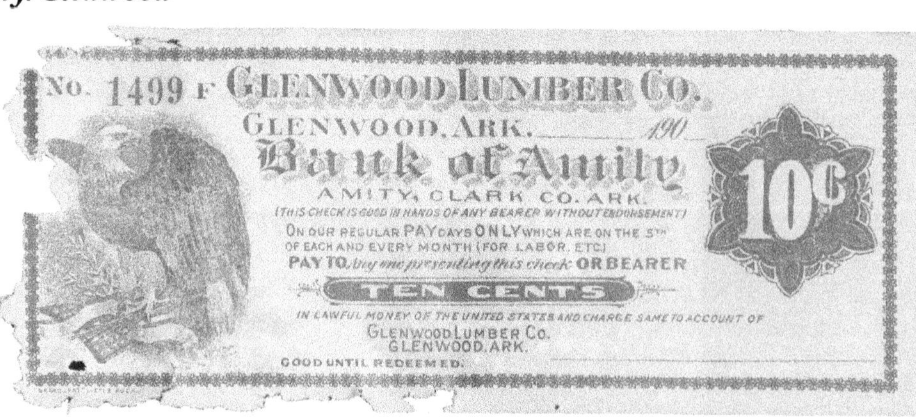

GLENWOOD LUMBER CO./BANK OF AMITY

AR3100-.10 10 Cents 190_. Brown. Eagle at left. Back green; ornate guilloche at left and right, arms at center. (shown at 80%)
d. Unissued, remainder. **R5**

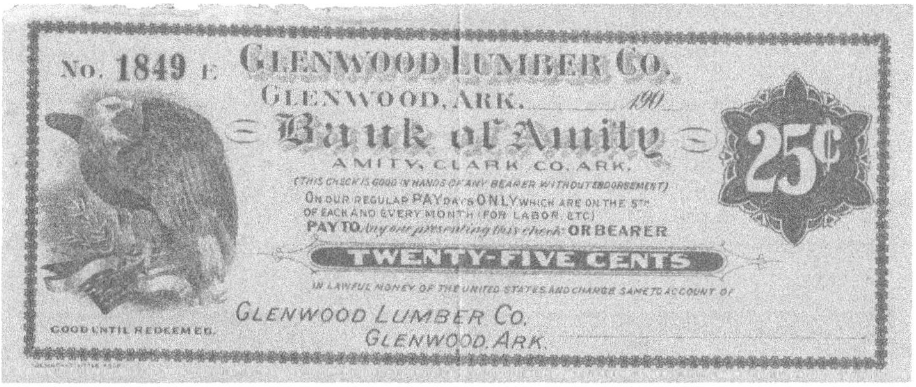

AR3100-.25 25 Cents 190_. Brown on light blue paper. Design as above. (shown at 72%)
d. Unissued, remainder. **R5**

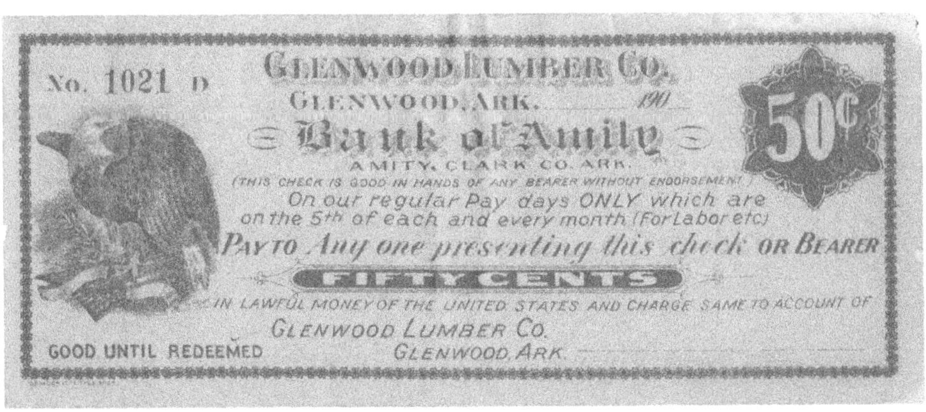

AR3100-.50 50 Cents 190_. Brown. As above pieces. (shown at 68%)
d. Unissued, remainder. **R5**

NOTE: Though at first glance the above notes appear to belong to the 1907 panic scrip period, the authors believe that they were not intended to be used as a means of alleviating the monetary emergency.

CALIFORNIA

Los Angeles

CLEARING HOUSE CERTIFICATE

CA3000-1000. 1,000 Dollars Mar. 1914. Black and gray. Five hand signatures at lower right. Uniface.
b. Issued, cancelled. R5

NOTE: This certificate was redeemed on Sept. 22, 1914.

WM. H. CARLSON

CA3100-5. 5 Dollars July 1, 1908. 8 percent interest bearing certificate. Eagle at left and right. (b/w)
a. Issued, not cancelled. R5

FLORIDA

Prairie

PRAIRIE PEBBLE PHOSPHATE CO.

FL3100-5. 5 Dollars Jan. 25, 1908. Black on tan paper. Back brown. (shown at 75%)
d. Unissued, remainder. R5

INDIANA

Fairbanks

U.S. CONSTRUCTION CO./FAIRBANKS TRUST CO.

IN3000-1. 1 Dollar ND (ca. 1908). Black. Eagle on shield at center. Back pale green, same design as face. 6 percent interest-bearing note. (shown at 71%)

a. Issued, not cancelled. **R3**

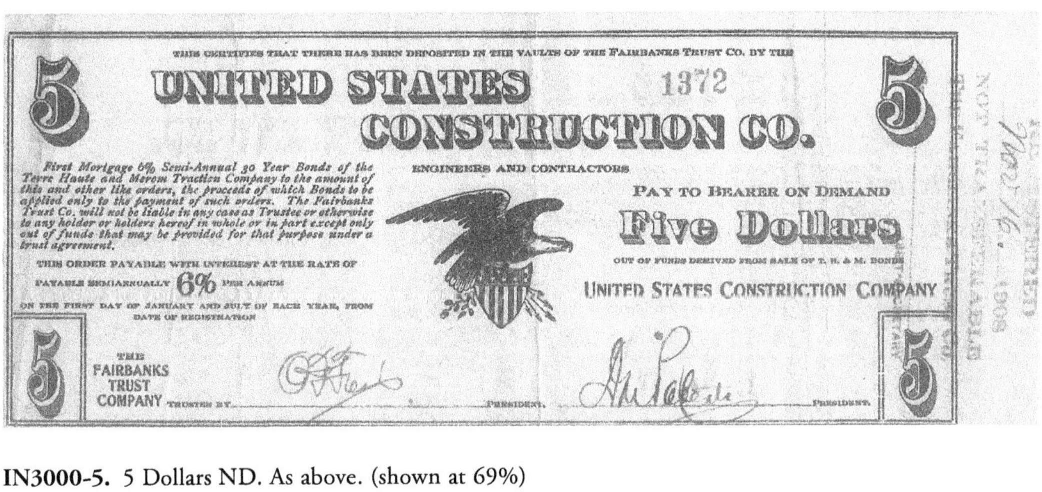

IN3000-5. 5 Dollars ND. As above. (shown at 69%)

a. Issued, not cancelled. **R3**

NOTE: The example of IN3000-5. illustrated has a registration date of Nov. 16, 1908.

Kansas

Girard

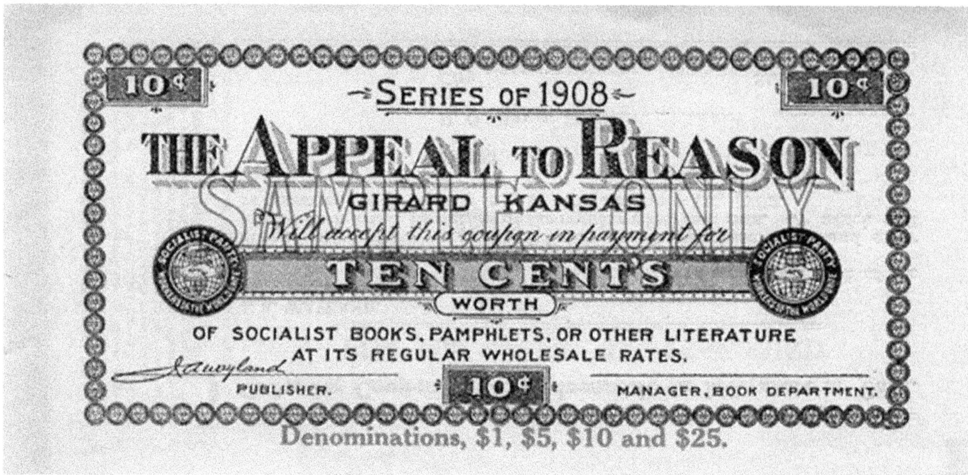

THE APPEAL TO REASON

KS3100-.10 10 Cents Series of 1908. Black text and two Socialist Party seals on brown paper. SAMPLE ONLY in outline letters across center. 115 × 55 mm. (shown at 75%)

e. Sample. **R5**

NOTE: Denominations of this issue listed in red on lower margin: $1, $5, $10 and $25. Scrip was usable for "Socialist books, pamphlets or other literature...."

Minnesota

St. Paul

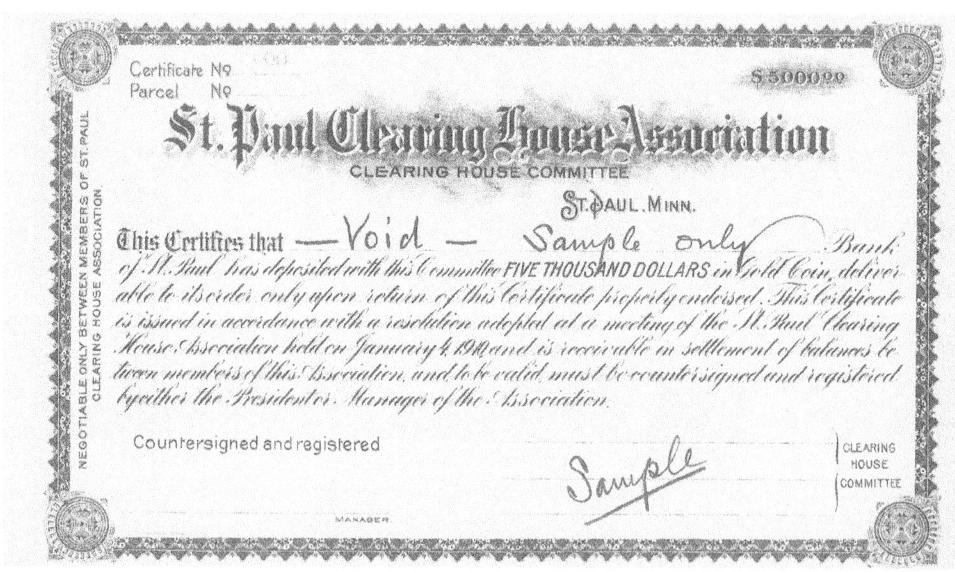

St. Paul Clearing House Association

MN3100-5000. 5,000 Dollars Jan. 4, 1910. Black on yellow paper. Large size. (shown at 52%)
e. Sample. **R5**

New Mexico

Cimarron

The Continental Tile & Lumber Company

NM3000-5. 5 Dollars Feb. 1, 1909. Black. Back green.
d. Unissued, remainder. **R5**

New York

Buffalo

The Bankers' Association of Buffalo

NY3000-1000. 1000 Dollars Jan. 22, 1890. Black on olive underprint. Pile of coins and value on back.
c. Unissued, cancelled. **R4**

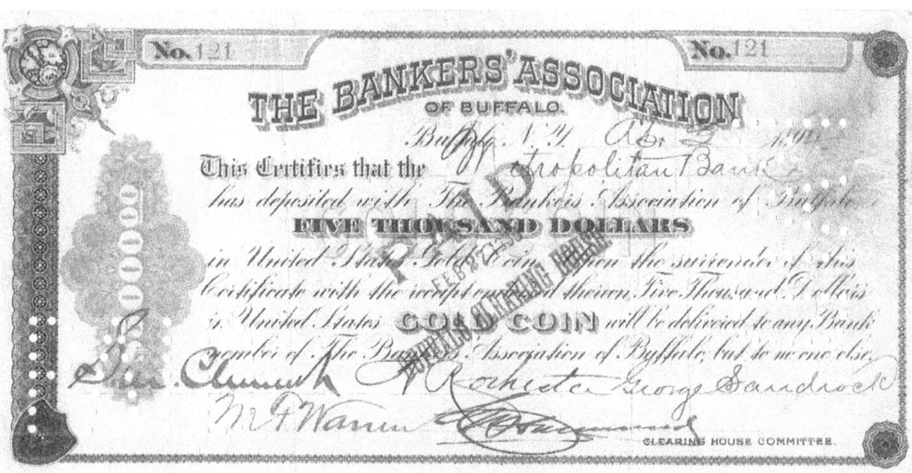

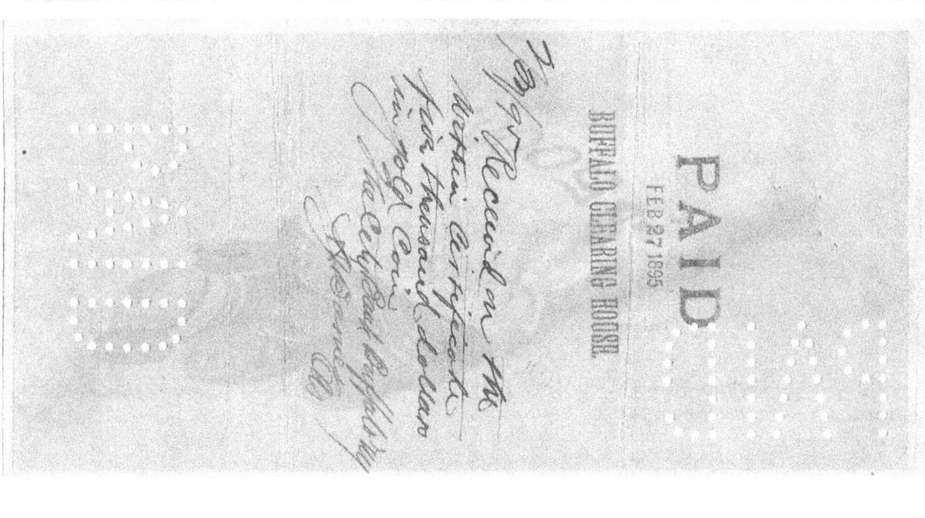

NY3000-5000. 5000 Dollars Nov. 6, 1893; Apr. 3, 1894 (and possibly later dates). Black with orange value guilloche at left. Orange back design as above. (shown at 53%)
b. Issued, cancelled. **R1**

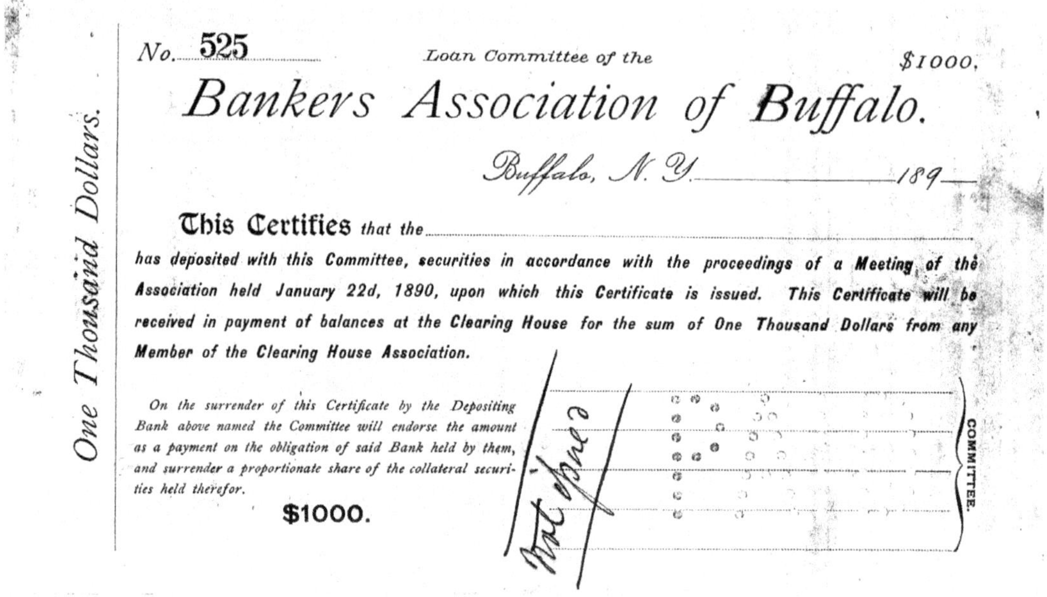
No. 525 Loan Committee of the $1000.
Bankers Association of Buffalo.
Buffalo, N. Y. 189
This Certifies that the
has deposited with this Committee, securities in accordance with the proceedings of a Meeting of the Association held January 22d, 1890, upon which this Certificate is issued. This Certificate will be received in payment of balances at the Clearing House for the sum of One Thousand Dollars from any Member of the Clearing House Association.
On the surrender of this Certificate by the Depositing Bank above named the Committee will endorse the amount as a payment on the obligation of said Bank held by them, and surrender a proportionate share of the collateral securities held therefor.
$1000.
One Thousand Dollars.
COMMITTEE.

Loan Committee of the Bankers Association of Buffalo

NY3020-1000. 1000 Dollars Jan. 22, 1890. Black on yellow paper. Uniface. Larger size. (shown at 57%)
c. Unissued, cancelled. **R4**

NY3020-5000. 5000 Dollars Jan. 22, 1890. Black on white paper. As above.
c. Unissued, cancelled. **R4**

Buffalo Clearing House Association

A. Issue without imprint

No. A 469 No. A 469
BUFFALO CLEARING HOUSE ASSOCIATION
Buffalo, N.Y. NOV 1912
This Certifies that the COLUMBIA NATIONAL BANK
has deposited with the Buffalo Clearing House Association
FIVE THOUSAND DOLLARS
in United States Gold Coin. Upon the surrender of this Certificate with the receipt endorsed thereon Five Thousand Dollars in United States GOLD COIN will be delivered to any Bank member of the Buffalo Clearing House Association but to no one else.
CLEARING HOUSE COMMITTEE.

NY3050-5000. 5000 Dollars Nov. 1, Dec. 1, 1912 (stamped dates). Black, with gold underprint design and denomination at center. (shown at 71%)
b. Issued, cancelled. **R1**

B. Issue with imprint

NY3075-5000. 5000 Dollars ND. Black, with orange underprint design and denomination at center. Back orange; denomination at center. Large stub at left. Imprint: American Bank Note Co. New York Litho. (shown at 75%)

f. Specimen. **R1**

PENNSYLVANIA

Scranton

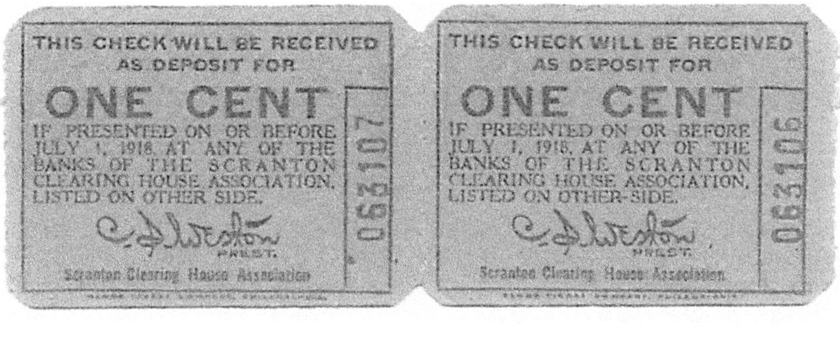

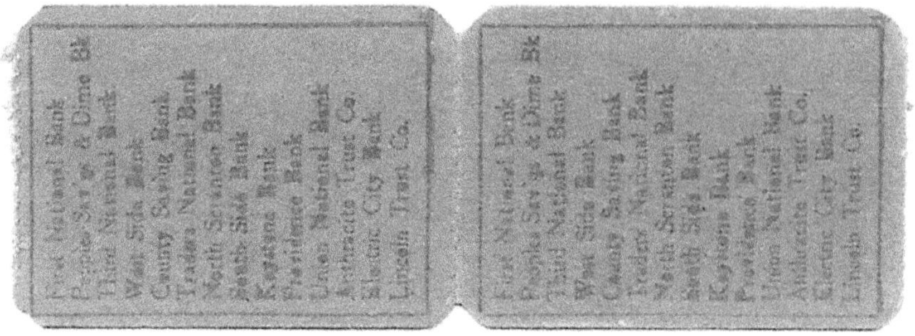

Scranton Clearing House Association

PA3100-.01 1 Cent ND (1918). Black on brown card. Redeemable by July 1, 1918. List of member banks on back. 53 × 38mm. Imprint: Globe Ticket Company, Philadelphia.(shown at 100%)
a. Issued, not cancelled. **EF, 10. Unc., 15.**

NOTE: This piece was issued because of a one-cent shortage caused by World War I.

Utah

Salt Lake City

Salt Lake City Clearing House

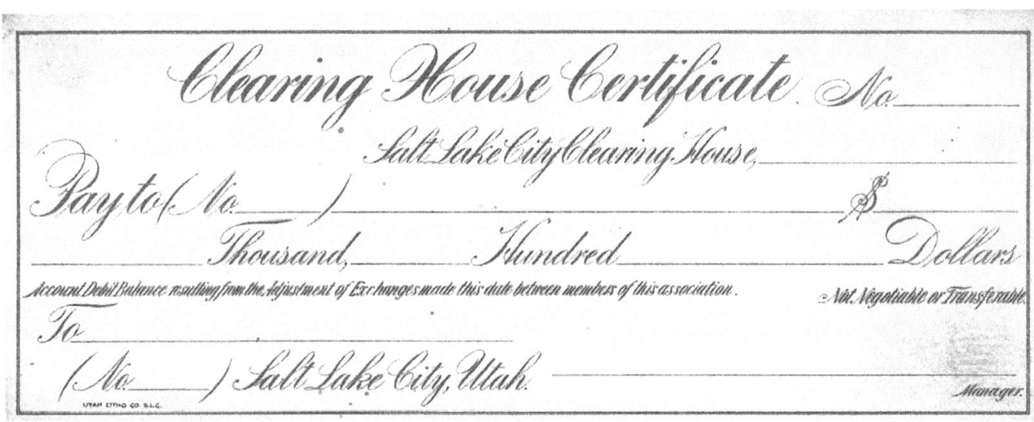
Clearing House Certificate No.
Salt Lake City Clearing House,
Pay to (No.) $
Thousand, Hundred Dollars
Account Debit Balance resulting from the Adjustment of Exchanges made this date between members of this association.
Not Negotiable or Transferable
To
(No.) Salt Lake City, Utah.
Manager.
Utah Litho Co. S.L.C.

UT3200-Var. Various amounts ND. Black form. Imprint: Utah Litho. Co. S.L.C. (shown at 64%)
d. Unissued, remainder. **R5**

WASHINGTON

State of Washington

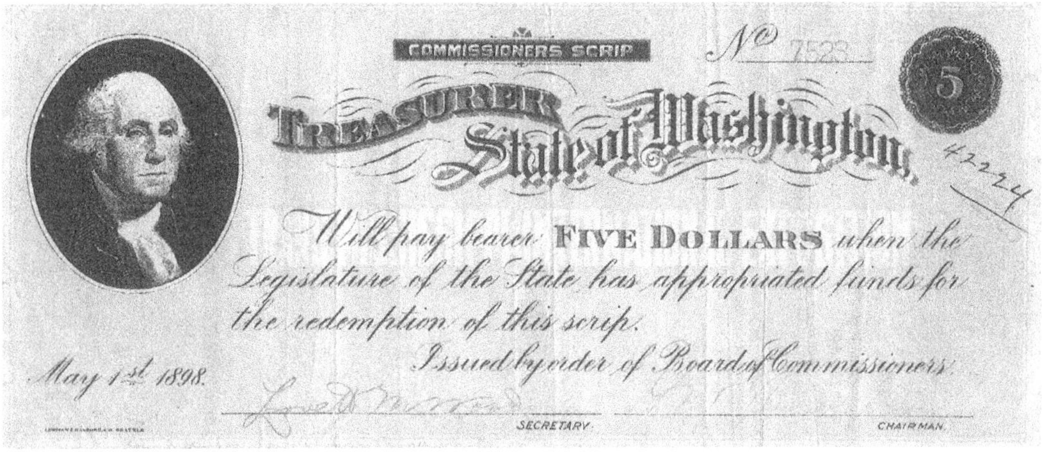

COMMISSIONERS SCRIP

WA3100-5. 5 Dollars May 1, 1898. Black on green. Washington at left. Wording across center in white: TRANS-MISSISSIPPI INTERNATIONAL EXPOSITION. Back green and brown; value in white at center. Large size. Imprint: Lowman & Hanford Co. Seattle. (shown at 62%)

b. Issued, cancelled. **R5**

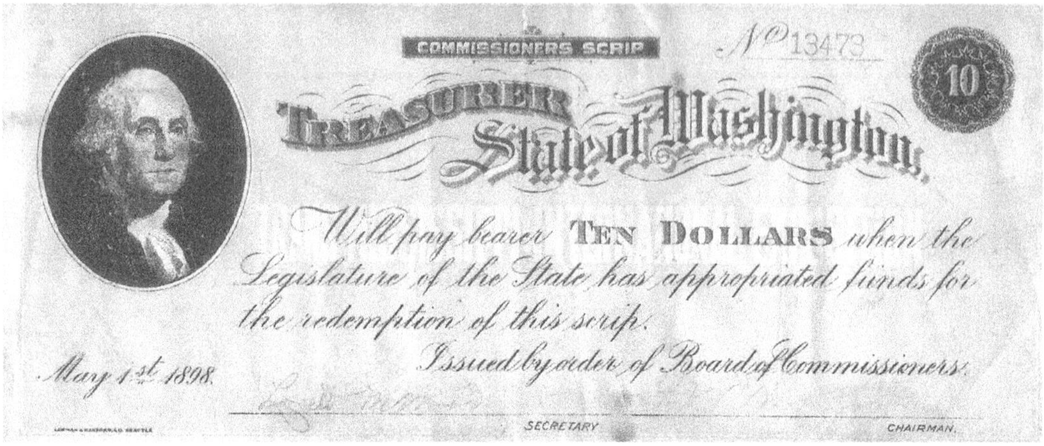

WA3100-10. 10 Dollars May 1, 1898. As above. (shown at 62%)
b. Issued, cancelled. **R5**

Seattle

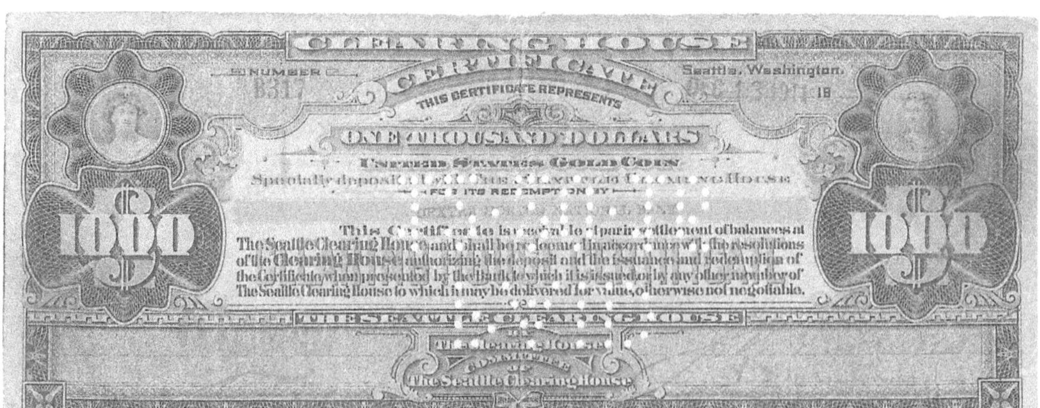

Clearing House Certificate

WA3200-1000. 1000 Dollars (various stamped dates, as Dec. 13, 1911). Brown on cream paper. Woman's head at upper corners. Uniface. Imprint: Western Bank Note and Engraving Company Chicago. (shown at 63%)

b. Issued, cancelled. **R4**

f. Specimen. **R4**

Wyoming

Cambria

Cambria Trading Company

WY3000-1. 1 Dollar January 1908. Blue. Miners working in center circle. Wide mining scene across back. Value at left and right. Imprint: Gast—St. Louis. (shown at 83%)

d. Unissued, remainder. **AU, 100. Unc., 150.**

Kilpatrick Bros. & Collins

WY3100-5. 5 Dollars January 1897. Gray. Similar to WY3000.

d. Unissued, remainder. **AU, 200. Unc., 300.**

Appendix C. The Clearing House Certificate as a Cash Substitute, 1857–1933

By Loren Gatch

Prior to the creation of the Federal Reserve System in 1913, major aspects of banking regulation lay in the hands of private bank clearing house associations. Formed initially for the limited purpose of facilitating the clearing of checks and other offsetting liabilities, clearing houses rapidly took on wider regulatory responsibilities including mutual protection against the contagion of bank runs. By the beginning of the twentieth century the New York Clearing House Association (NYCHA) in particular assumed central banking functions and responsibilities for the nation's financial system. Building upon early appreciations of the role clearing houses played in ameliorating the financial crises of the National Banking Era (Cannon 1910a; Sprague 1910; Spahr 1926), modern scholars have argued that the clearing house arrangement represented a viable private, market-oriented alternative to public regulation of the nation's monetary and financial systems (Timberlake 1984, 1993; Gorton 1985; Gorton and Mullineaux 1987).

As an outgrowth of their clearing activities, clearing houses introduced their own internal exchange media — large denomination certificates issued against gold and currency deposits — that enabled banks to settle without the bother of handling large amounts of coin and paper. In addition, to provide for mutual aid during financial stringencies, banks developed a distinctive financial instrument, the clearing house loan certificate. Also issued in large denominations ($1,000 to $100,000) and circulated only among members of the clearing house, loan certificates enabled members to extend to each other credit during periods of financial stress. Settlements via certificates enabled member banks to pool their legal reserves when financial markets grew tight, effectively expanding these reserves by eliminating the need to settle their mutual balances in cash, which could then be employed to satisfy the increased liquidity demands of depositors. Their use, according to the financial historian Fritz Redlich, "was the specifically American solution to a problem which central banks in other great commercial nations of the world were faced at every crisis throughout the second half of the nineteenth century" (Redlich 1951 Part II: 158).

Used successfully during periods of financial stress between 1860 and 1884, the clearing house loan certificate took on a new significance during the Panic of 1893 when small-denomination versions were issued by a few scattered bankers' associations to circulate amongst the general public. By the Panic of 1907, the clearing house certificate (the word "loan" was increasingly dropped) emerged as a cash substitute on a national scale, when upwards of $500 million worth of certificates, and variants thereof, were issued by dozens of clearing house associations across the country.

Of uncertain legality under federal law, these currency substitutes nonetheless met widespread public demand for liquidity, and their success in stemming the panic stimulated a policy debate about banking reform that led shortly to the Aldrich-Vreeland Act of 1908, which authorized the creation of National Currency Associations with the power to issue emergency notes. Invoked briefly at the outbreak of World War I, the Aldrich-Vreeland arrangement was overtaken by the founding of the Federal Reserve, which replaced clearing house associations as a source of emergency liquidity with its own discount facilities.

Despite the existence of the Federal Reserve, the stock market crash of 1929 and its aftermath ushered in a contraction of prices and output that the Fed proved unable or unwilling to counteract. Culminating in the banking holidays of 1932–1933, the economic crisis provoked one last brief issue of clearing house certificates in March 1933. By this time, however, the clearing house cer-

Loren Gatch is a professor in the Department of Political Science, University of Central Oklahoma, Edmond. He is interested in non-governmental emergency currencies of the type discussed in this book. He is a columnist for Paper Money *and his other articles on emergency money have appeared in various scholarly journals, such as* Essays in Business and Economic History, International Journal of Community Currency Research, *and* Chronicles of Oklahoma.

tificate had been rendered obsolete as a currency substitute, and quickly disappeared from the financial scene.

This appendix traces the evolution of the clearing house certificate from a device for interbank settlements to an important source of emergency liquidity and even a cash substitute for hand-to-hand transactions. It argues that the rise of the clearing house certificate as a private adjunct to the national money supply was abetted by two factors. First, the treatment of money both in economic thought and law defined money in a narrow enough way to exempt the clearing house certificate from sustained hostile scrutiny. Second, the legal status of clearing houses as private, unincorporated associations endowed them with a degree of flexibility and discretion that enabled them to mobilize their member banks' resources without fear of legal challenge. Indeed, recognizing these advantages, clearing houses resisted proposals to formalize their cooperative arrangements by incorporating under federal auspices.

The Origins and Significance of Clearing House Certificates

The NYCHA, founded in 1853, was the first bank clearing house in the nation, although the Suffolk System of New England had functioned for many years previously on analogous principles for clearing banknotes. Soon, banks in other major cities began establishing their own clearing house associations, including Boston (1856), Philadelphia (1858), Chicago (1865), and St. Louis (1868). By century's end, hundreds of cities, large and small, would feature similar associations of local banks (Cannon 1910a: 75–116).

Very early on, the NYCHA employed a device called the "clearing house certificate," issued against deposits of gold coin, which enabled banks to settle with each other on a routine basis without the effort and risk of transferring actual specie (Gibbons 1868: 340–1; Cleaveland and Hutchinson 1980 [1864]: 274–5). This practice was subsequently copied by other clearing houses. With the advent of the legal tender Greenback, certificates issued against deposits of legal tenders were also used in clearings. Federal legislation establishing the system of national banks in 1864 conferred official status upon these private clearing house certificates by deeming them "lawful money" for the purposes of calculating legal reserves. Further, the U.S. government authorized the issue of its own gold certificates in 1863, and currency certificates in 1872. While not legal tender, these notes could also serve as part of national banks' reserves, and served to settle clearing house balances (Knox 1885: 115–6; Dunbar 1969 [1897]: 209–10, 223). Up until 1888, the issue of coin and currency certificates for the NYCHA was managed by the Bank of America. In that year, the U.S. Treasury began issuing large-denomination gold coin certificates that supplanted these private certificates. In smaller clearing houses, standards were less strict as to what settled balances. Settlements could be made in non-legal tender national bank notes or even in exchange on New York, Boston, or Chicago.

A second, but similar, instrument, the clearing house "loan" certificate, emerged at the same time as a way for clearing house members to lend reserves to each other. This device was far more significant as a policy instrument. When the money market tightened and concerned depositors withdrew their funds, member banks could settle with each other not with scarce cash, but with interest-bearing certificates issued by a clearing house committee against approved collateral (loans, bonds, bills of exchange) hypothecated by the bank needing the certificates. Negotiable only amongst member banks, clearing house loan certificates effectively enabled banks to expand temporarily the money supply by eliminating the need to settle with each other in lawful money, which could then be used to meet withdrawals. Since these certificates paid interest, banks that drew them from the clearing house had an obvious incentive to retire the notes as soon as conditions permitted.

The use of clearing house loan certificates was often (but not always) associated with the sus-

A POWERLESS DEFENDER.

***Bankers' Magazine*, December 1907**

pension of payments by banks during financial crises. "Suspension" meant different things at different times during the 19th century, reflecting the progressive change in the nation's circulating medium from banknotes to bank deposits. Before the Civil War, when banks suspended (as in 1819, 1837, and 1857) they no longer redeemed their banknotes and deposits in specie. With the introduction of Greenbacks, the advent of the National Banking System, and the growth of deposit banking, suspension after the 1860s meant that banks would cease to redeem freely their deposits in either legal tender — gold, Greenbacks, silver dollars and silver certificates — or in national banknotes.

In neither period did suspension necessarily mean that banks were about to go out of business, although many did. Whereas in antebellum America suspension of specie payments cast into question the value of state bank-notes and implied a temporary departure from a metallic monetary standard, after the Civil War suspension increasingly cast into question the solvency of financial institutions, and implied an inability of banks to convert their deposits into hand-to-hand currency (Myers 1931 Vol. I: 235).

The National Banking System established during the Civil War was intended to provide a uniform and secure currency, and to support the Union war debt. Yet several features of this system predisposed it to stringency and even crisis. National banknotes were widely criticized for being "inelastic," meaning that their supply neither adjusted easily to seasonal needs (like agricultural harvests), nor to the immediate demands of depositors. Because the supply of banknotes was determined by the supply and price of the government bonds which banks had to deposit as collateral, the amount of notes in circulation did not respond easily to shifts in the public's liquidity preferences. Indeed with the growth of deposit banking currency, inelasticity emerged as a fundamental element of instability within the nation's financial structure. Stipulated reserves for national banks took the form of specie and legal tenders (state banks could also make use of national bank notes), while checkable deposits during normal times provided a flexible and workable circulating medium in addition to the relative stagnant supplies of paper currency. Yet to the extent that such currency also formed the monetary reserves of the banking system, sudden shifts in the currency-deposit ratio caused by heightened liquidity demands would only aggravate tight credit conditions. Customers who demanded currency reduced the reserve base and thus restricted the supply of credit to a multiple of their currency withdrawals. Lacking any easy way of meeting currency demands without reducing the supply of deposits by an even greater amount, banks lacked the flexibility to prevent tight credit conditions from tipping over into financial panics (Timberlake 1993: 210).

Other characteristics of the banking system compounded the instability caused by an inelastic currency. The lack of a national rediscount market made it difficult for individual banks to liquidate their portfolios at short notice. The increasing concentration of banking resources in a central reserve city like New York, and the practice of paying interest on bankers' balances, linked the nation's reserves to unstable and speculative money markets. As the nation's banks became increasingly interconnected, suspension disrupted the national payments system by making it hard for reserve cities to remit to outlying areas. Finally, the growth of correspondent banking relationships in the late 19th century increasingly knitted together three distinct types of institutions — state banks, national banks, and trust companies — that were regulated differently and which often viewed each other as commercial competitors (Sprague 1910: 228–30; Myers 1931 Vol. I: 240–250). By the end of the 19th century, as these three groups all turned to clearing houses during crises as a source of emergency liquidity and lender of last resort, their differences worsened the panic conditions that encouraged the use of clearing house certificates as a cash substitute.

The Clearing House Loan Certificate, 1860–1884

While a device similar to the clearing house loan certificate was employed by New York banks during the Panic of 1857, the instrument was first introduced during financial disturbances surrounding the election of 1860, when an issue of $10 million in certificates was authorized by the clearing house loan committee. Backed by deposits of federal and New York State debt, certificates paying seven percent interest were issued in amounts to seventy-five percent of the value of the underlying collateral, a formula which became fairly widespread in the following decades. In addition to accepting these certificates in clearing, the NYCHA banks also agreed to pool their reserves so as to protect their weaker brethren. With the outbreak of the Civil War, three more issues of clearing house certificates on similar terms in 1861, 1863, and 1864 increased the total amount issued to some $59 million.

Following the precedent set by New York, other cities' clearing house associations adopted the same device during the financial disturbances of 1873. By September of that year financial conditions were so difficult that the New York Stock Exchange closed its doors for two weeks. Between then and January of 1874, New York banks issued more than $26 million in clearing house loan certificates on terms similar to those of the 1860s. The banks also took the precaution of not publishing the financial statements of banks that were in bad shape, so as to discourage bank runs. The clearing houses of Boston, Philadelphia, Baltimore, St. Louis, Cincinnati, and New Orleans (but not Chicago) followed with their own issues. During this crisis, banks also began the practice of issuing certified checks, "payable through the clearing house," drawn on their balances. While these instruments could be deposited and checked against, banks would not pay out currency for them. This practice allowed banks to economize on the use of cash. Apart from a small issue of loan certificates in New Orleans in 1879, the next emission came in 1884, when the NYCHA put out nearly $25 million between May and September. In 1890, New York along with Boston and Philadelphia issued more than $30 million in clearing house loan certificates, much of which offset a drain of balances to smaller reserve cities and country banks (Cannon 1910a: 80–95).

The Clearing House (Loan) Certificates of 1893

Up to this point clearing house loan certificates served only to enlarge member banks' reserves by removing the need to settle in cash. With the Panic of 1893, however, clearing house loan certificates assumed a new role. Poor crops, uncertainty over the nation's commitment to the gold standard, and some prominent business failures led New York and eight other large cities in June 1893 to issue about $70 million in certificates, following precedent. As in 1890, demand for these certificates was heightened by the withdrawal by interior banks of their reserve balances, thus hastening the panic by anticipating it. By August, withdrawals and hoarding produced such tight money conditions that a premium of up to five percent emerged on the sale of currency (Lauck 1907: 102–3).

In the face of this demand for liquidity and the inelasticity of the national banknote circulation, private remedies burst forth. For the first time, clearing houses, particularly in the Southeast, began issuing certificates not for interbank settlements, but for general circulation, as in Atlanta and Birmingham, Alabama. In the latter city, the use of small denomination notes produced such a need for a further medium with which to make change for the notes that the clearing house eventually issued scrip to denominations as small as twenty-five cents. To meet withdrawals, other banks in Georgia and South Carolina issued "clearing house certificates" against their own assets, outside of any clearing house arrangement, as an emergency currency. Hoarding of currency by the public also became a problem. Jacksonville, Florida banks refused to rent safe deposit boxes to customers who withdrew cash from the banks only to store it in the banks' own vaults (Cannon 1910a: 98–116; Stevens 1894: 145–8; Warner 1895; Indianapolis Monetary Commission 1900: 221–2).

"Payable only through the clearing house" once again became a common caveat on bank checks. The Panic of 1893 also witnessed a variety of other temporary currency devices throughout the country, including certified checks, negotiable certificates of deposit, bond certificates, warrants, and payroll checks issued in round amounts. The use of unofficial media was hardly unusual in American financial history. However, the trend in 19th century financial crises towards ever-larger uses of such media as sources of emergency liquidity and circulation suggested structural flaws in the organization of American banking and finance. These flaws would become dramatically evident during the Panic of 1907.

The Clearing House Certificates of 1907

Prior to 1907, resort was again made, on a small scale, to clearing house loan certificates in Boston, Philadelphia, and New Orleans during 1895 and 1896. However, it was the Panic of 1907 that triggered the largest and most dramatic use of clearing house media, both for settlements and for general circulation. The defects in the nation's financial system illuminated by that crisis inaugurated a searching public debate over financial reform, leading to the Aldrich-Vreeland Act of 1908, and by 1913 to the establishment of the Federal Reserve System.

Unlike 1893, the Panic of 1907 emanated from New York outward. Unlike 1893, there was no political battle over the monetary standard to explain it. Brought on by badly-handled runs on major New York trust companies, the national rush to liquidity touched off a cascade of clearing house issues throughout the country. Even more so than in 1893, the events of late 1907 highlighted how the basic features of American finance — the network of correspondent banking; the uneven regulation of national banks, state banks, and trust companies; the pyramiding of reserves in New York City, and their investment in stock market loans — had produced a financial system that was highly sensitive to losses of public confidence, whatever the particular disturbance. As the NYCHA resorted in late October to clearing house certificates and restricted payments, banking associations in regional reserve cities and their outlying areas all hastened to adopt similar measures lest they too be confronted with currency drains. In effect, the Panic of 1907 expressed itself as much in the preemptive fears of bankers as it did in the behavior of depositors. Indeed, the rush to issue certificates was itself a stimulus to forming clearing house associations in the smallest locales. For example, in Oklahoma alone, where some two dozen emissions occurred, associations were formed with memberships as small as two banks simply to issue scrip (Gatch 2009).

The volume of clearing house loan certificates in 1907 surpassed all previous crises. New York alone issued more than $100 million; other major clearing house associations together issued a comparable amount. These large-denomination certificates did not circulate amongst the general public. Although banks in most states did not shut their doors, restrictions upon cash withdrawals were common throughout the country. What made this crisis distinctive was the explosion of cash substitutes issued by banks and others in lieu of scarce legal tender, even compared to 1893. In his early survey of the crisis, the economist A. Piatt Andrew (1908) distinguished seven different sorts of emergency media:

1. Clearing house loan certificates, issued in large denominations for bank settlements. Their use dated back to 1860, and were not a cash substitute in the sense that they never circulated as hand-to-hand currency;

2. Clearing house (loan) certificates, issued in small denominations for general circulation. Some clearing houses, such as Chicago's and Los Angeles's, used both large certificates for bank settlements and small certificates for circulation;

3. Clearing house Checks in round amounts. Similar to the small-denomination clearing house certificates in that they were issued against collateral deposited with the clearing house association, these were technically distinct in that they were a liability of the bank that drew them, and not of the association. In a few cases, the issue of clearing house checks in very small amounts for change making purposes (to $1 and less) complemented the use of circulating clearing house certificates of higher denominations;

4. Cashiers' Checks in round amounts. Unlike clearing house certificates and checks, cashiers' checks were not issued through, or in the name of, any association of banks. Favored by smaller institutions, they were instead circulated directly by individual banks, which sought to avoid overtly breaking the law against non-national banknotes by making the checks payable to fictitious persons, "or bearer."

5. Certificates of Deposit in round amounts. Less often, smaller banks styled their emergency circulations as unassigned evidences of deposit, with or without an interest feature, and payable at sight or within some specified period.

6. Bank Drafts on Eastern Exchange in round amounts. While correspondent balances may have been unavailable during the panic, interior banks circulated drafts on these balances in small denominations.

7. Payroll Checks in round amounts. Similar to cashiers' checks (no. 4 above), payroll checks enabled non-bank employers to effectively print their own currencies, subject to the tolerance and trust of their communities. This was done at the employer's own initiative, although bankers sometimes assisted, as in Philadelphia.

While the recent onset of the Panic made his survey incomplete, Andrew estimated that these various emergency media amounted to more than $500 million, half of which were clearly designed to circulate as cash substitutes. Andrew's estimates also show that the bulk of this emergency currency took the form of nos. 2–4: small denomination clearing house certificates, clearing house checks, and cashiers' checks.

James G. Cannon, a New York banker and a student of clearing houses, examined the various means by which banks created cash substitutes in 1907. Cannon found that, as a mark of their scrupulous attention to form, banks typically took care to back up these currency substitutes with some sort of collateral, however redundant the arrangement may have been in practice. Thus, in most instances small denomination clearing house notes, checks or scrip were "backed" by large denomination clearing house loan certificates, even though these large denomination certificates in turn merely represented the banks' own loan and discount portfolios. This was the case in Chicago, Cleveland, Kansas City, and many other large towns. Whatever their precise character, circulating notes themselves tended to be more utilitarian and check-like in appearance, and generally lacked the ornamentation typical of currency. Manufacturing centers with large payrolls like Pittsburgh and Canton issued both small denomination certificates down to $5, and even smaller denominations of bearer checks put out at the fiat of individual banks so as to make change for the larger notes. Philadelphia banks issued certified "payroll checks" in small round amounts against the encumbered deposits of employers (Cannon 1910a: 117–136; Cannon 1910b). In the parlance of the time, such cash substitutes were examples of "asset currency"—liabilities issued against the banks' portfolios of loans and discounts—as opposed to "bond-backed" currency, of which national banknotes were the major example. In effect, during disturbances like 1893 and 1907 banks were reverting to the issuing practices of the antebellum state banking era.

Given the vital service clearing house loan certificates provided during 1893 and 1907, it was understandable that their use would inform debate over reform of the nation's financial system. Beginning in the 1890s, a number of legislative proposals sought to formalize the clearing house role, including those of Senator Orville Platt (1903) and the New York Chamber of Commerce in 1906 (Redlich 1951 Part I: 167; Timberlake 1993: 205–7; Wicker 2005: 80–83). Other plans prominent at the time included Theodore Gilman's scheme for a federal system of incorporated clearing houses, and Cannon's own alternative that envisioned clearing houses organized around the existing regional Sub-Treasuries (Gilman 1896, 1903, 1904; Cannon 1910b: 25–31). Ultimately, though, the private bank clearing house and its certificates had no role in the arrangement provided by Federal Reserve Act of 1913. Richard Timberlake suggests that the questionable legal status of clearing house certificates (see below) imparted to them a "hucksterish quality"; moreover, the general idea of banks creating their own circulations without an identifiable reserve "smacked of Wall Street legerdemain" (Timberlake 1993: 211–2). O.M.W. Sprague faulted the New York banks for suspending too early in 1907, out of a misplaced fear for their reserve levels; the coincidence of suspension and the issue of clearing house loan certificates tarred the latter as part of the problem, not the solution (Sprague 1910: 273, 276).

In a more substantive sense, though, defining the solution also defined the problem. Advocating merely a more formal and preemptive version of clearing house certificate issuance presumed that the nation's financial problem lay primarily in its inelastic supply of currency, the (private) solution for which would require no fundamental reordering of the nation's financial system. Advocates of "asset" currency tended to cluster around this alternative, as did opponents of branch banking who (like Gilman) saw clearing house associations as a bulwark of unit banking. In contrast, advocating some kind of central bank with discount and note-issuing powers presumed that the problem lay not in the availability of currency during crises, but in the insufficient concentration of and control over reserves, the (public) solution for which would require institutional innovations of a Hamiltonian sort beyond what the Independent Treasury and National Banking Systems had yet achieved.

Were Clearing House Certificates and Other Emergency Monies Legal?

The legal status of emergency money, of which clearing house certificates were an example, must be appreciated in the context of the increasing standardization of American currency that occurred during the second half of the 19th century. If the state bank note reigned during the antebellum period, the Civil War imposed increased federal control over the provision and regulation of circulating media. Along with the issuance of government Greenbacks themselves — the nation's first legal tender fiat currency — the founding of the National Banking System standardized both the appearance and backing of bank notes. In response to the bane of "shinplasters" (fractional currency in paper form), a federal statute of 1862 proscribed the issue of currency notes in denominations less than one dollar. Shortly thereafter, state bank notes were driven out of existence by the so-called "death tax" of ten percent upon their circulation. The constitutionality of this tax was upheld in *Veazie Bank v. Fenno* (1869), while federal legal tender powers sustaining the Greenback were upheld by the Legal Tender cases between 1871 and 1884 (Dunbar 1969 [1897]: 170, 198; Dunne 1960: 49–50, 67–83).

Despite these measures, scrip payable in merchandise as well as forms of municipal debt with currency-like properties did survive, thanks to the permissive nature of 19th century court-based economic regulation. Without proactive enforcement of the law by agents of the state, complaints had to be made before the courts would take notice; otherwise, illegal monetary practices would persist with the consent of all parties. When disputes about the monetary quality of negotiable instruments did arise, 19th century federal courts looked to the intent of the issuer and even to the text on the notes themselves for interpretive guidance. If the presumed intent was to create exchange media for general use, then such media invited suppression. However, courts upheld the use of instruments if they had the character of an evidence of debt (*Poindexter v. Greenhow*, 114 U.S. 270 [1885]). If scrips promised redemption in goods and services and not in money, then they also passed muster (*United States v. Van Auken*, 96 U.S. 366 [1877]; *Hollister v. Zion's Cooperative Mercantile Institution*, 111 U.S. 62 [1884]).

In their rulings, courts could employ a definition of money that was so strict as to grant pragmatic acceptance to a wide array of media with money-like properties. As one judge declared in a 1900 case examining the monetary status of warrants issued by the state of Texas, "it must not only be that they are capable of sometimes being used instead of money, but they must have a fitness for general circulation in the community as a representative and substitute for money in the common transactions of business." As a standard for ascertaining moneyness, "fitness for general circulation" left ample scope for exchange media of a more limited nature (*Houston and Texas Central Railroad Company v. Texas*, 177 U.S. 66 [1900]: 84). Likewise, the limited negotiability of private scrip meant that it posed no meaningful competition to national currency. "Congress," the U.S. Attorney General's Office opined in 1888, "did not intend to clog the business of the country by repressing the giving of negotiable promissory notes, nor impose an additional indebtedness of 10 per cent. upon a debtor who, in the ordinary course of business, gives his creditor a promissory note for the amount he owes" (19 Op. Att'y Gen. 100 [1888]).

Given the widespread forbearance shown quasi-monetary exchange media, it is understandable that large-denomination clearing house loan certificates were never the object of serious legal questioning. While even the casual observer could note that by the late 19th century the nation's business was increasingly being conducted via checkable deposits, specie and currency continued to occupy a separate, iconic status in policymaking and economic analysis.

Despite its functional identity with bank deposit credit, paper currency continued to be regarded with special solicitude, even as credits increasingly constituted the bulk of the nation's circulating medium. This policy distinction between notes and deposits was also justified in terms of the different responsibilities attributed to their users. It was incumbent upon those making use of bank deposits to be an informed consumer of a bank's services. For those using currency, however, the presumption was that its integrity was the responsibility of the state. In New York, whose free banking law was later to become the model for other states, public authorities characterized this responsibility by distinguishing between deposit banks and banks of issue:

> Of those which issue no paper to be circulated as money, no danger can be apprehended, unless to the depositors who may perhaps be tempted, by offers of interest or competition in some other

> way, to extend to them an unmerited credit. Indeed, it would seem to be an unnecessary interference with individual right, to prohibit the establishment of offices, either by associations or individuals, for the purpose of lending actual capital and receiving deposites [sic]; but we can perceive no substantial grounds for any claim of natural right in any individual, to furnish by his own notes, the whole or any part of the currency of the country [Report of the Bank Commissioners 1837: 14–15].

While federalizing the provision of bank notes, the postbellum National Banking System still preserved the distinction between credit and currency, particularly insofar as the new system adopted the practices of New York State's Safety Fund, which had protected state bank notes but not deposits. Accordingly, national bank notes were to be issued against the deposit of approved bonds, with an additional gold redemption fund held by the Treasury. In contrast, not only did deposits not enjoy such protection, but schemes for deposit guarantees were opposed both by political and financial authorities as morally-enervating, socialistic, and worse.

These political and policy predispositions to treat currency and deposits differently were reinforced by the dominant currents of late 19th century American monetary thought. Most authorities cleaved to a distinction, inherited from the British "Banking School" tradition, between money and deposit credits. As the standard of value, money measured the value of commodities, while deposit credit and currency (properly issued) merely facilitated their exchanges. Indeed, some writers went so far as to deny that deposit credits had any influence at all on the level of prices, arguing that they were an endogenous effect of real economic activity and that their supply was thus self-regulating. When connected to a commitment to a metallic monetary standard, this doctrine led to typical condemnations of inconvertible paper currencies like the Greenback (see, e.g., Laughlin 1903; Scott 1910; Cleveland 1908; Conant 1906). Unfortunately for the contrary view, grounded upon the quantity theory of money, that the supply of specie, currency and deposit credits together did influence the price level, its contemporary associations with the radicalism of free-silver Populists tainted it too much to be taken seriously (Fisher 1911: 15).

Against this legal and intellectual backdrop, the use of the large-denomination clearing house loan certificate was not perceived as a monetary phenomenon. Indeed, even though it was a powerful device for expanding the reserve capacity of clearing house member banks, playing the functionally equivalent role of additional supplies of specie or Greenbacks, its use solely within the restricted confines of the clearing house caused it to be regarded as evidence of a loan between private parties with no monetary significance. Arguing that such certificates were not subject to the ten-percent "death tax," the *Banking Law Journal* contended that the tax "is designed as a prohibitive tax upon notes issued by persons or state banks which circulate among the people at large, and cannot be extended to embrace certificates, issued upon deposit of collateral, and available in the settlement of balances, only among a limited number of banks consenting thereto" (3 *Banking Law Journal* 451). According to another contemporary description,

> [loan certificates] are not in any sense to be considered as currency or as bank notes; they are not passed over the counter to bank depositors or check-holders; they do not pass between man and man as a medium of exchange. They do not in any way measure, determine, or express the value of commodities, nor is the value of anything quoted in their terms [Curtis 1897: 253].

In contrast, in the case of the small-denomination emergency currencies issued by banks, their semblance to Greenbacks and bank notes seemed obvious and inescapable. Even their friends presumed they were illegal. According to John Dewitt Warner, the measures of 1893 worked by "overriding and evading restrictive law" (Warner 1895). A. Barton Hepburn wrote of the 1893 issues that they were "clearly subject to the 10 percent tax enacted for the purpose of getting rid of state bank circulation. This temporary currency, however, performed so valuable a service ... that the government, after due deliberation, wisely forbore to prosecute" (Hepburn 1903: 374). As one South Carolinian newspaper defended its state's emissions, "we ask no more consideration for our clearing house certificates than has been given to those issued in New York. There they passed between the banks as money. Here they perforce passed between both the banks and the people" (*The State* [Columbia, S.C.] 1893: 4). Of 1907, A. Piatt Andrew concluded, "it was an inconvertible paper money issued without the sanction of law" (Andrew 1908: 516). *Bankers' Magazine* agreed: "without awaiting legal sanction—in fact, in the face of express statutory prohibitions—the country has lately been supplied with an abundance of 'checks' and 'clearing-house certificates,' constituting a real emergency currency" (*Bankers' Magazine* 1907: 888). While considering their issue to be of doubtful legality, Joseph Cannon (1910b: 8) contended that "no right thinking man would condemn either the purpose or the act" of issuing such currency. Cannon also noted that the Chicago Clearing House in 1907 took care to authorize the drawing of bearer checks only against national banks, since any state bank circulation would have been subject to the "death tax." It was widely assumed that, given their obvious value in meeting panics, the government simply chose not to prosecute issuers of emergency monies.

Indirect evidence for this forbearance can be found in the federal government's own legal interpretations. Commenting on a twenty-dollar certificate of deposit issued in 1893 by the First National Bank of Albany (Georgia) against collateral deposited with the Albany Clearing House, U.S. Attorney General Richard Olney argued that, since the wording of the note did not express any specific promise to pay, it was not illegal currency subject to the ten percent tax. Olney pointed out further, "the paper is not signed anywhere by the First National Bank. It is plainly not an instrument upon which either that bank or the Clearing House Association could be sued in an action at common law and a money judgment recovered by introducing the paper alone" (Op. Att'y Gen. 681 [1893]). Richard Timberlake quotes Comptroller James H. Eckel's somewhat facetious defense of certificates of that year: "if they had been used as currency ... the banks issuing them would have been fined" (207). Given that there were numerous examples of emergency currency that did make such promises to pay, the opinion seems conveniently disingenuous. In contrast, federal authorities did look less kindly upon emissions backed up by the assets of a single bank alone (23 *Banking Law Journal* 945, 1019). As for the issue of small-denomination certificates of deposit, as well as certified and cashiers' checks, case law on the applicability of the federal tax to these various devices was less than clear as to when they would be regarded as unauthorized currency (9 *Banking Law Journal* 203).

A more hypothetical legal problem was the banks' own customers. Under the law, checks presented or deposited had to be paid in legal tender, unless otherwise agreed. Not to do so violated contract and exposed the banks to damage claims. During general panics like 1893 and 1907, it was countered that payment restrictions reflected "a temporary rule of the bank not to pay any checks in currency. A refusal so generally understood and so universal in its application can in no wise impair the drawer's credit" (Angert 1908: 23). Given the widespread approval that state attorneys-general and governors gave to payment restrictions (including outright bank holidays during the Panic of 1907 in several states), banks could be confident that their actions would not give rise to suits for damage (White 1911: 228).

Yet another potential legal threat to clearing house certificates, whether used for interbank clearings or general circulation, came not from public authority but from private challenges to the ability of banks to hypothecate collateral to clearing house associations in exchange for their certificates, without that collateral being subject to prior claims by other creditors. Claims upon the collateral behind these certificates would have compromised their utility precisely under those panic conditions when they would have been needed most (*Yardley v. Philler* 167 U.S. 334 [1897]).

In any event, none of these emergency media circulated long enough to create the opportunities for legal challenges. Moreover, the fact that none of the hundreds of millions' worth was ever repudiated by its issuers took the fundamental legal cause of action off the table. Not everyone liked the ersatz money. Horace White's disdain for it was unsparing. "All were illegal. Some were engraved to resemble bank notes or government notes, and these were doubly illegal; some were as small as twenty-five cents, and these were trebly illegal" (White 1911: 229). Populists like Senators William A. Peffer of Kansas in 1894 and Benjamin R. Tillman of South Carolina in 1907 found it galling that banks were allowed this power to expand their circulation — what Tillman called "clearing-house shinplasters" — while farmers could not issue notes against their stored crops (Peffer 1894; Tilman 1908). Expressing the prevailing fear of concentrated private financial interests, the Money Trust Investigation of 1912 saw great hypothetical danger in the prospect of private clearing house associations issuing unregulated circulating media, and recommended the incorporation and regulation of such associations under federal law (U.S. House of Representatives 1912: 24–7, 107–113).

Even more sympathetic observers who envisioned a significant role for clearing houses in the nation's financial future urged that they incorporate and formalize their relationship with public authority. This unease captured an important part of the legal reality that made clearing houses such successful adaptors to financial crises in the first place. Thanks to their legal status as private, unincorporated associations, they could bind their members individually to agreements while minimizing their exposure collectively to legal action from other parties. A clearing house existed solely to facilitate settlements. While it could issue clearing house loan certificates, the clearing house itself was not a bank. (*Philler v. Patterson*, 168 Pa 468 [1895]; *Crane v. Fourth Street National Bank* 173 Pa 566 [1896]).

While other activities of a regulatory or policy nature might evolve from this initial cooperation, at the core of the clearing house was a function — the offsetting of credits and debits — that had no legal or material implication for other parties who might otherwise have relations with the member banks. These other parties were, in the legal argot, "strangers" to the activities of the clearing house, being neither helped nor harmed by it. In particular, the routine act of sending a check through a clearing house did not in itself imply its payment, since this only occurred when bank ascertained that the check was good and that sufficient funds existed. This occurred not on the premises of the clearing house, but at the individual member bank, just as if the check had been presented directly over the counter (Watson 1902: 22, 60, 67; Bryan 1915: 447–56). In addition to the flexibility and protection afforded by the unincorporated status of clearing houses, James L. Laughlin argued that banks were reluctant to make formal arrangements which, if readily available to clearing house members, might encourage excessive lending: "What is good medicine for a sharp attack of disease ... is not desirable as a regular diet" (Laughlin 1912: 185). In sum, given the advantages of remaining unincorporated, it is not surprising that clearing house associations remained lukewarm about measures to increase their supervision by public authority (8 *Banking Law Journal* 455; Redlich 1951: 167).

The Clearing House Certificates and Aldrich-Vreeland Notes of 1914

The Federal Reserve Act of 1913 was supposed to have solved the 19th century financial problems that had periodically given rise to clearing house emissions. Now that a national lender of last resort existed with powers to issue an elastic currency presumably at will and at need, clearing house loan certificates ought to have disappeared. The core function of clearing houses, the clearing of checks, migrated to the regional Federal Reserve banks as those banks accumulated reserve deposits from their new members and endeavored to enforce par clearing for checks. It became inevitable that settlements through local clearing houses would be replaced by the simple debiting and crediting of member banks' account with their Federal Reserve district bank (Spahr 1926: 172, 196–7, 226; Andrews 1942: 595).

The banking reform movement sparked by the Panic of 1907 did produce legislation that temporarily legalized one version of emergency asset currency, the Aldrich-Vreeland notes. To issue such emergency notes, banks had to organize themselves into National Currency Associations under federal authority, an arrangement that merely wrote into law the existing informal arrangement for issuing clearing house certificates. Before the Federal Reserve was up and running the financial stresses accompanying the outbreak of World War I provoked the first and only issue of Aldrich-Vreeland emergency notes. Fortuitously, the act establishing the Federal Reserve had temporarily extended for one year the Aldrich-Vreeland provisions for emergency currency. Between August and October 1914, forty-five National Currency Associations hurriedly formed under the 1908 statute issued some $370 million in emergency notes, mostly against commercial paper and corporate bonds. These were rapidly retired as the Federal Reserve opened for business. During the same time, New York and eleven other clearing house associations briefly issued over $200 million in loan certificates for their own settlements. None of these circulated amongst the public. (U.S. Comptroller of the Currency 1916: 99–100; Kemmerer 1914: 604–5). A few clearing houses in areas lacking National Currency Associations did issue low denomination certificates for general circulation. Otherwise, the Aldrich-Vreeland issues eliminated the need for any widespread resort to scrip on the level of 1907 (Commercial and Financial Chronicle 1915: 509). Shortly thereafter, a brief issue of Federal Reserve Bank Notes to replace existing silver certificates was occasioned by the provisions of the Pittman Act of 1918, which authorized the sale of silver to Great Britain. While not emergency notes, they bear mentioning because the terms of their issue resembled the Aldrich-Vreeland currency, and they later reappeared in 1933 under more trying circumstances (Nussbaum 1958: 166–7, 178, 200). In any event, with the Federal Reserve henceforth controlling the issue of currency, the role of clearing house certificates as a cash substitute seemed to be over.

The Clearing House Certificates of 1933

The stock market crash of September 1929 and the ensuing depression ushered in yet another episode of emergency currencies. Given the severity of the economic downturn, these currencies ranged from barter notes and tax warrants to the exotic fad of "stamp scrip." The increasing problem of insolvent banks led by early 1933 to the collapse of the nation's financial system, and to the declaration of a national banking holiday at the outset of the new Roosevelt Administration. Intended as a breathing space to prepare a program for the rescue of the banking system, the holiday of March 1933 was also the occasion for the last issue of clearing house certificates. Previous panics did not compare to the grinding liquidations of 1929 to 1932, although many country banks had already suffered through the agricultural depression of the early 1920s. Whereas a generation earlier, clearing house associations used certificates first for interbank clearings, and then as general-circulation currency, the advent of the Fed's discount window as well as its use of open-market operations meant that banks no longer looked to their clearing house associations for an emergency expansion of reserves. At the same time, so severe was the effect of price deflation upon banks' portfolios that, by 1932, banks were turning to the Reconstruction Finance Corporation to recapitalize their balance sheets. What banks needed at the height of the crisis was an emergency currency to counteract hoarding and meet the extraordinary demands of panicky depositors.

As state-level bank moratoria culminated in Roosevelt's decision to close all banks on March 4, 1933, the possibility of clearing house certificates once again arose. Despite the actual closure of banks, the president's declaration left open the use of certificates to meet immediate currency needs. It was symptomatic of the new situation that the NYCHA, which during previous crises through 1914 had never issued small-denomination scrip, now endeavored to produce an emergency circulation. After a few days' delay, Treasury Secretary William Woodin did give clearing houses permission to issue certificates. According to Vernon L. Brown, who wrote the first study of Depression-era emergency currency, forty-six clearing houses authorized nearly $650 million in such scrip, and many millions' worth were printed by the American Bank Note Company and other firms. Unlike their 1907 forbearers, the clearing house certificates of 1933 looked less like bank checks and more like currency. Yet before the use of certificates could gear up, the Federal Reserve used its new powers under the Emergency Banking Act of March 9, 1933, to create sufficient Federal Reserve Bank notes — descendents of the Aldrich-Vreeland and Pittman Act currencies — to meet anticipated public demands for cash once the banks reopened. Of the original amount of clearing house scrip authorized, less than $30 million was actually issued by fifteen associations, and most of this circulated for no longer than one month. Otherwise, the bulk of the scrip printed sat unused in bank vaults (Brown 1941: 129–147). Federal Reserve officials opposed the use of bank scrip, believing that it encouraged monetary radicals in Congress. In particular, the prospect of the New York Clearing House — the premier banking organization of the country — issuing scrip was too much for Washington, especially as the New York state legislature had also authorized the creation of an Emergency Certificate Corporation to issue a statewide scrip. Treasury Secretary Woodin forbade New York to undertake this, on the grounds that the emergency banking legislation represented a solution to the problem (Kennedy 1973: 172–3).

As in 1907, the events of 1933 produced variants on the clearing house certificate form. Though closed by the various bank holidays or even insolvent, banks outside of clearing houses sought some means of providing their depositors access to their funds. Banks did this by assigning some fraction of their assets as collateral for scrip, and using the notes to meet some of the demand for currency. The famous "wooden money" of Tenino, Washington, was issued in this fashion, and other banks individually produced scrip (particularly in Tennessee) for circulation. In Wisconsin, the state legislature authorized the issue of "State of Wisconsin Bank Scrip" against frozen deposits, which was clearly illegal under federal law. In other cases, banks worked with other business organizations to issue currency. For example, the Springfield, Illinois, "Credit Clearing Committee" issued notes in round amounts against the encumbered accounts of specific depositors. In New Bedford, Massachusetts numerous employers met their payrolls through small denomination checks issued through local banks, much like the earlier examples of 1907 (Gatch 2008).

All of these currency expedients disappeared quickly as monetary conditions moved back from the precipice of March 1933, and stability (if not prosperity) returned to the credit markets. Clearing house certificates and their variants had been displaced by the issue of emergency Federal Reserve Bank notes under the provisions of the March 9 legislation. In any event, the returning flood of dishoarded currency meant that most of these emergency notes were never put into circulation. As for the clearing house certificate, the events of 1933 marked its retirement into financial history.

Conclusion

The rise and fall of the clearing house certificate as a cash substitute over some seventy years was symptomatic of a financial system that remained permeable to the introduction of private exchange media, even as federal law and policy sought to impose uniformity upon the nation's money. Motives for the use of clearing house certificates, large and small, were afforded by the distinctive shortcomings of the postbellum National Banking System, especially its failure to provide an adequate supply of paper currency flexible enough to meet seasonal and emergency needs. Opportunities to issue this particular form of private money were afforded by the prevailing ideas about what money and currency were (and were not); in particular, enduring conceptual and legal distinctions between the form and function of specie, paper currency, and deposit credit encouraged a permissive regulatory atmosphere in which local bank scrip flourished. As private unincorporated voluntary associations, clearing houses enjoyed both flexibility and discretion in carrying out their monetary innovations within the interstices of the law.

The persistence of private clearing house certificates also illustrates nicely what the legal historian Arthur Nussbaum termed the "society theory of money"; namely that, despite the assumption by the modern state of monetary functions as an aspect of sovereignty, societal actors can and do provide private alternatives to legal tender when the state falls short (Nussbaum 1950: 5–10). Even in their disagreements, contemporary observers of the clearing house were sophisticated about the larger financial system and its shortcomings. They understood that, even if clearing house certificates were technically illegal (or, as Redlich put it, "extra-legal"), they served a purpose that was more important than conformity to an imperfect law.

Present-day scholars have rediscovered in the 19th century bank clearing house a plausible alternative to monetary regulation via a central bank under public (or, as Richard Timberlake [1984] would have it, "political") control. As Gary Gorton and Donald J. Mullineaux (1987) have contended, clearing houses solved information asymmetries peculiar to the dynamics of checkable deposits, especially as opposed to banknotes. Moreover, the episodic use of clearing house certificates represented "co-insurance" of members' bank deposits during panics. What the present article suggests is that such interpretations of the clearing house are best situated in the understandings and practices of late 19th century banking. In particular, a device like the clearing house certificate, which found function and purpose during this period, later lost its relevance as the mode and locus of financial regulation shifted from the private to the public sphere.

References

Andrew, A. Piatt (1908). "Substitutes for Cash in the Panic of 1907." *Quarterly Journal of Economics* 22 (August): 497–516.

Andrews, Fletcher R. (1942). "The Operation of the City Clearing House." *Yale Law Journal* 51 (February): 582–607.

Angert, Eugene H. (1908). "Liability of Banks for Refusal to Pay Checks in Currency." *Bankers' Magazine* (January): 22–7.

Bankers' Magazine (1907). "A Real Emergency Currency." (December): 888–889.

Banking Law Journal (1890). "Taxation of Clearing-House Certificates." 3 (May-December): 451–2.

_____ (1893). "Substitutes for Currency." 9 (July-December): 156–8.

_____ (1893). "Clearing House Associations in Minnesota." 8 (January-June): 455–6.

_____ (1893). "Taxation of Certificates of Deposit and Certified Checks." 9 (July-December): 203–4.

_____ (1907). "Tax on Circulation." 23 (January-December): 945–6.

_____ (1907) "Tax on Notes Used for Circulation" 23 (January-December): 1019.

Brown, Vernon L. (1941). "Scrip and Other Forms of Emergency Currency Issued in the United States During the Depression Years of 1931–1934," Vol. I (MBA Thesis, New York University).

Bryan, George (1915). "The Law of Clearing Houses," *Virginia Law Review* 2 (March): 447–456.

Cannon, James G. (1910a). *Clearing Houses.* Washington, D.C.: National Monetary Commission.

_____ (1910b). *Clearing House Loan Certificates and Substitutes for Money Used During the Panic of 1907.* New York: Trow.

Cleaveland, John, and G. S. Hutchinson (1980 [1864]). *The Banking System of the State of New York*, 2d ed. New York: Arno.

Cleveland, Frederick A. (1908). *The Bank and the Treasury.* New York: Longmans, Green.

Commercial and Financial Chronicle (1915). "The 1914 Issue of Clearing-House Loan Certificates" 100 (February 13): 508–10.

Conant, Charles A. (1906). *The Principles of Money and Banking*, 2 vols. New York: Harper and Bros.

Crane v. Fourth Street National Bank. 173 Pa 566 (1896).

Curtis, Charles E. (1897). "Clearing House Certificates, How Issued and Why." *Yale Review* 6: 251–66.

Dunbar, Charles F. (1969 [1897]). *Laws of the United States Relating to Currency, Finance and Banking.* New York: August M. Kelley.

Dunne, Gerald T. (1960). *Monetary Decisions of the Supreme Court.* New Brunswick, NJ: Rutgers University Press.

Fisher, Irving (1911). *The Purchasing Power of Money.* New York: Macmillan.

Gatch, Loren (2008). "Local Money in the United States During the Great Depression." *Essays in Economic and Business History* XXVI: 47–61.

_____ (2009) "'An' the West Jes' Smiled': Oklahoma Banking and the Panic of 1907." *Chronicles of Oklahoma* 87: 4–33.

Gibbons, J. S. (1868). *The Banks of New-York, Their Dealers, the Clearing House, and the Panic of 1857.* New York: D. Appleton.

Gilman, Theodore (1896). "The Incorporation of Clearing Houses and the Issue of a Clearing House Currency." *Banking Law Journal* 13: 141.
_____ (1903). "Clearing-House Emergency Circulation." *Bankers' Magazine* 67 (September): 416–23.
_____ (1904). "The Clearing-House System." *Journal of Political Economy* 12 (March): 208–224.
Gorton, Gary (1985). "Clearinghouses and the Origins of Central Banking in the United States." *Journal of Economic History* 45 (June): 277–283.
Gorton, Gary, and Donald J. Mullineaux (1987). "The Joint Production of Confidence: Endogenous Regulation and Nineteenth Century Commercial-Bank Clearinghouses." *Journal of Money, Credit and Banking* 19: 457–468.
Hepburn, A. Barton (1903). *History of Coinage and Currency in the United States and the Perennial Contest for Sound Money.* New York: Macmillan.
Hollister v. Zion's Co-operative Mercantile Institution, 111 U.S. 62 (1884).
Houston and Texas Central Railroad Company v. Texas, 177 U.S. 66 (1900).
Indianapolis Monetary Commission (1900). Report of the Monetary Commission of the Indianapolis Convention. Indianapolis: Hollenbeck.
Kemmerer, E. W. (1914). "Issue of Emergency Currency in the United States." *Economic Journal* 24 (December): 604–5.
Kennedy, Susan Estabrook (1973). *The Banking Crisis of 1933.* Lexington: University Press of Kentucky.
Knox, John Jay (1885). United States Notes, 2d ed. London: T. Fisher Unwin.
Lauck, W. Jett (1907). *The Causes of the Panic of 1893.* Boston and New York: Houghton Mifflin.
Laughlin, James L. (1903). *Principles of Money.* NY: Scribner's.
_____ (1912). *Banking Reform.* Chicago: National Citizens' League for the Promotion of a Sound Banking System.
Myers, Margaret (1931). *The New York Money Market, Vol. I Origins and Development.* New York: Columbia University Press.
New York State (1837). Report of the Bank Commissioners. New York Assembly Document 78 (January 27).
Nussbaum, Arthur (1950). *Money in the Law.* Brooklyn, NY: Foundation.
_____ (1958). *A History of the Dollar.* New York: Columbia University Press.
Peffer, Willaim A. (1894). Agricultural Depression: Causes and Remedies. Senate Report No. 787, 53rd Congress, 2rd sess. Washington, D.C., GPO.
Philler v. Patterson, 168 Pa 468 (1895).
Poindexter v. Greenhow, 114 U.S. 270 (1885).
Redlich, Fritz (1951). *The Molding of American Banking, Part II.* New York: Hafner.
Scott, William A. (1910). *Money and Banking*, 4th ed. New York: Henry Holt.
Spahr, Walter E. (1926). *The Clearing and Collection of Checks.* New York: Bankers.
Sprague, O.M.W. (1910). *A History of Crises Under the National Banking System.* Washington, D.C.: National Monetary Commission.
The State. Columbia, SC. October 29, 1893.
Stevens, Albert C. (1894). "Analysis of the Phenomena of the Panic in the United States in 1893." *Quarterly Journal of Economics* (January): 117–148.
Tillman, Benjamin R. (1908). Speech of the Hon. Benjamin R. Tillman ... Upon the Legality of Clearing House Certificates and Panama Bonds, December 16, 1907 (Washington D.C.).
Timberlake, Richard H., Jr. (1984). "The Central Banking Role of Clearinghouse Associations." *Journal of Money, Credit and Banking* 16: 1–15.
_____ (1993). *Monetary Policy in the United States.* Chicago: University of Chicago Press.
United States v. Van Auken, 96 U.S. 366 (1877).
U.S. Government (1888). 19 Op. Att'y Gen. 100.
U.S. Government (1893). 20 Op. Att'y. Gen. 681.
U.S. Government (1908). Annual Report of the Comptroller of the Currency, 1907. Washington, D.C.: GPO.
U.S. Government (1916). Annual Report of the Comptroller of the Currency, 1915, Vol. I. Washington, D.C.: GPO.
U.S. Government, House of Representatives (1912). Report of the Committee ... to Investigate the Concentration of Control of Money and Credit House of Representatives. Report No. 1593. 62nd Congress, 3rd sess. Washington, D.C.: GPO.
Warner, John DeWitt (1895). "The Currency Famine of 1893," *Sound Currency* 2 (February 15): 337–356.
Watson, Archibald Robinson (1902). *The Law of the Clearing House.* New York: Banks Law.
White, Horace (1911). *Money and Banking*, 4th ed. Boston: Ginn.
Wicker, Elmus (2005). *The Great Debate on Banking Reform. Nelson Aldrich and the Origins of the Fed.* Ohio State University.
Yardley v. Philler. 167 U.S. 334 (1897).

Appendix D. G. B. DeBernardi Labor Exchange Scrip of 1895–1905

By Steven K. Whitfield

Schingoethe Sale #9 in December 2006 brought to light many Labor Exchange notes that were simply not generally seen over the previous 30 years. Many of these notes never saw the light of day as dealers set them aside for the couple, who always bought a note if they didn't have it, and stuck it in the vault.

Although that kept many of the notes from being reported in numismatic circles, it served the purpose of gathering up most of the Labor Exchange notes that had surfaced; thereby making it easier to record them at a single sitting.

This listing updates a trial listing of these notes published in *Paper Money* several years ago (see *Paper Money*, Whole #197, page 147) after some research into the Labor Exchange organization, of branches that I had been able to record prior to the Schingoethe sale.

That research identified around 150 previously unreported branches of the 300 plus that were suspected from 34 states and Canada. (Arizona was listed in error.) Several collectors took advantage of the offer and requested reports on their states.

Since then, quite a few notes have surfaced in auctions or dealer listings that verified many branch names and numbers. The Schingoethe release was a bonanza of newly confirmed notes. It also included many previously unreported branch notes and corrected a couple of errors.

Since it is unlikely that such a grouping will ever be assembled again, in 2006 it seemed like a good time to publish what was known to make it a reference for collectors, past and present; and future auction catalogers. My updated listing appeared in *Paper Money*, Whole #252, pp. 242ff., with an addenda appearing in *Paper Money*, Whole #255, p. 295. Those updates are incorporated in the listing appearing here.

When I first got interested in these notes there was little known about them. Occasionally, one would appear at auction or on a dealer's list. The designs, although varying slightly, are all of a similar theme proclaiming the superiority of labor over capital. Notes were given out as a "balance due bearer in labor, or the products of labor." (A unique set of notes, so far, also surfaced in this sale; of blue, red and orange notes with entirely different designs from the "Self Reliance" branch in Cincinnati, Ohio.) The notes are denominated as fractions of a day's labor, from 1/100th to twenty units, known so far. (5/100ths are represented on some notes as 1/20th, but for uniformity's sake I have listed all reported notes of this denomination as 5/100ths.)

The notes are not especially attractive. The standard face design depicts a globe at center with time zones of longitude denoted in sunlight showing laborers or darkness depicting "rest." In addition many notes have pro-labor slogans such as "The Day of Equity," "The Reign of Liberty," "Capitalization of Labor," and "Emancipation of Industry." The branch number, location and date are stamped in red.

Backs generally show a symbolic vignette depicting Liberty riding the cow catcher on the locomotive "Progress," with a "Labor Exchange" tender, and hauling a carload of "Plenty." Liberty instructs capitalists who are stopping progress with their legal tender sacks of gold and silver interests to "Clear the track," and let the Labor Exchange train steam past the unprogressive "Legal Tender Toll Gate."

Steven K. Whitfield, collector and author, has written numerous articles for hobby publications, including Bank Note Reporter, Paper Money, and the Check List. *He also authored the* Society of Paper Money Collectors' state volume on Kansas, *and has made numerous presentations on the history of Kansas money to a variety of organizations. In 2009 McFarland & Company published Steve's* Kansas Paper Money: An Illustrated History, 1854–1935, *edited by Fred Reed. That book won a Numismatic Literary Guild Extraordinary Merit Award in 2010, and was named a runner up to the SPMC Wismer Award as "Book of the Year."*

However, these notes have one great quality that has increased their popularity, which is the wide variation of localities and branch names that appear on the notes. While it would be relatively easy to put together a denomination type set from 1/100th to 2 units, perhaps unique 3, 10 and 20 units have also surfaced in recent years. Another possibility would be to try to collect the different design variations. A denomination set, the common back design, plus several of the unique varieties are shown here.

A real challenge would be to attempt to collect a note from each of the 34 known issuing states (plus Canada). This may well be impossible as 14 of those have not surfaced a single note to date. Undoubtedly some of these will turn up as more and more information is widely disseminated about the hobby and collectors seek them out.

I believe the main attraction of these Labor Exchange notes will always be the great "Americana" locations, and names of the branch locations; such as: Dixie, Tennessee; Red Bluff, California; Malta Bend, Missouri; Gray Cloud Island, Minnesota; Science Hill, Kentucky; Vineyard Haven, Martha's Vineyard, Massachusetts; Freedom, Kansas, and many others. The greatest notes, to my way of thinking would be #157, Toronto, Canada; (SENC) #103, Bernardi, Oklahoma; (SENC) #1, Kansas City, Missouri; #318, Nashville, Illinois, and that "20" from Stevensville, Montana. It should also be noted that there are other collectibles related to DeBernardi's Labor Exchange besides the notes, such as receipts, checks and other related paper.

A few stats for those interested:

- The earliest date seen on a note is 1895 and the latest is 1905.
- The high branch number is now #335 from Detroit, Michigan, the Christian Industrial Exchange. About 186 branches have been identified so there may be another 130 branches or so remaining to be identified. It is also possible that most of those 130 never organized or issued notes.
- A unique 75/100th denomination was listed in the auction catalog for branch #219, Toledo, Oregon, but I believe this was a typo for 25/100ths.
- Only 14 of the former 48 continental United States do not have a known branch listed. Of the 34 states that have notes reported, 22 of them have 1 to 5 reported branches, 7 have 5 to 10 branches and 5 states (California, Colorado, Ohio, Oregon and Pennsylvania) have from 11 to 31 branches listed. California is the champ for number of branches started. If you want a place to start, pick one of these five.
- About 125 of the known branches remain unconfirmed by reported notes and there are still a lot of missing branches and numbers of the 318 suspected total, so there is a lot of work remaining for dealers and collectors to root these out.

I have recorded about 150 of these notes. I am sure there are more that I missed or logged incorrectly so if you can add to the list or correct errors, please do. Report any omissions or corrections to me, or one of the authors or the editor.

Denomination Set of Labor Exchange Scrip

TENTH
BALANCE DUE BEARER IN LABOR OR THE PRODUCTS OF LABOR
CAPITALIZATION OF LABOR.
By Labor Exchange
1/10
BRANCH
299
Vineyard Haven, Mass.
1898
REST
UNIT
The day of Equity.
8
Pres.
INDUSTRIAL LIBERTY.

QUARTER
BALANCE DUE BEARER IN LABOR OR THE PRODUCTS OF LABOR
CAPITALIZATION OF LABOR.
By Labor Exchange
1/4
BRANCH
266
Great Falls, Mont
1897
REST
UNIT
The day of Equity.
17
Pres.
Acct.
INDUSTRIAL LIBERTY.

HALF
BALANCE DUE BEARER IN LABOR OR THE PRODUCTS OF LABOR
CAPITALIZATION OF LABOR.
By Labor Exchange
1/2
BRANCH
256
Galveston, Texas
1897
REST
UNIT
The day of Equity.
2
John Owens Pres.
Acct.
INDUSTRIAL LIBERTY.

1
ONE
1
BALANCE DUE BEARER IN LABOR OR THE PRODUCTS OF LABOR BY
CAPITALIZATION OF LABOR.
Labor Exchange
REST
UNIT
1
BRANCH
289
Belt, Mont
The day of Equity
80
INDUSTRIAL LIBERTY.

TWO
BALANCE DUE BEARER IN LABOR, OR THE PRODUCTS OF LABOR
BY
LABOR EXCHANGE
The Day of Equity.
The Reign of Liberty
Capitalization of Labor
Emancipation of Industry
REST
UNIT
BRANCH No. 108
Salem, Oregon.
2
126

FIVE
BALANCE DUE BEARER IN LABOR, OR THE PRODUCTS OF LABOR
BY
LABOR EXCHANGE
The Day of Equity.
The Reign of Liberty.
Capitalization of Labor
Emancipation of Industry
REST
UNIT
BRANCH No. 162
Aspen, Colo.
1896.
5
15
AND MANAGER

Following is a listing of branch names with numbers, dates and "denominations" of notes reported, or seen.

State	*#*	*Name*	*Date*	*Reported Denominations*
AL	43	Branchville		
	298	Thomasville		
AR	82	Maple		
	280	Hot Springs		
	293	Fayetteville	1898	5/100, 1/4, 1/2, 1, 2, 5
CA	26	San Francisco	1898	1, 2, 5
	28	San Diego		
	29	Pleasant Valley (El Dorado)		
	32	Red Bluff		
	34	Farmington		
	39	Los Angeles		
	41	Arroyo Grande	1896	1/10
	46	Stockton	1896	1/10
	51	Fresno		
	64	Bakersfield		

State	*#*	*Name*	*Date*	*Reported Denominations*
	74	San Jose	1895	5/100
CA	77	Elsinore		
	88	Santa Paula		
	92	Venture		
	97	Tulare		
	106	Santa Cruz	1896	5/100
	127	Visalia		
	132	Williams		
	133	Eureka		
	135	Dos Palos		
	136	Portersville		2
	138	Carpenteria		
	144	Santa Barbara		
	167	San Francisco		
	177	Santa Maria (shown at 75%, p. 000)	1897	5/100
	208	Elgin		
	241	Tulare		
	257	San Francisco	1897	2
	267	Reedley	1897	1
	?	Hanford		
	25	?		
CANADA	157	Toronto		
CO	11?	Forsythe ? (11 is Pfafftown, NC)		
	66	Trinidad		
	81	Boulder ?		
	102	Monta Vista (possibly 202)		
	104	Fruita	1896	1/20, 1/10, 1/4, 1, 2, 5, 10
	151	Mosca		
	153	Hooper (Garrison?)	1896	5/100
	156	Hotchkiss	1896	1/10, 1/2
	158	Denver	1897	5/100, 1/10, 1/4, 1/2, 1, 5 (1896)

State	*#*	*Name*	*Date*	*Reported Denominations*
	162	Aspen (shown at 75%)	1896	5/100, 1/4, 5 (reverse shown at 75%)
	165	Del Norte		
	242	Denver	1897	1
FL	308	Bunnell		
	?	Daytona		
GA	16	Atlanta		
	189	Fitzgerald	1898	5/100, 1/4 (1897)
ID	42	Idaho Falls (shown at 75%, p. 000)	1895	5/100, 1/20, 1
IL	179	Chicago	1897	1/100, 1/10, 1, 5

State	*#*	*Name*	*Date*	*Reported Denominations*
	269	Englewood	1897	1/100, 5/100, 1/10, 1, 5
	318	Nashville	1899	1/4, 1/2, 1
IN	154	Elkhart	(20th Century Branch)	
	240	Kingstown (Knightstown?)		
IA	19	Center Point		
	288	High Creek		
	186	Mapleton		
	?	Avery		
KS	6	Olathe (shirts)		
	38	Olathe (Press & Mill)		
	54	Pittsburg		
	131	Salina		
	140	Harding		
	197	Edwardsville		
	199	Freedom	1898	1/10, 1/4, 1/2, 1
	223	Osage City (coal mining)	1898	5/100
	?	Beloit		
	?	Ft Scott		
	?	Peterton		
	?	Turner		
KY	134	Science Hill		
LA	170	Nugent		
	271	Lake Charles		
MA	150	Haverhill	1897	1/10, 1/4, 1, 2, 5
	291	Easthampton		
	299	Vineyard Haven (shown at 75%, p. 000)	1898	5/100, 1/10, 1 (fish)
	303	Weymouth		
MI	35	E. Lansing		
	67	Saginaw		
	233	Manistee		
	246	Bay City		
	249	Grand Rapids		
	252	Detroit		

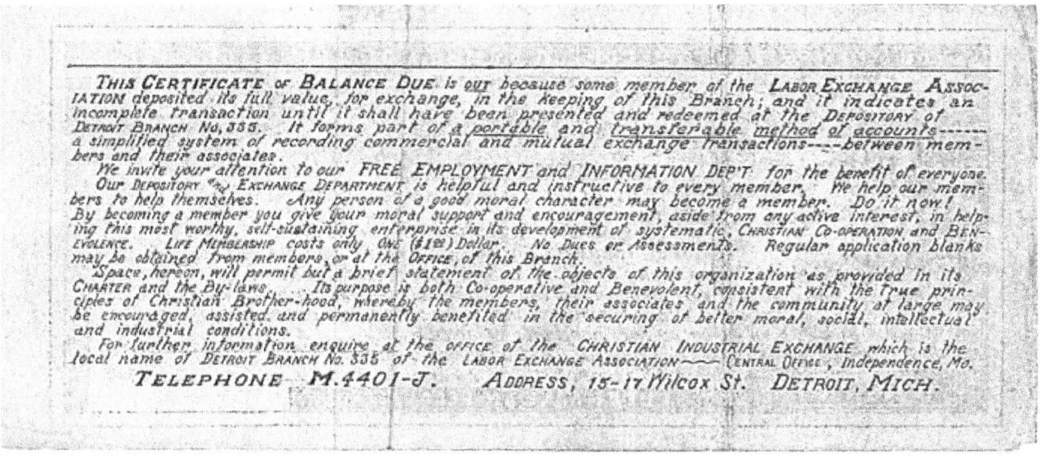
THIS CERTIFICATE OF BALANCE DUE is out because some member of the LABOR EXCHANGE ASSOCIATION deposited its full value, for exchange, in the keeping of this Branch; and it indicates an incomplete transaction until it shall have been presented and redeemed at the DEPOSITORY of DETROIT BRANCH No. 335. It forms part of a portable and transferable method of accounts------a simplified system of recording commercial and mutual exchange transactions-----between members and their associates.

We invite your attention to our FREE EMPLOYMENT and INFORMATION DEP'T for the benefit of everyone. Our DEPOSITORY and EXCHANGE DEPARTMENT is helpful and instructive to every member. We help our members to help themselves. Any person of a good moral character may become a member. Do it now! By becoming a member you give your moral support and encouragement, aside from any active interest, in helping this most worthy, self-sustaining enterprise in its development of systematic, CHRISTIAN CO-OPERATION and BENEVOLENCE. LIFE MEMBERSHIP costs only ONE ($1.00) Dollar. No Dues or Assessments. Regular application blanks may be obtained from members, or at the OFFICE, of this Branch.

Space, hereon, will permit but a brief statement of the objects of this organization as provided in its CHARTER and the By-laws. Its purpose is both Co-operative and Benevolent, consistent with the True principles of Christian Brother-hood, whereby the members, their associates and the community at large may be encouraged, assisted and permanently benefited in the securing of better moral, social, intellectual and industrial conditions.

For further information enquire at the OFFICE of the CHRISTIAN INDUSTRIAL EXCHANGE which is the local name of DETROIT BRANCH No. 335 of the LABOR EXCHANGE ASSOCIATION—— CENTRAL OFFICE, Independence, Mo.

TELEPHONE M.4401-J. ADDRESS, 15-17 Wilcox St. DETROIT, MICH.

State	*#*	*Name*	*Date*	*Reported Denominations*
	335	Detroit (shown at 78%)	1905	3 (unique denomination)
MN	25	Minneapolis		
	98	St. Paul	1896	1/100
	225	New Ulm		
	260	Duluth		

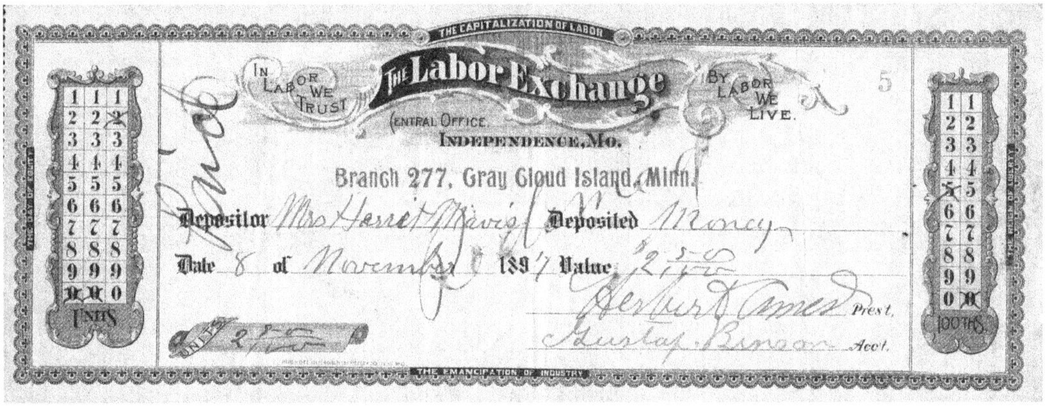

	277	Gray Cloud Island (shown at 75%)	1898	1.90 receipt, 2.50 receipt
	309	Garfield		
	?	Lamberton		
MS	260	Biloxi		
MO	1	Kansas City (#216 E. 15th ST, Tin cans & tailors)	1898	5/100
	2	Marshall		½
	36	St. Louis		
	40	Kansas City		
	78	Brookfield		
	183	Marshall	1897	½, 1
	268	Malta Bend		
	?	Sedalia (large fruit farm)		
MT	69	Hamilton		
	93	Lewiston		
	192	Grantsdale		
	207	Stevensville (shown at 75%, p. 000)	1897	20 (unique denomination)

State	*#*	*Name*	*Date*	*Reported Denominations*
	266	Great Falls (shown at 75%, p. 000)	1897	1/4, 1
	289	Belt (shown at 75%, p. 000)	1898	1
NE	20	?		
	286	Guide Rock		
NJ	195	Phillipburg		
	121	Patterson		
	125	Orange	1897	1/10, 1
	159	Rewnron		1/100, 5/100, 1/10, 1/4
NY	193	Jamestown		
	201	Jamestown	1897	1/100, 5/100, 1/4, 1/2, 1
	295	New York City		
NC	11	Pfafftown	1898	5/100, 1/4
	33	Taylorsville		
OH	84	Ashtabula	1897	1/100, 5/100, 1/10
	107	Columbus		
	109	Cleveland		
	163	New Philadelphia	1896	5/100
OH	191	Akron (shown at 75%, p. 000)	1897	1/100, 5/100, 1/4, 1
	210	Youngstown		
	213	Powell	1897	1/100, 5/100, 1

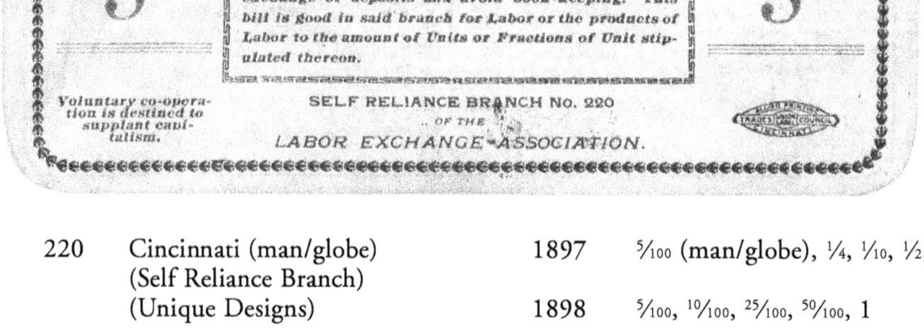

	220	Cincinnati (man/globe)	1897	5/100 (man/globe), 1/4, 1/10, 1/2, 1
		(Self Reliance Branch)		
		(Unique Designs)	1898	5/100, 10/100, 25/100, 50/100, 1

State	*#*	*Name*	*Date*	*Reported Denominations*
	224	Alliance (shown at 72%)	1897	1/100, 5/100, 1/10, 1/4, 1/2, 1, 2, 5
	245	Columbiana		
	262	Salem		
OK	3	Mine ? (nut butter)		
	103	Bernardi		
	160	Okarche ? (possibly "Forest")		
	311	Bellmont		
OR	14	Dilley		
	27	Pittsburg		
	85	Ukiah		
	9	McMinnville ? (possibly "Amity")		10
	89	Amity (shown at 75%, p. 000)	1896	10
	108	Salem (shown at 75%, p. 000)	1896	5/100, 1/10, 1/4, 1/2, 1, 2
	118	Detroit		
	122	LaGrande	1896	1/10, 1
	123	Salem (Lakeview)		
	147	Coquille		
	185	Oregon City		
	200	Corvallis	1897	1/10, 1/2, 1
	203	Falls City		
	218	Empire City		
	219	Toledo	1897	5/100, 1/10, 1/4, 1/2, 75/100, (note 75/100!), 1
	244	Harrisburg		
	253	Marshfield	1897	1/4
	?	The Dalles		
PA	12	Lititz	1897	5/100, 1/10, 1
	31	Monroeville		
	86	Erie 1897 (deposit certificate)		
	119	Reading	1896	5/100, 1/10
	171	Leechburg		
PA	216	Johnstown	1897	1/2, 1, 2
	217	Beaver Falls	1897	1
	230	Brunswick Valley (Kepner)	1897	1/100, 5/100, 1/4, 1, 2, 5
	?	Colony of Eastern PA		
	231	Sturgeon		
	255	Williamsport	1897	1
	264	Salem		
	265	Bellaire		
	274	Corry		
	?	Philadelphia		

State	*#*	*Name*	*Date*	*Reported Denominations*
SD	44	Aberdeen		
TN	10	?		
	175	Dixie		
TX	47	Caddo		
	239	Gainesville		
	256	Galveston (shown at 75%, p. 000)	1897	$\frac{5}{100}$, $\frac{1}{10}$, $\frac{1}{4}$, $\frac{1}{2}$, 1
	261	El Dorado		
	287	Houston		
	300	Cliffton		
UT	307	Salt Lake City	1898	$\frac{5}{100}$
VA	188	Danville		
WA	18	Port Angeles		
	61	Buckley	1895	$\frac{5}{100}$
	62	Marysville		1
	68	?		
	180	Vancouver		
	250	LaCenter	1897	$\frac{5}{100}$, $\frac{1}{4}$, 1, 2, 10
WI	187	Milwaukee		
	222	Stetsonville	1897	10

BIBLIOGRAPHY

Alaskan Token Collector & Polar Numismatist. December 1985 and August 1987.

Andrew, A. Piatt. "Substitutes for Cash in the Panic of 1907." *Quarterly Journal of Economics,* August 1908.

Auction catalogs, especially Lyn Knight, NASCA, R.M. Smythe, Heritage, and Currency Auctions of America.

Bank Note Reporter. Various articles, 1973–Present.

Bender, Bary. "Unreported Scrip Surfaces" (Washington–Alaska Bank of Fairbanks), *Alaskan Token Collector & Polar Numismatist,* Vol. XVIII, No. 1 (January 1996).

Benice, Ronald J. *Florida Paper Money: An Illustrated History, 1817–1934.* Edited by Fred Reed. Jefferson, NC: McFarland, 2008.

Bradfield, Elston G. "You Can't Get Your Money, but It's Safe." *Numismatic Scrapbook,* February 1950.

Bruner, Robert F., and Sean Carr. *The Panic of 1907: Lessons Learned from the Market's Perfect Storm.* New York: John Wiley, 2007.

Burgett, Maurice, and Steven Whitfield. *Indian Territory and Oklahoma Obsolete Notes and Scrip/Kansas Obsolete Notes and Scrip.* Harrisburg, PA: Society of Paper Money Collectors, 1980.

Cannon, James G. *Clearing House Loan Certificates and Substitutes for Money Used During the Panic of 1907.* New York: Trow, 1910.

Conant, Charles A. *A History of Modern Banks of Issue.* New York and London: G.P. Putnam's, 1927.

Criswell, Grover C. *North American Currency,* 2d ed. Citra, FL: Criswell's, 1969.

Chandler, Robert J. *San Francisco Clearing House Certificates.* Reno, NV: McDonald, 1986.

Corrigan, Douglas. *A Census of Emergency Money Used During the Panic of 1907: Clearing House Certificates, Clearing House Checks, Cashiers Checks, and Payroll Checks.* Various editions, 2002–09.

Currency Auctions of America. PCDA St. Louis Convention catalog, November 13, 1992, pp. 105–111.

Hoober, Richard T. "Emergency Currency of 1893," *The Numismatist,* January 1971.

Krueger, Kurt R. The William G. Bruce Ohio Currency Collection. Mail bid sale. July 29, 1992.

Mautz, Carl. "The Clearing House Currency of Portland, Oregon." *Paper Money,* Vol. 11, No. 4 (1972).

Mims, Nolan. "Clearing House Scrip of 1907." *Gulf Coast Numismatic Association Numismatic Views,* Vol. 4, No. 6 (August 2003).

Nevins, Allan. *History of the Bank of New York and Trust Company 1784–1934.* New York: Privately printed, 1934.

Northwest Token and Medal Society. A Trial Listing of Washington State Scrip, 1979.

Rochette, Ed. "A Plant as Obsolete as the Currency!" *Coins,* March 1994.

Sheehan, Thomas W. "The 1907 Nome Clearing House Issue." *Paper Money,* Vol. XXX, No. 6 (November-December 1991).

Sheheen, Austin M., Jr. *South Carolina Obsolete Notes and Scrip.* Camden, SC: Privately published, 2003.

Shull, Hugh. *A Guide Book of Southern States Currency.* Atlanta: Whitman, 2007.

Smythe, R.M. The Twentieth Annual Memphis International Paper Money Show auction catalog, June 22, 1996, pp. 58–63.

Walton, Gerome. *A History of Nebraska Banking and Paper Money.* Published by the author, 1978.

Whitfield, Steve. *Kansas Paper Money: An Illustrated History, 1854–1935.* Edited by Fred Reed. Jefferson, NC: McFarland, 2009.

Warner, John DeWitt. "The Currency Famine of 1893," *Sound Currency,* Vol. II, No. 6 (February 15, 1895).

Index

A. Hoen & Co., Lith. Richmond, VA 46
Abbeville (SC) Mercantile Association 43, 44
Abram Cox Stove Company (Philadelphia, PA) 266
Alamance (NC) Clearing House 222–223
Alamo National Bank (San Antonio, TX) 305
Alaska Banking & Safe Deposit Company (Nome, AK) 72–74
Albany (GA) Clearing House 14–15, 377
Alden Eng. Co. Cedar Rapids, IA 146
Aldrich-Vreeland Currency Act 59, 368, 372, 378–380
Allegheny (PA) National Bank 282–283
Allen County State Bank (Iola, KS) 158
Allied Banks of America 354
Altoona (PA) Clearing House 260–261
American Bank Note Company 268
American Bank Note Co., New York, Litho. 36, 39, 41, 261–262, 287, 290, 363–364
American Bank Note Co., Philada. 41, 265
American Bridge Company (Philadelphia, PA) 265
American Bridge Company of New York 216
American Car & Foundry Company (Detroit, MI) 170–171
American Exchange Bank (Duluth, MN) 177
American Exchange Bank (Greensboro, NC) 223
American Exchange Bank (Superior, WI) 333
American Lemon House Association 354
American National Bank (Bartlesville, OK) 250
American National Bank (Cincinnati, OH) 230–231
American National Bank (Everett, WA) 324
American National Bank (Hartford, CT) 13
American National Bank (Indianapolis, IN) 142–143
American National Bank (Lynchburg, VA) 315
American National Bank (McAlester, OK) 253
American National Bank (Nashville, TN) 300
American National Bank (New Orleans, LA) 23
American National Bank (Oklahoma City, OK) 254
American National Bank (Richmond, VA) 317
American National Bank (Spartanburg, SC) 294
American Numismatic Association 2
American Numismatic Society 1
American State Bank (Wichita, KS) 161
American Steel & Wire Company (Pittsburgh, PA) 269–271
American Trust & Banking Company (Atlanta, GA) 16
American Trust & Savings Bank (Birmingham, AL) 60
American Trust & Savings Bank (Cedar Rapids, IA) 144–145
American Trust Company (Coeur d'Alene, ID) 130–131
American Trust Company (South Bend, IN) 144
Amsterdam (NY) National Bank 34
Andrew, A. Piatt 354, 373, 377, 381
Any Old Bank 354
A.O. Hauge (Muscatine, IA) 150
Appeal to Reason (Girard, KS) 360
Arizona National Bank (Tucson, AZ) 77
Arlington (WA) State Bank 324
Arnold Print Works (North Adams, MA) 28–29
Artcraft Litho. Co. Detroit, MI 171
Asheville (NC) Clearing House 223
Associated Banks (Muscatine, IA) 150–152
Associated Banks Group No. 2 Ohio Bankers Association 228
Associated Banks of Blakely, GA 118
Associated Banks of Chase City, VA 312–313
Associated Banks of Chehalis County, WA 321
Associated Banks of Danville, VA 49, 314
Associated Banks of Eastern Knox County (NE) 209–210
Associated Banks of Ellensburg, WA 321–322
Associated Banks of Gaffney, SC 292 293
Associated Banks of Greensboro, NC 223–224
Associated Banks of Howard County, IN 142
Associated Banks of Lynchburg, VA 315
Associated Banks of Martinsville, VA 315–316
Associated Banks of Moline, IL 138
Associated Banks of Olympia, WA 322
Associated Banks of Pittsburg, KS 160
Associated Banks of Portsmouth, OH 247
Associated Banks of Riverside, CA 86–87
Associated Banks of Rock Hill, SC 46, 294
Associated Banks of Snohomish County, WA 324–325
Associated Banks of South Bend, WA 325
Associated Banks of South Boston & Houston, VA 317
Associated Banks of the City of Topeka, KS 160–161
Atchison (KS) Clearing House 155–156
Atchison (KS) Savings Bank 155
Atlanta (GA) Clearing House 15–16, 113–115, 372
Atlanta (GA) Litho Co. 17
Atlanta (GA) National Bank 16, 115
Atlanta (GA) Trust & Banking Company 16
Atlantic Crushed Coke Company (Pittsburgh, PA) 271
Atlantic National Bank (Jacksonville, FL) 110
Atlas National Bank (Cincinnati, OH) 231
Augusta (GA) Clearing House 115–117
A.W. Hyatt Stat'y Mfg. Co. N.O. (LA) 23

Bainbridge (GA) Clearing House 117–118
Baird, Jno. L. 64
Baker, S.H. 64
Baker Trust & Banking Company (Dothan, AL) 65
Baltimore (MD) Clearing House 23–24, 168, 391
Bank of Alabama (Ensley, AL) 66
Bank of America (New York City) 35
Bank of Amity (AR) 356
Bank of Benson (AZ) 75
Bank of Bristol (TN) 296
Bank of Chase City (VA) 312–313
Bank of Chester (SC) 44
Bank of Coffee Springs (AL) 65
Bank of Columbia (SC) 45
Bank of Commerce (Anacortes, WA) 318–319
Bank of Commerce (Dyersburg, TN) 297
Bank of Commerce (Everett, WA) 324
Bank of Commerce (Superior, WI) 333
Bank of Commerce, N.A. (Cleveland, OH) 235
Bank of Danville (VA) 314
Bank of Dawson (Dawson Springs, KY) 166
Bank of Eastern Arkansas (Forrest City, AR) 77
Bank of Elberton (GA) 20
Bank of Ensley (AL) 66–67
Bank of Forrest City (AR) 78
Bank of Gleason (Gleason, TN) 301
Bank of Grand Chain (IL) 140
Bank of Greenwood (SC) 293
Bank of Halifax (Halifax, VA) 317
Bank of Hanson (KY) 166
Bank of Joplin (MO) 190
Bank of Lunenburg (Blackstone, VA) 312
Bank of McAlester (OK) 253
Bank of Mecklenburg (VA) 312–313
Bank of Ninety-Six (Greenwood, SC) 293
Bank of Pinehurst (GA) 339–340
Bank of Pittsburgh (PA) N.A. 272, 275, 278–279, 282–283
Bank of Rock Hill (SC) 294
Bank of Sharon (Sharon, TN) 301
Bank of South Boston (VA) 317
Bank of South Greensboro (NC) 223
Bank of Spartanburg (SC) 294
Bank of Stanwood (WA) 324
Bank of Troy (Troy, SC) 293
Bank of Troy (Troy, TN) 301
Bank of Woodruff (Woodruff, SC) 294
Bankers' Association of Buffalo, NY 361
Bankers' Association of Yorkville, SC 295
Bankers' Dream Association (Windy City, i.e. Chicago) 355
Bankers Supply Co. Litho. Denver, CO 130
Barnard Mfg. Co. (Fall River, MA) 24–25
Barney, Charles T. 58
Bartlesville (OK) Clearing House 250
Bartlesville (OK) National Bank 250
Bayonne, NJ 214
Bellingham (WA) Clearing House 319–321
Belton (TX) State Bank 302
Berlin, NH 214
Bessemer (AL) National Bank 59–60
B.F. McCann (Pittsburgh, PA) 276–277
Big Five Company (Denver, CO) 97
Birmingham (AL) Clearing House 8–9, 60–62, 372
Birmingham (AL) Trust & Savings Company 60
Bishop (GA) Banking Company 118
Blakely (GA) Clearing House 118
Blatchly Company (Tacoma, WA) 55
Booth-Flynn Company (Pittsburgh, PA) 271
Border Grange Bank (Danville, VA) 49
Boston (MA) Clearing House 24, 169–170, 371–372
Boston Bank Note Co. (Boston, MA) 169–170
Boston National Bank (South Boston, VA) 317
Bower City Bank (Janesville, WI) 327
Bradt Printing Co. (Chattanooga, TN) 47
Braid & Button, Inc., Lithographers, Savannah, GA 340
Brandewie, J.P. 60–62
Brandon Printing Co., Nashville, TN 20–21, 46, 48, 49, 115, 164, 166, 188, 300, 350
Bristol (TN) Clearing House 295–296
Bristol (VA) Clearing House 312
Britton & Rey, Lith. (San Francisco) 87–88, 92–94, 213
Brooks-Griffiths Company (Minneapolis, MN) 3
Brown, Vernon L. 379, 381
Brown Printing Co., Montgomery, AL 68
Brunswick, 118
Brunt Mine, Pittsburg Iron Ore Company (Hibbing, MN) 184
Bryan, William Jennings 354
Buffalo (NY) Clearing House 34, 215–216, 361–362
Bullion & Exchange Bank (Carson City, NV) 34
Burgett, Maurice 1
Burnes National Bank of St. Joseph (Mo) 194
Bushong & Co. (Portland, OR) 258
Buxton & Skinner Lith. (St. Louis, MO) 198

The California (Fairbanks, AK) 69–70
Cambria (WY) Trading Company 367
Cambridge Bank (Cambridge, SC) 293
Canal Dime Savings Bank (Columbia, SC) 45
Cannon, James G. 373, 381
Canton (OH) Clearing House 228–230
Capital City Bank (Atlanta, GA) 16
Capital City State Bank (Des Moines, IA) 149
Capitol National Bank (Denver, CO) 97–98
Carnegie Steel Company (Pittsburgh, PA) 272
Carnegie Steel Company (Youngstown, OH) 248
Carney (OK) State Bank 251
Carolina National Bank (Columbia, SC) 45
C.C. Limerick Company (Sylvania, GA) 340
Cedar Rapids (IA) Clearing House 145–146
Cedar Rapids (IA) National Bank 145–146
Central Bank & Trust Corporation (Atlanta, GA) 115
Central National Bank (Cleveland, OH) 235–236
Central National Bank (Columbia, SC) 45
Central National Bank (Denver, CO) 98–99
Central National Bank (Portsmouth, OH) 247
Central National Bank (St. Louis, MO) 197
Central National Bank (Spartanburg, SC) 294
Central Railroad Company of New Jersey (New York City) 216
Central State Bank (Des Moines, IA) 149
Century Savings Bank (Des Moines, IA) 149
C.F. King 170
Chace Mills (Fall River, MA) 25
Charleston (SC) Clearing House 291–292
Chase City (VA) Clearing House 312–313
Chase National Bank (New York City) 61
Chatham Bank (Savannah, GA) 124–125
Chattanooga (TN) National Bank 47–48
Chattanooga (TN) Savings Bank 47–48
Chehalis County (WA) Clearing House 321
Chester (SC) Clearing House 44
Cheyenne (WY) Clearing House 334–335
Chicago, IL 342
Chicago Coated Board Company 133
Chicago (IL) Clearing House 131–134, 334–335, 342–343, 373–374, 377
Choctaw (OK) Commercial Bank 256
Christian Industrial Exchange 384

Christie Lithograph & Printing Co., Duluth, MN 175, 177, 327, 345
Cincinnati Lith. Co. (Cincinnati, OH) 165
Cincinnati (OH) Clearing House 36, 349–350, 371
Citizens & Screven County Bank (Sylvania, GA) 340
Citizens & Southern Bank (Savannah, GA) 124–125
Citizens Bank (Arlington, WA) 324
Citizens Bank (Bristol, TN) 296
Citizens Bank (Dyersburg, TN) 297
Citizens Bank (Nebo, KY) 166
Citizens Bank & Trust Company (Bartlesville, OK) 250
Citizens Bank & Trust Company (Chattanooga, TN) 47–48
Citizens Bank of Louisiana (New Orleans, LA) 167
Citizens National Bank (Cheyenne, WY) 334
Citizens National Bank (Cincinnati, OH) 231–232
Citizens National Bank (Des Moines, IA) 149
Citizens National Bank (East Liverpool, OH) 241–242
Citizens National Bank (Independence, KS) 157
Citizens National Bank (Johnstown, PA) 39–40
Citizens National Bank (Joliet, IL) 136–137
Citizens National Bank of Pensacola (FL) 110–111
Citizens National Bank (Riverside, CA) 86
Citizens National Bank (Sedalia, MO) 201
Citizens National Bank (South Bend, IN) 144
Citizens Savings & Trust Company (Cleveland, OH) 235–236
Citizens Savings & Trust Company (Mount Pleasant, PA) 265
Citizens Savings Bank (Danville, VA) 49
Citizens State Bank (Joplin, MO) 190
Citizens State Bank (Wichita, KS) 161
Citizens Trust & Savings Bank (Davenport, IA) 148
City Bank Company (Lorain, OH) 246
City Bank of Hartford (CT) 12, 108
City National Bank (Akron, OH) 36
City National Bank (Canton, OH) 228–229
City National Bank (Duluth, MN) 177–178, 182
City National Bank (Greensboro, NC) 223
City National Bank (Harrisburg, IL) 135–136
City National Bank (Knoxville, TN) 298
City National Bank (Lincoln, NE) 203
City National Bank (McAlester, OK) 253
City National Bank (Philadelphia, PA) 266
City of Brunswick (GA) 16–17
City of Richmond, VA 50
City of Tacoma (WA) 55
Claude O. Funk Printing Co. (Wichita, KS) 162
Clearing House Association of Hopkins County (KY) 166
Clearing House Association of Lexington, KY 165
Cleveland, Grover 7
Cleveland, OH 336, 374
Cleveland (OH) Clearing House 37, 235–241, 374
Cleveland (OH) Trust Company 237
Coal & Iron National Bank (New York City) 216–217
Coeur d'Alene (ID) Clearing House 130
Colorado National Bank (Denver, CO) 99
Columbia Bank & Trust Company (Oklahoma City, OK) 255
Columbia County (OR) Clearing House 257
Columbia (GA) Clearing House 119
Columbia National Bank (Pittsburgh, PA) 260, 284–285
Columbia (SC) Clearing House 44–45, 292
Columbian Bank Note Co., Chicago, IL 139
Columbus (GA) Clearing House 119
Columbus, OH 241
Combe Printing Co., St. Joseph, MO 157, 196
Commerce Trust Company (Kansas City, MO) 191–192
Commercial Bank (Albany, GA) 14
Commercial Bank (Danville, VA) 49, 314
Commercial Bank (Dawson Springs, KY) 166
Commercial Bank (Jacksonville, FL) 110
Commercial Bank (Savannah, GA) 124–125
Commercial Bank (Union City, TN) 301
Commercial Bank (Wausa, NE) 209–210
Commercial Bank & Trust Company (Fort Collins, CO) 104–105
Commercial Bank of Fargo (ND) 227
Commercial Bank of Snohomish (WA) 324
Commercial-Germania Trust & Savings Bank (New Orleans, LA) 167
Commercial National Bank (Chicago, IL) 133
Commercial National Bank (Independence, MO) 157
Commercial National Bank (Muskogee, OK) 253–254
Commercial National Bank (Pittsburgh, PA) 273–274
Commercial Printing Co., Pine Bluff, AR 81
Commercial State Bank (Birmingham, AL) 59–60
Conqueror Trust Company (Joplin, MO) 190
Consolidated Mines Company 211
Consolidated National Bank (Tucson, AZ) 77
Consolidated Warehouse Company (Sylvania, GA) 340–341
Continental Bank & Trust Company (Prosper, TX) 304–305
Continental National Bank (Chicago, IL) 133–135, 238
Continental Tie & Lumber Company (Cimarron, NM) 361
Cook, Musser & Company State Bank & Trust Company (Muscatine, IA) 150–151
Cordele (GA) Clearing House 119
Corn Exchange National Bank of Chicago (IL) 133–134
Corrigan, Douglas 1
Corrigan, McKinney & Company (Cleveland, OH) 238
Cortelyou, George 58
Cosgriff & Rumsey (Cheyenne, WY) 335
Council Bluffs (IA) Clearing House 147
Crane v. Fourth Street National Bank 378
Crisp County (GA) Cotton Association 339
Croxton Mining Company (Hibbing, MN) 182–183
C.T. Sampson Mfg. Co. (North Adams, MA) 29
Culbreth, W.G. 66

Dallas (TX) Clearing House 302
Danbury (CT) National Bank 11
Danville (VA) Clearing House 49, 314
Danville (VA) Savings Bank Loan & Improvement Company 49
Davenport (IA) Clearing House 148
Davies, G.R. 60
Dawson (GA) Clearing House 119–120
DeBernardi, G.B. 383
Delaware & Hudson Company (New York City) 217
Denver (CO) Clearing House 98–103
Denver (CO) National Bank 99–100
Depositors Savings & Trust (Cleveland, OH) 238
Deseret National Bank (Salt Lake City, UT) 310
Des Moines (IA) Clearing House 148–149
Des Moines (IA) National Bank 149
Des Moines (IA) Savings Bank 149
Detroit (MI) Clearing House 29, 171–172
Diamond National Bank (Pittsburgh, PA) 285
Dime Savings & Banking Company (Cleveland, OH) 239
D.M. Ferry & Company (Detroit, MI) 172

Dodd Lith. Co., Hartford, CT 109
Doe Run (MO)_Lead Company 189
Doeville (GA) Telephone Company 341
Dollar Savings & Trust Company (Youngstown, OH) 248
Dollar Savings Bank (East Liverpool, OH) 242
Dollar Savings Bank (Spartanburg, SC) 294
Dominion National Bank (Bristol, TN) 296
Dorsey Printing Co., Dallas, TX 250
Dothan (AL) Clearing House 66
Dothan (AL) National Bank 65
Dothan (GA) Clearing House 120
Douglas (GA) Clearing House 120
Drovers & Merchants Bank (St. Joseph, MO) 195
Duluth (MN) & Iron Range Railroad Company 177–178
Duluth (MN) Clearing House 177–185
Duluth (MN) Lithograph & Printing Company 177
Duluth (MN), Missabe & Northern Railway Co. 178–179
Dyersburg (TN) Clearing House 297

Earlington (KY) Bank 166
East Tennessee National Bank (Knoxville, TN) 298
Easton (PA) Clearing House 261–262
Eagle & Phoenix Manufacturing Company (Columbus, GA) 18
Ellensburg (WA) Clearing House 321
Ellsworth Collieries Company (Pittsburgh, PA) 272
Emergency Banking Act of 1933 380
Emergency Certificate Corporation 380
Enquirer Print, Yorkville, SC 295
Enterprise Print, Chester, SC 44
Erie, IL 135
Erie Railroad Company (New York City) 217
Eubank, P[eyton]. A. 66–67
Euclid Avenue National Bank (Cleveland, OH) 37
Eugene (OR) Clearing House 257
Eureka Warehouse Company (Doeville, GA) 341
Evanston (WY) Clearing House 335
Evanston (WY) National Bank 335
Everett (WA) Trust & Savings Bank 324
Exchange Bank (Albany, GA) 14–15
Exchange Bank (Chester, SC) 44
Exchange Bank (Macon, GA) 21
Exchange Bank (Savannah, GA) 124–125
Exchange National Bank (Atchison, KS) 155–156
Exchange National Bank (Little Rock, AL) 10
Exploitation Mercantile Company 355

Fairbanks (AK) Banking Company of Fairbanks 70–71
Fairbanks (MN) Trust Company 359
Fall River (MA) Clearing House 24–26
Fargo National Bank of Fargo, ND 227
Fargo (ND) Clearing House 227
Farmers & Mechanics Bank (Columbia, SC) 45
Farmers & Mechanics Savings Bank (Davenport, IA) 148
Farmers & Merchants Bank (Dothan, AL) 65
Farmers & Merchants Bank (Greenwood, SC) 293
Farmers & Merchants Bank (Lincoln, NE) 203–204
Farmers & Merchants Bank (Martin, TN) 301
Farmers & Merchants National Bank (Reno, NV) 212
Farmers Bank (White Plains, KY) 166
Farmers Bank & Trust Company (Henderson, KY) 164–165
Farmers Deposit National Bank (Pittsburgh, PA) 285
Farmers National Bank (Madisonville, KY) 166
Farmers Oil & Fertilizer Company (Sylvania, GA) 340
Farmers State Bank (Jonesboro, GA) 341
Federal National Bank (Pittsburgh, PA) 276, 279
Federal Reserve Act of 1913 374, 378
Federal Reserve System 59, 368, 372
Fidelity Loan & Trust Company (Spartanburg, SC) 294
Fidelity Trust & Savings Bank (Cedar Rapids, IA) 146
Financial Crisis of 1914 337
First National Bank (Albany, GA) 14, 377
First National Bank (Ambia, IN) 343–344
First National Bank (Atchison, KS) 156
First National Bank (Austin, MN) 176
First National Bank (Bartlesville, OK) 250
First National Bank (Beggs, OK) 250
First National Bank (Berkeley, CA) 81–82
First National Bank (Birmingham, AL) 61–62
First National Bank (Bradshaw, NE) 202–203
First National Bank (Bristol, TN) 296
First National Bank (Canton, OH) 229–230
First National Bank (Chattanooga, TN) 47
First National Bank (Cheyenne, WY) 334
First National Bank (Chicago, IL) 131, 135
First National Bank (Cincinnati, OH) 232
First National Bank (Cleveland, OH) 237, 239–240, 243
First National Bank (Columbia, AL) 65
First National Bank (Council Bluffs, IA) 147–148
First National Bank (Danville, VA) 314
First National Bank (Davenport, IA) 148
First National Bank (Denver, CO) 99–102
First National Bank (Detroit, MI) 171–172
First National Bank (Doeville, GA) 341
First National Bank (Dothan, AL) 65
First National Bank (Douglas, AZ) 76
First National Bank (Duluth, MN) 179–185
First National Bank (Dyersburg, TN) 297
First National Bank (East Liverpool, OH) 242–243
First National Bank (Ely, NV) 347–348
First National Bank (Everett, WA) 324
First National Bank (Fairbanks, AK) 71
First National Bank (Fargo, ND) 227
First National Bank (Ford City, PA) 262–263
First National Bank (Fort Collins, CO) 104
First National Bank (Gadsden, AL) 67
First National Bank (Grandview, TX) 302–303
First National Bank (Harrisburg, IL) 135–136
First National Bank (Headland, AL) 65
First National Bank (Hubbard, TX) 303–304
First National Bank (Independence, MO) 157–158
First National Bank (Joliet, IL) 136–137
First National Bank (Joplin, MO) 190
First National Bank (Lincoln, NE) 204
First National Bank (Lynchburg, VA) 315
First National Bank (Martinsville, VA) 315–316
First National Bank (McAlester, OK) 253
First National Bank (Memphis, TN) 298–299
First National Bank (Milwaukee, WI) 330–332
First National Bank (Moorhead, ND) 227
First National Bank (Mound City, IL) 140
First National Bank (Muscatine, IA) 151
First National Bank (Muskogee, OK) 254
First National Bank (Nashville, TN) 300

First National Bank (New Carlisle, IN) 143–144
First National Bank (Newnan, GA) 22
First National Bank (Newton, KS) 344–345
First National Bank (Ogden, UT) 308–309
First National Bank (Omaha, NE) 205–207
First National Bank (Parsons, KS) 159
First National Bank (Pensacola, FL) 111
First National Bank (Peoria, IL) 138–139
First National Bank (Philadelphia, PA) 267
First National Bank (Pittsburg, KS) 160
First National Bank (Pittsburgh, PA) 270–271, 279, 286
First National Bank (Portsmouth, OH) 247
First National Bank (Rhyolite, NV) 213
First National Bank (Riverside, CA) 86
First National Bank (Rock Hill, SC) 46
First National Bank (St. Augustine, FL) 112
First National Bank (Seattle, WA) 53
First National Bank (Sioux City, IA) 152
First National Bank (Slocomb, AL) 65
First National Bank (Snohomish, WA) 324
First National Bank (South Boston, VA) 317
First National Bank (Spartanburg, SC) 294
First National Bank (Superior, WI) 333–334
First National Bank (Sweet Water, TX) 306–307
First National Bank (Temple, TX) 307
First National Bank (Tombstone, AZ) 76–77
First National Bank (Ullin, IL) 140
First National Bank (Union City, TN) 301
First National Bank (Virginia, MN) 187
First National Bank (Wilkinsburg, PA) 290
First National Bank (Winsted, CT) 13
First National Bank (Yorkville, SC) 295
First National Bank (Youngstown, OH) 249
First National Bank of Buchanan County (St. Joseph, MO) 196
First National Bank of Idaho (Boise, ID) 129–130
First Scandia Bank (Everett, WA) 324–325
First State Bank (Chase City, VA) 312–313
First State Bank (Moorhead, ND) 227
First State Bank (Mounds, IL) 140
First State Bank (Nortonville, KY) 166
First State Bank (Pittsburg, KS) 160
First State Bank (Ullin, IL) 140
First State Bank of Mound City 140
First Trust & Savings Bank (Muscatine, IA) 151
Fitzgerald (GA) Clearing House 120
Florida East Coast Railway (St. Augustine, FL) 112
Florida National Bank (Jacksonville, FL) 110
Foote & Davies Co., Atlanta, GA 66, 110, 113–115, 117, 120–123, 126–129, 310–311, 358
Fort Collins (CO) Clearing House 104–105
Fort Wayne (IN) Clearing House 141
Foster Webb & Parkes, Nashville, TN 296–297
Fourth National Bank (Atlanta, GA) 115
Fourth National Bank (Cincinnati, OH) 233
Fourth National Bank (Detroit, MI) 171–172
Fourth National Bank (Grand Rapids, MI) 173–174
Fourth National Bank (Nashville, TN) 48, 300
Fourth National Bank (Wichita, KS) 161
Franklin Press Co., Pueblo, CO 107
Franklin Savings & Trust Company (Pittsburgh, PA) 272–273
Fresno (CA) Clearing House 83
Frost National Bank (San Antonio, TX) 306
Fruit Growers Bank (Greenfield, TN) 301

Gadsden (AL) Clearing House 67
Gadsden (AL) National Bank 67
Gadsden (GA) Clearing House 120
Gaffney (SC) Clearing House 292–293
Gast — St. Louis 18
Geo. D. Barnard & Co., St. Louis, MO) 81
George D. Harter Bank (Canton, OH) 230
George W. Brown (Pittsburgh, PA) 272
Gerlach Bank (Woodward, OK) 256
German-American Bank (Milwaukee, WI) 330–332
German-American National Bank (Fort Wayne, IN) 141
German-American Savings Bank of Muscatine (IA) 151
German-American State Bank (Merrill, WI) 328–330
German National Bank (Allegheny, PA) 276
German National Bank (Cincinnati, OH) 233
German Savings & Deposit Bank (Pittsburgh, PA) 287
German Savings Bank (Des Moines, IA) 149
Germania Bank (Savannah, GA) 124–125
Germania National Bank (Milwaukee, WI) 330–332
Germania Savings Bank (Pittsburgh, PA) 288
Gila Valley Bank & Trust Company (Globe, AZ) 76
Glass, Carter 58
Glenwood Lumber Company (Glenwood, AR) 357
Globe (AZ) Clearing House 76
Globe Ticket Co. (Philadelphia, PA) 363–364
G.M. Lauridsen (Port Angeles, WA) 52–53
Goes Litho Co. (Chicago, IL) 144
Gold Miners Union 211
Gold Mountain Consolidated Mining Company (Richfield, UT) 309–310
Goldfield Consolidated Mines Company 210–211, 355
Grand Rapids, MI 336
Grand Rapids (MI) Clearing House 172–174
Grand Rapids (MI) National Bank 173
Granite Falls (WA) State Bank 324
Great Lakes Coal Company (Pittsburgh, PA) 274
Greene, J.B., Jr. 60
Greenfield Bank (Greenfield, TN) 301
Greensboro (NC) Clearing House 223
Greensboro (NC) Commercial & Savings Bank 223
Greensboro (NC) Loan & Trust Company 223
Greensboro (NC) National Bank 223
Greenville (SC) Clearing House 293
Greenwood (SC) Clearing House 293
Griffin (GA) Clearing House 120–121
Grosvenor Dale Company (Providence, RI) 43, 291
Guaranty Trust Company (New York City) 67
Guardian Savings & Trust Company (Cleveland, OH) 237
Guthrie (OK) Clearing House 251–252
Guthrie (OK) National Bank 251
Guthrie (OK) Savings Bank 251–252

Hale & Kilburn Manfacturing Company (Philadelphia, PA) 267
Hall Litho. Co., Topeka, KS 160
Hamburger Cotton Mills (Columbus, GA) 19
Hamilton (OH) Clearing House 244–245
Hargraves Mills (Fall River, MA) 25
Harrisburg (IL) State Savings Bank 135–136

Harrisburg (PA) Clearing House 263–264
Harrisburg (PA) National Bank 263–264
Harrisburg (PA) Trust Company 264–265
Hartford Courant (CT) 108
Hartford (CT) Clearing House 12, 108–109
Hartford (CT) National Bank 109
Hartford (CT) Trust Company 12
Hartford Cycle Company 12
Hastings (NE) Clearing House 203
H.B. Walker & Company (Sylvania, GA) 340
H.C. Frick Coke Company (Pittsburgh, PA) 273
Heinze, F. August 57
Henderson (KY) Clearing House 164–165
Henderson (KY) National Bank 164–165
Henderson County (KY) Savings Bank 164–165
Hennepin County Savings Bank (Minneapolis, MN) 31
Hepburn, A. Barton 376
Hepner Press, N.Y. (New York City) 220
Hershey State Bank (Muscatine, IA) 151
Hibernia Bank of Savannah (GA) 124–125
Hine, J.H. 60
Hobart Mine, Pittsburg Iron Ore Company (Hibbing, MN) 184
Holister v. Zion's Co-operative Mercantile Institution 375
Holston National Bank (Knoxville, TN) 298
Home Savings & State Bank (Peoria, IL) 139
Home Savings Bank (Danville, VA) 314
Home Savings Bank (Des Moines, IA) 149
Home Savings Bank (Greensboro, NC) 223
Hopkins County Bank (Madisonville, KY) 166
Hopkins County (KY) Clearing House 166
Houston, TX 303
Houston & Texas Central Railroad Co. v. Texas 375
Howard County (IN) Clearing House 142
Howland Mills Corp. (New Bedford, MA) 27

Illinois Central Railroad Company 134
Illinois Trust & Savings Bank (Chicago, IL) 134
Indianapolis (IN) Clearing House 143
Iola (KS) Clearing House 158
Iola (KS) State Bank 158
Iowa Litho. Co., Des Moines, IA 148
Iowa National Bank (Davenport, IA) 148
Iowa National Bank (Des Moines, IA) 149
Iowa State Bank (Des Moines, IA) 149
Iowa State Savings Bank (Sioux City, IA) 154
Iowa Trust & Savings Bank (Des Moines, IA) 149
Iron Exchange Bank (Hurley, WI) 327
Iron River, MI 174
Irwin-Hodson Co. (Portland, OR) 257, 259

Jackson (GA) Clearing House 121
Jacksonville (FL) Clearing House 110
Jas. Johns & Company (Minneapolis, MN) 30
J.C. Hall Co., Prov. R.I. & S.F. 43
Jefferson County Savings Bank (Birmingham, AL) 63–64
Jefferson Trust Company (McAlester, OK) 253
J.M. Taylor (Wilkinsburg, PA) 290
John S. Cook & Company Bankers, (Goldfield, NV) 211
Johnson Company (Johnstown, PA) 39–40
Johnson Steel Street Rail Company 41
Johnston & Cheek (Danville, VA) 314
Joliet (IL) National Bank 136–137
Jones & Laughlin (Pittsburgh, PA) 274
Joplin (MO) Clearing House 190
Joplin (MO) National Bank 190
Joplin (MO) State Bank 190

Kalamazoo, MI 175
Kansas City (MO) Clearing House 192–193, 384
Kansas Printing Company 344–345
Kansas State Bank (Newton, KS) 344–345
Kentucky Bank & Trust Company (Madisonville, KY) 166
Key West (FL) Clearing House 110
Keystone Coal & Coke Company (Pittsburgh, PA) 275
Kilpatrick Bros. & Collins (Cambria, WY) 367
King, C.F. 170
Kingfisher, OK, Village of 38
Klopp & Bartlett Co., Omaha, NE 206
Knickerbocker Trust Company (New York City) 58
Knox County Bank & Trust Company (Knoxville, TN) 298
Knoxville (TN) Banking & Trust Company 298
Knoxville (TN) Clearing House 298
Krause, Chet 1

Labor Exchange (Appendix D) 383
Labor Exchange (Cincinnati, OH) 383
Larimer County (CO) Bank 106
Las Vegas (NM) Clearing House 214
Last Rational Bank of Trust Me Not 355
L.C. Smith & Bros. Typewriter Company (Pittsburgh, PA) 280
Lehigh Coal & Navigation Company (Philadelphia, PA) 267
Leo D. Burnard & Co., St. Louis, MO 53
Lester & Company, Printers 15
Levey, Ind'pls. 143
Lexington (KY) Clearing House 165
Liggett Spring & Axle Company (Pittsburgh, PA) 275
Lincoln National Bank (New York City) 220
Lincoln (NE) Clearing House 203
Lincoln Trust Company (New York City) 59
Lith. Britton & Rey, Lith. S.F. 87–88, 92–93
Little Rock (AR) Clearing House 81
Loan & Exchange Bank of South Carolina (Columbia, SC) 45
Loan & Savings Bank (Yorkville, SC) 295
Loomis & Hart Mfg. Co. (Chattanooga, TN) 47
Lorain County Banking Company (Elyria, OH) 243
Lorain (OH) Banking Company 247
Lorain (OH) Clearing House 246–247
Los Angeles (CA) Clearing House 83, 357, 375
Louisville (KY) Clearing House 165–166
Loveland (CO) National Bank 105–106
Lowman & Hanford Company (Seattle, WA) 365–366
Lowry Banking Company (Atlanta, GA) 16
Lowry National Bank (Atlanta, GA) 115
L.P. Pearson & Son (Sylvania, GA) 340
Lupfert Scales Company (Winston-Salem, NC) 225
Lutz & Schramm Company (Pittsburgh, PA) 276
Lyn Knight Currency Auctions (Lenexa, KS) 1, 211, 336, 348, 355
Lynchburg (VA) Clearing House 315
Lynchburg (VA) National Bank 315
Lynchburg (VA) Trust & Savings Bank 315
Lynn, MA 170

Macon (GA) Clearing House 121–122
Maddox-Rucker Banking Company (Atlanta, GA) 16, 115
Madisonville (KY) Savings Bank 166
Manufacturers Bank (Dothan, AL) 65
Manufacturers' Pay Check (Lansing, MI) 175
Marine Bank (Buffalo, NY) 34–35
Marine National Bank (Milwaukee, WI) 330–333
Marine National Bank (Pittsburgh, PA) 274

Market National Bank (Cincinnati, OH) 234
Market Street National Bank (Philadelphia, PA) 268
Marquardt Savings Bank (Des Moines, IA) 149
Marshall & Ilsley Bank (Milwaukee, WI) 330–332
Martin Bank (Martin, TN) 301
Martin Grogan (Pittsburgh, PA) 274
Martinsville (VA) Clearing House 315–316
Marysville (WA) State Bank 324
Massasoit National Bank (Fall River, MA) 25–26
McAdoo, William Gibbs 337
McAlester (OK) Clearing House 253
McAlester (OK) Trust Company 253
McCann & Company (Pittsburgh, PA) 277
McCormick & Company (Salt Lake City, UT) 311
McGill-Warner Co., St. Paul, MN 176
McKinley, William 7
Mechanics-American National Bank (St. Louis, MO) 199
Mechanics Bank & Trust Company 298
Mechanics National Bank (New York City) 220
Mechanics Savings Bank (Des Moines, IA) 149
Mellon National Bank (Pittsburgh, PA) 262–263, 272–273, 278, 281
Memphis (TN) Clearing House 298–299
Mercantile Bank & Trust Company (Dyersburg, TN) 297
Mercantile National Bank (New York City) 58, 99, 216
Merchants & Farmers Bank (Spartanburg, SC) 294
Merchants & Manufacturers Bank (Milwaukee, WI) 30–332
Merchants & Miners State Bank (Hibbing, MN) 183
Merchants & Planters Bank (Carrollton, GA) 17
Merchants Bank (Atlanta, GA) 16
Merchants Bank (Austin, MN) 176
Merchants Bank (Danville, VA) 49
Merchants Bank (Knoxville, TN) 298
Merchants Bank (St. Joseph, MO) 196
Merchants Loan & Trust Company (Chicago, IL) 134
Merchants National Bank (Cedar Rapids, IA) 146
Merchants National Bank (Cincinnati, OH) 234
Merchants National Bank (Fargo, ND) 227
Merchants National Bank (Fort Smith, AR) 78
Merchants National Bank (Omaha, NE) 206
Merchants National Bank (Savannah, GA) 124–125
Merchants National Bank (Sioux City, IA) 153
Miami Valley National Bank (Hamilton, OH) 244
Middle Georgia Bank (Eatonton, GA) 20
Middletown Car Works (Harrisburg, PA) 265
Midland National Bank (Newton, KS)344–345
Milledgeville (GA) Clearing House 122
Milner (ID) State Bank 131
Milwaukee (WI) Clearing House 174, 330–332
Milwaukee (WI) National Bank 330–332
Miners & Merchants Bank (Bisbee, AZ) 75–76
Miners & Merchants Bank (Nome, AK) 72–74
Miners Bank of Joplin (MO) 190
Minneapolis & Northern Elevator Company (MN) 30
Minneapolis Clearing House (MN) 186
Minneapolis Threshing Machine Company (MN) 30
Mississippi (state) 32–33
Mississippi River & Bonne Terre Railway 189
Missouri Savings Bank (Kansas City, MO) 193
M.J. Moroney (Pittsburgh, PA) 277
Model Printing Company (Muskogee, OK) 254
Moline (IL) Clearing House 138
Moline (IL) Trust & Savings Bank 138
Monongahela National Bank (Pittsburgh, PA) 277, 280
Monroe (WA) State Bank 324
Montgomery (AL) Clearing House 68–69
Moore, Waldo C. 245–246
Moore's Cheery Study (Lewisburg, OH) 245–246
Moore's Hennery (Lewisburg, OH) 245–246
Moorhead National Bank (Moorhead, ND) 227
Morgan, J. Pierpont 58–59
Morgan Litho. Co., Cleveland, OH 235, 239
Morse, C.F. 57
Morton's Bank & Trust Company (Madisonville, KY) 166
Mount Pleasant (PA) Business Men's Association 265
Mt. Vernon (WA) Shingle Script 51–52
Munson, Wm. 69–70
Muscatine (IA) Clearing House 150–152

Nashville (TN) Clearing House 300, 350
Nassau Ore Company (Hibbing, MN) 184
National Bank of Commerce (Denver, CO) 102–103
National Bank of Commerce (Hattiesburg, MS) 187–188
National Bank of Commerce (Lincoln, NE) 204–205
National Bank of Commerce (New Bedford, MA) 26–27
National Bank of Commerce (New York City) 58, 217
National Bank of Commerce (Pittsburg, KS) 160
National Bank of Commerce (St. Louis, MO) 200
National Bank of Jacksonville (FL) 110
National Bank of Merrill (WI) 328–329
National Bank of Pittsburg (KS) 160
National Bank of Riverside (CA) 86
National Bank of Savannah (GA) 124–125
National Bank of the Republic (New York City) 36
National Bank of Western Pennsylvania (Pittsburgh, PA) 271, 282, 288
National Bank of Wichita (KS) 161
National Banking System 370, 374–376, 380, 382
National City Bank (New York City) 222
National Commercial Bank (Cleveland, OH) 236
National Commercial Bank of Albany, NY 217
National Cordage Company 7
National Exchange Bank (Lynchburg, VA) 315
National Exchange Bank (Milwaukee, WI) 330–332
National Loan & Exchange Bank (Greenwood, SC) 293
National Pahquioque Bank (Danbury, CT) 11
National Park Bank (New York City) 11
National State Bank (Boulder, CO) 97
National Tube Company (Pittsburgh, PA) 278
National Union Bank (Rock Hill, SC) 294
Neal Bank (Atlanta, GA) 115
Neal Loan & Banking Company (Atlanta, GA) 16
Nebraska National Bank of Omaha, NE 206–207
New Bedford Manufacturing Company 27
New Farley National Bank (Montgomery, AL) 68
New Orleans (LA) Clearing House 22–23, 167, 371–372
New Orleans (LA) National Bank 167
New York & Cleveland Gas Coal Company (Pittsburgh, PA) 278
New York Central & Hudson River Rail Road Company 219–220
New York Chamber of Commerce 374
New York Clearing House 35, 61–

62, 67, 218–220, 368–369, 371–377, 379–380
New York, Lake Erie & Western Railroad Company 36
New York, Ontario & Western Railway Company (New York) 220
New York Stock Exchange ii, 58, 337, 371
New York Times 57
Newnan (GA) Clearing House 22, 122–123
Newton (KS) Clearing House 344–345
Nixon National Bank (Reno, NV) 212
Nome (AK) Bank & Trust Company 72–74
Nome (AK) Clearing House 72–74
Northern Electric Company (San Francisco) 91
Northern Trust Company of Fargo (ND) 227
Northrup National Bank (Iola, KS) 158
Northwestern Lith. & Pub. Co., Minneapolis 30
Northwestern Mutual Savings & Loan Association (Fargo, ND) 227
Northwestern National Bank (Sioux City, IA) 153
Northwestern Trust Company (St. Paul, MN) 186–187
N.P. Bank Note Co., Tacoma, WA 321–322, 325–326
N.R. Allen's Sons Co. 135

Oakland (CA) Clearing House 85–86
Obion County (TN) 301
Ocean Shore Railway Company (San Francisco) 93
Ogden (UT) Clearing House 309
Ohio Valley Bank (Allegheny, PA) 260
Ohio Valley Banking & Trust Company (Henderson, KY) 164–165
Oklahoma City (OK) Clearing House 255
Oklahoma City (OK) National Bank 255
Oklahoma Engraving & Printing Co., Oklahoma City, OK 254–255
Old Dominion Commercial Company (Globe, AZ) 76
Old National Bank (Detroit, MI) 173
Olds Motor Works (Lansing, MI) 175
Oliver Iron Mining Company (MN) 180
Olney, Richard 377
Olympia (WA) Clearing House 322
Omaha (NE) Clearing House 205–209
Orange Judd Company (Atlanta, GA) 341
Otis Steel Company (Cleveland, OH) 240

Packers National Bank (Omaha, NE) 209
Paducah, KY 336
Paducah (KY) Clearing House 167
Panic of 1857 368, 371, 381
Panic of 1893 1–55, 368, 372, 382
Panic of 1907 1, 6, 8, 57–336, 357, 368, 372–373, 377–378
Panic of 1914 337–351
Parsons (KS) Clearing House 159
Parsons (KS) Commercial Bank 159
Penn Iron Mining Company (Chicago, IL) 135
Penn National Bank (Philadelphia, PA) 266
Pennfield Bank (Lorain, OH) 247
Pennsylvania Railroad Company 41
Pensacola Bank & Trust Company of Pensacola (FL) 112
Peoples Bank (Aurora, MO) 188
Peoples Bank (Clifton, TN) 296–297
Peoples Bank (South Boston, VA) 317
Peoples Bank & Trust Company (Rock Hill, SC) 294
Peoples Bank of Earlington (KY) 166
People's Bank of Martinsville, VA 315–316
People's Banking Company (Ironwood, MI) 174
Peoples National Bank (Lynchburg, VA) 315
Peoples National Bank (Pittsburgh, PA) 276–277, 280–288
Peoples National Bank (Winston-Salem, NC) 225
Peoples Savings Bank (Des Moines, IA) 149
Peoples Savings Bank (Henderson, KY) 164–165
Peoples Savings Bank & Trust Company (Birmingham, AL) 8, 64
Peoples Savings Bank & Trust Company (Danville, VA) 314
Peoples Savings Bank & Trust Company (Moline, IL) 138
Peoples Savings Bank & Trust Company (Pine Bluff, AR) 81
People's State Bank (Detroit, MI) 171–172
Peoria (IL) Clearing House 138–139
Perkins Bros. Company (Sioux City, IA) 152
Pewabic Company (Iron Mountain, MI) 174
P.F. Pettibone & Company, Chicago, IL 333
Philadelphia & Reading Railway Company (Philadelphia, PA)268
Philadelphia (PA) Clearing House 41, 266–267, 369, 371–372
Philadelphia (PA) National Bank 265–266
Philler v. Patterson 378
Pickands, Mather & Company (Duluth, MN) 180–181
Pine Bluff (AR) Clearing House 81
Pittman Act of 1918 379
Pittsburg Iron Ore Company (Hibbing, MN) 184
Pittsburg (KS) Clearing House 160
Pittsburgh (PA) Clearing House 42268–269, 272, 275, 278–279, 282–283
Pittsburgh (PA) Printing Company 279
Planters & Merchants National Bank (South Boston, VA) 317
Planters Bank (Morton's Gap, KY) 166
Planters National Bank (Danville, VA) 49
Planters State Bank (Henderson, KY) 164–165
Platt, Orville 374
Pocasset National Bank (Fall River, MA) 26
Poindexter v. Greenbow 375
Portland (OR) Clearing House 258–259
Portsmouth (OH) Banking Company 247
Portsmouth (OH) Clearing House 247
Potters National Bank (East Liverpool, OH) 242
Poudre Valley National Bank (Fort Collins, CO) 105
P.P. Parsons & Co., Chicago, IL 135
Prairie Pebble Phosphate Company (Prairie, FL) 358
Pratt & Whitney Company 13
Providence (RI) Clearing House 43
Puget Sound National Bank (Seattle, WA) 54
Pulaski County (IL) Clearing House 140

Quaker National Bank (Philadelphia, PA) 268
Queen City Bank (Gadsden, AL) 67

Racine, WI 332
Rawhide, NV 211
Reconstruction Finance Corporation 379
Record Co., St. Augustine, FL 112
Red Cedar Shingle Company (Mt. Vernon, WA) 52
Red Wing (MN) Stoneware Company 32
Rees Printing Co., Omaha, NE 207, 209
Reno (NV) Clearing House 212–213
Republic Bank Note Co. 248, 268
Republic Iron & Steel Company (Duluth, MN) 182
Republican Clearing Script 354
Rhode Island Hospital Trust Company (Providence, RI) 42, 291
Rhode Island Locomotive Works 43
Rhode Island National Bank (Providence, RI) 43
Rhyolite (NV) Clearing House 213–214
Richfield (UT) Commercial & Savings Bank 309–310
Richmond (VA) Locomotive & Machine Works 50–51
Riverside (CA) Clearing House 86
Roberts & Son, Lith., Birmingham, AL 8–10, 66
Rochester (NY) Clearing House 348–349
Rock Hill (SC) Clearing House 46, 294

Rocky Mountain Bank Note Co., Denver, CO 97–99, 157
Rolfe, E.A. 78
Rome (GA) Clearing House 123
Roosevelt, Theodore 57, 59, 211
Rotch Spinning Corp. (New Bedford, MA) 27
Russell & Company (Massillon, OH) 37

S.A. Bristol Co., Cheyenne, WY 334–335
Sacramento (CA) Clearing House 87
St. Joseph (MO) Clearing House 195–197
St. Louis Bank Note Company 32
St. Louis (MN) County Bank 182
St. Louis (MO) Clearing House 197–201, 346, 369, 371
St. Paul (MN) Clearing House 186–187, 346, 360–361
Salchaket Trading Post & Roadhouse (Fairbanks, AK) 69–70
Saline Trust & Savings Bank (Harrisburg, IL) 1135–136
Salt Lake City (UT) Clearing House 310–311, 364
San Antonio (TX) Clearing House 305–306
San Francisco (CA) Clearing House 87–90
San Luis Obispo (CA) County Bankers' Association 93–94
Savannah (GA) Bank & Trust Company 124–125
Savannah (GA) Clearing House 123–125
Savannah (GA) Trust Company 124–125
Savings Deposit Bank & Trust Company (Elyria, OH) 243
S.C. Toof & Co., Memphis, TN 33
Scheeling Bank & Trust Company (Reno, NV) 212
Schingoethe, Herb 1
Schingoethe, Martha 1
Scott County Savings Bank (Davenport, IA) 148
Scranton (PA) Clearing House 364
Screven Telephone Company (Sylvania, GA) 340
Seattle (WA) Clearing House 322–324, 366
Second National Bank (Hamilton, OH) 244–245
Second National Bank (Pittsburgh, PA) 272, 281–282, 289
Second Ward Savings Bank (Milwaukee, WI) 330–332
Security National Bank (Sioux City, IA) 154
Security Savings Bank (Cedar Rapids, IA) 146–147
Security Savings Bank & Trust Company (Portsmouth, OH) 247
Sedalia (MO) Trust Company 202
Seventeenth National Bank (Philadelphia, PA) 42
Sharon Steel Hoop Company (Pittsburgh, PA) 279
Shaw-Borden Co., Spokane, WA 54
Shenango Furnace Company (Hibbing, MN) 185
Sherman Silver Purchase Act 7
Sherwood Lith. Co., Chicago, IL 151
Silver Belt Print., Globe, AZ 76
Sioux City (IA) Clearing House 152–155
Sisson, Pr., Atlanta, GA 20, 22
Skagit County (WA) Clearing House 319, 324
Slate Belt Clearing House (Bangor, PA) 261
Slocomb (AL) National Bank 65
Smithsonian Institution 1
Snohomish County (WA) Clearing House 324–325
Soakum & Slockum Bank 355
Social Manufacturing Company (Providence, RI) 43
Solvay Process Company (Detroit, MI) 172
Sonoma County (CA) Clearing House 94
South Bend (IN) Clearing House 144
South Bend (WA) Clearing House 325
South Boston & Houston (VA) Clearing House 317
South Boston (VA) Savings Bank 317
South Chattanooga (TN) Savings Bank 47
South Omaha National Bank (NE) 208
Southern Banking & Trust Company (Atlanta, GA) 16
Southern Iron Works (Warner, TN) 49
Southern Pacific Rail Road (New York City) 220
Southern Trust Company (Spartanburg, SC) 294
Spang, Chalfant & Company (Pittsburgh, PA) 280
Sparks, John 211
Sparta (GA) Clearing House 125–126
Spartanburg (SC) Clearing House 294
Spartanburg (SC) Savings Bank 294
Spokane (WA) Clearing House 323–326
Spokane (WA) Litho. Co. 325
(Spokane, WA) School Fund 54
Springfield (IL) Clearing House 140
Springs Bank of Rock Hill (SC) 46
Standard Engineering Co. (Pittsburgh, PA) 280
Standard Oil Company (Cleveland, OH) 37
Standard Oil Company of New York (New York City) 220–221
Standard Prtg. Co., Lith., Hannibal, MO 190
Standard Steel Car Co. (Pittsburgh, PA) 281
State Bank & Trust Company (Muscatine, IA) 151
State Bank of Edmonds, WA 324
State Bank of Florida (Jacksonville, FL) 110
State Bank of Greentown (Greentown, IN) 142
State Bank of Rocky Ford (CO) 107
State Capital Co., Guthrie, OK 252
State Journal Co., Lincoln, NE 209
State National Bank (Memphis, TN) 299
State National Bank (Oklahoma City, OK) 254
State of Mississippi 32–33
State Savings Bank & Trust Company (Moline, IL) 138
Staten Island Rapid Transit Railway (New York City) 221
Steele Ptg. Co., Harrisburg, IL 136
Steiner Bros. Bank (Birmingham, AL) 8, 64
Steiner Brothers, Banking House of (Birmingham, AL) 64
Stephens Litho & Eng. Co., St. Louis, MO 76, 256
Stevens, Frank 60
Stewart, Warren & Co., 29 Howard St., N.Y. (New York City) 108
Stiffel & Freeman (Philadelphia, PA) 268
Stock Growers National Bank (Cheyenne, WY) 334–335
Stockton (CA) Clearing House 95–96
Strobridge Litho. Co., Cin. O. (Cincinnati, OH) 230–234, 244–245
Superior (WI) Clearing House 333–334
Swedish American Bank (Minneapolis, MN) 30
Swift Manufacturing Co. (Columbus, GA) 19
Syl. Lester & Co., Atlanta, GA 15, 44
Sylvania & Girard Rail Road Co. (Sylvania, GA) 340
Sylvania Banking Company (Sylvania, GA) 340
Sylvester (GA) Clearing House 126

Tacoma (WA) Bituminous Paving Co. 55
Tacoma (WA) Clearing House 326
Taft, William Howard 354
Tampa (FL) Clearing House 113
Taunton, MA 170
Tecumseh Mills (Fall River, MA) 26
"Teddy Bear" scrip 355
Telephone Publishing Co. (Sylvania, GA) 340
Temple State Bank of Temple (TX) 308
Tenino, WA 380
Thaxter's Drug Store (Carson City, NV) 32
Third National Bank (Atlanta, GA) 115
Third National Bank (Chattanooga, TN) 47
Third National Bank (Dothan, AL) 65
Third National Bank (Knoxville, TN) 298
Third National Bank (Providence, RI) 43

Third National Bank of St. Louis (MO) 200
Thomas, Ransom H. 58
Thomaston (GA) Clearing House 126
Thomasville (GA) Clearing House 127
Thos. Gilbert, Printer (Columbus, GA) 18–19
Tifton (GA) Clearing Housse 127
Timken Roller Bearing Axle Company (Canton, OH) 230
Topeka (KS) Clearing House 160–161
Traders National Bank (Birmingham, AL) 65
Trans-Mississippi International Exposition 366
Trust Company of America (New York City) 59
Tucker, Hanford Company, Seattle, WA 320–321
Tucson (AZ) Clearing House 77
Twin Falls (ID) North Side Land & Water Company 131

Union & Planters Bank & Trust Company (Memphis, TN) 299
Union Bank (Knoxville, TN) 298
Union Bank & Trust Company (Asheville, TN) 46
Union Bank & Trust Company (Henderson, KY) 164–165
Union Bank & Trust Company (Nashville, TN) 300
Union Bank Note Co., K.C. Mo. (Kansas City, MO) 38, 155–156, 159, 201, 250, 253
Union Banking Company (Douglas, GA) 120
Union City (TN) Banking & Trust Company 301
Union County (TN) Association of Banks 300–301
Union Exchange Bank (Danville, VA) 314
Union Litho Co. L.A. (Los Angeles, CA) 75, 83–84
Union Litho Co. S.F. (San Francisco, CA) 82, 86, 94
Union National Bank (Cleveland, OH) 237, 240–241, 243
Union National Bank (Elyria, OH) 243
Union National Bank (Kansas City, MO) 193
Union Savings Bank (Davenport, IA) 148
Union Savings Bank & Trust Company (Macon, GA) 22
Union Stock Yards National Bank (Omaha, NE) 209
Union Switch & Signal Company (Pittsburgh, PA) 281
Union Trust Company (Doeville, GA) 341
Union Trust Company (Pittsburgh, PA) 278, 282,
United Engineering & Foundry Company (Pittsburgh, PA) 282
United States Cast Iron Pipe & Foundry Company (New York) 222
United States Construction Company (Fairbanks, IN) 359
U.S. House of Representatives, Banking & Currency Commission 23
United States National Bank (Denver, CO) 103–104
United States National Bank of Omaha (NE) 207
U.S. Steel Corp. 59
United States Sugar & Land Company (Garden City, KS) 157
United States v. Van Auken 375
Universal Bunco Bank of America 354
Utah Litho. Co., S.L.C. (Salt Lake City, UT) 308, 312, 347–348, 364

Valdosta (GA) Clearing House 128
Valley National Bank (Des Moines, IA) 149
Veazie Bank v. Fenno 375
Ventura County (CA) Bankers' Association 96
Vicksburg (MS) Clearing House 188
Victoria Elevator Company (Minneapolis, MN) 31

W.A. Mallory & Bro. (Sylvania, GA) 340
Wachovia Loan & Trust Company (New York City) 226
Wachovia Loan & Trust Company (Winston-Salem, NC) 225
Waid, C.H. 65
Walker Brothers (Salt Lake City, UT) 312
Walker, Evans & Cogswell Co. (Columbia, SC) 45
Walker, Evans & Cogswell Co., Shas'n, S.C. (Charleston, SC) 292
Walker's Mercantile Company (Doeville, GA) 341
Wampanoag Mills (Fall River, MA) 26
Washington (state) 365–366
Washington-Alaska Bank of Fairbanks (AK) 71–72
Washington (DC) Clearing House 337–338
Washington National Bank (St. Louis, MO) 201
Washington Trust & Savings Bank (Bristol, TN) 296
Washoe County Bank (Reno, NV) 212
Waycross (GA) Clearing House 128
Weakley County Bank (Breeden, TN) 301
Weakley County (TN) Bankers' Association 301–302
Weed Parsons Printing Co., Albany, NY 34
Weldon, Williams & Liew, Ft. Smith, AR 79
Werner Company (Akron, OH) 36
West Side Bank (Milwaukee, WI) 330–332
Western Bank Note and Engraving Company, Chicago, IL 131, 134, 140, 160, 162–163, 167, 173, 179, 197, 205–207, 235, 246, 249, 342, 367
Western Bank Note Co. Pgh (Pittsburgh, PA) 274
Western German Bank (Cincinnati, OH) 234
Western Litho. Co., Wichita, KS 162–163, 345
Western Pub. & Eng. Co., Detroit 29
W.H. Stanage & Co., Cin. O. (Cincinnati, OH) 228
Wheeling (WV) Clearing House 326
Wichita (KS) Clearing House 161–163, 345
Wiehl, Probasco & Company (Chattanooga, TN) 47
Wilber & Hastings Lith. 57 Fulton St. N.Y. (New York City) 220
Wilkes-Barre (PA) Clearing House 289–290
Wilkinsburg (PA) Trust Company 290–291
Will County National Bank (Joliet, IL) 136–138
Willacoochee (GA) Clearing House 129
Wilmington, DE 109
Wilson, S.N. 63
Wingfield, George 211, 355
Wisconsin National Bank (Milwaukee, WI) 330–332
W.J. Walker & Company (Sylvania, GA) 340
Wm. Flaccus Oak Leather Company (Pittsburgh, PA) 272
Wm. H. Carlson (Los Angeles, CA) 358
wooden money 380
Woodin, William 379–380
Woodland Ave. Savings & Trust Company (Cleveland, OH) 241
Wyoming Trust Company (Thermopolis, WY) 336

X-Co., Dallas, TX 303, 307

Youngstown, OH 336
Youngstown (OH) Clearing House 248–249
Youngstown Sheet & Tube Company (Youngstown, OH) 249

www.ingramcontent.com/pod-product-compliance
Ingram Content Group UK Ltd.
Pitfield, Milton Keynes, MK11 3LW, UK
UKHW051929100926
8556IPUK00022B/1448

9 780786 475773